Meet the *Southern Living* Foods Staff

On these pages we present the *Southern Living* Foods Staff (left to right in each photograph).

Susan Payne, Foods Editor; Dana Adkins Campbell, Assistant Foods Editor

Jean Wickstrom Liles, Senior Foods Editor

Patty Vann, Assistant Test Kitchens Director; Kaye Adams, Test Kitchens Director; Peggy Smith, Marketing Manager

Karen Brechin and Cathy Dunklin, Editorial Assistants

*Susan Dosier, Assistant Foods Editor; Helen Anne
Dorrough, Associate Foods Editor*

*Leslie Byars, Assistant Photo Stylist; Jan Wyatt,
Photographer*

*Charles Walton IV, Senior Foods Photographer; Beverly
Morrow Perrine, Senior Photo Stylist.*

*Judy Feagin, Diane Hogan, and Jane Cairns, Test
Kitchens Home Economists*

Southern Living®

1990 ANNUAL RECIPES

Oxmoor House®

Copyright 1990 by Oxmoor House, Inc.
Book Division of Southern Progress Corporation
P.O. Box 2463, Birmingham, Alabama 35201

Southern Living®, Summer Suppers®, and *Holiday Dinners®*
are federally registered trademarks of Southern Living, Inc.

Library of Congress Catalog Number: 79-88364
ISBN: 0-8487-1032-0
ISSN: 0272-2003

Manufactured in the United States of America
First printing 1990

Southern Living®
    Senior Foods Editor: Jean Wickstrom Liles
    Foods Editor: Susan Payne
    Associate Foods Editor: Helen Anne Dorrough
    Assistant Foods Editors: Dana Adkins Campbell,
      Susan Dosier
    Editorial Assistants: Karen Brechin, Cathy Dunklin
    Test Kitchens Director: Kaye Adams
    Assistant Test Kitchens Director: Patty Vann
    Test Kitchens Staff: Jane Cairns, Judy Feagin,
      Diane Hogan, Peggy Smith
    Senior Photo Stylist: Beverly Morrow Perrine
    Assistant Photo Stylist: Leslie Byars
    Senior Foods Photographer: Charles E. Walton IV
    Additional photography by *Southern Living* photographer
      Jan Wyatt, pages 37, 41 (lower photo), 188, 257,
      263, and 264.
    Production Manager: Clay Nordan
    Assistant Production Manager: Amy Cherner
    Production Traffic Manager: Vicki Weathers

Oxmoor House, Inc.
    Executive Editor: Ann H. Harvey
    Director of Manufacturing: Jerry R. Higdon
    Associate Production Manager: Rick Litton
    Art Director: Bob Nance
    Production Assistant: Theresa L. Beste

Southern Living® 1990 Annual Recipes

    Editor: Olivia Kindig Wells
    Copy Chief: Mary Ann Laurens
    Editorial Assistants: Pam Beasley Bullock, Kelly E. Hooper

    Designer: Carol Middleton
    Illustrator: Ray E. Watkins, Jr.

Cover: *Among our 25 best desserts from the past 25 years are (clockwise
from top) Perfect Chocolate Cake, Almond Cream Confections, Pecan
Pie, and Chocolate-Tipped Butter Cookies. (Recipes begin on page 305.)*

Back cover: *A clear-cut winner, Hummingbird Cake (page 305)
overwhelmingly takes the cake as number one of our 25 best desserts.*

Page 1: *Fresh fruit frames Luscious Flan (page 56) with an array of
vibrant colors.*

Page 4: *Traditional Mexican spices—cumin and chili powder—flavor
Tacoritos (page 133), a festive entrée wrapped in a flour tortilla.*

To find out how you can receive *Southern Living* magazine, write to
Southern Living®, P.O. Box 830119, Birmingham, AL 35283.

Table of Contents

January   11

Here's To The Lucky Year Ahead   12
QUICK! Serve Vegetables   13
On The Light Side:
   Quenchers: Cool And Light   14
Microwave Cookery: Fast And
   Fabulous Finales   15
Entertaining Is Easy For This Man   16
Wonderful Ways With Broccoli
   And Cauliflower   17
A Lesson On Poaching Fish   18
Super Bowl Sandwich   19
Microwave Puddings   19
Taco Salad For Two   20
The Jeweled Crown
   Of Mardi Gras   20
Sip A Hot Cider   21
From Our Kitchen To Yours   22

February   23

Savory Pot Pies   24
On The Light Side: Cook It Light,
   Cook It Cajun   26
Light Menu: A Heart-Healthy Menu
   For Two   29
Light Favorite: Trimmed-Down
   Macaroni And Cheese   30

Homemade Stocks Make Savory
   Soups And Stews   30
Homemade Soups—
   Warm And Delicious   31
Put The Chill On Winter Salads   32
Microwave Cookery:
   Weeknight Entrées   33
Serve Onions On The Side   34
QUICK! Dinner In A Skillet   35
Tease Appetites With A Party
   Spread   36
A Novel Look At Nobility   45
One Recipe, Three Batches
   Of Bread   46
Savory Dough Conceals
   The Cheese   47
Snack-In-The-Box   47
Treat Yourself To Kumquats   48
Pralines For Dessert   48
Cookie By The Slice   49
Pastries For Breakfast   49
From Our Kitchen To Yours   50

March   51

A Wellspring Of Entrée Ideas   52
Toss The Salad, But Don't Mix Up
   The Greens   54

On The Light Side: Spectacular
   Light Desserts   56
Light Menu: Plan The Meal Around
   Healthy Soup   58
Light Favorite: A Healthier
   Corn Pudding   60
Sporty Appetizers For Active
   Appetites   60
Microwave Cookery: Potatoes
   In Minutes   61
QUICK! Toss A Pasta Salad   62
The Luck Of The Irish To You   63
Cure The Chicken Doldrums   64
Quick Breads, Faster Than Yeast   65
Crispy, Delicious Popovers   66
Make Ahead And Freeze   67
Beefed Up Dishes For
   Globe-Trotters   68
The Best Of Seafood In A Salad   69
Bar Cookies Are Welcome Anytime   69
Time Enough For Doughnuts   70
Crab—A Southern Delicacy   71
From Our Kitchen To Yours   72

April   73

Tease The Palate With Eggplant   74
QUICK! Rely On Fish Fillets   75

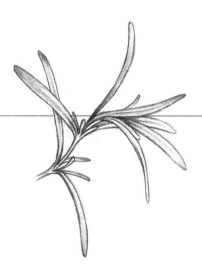

Brunches & Lunches Special
  Section   81
  Toast The Morning, And Greet
    Midday   81
  Share This Menu With Friends   84
  Invite Friends To A Coffee   85
  Country Ham, From Start To
    Finish   87
  Soup And Salad Specials   88
  A Lunch For A Southern
    Celebration   89
  Lunches, Boxed To Go   91
  The Races Start With Brunch   92
  Kids Kindle The Derby Spirit   94
  Reach For The Granola   95
Medaillons Make A Showy Entrée   96
Something Different With Steak   97
Microwave Cookery: The Microwave
  Is A Natural For Vegetables   98
Outstanding Standbys   99
On The Light Side: Toss
  A Healthy Stir-Fry   100
Light Menu: Serve
  A Hearty Supper   101
Light Favorite: Trimmed-Down
  Cheese Grits   102
Sit Down To Some Crawfish   102
Hats Off To Spring Beverages   103
Not Such A Tough Nut To Crack   104
Desserts Tailored For Passover   106
Fancy Cakes From Basic Layers   106
From Our Kitchen To Yours   108

May   109

On The Light Side: Host A Healthy
  Springtime Get-Together   110
Blue-Ribbon Cookies   111
Microwave Cookery:
  Shellfish: Fast And Flavorful   112
QUICK! Team Chicken And Sauces   117
Make A Meal Of Tex-Mex
  Appetizers   118

Enjoy Barbecue, Memphis Style   120
On The Light Side: Celebrate
  Cinco De Mayo   121
Light Favorite: Better-Than-Ever
  Potato Salad   122
Embellish Pasta For
  An Entrée   122
Mold A Salad Ahead Of Time   123
Serve Fruit On The Side   124
Feast On Fresh Strawberries   125
From Our Kitchen To Yours   126

June   127

Relax! The Entrées Are Easy   128
From Our Kitchen To Yours   130
On The Light Side Special Section   131
  Do Your Heart A Favor; Adopt
    A Healthy Lifestyle   131
  A Fiesta Of Mexican Food   133
  Triglycerides: Why Are They
    Important?   134
  Fiber For Your Arteries   134
  Homegrown Sprouts   136
  A Heart-Healthy Feast For
    Guests   137
  Pizza Goes Light   139
QUICK! These Eggs Can't Be
  Beat   140
Burstin' With Blueberries   140
Microwave Cookery: Poaching
  Imparts Flavor   141
Picture Perfect, From Garden
  To Table   142
A Taste Of English Peas
  In A Salad   143
The Time Is Ripe For Cucumbers   143
A Hero, Any Way You Stack It   144
Meaty Ways With Rice   145
Chicken Salad, Better Than Ever   146
Appetizers From The Vegetable
  Patch   147
Fired Up About Grilled Entrées   148

July   153

Vegetables That Signal The Season   154
Summer's Sweet Traditions   156
Summer Suppers® Special Section   157
  Treasured Reunion Recipes   157
  Gather Around The
    Porter Table   158
  Reunion Samplings   160
  A Taste Of Tennessee   161
  Stop Talking And Start
    Planning!   162
  From Generation To Generation   163
  Publish Your Family Recipes   163
On The Light Side:
  Herbs—Nature's Own Seasonings   164
Light Menu: Invite Friends For A
  Healthy Cookout   166
Light Favorite: Lean Butterbeans   166
Microwave Cookery: Play It Cool
  With Soup   167
QUICK! Sauces Take The Lead   168
Drinks With A Taste Of The
  Tropics   169
The Best Berries Of The Season   170

August   171

Contemporary Cuisine With A
  Southern Accent   172
New Choices For Cheesecake   174
QUICK! Olé, It's Mexican   175
On The Light Side: Healthy
  Sandwiches That Satisfy   176
Light Menu: A Breakfast For Kids   178
Light Favorite: A Peach Of A
  Sherbet   179
In The Mood For A Soda?   179
Celebrating The Fruits Of Summer   180
Toss Around New Ideas For Salads   180
Pastries Are Her Cup Of Tea   181
From Our Kitchen To Yours   182
Around The World With Rice   183
Pecans Make The Pie   184

September   189

Meet Our Cooks Across The South 190
Sweet Rolls On The Rise   194
Microwave Cheesecake   196
On The Light Side: Spilling The
  Beans About Legumes   197
Light Menu: A Healthy Salute To
  Summer   198
Light Favorite: Serve This Bread
  With A Spoon   200
Squash Side Dishes To Savor   200
QUICK! Ladle Up Some Soup   201
Dried Tomatoes Burst With Flavor 202
A Banker Lends His Culinary
  Talents   204
From Our Kitchen To Yours   205
Appetizers To Cheer For   206
Here's To The Game   206
Speedy Vegetables   207

October   209

Ladle Up The Cream Of The Crop   210
Fruit Makes It Fancy   211
It's Apple Season   212
Classic Creations With Cornmeal 213
Usher In Autumn With Breads   214
Yogurt Adds Culture To These
  Dishes   215
Introducing Mirlitons   217
Sweet Send-Offs   218
Quick Southern Classics   218
From Our Kitchen To Yours   225
No Trick To Treats For Teens   225
Crazy About Caramel   227
Plump And Delicious   227
On The Light Side: Fight Cancer
  With Your Fork   228
Light Menu: A Healthy Meal With
  A Cajun Flair   229
Light Favorite: Beef Stew Minus
  All The Fat   230

Tastefully Tossed Salad   231
Fiesta Supper In A Snap   231
A Southern Menu With A Few
  Surprises   232
QUICK! Supper From The Sea   233
Pick An Entrée For Two   234
Ham With New Appeal   235
Side Dishes That Satisfy   236
Artichokes Fill This Strata   236

November   237

Company's Coming For Casseroles 238
Holiday Dinners® Special Section 241
  Holiday Entertaining At Its
    Best   241
  Open House Planning Guide   244
  It's Easy To Host A Buffet   246
  Set The Mood For A Party   247
  Dishes That Make Holiday
    Tradition   249
  Taste A Sentimental Journey   251
  Tasty, Timeless Hanukkah
    Treats   254
  Longing For Louisiana Flavor   255
  A Grand Finale   265
  Drop By For Dessert   266
  Gifts Say "Thank You"   267
  Entertain Young Adults With A
    Festive Menu   268
  Invite Kids To The Party   269
  Beverages Brewed For The
    Season   272
  Beverages For All Ages   273
  A Clear Look At Glassware   274
  From Our Kitchen To Yours   276
  Innovative Invitations   277
On The Light Side: Simmer A
  Pot Of Soup   278
Light Menu: Dinner For The
  Health-Conscious   279
Decorate The Door Naturally   280
Accent With Light   282

QUICK! No-Fret Breads   283
A Passion For Pound Cake   284
Making The Best Pound Cakes   285
Choose A Better Salad   286
Tasty Turkey Soup   287
Crimson Cranberries   287
Elegant Charlotte Russe   288

December   289

Side Dishes With A Holiday Dash 290
QUICK! Easy Appetizers   292
On The Light Side: Cranberries:
  Jewels Of The Season   293
Light Menu: A Menu For The Two
  Of You   294
Light Favorite: Heart-Smart
  Pumpkin Pie   296
Pair Citrus And Cream   296
Our All-Time Best Desserts   305
From Our Kitchen To Yours   314
Stir In The Champagne   315
An Easy But Superb Dinner
  For Four   315
Entrées For Any Occasion   316
Stir Leftovers Into A Salad   318
After The Slopes, The Feast   319
Roast Turkey: Something To
  Squawk About   320
Bread With Italian Roots   321
Sip The Holiday Spirit   322
Ease Into Morning   323

Roots Of
  Southern Food   324

Appendices   329

Recipe Index Section   334

Our Year At Southern Living®

The year 1990 has been an exciting time for us at *Southern Living*. We celebrated our 25th year—our Silver Jubilee. Surviving 25 years in today's publishing world is a remarkable accomplishment, but much of our success is due to the unique relationship we have with you, our readers.

The foods staff is proud of its history and accomplishments during this quarter of a century. Since the magazine's first issue in 1966, we've shared thousands of wonderful recipes and entertaining ideas from some of the South's best cooks.

To celebrate the anniversary throughout the year, the foods staff offered several special features in the magazine with you in mind. We invited John Egerton, a native Southerner and noted food authority, to trace the history of foods indigenous to the South. You'll find his story "Roots of Southern Food" on page 324.

Because much of the popularity of our section is attributed to the sharing of favorite recipes by our readers, we selected 12 recipe contributors from nine states to be honored as "Cooks Across the South." Their visit to Birmingham was the highlight of our anniversary activities. These honorees had consistently submitted outstanding recipes and represented a cross section of our readers and the South. After three days of whirlwind activities, our guests confirmed that their favorite recipes are not only quick and easy but also nutritious and great tasting. (Their recipes begin on page 190.)

Speaking of favorite recipes, in 1989 we invited all our readers to cast a vote for their favorite recipes featured in *Southern Living* during the past 25 years. After all the ballots were tallied, it was obvious that Southern desserts are still special, even though we're trying to trim calories. As a grand finale for our Silver Jubilee, in December we spotlighted the 25 all-time best dessert recipes. In my opinion, each of those recipes is a blue-ribbon winner, but this smorgasbord includes two recipes that have been special to me for 25 years or longer. The Pecan Pie came from Jane Brittain, a longtime friend, and the Holiday Coconut Cake has been a specialty of my mother longer than I can remember.

The foods staff is very proud of *1990 Annual Recipes*. In addition to the above Silver Jubilee features, each of our special sections focused on a specific theme. "Brunches & Lunches" centered around one of the South's most famous events, the Kentucky Derby. This entertaining guide had something for everyone—from elaborate brunches to delicious box lunches.

"On the Light Side" featured a guide for heart-healthy living. This section focused on cholesterol and included low-cholesterol, low-fat recipes.

Our region has many traditions that celebrate the family, but none is more Southern than a reunion. Thus we devoted "Summer Suppers" to family reunions, offering hints for organizing a reunion, planning activities for all ages, and publishing a family cookbook.

"Holiday Dinners" offered a complete party guide with an array of recipes, menus, and entertaining ideas. The tips included everything from entertaining a crowd to lighting your home for special evenings.

We hope you've enjoyed celebrating our Silver Jubilee with us! Having been at *Southern Living* over 18 years, I assure you this has been the most exciting and rewarding year ever. In all those years, I've taste-tested more than 50,000 recipes in our kitchens. I'm glad I didn't keep a tally on the calories!

Jean Wickstrom Liles

JANUARY

Usher in the New Year with a celebration. As you make plans, turn to our New Year's Eve menu; then set the table, light the candles, and serve a dinner with flair. The next day, be prepared to offer a lucky menu featuring a hearty helping of greens and some old-fashioned black-eyed peas to start the New Year right.

Here's To The Lucky Year Ahead

In the South a lucky menu requires a hearty helping of greens and some old-fashioned black-eyed peas. For this New Year's Day we offer you a menu of traditional dishes to start your new year off right.

Be sure to serve turnip greens—fresh or frozen, it doesn't matter, as long as they're green and hint at all the money that's *sure* to come your way. Offer vinegar and hot pepper sauce on the side.

Culled from Louisiana's Spanish culture, Hopping John is a delicious combination of rice, black-eyed peas, and a little pork. For this menu it is intended as a side dish, but it can be served as a main dish.

Tomato Juice Cocktail
Ribs With Blender Barbecue Sauce
Hopping John
Turnip Greens
Skillet Cornbread

TOMATO JUICE COCKTAIL
(pictured on page 41)

1 (46-ounce) can tomato juice
1 tablespoon instant minced onion
1 tablespoon sugar
1 teaspoon bon appétit seasoning
1 teaspoon powdered horseradish
⅛ teaspoon pepper
1 bay leaf
6 whole cloves
2 whole allspice
3 tablespoons white vinegar

Combine all ingredients except vinegar in a large saucepan; bring to a boil. Reduce heat, and simmer 15 minutes, stirring occasionally.

Remove from heat; stir in vinegar, and let cool. Strain and discard bay leaf, cloves, and allspice. Cover and chill 3 to 4 hours. Pour beverage into glasses. Yield: about 6 cups.
Robbie Ann Colopy
Shenandoah, Virginia

Tip: *Compare costs of fresh, frozen, canned, and dried foods. To compute the best buy, divide the price by the number of servings. The lower price per serving will be the thriftiest buy.*

RIBS WITH BLENDER BARBECUE SAUCE
(pictured on page 43)

5 pounds country-style pork ribs
  or loin spare ribs
1 (16-ounce) can apricots, drained
¼ cup firmly packed brown sugar
1 teaspoon chili powder
½ cup catsup
½ cup white vinegar
2 teaspoons Worcestershire sauce

Place ribs in a large Dutch oven; cover with water. Bring water to a boil; cover, reduce heat, and simmer 30 minutes. Drain ribs, and arrange in a large shallow dish.

Combine apricots and remaining ingredients in container of an electric blender; blend until smooth. Pour sauce over ribs, turning to coat; cover and marinate in refrigerator 8 hours, turning occasionally.

Remove ribs from marinade, and place on a lightly greased rack in broiler pan, reserving marinade for basting. Bake at 425° for 40 minutes, basting twice. Yield: 6 servings.
Marjorie Henson
Benton, Kentucky

HOPPING JOHN
(pictured on page 43)

1 cup sliced celery
⅔ cup chopped onion
1 clove garlic, minced
1 tablespoon vegetable oil or
  bacon drippings
4 cups water
2 (10¾-ounce) cans condensed
  chicken broth, undiluted
1 (16-ounce) package frozen
  black-eyed peas
½ pound cooked ham, cut into
  cubes
¼ teaspoon crushed red pepper
1 bay leaf
3 cups cooked long-grain rice

Sauté celery, onion, and garlic in vegetable oil in a large Dutch oven until tender. Add water and remaining ingredients except rice. Bring to a boil; cover, reduce heat, and simmer 40 minutes or until peas are tender. Remove and discard bay leaf, and serve mixture over rice. Yield: 12 side dish servings or 6 main dish servings.

Note: To cook rice with black-eyed peas, stir 1 cup uncooked long-grain rice into peas after 40 minutes, and simmer an additional 35 minutes.
Dot Cordell
Gadsden, Alabama

TURNIP GREENS
(pictured on page 43)

2 pounds fresh turnip greens
5 slices bacon
4 cups water
1 tablespoon white vinegar
1 teaspoon salt
¼ to ½ teaspoon red pepper
  flakes
¼ teaspoon pepper

Wash greens thoroughly; drain. Tear into bite-size pieces. Combine greens, bacon, and water in a Dutch oven, and bring to a boil. Cover, reduce heat, and simmer 30 minutes. Add vinegar, salt, pepper flakes, and pepper. Cover and cook 1 hour. Remove bacon slices before serving. Yield: 6 servings.

Note: One (16-ounce) package of frozen turnip greens can be substituted for fresh turnip greens. Cook according to package directions, adding seasonings.
Aimee Goodman
Corryton, Tennessee

SKILLET CORNBREAD
(pictured on page 43)

1¼ cups yellow cornmeal
½ cup all-purpose flour
1 to 2 tablespoons sugar
1½ teaspoons baking powder
½ teaspoon baking soda
½ teaspoon salt
1 egg, beaten
1 cup buttermilk
¼ cup vegetable oil, divided

Combine first 6 ingredients in a large bowl; add egg, buttermilk, and 3 tablespoons oil, stirring just until dry ingredients are moistened.
Pour remaining 1 tablespoon oil into an 8-inch cast-iron skillet, and place in a 425° oven for 5 minutes or until hot. Remove from oven; spoon batter into skillet. Bake at 425° for 20 minutes or until lightly browned. Yield: about 6 servings.
Maxine Compton
Lampasas, Texas

QUICK!

Serve Vegetables

Vegetable side dishes add a lot to a meal, including color, texture, and nutrition. In many cases canned or frozen vegetables may work as well as fresh ones.

And don't hesitate to rely on convenience products or easy sauces, such as the one for Peach-Glazed Carrots, which combines peach preserves and melted butter.

QUICK CORN RELISH
(pictured on page 37)

1 (12-ounce) can Mexican-style
  corn
⅓ cup sugar
⅓ cup cider vinegar
⅓ cup sweet pickle relish
2 tablespoons instant minced
  onion
½ teaspoon celery seeds
Garnishes: Bibb lettuce, radicchio

Combine first 6 ingredients in a small saucepan; bring to a boil over medium heat. Reduce heat; cover and simmer 10 minutes.
Remove to a serving bowl; cover and refrigerate 4 to 8 hours, if desired. Serve with meat; garnish, if desired. Yield: 2 cups.
Microwave Directions: Combine first 6 ingredients in a 1-quart casserole. Cover and microwave corn mixture at MEDIUM HIGH (70% power) 5 to 7 minutes. Cover and refrigerate 4 to 8 hours, if desired.
Virginia McIntyre
Tampa, Florida

PEACH-GLAZED CARROTS

1 pound carrots, scraped and
  sliced
Water
⅓ cup peach preserves
1 tablespoon butter or margarine,
  melted

Cook carrots in 1 cup boiling water in a saucepan 5 minutes or until crisp-tender; drain.
Combine peach preserves and butter; stir into carrots. Cook over low heat until carrots are thoroughly heated. Yield: 4 servings.
Microwave Directions: Combine carrots, 2 tablespoons water, peach preserves, and butter in a 1-quart casserole. Cover and microwave at HIGH 7 to 8 minutes or until crisp-tender, stirring once. Serve with a slotted spoon.
Barbara Hill
Miami, Florida

JULIENNE ZUCCHINI AND CARROTS

1 tablespoon vegetable oil
1 tablespoon lemon juice
1 tablespoon white vinegar
1 teaspoon salt-free
   herb-and-spice blend
⅛ teaspoon garlic salt
2 large carrots
1 large zucchini

Combine first 5 ingredients; stir well, and set aside.

Cut carrots and zucchini into 2-inch-long x ½-inch-wide x ½-inch-thick sticks. Arrange carrots on a steaming rack, and place over boiling water; cover and steam 2½ minutes. Add zucchini to steaming rack, and steam an additional 2 minutes. Place vegetables in serving bowl. Pour sauce mixture over vegetables; toss gently to coat. Yield: 4 servings.

Microwave Directions: Combine first 5 ingredients in an 8-inch square baking dish; add carrot sticks, and toss gently to coat. Cover tightly with heavy-duty plastic wrap; fold back a small corner of wrap to allow steam to escape. Microwave at HIGH 5 minutes, stirring once. Add zucchini sticks, stirring gently. Cover and microwave at HIGH 2 to 2½ minutes or until vegetables are crisp-tender.

Joan E. Schultz
Maitland, Florida

SOUFFLÉ POTATOES

2⅔ cups mashed potato mix
1 egg, beaten
1 (2.8-ounce) can French-fried
   onions
¼ teaspoon salt
½ cup (2 ounces) shredded
   Cheddar cheese

Prepare mashed potato mix according to package directions. Add egg, onions, and salt, stirring until blended. Spoon mixture into a lightly greased 2-quart baking dish; sprinkle with cheese. Bake, uncovered, at 350° for 5 minutes or until cheese melts. Yield: 8 servings.

Microwave Directions: Prepare mashed potato mix in microwave according to package directions. Add egg, onions, and salt, stirring until blended. Spoon mixture into a lightly greased 2-quart baking dish. Microwave at HIGH 4 to 5 minutes. Sprinkle with cheese; cover and let stand 2 minutes or until cheese melts.

Shirley A. Edwards
Gainesville, Florida

ON THE LIGHT SIDE

Quenchers: Cool And Light

Exercising regularly and eating healthier top the list of New Year's resolutions for folks who want to get back into shape. To help them, we've put together a collection of beverages that will quench tall thirsts and replace fluids and minerals lost during long workouts. And each drink is satisfying enough to be a nutritious, low-calorie snack.

STRAWBERRY SPRITZER

2 (16-ounce) packages frozen
   unsweetened strawberries,
   thawed
2 (24-ounce) bottles white grape
   juice, chilled
1 (28-ounce) bottle unsweetened
   carbonated water, chilled

Place strawberries in container of an electric blender; process until smooth. Combine strawberry puree, white grape juice, and carbonated water. Yield: 12½ cups (122 calories per 1¼-cup serving).

☐ *0.4 gram protein, 0.1 gram fat, 31.4 grams carbohydrate, 0 milligrams cholesterol, 24 milligrams sodium, and 36 milligrams calcium.*

Christine McQueen
Annville, Kentucky

PINEAPPLE-BANANA SLUSH

1 medium-size ripe banana
1½ cups pineapple juice
2 tablespoons honey
Ice cubes

Combine first 3 ingredients in container of an electric blender. Add enough ice cubes to measure 3 cups; blend until smooth. Serve immediately. Yield: 3 cups (149 calories per 1-cup serving).

☐ *0.8 gram protein, 0.3 gram fat, 38.1 grams carbohydrate, 0 milligrams cholesterol, 2 milligrams sodium, and 24 milligrams calcium.*

APPLE COOLER

2 cups apple juice
1 (12-ounce) can apricot nectar
¼ cup lemon juice
¼ teaspoon bitters
2 (6½-ounce) bottles carbonated
   water, chilled

Combine first 4 ingredients; chill. Stir in carbonated water just before serving. Yield: 5 cups (89 calories per 1-cup serving).

☐ *0.3 gram protein, 0.1 gram fat, 22.6 grams carbohydrate, 0 milligrams cholesterol, 21 milligrams sodium, and 16 milligrams calcium.*

Mrs. Milton E. Miller
Orange Park, Florida

LEMON VELVET

1 (8-ounce) container lemon
  low-sugar, low-fat yogurt
1 (6-ounce) can frozen orange
  juice concentrate, undiluted
2½ cups skim milk
1 teaspoon vanilla extract
Ice cubes

Place half each of yogurt, orange
juice concentrate, skim milk, and vanilla in container of an electric
blender. Add enough ice cubes to
measure 3½ cups; blend until
smooth. Repeat procedure with remaining ingredients. Serve immediately. Yield: 7 cups (100 calories per
1-cup serving).

□ *4.9 grams protein, 0.6 gram fat,
18.5 grams carbohydrate, 2 milligrams cholesterol, 66 milligrams sodium, and 161 milligrams calcium.*

WHITE GRAPE PUNCH

1 (48-ounce) bottle apple juice
1 (24-ounce) bottle white grape
  juice
1 (12-ounce) can frozen lemonade
  concentrate, thawed and
  undiluted
1 (33.8-ounce) bottle club soda,
  chilled

Combine first 3 ingredients; chill
well. Stir in club soda just before
serving. Yield: 3½ quarts (122 calories per 1-cup serving).

□ *0.1 gram protein, 0.1 gram fat,
31.1 grams carbohydrate, 0 milligrams cholesterol, 20 milligrams sodium, and 18 milligrams calcium.*
June H. Johnson
Mocksville, North Carolina

MICROWAVE COOKERY

Fast And Fabulous Finales

Is dessert reserved just for special
occasions in your household? If preparation time is the deciding factor,
these microwave desserts can
quickly turn *any* meal into a special
occasion.

Your family will be delighted with
Microwave Chocolate Pie on an otherwise ordinary weeknight. Marshmallows add delicious flavor to this
dessert.

MICROWAVE CHOCOLATE PIE

2 cups miniature marshmallows
1 cup milk chocolate morsels
1 cup milk
1 (1-ounce) square unsweetened
  chocolate
1 cup whipping cream, whipped
Chocolate Crust

Combine marshmallows, chocolate
morsels, milk, and unsweetened
chocolate in a 2-quart glass mixing
bowl. Microwave at HIGH 4 to 5
minutes, stirring once. Cool. Fold in
whipped cream, and pour into prepared Chocolate Crust. Freeze until
firm. Yield: one 9-inch pie.

Chocolate Crust

⅓ cup butter or margarine
1½ cups chocolate wafer crumbs

Place butter in a small glass mixing
bowl. Microwave at HIGH 1 minute.
Add chocolate crumbs; mix well.
Press chocolate crumb mixture into a
9-inch pieplate. Microwave at HIGH
1 minute or until firm. Cool. Yield:
one 9-inch crust.   *Dorothy Grant*
Pensacola, Florida

CHOCOLATE-MINT PARFAITS
(pictured on page 44)

¼ cup butter or margarine
1½ cups chocolate wafer crumbs
  (about 30 wafers)
1 (10-ounce) package large
  marshmallows
¼ cup milk
¼ cup green crème de menthe
1 cup whipping cream, whipped
Garnishes: sweetened whipped
  cream, chocolate wafer crumbs

Place butter in a microwave-safe
bowl; microwave at HIGH 55 seconds or until butter melts. Stir in
chocolate wafer crumbs, mixing well.
Set aside.

Combine marshmallows and milk in
a microwave-safe bowl. Microwave
at HIGH 1½ to 2 minutes or until
marshmallows melt, stirring with a
wire whisk at 30-second intervals.
Cool until mixture is slightly thickened. Gently fold in crème de
menthe and whipped cream.

Spoon alternate layers of crumb
mixture and marshmallow mixture
into chilled parfait glasses. Garnish, if
desired. Yield: 6 servings.

Microwave Tips

■ To determine whether or not
a dish is microwave-safe, pour 1
cup water into a glass measure.
Place the measure in the microwave in the dish being tested.
Then microwave at HIGH for 1
minute. If the dish being tested
is warm and the water cool, the
dish is unsafe.

■ For a quick way to warm liqueurs for flaming, place the liqueur in your microwave oven
at HIGH; allow about 15 seconds for 2 tablespoons to ¼ cup
liqueur.

OATMEAL CHERRY-APPLE CRISP

1 cup regular oats, uncooked
1 cup all-purpose flour
1 cup firmly packed brown sugar
½ cup butter or margarine,
 softened
1 (16-ounce) can sour red
 cherries, drained
2 medium Granny Smith apples,
 peeled and chopped
1½ tablespoons quick-cooking
 tapioca
½ cup apple juice

Combine oats, flour, and brown sugar in a medium mixing bowl; mix well. Cut butter into oat mixture with a pastry blender until mixture resembles coarse meal. Spoon half of mixture into a lightly greased 8-inch square baking dish. Microwave at HIGH 3 minutes. Let crust cool 15 minutes.

Combine cherries, chopped apple, tapioca, and apple juice, mixing well; spoon over crust. Sprinkle remaining oat mixture over filling. Microwave at HIGH 13 to 14 minutes, giving dish a half-turn after 6 minutes. Yield: 8 servings.

Gayle Nicholas Scott
Chesapeake, Virginia

Entertaining Is Easy For This Man

Entertaining a large group sounds easy when Dale Safrit of Raleigh, North Carolina, explains how he coordinates meal preparation. "I clean the house and style the table the day before the event, and I always choose a dessert that I can make ahead of time, too."

He frequently marinates vegetables a day or two early, and he also bakes the bread and freezes it until needed. "The main thing I have to do the day of my party is prepare the main course," he explains proudly.

According to Dale, one reason he enjoys cooking is because he sticks to recipes that are easy to prepare. Here is Dale's menu designed to usher in the New Year.

**New Year's Eve Dinner
For Four**

**Spinach Salad
With Honey Dressing
Roast Duckling
With Tangerine Stuffing
Asparagus With Curry Sauce
Dilled Carrots
Sour Cream Yeast Rolls**

SPINACH SALAD WITH HONEY DRESSING

¼ teaspoon salt
1 clove garlic, crushed
⅓ cup honey
⅓ cup light olive oil
1 tablespoon lemon juice
¾ pound fresh spinach, torn
1 (8-ounce) can mandarin
 oranges, drained
¾ cup coarsely chopped walnuts,
 toasted

Sprinkle salt in a salad bowl; rub garlic into salt, using the back of a wooden spoon. Add honey, oil, and lemon juice to salad bowl; beat with a wire whisk. Refrigerate.

Add spinach and remaining ingredients to dressing; toss gently. Serve immediately. Yield: 4 to 6 servings.

ROAST DUCKLING WITH TANGERINE STUFFING

1 (5-pound) dressed duckling
¼ teaspoon salt
⅛ teaspoon pepper
½ lemon
Tangerine Stuffing
¼ teaspoon lemon-pepper
 seasoning
Garnishes: grapes, oranges,
 lemons, limes

Remove giblets and neck from duckling, and reserve for use in other recipes, if desired.

Rinse duckling with cold water, and pat dry with paper towels. Sprinkle cavity evenly with salt and pepper. Rub skin with lemon.

Spoon Tangerine Stuffing into cavity of duckling; close cavity with skewers, and truss. Prick skin with a fork at 2-inch intervals.

Place duckling, breast side up, on rack in a shallow roasting pan. Insert meat thermometer into thigh, making sure it does not touch bone.

Bake, uncovered, at 325° for 1½ hours. Sprinkle duckling with lemon-pepper seasoning; bake an additional 30 minutes or until meat thermometer registers 185°. Transfer duckling to a serving platter, and garnish with grapes, oranges, lemons, and limes, if desired. Yield: 4 servings.

Tangerine Stuffing

⅓ cup chopped celery
3 tablespoons butter or
 margarine, melted
2 tangerines
2⅔ cups herb-seasoned
 stuffing mix
2 cups cooked wild rice
⅓ cup cranberries
⅓ cup chicken broth
¼ teaspoon poultry
 seasoning

Sauté celery in butter until tender; set aside.

Peel, section, and chop tangerines; place in a large bowl. Add celery mixture, stuffing mix, wild rice, cranberries, chicken broth, and poultry seasoning; stir well. Yield: 5 cups.

ASPARAGUS WITH CURRY SAUCE

½ cup mayonnaise or salad
    dressing
2 to 3 teaspoons curry powder
1½ teaspoons lemon juice
1 pound fresh asparagus spears
    or 2 (10-ounce) packages
    frozen asparagus spears,
    thawed
2 tablespoons capers

Combine first 3 ingredients; cover and chill.

Snap off tough ends of asparagus; remove scales with a knife or vegetable peeler, if desired. Cook asparagus, covered, in a small amount of boiling water 6 to 8 minutes or until crisp-tender; drain.

Arrange asparagus spears on a serving plate; top with curry sauce, and sprinkle with capers. Yield: 4 servings.

DILLED CARROTS

2 (10-ounce) packages frozen
    whole baby carrots
1 teaspoon sugar
1 tablespoon butter or margarine
2 teaspoons dried whole dillweed

Cook carrots according to package directions, adding sugar to the water. Drain well. Add butter and dillweed, tossing gently until carrots are evenly coated. Yield: 4 to 6 servings.

Tip: *Use finely chopped fresh herbs whenever possible. Dried whole herbs are usually the next best choice since they maintain their strength longer than the commercially ground form. Remember to use 3 times more fresh herbs in a recipe if it calls for the more potent dried form.*

SOUR CREAM YEAST ROLLS

¼ cup butter or margarine
½ cup sour cream
¼ cup sugar
½ teaspoon salt
1 package dry yeast
¼ cup warm water (105° to 115°)
1 egg, beaten
2 cups all-purpose flour
2 egg whites, lightly beaten

Combine first 4 ingredients in a small saucepan; cook over low heat until butter melts. Cool to 105° to 115°.

Dissolve yeast in warm water in a large mixing bowl; let stand 5 minutes. Stir in sour cream mixture and egg. Gradually add flour to yeast mixture, mixing well. Cover and refrigerate at least 8 hours.

Punch dough down, and divide in half. Roll each portion to a 12-inch circle on a floured surface. Cut each circle into 12 wedges; roll each wedge, jellyroll fashion, beginning at wide end. Place on greased baking sheets, point side down.

Cover and let rise in a warm place (85°), free from drafts, 1 hour or until doubled in bulk. Brush with egg white. Bake at 375° for 12 minutes or until rolls are golden brown. Yield: 2 dozen.

Wonderful Ways With Broccoli And Cauliflower

Just to name a few attributes of those year-round favorites broccoli and cauliflower, let's start with versatility, nutrition, and flavor.

Take care to preserve the nutritional value and color of these excellent sources of water-soluble vitamin C by cooking them in as little water and for as short a time as possible. Save the vitamin-packed cooking water for later use in soups. To keep the true green of fresh broccoli, try leaving the lid off during the first five minutes of cooking time. And a little lemon juice or white vinegar added to the cooking water will keep cauliflower's white bright.

CAULIFLOWER SOUFFLÉ

1 (2¼-pound) cauliflower
2 eggs, separated
2 green onions, chopped
½ cup (2 ounces) shredded
    Cheddar cheese
2 tablespoons milk
2 tablespoons butter or
    margarine, melted
½ teaspoon salt
¼ teaspoon white pepper
2 tablespoons grated Parmesan
    cheese

Cook cauliflower in a small amount of boiling water 6 to 8 minutes or until crisp-tender; drain well. Cut cauliflower into 4 sections.

Position knife blade in food processor bowl; add cauliflower, and process until smooth. Set aside.

Cut a piece of aluminum foil long enough to fit around a 1-quart soufflé dish, allowing a 1-inch overlap; fold foil lengthwise into thirds. Lightly oil one side of foil and bottom of dish. Wrap foil around outside of dish, oiled side against dish, allowing it to extend 3 inches above rim to form a collar; secure with string.

Beat egg yolks until thick and lemon colored; combine yolks, cauliflower, chopped green onions, shredded cheese, milk, melted butter, salt, and pepper.

Beat egg whites (at room temperature) until stiff but not dry; gently fold into cauliflower mixture. Pour into prepared soufflé dish, and sprinkle with Parmesan cheese. Bake at 350° for 50 to 55 minutes or until soufflé is puffed and set. Remove collar, and serve soufflé immediately. Yield: 6 servings.   *Gwen Louer*
Roswell, Georgia

FRIED CAULIFLOWER

2 eggs, beaten
1 cup all-purpose flour
½ teaspoon salt
2 tablespoons olive oil
¾ cup beer
1 large cauliflower, cut into
    flowerets
2 tablespoons lemon juice
3 tablespoons minced fresh
    parsley
Vegetable oil

Combine first 4 ingredients in a bowl; stir in beer. Refrigerate 2 to 3 hours.

Place cauliflower in vegetable steamer over boiling water; cover and steam 3 to 5 minutes or until crisp-tender. Drain and cool. Combine lemon juice and parsley in a large bowl; add cauliflower, and toss gently. Cover and marinate 1 hour.

Pour oil to a depth of 2 to 3 inches into a Dutch oven; heat to 375°. Dip cauliflower in batter; fry in oil until golden. Drain on paper towels. Serve immediately. Yield: 6 to 8 servings.
Mary B. Quesenberry
Dugspur, Virginia

RED, WHITE, AND GREEN SALAD

½ cup sour cream
½ cup mayonnaise or salad
    dressing
⅛ teaspoon salt
⅛ teaspoon pepper
2½ cups broccoli flowerets
2½ cups cauliflowerets
1 medium tomato, chopped
2 green onions, chopped
Lettuce leaves

Combine first 4 ingredients; stir well. Combine broccoli, cauliflower, tomato, and green onions. Add mayonnaise mixture, and toss gently. Chill 3 to 4 hours. Line a serving bowl with lettuce leaves, and fill with salad just before serving. Yield: 10 to 12 servings.
Phyllis McCalop
Cleveland, Mississippi

SWISS ALPINE QUICHE

Pastry for 9-inch pie
1 (10-ounce) package frozen
    chopped broccoli
2 cups cubed cooked ham
2 cups (8 ounces) shredded Swiss
    cheese
3 tablespoons minced onion
1½ cups milk, heated
3 eggs, beaten
⅛ teaspoon salt
⅛ teaspoon pepper

Roll dough to ⅛-inch thickness on a lightly floured surface. Place in a 9-inch quiche dish; trim off excess pastry along edges. Set aside.

Cook broccoli according to package directions, omitting salt; drain well. Layer half each of broccoli, ham, and cheese in pastry shell; repeat layers. Sprinkle onion over top. Combine milk and eggs; add salt and pepper, mixing well. Pour egg mixture into pastry shell.

Bake at 450° for 10 minutes. Reduce heat to 325°, and bake 30 to 35 minutes. Let stand 5 to 10 minutes before serving. Yield: one 9-inch quiche.
Dee Christensen
Cockeysville, Maryland

A Lesson On Poaching Fish

Poaching is an excellent low-fat cooking method for fish. It preserves the delicate texture of the fish and enhances its deep flavor. It's important to immerse the fish completely in the poaching liquid so that an exchange of flavors between the fish and the cooking liquid will take place.

Large fish are most easily cooked in a fish poacher, a long narrow piece of cookware with a removable tray. Or they can be cut in half crosswise so that they will fit in a smaller container. A large skillet, saucepan, or small turkey roaster can be used to poach smaller fish, fish steaks, and fillets. Most firm-fleshed fish can be poached.

To poach fish, wrap in cheesecloth so that it can be removed from the poaching liquid without breaking. Have the poaching liquid simmering when fish is lowered into it; then reheat the liquid to barely simmering for cooking. Poach 10 minutes per inch of thickness, turning halfway through the cooking time. (To determine thickness, measure thickest part of fish with a ruler.) Fish is done when the flesh becomes opaque and flakes easily with a fork.

POACHED FISH WITH VEGETABLES

2 quarts water
2 cups dry white wine
1 (8-ounce) bottle clam juice
3 medium onions, sliced
2 carrots, cut into 1-inch pieces
3 celery stalks with leaves, cut
    into 1-inch pieces
2 teaspoons salt
Bouquet garni (recipe follows)
1 (3½-pound) dressed red snapper
1 pound baby carrots, steamed
1 pound snow pea pods, steamed
1 pound new potatoes, steamed
1 pound green beans, steamed
1 pint cherry tomatoes
½ pound fresh mushrooms
Mustard Sauce

Combine first 8 ingredients in a fish poacher; bring to a boil. Cover, reduce heat, and simmer 30 minutes. Cool to room temperature; strain. Discard vegetables and bouquet garni. Return liquid to poacher.

Wrap fish in cheesecloth; tie ends with string. Place fish in poaching liquid; add water to cover fish 1 to 1½ inches. Cover and bring to a slow simmer; simmer 15 minutes. Remove from heat, leaving fish in liquid 15 minutes. Remove fish from liquid, and remove cheesecloth. Remove and discard skin, and place fish on a large platter. Arrange vegetables around fish. Serve with Mustard Sauce. Yield: 6 servings.

Bouquet Garni

4 fresh parsley sprigs
1 fresh tarragon sprig
1 fresh thyme sprig
2 bay leaves
10 peppercorns

Tie all ingredients in a cheesecloth bag. Yield: 1 bouquet garni.

Mustard Sauce

⅔ cup mayonnaise or salad
  dressing
2 tablespoons Dijon mustard
¾ teaspoon minced fresh tarragon

Combine all ingredients, stirring well; cover and chill. Yield: ¾ cup.

Judy McFarlin
Potomac, Maryland

Fish Tips

■ When buying whole fish, don't discard the head and tail; when cooked with the fish or by themselves, they make good fish stock for sauces, aspics, and chowders or other soups.

■ As a rule, thawed fish should not be kept longer than one day before cooking; the flavor is better if it is cooked immediately after thawing.

■ Fresh fish has practically no "fish" odor. The fish odor becomes more pronounced with the passage of time, but should not be strong when fish are bought.

Super Bowl Sandwich

Attention sports fans! Here's just the fare for big gridiron action. Mike Singleton's Sausage-Stuffed French Loaf fits the fun mood of the day, and you can bet he'll be serving it to his Memphis, Tennessee, friends during the game.

SAUSAGE-STUFFED FRENCH LOAF

1 (16-ounce) loaf French bread
½ pound bulk pork sausage
½ pound ground chuck
1 medium onion, chopped
1 cup (4 ounces) shredded
  mozzarella cheese
1 egg
¼ cup chopped fresh parsley
1 teaspoon Dijon mustard
¼ teaspoon fennel seeds
¼ teaspoon salt
¼ teaspoon pepper
2 tablespoons butter or
  margarine
1 clove garlic, crushed

Cut off ends of French bread loaf, and set ends aside. Hollow out the center of loaf with a long serrated bread knife, leaving a ½-inch-thick shell. Position knife blade in food processor bowl; add bread removed from inside the loaf. Process to make coarse crumbs. Set bread shell and crumbs aside.
  Cook sausage, beef, and onion in a skillet until meat is browned, stirring to crumble meat; drain well. Add 1 cup reserved breadcrumbs, cheese, and next 6 ingredients, mixing well. Spoon meat mixture into bread shell, and replace loaf ends, securing with wooden picks.
  Melt butter in a small saucepan; add garlic, and cook about 1 minute.

Brush butter mixture over loaf. Wrap loaf in aluminum foil, leaving open slightly on top. Bake at 400° for 20 minutes or until thoroughly heated and cheese is melted. Cut into 4 pieces. Yield: 4 servings.

Microwave Puddings

Introduce your family and friends to these microwave puddings, which take advantage of fresh fall produce.

BUTTERNUT SQUASH PUDDING

1 medium butternut squash
  (about 2½ pounds)
2 eggs, beaten
½ cup half-and-half
⅓ cup sugar
2 tablespoons butter or margarine
½ teaspoon ground cinnamon
⅛ teaspoon ground nutmeg
½ teaspoon grated lemon rind
2 teaspoons lemon juice
Sweetened whipped cream

Pierce squash 6 or 8 times with a fork. Place squash on paper towels in microwave oven. Microwave, uncovered, at HIGH 16 to 18 minutes, turning squash after 8 minutes. Let stand 5 minutes.
  Cut squash in half, and remove and discard seeds. Scoop out pulp, and discard shell.
  Combine squash pulp, eggs, and next 7 ingredients in a mixing bowl; beat at medium speed of an electric mixer until smooth. Spoon squash mixture into an 8-inch square baking dish. Microwave, uncovered, at HIGH 15 minutes; stir. Microwave at MEDIUM (50% power) 5 minutes. Let stand 5 minutes. Serve with sweetened whipped cream. Yield: 4 to 6 servings.

PUMPKIN PUDDING

½ cup pecans
¾ cup vanilla wafer crumbs
2 tablespoons sugar
1 teaspoon grated orange rind
2 tablespoons butter or
    margarine, melted
1 (3-ounce) package cream
    cheese, softened
½ cup firmly packed brown sugar
3 eggs
⅓ cup orange juice
1 teaspoon grated orange rind
½ teaspoon ground cardamom
1 cup cooked, mashed pumpkin
Garnishes: whipped cream,
    vanilla wafers, orange rind

Spread pecans in a single layer in a pieplate. Microwave at HIGH 2 minutes, stirring after 1 minute. Chop pecans, and set ¼ cup chopped pecans aside.

Combine ¼ cup chopped pecans and next 4 ingredients, mixing well. Divide mixture into 8 (6-ounce) greased custard cups or ramekins. Press crumb mixture evenly over bottom of custard cups. Microwave at HIGH 2 minutes; set aside.

Beat cream cheese with an electric mixer until light and fluffy; gradually add brown sugar, mixing well. Add eggs and orange juice, mixing well. Add 1 teaspoon orange rind, cardamom, and pumpkin; mix until smooth. Pour pumpkin mixture into prepared custard cups.

Arrange custard cups in a circle in oven. Microwave, uncovered, at MEDIUM HIGH (70% power) 6 to 7 minutes or until pudding is set, rearranging cups halfway through cooking time. Garnish with reserved ¼ cup chopped pecans and whipped cream, vanilla wafers, or orange rind, if desired. Serve pudding warm or chilled. Yield: 8 servings.

Taco Salad For Two

Taco salad is a popular item found on restaurant menus. This recipe for Taco Salad is just the right amount for two. The meat is served in a sunburst-shaped taco shell and placed on layers of lettuce, tomato, olives, and avocado.

TACO SALAD

2 (9-inch) flour tortillas
Vegetable oil
½ pound ground beef
½ cup water
2 tablespoons taco seasoning mix
2 tablespoons chopped green
    onions
½ medium head iceberg lettuce,
    shredded
1 small tomato, chopped
¼ cup ripe olives, sliced
1 small avocado, sliced
Garnishes: chopped tomatoes,
    shredded Cheddar cheese,
    sliced ripe olives, and sour
    cream
Commercial picante sauce

Cut tortillas into sunburst design, using scissors. Pour oil to a depth of 3 inches into a medium saucepan 1 to 1½ inches smaller than the diameter of the tortilla; heat to 375°. Push 1 tortilla into oil, using ladle, and press down in center. Cook 45 to 60 seconds or until golden brown. Drain. Repeat cooking procedure with remaining tortilla.

Cook beef in a skillet until meat is browned, stirring to crumble; drain. Return meat to skillet; add water and taco seasoning. Simmer mixture 10 minutes; stir in onions.

Layer half each of lettuce, chopped tomato, ¼ cup sliced olives, and avocado on serving plates. Fill tortilla cups with meat mixture, and place on top of salads. Garnish, if desired. Serve with picante sauce. Yield: 2 servings.

The Jeweled Crown Of Mardi Gras

The twelfth day of Christmas ends a celebration for many, but in New Orleans and other Southern cities near the Gulf, the party is just beginning. Whether known as Twelfth Night, Epiphany, or King's Day, one thing is certain: On January 6, centuries-old traditions once again come to life and reign for several fun-filled weeks of merrymaking. This season even boasts its own dessert, King Cake—a confection as rich in history as it is in flavor.

The cake is decorated in the royal colors, honoring the three kings who visited the Christ Child on Epiphany.

The King Cake tradition is thought to have been brought to New Orleans from France in 1870. The Creoles placed a bean or pea inside the cake before serving it, and the favor's finder was named king or queen for a day. Today a tiny plastic doll is the common prize, and the honored recipient is bound by custom to host the next party and provide the King Cake.

KING CAKE

¼ cup butter or margarine
1 (16-ounce) carton sour cream
⅓ cup sugar
1 teaspoon salt
2 packages dry yeast
1 tablespoon sugar
½ cup warm water (105° to 115°)
2 eggs
6 to 6½ cups all-purpose flour,
    divided
½ cup sugar
1½ teaspoons ground cinnamon
⅓ cup butter or margarine,
    softened
Colored Frostings
Colored Sugars

Combine first 4 ingredients in a saucepan; heat until butter melts, stirring occasionally. Let mixture cool to 105° to 115°.

Dissolve yeast and 1 tablespoon sugar in warm water in a large bowl; let stand 5 minutes. Add butter mixture, eggs, and 2 cups flour; beat at medium speed of an electric mixer 2 minutes or until smooth. Gradually stir in enough remaining flour to make a soft dough.

Turn dough out onto a lightly floured surface, and knead until smooth and elastic (about 10 minutes). Place in a well-greased bowl, turning to grease top. Cover and let rise in a warm place (85°), free from drafts, 1 hour or until dough is doubled in bulk.

Combine ½ cup sugar and cinnamon; set aside.

Punch dough down, and divide in half. Turn one portion of dough out onto a lightly floured surface, and roll to a 28- x 10-inch rectangle. Spread half each of butter and cinnamon mixture on dough. Roll dough, jellyroll fashion, starting at long side. Gently place dough roll, seam side down, on a lightly greased baking sheet. Bring ends of dough together to form an oval ring, moistening and pinching the edges together to seal. Cover and let rise in a warm place, free from drafts, 20 minutes or until doubled in bulk. Bake at 375° for 15 to 20 minutes or until golden.

Repeat procedure with remaining dough, butter, and cinnamon mixture. Decorate each cake with bands of Colored Frostings, and sprinkle with Colored Sugars. Yield: 2 cakes.

Colored Frostings

3 cups sifted powdered sugar
3 tablespoons butter or
  margarine, melted
3 to 5 tablespoons milk
¼ teaspoon vanilla extract
1 to 2 drops each of green,
  yellow, red, and blue food
  coloring

Combine powdered sugar and melted butter. Add milk (at room temperature) to reach desired consistency for drizzling; stir in vanilla. Divide frosting into 3 batches, tinting one green, one yellow, and combining red and blue food coloring for purple frosting. Yield: about 1½ cups.

Colored Sugars

1½ cups sugar, divided
1 to 2 drops each of green,
  yellow, red, and blue food
  coloring

Combine ½ cup sugar and drop of green food coloring in a jar. Place lid on jar, and shake vigorously to evenly mix color with sugar. Repeat procedure with ½ cup sugar and yellow food coloring. For purple, combine 1 drop red and 1 drop blue food coloring before adding to ½ cup sugar. Yield: ½ cup of each color.

Fran Ginn
Columbia, Mississippi

Sip A Hot Cider

Whether it's for large crowds or single servings, hot cider takes the chill off a cold winter day and leaves all who partake warm and satisfied. Often thought to be made exclusively from apples, cider actually describes the juice pressed from any fruit.

Several of these recipes make large yields of steaming beverage. If any is left over, just cover and chill it up to a week. Reheat it in a saucepan or in the microwave oven; 1 cup of cider will reheat in 1½ to 2 minutes at HIGH.

MULLED GRAPE JUICE

1 quart grape juice
1 lemon, sliced
1 orange, sliced
2 (4-inch) sticks cinnamon
Dash of ground allspice

Combine all ingredients in a Dutch oven. Bring to a boil; reduce heat, and simmer 5 minutes. Remove and discard cinnamon sticks before serving. Yield: 5 cups.

Mrs. Edward R. Haug
Sulphur, Louisiana

HOT PINEAPPLE NECTAR

1 quart pineapple juice
2 cups apple cider
1 cup orange juice
1 (12-ounce) can apricot nectar
2 (3-inch) sticks cinnamon,
  broken into pieces
1 teaspoon whole cloves
4 whole cardamom seeds, crushed

Combine first 4 ingredients in a Dutch oven. Tie broken cinnamon sticks, cloves, and cardamom in a cheesecloth bag; add spice bag to juice mixture, and bring to a boil. Reduce heat, and simmer 5 minutes. Remove and discard spice bag before serving beverage. Yield: 2 quarts.

Dorothy Burgess
Huntsville, Texas

HOT APPLE CIDER

7 cups apple cider
2 cups orange juice
½ cup honey
3 whole cloves
1 apple, peeled
1 orange, sliced

Combine first 3 ingredients in a Dutch oven. Insert cloves into apple; add apple and orange slices to juice mixture, and bring to a boil. Reduce heat, and simmer 15 minutes. Remove cider from heat, and let stand about 5 minutes. Yield: 2 quarts.

Frieda Wolf
Laporte, Texas

HOT CRANAPPLE GLOGG

½ cup sugar
1 (32-ounce) bottle
  cranberry-apple drink
2 cups Burgundy or other dry red
  wine
½ cup water
½ cup raisins
4 whole cloves
1 (2-inch) stick cinnamon
3 whole cardamom seeds, lightly
  crushed
½ cup slivered almonds (optional)
Garnish: orange slices

Combine first 4 ingredients in a large
Dutch oven; let stand until sugar dissolves, stirring often.

Tie raisins, cloves, cinnamon stick,
cardamom, and, if desired, almonds
in a cheesecloth bag; add spice bag
to juice mixture, and cook over low
heat just until hot. Discard spice bag.
Serve glogg with orange slices as
garnish, if desired. Yield: 1½ quarts.

Note: To make glogg without alcohol, omit Burgundy and sugar, and
add 2 cups cranberry-apple drink.
A. Irving
Gainesville, Florida

PERKY CINNAMON-APPLE JUICE

1 gallon apple juice
1 (33.8-ounce) bottle ginger ale
1 teaspoon whole cloves
2 (3-inch) sticks cinnamon,
  broken into pieces
¾ cup red cinnamon candies

Pour apple juice and ginger ale into a
30-cup electric percolator; place
spices and candy in percolator basket. Perk through complete cycle.
Yield: 7½ quarts. *Deryle Harsell*
Spring, Texas

FOUR-FRUIT WASSAIL

1 gallon apple juice
2 cups orange juice
2 cups pineapple juice
⅔ cup lemon juice
4 (4-inch) sticks cinnamon
1 cup bourbon or brandy
Cinnamon sticks
  (optional)

Combine apple juice, orange juice,
pineapple juice, lemon juice, and 4
cinnamon sticks in a large Dutch
oven. Bring mixture to a boil; reduce
heat, and simmer 30 minutes. Stir in
bourbon.

Remove 4 cinnamon sticks from
hot juice mixture. Serve wassail with
fresh cinnamon sticks, if desired.
Yield: 5 quarts.

Anne Fowler Newell
Johnsonville, South Carolina

From Our Kitchen To Yours

Whether you are a novice or an experienced cook, kitchen accidents can
happen without warning. Among re-
sulting injuries, burns are the number
one cause of disfigurement and pain.
For that reason, a knowledge of first
aid for burns and an awareness of
safety precautions are important.

First Aid Treatment

If you get burned, follow the ad-
vice of Dr. Robert E. Howe, a Birmingham, Alabama, plastic surgeon:
"Before seeking medical help, the
important factor in treating burns is
to minimize the problem by initially
treating them with cool water."

Some household burns are classi-
fied as first-degree burns. Most per-
sons have experienced a sunburn,
the most common first-degree burn.
The skin turns red, bringing discomfort and mild pain. Unless the expo-
sure is extensive, the burn isn't too
serious. Cool, wet dressings and a
soothing ointment usually bring relief.

A more serious second-degree
burn blisters the skin and causes intense pain. Unless the burn covers a
very small area, medical attention is
essential. Run cool water over the
affected area until the pain lessens;
then wrap in a clean, dry cloth, and
seek medical attention. Don't apply
lotion or ointment; it will trap the
heat and can cause infection. The
area needs treatment with an antibi-
otic ointment and a gauze bandage.

Immediate attention and medical
treatment should be given to a third-
degree burn—the most serious. Immerse the injured area in a tub of
clean, cool water, or wrap the area
in towels saturated with clean, cool
water, and call for emergency help.

Preventive Steps

For safety, deep-fat frying or
cooking with a hot liquid requires
good judgment. If grease catches
fire, place a lid over the Dutch oven
or skillet to smother the flames; then
turn off the burner. Do not throw
water or anything else on a grease
fire, and do not risk scalding a child
or catching your clothes on fire by
picking up the pan and running to the
sink or out the back door.

Following basic safety rules and
eliminating any hazards can make
your kitchen a safer place and reduce
the risk of a burn injury. For example, never store tempting treats near
the cooktop because a child looking
for a snack could reach across a
burner. And when cooking, don't
leave the kitchen unattended. Turn
pot handles inward, and when possible, use the back burners so that
saucepans are less likely to be
knocked off the edge. Avoid using
towels or other cloths in place of pot
holders or oven mitts, and avoid
wearing long, loose-fitting sleeves.
Keep young children out of the way
by designating a safe play area away
from the cooktop, oven, and sink;
then give them toy pans for play.

FEBRUARY

Hot cooked rice topped with spicy red beans, vegetable-rich gumbo, savory Jambalaya—imagine these Cajun-Creole recipes made light and healthy. Even our romantic dinner for two offers a heart-healthy menu with calories trimmed down. And opening this chapter are delicious home-baked pot pies, dressed up with fancy pastry designs.

Savory Pot Pies

We look to the winners of the test of time for security, and clinging to Mama's apron strings is just fine as long as they lead to her dependable home-cooked favorites—one of the greatest comforts life has to offer.

Many generations have put tender, flaky pot pies at the top of the list of dependable home-cooked favorites. These savory, filled pastries long ago found a permanent niche in Southern cuisine.

TURKEY POT PIE

1¼ pounds turkey tenderloins
8 cups water
1 medium onion, quartered
1 stalk celery, cut into fourths
1 bay leaf
1 teaspoon salt
½ teaspoon pepper
¼ teaspoon dried whole thyme
¼ teaspoon poultry seasoning
4 small red potatoes, peeled and cubed
1 (16-ounce) package frozen mixed vegetables
¼ cup butter or margarine
⅓ cup all-purpose flour
3 hard-cooked eggs, sliced
½ teaspoon salt
¼ teaspoon pepper
Pastry for 9-inch pie

Combine first 9 ingredients in a Dutch oven; cover and cook over medium heat 30 minutes. Remove turkey, and chop meat into bite-size pieces; set aside. Strain broth, reserving 2¾ cups.

Return broth to Dutch oven; bring to a boil. Add potatoes and mixed vegetables; cover and cook 10 to 12 minutes or until potatoes are tender. Drain, reserving broth.

Melt butter in a heavy saucepan over low heat; add flour, stirring until mixture is smooth. Cook 1 minute, stirring constantly. Gradually add broth; cook over medium heat, stirring constantly, until mixture is thickened and bubbly. Stir in turkey, vegetables, eggs, salt, and pepper.

Spoon mixture into a lightly greased 2½-quart casserole. Place pastry over filling. Trim edges; seal, and flute. Cut several slits in top pastry to allow steam to escape. Bake at 375° for 20 to 25 minutes or until golden brown. Yield: 6 to 8 servings.
Delana Smith
Birmingham, Alabama

SAVORY SOUTHERN CHICKEN PIE
(pictured on pages 38 and 39)

½ pound bulk pork sausage
¼ cup butter or margarine
⅓ cup all-purpose flour
¼ teaspoon salt
⅛ teaspoon pepper
1 (14½-ounce) can ready-to-serve chicken broth
1 cup milk
2 cups chopped cooked chicken
1 (10-ounce) package frozen English peas, thawed and drained
Savory Pastry

Cook sausage in a skillet over medium heat until browned, stirring to crumble meat. Drain on paper towels; set aside.

Melt butter in a 3-quart heavy saucepan over low heat; add flour, salt, and pepper, stirring until smooth. Cook 1 minute, stirring constantly. Gradually add broth and milk; cook over medium heat, stirring constantly, until thickened and bubbly. Stir in chicken, peas, and sausage; cook until thoroughly heated. Pour chicken mixture into 4 individual 1½-cup baking dishes or an 8-inch square baking dish.

Roll Savory Pastry on a lightly floured surface to ¼-inch thickness in a slightly smaller shape than the individual dishes or large dish; scallop edges. Place pastry over chicken mixture (edges should not touch side of dish). Decorate with pastry cutouts, if desired. Bake at 425° for 20 to 25 minutes or until crust is browned. Yield: 4 servings.

Savory Pastry

1 cup all-purpose flour
1 teaspoon celery seeds
½ teaspoon salt
½ teaspoon paprika
⅓ cup shortening
2 to 3 tablespoons water

Combine flour, celery seeds, salt, and paprika in a large bowl; cut in shortening with a pastry blender until mixture resembles coarse meal. With a fork, stir in enough water, 1 tablespoon at a time, to moisten dry ingredients. Shape dough into a ball. Yield: enough pastry to top 4 individual pies or one 8-inch square pie.
Linda Magers
Clemmons, North Carolina

NANA'S CHICKEN PIE

(pictured on pages 38 and 39)

½ cup pearl onions
½ cup chopped carrots
¼ cup chopped green pepper
½ cup frozen English peas,
    thawed
½ cup chopped onion
¼ cup vegetable oil
¼ cup all-purpose flour
2 cups chicken broth
¼ teaspoon pepper
2 cups chopped cooked
    chicken
1½ cups all-purpose flour
2¼ teaspoons baking powder
½ teaspoon salt
⅓ cup shortening
½ cup milk

Cook pearl onions and carrots in boiling water to cover 5 minutes. Add green pepper; continue to cook 3 minutes. Remove from heat, and drain. Add peas; set aside.

Sauté ½ cup chopped onion in oil in a large skillet until tender and lightly browned. Remove half of onions to a paper towel; set aside for use in biscuits.

Add ¼ cup flour to onion and oil in skillet, stirring until smooth. Cook 1 minute, stirring constantly. Gradually add broth, and cook, stirring constantly, until mixture is thickened and bubbly. Stir in pepper. Add vegetables and chicken; simmer 5 minutes, stirring often. Pour into a lightly greased 9-inch square baking dish; set aside.

Combine 1½ cups flour, baking powder, and salt; cut in shortening with a pastry blender until mixture resembles coarse meal. Add milk and reserved onion, stirring just until dry ingredients are moistened. Turn dough out onto a lightly floured surface, and knead 4 or 5 times.

Roll dough to ¼-inch thickness; cut with a 2-inch chicken-shaped or round cutter.

Arrange biscuits on top of chicken mixture; bake at 450° for 10 to 12 minutes or until biscuits are lightly browned. Yield: 4 servings.

Carolyne M. Carnevale
Ormond Beach, Florida

HAM POT PIE

2 cups water
1½ teaspoons vegetable-flavored
    bouillon granules
¼ cup butter or margarine
¼ cup all-purpose flour
1 (5-ounce) can evaporated milk
3 cups cubed cooked ham
1 (16-ounce) can peas and
    carrots, drained
1 (4-ounce) can sliced
    mushrooms, drained
1 teaspoon onion powder
½ teaspoon dried whole thyme
¼ teaspoon pepper
2 cups all-purpose flour
¾ cup cornmeal
1 tablespoon baking powder
1 teaspoon salt
½ cup shortening
1 cup milk
Paprika
1 cup (4 ounces) shredded
    Cheddar cheese

Combine water and bouillon granules; set aside.

Melt butter in a skillet over low heat; add ¼ cup flour, stirring until smooth. Cook 1 minute, stirring constantly. Gradually add bouillon mixture and evaporated milk; cook over medium heat, stirring constantly, until mixture is thickened and bubbly. Add ham and next 5 ingredients; cook over low heat, stirring constantly, until thoroughly heated. Spoon into a lightly greased 13- x 9- x 2-inch baking dish.

Combine 2 cups flour, cornmeal, baking powder, and salt; cut in shortening with a pastry blender until mixture resembles coarse meal. Add 1 cup milk, stirring just until dry ingredients are moistened. Turn dough out onto a lightly floured surface, and knead 4 or 5 times.

Roll dough to a 12- x 10-inch rectangle; sprinkle with paprika. Sprinkle cheese over paprika. Starting with a long side, roll jellyroll fashion, turning seam side down. Slice into 15 biscuits; arrange over ham mixture. Bake at 425° for 15 minutes or until biscuits are golden. Yield: 8 servings.

Roberta McPherson
Birmingham, Alabama

SAUSAGE-AND-CORNBREAD PIE

1 pound bulk pork sausage
1 cup chopped onion
1 clove garlic, crushed
1 (28-ounce) can tomatoes,
    undrained
1 (4-ounce) can chopped green
    chiles, undrained
1 cup frozen whole kernel corn
1 teaspoon chili powder
1 cup yellow cornmeal
⅔ cup all-purpose flour
2 teaspoons baking powder
½ teaspoon salt
2 teaspoons sugar
1 egg, beaten
⅔ cup milk
¼ cup vegetable oil

Cook sausage, onion, and garlic in a large skillet over medium heat until meat is browned, stirring to crumble meat; drain. Add tomatoes, chiles, corn, and chili powder; simmer 20 minutes. Spoon mixture into a lightly greased 8-inch square baking dish, and set aside.

Combine cornmeal and next 4 ingredients in a medium bowl, mixing well. Combine egg, milk, and oil in a small bowl; add to dry ingredients, stirring just until moistened. Spread cornmeal mixture evenly over sausage mixture. Bake at 375° for 40 minutes or until golden brown. Yield: 4 to 6 servings.

Nora Henshaw
Okemah, Oklahoma

Tip: *Avoid using together two strong-flavored herbs, such as bay, rosemary, or sage, as the flavors will fight each other. Instead, use a strong herb in combination with a milder one. The accent herbs are slightly milder than the strong herbs and include basil, tarragon, and oregano. Medium herbs are dillweed, marjoram, winter savory, fennel, mint, and lemon thyme. The group of delicate herbs includes chervil, chives, parsley, and summer savory.*

LAMB PIE
(pictured on pages 38 and 39)

1 (4- to 5-pound) lamb shoulder
6 cups water
1 teaspoon salt
½ teaspoon pepper
1 cup pearl onions
½ cup water
⅓ cup vegetable oil
⅓ cup all-purpose flour
½ teaspoon salt
½ teaspoon pepper
1 teaspoon browning-and-
   seasoning sauce
1 (10-ounce) package frozen
   English peas, thawed
Pastry for 9-inch pie
Poppyseeds

Place first 4 ingredients in a large Dutch oven. Bring to a boil; cover, reduce heat, and simmer 1½ hours or until tender. Remove lamb, reserving broth. Cut lamb into ½-inch cubes. Set aside. Chill broth, and remove fat. Add water, if necessary, to equal 3 cups. Set aside.

Combine onions and ½ cup water in a small saucepan; bring to a boil. Reduce heat, and simmer 10 to 15 minutes or until onions are tender. Drain and set aside.

Heat oil in a heavy saucepan; add flour, ½ teaspoon salt, and ½ teaspoon pepper. Cook 1 minute, stirring constantly. Gradually add 3 cups reserved lamb broth; cook over medium heat, stirring constantly, until thickened and bubbly. Add browning-and-seasoning sauce, onions, lamb, and peas, mixing well. Pour into a lightly greased 2-quart casserole.

Roll pastry to a 9-inch circle. Sprinkle with poppyseeds, and continue to roll pastry until poppy seeds are pressed into pastry. Place on top of pie; fold edges under, and flute. Cut an "X" in center of pastry. Starting with four points in center, roll flaps of pastry toward outer edges, exposing lamb filling. Bake at 400° for 25 to 30 minutes. Yield: 6 servings.
Mike Singleton
Memphis, Tennessee

ON THE LIGHT SIDE

Cook It Light, Cook It Cajun

For cooks interested in healthy cooking, Cajun-Creole recipes are often the last ones to be trimmed. Basic modification, however, can yield light results. For example, try substituting vegetable oil for bacon grease in the roux for gumbo. Or make a fat-free roux like the one in our Chicken Gumbo recipe. Both methods give gumbos the rich, nutty flavor they're known for.

To make Jambalaya healthier, brown the chicken in a little vegetable oil instead of fat rendered from browning sausage. And to give the savory flavor that only sausage can, use Italian turkey sausage.

JAMBALAYA

4 (6-ounce) skinned chicken
   breast halves
1 tablespoon vegetable oil
2 cups chopped onion
⅓ cup chopped green pepper
⅓ cup sliced green onions
½ pound lean pork, cut into
   cubes
¼ cup (1½ ounces) chopped
   cooked lean ham
2 tablespoons chopped fresh
   parsley
5 cloves garlic, minced
½ pound Italian turkey sausage
1 teaspoon salt
¼ teaspoon pepper
¼ teaspoon chili powder
⅛ teaspoon dried whole thyme
⅛ teaspoon ground cloves
6 bay leaves, finely crushed
Dash of mace
1 cup uncooked long-grain rice
2 cups canned ready-to-serve,
   no-salt-added chicken broth

Cook chicken breast halves in oil in a large Dutch oven over medium-high heat until browned. Remove chicken, and cool slightly.

Add onion and next 6 ingredients to Dutch oven; cook over medium-high heat 15 minutes, stirring every 5 minutes. Add sausage and next 7 ingredients, stirring to crumble meat.

Cut chicken breast halves in half, using a sharp knife or kitchen shears. Place chicken in a single layer in Dutch oven; add rice and chicken broth. Bring mixture to a boil; cover, reduce heat, and cook 35 to 40 minutes or until rice is tender. Toss gently before serving. Yield: 8 servings (380 calories per 1-cup serving).

☐ *34.6 grams protein, 14.9 grams fat, 24.1 grams carbohydrate, 98 milligrams cholesterol, 645 milligrams sodium, and 76 milligrams calcium.*

CHICKEN GUMBO

¾ cup all-purpose flour
4 (6-ounce) skinned chicken
   breast halves
2 quarts water
1 cup chopped onion
½ cup chopped green pepper
½ cup chopped celery
3 cloves garlic, minced
½ cup sliced green onions
¼ cup chopped fresh parsley
2 bay leaves
2 teaspoons creole seasoning
½ teaspoon salt
1½ tablespoons reduced-sodium
   Worcestershire sauce
1 teaspoon hot sauce
2 (10-ounce) packages frozen cut
   okra, thawed
3⅓ cups hot cooked rice (cooked
   without salt or fat)

Place flour in a 10-inch cast-iron skillet. Bake at 400° for 1 hour or until dark brown, stirring every 10 minutes. Remove skillet from oven, and set aside.

Combine chicken and water in a large Dutch oven; cook 20 minutes or until chicken is tender. Remove chicken and broth from Dutch oven, and set aside.

Combine onion, green pepper, celery, garlic, and ⅓ cup chicken broth in Dutch oven. Cook over medium heat 10 to 12 minutes or until vegetables are tender. Add browned flour and 1 cup chicken broth; stir until blended. Gradually stir in remaining broth; add green onions and next 7 ingredients.

Remove chicken from bones, and chop into bite-size pieces; add to Dutch oven. Cover and simmer 1 hour, stirring occasionally. Remove bay leaves. Serve gumbo with rice. Yield: 10 servings (228 calories per 1-cup serving with ⅓ cup rice).

☐ *20.7 grams protein, 2.4 grams fat, 30.1 grams carbohydrate, 46 milligrams cholesterol, 247 milligrams sodium, and 76 milligrams calcium.*

RED BEANS AND RICE

1 pound dried red beans
Vegetable cooking spray
2½ cups chopped celery
2 cups diced onion
1 cup sliced green onions
1 cup chopped green pepper
4 cloves garlic, minced
1½ cups (6 ounces) diced cooked
   lean ham
1 teaspoon salt
1 teaspoon red pepper
1 teaspoon dried Italian
   seasoning
½ teaspoon pepper
1 teaspoon hot sauce
2 bay leaves
2 quarts water
4½ cups hot cooked rice (cooked
   without salt or fat)

Sort and wash beans; place in a large Dutch oven. Cover with water 2 inches above beans; let soak 8 hours. Drain well.

Coat a Dutch oven with cooking spray; place over medium-high heat until hot. Add celery, onion, green

onions, green pepper, and garlic; sauté until tender. Add beans, ham, and remaining ingredients except rice, and cook, uncovered, over medium heat 1 hour, stirring occasionally. Remove bay leaves; serve bean mixture over rice. Yield: 9 servings (309 calories per 1 cup beans and ½ cup rice).

☐ *17.1 grams protein, 2.1 grams fat, 56 grams carbohydrate, 13 milligrams cholesterol, 309 milligrams sodium, and 83 milligrams calcium.*

BAKED OYSTERS BIENVILLE

Rock salt
Vegetable cooking spray
2 teaspoons reduced-calorie
   margarine
2 cloves garlic, minced
¼ cup sliced green onions
¼ cup chopped fresh parsley
⅛ teaspoon hot sauce
¼ cup soft breadcrumbs
¼ cup freshly grated Parmesan
   cheese
1 tablespoon lemon juice
⅛ teaspoon freshly ground black
   pepper
1 dozen oysters on the half shell

Sprinkle a thin layer of rock salt in a shallow pan; set aside.

Coat a nonstick skillet with cooking spray; place over medium-high heat until hot. Add margarine and next 3 ingredients; sauté until onions are tender. Add hot sauce, breadcrumbs, Parmesan cheese, lemon juice, and pepper; stir well.

Arrange oysters (in shells) over salt. Spoon green onion mixture evenly over oysters. Bake at 425° for 6 to 8 minutes or until edges of oysters begin to curl. Yield: 1 dozen (31 calories per oyster).

☐ *2 grams protein, 1.4 grams fat, 2.6 grams carbohydrate, 9 milligrams cholesterol, 69 milligrams sodium, and 36 milligrams calcium.*

BLACKENED RED SNAPPER

Vegetable cooking spray
1 tablespoon olive oil
¼ cup minced onion
2 cloves garlic, minced
½ tablespoon paprika
¼ teaspoon white pepper
¼ teaspoon red pepper
¼ teaspoon black pepper
¼ teaspoon dried whole oregano
4 (5-ounce) skinned red snapper
   fillets

Coat a nonstick skillet with cooking spray; place over medium-high heat until hot. Add olive oil, onion, and garlic; sauté until tender.

Stir in paprika and next 4 ingredients; set aside to cool. Spread cooled spice mixture on both sides of fish fillets.

Place fish on rack coated with cooking spray; place rack in a broiler pan. Broil 3 inches from heat 7 to 9 minutes or until fish flakes easily when tested with a fork (fish will be lightly charred). Yield: 4 servings (183 calories per serving).

☐ *29.5 grams protein, 5.6 grams fat, 2.1 grams carbohydrate, 52 milligrams cholesterol, 64 milligrams sodium, and 54 milligrams calcium.*

Spice Tips

■ When seasoning foods with curry powder, keep in mind that it is a rich blend of turmeric, coriander, cumin, red pepper, and fenugreek.

■ Store spices in a cool place and away from any direct source of heat, because the heat will destroy their flavor. Red spices will maintain flavor and retain color longer if they are stored in the refrigerator.

BARBECUED SHRIMP

Olive oil-flavored vegetable
  cooking spray
¼ cup diced onion
1 tablespoon brown sugar
1 tablespoon dry mustard
¼ teaspoon garlic powder
1 tablespoon white vinegar
½ cup reduced-calorie catsup
Dash of hot sauce
2 tablespoons fresh rosemary,
  chopped
24 unpeeled jumbo fresh shrimp
4 (8-inch) wooden skewers
1 lemon, cut into wedges

Coat a nonstick skillet with cooking spray; place over medium-high heat until hot.

Add onion to skillet, and sauté until tender; remove from heat. Add brown sugar, dry mustard, garlic powder, vinegar, catsup, hot sauce, and rosemary; stir until well blended. Let stand 2 to 3 hours.

Peel and devein shrimp; place in a shallow dish. Pour marinade over shrimp, turning to coat both sides. Cover and chill 1 hour.

Soak wooden skewers in water at least 30 minutes. Thread tail and neck of six shrimp onto each skewer so that shrimp will lie flat. Grill kabobs over medium-hot coals 3 to 4 minutes on each side or until shrimp turn pink. Squeeze lemon over shrimp, and serve immediately. Yield: 4 servings (156 calories per serving of 6 shrimp).

☐ *22.7 grams protein, 2.6 grams fat, 9.5 grams carbohydrate, 166 milligrams cholesterol, 384 milligrams sodium, and 72 milligrams calcium.*

Tip: *When cooking on the grill, never allow the coals to flame during cooking, because the flames may either burn the food or cause it to dry out. Just remember to keep a container of water nearby so that you can douse flames as they appear.*

BREADED CATFISH WITH CREOLE SAUCE

½ cup yellow cornmeal
¼ teaspoon pepper
2 tablespoons evaporated
  skimmed milk
4 (4-ounce) farm-raised catfish
  fillets
Olive oil-flavored vegetable
  cooking spray
Creole Sauce

Combine cornmeal and pepper; set aside. Pour milk into a shallow dish. Dip fillets in milk; dredge in cornmeal mixture. Place fish on a baking sheet coated with cooking spray. Spray each fillet lightly with cooking spray. Bake at 425° for 10 minutes or until fish flakes easily when tested with a fork. Broil fish 3 inches from heat 1 minute or until browned. Serve fish with Creole Sauce. Yield: 4 servings (229 calories per fillet with ¾ cup Creole Sauce).

☐ *23.5 grams protein, 5.8 grams fat, 19.5 grams carbohydrate, 66 milligrams cholesterol, 129 milligrams sodium, and 84 milligrams calcium.*

Creole Sauce

Olive oil-flavored vegetable
  cooking spray
1 teaspoon reduced-calorie
  margarine
¾ cup chopped onion
½ cup chopped celery
2 cloves garlic, minced
1 cup coarsely chopped tomatoes
1 cup sliced fresh okra
½ cup chopped green pepper
½ teaspoon dried whole basil
½ teaspoon dried whole oregano
½ teaspoon dried whole thyme
¼ teaspoon salt
¼ teaspoon red pepper
¼ teaspoon freshly ground pepper
1 (10½-ounce) can ready-to-serve,
  no-salt-added chicken broth
1 (8-ounce) can no-salt-added
  tomato sauce
Dash of hot sauce

Coat a large nonstick skillet with cooking spray; place skillet over medium-high heat. Add margarine and next 3 ingredients; sauté until vegetables are tender. Add tomatoes and remaining ingredients; bring to a boil. Reduce heat, and simmer, uncovered, 20 minutes, stirring occasionally. Yield: 3 cups (77 calories per ¾-cup serving).

☐ *2.7 grams protein, 1.2 grams fat, 14.8 grams carbohydrate, 0 milligrams cholesterol, 191 milligrams sodium, and 57 milligrams calcium.*

ANGEL BISCUITS

1 package dry yeast
¼ cup warm water (105° to 115°)
3¼ cups all-purpose flour
1 teaspoon baking powder
½ teaspoon baking soda
1 teaspoon salt
1 tablespoon sugar
½ cup vegetable oil
1 cup nonfat buttermilk

Dissolve yeast in warm water; let stand 5 minutes. Combine flour and next 4 ingredients; make a well in center of mixture. Add yeast mixture, oil, and buttermilk; stir until dry ingredients are moistened.

Turn dough out onto a lightly floured surface; roll to ½-inch thickness. Cut with a 2-inch biscuit cutter; place on ungreased baking sheets. Cover; let rise in a warm place (85°), free from drafts, 1 hour. Bake at 400° for 8 minutes or until lightly browned. Yield: 2 dozen (100 calories per biscuit).

Note: Dough may be stored in refrigerator 5 days. Roll and cut; place on baking sheet, and keep at room temperature 1 hour before baking.

☐ *2 grams protein, 4.7 grams fat, 12.3 grams carbohydrate, 0 milligrams cholesterol, 138 milligrams sodium, and 27 milligrams calcium.*

Judi Grigoraci
Charleston, West Virginia

A Heart-Healthy Menu For Two

Valentine's Day and the American Heart Association's (AHA) national campaign against heart disease during February set the stage to kick off the expansion of our monthly "On the Light Side" section. Each month we'll feature a healthy, low-cholesterol menu that meets the AHA's recommendations of 50% of calories from carbohydrates, 20% from protein, and 30% (or less) from fat. We'll end with a light version of a Southern favorite.

**Baked Halibut
With Champagne Sauce
Stuffed Scalloped Tomatoes
Steamed Vegetable Medley
Commercial Whole Wheat Rolls
Strawberries 'n' Cream
Champagne (6 ounces)**

BAKED HALIBUT
WITH CHAMPAGNE SAUCE

2 (4-ounce) halibut steaks
Vegetable cooking spray
Champagne Sauce
Garnishes: fresh parsley, lemon
  slices

Place halibut in a baking dish coated with cooking spray. Bake at 350° for 20 minutes or until fish flakes easily when tested with a fork. Remove to serving plate; keep warm. Serve with Champagne Sauce. Garnish, if desired. Yield: 2 servings (174 calories per serving with ¼ cup sauce).

☐ *24.9 grams protein, 4.8 grams fat, 6.6 grams carbohydrate, 37 milligrams cholesterol, 108 milligrams sodium, and 102 milligrams calcium.*

Champagne Sauce

2 teaspoons cornstarch
2 tablespoons evaporated
  skimmed milk
½ teaspoon lemon juice
¼ cup champagne
½ tablespoon reduced-calorie
  margarine
¼ teaspoon lemon rind

Combine cornstarch, milk, and lemon juice in a small saucepan; stir in champagne. Cook over medium heat, stirring constantly, until mixture begins to boil; boil 1 minute, stirring constantly. Remove from heat. Add margarine and lemon rind; stir until margarine melts. Yield: 2 servings (12 calories per tablespoon).

☐ *0.3 gram protein, 0.5 gram fat, 6.6 grams carbohydrate, 0 milligrams cholesterol, 12 milligrams sodium, and 12 milligrams calcium.*

STUFFED SCALLOPED
TOMATOES

2 medium tomatoes (¾ pound)
Vegetable cooking spray
2 tablespoons diced onion
½ teaspoon brown sugar
¼ teaspoon salt
¼ teaspoon pepper
⅔ cup soft breadcrumbs, toasted
1 tablespoon grated Parmesan
  cheese

Cut tops from tomatoes; chop tops, and set aside. Scoop out pulp, leaving shells intact. Reserve pulp.
Coat a nonstick skillet with cooking spray; place over medium-high heat until hot. Add onion, and sauté until tender. Add chopped tomato tops, reserved tomato pulp, brown sugar, and next 3 ingredients; stir well, and remove from heat.
Spoon stuffing mixture into tomato shells, and place in an 8-inch square baking dish coated with cooking spray. Sprinkle with Parmesan cheese, and bake at 350° for 10 minutes or until thoroughly heated. Yield: 2 servings (184 calories per tomato).

☐ *6.9 grams protein, 3 grams fat, 33.6 grams carbohydrate, 4 milligrams cholesterol, 599 milligrams sodium, and 93 milligrams calcium.*

STEAMED VEGETABLE
MEDLEY

1 cup julienne-sliced zucchini
½ cup julienne-sliced carrots
1 teaspoon reduced-calorie
  margarine, melted
½ teaspoon lemon-pepper
  seasoning

Combine zucchini and carrots in a steaming rack. Place rack over boiling water; cover and steam 3 to 5 minutes or until vegetables are crisp-tender.
Transfer vegetables to a serving dish. Add melted margarine and lemon-pepper seasoning, and toss gently. Yield: 2 servings (32 calories per ¾-cup serving).

☐ *1.1 grams protein, 1.4 grams fat, 5 grams carbohydrate, 0 milligrams cholesterol, 115 milligrams sodium, and 17 milligrams calcium.*

STRAWBERRIES 'N' CREAM

2 tablespoons light process cream
  cheese product
1 tablespoon Cointreau or other
  orange-flavored liqueur
¼ cup vanilla low-fat yogurt
1½ cups fresh strawberries,
  washed and hulled

Combine cream cheese and Cointreau; fold in yogurt, and chill. Divide
strawberries into compotes; chill.
Before serving, spoon sauce evenly
over strawberries. Yield: 2 servings
(112 calories per serving).

☐ *3.6 grams protein, 3.2 grams fat,
16.2 grams carbohydrate, 1 milligram
cholesterol, 99 milligrams sodium,
and 84 milligrams calcium.*

LIGHT FAVORITE

Trimmed-Down Macaroni And Cheese

For years dietitians have warned
folks with cholesterol problems to
stay away from macaroni and cheese.
Butter, whole milk, high-fat cheese,
and eggs kept it off their "acceptable
foods" lists—until now.

This recipe takes advantage of the
low-cholesterol products on the market to keep fat, calories, and cholesterol low without sacrificing flavor.

MACARONI AND CHEESE

1 (8-ounce) package elbow
  macaroni
2 tablespoons reduced-calorie
  margarine
2 tablespoons all-purpose flour
2 cups skim milk
½ teaspoon salt
1½ cups (6 ounces) shredded
  ⅓-less-fat sharp Cheddar
  cheese
3 tablespoons egg substitute
Vegetable cooking spray
¼ teaspoon paprika

Cook macaroni according to package
directions, omitting salt and fat.
Drain well, and set aside.

Melt margarine in a heavy saucepan over low heat; add flour, stirring
until smooth. Cook 1 minute, stirring
constantly. Gradually add milk; cook
over medium heat, stirring constantly, until thickened and bubbly.
Stir in salt and cheese, stirring until
cheese melts. Gradually stir about
one-fourth of hot mixture into egg
substitute; add to remaining hot mixture, stirring constantly.

Stir cheese sauce into macaroni;
pour into a 2-quart baking dish

---

coated with cooking spray. Sprinkle
with paprika. Bake at 350° for 25 to
30 minutes. Yield: 5½ cups (160 calories per ½-cup serving).

☐ *9 grams protein, 4.5 grams fat,
19.5 grams carbohydrate, 12 milligrams cholesterol, 265 milligrams sodium, and 226 milligrams calcium.*

COMPARE THE NUTRIENTS (per serving)		
	Traditional	Light
Calories	242	160
Fat	13.2g	4.5g
Cholesterol	53mg	12mg

Homemade Stocks Make Savory Soups And Stews

Soups and stews are only as good as
the stock on which they are built.
The stock will not only improve your
cooking, but it will also make dishes
healthier. Luckily, making a good,
rich stock is relatively simple, though
lengthy.

Stockmaking is basically a matter
of dissolving the protein and minerals
from bones and vegetables in water.
Start with the freshest ingredients;
dice vegetables so that the most flavor can be extracted from them. Remove excess fat from bones, and
crack large bones. During cooking,
skim off the foam or scum that rises
to the top.

Simmer stocks slowly for several
hours to get all the nutrients and
taste from the meat and vegetables.

As water evaporates during cooking, the flavor becomes intense. Once the stock is made, strain it through a paper towel- or cheesecloth-lined sieve. Then chill thoroughly to allow fat to solidify on top. Skim solidifed fat from the surface.

Ice-cube trays offer a convenient way to freeze stocks. Each cube is about 2 tablespoons, so measuring is simple. When stock is frozen, transfer cubes to plastic bags for storage in the freezer.

BROWN MEAT STOCK

5 to 6 pounds beef or veal bones
6 quarts water
1 pound carrots, diced
2 medium onions, diced
4 stalks celery, diced
3 cloves garlic, quartered
3 bay leaves
8 peppercorns
2 cups chopped fresh parsley

Place bones in a shallow roasting pan; bake at 450° for 45 minutes or until bones are well browned, turning occasionally. Combine browned bones and 6 quarts water in a large stockpot. Bring to a boil; cover, reduce heat, and simmer 1½ to 2 hours. (Skim surface frequently to remove scum.) Uncover and continue cooking 4 hours.

Add carrots and remaining ingredients. Reduce heat to low, and cook, uncovered, 6 hours. Remove from heat, and cool.

Strain stock through a cheesecloth- or paper towel-lined sieve into a large bowl; discard bones, vegetables, and seasonings. Cover and chill stock. Skim and discard solidified fat from top of stock. Yield: 2½ cups.

Tip: *When buying garlic, select firm, plump bulbs that have dry, unbroken skins. Store in a cool, dry place that is well ventilated. The flavor will remain sharp up to four months.*

LIGHT POULTRY STOCK

1 turkey or chicken carcass
5 quarts water
1 pound carrots, diced
2 medium onions, diced
2 stalks celery, diced
1½ cups chopped fresh parsley
3 cloves garlic, quartered
2 bay leaves
1 teaspoon dried whole thyme
8 peppercorns
6 whole cloves

Combine all ingredients in a large stockpot. Bring to a boil; cover, reduce heat, and simmer 1½ to 2 hours. Uncover and continue cooking 4 hours (skim surface frequently for the first 2 hours to remove scum.) Remove from heat, and cool.

Strain stock through a cheesecloth- or paper towel-lined sieve into a large bowl; discard bones, vegetables, and seasonings. Cover stock, and chill thoroughly. Skim and discard solidified fat from top of stock. Yield: about 1½ quarts.

VEGETABLE STOCK

4½ quarts water
3 medium onions, diced
5 stalks celery, diced
1 pound carrots, scraped and diced
1 small bunch parsley
1 medium turnip, diced
3 cloves garlic, quartered
3 bay leaves
1 teaspoon dried whole thyme

Combine all ingredients in a stockpot. Bring mixture to a boil; cover, reduce heat, and simmer 1½ to 2 hours. Uncover stockpot, and continue cooking 2 hours.

Strain stock through a cheesecloth- or paper towel-lined sieve into a large bowl; discard vegetables and seasonings. Cover and chill stock. Yield: 4 cups.

Homemade Soups—Warm And Delicious

Nothing is better than a bowl of hot soup for satisfying the appetite on a cold, crisp day. You may want to round out the menu with a sandwich or salad.

FRENCH ONION SOUP

6 (¾-inch-thick) slices French bread
1 tablespoon butter or margarine, softened
¾ teaspoon garlic powder
1 tablespoon grated Parmesan cheese
1½ pounds onions, sliced (about 5 cups)
¼ cup butter or margarine, melted
2 (10½-ounce) cans condensed beef broth, undiluted
1⅓ cups water
2 teaspoons Worcestershire sauce
⅛ teaspoon cracked pepper
⅛ teaspoon curry powder
Pinch of garlic powder
½ cup (2 ounces) shredded mozzarella cheese

Butter each slice of bread on one side with ½ teaspoon softened butter; sprinkle with ⅛ teaspoon garlic powder. Place bread on a baking sheet; bake at 300° for 15 to 20 minutes. Sprinkle with ½ teaspoon Parmesan cheese. Set aside.

Separate onions into rings; cook in ¼ cup butter in a Dutch oven over medium heat 25 to 30 minutes, stirring frequently. Add broth and next 5 ingredients; bring to a boil. Cover, reduce heat, and simmer 30 minutes.

Ladle soup into 6 soup bowls. Sprinkle each with 1 heaping tablespoon mozzarella cheese, and top with a French bread slice. Yield: about 6 cups.
Mildred Bickley
Bristol, Virginia

MUSHROOM-RICE SOUP

1 pound fresh mushrooms,
  sliced
¼ cup butter, melted
4 chicken-flavored bouillon cubes
1½ cups hot water
3 quarts chicken broth
2 carrots, sliced
1 cup chopped onion
2 stalks celery, sliced
¾ cup uncooked long-grain rice
¾ cup macaroni, uncooked
¼ cup chopped fresh parsley
¼ teaspoon pepper

Sauté sliced mushrooms in melted butter in a skillet until tender (about 10 minutes). Drain.

Dissolve bouillon cubes in hot water; set aside.

Combine chicken broth, carrot, onion, and celery in a Dutch oven. Bring to a boil; reduce heat, and simmer, uncovered, 10 minutes or until vegetables are tender. Add rice, and simmer 10 minutes. Add macaroni, parsley, bouillon, and pepper; cook 10 minutes. Stir in mushrooms, and serve. Yield: 3¼ quarts.

Barbara Carson
Hollywood, Florida

DOWN-HOME VEGETABLE SOUP

2 medium onions, chopped
1 medium-size green pepper,
  chopped
½ cup chopped celery
2 tablespoons bacon drippings
3 cups frozen English peas
3 carrots, thinly sliced
2 medium potatoes, cubed
2 (16-ounce) cans whole
  tomatoes, undrained and
  coarsely chopped
1 (8-ounce) bottle French salad
  dressing
1 cup water
1 (4-ounce) can sliced
  mushrooms, drained
¼ teaspoon pepper

Sauté onion, green pepper, and celery in bacon drippings. Add remaining ingredients; bring to a boil. Cover, reduce heat, and simmer 1 hour. Yield: 2½ quarts.

Mary Kay Menees
White Pine, Tennessee

SPICY TORTILLA SOUP

½ cup chopped onion
1 clove garlic, minced
1 tablespoon vegetable oil
3 medium zucchini, sliced
4 cups chicken broth
1 (16-ounce) can stewed
  tomatoes, undrained
1 (15-ounce) can tomato sauce
1 (12-ounce) can whole kernel
  corn, undrained
1 teaspoon ground cumin
½ teaspoon pepper
Tortilla chips
½ cup (2 ounces) shredded
  Monterey Jack or Cheddar
  cheese

Sauté onion and garlic in oil in a Dutch oven. Add zucchini, chicken broth, tomatoes, tomato sauce, corn, cumin, and pepper; bring to a boil. Cover, reduce heat, and simmer 15 to 20 minutes.

Spoon soup into individual soup bowls, and add tortilla chips and shredded cheese. Yield: 2¼ quarts.

Linda J. Jones
Longview, Texas

Tip: *Onions offer outstanding nutritive value. They are a good source of calcium and vitamins A and C. They contain iron, riboflavin, thiamine, and niacin; have a high percentage of water; and supply essential bulk. They are low in calories and have only a trace of fat.*

Put The Chill On Winter Salads

Although most backyard gardens have fallen prey to frost and freeze by February, fresh produce is still available at the grocery store.

MARINATED ZUCCHINI SALAD

3 medium zucchini, thinly sliced
⅓ cup cider vinegar
¼ cup sweet pickle relish
3 tablespoons vegetable oil
1 clove garlic, crushed
1 (2-ounce) jar diced pimiento,
  drained
2 tablespoons minced onion
½ teaspoon salt
¼ teaspoon pepper
Lettuce leaves

Place zucchini in a bowl. Combine vinegar and next 7 ingredients; stir. Pour over zucchini; toss. Cover and chill 8 hours. Serve on lettuce-lined salad plates. Yield: 6 to 8 servings.

Marie H. Webb
Roanoke, Virginia

BROCCOLI 'N' CAULIFLOWER SALAD

1 small cauliflower, broken into
  flowerets
1 pound broccoli, broken into
  flowerets
½ pound fresh mushrooms, sliced
1 small purple onion, sliced and
  separated into rings
2 stalks celery, sliced
1 cup vegetable oil
½ cup white wine vinegar
½ cup sugar
1 tablespoon dried Italian
  seasoning
2 teaspoons dry mustard
1 teaspoon salt
Lettuce leaves (optional)

Combine cauliflower, broccoli, sliced mushrooms, onion rings, and sliced celery in a large bowl; set aside.

Combine oil and next 5 ingredients in a small bowl; stir well, and pour over vegetables. Toss gently to coat; cover and chill 3 hours, stirring occasionally. Serve salad with a slotted spoon over lettuce leaves, if desired. Yield: 8 to 10 servings.

Carolyn Gower
Columbia, South Carolina

OVERNIGHT VEGETABLE SALAD

2 cups shredded cabbage
1 (17-ounce) can English peas, drained
1 (8-ounce) can sliced water chestnuts, drained
¼ cup chopped onion
¾ cup chopped celery
1 large red apple, cored and chopped
¼ teaspoon salt
½ cup sour cream
½ cup mayonnaise or salad dressing
1 teaspoon sugar
1 cup (4 ounces) shredded Cheddar cheese
1 cup pecans, finely chopped

Combine cabbage, peas, water chestnuts, onion, celery, apple, and salt in a large bowl; toss well.

Combine sour cream, mayonnaise, and sugar, stirring until blended. Spread sour cream mixture over cabbage mixture, sealing edges. Layer cheese and pecans on top. Cover and chill 8 hours. Toss before serving. Yield: 8 servings. *Jean M. Lumley*
Pfafftown, North Carolina

MICROWAVE COOKERY

Weeknight Entrées

Many folks shy away from cooking meats in the microwave because meats don't brown as they would using conventional methods. But you can use a browning dish to sear meat in the microwave or select meats that do not require browning.

For example, Burgandy Round Steak Over Rice is easy to prepare and browns nicely in the microwave, thanks to the use of a browning dish.

Ginger-Nut Chicken is a quick recipe that doesn't require browning and is a great choice for busy nights.

BURGUNDY ROUND STEAK OVER RICE

1 (1½-pound) boneless round steak
¼ cup all-purpose flour
⅛ teaspoon ground cinnamon
⅛ teaspoon ground cloves
⅛ teaspoon pepper
2 tablespoons bacon drippings
1 medium onion, chopped
2 cloves garlic, minced
1 (8-ounce) can tomato sauce
½ cup Burgundy or other dry red wine
¼ teaspoon salt
Hot cooked rice

Trim excess fat from steak; slice diagonally across grain into ¾-inch-wide strips. Cut strips into 2-inch pieces.

Combine flour, cinnamon, cloves, and pepper; dredge steak in flour mixture.

Preheat a 10-inch browning dish in microwave at HIGH 8 to 9 minutes. Add bacon drippings; let stand until drippings melt. Add steak, onion, and garlic, stirring well. Microwave at HIGH 4 minutes, stirring after 1½ minutes. Add tomato sauce, wine,

and salt, stirring well. Cover with heavy-duty plastic wrap; fold back a small edge of wrap to allow steam to escape. Microwave at MEDIUM (50% power) 30 to 35 minutes, stirring at 10-minute intervals. Serve over rice. Yield: 6 servings.

GINGER-NUT CHICKEN

1 tablespoon butter or margarine
2 chicken breast halves, skinned and boned
1½ cups broccoli, cut into 1½-inch pieces
½ cup green onions, cut into 1-inch pieces
½ cup celery, cut into 1-inch pieces
3 (⅛-inch) slices fresh gingerroot
2 tablespoons cornstarch
½ cup water, divided
1 tablespoon soy sauce
¼ teaspoon lemon-pepper seasoning
⅛ teaspoon garlic salt
⅓ cup dry roasted peanuts
Hot cooked rice

Place butter in a 1½-quart casserole. Microwave at HIGH 45 seconds or until melted.

Cut chicken into bite-size pieces. Add to casserole, and coat with butter. Cover and microwave at HIGH 4 minutes, stirring after 2 minutes Add broccoli, green onions, celery, and gingerroot. Microwave at HIGH 2 minutes.

Combine cornstarch and ¼ cup water in a glass measuring cup, stirring well. Add remaining ¼ cup water, soy sauce, lemon-pepper seasoning, and garlic salt; stir well. Pour cornstarch mixture over chicken and vegetables. Cover and microwave at HIGH 2 to 3 minutes or until sauce is slightly thickened; stir once. Stir in peanuts. Remove gingerroot, and serve over rice. Yield: 2 to 3 servings. *Carolyn Bond*
Pensacola, Florida

CREAMY TURKEY DIVAN

2 (10-ounce) packages frozen
   broccoli spears, thawed
1 (10¾-ounce) can cream of
   chicken soup, undiluted
2 cups cubed cooked turkey
1 (8-ounce) carton sour cream
1 cup (4 ounces) shredded
   Cheddar cheese, divided

Place broccoli in a shallow 2-quart
baking dish. Cover tightly with
heavy-duty plastic wrap; fold back a
small corner of wrap to allow steam
to escape. Microwave at HIGH 11 to
12 minutes, separating spears with a
fork. Drain broccoli, and return to
dish; set aside.

Place soup in a shallow 2-quart
baking dish; cover and microwave at
HIGH 2½ to 3 minutes or until very
hot. Stir in turkey; cover and microwave at HIGH 1½ to 2 minutes. Stir
in sour cream and ½ cup cheese;
microwave at HIGH 2 minutes.
Spoon sauce over broccoli; sprinkle
remaining ½ cup cheese on top. Microwave at HIGH, uncovered, 1 minute. Yield: 6 servings.

Pamela Deutsch
Dallas, Texas

Serve Onions On The Side

Too often relegated to the background flavor of a dish, onions can
play a feature role on the menu.
Cooking tames their pungent flavor,
tenderizing and positioning them for
many uses.

Select quality onions based on how
they look and feel. Their skins should
be clean, dry, and paper-thin. The
onions themselves should be firm. Be
sure to store them in a cool, dry,
well-ventilated place. Keep them
away from potatoes, as the moisture
in potatoes will cause a more rapid
decay of the onions.

ONION KUCHEN

2 medium onions, sliced and
   separated into rings
3 tablespoons butter or
   margarine, melted
2 (4.5-ounce) cans refrigerated
   biscuits
1 egg, beaten
1 (8-ounce) carton sour cream
¼ teaspoon salt
1 teaspoon poppyseeds

Sauté onions in butter 5 minutes or
until tender; set aside.

Separate biscuits, and arrange in
bottom of a lightly greased 8-inch
round cakepan. Press biscuits together, covering bottom of pan completely; bake at 375° for 5 minutes.
Spoon onions evenly over biscuit
layer, and set aside.

Combine egg, sour cream, and
salt; stir well. Pour over onion layer;
sprinkle with poppyseeds. Bake at
375° for 30 minutes or until set. Let
dish stand 5 minutes before serving.
Yield: 8 servings.   *Kathleen Stone*
Houston, Texas

CURRIED ONIONS

4 medium onions, sliced and
   separated into rings
1 cup water
1 teaspoon salt
3 tablespoons all-purpose flour
½ teaspoon curry powder
½ cup water
½ cup milk
1 tablespoon butter or margarine

Combine onions, 1 cup water, and
salt in a saucepan; bring to a boil.
Cover, reduce heat, and simmer 5
minutes.

Combine flour, curry powder, and
½ cup water; stir until smooth. Add
flour mixture to onions, stirring well.
Gradually stir in milk; cook until
thickened, stirring constantly. Add
butter, stirring until melted. Yield: 8
servings.   *Mrs. Thomas Lee Adams*
Kingsport, Tennessee

CHEESE-STUFFED ONIONS

4 large onions
4 ounces Havarti cheese with dill
   or other herb, cubed
½ cup dry breadcrumbs
Paprika
½ cup water
Garnish: fresh parsley

Peel onions, and cut a thin slice from
top; discard slice. Cook onions in
boiling salted water to cover 20 minutes or until tender but not mushy.
Remove centers of onions, leaving
¾-inch shells intact; chop centers.

Combine chopped onion, cheese,
and breadcrumbs; stir well. Fill shells
with cheese mixture. Place stuffed
onions in an 8-inch square baking
dish. Sprinkle with paprika. Pour ½
cup water into baking dish. Bake at
350° for 20 to 25 minutes. Garnish, if
desired. Yield: 4 servings.

Mary B. Quesenberry
Dugspur, Virginia

SWEET-AND-SOUR BAKED ONIONS

6 medium onions
¼ cup sugar
¼ cup white vinegar
¼ cup boiling water
¼ cup butter or margarine

Peel onions; cut a thin slice from
tops, and slash cut surfaces of onions
with a shallow x. Place onions in a
12- x 8- x 2-inch baking dish.

Combine sugar and remaining ingredients, stirring until sugar dissolves; pour over onions. Cover and
bake at 350° for 1 hour or until
tender. Yield: 6 servings.

Dolly G. Northcott
Fairfield, Alabama

QUICK!

Dinner In A Skillet

Recipes for entrées that cook in a flash may be the ones you use most. At the end of a busy weekday, prepare and serve one of these skillet dinners over hot cooked noodles or rice, and add a tossed green salad and commercial rolls for a fast meal that's high in taste appeal.

LEMON-GARLIC CHICKEN

¼ cup butter or margarine
6 chicken breast halves, skinned and boned
4 cloves garlic, crushed
½ cup chicken broth
½ cup white wine
3 tablespoons lemon juice
¼ teaspoon salt
⅛ teaspoon pepper
Hot cooked noodles or rice

Melt butter in a large skillet over medium heat. Add chicken and garlic, and cook 3 to 4 minutes on each side or until golden brown. Add broth and next 4 ingredients. Bring to a boil. Cover, reduce heat, and simmer 20 minutes or until chicken is tender. Serve with hot noodles or rice. Yield: 6 servings.
Donna Ann Smith
Springfield, Missouri

PORK MARSALA

1 (1-pound) pork tenderloin
1 tablespoon butter or margarine
1 tablespoon vegetable oil
1 clove garlic, minced
½ cup marsala
½ cup dry red wine
1 tablespoon tomato paste
½ pound fresh mushroom caps
1 tablespoon chopped fresh parsley
Hot cooked noodles or rice

Cut tenderloin into 4 equal pieces. Place each piece between two sheets of wax paper, and flatten to ¼-inch thickness, using a meat mallet or rolling pin.

Heat butter and oil in a large, heavy skillet over medium heat. Add pork, and cook 3 to 4 minutes on each side or until browned. Remove pork from skillet, and keep warm. Sauté garlic in pan drippings in skillet; add wines and tomato paste, stirring until blended. Add mushroom caps, and simmer 3 to 5 minutes. Return pork to skillet, and cook until thoroughly heated. Sprinkle with parsley, and serve over noodles or rice. Yield: 4 servings.
Schatzi Mosley
Meeker, Oklahoma

ZIPPY STEAK AND GRAVY

¼ cup all-purpose flour
⅛ teaspoon salt
¼ teaspoon pepper
4 cubed beef steaks (about 1⅓ pounds)
¼ cup vegetable oil
1 (10-ounce) can diced tomatoes with chiles, undrained
Hot cooked rice or noodles

Combine flour, salt, and pepper in a plastic bag. Add steaks, one at a time; close bag securely, and shake until well coated.

Brown steaks on both sides in hot oil. Drain all but 1 tablespoon drippings from pan. Pour tomatoes and chiles over steaks. Bring to a boil; cover, reduce heat, and simmer 15 minutes or until steaks are tender. Serve over hot cooked rice or noodles. Yield: 4 servings.

Janice Godfrey
Cherokee, Alabama

CHICKEN WITH ARTICHOKES AND MUSHROOMS

4 chicken breast halves, skinned and boned
¼ cup all-purpose flour
2 tablespoons butter or margarine
1 (16-ounce) can artichoke hearts, drained and quartered
1 (4-ounce) can sliced mushrooms
1 cup whipping cream
½ teaspoon cracked pepper
Hot cooked noodles or rice

Place each piece of chicken between two sheets of wax paper; flatten to ¼-inch thickness, using a meat mallet or rolling pin. Dredge chicken lightly in flour.

Melt butter in a large skillet over medium heat. Add chicken, and cook 5 minutes on each side or until golden brown; cover and cook 5 minutes. Drain drippings from pan. Add artichokes and next 3 ingredients; cook, stirring constantly, over low heat until sauce is thickened. Serve over hot cooked noodles or rice. Yield: 4 servings.
Susie Lavenue
Alamo, Tennessee

Tease Appetites
With A Party Spread

Guests like party spreads because of the varied and distinctive tastes they offer, while cooks praise them for their easy preparation. These recipes are simple to stir together, and most can be made ahead.

Gouda Cheese Spread, for example, contains only three ingredients—not counting the paprika and leaf lettuce garnish. This spread can be served immediately after preparation, or it can be chilled until it is needed.

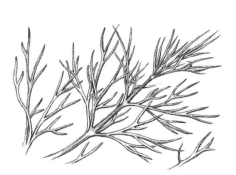

GOUDA CHEESE SPREAD

1 (10-ounce) round of Gouda
   cheese
½ cup sour cream
1 tablespoon dry Italian dressing
   mix
Leaf lettuce
Paprika

Cut a ½-inch slice off top of Gouda cheese. Remove red wrapping. Carefully scoop out cheese, leaving ¼-inch shell intact; set cheese shell aside. Grate remaining cheese.

Combine grated cheese, sour cream, and Italian dressing mix, stirring well. Spoon cheese mixture into lettuce-lined shell. Sprinkle with paprika. Serve with assorted crackers. Yield: 1 cup.   *Pamela Eva*
Huntsville, Alabama

CREAMY RAISIN SPREAD

1 egg, beaten
1 cup sugar
1 cup chopped raisins
1 cup mayonnaise or salad
   dressing
3 tablespoons lemon juice
1 tablespoon butter or margarine
¼ teaspoon grated lemon rind
½ cup finely chopped pecans

Combine first 7 ingredients in a saucepan; cook over low heat until thickened and bubbly, stirring constantly. Stir in pecans; cool. Serve with melba crackers. Yield: 2¼ cups.   *Mrs. Joe M. Campbell*
Spartanburg, South Carolina

ZIPPY SHRIMP SPREAD

3 cups water
1 pound unpeeled medium-size
   fresh shrimp
2 (3-ounce) packages cream
   cheese, softened
⅓ cup catsup
1 teaspoon grated onion
1 teaspoon prepared horseradish
½ teaspoon red pepper
½ teaspoon Worcestershire sauce

Bring water to a boil; add shrimp, and cook 3 to 5 minutes. Drain well; rinse with cold water. Chill. Peel and devein shrimp. Set aside 3 shrimp for garnish; coarsely chop remainder.

Combine cream cheese and remaining ingredients in a mixing bowl; beat at medium speed of an electric mixer. Stir in chopped shrimp. Cover and chill at least 2 hours. Garnish with whole shrimp, and serve with assorted crackers. Yield: 1¼ cups.
   Ella C. Sharpe
Williamston, North Carolina

WINE PÂTÉ

¼ cup butter or margarine
1 pound chicken livers
½ cup sliced fresh mushrooms
⅓ cup chopped green onions
1 clove garlic, minced
¾ teaspoon salt
½ cup dry white wine
½ cup butter or margarine,
   softened
Pinch of dried whole dillweed
3 to 4 drops of hot sauce

Melt ¼ cup butter in a skillet. Add livers and next 4 ingredients; sauté 5 minutes. Add wine and remaining ingredients; cover and simmer 10 minutes. Cool slightly.

Pour mixture into container of an electric blender; blend until smooth. Pour into a lightly oiled 3-cup mold; cover and chill at least 8 hours. Unmold and serve pâté with assorted crackers. Yield: 3 cups.
   Monica C. Foster
Harmony, North Carolina

Right: *Quick Corn Relish (page 13) is an appetizing complement to beef.*

Pages 38 and 39: *Enjoy the goodness of (clockwise from bottom) Savory Southern Chicken Pies, Nana's Chicken Pie, and Lamb Pie. (Recipes begin on page 24.)*

Above: *Greet guests with Tomato Juice Cocktail (page 12). A variety of seasonings gives this beverage a robust flavor.*

Above left: *Invite a group of friends to join you in heralding spring's coming with Baked Ham With Orange-Honey Glaze (page 53).*

Left: *Caesar salad dressing seasons Caesar's Fish (page 76), a 20-minute entrée that's special enough to serve company.*

Far left: *Serve (from front) Goat Cheese and Greens, Leafy Cheese Sandwiches, or Colorful Tossed Salad. (Recipes begin on page 54.)*

Above: *Spin a cage of caramelized sugar around Vanilla Poached Pears (page 57).*

Right: *Reminisce about old times, and speculate about the year ahead over (from left to right) Skillet Cornbread, Hopping John, Ribs With Blender Barbecue Sauce, and Turnip Greens. (Recipes begin on page 12.)*

Above: *Layers of crunchy chocolate crumbs and satiny, crème de menthe-laced whipping cream stack up to a rising success in Chocolate-Mint Parfaits (page 15).*

A Novel Look At Nobility

Here we present a pair of the South's grandest cakes, a couple only fate could bring together—Lord and Lady Baltimore.

LORD BALTIMORE CAKE

¾ cup shortening
2¼ cups sugar
8 egg yolks
3¾ cups sifted cake flour
1½ tablespoons baking powder
½ teaspoon salt
1¾ cups milk
½ teaspoon almond extract
½ teaspoon vanilla extract
Frosting (recipe follows)
1 cup chopped mixed candied fruit
1 cup chopped pecans or walnuts
½ cup macaroon crumbs
1 teaspoon vanilla extract
½ teaspoon almond extract

Cream shortening; gradually add sugar, beating well at medium speed of an electric mixer. Add egg yolks, one at a time; beat well after each addition.

Combine flour, baking powder, and salt; add to creamed mixture alternately with milk, beginning and ending with flour mixture. Mix just until blended after each addition. Stir in ½ teaspoon almond extract and ½ teaspoon vanilla.

Pour batter into 3 greased and floured 9-inch round cakepans. Bake at 350° for 20 to 25 minutes or until a wooden pick inserted in center comes out clean. Cool in pans 10 minutes. Remove from pans; cool completely on wire racks.

Combine 2 cups frosting, candied fruit, and remaining ingredients; spread between layers. Spread remaining frosting on top and sides of cake. Yield: one 3-layer cake.

Frosting

1½ cups sugar
½ cup water
1 tablespoon light corn syrup
4 egg whites

Combine sugar, water, and syrup; cook over low heat until mixture reaches soft ball stage (240°).

Beat egg whites (at room temperature) until soft peaks form. Continue to beat, slowly adding hot syrup mixture. Beat 1 minute. Yield: 7 cups.

LADY BALTIMORE CAKE

1 cup butter or margarine, softened
2 cups sugar
½ cup water
½ cup milk
3 cups sifted cake flour
2¾ teaspoons baking powder
½ teaspoon salt
½ teaspoon almond extract
6 egg whites
1 cup chopped raisins or currants
1 cup chopped dried figs
1 cup chopped almonds or walnuts
½ cup sherry or brandy
Boiled Frosting

Cream butter; gradually add sugar, beating well at medium speed of an electric mixer.

Combine water and milk in a small bowl; set aside.

Combine flour, baking powder, and salt; add to creamed mixture alternately with milk mixture, beginning and ending with flour mixture. Mix just until blended after each addition. Stir in almond extract.

Beat egg whites (at room temperature) until stiff peaks form; fold into batter. Pour batter into 3 greased and floured 9-inch round cakepans. Bake at 350° for 25 to 30 minutes or until a wooden pick inserted in center comes out clean. Cool in pans 10 minutes; remove from pans, and let cool completely on wire racks.

Combine raisins, figs, almonds, and sherry; let stand 30 minutes. Drain well, discarding sherry; set raisin mixture aside.

Combine 2 cups Boiled Frosting and raisin mixture; spread between layers. Spread remaining frosting on top and sides of cake. Yield: one 3-layer cake.

Boiled Frosting

1½ cups sugar
½ teaspoon cream of tartar
⅛ teaspoon salt
½ cup water
4 egg whites
½ teaspoon almond extract
½ teaspoon vanilla extract

Combine first 4 ingredients in a heavy saucepan. Cook over medium heat, stirring constantly, until clear. Cook, without stirring, to soft ball stage (240°).

Beat egg whites (at room temperature) until soft peaks form. Continue to beat, slowly adding hot syrup mixture. Add flavorings; beat until stiff peaks form and frosting is thick enough to spread. Yield: 7 cups.

Cake Tips

■ If a cake recipe calls for beaten egg whites, beat them first and then use beaters without washing for beating egg yolks. Saves on cleanup.

■ Use shiny cookie sheets and cakepans for baking. Dark pans absorb more heat and cause baked products to overbrown.

■ When baking a layer cake, don't let pans touch each other or sides of oven; stagger their placement so that heat can circulate evenly around pans.

One Recipe, Three Batches Of Bread

In Montgomery, Alabama, Susan Cheek is known for her variety of sweet yeast breads. The secret is that they all come from one recipe of dough for Best-Ever Yeast Rolls, which can be shaped into pan rolls, filled pinwheel rolls, braided loaves, or rolled loaves.

Each recipe of dough makes enough for three of each, or you can bake one each of three of the variations. Susan even provides three cream cheese fillings—cinnamon, orange, or chocolate—so that you can pick your favorite flavor or mix and match different flavors with the varied shapes to personalize the breads as you please.

A basket of rolls and the filled breads and some gourmet jellies make wonderful gifts throughout the year. But don't wait for a special occasion. You can bake one pan of rolls or a loaf for your family to enjoy now, and freeze the others for later or to serve for drop-in company.

Freeze the bread in airtight plastic freezer bags. It's best to freeze the baked bread without the Sugar Glaze. Just drizzle it on after the bread is thawed and reheated.

BEST-EVER YEAST ROLLS

2 packages dry yeast
⅔ cup sugar, divided
1 cup warm water (105° to 115°)
1 teaspoon salt
½ cup butter or margarine, softened
½ cup shortening
1 cup boiling water
2 eggs, beaten
6 to 7 cups all-purpose flour, divided
Cinnamon-Cheese Filling (optional)
Orange-Cheese Filling (optional)
Chocolate-Cheese Filling (optional)
Sugar Glaze (optional)

Dissolve yeast and 1 teaspoon sugar in 1 cup warm water; let stand about 5 minutes.

Combine remaining sugar, salt, butter, and shortening in a large bowl. Add boiling water, stirring until butter and shortening melt. Cool slightly. Add dissolved yeast, stirring well. Add eggs and 3 cups flour, beating until smooth. Gradually stir in enough remaining flour to make a soft dough. Place in a well-greased bowl, turning to grease top. Cover and let rise in a warm place (85°), free from drafts, 1 to 1½ hours or until doubled in bulk.

Punch dough down; turn dough out onto a well-floured surface, and knead several times. Shape into 2-inch balls, and place in 3 greased 9-inch round pans. Cover and let rise in a warm place, free from drafts, 30 to 40 minutes or until doubled in bulk. Bake at 325° for 20 to 25 minutes or until golden. Yield: 3 dozen.

Sweet Pinwheel Rolls: Place 1 recipe of Best-Ever Yeast Rolls dough in a large bowl; cover and let rise in a warm place (85°), free from drafts, 1 to 1½ hours or until dough is doubled in bulk. Punch dough down; divide into 4 equal portions. Turn each portion out onto a heavily floured surface, and knead 4 or 5 times. Roll each portion to a 12- x 10-inch rectangle.

Spread ¾ cup of desired filling over each rectangle. Carefully roll up dough, jellyroll fashion, starting at long side; pinch seam to seal (do not seal ends). Cut each roll into 1-inch slices; place slices, cut side down, in greased muffin pans.

Cover and let rise in a warm place, free from drafts, 40 minutes or until doubled in bulk. Bake at 325° for 25 minutes or until golden. Drizzle or spread Sugar Glaze over warm rolls. Yield: 4 dozen.

Sweet Yeast Braid: Place 1 recipe of Best-Ever Yeast Rolls dough in a large bowl; cover and let rise in a warm place (85°), free from drafts, 1 to 1½ hours or until doubled in bulk. Punch dough down; divide into 4 equal portions. Turn each portion

out onto a heavily floured surface, and knead 4 or 5 times. Roll each portion to a 12- x 9-inch rectangle. Cut each rectangle into 3 equal lengthwise strips. Spread about ¼ cup desired filling down center of each strip, leaving a 1-inch margin at each end.

Fold edge of dough over filling; pinch loose ends of ropes at one end to seal. Braid ropes; firmly pinch loose ends to seal.

Carefully transfer braids to greased baking sheets. Cover and let rise in a warm place, free from drafts, 40 minutes or until doubled in bulk. Bake at 325° for 35 to 45 minutes or until loaves sound hollow when tapped. Cool on wire racks; drizzle Sugar Glaze over warm loaves. Yield: four 12-inch loaves.

Sweet-Filled Yeast Loaves: Place 1 recipe of Best-Ever Yeast Rolls dough in a large bowl; cover and let rise in a warm place (85°), free from drafts, 1 to 1½ hours or until doubled in bulk. Punch dough down; divide into 4 equal portions. Turn each portion out onto a heavily floured surface, and knead 4 or 5 times. Roll each portion to a 12- x 10-inch rectangle.

Spread ¾ cup of desired filling over each rectangle. Roll up dough, jellyroll fashion, starting at long side; pinch seam and ends to seal. Transfer loaves, seam side down, to greased baking sheets. Cover; let rise in a warm place, free from drafts, 40 minutes or until doubled in bulk. Bake at 325° for 35 to 45 minutes or until loaves sound hollow when tapped. Cool on wire racks; drizzle Sugar Glaze over warm loaves. Yield: four 12-inch loaves.

Cinnamon-Cheese Filling

2 (8-ounce) packages cream cheese, softened
½ cup butter or margarine, softened
¾ cup firmly packed brown sugar
2 teaspoons ground cinnamon
1 teaspoon vanilla extract
½ cup chopped pecans

Combine all ingredients except chopped pecans; beat at medium speed of an electric mixer until smooth. Stir in pecans. Yield: about 3 cups.

Orange-Cheese Filling

2 (8-ounce) packages cream
   cheese, softened
½ cup butter or margarine,
   softened
½ cup orange marmalade
½ cup sugar
3 tablespoons grated orange rind

Combine all ingredients; beat at medium speed of an electric mixer until smooth. Yield: about 3 cups.

Chocolate-Cheese Filling

2 (8-ounce) packages cream
   cheese, softened
½ cup butter or margarine,
   softened
½ cup sugar
1 teaspoon vanilla extract
1 cup semisweet chocolate
   mini-morsels

Combine all ingredients except mini-morsels; beat at medium speed of an electric mixer until smooth. Spread filling over dough, and sprinkle with chocolate mini-morsels. Yield: about 3 cups.

Sugar Glaze

¼ cup butter or margarine,
   softened
1 (16-ounce) package powdered
   sugar, sifted
⅓ to ½ cup milk or orange juice
1 teaspoon vanilla extract

Cream butter; gradually add powdered sugar alternately with milk, beating at medium speed of an electric mixer until mixture reaches desired consistency. Stir in vanilla. Yield: about 2 cups.

Savory Dough Conceals The Cheese

Golden Bread offers several serving options. The thick cheese layer and peppery flavor complement a cool, crisp salad. As an hors d'oeuvre or afternoon repast on a chilly day, Golden Bread is delicious. Bread, wine, and cheese are naturally good partners. You may wish to serve beer, a robust red wine, port, or sherry to balance the rich, blue cheese flavor of the bread.

GOLDEN BREAD

¾ cup milk
½ cup butter or margarine
½ teaspoon salt
1 package dry yeast
1 tablespoon sugar
¼ cup warm water (105° to 115°)
2 eggs
½ teaspoon ground coriander
½ teaspoon pepper
3½ cups all-purpose flour, divided
½ cup cracked wheat
2 cups (8 ounces) shredded
   Cheddar cheese
⅔ cup crumbled blue cheese
1 egg, beaten
1 to 1½ teaspoons caraway seeds

Combine milk, butter, and salt in a medium saucepan; cook until butter melts, stirring occasionally. Cool to 105° to 115°.

Dissolve yeast and sugar in warm water in a large mixing bowl; let stand 5 minutes. Add milk mixture, 2 eggs, coriander, pepper, and 2 cups flour; beat at medium speed of an electric mixer until blended. Add remaining 1½ cups flour and cracked wheat; beat at medium speed 1 minute. Cover and refrigerate 8 hours.

Turn dough out onto a lightly floured surface, and roll to an 18- to 20-inch circle. Place dough in a greased 9-inch round cakepan, letting excess hang evenly over edges.

Combine Cheddar cheese and blue cheese, and spoon over dough. Fold and pleat excess dough over filling; gather edge together in center, and twist to form a topknot.

Cover and let rise in a warm place (85°), free from drafts, 1 hour. Brush surface with beaten egg, and sprinkle with caraway seeds. Bake at 350° for 50 to 60 minutes. Yield: 1 loaf.

Linda Corley
Sperry, Oklahoma

Snack-In-The-Box

Your schedule is a busy one, and whether working hard or playing hard, you often need a quick pick-me-up. These tasty munchies fit right in to your plans; they're easy to make and travel well, too.

SNOWY CHOCOLATE BITES

1 (6-ounce) package semisweet
   chocolate morsels
½ cup peanut butter
½ cup butter or margarine
8 cups crispy rice cereal squares
1 cup sifted powdered sugar

Combine first 3 ingredients in a saucepan; cook over low heat until morsels and butter melt, stirring occasionally. Remove from heat, and stir until smooth. Pour chocolate mixture over cereal, stirring to coat evenly. Spread cereal mixture on 2 wax paper-lined 15- x 10- x 1-inch jellyroll pans; let cool 1 hour. Sprinkle mixture with powdered sugar; stir to coat evenly. Yield: 8 cups.

Bonnie Taylor
Jackson, Tennessee

CRUNCHY PEANUT GRANOLA

4 cups regular oats, uncooked
2 cups unsalted dry roasted
  peanuts
1 cup wheat germ
½ cup honey
⅓ cup butter or margarine
1 teaspoon vanilla extract
1 cup raisins

Combine first 3 ingredients in a large mixing bowl; set aside. Combine honey, butter, and vanilla in a small saucepan; cook over medium heat until thoroughly heated (do not boil). Pour over oat mixture; stir to coat evenly. Divide into two 15- x 10- x 1-inch jellyroll pans. Bake at 300° for 20 to 25 minutes or until golden brown, stirring often. Remove from oven, and cool. Stir in raisins. Store granola in an airtight container. Yield: 9 cups.
Phyllis A. Moyers
Lutesville, Missouri

Treat Yourself To Kumquats

Though small in size, they're big on flavor. Kumquats, the smallest of citrus fruits, taste like a tart cross between an orange and a lemon.

Kumquats are available in the grocery store during the winter months—December, January, and February.

KUMQUAT MARMALADE

3 quarts kumquats (about 5½
  pounds)
2 lemons, peeled
2 cups water
3¼ cups plus 2 tablespoons sugar
1 (3-ounce) package liquid pectin

Cut kumquats lengthwise, and remove outer rind. Set rind aside.

Combine kumquat pulp, peeled lemons, and 2 cups water in a large Dutch oven; bring mixture to a boil, reduce heat, and simmer, uncovered, 45 minutes.

Thinly slice kumquat rinds; place in a large Dutch oven, and cover with water. Bring mixture to a boil. Boil, uncovered, 5 minutes; drain well, and set aside.

Press kumquat pulp mixture through a sieve or food mill. Measure 4½ cups of puree into Dutch oven; add sugar and cooked kumquat rind. Bring to a full rolling boil; boil 1 minute, stirring constantly. Remove from heat. Add pectin, stirring until well blended.

Pour marmalade into hot sterilized jars, leaving ¼ inch headspace; wipe jar rims. Cover with metal lids; screw on bands. Process marmalade in boiling-water bath 10 minutes. Yield: 12 half pints.
Bruce M. Beard, Jr.
Washington, North Carolina

Pralines For Dessert

If you like the flavor of homemade pralines, don't just enjoy them as a sugary-flavored candy. Carol Barclay of Portland, Texas, crumbles the pecan-studded candy to serve in her recipe for Praline Freeze. Even without adding the homemade pralines, the praline-flavored ice cream mixture is a great dessert to have on hand for drop-in guests.

Remember that it's important to cook the candy mixture in a heavy saucepan. Also, if it's a humid day, the candy may have a more sugary texture. Best results generally occur when the weather is dry.

PRALINE FREEZE

½ gallon vanilla ice cream,
  softened
½ cup praline liqueur
1 cup whipping cream
2 tablespoons sugar
Pralines

Combine vanilla ice cream and praline liqueur in a large bowl; stir well. Spoon mixture into a 13- x 9- x 2-inch pan, and freeze.

Beat whipping cream at high speed of an electric mixer until foamy; gradually add sugar, beating until soft peaks form.

Using an ice cream scoop, spoon ice cream mixture into individual compotes. Sprinkle desserts evenly with crumbled Pralines, and top with sweetened whipped cream. Yield: 8 servings.

Pralines

1½ cups sugar
¾ cup firmly packed brown
  sugar
½ cup half-and-half
¼ cup plus 2 tablespoons
  butter or margarine
2 cups pecan halves

Combine all ingredients in a large heavy saucepan. Cook over low heat, stirring gently, until sugar dissolves. Cover and cook over medium heat 2 to 3 minutes to wash down sugar crystals from sides of pan. Uncover and cook to soft ball stage (235°), stirring constantly.

Remove saucepan from heat, and beat mixture with a wooden spoon just until mixture begins to thicken. Working rapidly, drop candy mixture by tablespoonfuls onto greased wax paper; let stand until candy is firm. Yield: 1½ dozen.

Cookie By The Slice

Sherry Marr of Burke, Virginia, combined several recipes to come up with her Pizza Cookie. It's popular at spend-the-night parties where she lets the kids decorate their own cookie.

PIZZA COOKIE

¾ cup butter or margarine, softened
1 cup sugar
1 egg
1½ cups all-purpose flour
½ teaspoon baking soda
¼ teaspoon salt
¼ cup cocoa
1 teaspoon vanilla extract
¾ cup candy-coated chocolate pieces, divided
½ cup chopped pecans, divided
¼ cup flaked coconut
½ cup miniature marshmallows

Line a 12-inch pizza pan with heavy-duty aluminum foil; grease foil, and set aside.

Cream butter; gradually add sugar, beating well at medium speed of an electric mixer. Add egg, and beat well. Combine flour and next 3 ingredients; add to creamed mixture, mixing well. Add vanilla, and mix well. Stir in ½ cup chocolate pieces and ¼ cup chopped pecans.

Spoon batter onto prepared pan, spreading to within 1 inch of edge. Sprinkle with coconut and remaining ¼ cup pecans. Bake at 350° for 15 minutes. Sprinkle marshmallows and remaining ¼ cup chocolate pieces on top; bake an additional 5 to 7 minutes. Cool on a wire rack. To serve, cut into wedges. Yield: one 12-inch cookie.

Pastries For Breakfast

Contrast the frenzy of the typical workday morning with a leisurely weekend Continental breakfast. Just put one of these pastries on the menu and you'll feel like lingering over a cup of coffee or serving the meal in bed.

Although rich with sauces and sweet surprises, these pastries are easy to make for the morning meal. They all bake in 20 to 35 minutes.

If you'd like to make one of these pastries ahead of time, try baking and freezing Butterscotch Pinwheels according to the directions given. You'll only have to reheat them 10 minutes.

BUTTERSCOTCH PINWHEELS

2 cups all-purpose flour
2 teaspoons baking powder
½ teaspoon salt
⅓ cup shortening
⅔ cup milk
3 tablespoons butter or margarine, softened
½ cup firmly packed light brown sugar

Combine flour, baking powder, and salt; cut in shortening with a pastry blender until mixture resembles coarse meal. Add milk, stirring until dry ingredients are moistened. Turn dough out onto a lightly floured surface, and knead lightly 4 or 5 times.

Roll dough to a 12-inch square on a lightly floured surface. Spread dough with butter, and sprinkle with brown sugar. Roll up jellyroll fashion; pinch seam to seal. Cut into 1-inch slices, and place cut side up in greased muffin pans. Bake at 375° for 25 to 30 minutes or until golden brown. Yield: 1 dozen.

Note: To freeze, bake rolls at 375° for 20 minutes; cool. Wrap in aluminum foil; freeze. To serve, unwrap rolls, and place on a lightly greased baking sheet; thaw. Bake at 375° for 10 minutes or until heated.

Mrs. Paul Raper
Burgaw, North Carolina

DATE SQUARES

6 eggs
1½ cups firmly packed brown sugar
1 teaspoon vanilla extract
1½ cups graham cracker crumbs
1 teaspoon baking powder
½ teaspoon salt
1 (8-ounce) package whole pitted dates, finely chopped
1 cup finely chopped walnuts or pecans
Sifted powdered sugar

Beat eggs at high speed of an electric mixer until thick and lemon colored (about 5 minutes). Gradually add brown sugar; mix well. Add vanilla, and stir well.

Combine graham cracker crumbs, baking powder, and salt; add to creamed mixture. Stir in dates and walnuts. Pour batter into a greased and floured 13- x 9- x 2-inch pan. Bake at 350° for 30 minutes or until a wooden pick inserted in center comes out clean. Cool and cut into squares. Sprinkle with powdered sugar. Yield: 2 dozen.

Velma McGregor
Gretna, Virginia

MAPLE CREAM COFFEE TREAT

1 cup firmly packed brown sugar
⅓ cup maple-flavored syrup
¼ cup butter or margarine, melted
½ cup chopped pecans
1 (8-ounce) package cream cheese, softened
¼ cup sifted powdered sugar
2 tablespoons butter or margarine, softened
½ cup flaked coconut (optional)
2 (10-ounce) cans refrigerated flaky biscuits

Combine first 4 ingredients in a bowl, stirring well. Spread mixture in an ungreased 13- x 9- x 2-inch pan.

Combine cream cheese, powdered sugar, and 2 tablespoons butter in a small mixing bowl. Beat at medium speed of an electric mixer until blended. Stir in coconut, if desired.

Separate biscuit dough into 20 pieces. Roll each biscuit on a lightly floured surface to a 4-inch circle. Spread about 1 tablespoon cream cheese mixture evenly on biscuit, and roll up jellyroll fashion. Place in prepared pan, seam side down, in two rows. Bake at 350° on lowest rack in oven for 20 to 25 minutes or until golden brown. Cool in pan 3 minutes. Turn biscuits out onto a serving platter. Yield: 20 pastries.

Laura Bailey
Brownsboro, Texas

DEEP-DISH CHEESECAKE COFFEE CAKE

3 cups biscuit mix
¼ cup sugar
½ cup milk
¼ cup butter or margarine, melted
1 (8-ounce) package cream cheese, softened
2 eggs
½ cup sugar
½ teaspoon vanilla extract
¼ cup strawberry preserves

Combine biscuit mix, ¼ cup sugar, milk, and butter; stir vigorously 30 seconds. Turn dough out onto a lightly floured surface; knead 4 or 5 times. Pat evenly in the bottom and up the sides of an ungreased 9-inch round cakepan; set aside.

Combine cream cheese, eggs, ½ cup sugar, and vanilla; beat at medium speed of an electric mixer until smooth. Pour over dough; bake at 350° for 30 to 35 minutes. Remove from oven; let stand 10 minutes. Spread preserves over top. Serve warm. Yield: 8 servings.

Ernestine Elder
Gainesville, Texas

From Our Kitchen To Yours

Whether you're planning a kitchen for the first time or adding to your current inventory, investing in the necessary tools makes cooking easier and more fun. Our staff compiled a basic guide for a well-equipped kitchen.

Preparation Equipment

When purchasing preparation equipment, invest in the best you can afford.
Mixing bowls in graduated sizes
Dry measuring cup set
Liquid measuring cups (1-, 2-, and 4-cup)
Measuring spoons
Set of quality knives
Mixing spoons (plastic, metal, and wooden)
Kitchen shears
Pastry blender
Thermometer (candy/deep fry, meat, and instant read)
Openers (electric, hand, and bottle)
Wire whisk
Vegetable parer
Timer
Mallet
Colander
Rolling pin
Sifter
Spatulas (rubber and metal)
Wire mesh strainer
Scales
Chopping board
Grater
Basting brush
Metal turners (small and large)
Meat fork
Tongs
Juicer
Garlic press
Bulb baster
Ladle
Funnel
Biscuit cutter
Potato masher
Ruler
Pastry board
Pie weights
Optional: pastry bag and tips, shaped cutters

Cookware

Be sure to purchase pots and pans of heavy gauge (thickness) and sturdy construction.
Saucepans (1-, 2-, and 3-quart with lids)
Large Dutch oven (with lid)
Skillets (6- or 8-inch)
Skillet (10-inch with lid)
Optional: steamer, double boiler, nonstick skillet

Bakeware

With these suggested bakeware pieces, you'll be prepared for almost any task.
Two or three 9-inch round cakepans
8- and 9-inch square pan
13- x 9- x 2-inch pan
10-inch tube pan
Bundt pan
13- x 9- x 2-inch baking dish
12- x 8- x 2-inch baking dish
8-inch square baking dish
1-quart baking dish
Two cookie sheets
15- x 10- x 1-inch jellyroll pan
Wire cooling racks
9- x 5- x 3-inch loafpan
Muffin pan
9-inch glass pieplate
Optional: springform pan, tart pan, miniature muffin pan, pizza pan

MARCH

*Whether you are looking for appetizers or breads, salads or
side dishes, entrées or desserts, you'll find them in this
chapter—many served in new ways. Desserts are light and
delectable. Pasta salads are tossed with vegetables, meat,
and dressings in a variety of robust flavors. Other salads
get a boost from new types of greens, easily identified once
you see our sampler of salad greens.*

A Wellspring Of Entrée Ideas

There comes a day when the sun's gentle warmth seems more sincere, and we revel in the knowledge that spring will soon arrive.

Anticipating the arrival of spring's edible gifts on our market shelves, we plan gatherings of all sorts and sizes to enjoy the freshest foods of the season. We bid farewell to hearty soups and stews for now and get ready for lightly flavored entrées.

A large luncheon buffet on a sunny day is a perfect event for Baked Ham With Orange-Honey Glaze, and any leftovers can be used in Ham and Apricots, a quick weeknight dish. Either of the following leg of lamb recipes is just right for a big Sunday dinner, and Marinated Chicken Breasts or Pecan Chicken serves as a more intimate meal.

CRANBERRY LEG OF LAMB

1 (3- to 5-pound) half leg of lamb
1 clove garlic, sliced
1 teaspoon ground ginger
1 teaspoon dry mustard
½ cup whole-berry cranberry sauce
¼ cup cherry preserves
1 tablespoon port wine
2 tablespoons all-purpose flour
¼ cup water
¼ teaspoon salt
⅛ teaspoon pepper

Place lamb, fat side up, on a rack in a shallow roasting pan. Make several slits on outside of lamb, and insert garlic slices.

Combine ginger and mustard in a small bowl, and rub on outside of lamb. Insert meat thermometer, making sure it does not touch fat or bone. Bake at 325° for 1 hour.

Combine cranberry sauce and preserves in a small saucepan, mixing well. Cook over low heat until melted; stir in wine. Spoon over lamb, and bake 1 hour and 15 minutes or until meat thermometer registers 160°. Remove lamb to a serving platter, reserving drippings in pan, and let lamb stand 10 minutes before carving.

Skim fat from pan drippings; measure remaining liquid, adding enough water to measure 1¼ cups, and pour into saucepan.

Combine flour and ¼ cup water, stirring well, and add to pan drippings. Cook over medium heat, stirring constantly, until gravy is thickened and bubbly. Stir in salt and pepper. Serve gravy with lamb. Yield: 4 to 6 servings.

Note: A boneless leg of lamb, rolled and tied, may be substituted. Bake 32 to 34 minutes per pound or until meat thermometer reaches 160°.

Velma Kestner
Berwind, West Virginia

HONEY-MUSTARD GLAZED LAMB

1 (3- to 4-pound) half leg of lamb
¼ cup prepared mustard
¼ cup honey
½ teaspoon salt
⅛ teaspoon pepper

Place lamb, fat side up, on a rack in a shallow roasting pan. Insert meat thermometer, making sure it does not touch fat or bone. Bake at 325° for 1 hour. Combine mustard, honey, salt, and pepper; mix well, and spoon over lamb. Bake an additional 45 minutes to 1 hour or until meat thermometer registers 160°. Let stand 10 minutes before carving. Yield: 4 to 6 servings.

Faye Hicks
Charleston, West Virginia

HAM AND APRICOTS

1 (16-ounce) can apricot halves,
   undrained
¾ cup chicken broth
⅓ cup sugar
¼ cup white vinegar
3 tablespoons soy sauce
3 tablespoons butter or margarine
1 pound cooked ham, cut into
   strips
1 green pepper, cut into 1-inch
   pieces
¼ cup cornstarch
¼ cup chicken broth
Hot cooked rice

Drain apricots, reserving juice; set
apricots aside. Combine juice, ¾ cup
chicken broth, and next 4 ingredients
in a large saucepan. Stir in ham and
green pepper. Bring to a boil; cover,
reduce heat, and simmer 10 minutes.

Combine cornstarch and ¼ cup
broth, stirring until smooth; add to
ham mixture. Bring to a boil; cook 1
minute or until thickened, stirring
constantly. Stir in apricots, and serve
over rice. Yield: 4 servings.
Pat Lubas
Tulsa, Oklahoma

BAKED HAM WITH
ORANGE-HONEY GLAZE
(pictured on page 41)

1 (6-ounce) can frozen orange
   juice concentrate, thawed and
   undiluted
1¾ cups water
½ cup honey
3 tablespoons cornstarch
1 teaspoon dry mustard
½ teaspoon salt
½ teaspoon ground nutmeg
1 (3-inch) stick cinnamon
1 (7- to 9-pound) smoked, fully
   cooked, whole boneless ham
Whole cloves
2 oranges, peeled and sectioned
Garnishes: orange rind strips,
   fresh parsley sprigs

Combine first 3 ingredients in a medium saucepan. Remove ¼ cup mixture, and combine with cornstarch,
stirring until smooth. Add cornstarch
mixture to orange juice mixture in
saucepan, stirring until smooth. Add
mustard and next 3 ingredients.
Cook over medium heat, stirring constantly, until mixture comes to a boil;
cook 1 minute. Remove cinnamon
stick. Remove mixture from heat,
and set aside.

Score fat on ham in a diamond design, and stud with cloves. Place
ham, fat side up, on rack in a shallow
roasting pan. Insert meat thermometer, making sure it does not touch
fat. Bake, uncovered, at 325° for 2
hours or until meat thermometer
registers 140° (18 to 24 minutes per
pound).

After the first hour, baste the ham
every 15 minutes with orange-honey
sauce. Heat remaining sauce; add orange sections, and serve with ham.
Garnish, if desired. Yield: 20 to 24
servings.
Trenda Leigh
Richmond, Virginia

CRANBERRY PORK CHOPS

4 (¾-inch-thick) pork chops
1 tablespoon vegetable oil
¼ teaspoon salt
⅛ teaspoon pepper
1 (8-ounce) can pineapple slices,
   undrained
½ cup hot water
½ cup whole-berry cranberry
   sauce
1 chicken-flavored bouillon cube
2 tablespoons brown sugar
2 tablespoons white vinegar
1 sweet red or green pepper, cut
   into rings
2 tablespoons cornstarch
2 tablespoons water

Brown pork chops in oil in a large
skillet; drain pan drippings. Sprinkle
pork chops with salt and pepper.

Drain pineapple, reserving juice;
set pineapple aside. Combine juice,

½ cup hot water, and next 4 ingredients; pour over pork chops. Cover
and simmer 20 minutes.

Place pineapple slices and pepper
rings on top of pork chops; cover and
simmer an additional 10 minutes.
Transfer chops, pineapple, and pepper rings to a serving platter, reserving pan drippings.

Combine cornstarch and 2 tablespoons water, stirring until smooth;
stir into pan drippings. Bring to a
boil, and cook 1 minute or until thickened, stirring constantly. Spoon over
chops. Serve immediately. Yield: 4
servings.
Jean Voan
Shepherd, Texas

ORANGE-TURKEY SLICES

½ cup grated Parmesan cheese
1 teaspoon salt
½ teaspoon pepper
2 pounds uncooked turkey breast
   slices
3 tablespoons butter or margarine
1 cup julienne carrots
1 cup chicken broth
2 oranges, peeled and cut into
   ¼-inch-thick slices
3 tablespoons orange juice
Garnish: fresh parsley sprigs

Combine cheese, salt, and pepper;
dredge turkey slices in mixture. Melt
butter in a large nonstick skillet over
medium heat; add turkey, and cook 1
to 2 minutes on each side. Place turkey in a lightly greased 13- x 9- x
2-inch baking dish; set aside.

Add carrots and broth to skillet;
bring to a boil. Reduce heat, and
simmer 5 minutes. Pour carrot mixture over turkey; top with orange
slices. Cover and bake at 350° for 25
minutes. Add orange juice, and bake
an additional 5 minutes. Arrange turkey on a serving platter with oranges
and carrots, and garnish, if desired.
Yield: 8 servings.
Charlotte Watkins
Lakeland, Florida

MARINATED CHICKEN BREASTS

6 chicken breast halves, skinned
  and boned
½ cup firmly packed brown sugar
⅓ cup olive oil
¼ cup cider vinegar
3 cloves garlic, crushed
3 tablespoons coarse-grain
  mustard
1½ tablespoons lemon juice
1½ tablespoons lime juice
1½ teaspoons salt
¼ teaspoon pepper

Place chicken breasts in a large shallow dish. Combine remaining ingredients; stir well, and pour over chicken. Cover and marinate chicken in the refrigerator 2 hours.

Remove chicken from marinade, discarding marinade. Grill chicken over hot coals about 8 minutes on each side. Yield: 6 servings.

Bettye Cortner
Cerulean, Kentucky

PECAN CHICKEN

4 chicken breast halves, skinned
  and boned
¼ cup honey
¼ cup Dijon mustard
1 cup finely chopped pecans

Place each piece of chicken between 2 sheets of wax paper; flatten to ¼-inch thickness, using a meat mallet or rolling pin. Set aside.

Combine honey and mustard; spread on both sides of chicken, and dredge chicken in chopped pecans. Arrange chicken in a lightly greased shallow baking dish. Bake at 350° for 30 minutes or until tender. Yield: 4 servings.

Dorothy Toombs
Richmond, Virginia

Toss The Salad, But Don't Mix Up The Greens

Shopping for salad greens can be confusing with the new types available. If you are puzzled about which lettuce to select for salads or sandwiches, the information in the box below right and the recipes on these pages will guide you.

When mixing greens for a salad, aim for a contrast in texture, color, and flavor. It takes only two or three greens to make a nice combination.

For an unusually tender blend of salad greens try mesclun, which is a combination of several baby lettuces torn and blended. If it is unavailable in your area, you can simulate mesclun by mixing your own blend of tender young leaves of watercress, endive, oakleaf, baby leaf, or baby romaine lettuce.

When selecting greens, look for those that are crisp and well colored. Rinse greens under cold water. Pluck the leaves from the head, rinsing the bases well where soil tends to cling. Discard wilted or blemished leaves. Drain the greens, and pat them between paper towels, or whirl them in a salad spinner to dry them.

If the greens are not to be used immediately, wrap a paper towel around them to absorb excess moisture, and store them in a plastic bag in the refrigerator.

GOAT CHEESE AND GREENS
(pictured on page 40)

1 (11-ounce) log goat cheese, cut
  into 12 rounds
½ cup herb-seasoned dry
  breadcrumbs
Vegetable cooking spray
⅓ cup olive oil
3 tablespoons lemon juice
1 teaspoon dried whole basil
¼ teaspoon salt
⅛ teaspoon pepper
1 head radicchio, torn
2 bunches arugula, torn

Dredge cheese in breadcrumbs, and spray lightly with vegetable cooking table cooking spray. Place on a lightly greased baking sheet, and bake at 400° for 7 minutes or until cheese is golden brown.

Combine olive oil and next 4 ingredients in a jar; cover tightly, and shake vigorously.

Arrange radicchio and arugula on individual salad plates, and top each with 2 slices goat cheese. Drizzle dressing over top, and serve immediately. Yield: 6 servings.

Tip: *Wash most vegetables; trim any wilted parts or excess leaves before storing in refrigerator.*

RED-AND-GREEN SALAD

1 (16-ounce) can sliced beets,
　drained and diced
Honey-Mustard Dressing
2 cups torn curly endive
2 cups torn escarole

Combine beets and about 2 tablespoons of Honey-Mustard Dressing,
tossing gently.

Toss torn endive and escarole with
remaining Honey-Mustard Dressing.
Arrange salad on individual salad
plates, and spoon beets on top.
Yield: 4 to 6 servings.

Honey-Mustard Dressing

¼ cup olive oil
2 tablespoons raspberry or red
　wine vinegar
1 tablespoon Dijon mustard
1 tablespoon honey
⅛ teaspoon salt
⅛ teaspoon pepper
⅛ teaspoon ground nutmeg

Combine all ingredients in a jar;
cover tightly, and shake vigorously.
Yield: ½ cup.

ROASTED RED PEPPER AND WATERCRESS SALAD

3 large sweet red peppers
¼ cup olive oil
2 tablespoons white vinegar
⅛ teaspoon salt
⅛ teaspoon pepper
1 clove garlic, minced
4 cups loosely packed trimmed
　fresh watercress
½ small onion, sliced and
　separated into rings

Place whole peppers on their sides
on a large baking sheet. Bake at 500°
for 20 minutes or until skin is blackened and charred. Transfer peppers
immediately to a paper bag, and seal
top. Refrigerate 10 minutes or until
peppers cool. Peel and seed peppers,
discarding seeds and charred skin.
Slice peppers into thin strips. Set
peppers aside.

Combine olive oil and next 4 ingredients in a jar; cover tightly, and
shake vigorously. Toss watercress
with dressing. Arrange watercress
on salad plates; arrange pepper strips
and onion over watercress. Serve
immediately. Yield: 6 servings.

COLORFUL TOSSED SALAD
(pictured on page 40)

1 head radicchio, torn
2 bunches arugula, torn
2 heads Belgian endive, torn
Blue Cheese Vinaigrette

Combine greens, and toss with
enough Blue Cheese Vinaigrette to
coat. Serve immediately. Yield: 8
servings.

Blue Cheese Vinaigrette

⅔ cup olive oil
2 ounces crumbled blue cheese
　(½ cup)
3 tablespoons white wine vinegar
1 teaspoon dried whole oregano
¼ teaspoon salt
¼ teaspoon freshly ground pepper

Combine all ingredients in a jar;
cover tightly, and shake vigorously.
Yield: 1 cup.

MESCLUN WITH TARRAGON DRESSING

6 cups torn mesclun
¼ cup pine nuts, toasted
¼ cup raisins
Tarragon Dressing

Combine first 3 ingredients in a large
salad bowl; toss with Tarragon
Dressing, and serve immediately.
Yield: 6 servings.

Tarragon Dressing

½ cup olive oil
⅓ cup white wine vinegar
¼ teaspoon salt
⅛ teaspoon pepper
2 tablespoons chopped fresh
　tarragon or 2 teaspoons dried
　whole tarragon

Combine all ingredients in a jar;
cover tightly, and shake vigorously.
Yield: ¾ cup.

A Sampler of Greens

Look for these new greens in
Southern supermarkets:
Escarole—A broad-leafed
cousin of curly endive, escarole
has a pleasantly bitter flavor and
a firm texture.
Belgian endive—The leaves
are slightly bitter and pale green
or yellow in color.
Watercress—Peppery greens
often blended with lettuces for
salads. Store in the refrigerator
with stems in a cup of water to
stay fresh; loosely cover leaves
with plastic wrap.
Oakleaf—A nut-flavored lettuce, oakleaf's availability is spo-
radic because the lettuce does

not ship well. If oakleaf lettuce
is not available in your market,
it can often be ordered through
the produce department.
Curly endive—This thick bun-
dle of greens has firm, curly
leaves that add an interesting
texture and tangy flavor to
salads.
Radicchio—Deep burgundy in
color, radicchio adds a chewy
texture and slightly bitter taste
to salads. Radicchio grows in
tight, round heads.
Arugula—This green has a
pleasantly bitter, pungent flavor.
Small, narrow leaves signal a
young, tender plant.

LEAFY CHEESE SANDWICHES
(pictured on page 40)

2 medium tomatoes, sliced
½ pound fresh mozzarella cheese
   in brine or 1 (6-ounce) package
   chèvre cheese, drained and
   thinly sliced
2 tablespoons vegetable oil
2 tablespoons white wine
   vinegar
½ teaspoon salt
¼ teaspoon freshly ground
   pepper
1 (3-ounce) package cream
   cheese, softened
2 tablespoons chopped fresh
   chives
4 individual French bread loaves,
   cut in half horizontally and
   toasted
2 ounces oakleaf or arugula
Garnishes: cornichons,
   pimiento-stuffed olives

Arrange tomato slices and mozzarella cheese slices in a 13- x 9- x 2-inch baking dish.

Combine vegetable oil, vinegar, salt, and pepper in a jar; cover tightly, and shake vigorously. Pour dressing over tomatoes and cheese. Cover and chill at least 2 hours.

Combine cream cheese and chives in a small bowl; spread evenly over cut surface of each piece of bread. Arrange half of lettuce leaves on bottom halves of bread. Drain tomatoes and cheese; arrange evenly over lettuce. Top with remaining lettuce and tops of bread. If desired, garnish sandwiches with cornichons and olives. Serve immediately. Yield: 4 servings.

ON THE LIGHT SIDE

Spectacular Light Desserts

A delectable dessert embellishes a meal like a beautiful frame sets off an artist's work. And we've created a gallery of dazzling light desserts that will please the eye as well as the palate. Each one conquers the myth that dessert must be high in calories, sugar, and fat to be delicious.

LUSCIOUS FLAN
(pictured on page 1)

¼ cup sugar
1 (12-ounce) can evaporated
   skimmed milk
½ cup skim milk
¾ cup egg substitute
¼ cup sugar
⅛ teaspoon salt
½ teaspoon almond extract
2 cups assorted fresh fruit

Sprinkle ¼ cup sugar in a heavy saucepan; place over medium heat. Cook, stirring constantly, until sugar melts and syrup is light golden brown. Pour syrup into six 6-ounce custard cups; let cool.

Combine milks in a medium saucepan, and heat until bubbles form around edge of pan.

Combine egg substitute, ¼ cup sugar, salt, and almond extract; beat well. Gradually stir about 1 cup hot milk into egg mixture; add to remaining milk, stirring constantly. Pour mixture evenly into custard cups; cover with aluminum foil. Place custard cups in a shallow pan; pour hot water to a depth of 1 inch into pan. Bake at 325° for 25 minutes or until a knife inserted near center comes out clean. Remove cups from water, and chill at least 4 hours.

To serve, loosen edges of custard with a spatula; invert onto plates. Arrange assorted fresh fruit around sides. Yield: 6 servings (154 calories per serving with ⅓ cup fruit).

☐ *8.3 grams protein, 0.3 gram fat, 30.4 grams carbohydrate, 3 milligrams cholesterol, 172 milligrams sodium, and 205 milligrams calcium.*

FROZEN CHOCOLATE ROULAGE

Vegetable cooking spray
1 tablespoon sifted cake flour
¾ cup sifted cake flour
1 teaspoon baking powder
½ teaspoon baking soda
¼ teaspoon salt
⅓ cup unsweetened cocoa
⅓ cup sugar
½ cup water
⅓ cup vegetable oil
2 teaspoons vanilla extract
5 egg whites
⅓ cup sugar
¼ cup sifted cake flour
2 tablespoons unsweetened cocoa,
   divided
2 cups frozen raspberry yogurt,
   softened

Coat bottom and sides of a 15- x 10- x 1-inch jellyroll pan with cooking spray; line with wax paper. Coat wax paper with cooking spray and 1 tablespoon flour; remove excess flour. Set aside.

Combine ¾ cup flour and next 5 ingredients in a large bowl. Add water, oil, and vanilla; stir until smooth. Set aside.

Beat egg whites (at room temperature) until foamy. Gradually add ⅓ cup sugar, 1 tablespoon at a time, beating until stiff peaks form. Fold egg whites into chocolate mixture. Sift ¼ cup flour over batter, and fold until combined.

Pour batter into prepared pan, spreading evenly. Bake at 325° for

12 minutes or until cake pulls away from sides of pan. Cool cake in pan on a wire rack 10 minutes. Quickly invert jellyroll pan onto a towel sprinkled with 1 tablespoon cocoa. Peel off wax paper. Starting at long side, roll up cake and towel together; cool seam side down on wire rack.

Carefully unroll cake, and sprinkle with remaining 1 tablespoon cocoa. Spread cake with frozen yogurt within ½ inch of edge, and reroll cake, without towel. Place cake on heavy-duty plastic wrap, seam side down. Wrap in plastic wrap, and freeze until firm. Yield: 14 servings (about 164 calories per 1-inch slice).

□ *3.2 grams protein, 6.2 grams fat, 23.8 grams carbohydrate, 3 milligrams cholesterol, 110 milligrams sodium, and 32 milligrams calcium.*

VANILLA POACHED PEARS
(pictured on page 42)

4 medium-size firm, ripe pears
1 tablespoon lemon juice
4 cups water
3 tablespoons vanilla extract
2 tablespoons honey
½ cup sugar
2 to 3 drops hot water
Chocolate Sauce
Garnish: fresh mint sprigs

Peel pears, and core from bottom, cutting to, but not through, the stem end. Cut a thin slice from bottoms so that pears stand upright. Rub lemon juice over pears.

Combine 4 cups water, vanilla, and honey in a large saucepan; bring to a boil. Add pears; cover, reduce heat, and simmer 15 to 20 minutes or until pears are tender. Remove pears, and let cool.

Up to 30 minutes before serving, place sugar in a heavy 1-quart saucepan and cook over medium heat, stirring constantly, until sugar melts and syrup is light golden brown. Stir in drops of water; let stand 1 minute.

Insert a meat fork at base of pear to hold. Drizzle caramelized sugar from a spoon, and quickly wrap threads around pears until a delicate web is formed. Repeat with remaining pears. To serve, spoon 2 tablespoons Chocolate Sauce on each serving plate; place pears on sauce. Garnish, if desired. Serve immediately. Yield: 4 servings (197 calories per pear with 2 tablespoons Chocolate Sauce).

□ *0.7 gram protein, 0.9 gram fat, 50.1 grams carbohydrate, 0 milligrams cholesterol, 0 milligrams sodium, and 22 milligrams calcium.*

Chocolate Sauce

2 tablespoons sugar
2 tablespoons unsweetened cocoa
1 teaspoon cornstarch
½ cup water
½ teaspoon vanilla extract

Combine all ingredients in a small saucepan; bring to a boil over medium heat, stirring constantly. Boil mixture 1 minute, stirring constantly. Remove from heat, and let sauce cool. Yield: ½ cup (18 calories per tablespoon).

□ *0.1 gram protein, 0.2 gram fat, 3.9 grams carbohydrate, 0 milligrams cholesterol, 0 milligrams sodium, and 4 milligrams calcium.*

CHOCOLATE-DRIZZLED
PINEAPPLE
WITH RASPBERRY SAUCE

2 cups frozen unsweetened
  raspberries, thawed
¼ cup water
1 tablespoon cornstarch
2 tablespoons honey
Chocolate Sauce
4 (1-inch-thick) fresh pineapple
  slices
Garnish: fresh mint sprigs

Combine raspberries and water in food processor or electric blender. Process until pureed. Strain puree, discarding seeds.

Combine raspberry puree, cornstarch, and honey in a saucepan. Bring to a boil over medium heat, stirring constantly. Boil 1 minute, stirring constantly. Cover and chill.

Spoon ¼ cup raspberry sauce and 1 tablespoon Chocolate Sauce on each serving plate; set aside.

Spoon remaining Chocolate Sauce into a heavy-duty zip-top plastic bag; seal bag. Snip a tiny hole in the end of bag, using scissors. Place pineapple slices on baking sheet; drizzle chocolate over pineapple.

Place pineapple over raspberry and chocolate sauces. Garnish, if desired. Yield: 4 servings (119 calories per serving with ¼ cup raspberry sauce, 2 tablespoons Chocolate Sauce, and one slice pineapple).

□ *0.8 gram protein, 0.8 gram fat, 25.5 grams carbohydrate, 0 milligrams cholesterol, 2 milligrams sodium, and 15 milligrams calcium.*

Chocolate Sauce

1 teaspoon cornstarch
½ cup water
2 tablespoons unsweetened cocoa
3 tablespoons honey
½ teaspoon vanilla extract

Combine cornstarch and water in a small saucepan; add remaining ingredients, stirring until smooth.

Cook over medium heat, stirring constantly, until mixture begins to boil; boil 1 minute, stirring constantly. Remove from heat.

Cover and chill. Yield: ½ cup (30 calories per 1 tablespoon).

□ *0.2 gram protein, 0.2 gram fat, 7.3 grams carbohydrate, 0 milligrams cholesterol, 0 milligrams sodium, and 5 milligrams calcium.*

FRESH FRUIT TART

1 (8-ounce) carton strawberry
  low-sugar, low-fat yogurt
Tart Crust
3 cups assorted fresh fruit
  (raspberries, sliced
  strawberries, and sliced
  kiwifruit)
¼ cup low-sugar apple jelly,
  melted

Spread yogurt evenly over pre-baked Tart Crust. Arrange fruit over yogurt. Brush with apple jelly. Chill thoroughly. Yield: 8 servings (154 calories per serving).

☐ *3.4 grams protein, 6.5 grams fat, 20.8 grams carbohydrate, 2 milligrams cholesterol, 78 milligrams sodium, and 51 milligrams calcium.*

Tart Crust

1 cup all-purpose flour
¼ cup corn oil margarine
2 to 3 tablespoons cold water

Place flour in a small bowl; cut in margarine with a pastry blender until mixture resembles coarse meal. Sprinkle water evenly over surface of mixture; stir with a fork until dry ingredients are moistened. Shape into a ball; place between 2 sheets of heavy-duty plastic wrap, and gently press to a 4-inch circle.
  Chill dough 15 minutes. Roll dough to a 10-inch circle, and freeze 5 minutes or until plastic wrap can be removed easily. Remove top sheet of plastic wrap; invert and fit pastry in an ungreased 9-inch tart pan. Prick bottom and sides of crust generously with a fork.
  Bake at 425° for 15 to 20 minutes or until edges of pastry are golden brown. Let cool on a wire rack. Yield: one 9-inch tart crust.

Tip: *To prepare kiwifruit, first chill the fruit; then peel and thinly slice crosswise for use in recipes or as an eye-catching garnish.*

AMARETTO PEARS WITH MERINGUE

3 tablespoons water
2 teaspoons lemon juice
3 medium pears
¼ cup amaretto
2 tablespoons light corn syrup
1 (2-inch) stick cinnamon
2 egg whites
¼ teaspoon cream of tartar
2 tablespoons sugar
¼ teaspoon grated lemon rind

Combine water and lemon juice in a medium bowl. Peel and core pears. Dip pears in lemon juice mixture; drain well. Cut pears in half vertically; cut into ⅛-inch-thick lengthwise slices, keeping slices in order as they are cut.
  Transfer sliced pear halves to a 9-inch pieplate, letting slices fan out slightly. Add amaretto and corn syrup to remaining lemon mixture; stir well, and pour into center of dish. Place cinnamon stick in center of dish. Cover dish tightly with heavy-duty plastic wrap, folding back a small edge of wrap to allow steam to escape. Microwave at HIGH 6 minutes, giving dish a quarter-turn after 3 minutes. Remove dish from microwave.
  Beat egg whites (at room temperature) and cream of tartar at high speed of an electric mixer until foamy. Gradually add sugar, beating until stiff peaks form. Add lemon rind; beat well.
  Dollop meringue around pears. Bake at 400° for 6 minutes or until golden brown. Serve warm. Yield: 6 servings (99 calories per serving).

☐ *1.4 grams protein, 0.4 gram fat, 24.3 grams carbohydrate, 0 milligrams cholesterol, 30 milligrams sodium, and 15 milligrams calcium.*

Plan The Meal Around Healthy Soup

Cool nights linger as winter wanes, making a supper of heartwarming, healthy Roasted Pepper-and-Chicken Soup welcome.

Roasted Pepper-and-Chicken
  Soup
Spicy Cornbread Muffins
Citrus Spinach Salad
Apricot Sponge Torte

ROASTED PEPPER-AND-CHICKEN SOUP

4 large sweet red peppers
4 large sweet yellow peppers
2 large green peppers
Vegetable cooking spray
1 tablespoon olive oil
4 (4-ounce) chicken breast halves,
  skinned and boned
5 (10½-ounce) cans
  ready-to-serve, no-salt-added
  chicken broth
½ teaspoon salt
¼ teaspoon pepper
½ teaspoon dried whole basil
½ teaspoon dried whole
  marjoram

Wash and dry peppers; place on a baking sheet, and broil 4 inches from heat 3 to 4 minutes on each side. Put peppers in a plastic bag; close tightly, and let stand 10 minutes to loosen skins.
  Peel peppers; remove and discard core and seeds. Cut peppers into ¼- x 2-inch strips; set aside.

Coat a large nonstick skillet with cooking spray; add olive oil, and place over medium-high heat until hot. Add chicken, and cook 15 minutes or until golden brown, turning once. Remove chicken from skillet, and cool slightly; cut into thin strips. Add pepper strips to skillet, and cook 2 to 3 minutes or just until tender, stirring often.

Bring broth to a boil in a Dutch oven. Add salt, pepper, basil, marjoram, chicken, and peppers; simmer 5 minutes. Yield: 10½ cups (182 calories per 1¾-cup serving).

☐ *19.2 grams protein, 5.2 grams fat, 12.1 grams carbohydrate, 47 milligrams cholesterol, 247 milligrams sodium, and 24 milligrams calcium.*

Kimberly Orr
Fort Worth, Texas

SPICY CORNBREAD MUFFINS

1½ cups yellow cornmeal
1 teaspoon baking soda
1 teaspoon sugar
½ teaspoon salt
2 egg whites
¼ cup picante sauce
¼ cup vegetable oil
1 (8-ounce) carton plain nonfat yogurt
Vegetable cooking spray

Combine first 4 ingredients in a large bowl; make a well in center of mixture. Combine egg whites and next 3 ingredients; add to dry ingredients, stirring just until moistened. Spoon into muffin pans coated with cooking spray, filling two-thirds full. Bake at 425° for 18 to 20 minutes. Remove from pans. Yield: 1 dozen (115 calories per muffin).

☐ *3.1 grams protein, 5 grams fat, 14.1 grams carbohydrate, 0 milligrams cholesterol, 257 milligrams sodium, and 55 milligrams calcium.*

Janette Reddig
Kerrville, Texas

CITRUS SPINACH SALAD

2 tablespoons orange juice
2 tablespoons rice vinegar
1 tablespoon vegetable oil
1 tablespoon honey
¼ teaspoon grated orange rind
6 cups torn spinach
2 oranges, peeled, seeded, and sectioned
1 small purple onion, sliced and separated into rings
1 tablespoon pine nuts, toasted

Combine first 5 ingredients in a jar; cover tightly, and shake vigorously. Chill thoroughly. Combine spinach, orange sections, and onion rings in a salad bowl. Drizzle dressing over spinach mixture; toss gently. Sprinkle with pine nuts before serving. Yield: 6 servings (86 calories per 1-cup serving).

☐ *2.5 grams protein, 4 grams fat, 12.6 grams carbohydrate, 0 milligrams cholesterol, 47 milligrams sodium, and 78 milligrams calcium.*

APRICOT SPONGE TORTE

Vegetable cooking spray
2 eggs
¼ cup sugar
½ teaspoon vanilla extract
½ teaspoon almond extract
⅓ cup sifted cake flour
½ teaspoon baking powder
Dash of salt
1 (16-ounce) can apricot halves in lite syrup, undrained
1 teaspoon cornstarch

Coat a 9-inch torte pan with removable bottom with cooking spray, and set aside.

Beat eggs at medium speed of an electric mixer until foamy. Gradually add sugar, 1 tablespoon at a time, beating until soft peaks form and sugar dissolves (about 10 minutes). Stir in vanilla and almond extracts. Combine cake flour, baking powder, and salt; fold into egg mixture.

Spoon into prepared pan. Bake at 325° for 25 minutes. Remove torte from oven.

Drain apricots, reserving ⅔ cup syrup; set aside. Arrange apricot halves, cut side down, around outside edge and center of torte. Combine cornstarch and reserved syrup in a small saucepan. Cook over medium heat, stirring constantly, until mixture boils. Cook 1 additional minute; remove from heat.

Spoon sauce over apricots. Return torte to oven, and bake an additional 5 minutes or until torte pulls away from sides of pan. Cool on a wire rack 5 minutes; remove outside rim from pan. Serve warm. Yield: 6 servings (133 calories per serving).

☐ *2.9 grams protein, 2.1 grams fat, 25.9 grams carbohydrate, 91 milligrams cholesterol, 98 milligrams sodium, and 35 milligrams calcium.*

Mrs. Gordon Watters
El Paso, Texas

Light Cooking Tips

■ Salt can be eliminated from almost any recipe (except yeast bread and pickles) without affecting the quality of the product. (Salt is added to yeast breads for a smooth texture, and it is added to pickles for prevention of bacterial growth.)

■ Remove the skin from chicken before, rather than after, cooking. Otherwise, the fat from the skin will be absorbed by the meat as it cooks.

■ By using vegetable cooking spray instead of margarine or oils to grease baking pans and skillets, you'll save fat calories.

A Healthier Corn Pudding

The recipe below for Creamy Baked Corn is a light version of a Southern favorite—corn pudding. Skim milk and egg substitute keep the amount of fat and cholesterol low.

CREAMY BAKED CORN

2 tablespoons reduced-calorie margarine
2 tablespoons all-purpose flour
1 cup skim milk
½ cup egg substitute
¾ teaspoon salt
½ teaspoon white pepper
2 (11-ounce) cans no-salt-added whole kernel corn, drained
1 tablespoon chopped pimiento
Vegetable cooking spray
⅛ teaspoon paprika

Melt margarine in a heavy saucepan over low heat; add flour, stirring until smooth. Cook 1 minute, stirring constantly. Gradually add milk; cook over medium heat, stirring constantly, until mixture is thickened and bubbly.

Remove from heat. Stir in egg substitute, salt, and pepper; add corn and pimiento. Spoon mixture into a baking dish coated with cooking spray. Sprinkle with paprika. Place dish in a shallow pan; add water to a depth of 1 inch. Bake at 350° for 45 minutes. Yield: 7 servings (103 calories per ½-cup).

☐ *4.6 grams protein, 2.9 grams fat, 14.7 grams carbohydrate, 1 milligram cholesterol, 330 milligrams sodium, and 52 milligrams calcium.*

Judy Grigoraci
Charleston, West Virginia

COMPARE THE NUTRIENTS (per serving)		
	Traditional	Light
Calories	161	103
Fat	7.1g	2.9g
Cholesterol	94mg	1mg

Healthy Substitutes

■ Instead of serving sauces or creams over vegetables, use seasonings such as bouillon, lemon juice, herbs, spices, or butter substitutes.

■ Reduce calories in recipes that call for ricotta cheese by substituting 1% low-fat or dry-curd cottage cheese.

Sporty Appetizers For Active Appetites

The appetizers here lend themselves to sporty entertaining. A combination of Swiss cheese and purple onion makes Swiss Cheese Spread a favorite with flair. Mayonnaise or salad dressing gives the spread its creamy consistency. Any that is left over makes a great sandwich spread when topped with bacon and broiled on an English muffin.

CLAM PUFFS

1 to 1¼ cups all-purpose flour, divided
2 teaspoons baking powder
1 teaspoon Old Bay seasoning
¼ teaspoon salt
¼ teaspoon pepper
2 eggs, beaten
⅓ cup milk
½ cup minced onion
4 (6½-ounce) cans minced clams, drained
Vegetable oil

Combine 1 cup flour and next 4 ingredients in a medium bowl; stir well. Make a well in center of mixture, and set aside.

Combine eggs, milk, onion, and clams; stir into dry ingredients. Add up to ¼ cup flour, if necessary, for a less sticky batter.

Pour oil to a depth of 2 to 3 inches in a Dutch oven or heavy saucepan. Heat to 375°. Carefully drop mixture by rounded tablespoonfuls into oil. Fry 1 to 2 minutes on each side or until golden brown. Drain on paper towels. Serve immediately with cocktail or tartar sauce. Yield: 2 dozen.

Note: Old Bay Seasoning, a blend of several spices, is available in the spice section or seafood counter of most supermarkets.

Sandra Rhodes Potter
Cambridge, Maryland

SWISS CHEESE SPREAD

1½ cups (6 ounces) shredded Swiss cheese
½ cup chopped purple onion
⅓ cup salad dressing or mayonnaise

Combine all ingredients; chill. Serve with assorted crackers or breadsticks. Yield: 1½ cups.

Nancy Seamon
Hilton Head, South Carolina

PARTY REUBENS

¼ cup commercial Thousand
  Island salad dressing
2 teaspoons Dijon mustard
1 teaspoon prepared horseradish
2 tablespoons butter or
  margarine, softened
24 slices party rye bread
12 thin slices corned beef, cut in
  half (about ¾ pound)
½ cup sauerkraut, drained
6 (1-ounce) slices Swiss cheese,
  quartered

Combine first 3 ingredients, and set
mixture aside.

Spread ¼ teaspoon butter on each
slice of bread. Place a half slice of
corned beef on each piece of buttered bread, folding beef to fit. Top
each with about ½ teaspoon sauce
mixture, 1 teaspoon sauerkraut, and
a piece of cheese.

Place bread slices on baking
sheets; broil 8 inches from heat 2 to
3 minutes or until cheese melts.
Yield: 2 dozen.   *Dottie Clark*
                Midwest City, Oklahoma

BLACK PEPPER CHEESE
LOGS

1 (8-ounce) package cream
  cheese, softened
1 tablespoon milk
1 clove garlic, crushed
1 teaspoon chopped fresh chives
2 tablespoons dried parsley flakes
Coarsely ground pepper

Combine first 5 ingredients. Shape
mixture into two 5-inch logs; roll in
coarsely ground pepper. Cover and
chill at least 3 hours. Serve with assorted crackers. Yield: about 1 cup.
             Rublelene Singleton
             Scotts Hill, Tennessee

MICROWAVE COOKERY

Potatoes
In Minutes

Potatoes take longer to cook than
most other vegetables when prepared in a conventional oven, but
they become a vegetable of convenience when cooked in the microwave oven.

The most important thing to remember when microwaving potatoes
is to arrange them evenly around the
dish so that all pieces cook uniformly.
Remember that if you change the
size of the potatoes called for in
these recipes, the length of cooking
time will change proportionally.
Large potatoes weigh about 10
ounces each; medium potatoes weigh
6 to 7 ounces each.

LEMONY POTATO
WEDGES

2 tablespoons butter or
  margarine
2 tablespoons lemon juice
3 tablespoons grated Parmesan
  cheese
1½ teaspoons grated lemon
  rind
½ teaspoon paprika
⅛ teaspoon salt
3 medium baking potatoes,
  unpeeled
Garnishes: fresh parsley sprigs,
  lemon rose

Place butter in a 1-cup glass measure. Microwave at HIGH 45 seconds. Add lemon juice. Set aside.
Combine Parmesan cheese, grated
lemon rind, paprika, and salt in a
small bowl.

Cut potatoes lengthwise into quarters. Brush potatoes with butter mixture, and sprinkle with cheese

mixture. Arrange potatoes, spoke
fashion, on a 12-inch pizza plate.
Cover loosely with wax paper. Microwave at HIGH 11 to 12 minutes
or until potatoes are tender, rotating
dish one-half turn after 5 minutes.
Arrange on platter, and garnish, if
desired. Yield: 4 servings.
                    Debbie Wall
                    Richmond, Texas

Try Baked Potatoes,
Too

Probably the biggest timesaver of
all between conventional and microwave cooking of potatoes is
the baked potato. One potato
takes an hour to bake convention-
ally, but it takes only 4 to 6 minutes in the microwave.

To bake potatoes in the microwave, rinse them, and pat dry;
prick several times with a fork.
Arrange potatoes in microwave
oven, leaving 1 inch between
each. (If microwaving more than
two potatoes, arrange them in a
circle.)

Microwave potatoes at HIGH
according to the times indicated
below, turning and rearranging
them once. Let potatoes stand 5
minutes before serving. (If potatoes are not done after standing,
microwave briefly, and let stand 2
minutes.)

Microwave-Baked Potatoes

Number of potatoes	Minutes at HIGH power
1	4 to 6
2	7 to 8
3	9 to 11
4	12 to 14
6	16 to 18

Note: These times are for cooking medium-size potatoes (6 to 7
ounces). If potatoes are larger,
allow more time.

CHILI-CHEESE POTATOES

3 medium baking potatoes,
   unpeeled and cut into ½-inch
   slices
1 tablespoon vegetable oil
2 tablespoons minced fresh
   parsley
1 teaspoon chili powder
½ teaspoon salt
¼ teaspoon pepper
1 cup (4 ounces) shredded
   Cheddar cheese
1 small green onion, chopped

Combine potatoes and oil in a 12- x
8- x 2-inch baking dish; toss well.
Sprinkle potatoes with parsley, chili
powder, salt, and pepper. Cover
tightly with heavy-duty plastic wrap;
fold back a small corner of wrap to
allow steam to escape. Microwave at
HIGH 9 to 10 minutes or until
tender, stirring gently every 3 minutes. Sprinkle potatoes with cheese
and onion. Let stand, covered, 5
minutes. Yield: 4 servings.

Jackie Broome
Greenville, South Carolina

HIGH 5 to 6 minutes. Uncover; stir
in green pepper, salt, and pepper.
Cover and microwave at HIGH 5 to
6 minutes. Uncover; stir in cheese.
Microwave, uncovered, an additional
2 minutes or until potatoes are
tender. Sprinkle with parsley. Yield:
4 servings. *Frances Christopher*
Iron Station, North Carolina

QUICK!

Toss A Pasta Salad

For versatility and ease of preparation, it's hard to beat pasta. And our
readers are tossing it with a wide
variety of vegetables, meats, and
dressings for tasty combinations that
can be made in less than 30 minutes.

HAM-PECAN-BLUE CHEESE PASTA SALAD

3 cups uncooked bow tie pasta
4 ounces cooked ham, cut into
   strips
1 cup coarsely chopped pecans
1 (4-ounce) package blue cheese,
   crumbled
⅓ cup chopped fresh parsley
2 tablespoons minced fresh
   rosemary or 2 teaspoons dried
   whole rosemary
1 clove garlic, minced
½ teaspoon coarsely ground
   pepper
¼ cup olive oil
⅓ cup grated Parmesan cheese

Cook pasta according to package directions; drain. Rinse with cold
water, and drain.
   Combine pasta and remaining ingredients except Parmesan cheese,
tossing well. Sprinkle with Parmesan
cheese. Serve immediately or chill, if
desired. Yield: 6 servings.

Travis Baker
Meeker, Oklahoma

PARMESAN POTATOES

2 tablespoons butter or margarine
3 medium potatoes, unpeeled and
   sliced
½ cup chopped onion
1 clove garlic, minced
⅓ cup chopped green pepper
½ teaspoon salt
⅛ teaspoon pepper
¼ cup grated Parmesan cheese
1 tablespoon chopped fresh
   parsley

Place butter in a 9-inch square baking
dish; microwave at HIGH 45 seconds
or until melted. Add potatoes, onion,
and garlic; toss gently. Cover tightly
with heavy-duty plastic wrap; fold
back a small corner of wrap to allow
steam to escape. Microwave at

SEAFOOD PASTA SALAD

1 (1-pound) package vegetable
   rotini
1 (6-ounce) can pitted ripe olives,
   drained
1 (10-ounce) package frozen
   chopped broccoli, thawed and
   drained
1 (1-pound) package frozen
   seafood mix, thawed
1 (8-ounce) bottle commercial
   Italian salad dressing

Cook rotini according to package directions; drain. Rinse with cold
water; drain.
   Combine pasta and remaining ingredients; toss well. Serve immediately or chill, if desired. Yield: 10 to
12 servings. *Debbie Collard Estes*
Vine Grove, Kentucky

PASTA SALAD

4 cups uncooked rotini
1 medium zucchini, sliced
2 carrots, scraped and sliced
½ sweet red pepper, cut into
   thin strips
1 cup broccoli flowerets
1 (6-ounce) can sliced ripe
   olives
1 (8-ounce) bottle commercial
   Italian salad dressing

Cook rotini according to package directions; drain. Rinse with cold
water, and drain.
   Combine cooked pasta and remaining ingredients in a large bowl, tossing well to coat pasta and vegetables.
   Serve salad immediately or chill, if
desired. Yield: 6 to 8 servings.

Marietta Marx
Louisville, Kentucky

PRESTO PASTA SALAD

1 (16-ounce) package fusilli
1 medium-size sweet red pepper,
   cut into strips
1 cup fresh mushrooms, sliced
1 cup broccoli flowerets
1 (12-ounce) bottle Caesar salad
   dressing

Cook pasta according to package directions; drain. Rinse with cold water, and drain.

Combine pasta and remaining ingredients; toss well. Serve immediately or chill, if desired. Yield: 10 to 12 servings.   *Cindy Ward*
Winston-Salem, North Carolina

ORIENTAL PASTA SALAD

8 ounces linguine, broken into
   thirds
4 green onions, sliced
2 carrots, scraped and thinly
   sliced
12 cherry tomatoes, halved
1 pound fresh broccoli, thinly
   sliced
½ cup vegetable oil
½ cup soy sauce
1 clove garlic, minced
¼ cup lemon juice
¼ teaspoon hot sauce
2 tablespoons sesame seeds

Cook linguine according to package directions; drain. Rinse with cold water; drain. Add green onions, carrots, cherry tomatoes, and broccoli.

Combine oil and remaining ingredients in a jar; cover tightly, and shake vigorously. Pour over salad, and toss gently to coat. Serve immediately. Yield: 8 servings.
Kay Castleman Cooper
Burke, Virginia

Tip: *Adding 1 or 2 tablespoons of vegetable oil to the cooking water keeps pasta separated.*

The Luck Of The Irish To You

O'Malley, O'Reilly, O'Brien . . . O, to be Irish! Southerners whose ancestries began on the Emerald Isle have an unmistakable pride in their heritage that, for at least one day a year, can make folks of other backgrounds leprechaun green with envy.

Here, our readers share a bit of their culture—dishes eaten often throughout the year, but certainly on March 17.

■ For more than 20 years, family and friends have enjoyed Barbara and Chuck Herlihy's annual Dugan's Dew and Irish Stew dinner in Birmingham, Alabama. The menu often includes the following recipes.

POACHED SALMON WITH EMERALD SAUCE

6 medium leeks
2 quarts water
¾ teaspoon salt
6 medium potatoes
2 cups water
½ cup cider vinegar
1 teaspoon salt
½ teaspoon ground allspice
6 salmon steaks (2 pounds)
2 tablespoons butter or
   margarine, melted
2 tablespoons chopped fresh
   parsley
Emerald Sauce

Remove roots, tough outer leaves, and tops from leeks, leaving 2 inches of dark leaves. Wash leeks well; split in half lengthwise to within 1 inch of bulb end. Rinse again. Bring 2 quarts water and ¾ teaspoon salt to a boil in a large Dutch oven; add leeks and potatoes. Cover, reduce heat, and simmer 10 to 15 minutes or until leeks are tender; remove leeks, and keep warm. Cook potatoes an additional 20 to 25 minutes or until tender. Drain and keep warm.

Combine 2 cups water and next 3 ingredients in a large skillet; bring to a boil. Add salmon; cover, reduce heat, and simmer 8 to 10 minutes or until fish flakes easily when tested with a fork. Cut potatoes into quarters; drizzle with butter, and sprinkle with parsley. Place potatoes, leeks, and salmon on a serving platter. Pour Emerald Sauce over salmon. Yield: 6 servings.

Emerald Sauce

2 tablespoons butter or margarine
2 tablespoons all-purpose flour
1 cup milk
½ cup pureed fresh spinach
   (about ¼ pound)
1 egg yolk
¼ cup half-and-half
½ teaspoon salt
¼ teaspoon white pepper

Melt butter in a heavy saucepan over low heat; add flour, stirring until smooth. Cook 1 minute, stirring constantly. Gradually add milk; cook over medium heat, stirring constantly, until mixture is thickened. Add spinach; cook 1 minute, stirring constantly.

Pour mixture into container of an electric blender; process until smooth. Return to saucepan.

Combine egg yolk and half-and-half. Gradually stir about one-fourth of hot mixture into yolk mixture; add to remaining hot mixture, stirring constantly. Cook over medium heat 1 minute, stirring constantly. Stir in salt and pepper. Yield: 1½ cups.

Note: Frozen chopped spinach, thawed and drained, may be substituted for fresh spinach.

IRISH STEW

1 cup Burgundy or other dry red
 wine
1 clove garlic, minced
2 bay leaves
1 teaspoon salt
½ teaspoon freshly ground pepper
¼ teaspoon dried whole thyme
3 pounds lean beef for stewing,
 cut into 1-inch cubes
¼ cup olive oil
2 (10½-ounce) cans condensed
 beef broth, undiluted
6 carrots, scraped and cut into
 2-inch slices
12 small boiling onions
6 medium potatoes, peeled and
 halved

Combine first 6 ingredients; pour
over beef in a shallow dish. Cover
and refrigerate 8 hours. Drain meat,
reserving marinade. Remove and discard bay leaves.

Heat oil in a Dutch oven over medium heat; brown beef in oil. Add
broth and reserved marinade; bring
to a boil. Cover, reduce heat, and
simmer 1½ hours. Add carrots,
onions, and potatoes; cover and cook
30 minutes. Yield: 2½ quarts.

■ Both native Irishmen, Henry and
Christiana Courtenay now live near
Dublin, Georgia, but return to their
homeland part of each year. Their
recipe, like many Irish recipes, dates
back to Ireland's darker days when
such frugal menu items were an eco-
nomic necessity, but are still popular
in today's better times.

COLCANNON

1 medium cabbage, coarsely
 shredded
6 medium potatoes, peeled and
 cut into eighths
¼ cup butter or margarine
1½ cups milk
1 teaspoon salt
¼ teaspoon pepper

Cook cabbage, covered, in a small
amount of boiling salted water 5 to 7
minutes or until tender. Drain and
set aside.

Cook potatoes in boiling salted
water to cover 15 minutes or until
tender. Drain and mash. Add butter
and remaining ingredients; mix well.
Add cabbage, stirring well. Serve immediately. Yield: 8 to 10 servings.

■ There's a little bit of Ireland in
Staunton, Virginia, at the Museum of
American Frontier Culture. Having
researched the Emerald Isle's cuisine, the museum gives us a recipe
for a favorite beverage using Irish
whiskey, often called "the water of
life" in that country.

WHISKEY PUNCH

2 cups water
¾ to 1 cup sugar
6 whole cloves
4 (2- x ¼-inch) strips lemon rind
1 (3-inch) stick cinnamon
2 cups Irish whiskey
1 lemon, sliced

Combine first 5 ingredients in a
saucepan, and bring to a boil. Boil
until sugar dissolves. Reduce heat;
remove cloves, lemon rind, and cinnamon stick.

Add whiskey to sugar mixture, and
cook until thoroughly heated, but not
boiling. Pour into cups, and float a
lemon slice in each. Serve immediately. Yield: 4 cups.

Cure The Chicken Doldrums

These recipes perk up menus and
offer a variety of new flavor combinations for chicken. They're all baked
in the oven, too, so you can prepare
the remainder of the meal while the
chicken is cooking.

FONTINA-BAKED CHICKEN

½ cup all-purpose flour
¼ teaspoon dried whole oregano
¼ teaspoon pepper
¼ teaspoon paprika
¼ teaspoon poultry seasoning
⅛ teaspoon red pepper
2 tablespoons Parmesan cheese
6 chicken breast halves, skinned
 and boned
2 eggs, beaten
½ cup butter or margarine,
 divided
½ pound fresh mushrooms,
 halved
½ pound cooked ham, diced
2 cups (8 ounces) shredded
 fontina cheese, divided

Combine first 7 ingredients, mixing
well. Dip chicken breasts in beaten
egg; dredge in flour mixture.

Melt ¼ cup butter in a large skillet
over medium heat. Add chicken, and
cook 10 minutes on each side or until
golden brown. Remove chicken, and
drain on paper towels. Place in a 12-
x 8- x 2-inch baking dish or individual
au gratin dishes.

Melt remaining ¼ cup butter in
skillet. Sauté mushrooms in butter 4
minutes or until tender; drain. Layer
mushrooms and ham over chicken.
Sprinkle with 1 cup shredded fontina
cheese. Cover and bake at 350° for
35 minutes. Uncover; sprinkle with
remaining 1 cup cheese, and bake an
additional 5 minutes. Yield: 6
servings.
Mitzi Amato
Kenner, Louisiana

GREEK LEMON CHICKEN

1 teaspoon garlic powder
1 teaspoon salt
2 teaspoons dried whole oregano
¼ teaspoon pepper
¼ cup lemon juice
¾ cup water
3 pounds chicken breasts, thighs,
  and legs, skinned
¾ cup all-purpose flour
3 to 4 tablespoons vegetable oil
Lemon slices

Combine first 6 ingredients in a large bowl; stir well. Add chicken; cover and chill 8 hours.

Remove chicken from marinade; reserve marinade. Place flour in a plastic bag; add chicken, and shake to coat.

Heat oil in a large skillet; add chicken, and brown on all sides. Drain chicken on paper towels. Place in a 12- x 8- x 2-inch baking dish; pour marinade over chicken, and cover with foil. Bake at 350° for 50 minutes or until tender.

Transfer chicken to a serving dish; garnish with lemon slices. Yield: 4 servings.   *Shirley Draper*
Winter Park, Florida

DILLY CHICKEN

½ cup sliced fresh mushrooms
1 tablespoon butter or margarine,
  melted
6 chicken breast halves, skinned
  and boned
12 slices dried beef
1 (10¾-ounce) can golden
  mushroom soup, undiluted
¼ cup red wine
½ cup plain yogurt
1 teaspoon dried whole dillweed
Hot cooked rice

Sauté mushrooms in butter; drain and set aside.

Place chicken in a lightly greased 12- x 8- x 2-inch baking dish. Layer dried beef and mushrooms over chicken.

Combine mushroom soup, wine, and yogurt, mixing well; spoon evenly over dried beef. Sprinkle with dillweed. Cover with aluminum foil. Bake at 350° for 1 hour. Serve over hot cooked rice. Yield: 6 servings.
Lana W. Fuller
Martinsville, Virginia

PARSLIED CHICKEN BAKE

¾ cup fine, dry breadcrumbs
2 tablespoons grated Parmesan
  cheese
3 tablespoons chopped fresh
  parsley
½ clove garlic, crushed
¼ teaspoon salt
¼ teaspoon pepper
1 (2½- to 3-pound) broiler-fryer,
  cut up and skinned
½ cup vegetable oil

Combine first 6 ingredients in a plastic bag; shake to mix. Place 2 pieces of chicken in bag, and shake to coat. Repeat procedure with remaining chicken. Place oil in a 15- x 10- x 1-inch jellyroll pan; heat at 400° for 5 to 8 minutes or until very hot. Add chicken; bake at 400° for 40 minutes or until done, turning once. Yield: 4 servings.   *Sue-Sue Hartstern*
Louisville, Kentucky

Quick Breads, Faster Than Yeast

Quick breads have one distinctive ingredient—baking powder. It makes them easy to mix and eliminates the need to let them rise.

It's important to make sure baking powder is fresh. Most brands have an expiration date stamped on the can. If there isn't a date, check for freshness by adding a teaspoon of baking powder to a half cup of hot water. The mixture should foam vigorously. If it doesn't, throw the can away. There is no need to waste the other ingredients and your time.

For moist and tender breads, be careful not to overmix the batter. Stir the liquid ingredients into the dry ingredients just enough to moisten them. Lumps are fine; the batter is not supposed to be smooth. And a crack in the top of the loaf is typical.

NUTTY WHEAT LOAF

1¼ cups unbleached flour
1 cup whole wheat flour
2 teaspoons baking powder
¾ teaspoon salt
½ cup wheat germ
1 cup firmly packed dark brown
  sugar
1 teaspoon ground cinnamon
½ teaspoon ground nutmeg
½ cup coarsely chopped walnuts
2 eggs, beaten
1¼ cups milk
½ cup butter or margarine,
  melted

Combine first 9 ingredients in a large mixing bowl, stirring well.

Combine eggs, milk, and butter; add to dry ingredients, stirring just until moistened. Spoon batter into a greased and floured 8½- x 4½- x 3-inch loafpan; bake at 350° for 50 to 55 minutes or until a wooden pick inserted in center comes out clean. Yield: 1 loaf.   *Nan Ashcraft*
Little Rock, Arkansas

Tip: *Measure ingredients accurately. For liquids, use a glass measuring cup; this allows you to see that you are measuring correctly. Use a metal or plastic measuring cup for solids or dry ingredients; fill the measuring cup to overflowing, and level off with a knife or a spatula.*

APPLESAUCE-PECAN BREAD

2 cups all-purpose flour
1 tablespoon baking powder
½ teaspoon baking soda
½ teaspoon salt
¾ cup sugar
½ teaspoon ground cinnamon
¼ teaspoon ground nutmeg
½ cup chopped pecans
½ cup raisins
1 egg, beaten
1 cup applesauce
¼ cup vegetable oil

Combine first 7 ingredients in a large bowl; stir in pecans and raisins. Make a well in center of mixture. Combine egg, applesauce, and oil; add to dry ingredients, stirring just until moistened. Spoon mixture into a greased and floured 8½- x 4½- x 3-inch loafpan. Bake at 350° for 40 to 45 minutes or until a wooden pick inserted in center comes out clean. Cool in pan 10 minutes; remove from pan, and let cool on a wire rack. Yield: 1 loaf.   *Mrs. Paul Raper*
Burgaw, North Carolina

MAPLE-BRAN MUFFINS

1 cup all-purpose flour
1 teaspoon baking soda
½ teaspoon baking powder
1 egg, beaten
¾ cup maple syrup
2½ cups bran flakes, crushed
1 (8-ounce) carton sour cream

Combine first 3 ingredients in a large bowl; make a well in center of mixture. Combine egg and syrup in a small bowl, stirring well; add bran flakes, and let stand 5 minutes. Stir in sour cream. Add liquid mixture to dry ingredients, stirring just until moistened. Spoon into greased muffin pans, filling two-thirds full. Bake at 400° for 18 to 20 minutes. Remove from pans immediately. Yield: 15 muffins.   *Eileen R. MaCutchan*
Largo, Florida

Crispy, Delicious Popovers

Popovers are crisp, crusty, hot breads with a hollow, slightly moist center. Recipes start with a smooth batter of eggs, flour, and milk. The addition of whole wheat flour, cinnamon, or Parmesan cheese gives these popovers special character and flavor. Served piping hot, the puffy creations are a delicious treat.

WHOLE WHEAT POPOVERS

2 eggs, slightly beaten
⅔ cup whole wheat flour
⅓ cup all-purpose flour
¼ teaspoon salt
1 teaspoon sugar
1 cup milk
1 tablespoon butter or margarine, melted
Cranberry Cream

Combine beaten eggs, flours, salt, sugar, milk, and melted butter; beat at low speed of an electric mixer just until smooth.
Place well-greased muffin pans in a 425° oven 3 minutes or until a drop of water sizzles when dropped in them. Remove pans from oven; fill each muffin cup half full with batter. Bake at 425° for 15 minutes. Reduce heat to 350°, and bake 15 minutes or until popovers are firm. Serve immediately with Cranberry Cream. Yield: 1 dozen.

Cranberry Cream

1 (3-ounce) package cream cheese, softened
¼ cup whole-berry cranberry sauce

Beat cream cheese at medium speed of an electric mixer until smooth; stir in cranberry sauce. Yield: ½ cup.
Yvonne M. Greer
Greenville, South Carolina

PARMESAN POPOVERS

2 eggs, slightly beaten
1 cup all-purpose flour
¼ teaspoon salt
1 cup milk
¼ cup grated Parmesan cheese

Combine all ingredients in a medium bowl; beat at low speed of an electric mixer until blended.
Place well-greased muffin pans in a 425° oven for 3 minutes or until a drop of water sizzles when dropped in them. Remove pans from oven; fill each muffin cup three-fourths full with batter. Bake at 425° for 15 minutes. Reduce heat to 350°, and bake 18 to 20 minutes or until popovers are firm. Serve immediately. Yield: 1 dozen.   *Erma Jackson*
Huntsville, Alabama

CINNAMON POPOVERS

3 eggs, slightly beaten
1 cup all-purpose flour
1 tablespoon sugar
1 teaspoon ground cinnamon
¼ teaspoon salt
1 cup milk
3 tablespoons butter or margarine, melted

Combine all ingredients in container of an electric blender; blend just until batter is smooth.
Place well-greased muffin pans in a 425° oven 3 minutes or until a drop of water sizzles when dropped in them. Remove pans from oven; fill each muffin cup half full with batter. Bake at 425° for 15 minutes. Reduce heat to 350°, and bake 12 to 15 minutes or until popovers are firm. Serve immediately. Yield: 1 dozen.
Mrs. Roy Nieman
Dunnellon, Florida

Make Ahead And Freeze

Each of these dishes should retain maximum texture and flavor when frozen three to six months. If food is frozen longer, flavor, texture, and color losses may occur, but the food will still be safe to eat.

Several items make good freezer containers, including freezer bags, plastic containers, or foil-lined baking dishes. Use of aluminum foil frees baking dishes for other uses while food is in the freezer. First, line the baking dish with foil, leaving at least a 1½-inch foil collar. Fill the foil-lined dish with food. Cover the dish with a sheet of foil, and fold the edges together, sealing tightly and pressing out air; freeze. When the mixture is frozen solid, lift the foil package from the dish, and return it to the freezer.

You may remove the foil and return the recipe to the same baking dish when ready to reheat and serve. Several manufacturers have introduced oven-to-freezer-to-microwave containers that work well, also.

ITALIAN SAUCE

2 pounds ground beef
1½ cups chopped onion
1 clove garlic, chopped
2 (16-ounce) cans plum tomatoes, undrained and chopped
1 (6-ounce) can tomato paste
1 cup water
2 tablespoons chopped fresh parsley or 2 teaspoons dried parsley flakes
1 tablespoon sugar
1½ teaspoons salt
1 teaspoon dried whole oregano
1 teaspoon dried whole basil
½ teaspoon pepper

Cook ground beef, onion, and garlic in a large skillet until meat is browned, stirring to crumble meat; drain well. Stir in tomatoes and remaining ingredients. Bring to a boil over medium heat, stirring occasionally. Reduce heat, and simmer, uncovered, 45 minutes. Serve sauce with spaghetti, lasagna, or manicotti. Yield: 7½ cups.

To freeze: Prepare recipe as directed above, and freeze in two 1½-quart airtight plastic containers or freezer bags.

To defrost and reheat: For **conventional** method, thaw sauce in refrigerator, and cook in saucepan 15 minutes or until thoroughly heated. For **microwave** oven, cover and defrost one container of sauce in a 1½-quart baking dish at MEDIUM (50% power) 20 minutes, rotating dish after 10 minutes. Microwave at HIGH 5 minutes or until thoroughly heated, stirring after 3 minutes.
Ashley Adams
Birmingham, Alabama

SWISS CHICKEN CASSEROLE

6 chicken breast halves, skinned and boned
6 (4- x 4-inch) slices Swiss cheese
1 (10¾-ounce) can cream of chicken soup, undiluted
¼ cup milk
2 cups herb-seasoned stuffing mix
¼ cup butter or margarine, melted

Arrange chicken in a greased 12- x 8- x 2-inch baking dish. Top with cheese. Combine soup and milk; stir well. Spoon over chicken; sprinkle with stuffing mix. Drizzle butter over crumbs; cover and bake at 350° for 50 minutes. Yield: 6 servings.

To freeze: Prepare recipe as directed above, and place in aluminum foil-lined dish. Cover tightly, and freeze.

To defrost and reheat: For **conventional** oven, thaw casserole in refrigerator; cover and reheat at 350° for 45 minutes or until thoroughly heated. For **microwave** oven, cover casserole tightly with heavy-duty plastic wrap; fold back a small corner of wrap to allow steam to escape. Defrost at MEDIUM LOW (30% power) 20 to 25 minutes, giving dish a half-turn after 10 minutes. Microwave at MEDIUM HIGH (70% power) 10 minutes or until bubbly, giving dish a half-turn after 5 minutes.
Mary Sears
Bixby, Oklahoma

Tip: *Read labels to learn the weight, quality, and size of food products. Don't be afraid to experiment with new brands. Store brands can be equally good in quality and nutritional value, yet lower in price than well-known brands. Lower grades of canned fruit and vegetables are as nutritious as higher grades. Whenever possible, buy most foods by weight or cost per serving rather than by volume or package size.*

CHICKEN CHOW MEIN

1 (3- to 3½-pound) broiler-fryer,
   cut up and skinned
2 chicken-flavored bouillon cubes
1 large onion, chopped
¾ cup thinly sliced celery
¼ pound fresh mushrooms,
   coarsely chopped
1 carrot, scraped and grated
1 green pepper, cut into strips
1 (14-ounce) can bean sprouts,
   drained
1 (8-ounce) can sliced water
   chestnuts, drained
1 (2-ounce) jar diced pimiento,
   drained
2 tablespoons soy sauce
1 teaspoon hot sauce
3 tablespoons cornstarch
¼ cup water
Hot cooked rice
1 (5-ounce) can chow mein
   noodles

Place chicken in a large Dutch oven; add enough water to cover chicken. Bring to a boil; cover, reduce heat, and simmer 40 minutes or until tender. Remove chicken, and let cool slightly. Bone chicken, cutting meat into bite-size pieces; set aside. Reserve 4 cups chicken broth.

Add bouillon cubes to reserved broth, and bring to a boil. Add onion, celery, mushrooms, and carrot; simmer 10 minutes or until vegetables are tender. Add green pepper and next 5 ingredients.

Combine cornstarch and ¼ cup water, stirring until smooth; add to chow mein. Cook over medium heat, stirring constantly, until thickened and bubbly. Serve over hot rice, and top with chow mein noodles. Yield: 8 to 10 servings.

To freeze: Prepare recipe as directed above, omitting rice and chow mein noodles. Place in two 1½-quart airtight plastic containers. Freeze.

To defrost and reheat: For **conventional** method, thaw chow mein, and cook in saucepan until thoroughly heated. For **microwave** oven, cover and defrost 1½-quart chow mein at MEDIUM (50% power) 20 minutes, rotating container after 10 minutes. Microwave at HIGH 10 minutes or until thoroughly heated, stirring after 3 minutes.
Jenny Heinzmann
Lothian, Maryland

Beefed Up Dishes For Globe-Trotters

Ground beef's versatility and low cost make it a popular choice. One pound will serve three or four people, and put into a casserole or sauce, it can be stretched to feed more. Uncooked ground beef will keep one or two days in your refrigerator's meat drawer or coldest section and three to four months in your freezer.

MOUSSAKA

1 pound ground beef
3 cups chopped onion
¼ cup tomato paste
1 tablespoon dried parsley flakes
¼ teaspoon salt
¼ teaspoon pepper
1 cup water
3 medium eggplants
2 teaspoons salt
Olive oil
½ cup cracker crumbs, divided
1 egg, slightly beaten
¼ cup plus 2 tablespoons butter
   or margarine
¼ cup plus 2 tablespoons
   all-purpose flour
3 cups milk
½ teaspoon salt
¼ teaspoon pepper
⅛ teaspoon ground nutmeg
2 eggs, slightly beaten
1 cup freshly grated Parmesan
   cheese

Cook ground beef and chopped onion in a large skillet until meat is browned, stirring to crumble meat; drain well. Stir in tomato paste and next 4 ingredients. Cover and simmer 30 minutes.

Peel eggplants, and cut into ¼-inch slices. To extract bitterness, sprinkle 1 teaspoon salt on each side of slices; let stand 30 minutes. Rinse and pat dry with a paper towel. Brush eggplant slices with olive oil; place on lightly greased rack of a broiler pan. Broil 4 inches from heat 3 to 5 minutes. Turn, brush with olive oil, and broil an additional 3 to 5 minutes or until tender.

Layer half of eggplant slices in a lightly greased 13- x 9- x 2-inch baking dish. Sprinkle ¼ cup cracker crumbs over eggplant. Set aside.

Add 1 egg and remaining ¼ cup cracker crumbs to meat sauce. Spoon half of meat sauce over eggplant. Repeat layers with remaining eggplant and meat sauce. Set aside.

Melt butter in a heavy saucepan over low heat; add flour, stirring until smooth. Cook 1 minute, stirring constantly. Gradually add milk; cook over medium heat, stirring constantly, until thickened and bubbly. Stir in ½ teaspoon salt, ¼ teaspoon pepper, and nutmeg. Gradually stir about 1 cup white sauce into 2 eggs; return to remaining white sauce, stirring well. Pour sauce over meat. Bake at 350° for 40 minutes. Sprinkle with cheese; bake an additional 5 minutes. Yield: 6 to 8 servings.

CHILI IN PASTRY CUPS

¾ pound ground beef
⅓ cup chopped green pepper
⅓ cup chopped onion
1 (7½-ounce) can tomatoes,
   pureed
1 (4-ounce) can chopped green
   chiles, drained
¼ cup tomato paste
1 teaspoon sugar
¼ teaspoon salt
¾ teaspoon chili powder
Cornmeal Pastry Cups

Cook ground beef, green pepper, and onion in a skillet until meat is browned, stirring to crumble meat; drain well.

Add tomatoes and next 5 ingredients, stirring well; simmer 10 minutes. Serve hot in Cornmeal Pastry Cups. Yield: 4 dozen appetizers.

Cornmeal Pastry Cups

1¾ cups all-purpose flour
¼ cup yellow cornmeal
½ teaspoon salt
½ cup shortening
4 to 6 tablespoons cold water

Combine flour, cornmeal, and salt; cut in shortening with a pastry blender until mixture resembles coarse meal. Sprinkle cold water (1 tablespoon at a time) evenly over surface; stir with a fork until dry ingredients are moistened. Shape dough into 48 balls. Place in greased 1¾-inch tart pans, shaping each ball into a shell. Bake at 350° for 20 minutes or until lightly browned. Cool on wire racks. Yield: 4 dozen pastry cups.
Mildred Bickley
Bristol, Virginia

MINI-TERIYAKI MEAT LOAF

1 (8¼-ounce) can crushed
  unsweetened pineapple,
  undrained
½ pound ground beef
¼ cup soft breadcrumbs
2 tablespoons finely chopped
  onion
2 tablespoons soy sauce
1 tablespoon milk
1 clove garlic, minced
¼ teaspoon pepper
1 teaspoon cornstarch
¼ teaspoon ground ginger
1 tablespoon soy sauce

Drain pineapple, reserving ¼ cup juice and 2 tablespoons pineapple. Set aside.

Combine ground beef and next 6 ingredients; stir in remaining pineapple. Shape mixture into a 6- x 3-inch loaf. Place on lightly greased rack of

a broiler pan. Bake at 350° for 45 minutes or until done.

Combine cornstarch, ginger, 1 tablespoon soy sauce, and reserved pineapple juice in a small saucepan. Bring to a boil; reduce heat, and cook 1 minute, stirring constantly. Remove from heat; stir in reserved pineapple. Spoon mixture over meat loaf. Yield: 2 servings.
Mrs. C. W. Horton
Demopolis, Alabama

The Best Of Seafood In A Salad

Mildred Sherrer of Bay City, Texas, was right when she said her Lobster Salad was special. We made it with lobster as well as a less-expensive seafood mix and liked it both ways.

LOBSTER SALAD

2½ quarts water
4 (10-ounce) lobster tails, fresh
  or frozen, thawed or 1 pound
  seafood mix
½ cup commercial French
  dressing
¼ cup dry sherry
1 cup chopped celery
⅓ pound fresh asparagus, cut
  into 1-inch pieces
½ to ¾ cup mayonnaise
¼ teaspoon pepper
Garnishes: Bibb lettuce leaves,
  tomato wedges

Bring water to a boil; add lobster tails. Cover, reduce heat, and simmer 12 to 15 minutes. Drain. Rinse with cold water. Split and clean tails. Cut lobster into ½-inch pieces; press between layers of paper towels to remove excess water.

Combine lobster, French dressing, and sherry; stir gently. Cover and refrigerate 3 to 4 hours. Drain mixture, if necessary.

Combine lobster mixture, celery, and next 3 ingredients; stir gently until coated.

If desired, serve on lettuce leaves, and top with tomato wedges. Yield: 6 servings.

Bar Cookies Are Welcome Anytime

When you need a special treat for special guests and you're in a hurry, this assortment of bar cookies will come to your rescue. A little fancier than basic bar cookies, these multi-layer timesavers are still deliciously simple—and simply delicious.

PECAN SQUARES

2 cups all-purpose flour
½ cup sifted powdered sugar
1 cup butter or margarine
1 (14-ounce) can sweetened
  condensed milk
1 egg
1 teaspoon vanilla extract
1 (6-ounce) package almond
  brickle chips
1 cup chopped pecans

Combine flour and sugar in a medium bowl. Cut in butter with a pastry blender until mixture resembles coarse meal. Press mixture evenly into a greased 13- x 9- x 2-inch pan. Bake at 350° for 15 minutes.

Combine condensed milk, egg, and vanilla, stirring well. Stir in brickle chips and pecans. Pour mixture over crust. Bake at 350° for 25 minutes or until golden. Let cool, and cut into squares. Yield: 4 dozen.
Betty Sue Adams
Fort Payne, Alabama

CHOCOLATE-COCONUT SQUARES

1½ cups graham cracker crumbs
½ cup firmly packed brown sugar
⅓ cup all-purpose flour
½ cup butter or margarine, melted
1 (14-ounce) can sweetened condensed milk
1 (7-ounce) package flaked coconut
1 (12-ounce) package semisweet chocolate morsels
2 tablespoons chunky peanut butter
Garnish: chopped peanuts

Combine first 4 ingredients in a medium bowl. Press mixture into an ungreased 13- x 9- x 2-inch pan. Bake at 350° for 10 minutes.

Combine condensed milk and coconut, mixing well; spread over crust. Bake at 350° for 10 to 12 minutes.

Combine chocolate morsels and peanut butter in a small saucepan. Cook over low heat, stirring constantly, until chocolate melts; spread over coconut layer. Garnish, if desired. Cool and cut into bars. Yield: 4 dozen.
Christine Chamblin
St. Petersburg, Florida

BUTTER PECAN TURTLE BARS

½ cup butter or margarine, softened
1 cup firmly packed brown sugar
2 cups all-purpose flour
1 cup chopped pecans
⅔ cup butter or margarine, melted
½ cup firmly packed brown sugar
1 cup milk chocolate morsels

Cream ½ cup butter; add 1 cup brown sugar, beating at medium speed of an electric mixer. Gradually add flour, mixing well. Press mixture into an ungreased 13- x 9- x 2-inch pan. Sprinkle with pecans; set aside.

Combine ⅔ cup butter and ½ cup brown sugar in a small saucepan.

Bring to a boil over medium heat, stirring constantly. Boil 30 seconds, stirring constantly. Remove from heat, and pour hot mixture over crust. Bake at 350° for 18 minutes or until bubbly. Remove from oven; immediately sprinkle with chocolate morsels. Let stand 2 to 3 minutes; cut through chocolate with a knife to create a marbled effect. Cool. Cut into squares. Yield: 4 dozen.
Mrs. P. B. Brothers
Richmond, Virginia

NOVELTY LAYER SQUARES

½ cup shortening
¾ cup sugar
2 eggs, separated
½ teaspoon vanilla extract
1½ cups all-purpose flour
1 teaspoon baking powder
¼ teaspoon salt
¾ cup firmly packed brown sugar
½ teaspoon vanilla extract
¾ cup chopped pecans

Cream shortening; gradually add ¾ cup sugar, beating well at medium speed of an electric mixer. Add egg yolks and ½ teaspoon vanilla; beat mixture well.

Combine flour, baking powder, and salt; gradually add to creamed mixture, and mix well. Press mixture into a lightly greased 13- x 9- x 2-inch pan. Bake at 350° for 8 minutes.

Beat egg whites (at room temperature) at high speed of an electric mixer just until foamy. Gradually add brown sugar, and beat 2 minutes. Add ½ teaspoon vanilla, mixing well. Spread mixture evenly over crust; sprinkle with pecans. Bake at 350° for 20 to 25 minutes. Let cool 30 minutes, and cut into squares. Remove from pan, and let cool completely on wire racks. (Cookies will fall while cooling.) Yield: 4 dozen.
Diane L. Watson
Thomson, Georgia

Time Enough For Doughnuts

Make Applesauce Drop Doughnuts in a fraction of the time that it takes to prepare the traditional kind. Baking powder and soda help these doughnuts rise rather than yeast, which requires a waiting period. And instead of hand-cutting each one, drop the batter into hot oil by heaping tablespoonfuls. The result is a pretty, round doughnut that cooks in only 4 minutes. Sprinkle the doughnuts with powdered sugar, and enjoy breakfast!

APPLESAUCE DROP DOUGHNUTS

½ cup sugar
¼ cup firmly packed brown sugar
2 eggs
2 tablespoons vegetable oil
2¾ cups all-purpose flour
1½ teaspoons baking powder
½ teaspoon baking soda
¼ teaspoon salt
½ teaspoon ground cinnamon
½ teaspoon ground nutmeg
¼ cup milk
1 cup applesauce
½ teaspoon vanilla extract
Vegetable oil
Powdered sugar

Combine first 4 ingredients in a large bowl; beat at medium speed of an electric mixer until blended. Combine flour and next 5 ingredients; add to sugar mixture alternately with milk, beginning and ending with flour mixture. Stir in applesauce and vanilla.

Pour oil to a depth of 2 to 3 inches in a heavy saucepan; heat to 375°. Drop batter by heaping tablespoonfuls into oil; cook 3 or 4 at a time. Cook 2 minutes on each side or until golden. Drain doughnuts on paper towels; sprinkle with powdered sugar. Yield: 3 dozen.
Dorothy Nieman
Dunnellon, Florida

Crab—A Southern Delicacy

Although fresh crabmeat is available almost all year, you'll find the freshest crab in the spring and summer months. From the Eastern Shore of Maryland to the sandy shores stretching from Florida to Texas, crab varies from region to region.

Full of barley and healthy vegetables, Old-Fashioned Crab Soup touts one telltale sign that it's from Maryland. It's the Old Bay seasoning, a blend of several spices available at the seafood counter or in the spice section of large supermarkets.

Before using any fresh crabmeat, be sure to remove the cartilage from the fresh meat. Cartilage is opaque and feels a little like bits of small broken sea shells.

CRAB CAKES

1 egg, beaten
½ teaspoon seasoned salt
½ teaspoon Old Bay seasoning
⅛ teaspoon pepper
½ teaspoon dry mustard
2 drops of hot sauce
1 teaspoon prepared horseradish
1 teaspoon Worcestershire sauce
1 pound fresh crabmeat, drained and flaked
3 tablespoons fine, dry breadcrumbs
Vegetable oil
Garnishes: lemon rind and wedges, tomato slices, lettuce

Combine first 8 ingredients; stir well. Stir in crabmeat and breadcrumbs. Shape mixture into 6 patties. Pour oil to a depth of 2 inches into a Dutch oven; heat to 375°. Fry until patties are golden brown. Drain on paper towels. Garnish, if desired. Yield: 6 servings.
Phyllis Murphy
Cambridge, Maryland

OLD-FASHIONED CRAB SOUP

8 cups water
8 slices bacon, cut into 1-inch pieces
1 pound carrots, diced
6 stalks celery, diced
2 medium onions, diced
1 large green pepper, diced
1½ pounds cabbage, chopped
1½ pounds potatoes, diced
1 (10-ounce) package frozen baby lima beans
¼ cup barley
1 (28-ounce) can tomato puree
1 (17-ounce) can English peas, drained
1 (12-ounce) can shoepeg whole kernel corn, drained
1 tablespoon Old Bay seasoning
2 pounds fresh crabmeat, drained and flaked

Combine water and bacon in a large Dutch oven. Bring to a boil, and cook about 20 minutes. Add carrots and next 8 ingredients; return to a boil, and cook 30 minutes or until vegetables are tender. Stir in peas, corn, and seasoning; return to a boil. Add crabmeat; cook until thoroughly heated. Yield: 8 quarts.
Charlotte Booze
Cambridge, Maryland

CREAM CHEESE-CRABMEAT MOLD

1 envelope unflavored gelatin
¼ cup cold water
1 (10¾-ounce) can cream of mushroom soup, undiluted
1 (8-ounce) package cream cheese, softened
¾ cup mayonnaise or salad dressing
1 cup chopped celery
1 small onion, grated
¾ cup fresh crabmeat, drained and flaked

Sprinkle gelatin over cold water; let stand 1 minute.

Heat soup in a large saucepan. Add softened gelatin mixture to soup. Cook over low heat, stirring constantly, until gelatin dissolves and mixture is thoroughly heated (do not boil). Remove from heat.

Combine cream cheese and mayonnaise, mixing well at medium speed of an electric mixer. Add cream cheese mixture to soup mixture, mixing well. Stir in celery and remaining ingredients. Spoon into a lightly oiled 4-cup mold; cover and chill until firm. Yield: 3½ cups.
Yolanda Trahan
Houma, Louisiana

What's What When Buying Crabmeat

- **Lump or backfin**—large, whole lumps of meat from the body of the crab. This is usually the most expensive meat and is often used in salads and special dishes.

- **Flake (regular)**—all meat from the body portion of the crab except lump.

- **Claw**—all meat from the claw appendages.

- **Crab claws**—claws of the crab with the shell partially removed. These are most often used as appetizers.

- **Pasteurized crabmeat**—canned lump crabmeat, which is found in the refrigerated section of the supermarket. It will keep for about 6 months, unopened, in the refrigerator. Once opened, the crabmeat will stay fresh three to five days in the refrigerator.

From Our Kitchen To Yours

When families gather, conversation often turns to health and diet. A current topic is how to avoid or limit specific ingredients, primarily cholesterol, saturated fat, and sodium. One of the most important ways to make the right nutritional choices is to read food labels carefully. Since food labels can be confusing, here is some information that may help.

What is the first step toward a healthier diet?

If you are not on a restricted diet, the aim for a light and healthy diet is to keep your fat intake under 30% of your daily calories with only 10% of that coming from saturated fat. Carbohydrates should make up at least 50% of your diet, and protein the remainder. Keep your sodium intake under 3,000 milligrams a day.

How can these goals be met?

Reading the complete label is an important step. The nutritional information on the label tells you the number of calories, the amount of protein, fat, carbohydrates, and sodium per serving, plus the percentage of seven essential vitamins and minerals. Few labels give the percent of calories from fat. However, by using the simple chart given here, you can calculate this percentage.

How do you know what a food product contains?

Ingredients are listed in order of their weight with the ingredient in the largest amount listed first. By reading the label you can determine what is in the product.

For example, wheat flour, butter, sugar, whole eggs, and salt are the listed ingredients for a commercial shortbread cookie. Wheat flour is the main ingredient. The other ingredients follow in order by weight. A cereal that lists sugar first and corn second is not as nutritious as one that lists corn first and sugar second.

Can labels be misleading?

You may be noticing the increasing number of health claims about many products on the market. Don't be misguided by reading just these claims; read all the nutritional information. The United States Department of Agriculture sets standards for labeling meat and poultry, and the Food and Drug Administration regulates the labeling of other foods.

When the **sodium** has been reduced, the words on the label are "sodium-free," "very low-sodium," "low-sodium," or "reduced-sodium." Foods that have been processed without salt are labeled "unsalted," "salt-free," and "no-salt-added"; however, keep in mind that the food may still have significant levels of sodium from substances used to prepare the product.

Be cautious of phrases such as "no-cholesterol" and "100% vegetable shortening." Although they may not contain **cholesterol,** the product may be high in undesirable saturated fat, which stimulates the body's production of cholesterol. Check ingredient lists for highly saturated tropical oils such as coconut, palm, and palm-kernel oils that are unacceptable for light and healthy eating.

The acceptable unsaturated oils include safflower, sunflower, corn, olive, sesame, soybean, peanut, canola, and cottonseed.

You'll notice just about everything on the supermarket shelves has a light version. The FDA has set guidelines in regard to **calories**; however, there is presently no legal definition of "light." A food marked "low-calorie" cannot contain more than 40 calories per serving. Foods labeled "reduced-calorie" must be at least one-third lower in caloric content than a similar food in which calories have not been reduced. Not every food labeled **"light"** or **"lite"** is low in calories. These terms are often used to describe products that are light in color or density. You should be aware that products lower in fat and calories may not necessarily be what you should select. For example, some "light" frozen entrées derive less than 30% of calories from fat, yet they are high in sodium.

However, manufacturers are introducing products labeled "light" that are lower in fat, calories, and sodium than their regular counterparts. By reading and understanding the information on labels, you will be able to choose those products which are truly healthful.

Nutrition information per serving of plain nonfat yogurt:

Serving size.....................1 cup
Calories.............................140
Protein..............................12g
Carbohydrates.....................17g
Fat.................................... 2g
Sodium........................ 180mg

To calculate the percentage of total calories from fat, just use the following formula: Multiply the total number of grams of fat in a serving by nine, the total number of calories in one gram of fat. Then divide the calories from fat by the number of calories per serving to give you the percentage of fat per serving.

2	X	9	=	18	÷	140	=	12.8%
Grams of fat		Calories in 1 gram fat		Calories from fat		Total calories per serving		Percentage of fat per serving

APRIL

Welcome spring with a celebration. "Brunches & Lunches,"
our new special section, offers a rich variety of daytime
entertaining ideas and menus, ranging from fancy boxed
lunches to large lavish brunches. There is even a special
lunch for children and a morning coffee menu featuring a
coffee bar and a sampler of bite-size goodies.

Tease The Palate With Eggplant

Eggplant's satiny, rich purple skin and interesting shape are as pleasing to look at as the distinctive flavor and texture are to savor. The small, young eggplants that are in the market during late summer are particularly delectable.

When shopping for eggplant, avoid large ones (more than 1½ pounds); they can be watery and lack flavor. Look for dark, rich-colored, glossy, unscarred skin. Check firmness by pressing the eggplant with your fingers. If ripe, it should spring back when pressed; the eggplant should not be as hard as a rock or so soft that your fingers leave an indentation. Store fresh, firm eggplant for up to four days sealed in a plastic bag and refrigerated. Bitterness develops if the vegetable is overripe or stored too long. Salting is not necessary, but it does remove any bitterness that may be in the flesh.

ITALIAN-STUFFED EGGPLANT
(pictured on page 77)

4 medium eggplants (about 1
   pound each)
2 teaspoons salt
Salt
2 pounds ground beef
½ cup chopped onion
1 clove garlic, minced
3 tablespoons butter or
   margarine, melted
1 (8-ounce) can tomato sauce
1 tablespoon sugar
1 tablespoon dried Italian herb
   seasoning
1 teaspoon dried whole basil
1 teaspoon salt
½ teaspoon pepper
1 tablespoon chopped fresh
   parsley
2 tablespoons Worcestershire
   sauce
¾ cup Italian-seasoned
   breadcrumbs, divided
½ cup grated Parmesan cheese,
   divided
Garnish: fresh basil sprigs

Cut eggplants in half lengthwise. Cut into pulp around perimeter of shell, cutting to but not through the skin, leaving ¼ inch of pulp intact with skin. Make diagonal cuts into pulp, cutting to but not through the skin. Scoop out pulp with a spoon to form a shell for stuffing.

Chop pulp, discarding large seeds, if desired. In a medium bowl, combine pulp with 2 teaspoons salt and water to cover; let stand. Sprinkle inside of eggplant shell with salt; let stand, cut side down, on paper towels to drain.

Cook ground beef in a large skillet until browned, stirring to crumble meat. Drain well.

Sauté onion and garlic in butter over medium heat until tender; add tomato sauce and next 7 ingredients stirring well.

Drain and rinse chopped eggplant pulp; add eggplant and meat to sauce. Cover, reduce heat, and simmer 20 minutes or until eggplant is tender, stirring often. (Add water if mixture becomes too dry.) Stir in ½ cup breadcrumbs and ¼ cup Parmesan cheese.

Rinse shells; pat dry, and place in a large shallow pan. Spoon eggplant mixture into shells. Combine remaining breadcrumbs and cheese; sprinkle over stuffing. Bake at 350° for 20 minutes. Garnish with fresh basil, if desired. Yield: 8 servings.
Frances Berga-Rigsby
Daphne, Alabama

RATATOUILLE PASTA SALAD
(pictured on page 77)

8 ounces uncooked rotelle pasta
1 large eggplant (about 1½
   pounds)
½ teaspoon salt
½ cup chopped onion
2 medium zucchini, sliced
1 teaspoon minced garlic
½ green pepper, cut into 1-inch
   strips
½ sweet red pepper, cut into
   1-inch strips
¼ cup olive oil, divided
¼ teaspoon freshly ground pepper
½ cup chopped fresh basil
1 tablespoon chopped fresh
   parsley
3 tablespoons lemon juice
Garnish: fresh basil sprigs

Cook rotelle in salted water according to package directions; rinse, drain, and set aside.

Peel eggplant, and cut into ¾-inch cubes; sprinkle evenly with salt. Place in a large shallow pan. Cover and bake at 400° for 20 to 25 minutes or until eggplant is tender. Uncover and set aside.

Sauté onion and next 4 ingredients in 2 tablespoons olive oil in a large Dutch oven until vegetables are crisp-tender. Add pasta, remaining olive oil, and next 4 ingredients, tossing gently. Cover and chill at least 1 hour. Garnish, if desired. Yield: 8 to 10 servings.
Mrs. Marshall Rogers
Columbia, Mississippi

QUICK EGGPLANT SLICES

(pictured on page 77)

1 large eggplant, unpeeled (about
   1½ pounds)
¼ cup oil-and-vinegar dressing
2 tablespoons lemon juice
2 cloves garlic, crushed
¼ teaspoon salt
½ teaspoon freshly ground pepper
1 tablespoon fresh thyme leaves
   or 1 teaspoon dried whole
   thyme
1 tablespoon fresh rosemary
   leaves or 1 teaspoon dried
   whole rosemary
2 tablespoons grated Parmesan
   cheese (optional)

Cut eggplant into ¾-inch slices.
Combine dressing, lemon juice, and
garlic; brush on each side of eggplant, and sprinkle with salt, pepper,
and herbs.

Broil 4 inches from heat 5 minutes. Brush with dressing mixture;
turn eggplant, and broil 5 additional
minutes or to desired degree of
doneness. Brush with dressing mixture; sprinkle with cheese, if desired.
Yield: 4 to 6 servings.

Note: Eggplant may be grilled, covered, over medium-hot coals 5 minutes on each side or to desired
degree of doneness. Proceed as
directed above.

CHEESY FRIED EGGPLANT

(pictured on page 77)

1 large eggplant (about 1½
   pounds)
Salt
1 cup dry breadcrumbs
¼ teaspoon salt
1 (6-ounce) package sliced
   mozzarella cheese
2 eggs, beaten
½ cup vegetable oil
1 (16-ounce) loaf French bread
Lettuce
1 tomato, sliced

Peel eggplant, and cut lengthwise
into eight ¼-inch slices. Sprinkle
both sides of slices with salt; allow to
sit 30 minutes. Rinse eggplant slices,
and pat both sides dry.

Combine breadcrumbs and ¼ teaspoon salt. Place 1 slice of cheese
between 2 slices of eggplant, trimming cheese to fit. Dip eggplant-
cheese sandwich in egg, and dredge
in breadcrumb mixture. Fry in hot oil
until golden brown, cooking a few
slices at a time.

Cut French bread into 5- to 6-inch
portions (to fit length of eggplant).
Split in half lengthwise; toast.

Place lettuce and tomato on 4
slices of French bread; top with eggplant and remaining bread slices.
Yield: 4 servings.

Note: Fried eggplant slices may be
served as a side dish or quartered
and served as an appetizer with commercial pizza sauce.

Charlotte Watkins
Lakeland, Florida

QUICK!

Rely On Fish Fillets

Baking fish is not only quick—it's
healthier than frying. A variety of
breadings and seasonings offers all
kinds of flavor combinations, too.
You can learn about the thickness of
fillets, the appearance of various fish,
and other factors by examining the
seafood counter, but the best way to
learn the distinctions is to eat different kinds of fish.

Often, fish fillets are packaged and
ready for purchase in the seafood
case. If not, ask the salesperson to
bone and fillet the fish for you. It's
easiest to purchase fish by the

pound—or ask for a specific number
of fillets, if you prefer.

Prepare fish the day of purchase, if
possible. If you buy it the day it arrives at the market, it will keep for
two days. Consider buying frozen fillets, too. Frozen-at-sea items are
sometimes fresher than fresh fish because they're frozen immediately
after they're caught. To cook frozen
fish, thaw fillets in the refrigerator or
microwave, and cook as instructed.

OVEN-FRIED SNAPPER

¼ cup vegetable oil
1 teaspoon sea salt
2 cloves garlic, crushed
½ cup Italian-seasoned
   breadcrumbs
½ cup grated Parmesan cheese
2 pounds snapper fillets

Combine oil, salt, and garlic in a
large dish; set aside.

Combine breadcrumbs and cheese.
Dredge each side of fillet in oil mixture, and dredge in breadcrumb mixture. Place fillets in a lightly greased
15- x 10- x 1-inch jellyroll pan. Bake
at 500° for 12 to 15 minutes or until
fish flakes easily when tested with a
fork. Yield: 6 servings.

Note: Sea salt is available in the
spice section of most supermarkets.

Patsy Bell Hobson
Liberty, Missouri

Tip: *When buying seafood for two,
use these amounts as a guideline:
1⅓ pounds of whole fish or ½ to ⅔
pound of fish fillets; ½ to 1 pound
of shucked or shelled crab, lobsters,
scallops, oysters, and shrimp.*

QUICK CRUNCHY FLOUNDER

2 cups corn flakes cereal
¼ cup mayonnaise or salad
    dressing
2 tablespoons lemon juice
3 to 4 teaspoons salt-free
    herb-and-spice blend
1 pound flounder fillets

Crush corn flakes. Set aside. Combine mayonnaise, lemon juice, and herb-and-garlic blend; spread on both sides of fillets, and coat with crushed corn flakes. Place fillets on rack of a lightly greased broiler pan. Bake at 400° for 10 to 15 minutes or until fish flakes easily when tested with a fork. Yield: 3 to 4 servings.

George Schultz
Maitland, Florida

CAESAR'S FISH
(pictured on page 41)

1 pound flounder fillets
½ cup golden Caesar salad
    dressing
1 cup round buttery cracker
    crumbs
½ cup (2 ounces) shredded
    Cheddar cheese

Arrange fillets in a single layer in a lightly greased 13- x 9- x 2-inch baking dish. Drizzle Caesar dressing over fillets; sprinkle cracker crumbs over top of fillets.

Bake fillets at 400° for 10 minutes; top with cheese, and bake an additional 5 minutes or until fish flakes easily when tested with a fork. Yield: 4 servings.

Debbie Wall
Richmond, Texas

MEXI-STYLE, OVEN-FRIED FISH

⅓ cup sour cream
1 tablespoon lemon juice
½ teaspoon chili powder
1 pound orange roughy or red
    snapper fillets
1¼ cups crushed corn chips
2 tablespoons butter or
    margarine, melted
Avocado slices (optional)
Tomato slices (optional)

Combine first 3 ingredients; dip fillets in sour cream mixture, and dredge in corn chips, coating well. Place fillets in a lightly greased 13- x 9- x 2-inch pan; drizzle with butter. Bake at 450°

for 12 to 15 minutes or until fish flakes easily when tested with a fork. If desired, serve with avocado and tomato slices. Yield: 4 servings.

Ann Rabito
Webster, Texas

HADDOCK FILLETS IN WHITE WINE

1½ pounds haddock fillets
¼ teaspoon salt
¼ teaspoon pepper
½ cup all-purpose flour
1 tablespoon butter or margarine
¼ cup chopped fresh parsley
2 tablespoons chopped green
    onions
½ cup dry white wine

Sprinkle fillets with salt and pepper; dredge lightly in flour. Place fillets in a lightly greased 13- x 9- x 2-inch baking dish; dot with butter, and sprinkle with chopped parsley and green onions. Pour wine around fillets in dish; bake at 400° for 12 to 14 minutes or until fish flakes easily when tested with a fork. Yield: 4 servings.

Terri Cohen
North Potomac, Maryland

More about Fish

■ Use fish as an economical dish. It has very little waste. A pound of fish, dressed or filleted, will yield two full-size servings.

■ "Light meat" tuna is less expensive than "white meat" tuna. Prices also descend according to the pack—from fancy or solid, to chunks, to flaked or grated. When you intend to use tuna for salads, sandwich fillings, creamed dishes, or casserole

dishes, you can always save money by buying the less expensive packs of tuna.

■ You should not thaw fish at room temperature or in warm water; it will lose moisture and flavor. Instead, place the fish in the refrigerator to thaw. Keep in mind that you should allow 18 to 24 hours for thawing a 1-pound package. You should never refreeze thawed fish.

Right: *To demonstrate eggplant's versatility, we present the vegetable in myriad ways: (front to back) Quick Eggplant Slices, Cheesy Fried Eggplant, Ratatouille Pasta Salad, and Italian-Stuffed Eggplant. (Recipes begin on page 74.)*

Page 80: *Accompany Smoked Turkey Pasta Primavera with Tasty Rolls and Very Berry Sorbet for a lunch guests will rave about. (Recipes begin on page 84.)*

Right: *Tempt appetites with Lobster Medaillons in Garlic-Chive Butter Sauce (page 96). Use fresh chives for an attractive garnish.*

Right: *Pork Medaillons in Mustard Sauce (page 96) provides an impressive entrée from a simple recipe.*

Left: *Colorful and delicately flavored julienne carrot strips complement Medaillons of Beef With Horseradish Cream (page 96).*

Left: *Use red and yellow peppers in Chicken-Rice Medaillons in Pepper Pesto (page 97) for a showy presentation.*

Brunches & Lunches

Toast The Morning, And Greet Midday

If you delight in entertaining at the noon hour, we hope you'll like our new approach to what has traditionally been called "Breakfasts & Brunches." In order to offer a broader range of recipes and menu suggestions, we've changed this 12th annual spring section to "Brunches & Lunches." We want to showcase the numerous luncheon ideas our readers have shared with us.

Southerners can make a day out of any sporting event, often starting with a before-noon gathering. Our Kentucky brunches give you a taste of what happens prior to one of the most famous Southern events, the Kentucky Derby. The menus begin with the one below served by Missy and Graeme Lang in Goshen, Kentucky, on Oaks Day, the Friday preceding the Derby.

Mint Juleps
Cucumber Sandwiches   Watercress Sandwiches
Creamed Sweetbreads
Baked Sausage Patties
Creamy Scrambled Eggs
Asparagus Vinaigrette
Kentucky Ham 'n' Angel Biscuits
Chess Tarts
Bourbon Balls
Strawberries Dipped in White Chocolate
Bluegrass Chocolate Tarts
White Wine

MINT JULEPS

1 cup sugar
1 cup water
1 cup fresh mint sprigs
Bourbon
Garnish: fresh mint sprigs

Combine sugar and water in a saucepan; bring to a boil, and cook, covered, 5 minutes (do not stir). Let syrup cool. Crush 1 cup mint with fingers, or bruise mint with the back of a spoon.

Place crushed mint in a jar; add syrup, cover, and chill 12 hours. Strain mixture, and discard mint. To serve, fill frosted julep cups or glasses with crushed ice; add 1 tablespoon syrup and 1 ounce bourbon for each serving, and stir well. Garnish, if desired. Yield: 21 servings.

CUCUMBER SANDWICHES

1 cup Homemade Mayonnaise
1 teaspoon fresh dillweed
24 slices thin-sliced white or
   wheat bread
1 large cucumber, peeled and
   sliced
Garnishes: fresh dillweed sprigs,
   fresh strawberries

Combine Homemade Mayonnaise and 1 teaspoon dillweed; set aside. Remove crust from bread; cut each slice into 2 triangles. Spread each with 1 teaspoon mayonnaise. Arrange cucumber on half of bread. Top with remaining bread. Garnish, if desired. Yield: 2 dozen party sandwiches.

Homemade Mayonnaise

1 egg
1 teaspoon sugar
¾ teaspoon salt
1 teaspoon dry mustard
½ teaspoon paprika
Dash of pepper
2 cups vegetable oil, divided
1½ tablespoons lemon juice
1 tablespoon boiling water

Beat egg in a deep bowl at high speed of an electric mixer until thick and lemon colored. Add sugar, salt, dry mustard, paprika, and pepper, mixing well. Add 1 cup oil in a very thin stream, beating at high speed until mixture begins to thicken. Add lemon juice, mixing well. Add remaining 1 cup oil in a very thin stream, beating until thickened. Add water, mixing well. Spoon mayonnaise into a glass or plastic container; cover and chill. Yield: 2 cups.

Brunches & Lunches

WATERCRESS SANDWICHES

1 (3-ounce) package cream
  cheese, softened
⅓ cup sour cream
1 tablespoon Homemade
  Mayonnaise (recipe, page 81)
1 tablespoon chopped chives
18 slices thin-sliced white or
  wheat bread
1 bunch fresh watercress
Garnish: fresh watercress sprigs

Combine cream cheese, sour cream, and Homemade Mayonnaise in a small bowl, and stir until blended; stir in chives.

Remove crust from bread, and cut each slice into 2 rectangles. Spread each rectangle with 1 teaspoon cream cheese mixture.

Arrange watercress on half of rectangles. Top with remaining rectangles. Garnish, if desired. Yield: 18 party sandwiches.

CREAMED SWEETBREADS

2 pounds veal sweetbreads
1 teaspoon salt
1 tablespoon white vinegar
¾ pound fresh mushrooms, diced
½ cup diced shallots
Vegetable cooking spray
½ cup butter or margarine
¼ cup all-purpose flour
2 cups half-and-half
2 cups chicken broth
½ teaspoon salt
½ teaspoon white pepper
Toast points

Soak sweetbreads in cold water 1 hour, changing water several times; drain. Place sweetbreads in a large saucepan; add 1 teaspoon salt, vinegar, and water to cover. Bring to a boil, and cook 10 minutes. Drain and immediately submerge in ice water. When cool, drain well, and remove thin outer covering and membrane. Carefully separate into small sections, keeping thinner coverings of sweetbreads intact. Set aside.

Sauté mushrooms and shallots in a large skillet coated with cooking spray. Remove mushroom mixture from skillet, and set aside. Melt butter in skillet; add flour, stirring until smooth. Cook 1 minute, stirring constantly. Gradually add half-and-half and chicken broth. Cook until thickened, stirring constantly. Stir in salt, pepper, mushroom mixture, and sweetbreads. Cook until thoroughly heated. Serve on toast points. Yield: 12 servings.

To make ahead: Prepare as directed. Cover and chill up to 2 days. Cook over low heat, stirring constantly, until thoroughly heated.

BAKED SAUSAGE PATTIES

1 (16-ounce) package bulk pork
  sausage

Shape sausage into 8 patties about ¾-inch thick; place on a rack in a broiler pan. Bake at 375° for 15 to 20 minutes or until done. Drain on paper towels. Yield: 8 servings.

To make ahead: Prepare as directed; let cool. Wrap in aluminum foil; refrigerate. To serve, let stand at room temperature 1 hour. Bake at 350° in foil 10 minutes or until thoroughly heated.

CREAMY SCRAMBLED EGGS

12 eggs, slightly beaten
1 teaspoon chopped fresh dillweed
½ teaspoon salt
¼ teaspoon pepper
¼ cup butter or margarine
½ cup sour cream

Combine first 4 ingredients, and set aside. Melt butter in a large nonstick skillet over medium heat. Add egg mixture; cook, without stirring, until mixture begins to set on bottom. Draw a spatula across bottom of pan to form large curds. Continue until eggs are thickened but still moist; do not stir constantly. Fold in sour cream. Yield: 12 servings.

ASPARAGUS VINAIGRETTE

3 pounds fresh asparagus spears
1 sweet red pepper, cut into
  strips
1 tablespoon vegetable oil
¾ cup vegetable oil
¼ cup white vinegar
2 tablespoons water
1 tablespoon grated onion
1 teaspoon hot dry mustard
½ teaspoon salt
Pinch of pepper

Snap off tough ends of asparagus. Remove scales from stalks with a knife or vegetable peeler, if desired. Cook asparagus, covered, in a small amount of boiling water 4 to 6 minutes or until crisp-tender. Drain. Rinse in cold water; drain.

Sauté red pepper strips in 1 tablespoon oil until crisp-tender; drain well, and let cool.

Place asparagus and pepper strips in a 13- x 9- x 2-inch dish. Combine ¾ cup oil and remaining ingredients;

stir well, and pour over vegetables. Cover and chill at least 8 hours. Remove from marinade, and arrange on serving platter. Yield: 12 servings.

KENTUCKY HAM 'N' ANGEL BISCUITS

1 package dry yeast
½ cup warm water (105° to 115°)
2 cups buttermilk
4½ cups all-purpose flour
1½ teaspoons baking soda
1 teaspoon salt
3 tablespoons sugar
¾ cup shortening
About 3 pounds cooked country ham, thinly sliced

Combine yeast and warm water; let stand 5 minutes. Add buttermilk, and set aside.

Combine flour and next 3 ingredients in a large bowl; cut in shortening with a pastry blender until mixture resembles coarse meal. Add buttermilk mixture, stirring with a fork until dry ingredients are moistened. Turn biscuit dough out onto a heavily floured surface, and knead lightly 4 or 5 times.

Roll dough to ⅓-inch thickness; cut with a 1¾-inch biscuit cutter. Place on lightly greased baking sheets, and bake at 400° for 8 to 10 minutes or until done. Serve with ham. Yield: 6 dozen.

To freeze: Bake biscuits at 400° for 8 minutes; cool. (Do not split and fill with ham.) Wrap biscuits in heavy-duty plastic wrap; place in freezer bags, and freeze. To serve, let thaw. Place on lightly greased baking sheets. Bake at 400° for 5 minutes or until biscuits are thoroughly heated and lightly browned.

CHESS TARTS

2 cups all-purpose flour
½ teaspoon salt
½ cup butter, chilled and cut into pieces
¼ cup shortening
⅓ cup ice water
2 eggs, beaten
1 cup sugar
1 tablespoon cornmeal
2 teaspoons white vinegar
⅓ cup butter or margarine, melted
¼ teaspoon vanilla extract
Garnish: fresh raspberries

Combine flour and salt in a bowl; cut in ½ cup butter and shortening with a pastry blender until mixture resembles coarse meal. Sprinkle ice water (1 tablespoon at a time) over surface; stir with a fork until ingredients are moistened.

Shape dough into 36 balls. Place in miniature (1¾-inch) muffin pans, shaping each ball into a shell. Cover and chill pastry shells 30 minutes.

Combine eggs and next 5 ingredients; stir well. Spoon evenly into pastry shells; bake at 350° for 20 to 25 minutes or until golden brown. Remove from oven. Remove tarts from pans; let cool on wire racks. Garnish, if desired. Yield: 3 dozen.

BOURBON BALLS

½ cup butter, softened
1 (16-ounce) package powdered sugar, sifted
¼ cup bourbon
1 cup chopped pecans
4 (1-ounce) squares semisweet chocolate
4 (1-ounce) squares unsweetened chocolate
4 dozen pecan halves

Cream butter; gradually add sugar, beating well at medium speed of an electric mixer. Add bourbon; beat until smooth. Stir in chopped pecans. Shape into 1-inch balls; cover and chill 8 hours.

Combine chocolate squares in top of a double boiler; bring water to a boil. Reduce heat to low, and cook until chocolate melts, stirring often. Dip bourbon balls in chocolate; place on wax paper, and gently press a pecan half on top of each. Chill until chocolate hardens. Yield: 4 dozen.

STRAWBERRIES DIPPED IN WHITE CHOCOLATE

2 pints fresh strawberries
6 ounces white chocolate or white chocolate-flavored baking bar, grated
Vegetable cooking spray

Rinse strawberries, and dry thoroughly with paper towels (chocolate will not stick to wet strawberries). Set berries aside.

Place white chocolate in top of a double boiler; bring water to a boil. Reduce heat to low; cook until chocolate melts.

Grasp strawberries by the stem, and dip into melted chocolate; place on a wire rack sprayed with vegetable cooking spray, and chill until chocolate is firm. Serve within 8 hours. Yield: 3 to 4 dozen.

Note: For larger parties, increase amount of strawberries and chocolate. Melt chocolate, and transfer to a chafing dish. Let guests dip their own strawberries.

BLUEGRASS CHOCOLATE TARTS

½ cup butter or margarine,
   softened
1 cup sugar
2 eggs
½ cup all-purpose flour
Pinch of salt
2 tablespoons bourbon
1 cup semisweet chocolate
   morsels
1 cup chopped pecans
Tart Shells

Cream butter and sugar; add eggs, mixing well. Add flour, salt, and bourbon, stirring until blended. Stir in chocolate morsels and pecans. Spoon mixture into Tart Shells, filling three-fourths full. Bake at 350° for 25 minutes or until lightly browned. Yield: 6 dozen.

Tart Shells

3 cups all-purpose flour
3 (3-ounce) packages cream
   cheese, softened
1¼ cups butter or margarine,
   softened

Combine all ingredients; stir until blended. Shape dough into 72 balls; chill. Place in greased miniature (1¾-inch) muffin pans, shaping each ball into a shell. Yield: 6 dozen.

To freeze: Bake as directed; let cool. Place tarts in freezer container; cover and freeze up to 2 weeks. To serve, let thaw.

Share This Menu With Friends

Celebrate spring with a luncheon for friends and neighbors. The entire menu below can be prepared ahead freeing you for the day of the luncheon to enjoy your guests.

Meet your guests at the door with Grapefruit Drink, a refreshing spring beverage. Then serve this delightful meal, which features Smoked Turkey Pasta Primavera.

Grapefruit Drink
Smoked Turkey Pasta Primavera
Tasty Rolls
Very Berry Sorbet

GRAPEFRUIT DRINK

1½ cups sugar
4 cups water
2 cups grapefruit juice
1 cup chopped grapefruit sections
¼ cup maraschino cherries,
   drained and halved
4 to 6 tablespoons lemon juice
4 cups sparkling mineral water,
   chilled

Combine sugar and 4 cups water in a medium saucepan; bring to a boil, stirring until sugar dissolves. Remove from heat, and let cool. Combine syrup, grapefruit juice, and next 3 ingredients. Chill.
   To serve, add chilled sparkling mineral water, stirring gently. Yield: 3 quarts.
                            Jane Noe
                        Sandia, Texas

Tip: *If stored at room temperature, grapefruit will keep for a day or two; when refrigerated, they will keep up to four months.*

SMOKED TURKEY PASTA PRIMAVERA
(pictured on page 80)

1 (12-ounce) package fettuccine
1½ pounds fresh broccoli, cut
   into flowerets
2 medium zucchini, thinly sliced
6 green onions, thinly sliced
1 sweet red pepper, sliced into
   thin strips
1 (6-ounce) can pitted ripe olives,
   drained and sliced
4 cups chopped cooked smoked
   turkey
⅔ cup grated Parmesan cheese
½ teaspoon salt
½ teaspoon freshly ground pepper
⅔ cup Basil Sauce
2 cups cherry tomatoes, halved
Lettuce leaves

Cook fettuccine according to package directions; drain. Rinse with cold water; drain.
   Combine fettuccine and next 9 ingredients, tossing well. Add ⅔ cup Basil Sauce and cherry tomatoes; toss gently. Chill. Serve on lettuce leaves. Yield: 12 servings.

Basil Sauce

¼ cup chopped fresh basil
1 clove garlic
2 eggs
½ teaspoon dry mustard
½ teaspoon salt
½ teaspoon lemon juice
1 tablespoon wine vinegar
1½ cups vegetable oil
½ cup sour cream

Combine basil and garlic in container of an electric blender or food processor; process 30 seconds or until basil is minced. Add eggs and next 4 ingredients. Process 20 seconds, scraping sides of processor bowl once. With motor running, gradually add oil in a slow, steady stream, mixing just until well blended. Add sour cream, and process 5 seconds or until blended. Yield: 2¼ cups.

TASTY ROLLS
(pictured on page 80)

2 packages dry yeast
2¼ cups warm water (105° to 115°), divided
2 tablespoons instant potato flakes
1 tablespoon sugar
1 teaspoon salt
2 tablespoons vegetable oil
2 tablespoons honey
2 tablespoons molasses
1 teaspoon caraway seeds
3½ to 4 cups bread flour, divided
½ cup oat bran
½ cup rye flour
½ cup whole wheat flour

Dissolve yeast in ¾ cup warm water in a large mixing bowl; let stand 5 minutes. Add remaining water, potato flakes, and next 6 ingredients, stirring well. Add 1 cup bread flour; beat until well blended. Gradually stir in oat bran, rye flour, whole wheat flour, and enough remaining bread flour to make a soft dough.

Turn dough out onto a floured surface, and knead until smooth and elastic (about 5 minutes). Place in a well-greased bowl, turning to grease top. Cover and let rise in a warm place (85°), free from drafts, 45 minutes or until doubled in bulk.

Punch dough down, and divide in half. Shape each half into 12 (3½- x 1½-inch) loaf-shaped rolls. Place on greased baking sheets. Cover and let rise in a warm place, free from drafts, 20 minutes or until doubled in bulk. Bake at 350° for 18 minutes or until golden brown. Yield: 2 dozen.
Rosa Marie Rudd
Spotsylvania, Virginia

VERY BERRY SORBET
(pictured on page 80)

2 envelopes unflavored gelatin
1 cup sugar
3 cups water
1 quart pureed strawberries (about 3 pints fresh)
1 cup cranberry juice cocktail
¼ cup lemon juice

Combine gelatin and sugar in a medium saucepan; stir in water. Let stand 1 minute. Cook over low heat, stirring constantly, until gelatin dissolves. Remove from heat; cool. Stir in strawberries and remaining ingredients. Pour into a 13- x 9- x 2-inch pan. Cover and freeze 8 hours.

Spoon about one-fourth of frozen mixture into container of an electric blender or food processor. Top with cover, and process until smooth; return to pan. Repeat until all mixture is processed. Return pan to freezer; freeze 4 hours or until firm. Let stand at room temperature 15 to 20 minutes. Yield: 2½ quarts.
Edith Askins
Greenville, Texas

Invite Friends To A Coffee

When you plan a party for the morning hours, it's usually called a coffee, in honor of the tasty beverage sipped by so many folks to start the day.

A morning party doesn't leave much time for same-day preparation, so it helps to have some recipes that can be made earlier in the week. Almost all of these can be prepared ahead of time. The cream dip for fresh strawberries tastes best chilled, so make it the day before, and pour it into the serving container before chilling.

Of course coffee served with cream and sugar is a must. Our Cappuccino Mix makes a nice addition to the coffee tray for guests who like a change from the usual. If you want to be even more creative, arrange a coffee bar for guests to fix their own flavored coffees.

Sausage-Apple Balls
Fresh Strawberries
With Cream Dip
Raisin Pastry Bites
Daisy Biscuits
Basic Cupcake Muffins
Cappuccino

SAUSAGE-APPLE BALLS

1 pound bulk pork sausage
2 cups biscuit mix
1 cup raisins, chopped
1 cup grated unpeeled apple
½ cup chopped walnuts
½ teaspoon apple pie spice

Combine all ingredients, mixing well. Shape into 1-inch balls. Place on ungreased baking sheets; bake at 350° for 20 minutes or until lightly browned. Yield: about 4½ dozen.

Brunches & Lunches

FRESH STRAWBERRIES WITH CREAM DIP

1 (8-ounce) package cream cheese, softened
1 cup sour cream
⅓ cup sifted powdered sugar
2 teaspoons Cointreau or other orange-flavored liqueur
1 quart fresh strawberries

Combine cream cheese and sour cream in a small bowl; beat at medium speed of an electric mixer until smooth. Add powdered sugar and Cointreau, mixing well. Chill 1 hour. Serve with fresh strawberries. Yield: 2 cups.
Bettye Cortner
Cerulean, Kentucky

RAISIN PASTRY BITES

1 package dry yeast
¼ cup warm water (105° to 115°)
3 cups all-purpose flour
¾ teaspoon salt
1 cup butter
2 egg yolks, slightly beaten
⅔ cup sour cream
1 teaspoon vanilla extract
Raisin Filling
Powdered sugar

Dissolve yeast in warm water in a small mixing bowl; let yeast mixture stand 5 minutes.

Combine flour and salt in a mixing bowl; cut in butter until mixture resembles coarse meal.

Combine egg yolks, sour cream, and vanilla; stir well. Add egg mixture and dissolved yeast to flour mixture; stir until mixture leaves the sides of bowl. Knead dough 4 or 5 times, and shape into a ball. Cover and chill two hours.

Divide dough in half. Turn out 1 portion onto a lightly floured surface; roll dough to a 14- x 12-inch rectangle. Cut rectangle into six 14- x 2-inch strips. Thinly spread Raisin Filling over each strip, leaving ¼-inch border down each long side. Moisten edges of long sides with water. Bring moistened edges together, pressing securely to seal and forming a log shape. Cut each log into 1½-inch pieces, and place seam side down on ungreased baking sheets. Repeat with remaining portion of dough. Bake at 375° for 10 to 12 minutes or until lightly browned.

Cool slightly; sprinkle with powdered sugar. Cool. Yield: 9 dozen.

Raisin Filling

2 cups raisins, ground
½ cup water
¼ cup sugar
2 tablespoons lemon juice
½ cup finely chopped pecans

Combine first 4 ingredients in a small saucepan; bring to a boil. Reduce heat, and simmer 4 to 5 minutes or until thickened, stirring often. Remove from heat; stir in pecans. Cool. Yield: about 2½ cups.
Mrs. Curtis H. Ward
Auburn, Alabama

DAISY BISCUITS

1 (3-ounce) package cream cheese
¼ cup butter or margarine
2½ cups self-rising flour
¾ cup milk
2½ tablespoons orange marmalade
2½ tablespoons raspberry jam

Cut cream cheese and butter into flour with a pastry blender until mixture resembles coarse meal. Add milk, stirring just until dry ingredients are moistened. Turn dough out onto a floured surface, and knead 3 or 4 times.

Roll dough to ½-inch thickness; cut with a 2-inch biscuit cutter. Place on ungreased baking sheets. Make 6 slits through dough around edges of each biscuit to ¼ inch from center. Press thumb in center of each biscuit, leaving an indentation. Spoon ½ teaspoon marmalade or jam into each biscuit indentation. Bake at 450° for 10 to 12 minutes or until golden brown. Yield: 28 biscuits.

Nora Hendrix
Augusta, Georgia

BASIC CUPCAKE MUFFINS

1 cup self-rising flour
¼ cup sugar
1 egg, beaten
½ cup milk
¼ cup vegetable oil
½ teaspoon vanilla extract
Sifted powdered sugar

Combine flour and ¼ cup sugar in a mixing bowl; make a well in center of mixture. Combine egg and next 3 ingredients; add to dry ingredients, stirring just until moistened. Spoon into greased and floured 1½-inch muffin pans, filling about two-thirds full. Bake at 400° for 12 to 14 minutes or until edges are lightly browned. Remove from pans; sprinkle with powdered sugar. Yield: 2½ dozen.

Cherry-Nut Muffins: Stir ¼ cup chopped maraschino cherries and ¼ cup chopped pecans into basic muffin batter.

Rum-Nut Muffins: Stir 2 tablespoons rum and ¼ cup chopped pecans into basic muffin batter.

Chocolate Chip Muffins: Stir ¼ cup semisweet chocolate mini-morsels and ¼ cup chopped walnuts into basic muffin batter.

Almond Muffins: Stir 2 tablespoons amaretto and ¼ cup chopped toasted almonds into basic muffin batter.

Mrs. Lawrence A. Angelo
Birmingham, Alabama

CAPPUCCINO MIX

1 cup powdered instant non-dairy creamer
1 cup chocolate milk mix
⅔ cup instant coffee granules
½ cup sugar
½ teaspoon ground cinnamon
¼ teaspoon ground nutmeg

Combine all ingredients; mix well. Store in an airtight container.

To serve, place 1 tablespoon plus 1 teaspoon mix in a cup. Add 1 cup boiling water; stir well. Yield: about 33 servings.

BariLynn Mitchell
St. Peters, Missouri

Country Ham, From Start To Finish

Many folks across the South serve country ham when a crowd gathers for a special occasion, whether it's for breakfast, brunch, or lunch. This full-flavored meat makes a tasty entrée and often provides leftovers for other recipes.

OVEN-BRAISED COUNTRY HAM

6 (4-ounce) slices cooked country ham
2 tablespoons brown sugar
¼ cup water

Place ham slices in a lightly greased 13- x 9- x 2-inch baking dish; sprinkle with brown sugar. Pour water around ham. Cover with aluminum foil, and bake at 350° for 30 minutes. Serve immediately. Yield: 6 servings.

Dorothy Martin
Woodburn, Kentucky

Preparing Country Ham

Many country hams are covered with mold when purchased. Scrub or cut off the mold when you receive the ham. Then rinse it with a mixture of equal parts of white vinegar and water, and hang it in a cool place. Repeat the process if mold reoccurs. The ham will continue to age during storage; the cooler the temperature, the less it will age.

Country hams taste salty. You can remove some of the salt and add moisture back to the cured ham by soaking it in water 24 hours. Salt-conscious people sometimes soak them up to 72 hours, changing the water daily. This removes some of the salty taste.

Once the ham is cooked, it should be wrapped tightly in brown paper or aluminum foil and refrigerated. Don't use plastic wrap because it holds in too much moisture and speeds spoilage. Cooked cured ham will keep in the refrigerator up to six weeks.

CHEESY COUNTRY HAM PUFF

4 slices white bread, torn into
  bite-size pieces
2 cups milk
3 eggs
½ teaspoon spicy mustard
⅛ teaspoon paprika
Dash of garlic powder
2 cups (8 ounces) shredded
  Cheddar cheese
1½ cups diced country ham
½ cup chopped onion
4 slices bacon, cooked and
  crumbled
2 tablespoons chopped fresh
  parsley or 2 teaspoons dried
  parsley flakes

Combine first 6 ingredients in a large
mixing bowl. Beat at medium speed
of an electric mixer 1 minute or until
smooth. Stir in cheese and remaining
ingredients. Pour into a greased 12-
x 8- x 2-inch baking dish. Bake at
375° for 30 minutes or until center is
set. Let stand about 10 minutes before serving. Yield: 8 servings.

Donna Hill
Belden, Mississippi

COUNTRY HAM WITH BROWN
SUGAR COATING

1 (10- to 12-pound) uncooked
  country ham
1 (64-ounce) bottle apple juice
2 teaspoons ground cloves
⅔ cup firmly packed brown sugar
2½ tablespoons dry sherry, red
  wine, or cider vinegar

Place ham in a large container. Cover
with water, and let soak 24 hours.
Drain. Scrub ham in warm water
with a stiff brush, and rinse well.
  Place ham in a large cooking container. Insert meat thermometer,
making sure it does not touch fat or
bone. Add apple juice. Add enough
hot water to cover ham. Bring to a
boil; cover, reduce heat, and simmer
2 hours or until meat thermometer
registers 142°. Let ham cool in drippings 3 hours. Remove from drippings. Cover and refrigerate ham at
least 8 hours.
  Trim skin from ham. Place ham,
fat side up, on a rack in a shallow
roasting pan. Sprinkle fat with ground
cloves. Combine brown sugar and
sherry; brush over ham. Bake at
425° for 10 to 15 minutes or until
coating is golden and crusty (ham will
be cool). Slice thinly to serve. Yield:
30 servings.

Note: To serve ham warm, bake
ham as directed above to brown the
coating; then cover with aluminum
foil, reduce heat to 350°, and bake 1
hour or until thoroughly heated.

Soup And Salad
Specials

An easy but elegant luncheon built
around well-paired soups and salads
is a great accompaniment for lots of
spring events.
  Just add bread sticks, whole wheat
rolls, or crisp crackers on the side
and sherbet or other light dessert to
complete our soup-and-salad teams.
  Creamy, rich Seafood Salad can be
made the night before; its partner,
Dilled Zucchini Soup, with only five
ingredients, takes about half an hour
to prepare. When the morning before
the luncheon is a busy one, these
two fit the bill. For a lighter taste,
try Turkey-Rice Soup and Spinach-
Apple Salad. Both menus are planned
to serve four.

DILLED ZUCCHINI SOUP

4 medium zucchini, sliced
1 (14½-ounce) can ready-to-serve
  chicken broth
¼ teaspoon garlic salt
1 tablespoon fresh dillweed or 1
  teaspoon dried whole dillweed
2 cups half-and-half
Garnishes: zucchini slices, fresh
  dillweed sprigs

Combine zucchini and broth in a large
saucepan. Bring to a boil; cover, reduce heat, and simmer 12 to 15 minutes or until tender. Pour into
container of an electric blender, and
process until smooth.
  Return zucchini mixture to saucepan; stir in seasonings and half-and-
half. Cook over low heat, stirring
constantly, until heated. Garnish
soup, if desired. Yield: 6 cups.

Azine Rush
Monroe, Louisiana

SEAFOOD SALAD

4 ounces fine egg noodles
½ cup sour cream
½ cup plain yogurt
1 tablespoon plus 1 teaspoon
  lemon juice
1 teaspoon Worcestershire sauce
1 (16-ounce) package frozen
  seafood mix, thawed
½ cup chopped celery
2 tablespoons capers, drained
1½ tablespoons minced onion
2 teaspoons dried parsley flakes
2 teaspoons freeze-dried chives
¼ teaspoon seasoned salt
Leaf lettuce
Garnishes: tomato wedges, fresh
  parsley sprigs

Cook egg noodles according to package directions; drain. Rinse with cold
water; drain. Set aside.

Combine sour cream, yogurt, lemon juice, and Worcestershire sauce, mixing well. Combine noodles, sour cream mixture, seafood mix, and next 6 ingredients, mixing well. Chill 8 hours. Arrange on lettuce-lined plates. Garnish, if desired. Yield: 4 servings. *Gail McDaniel*
Springfield, Missouri

TURKEY-RICE SOUP

¾ pound turkey tenderloin, cut into bite-size pieces
1½ quarts water
2 stalks celery, sliced
1 medium onion, chopped
2 chicken-flavored bouillon cubes
1 teaspoon salt
¼ teaspoon poultry seasoning
1 bay leaf
½ cup uncooked long-grain rice
2 carrots, scraped and sliced

Combine first 8 ingredients in a Dutch oven. Bring to a boil; cover, reduce heat, and simmer 40 minutes. Add rice and carrots; cover and simmer an additional 20 minutes or until rice is tender. Remove bay leaf. Yield: 1½ quarts. *Billie Taylor*
Wytheville, Virginia

SPINACH-APPLE SALAD

½ pound fresh spinach
⅓ cup mayonnaise or salad dressing
¼ cup frozen orange juice concentrate, thawed
1 large red apple, unpeeled
2 teaspoons lemon juice
4 slices bacon, cooked and crumbled
Freshly ground pepper to taste

Remove stems from spinach; wash leaves thoroughly, and pat dry. Tear into bite-size pieces. Set aside. Combine mayonnaise and orange concentrate; stir well, and set aside.

Just before serving, core apple; cut into wedges. Sprinkle with lemon juice; toss gently to coat. Arrange spinach, apple, and bacon on plates. Drizzle with dressing; sprinkle with pepper. Yield: 4 servings.

A Lunch For A Southern Celebration

This menu makes Sunday dinner easy on the cook and satisfying to the palate. Mint Tea, salad, rolls, and dessert can all be made ahead of time. Crispy Walnut Chicken and Baked New Potatoes both bake in a 350° oven, so preparation right before the meal is easy.

Mint Tea
Crispy Walnut Chicken
Baked New Potatoes
Zesty Marinated Salad
Hurry-Up Yeast Rolls
Lemon Cloud Mousse
or
Orange-Coconut Pie

MINT TEA

1 quart boiling water
3 family-size tea bags and 2 regular-size tea bags
Mint Syrup
2½ quarts water
Garnishes: fresh mint sprigs, lemon slices

Pour boiling water over tea bags; cover and steep 5 minutes. Remove tea bags, squeezing gently. Stir in Mint Syrup and 2½ quarts water. Serve over ice. Garnish, if desired. Yield: 1 gallon.

Mint Syrup

3 cups water
2¼ cups sugar
3 cups fresh mint leaves

Combine all ingredients in a saucepan; stir well. Bring to a boil, and cook 10 minutes or until mixture is reduced to 2¼ cups, stirring often. Remove from heat; cool. Strain. Yield: 2 cups.

Note: Syrup may also be served over fresh fruit. *Georgianne McGee*
Waycross, Georgia

CRISPY WALNUT CHICKEN

3 cups crispy rice cereal
½ cup walnuts
½ cup butter or margarine, melted
1 teaspoon garlic powder
½ teaspoon salt
½ teaspoon pepper
3 pounds chicken pieces, skinned

Position knife blade in food processor bowl. Add cereal and walnuts; top with cover, and process until finely ground. Set aside.

Combine butter, garlic powder, salt, and pepper; stir well. Dredge chicken in butter mixture, then in cereal mixture. Arrange chicken in a 15- x 10- x 1-inch jellyroll pan; pour any remaining butter mixture over chicken. Bake at 350° for 1 hour or until done. Yield: 6 servings.
La Juan Coward
Jasper, Texas

BAKED NEW POTATOES

2¼ pounds new potatoes,
 unpeeled and quartered
¼ cup butter or margarine,
 melted
2 tablespoons vegetable oil
½ teaspoon salt
½ teaspoon dried whole thyme

Arrange potatoes in a 13- x 9- x 2-inch baking dish. Combine melted butter and remaining ingredients in small bowl; pour mixture over potatoes, and turn potatoes to coat evenly. Bake, uncovered, at 350° for 35 minutes or until potatoes are tender. Yield: 6 servings.

Note: Cooking time will vary depending on size of potatoes.

ZESTY MARINATED SALAD

2 tomatoes, sliced
2 medium zucchini, sliced
1½ cups sliced fresh mushrooms
¼ cup chopped fresh parsley
1 (8-ounce) bottle commercial
 Italian salad dressing
Bibb lettuce

Combine first 4 ingredients in an 8-inch square baking dish. Pour dressing over vegetables, tossing to coat. Cover and chill 8 hours. Drain, reserving dressing.
 Arrange vegetables over lettuce. Serve with reserved dressing. Yield: 6 servings.   *Linda Sanders*
Raleigh, North Carolina

HURRY-UP YEAST ROLLS

1 package dry yeast
¾ cup warm water (105° to 115°)
3 to 3½ cups biscuit mix
2 tablespoons sugar

Dissolve yeast in warm water in a large mixing bowl; let yeast mixture stand 5 minutes. Combine biscuit mix and sugar; gradually add biscuit mix to yeast mixture, stirring well.
 Turn dough out onto a floured surface, and knead until smooth (about 10 minutes). Roll dough to a 12-inch circle on a floured surface. Cut circle of dough into 12 wedges; roll up each wedge, beginning at wide end. Place rolls on a greased baking sheet, point side down.
 Cover and let rise in a warm place (85°), free from drafts, 1 hour or until doubled in bulk. Bake at 425° for 10 to 12 minutes or until golden brown. Yield: 1 dozen.

Note: Rolls may be frozen. Prepare as directed, and bake at 425° for 5 minutes; cool. Wrap in aluminum foil, and place in freezer bag; freeze up to 2 months. To reheat, let thaw to room temperature. Place on baking sheet, and bake at 425° for 7 to 8 minutes or until golden brown.
Eula Cox
Columbus, Mississippi

LEMON CLOUD MOUSSE

3 egg yolks
1 (14-ounce) can sweetened
 condensed milk
¾ cup lemon juice
1 cup whipping cream, whipped
 and divided
½ cup graham cracker crumbs

Beat egg yolks in a small bowl at high speed of an electric mixer until thick and lemon colored; gradually add condensed milk, beating until well blended. Gradually add lemon juice; mix well.
 Fold 1¼ cups whipped cream into lemon mixture, reserving remaining whipped cream for garnish. Spoon about ¼ cup lemon mixture into each of six 6-ounce parfait glasses; top with 2 teaspoons graham cracker crumbs. Repeat layers, ending with lemon mixture. Garnish with remaining whipped cream. Chill 8 hours. Yield: 6 servings.   *Dorsella Utter*
Louisville, Kentucky

ORANGE-COCONUT PIE

¼ cup butter or margarine,
 softened
1 cup sugar
3 eggs, beaten
½ cup orange juice
1 teaspoon lemon extract
Dash of salt
1 cup flaked coconut
1 unbaked 9-inch pastry shell

Cream butter; gradually add sugar, beating well at medium speed of an electric mixer. Add eggs, and beat until blended. Stir in orange juice, lemon extract, salt, and coconut, mixing well.
 Pour into pastry shell. Bake at 350° for 45 to 50 minutes or until a knife inserted in center comes out clean. Yield: one 9-inch pie.
Velma McGregor
Gretna, Louisiana

Tip: *Every time the door is opened to the oven, the temperature drops 25 to 30 degrees. Use the oven window so as not to waste energy.*

Lunches, Boxed To Go

Some Derby fans are definitely winners if they happen to be the all-day guests of Curtis and Linda Green. After a brunch, the Greens charter a bus to Churchill Downs from their farm near Lexington, Kentucky. Delicious box lunches packed in coolers are enjoyed after the races.

Why not borrow some ideas from the Greens? Your box lunches can be as attractive to the eye as they are to the palate. Just spoon individual servings of food into small plastic containers; then pack into assorted boxes. (See Fancy Touches for Box Lunches, below.)

Beef Tenderloin Picnic
Sandwiches
Marinated Asparagus
and Hearts of Palm
Pasta Salad
Fresh strawberries
Miniature Derby Tarts

BEEF TENDERLOIN PICNIC SANDWICHES

½ cup butter or margarine,
    melted
1 tablespoon seasoned salt
2 teaspoons garlic powder
2 teaspoons ground red pepper
1 (4- to 5-pound) beef tenderloin
Party rolls
Sour cream
Prepared horseradish

Combine first 4 ingredients; mix well. Place tenderloin on a rack in a roasting pan; brush with butter mixture. Insert meat thermometer, making sure it does not touch fat. Bake at 425° for 30 to 45 minutes or until thermometer registers 140° for rare, 150° for medium rare, or 160° for medium. Slice tenderloin. Serve on party rolls with sour cream and prepared horseradish. Yield: 16 to 20 servings.

MARINATED ASPARAGUS AND HEARTS OF PALM

3 pounds fresh asparagus
2 (14-ounce) cans hearts of palm,
    drained and cut into ½-inch
    slices
1 cup vegetable oil
½ cup cider vinegar
3 cloves garlic, crushed
1½ teaspoons salt
1 teaspoon pepper
Cherry tomatoes

Snap off tough ends of asparagus. Remove scales from stalks with a knife. Place asparagus in steaming rack over boiling water; cover and steam 4 minutes. Drain and submerge in ice water to cool. Drain asparagus well.

Combine asparagus and hearts of palm in a zip-top, heavy-duty plastic bag. Combine oil and next 4 ingredients in a jar; cover tightly, and shake vigorously. Pour dressing over vegetables. Seal bag, and marinate in refrigerator 8 hours; turn bag occasionally. Add tomatoes. Yield: 12 servings.

PASTA SALAD

1 pound uncooked vegetable
    rotini
1 green pepper, chopped
1 sweet red pepper, chopped
1 (8-ounce) can sliced water
    chestnuts, drained
1 bunch green onions, chopped
Cherry tomatoes (optional)
¾ cup vegetable oil
¼ cup cider vinegar
1½ teaspoons salt
1½ teaspoons pepper
1 clove garlic, crushed

Cook pasta according to package directions, omitting salt; drain. Rinse with cold water; drain.

Combine pasta, peppers, water chestnuts, green onions and, if desired, cherry tomatoes in a bowl. Combine oil and remaining ingredients, mixing well. Pour over pasta mixture, stirring to coat well. Cover and chill 8 hours; stir occasionally. Yield: 12 servings.

Fancy Touches for Box Lunches

■ Line assorted boxes with colorful napkins or tissue paper.

■ Tie color-coordinated ribbons in gift-wrap fashion around boxes.

MINIATURE DERBY TARTS

Tart Pastry
⅓ cup chopped pecans
1½ tablespoons bourbon
⅔ cup sugar
½ cup light corn syrup
2 eggs
2 tablespoons butter or
   margarine, melted
⅓ cup semisweet chocolate
   morsels
⅓ cup flaked coconut
½ teaspoon vanilla extract

Roll pastry to ⅛-inch thickness on a lightly floured surface. Cut with a 2-inch round cutter, and fit into miniature (1¾-inch) muffin pans.

Soak pecans in bourbon. Combine sugar, corn syrup, eggs, and butter; mix until blended. Stir in morsels, coconut, vanilla, and bourbon-pecan mixture. Spoon mixture into pastry-lined muffin pans, filling three-fourths full. Bake at 350° for 15 to 20 minutes or until golden. Yield: 3 dozen.

Tart Pastry

1½ cups all-purpose flour
½ teaspoon baking powder
½ teaspoon salt
¼ cup butter or margarine
¼ cup shortening
4 to 6 tablespoons milk

Combine flour, baking powder, and salt; cut in butter and shortening with pastry blender until mixture resembles coarse meal. Sprinkle milk evenly over surface of mixture; stir with a fork just until dry ingredients are moistened. Shape dough into a ball; chill. Yield: enough pastry for 3 dozen tarts.

The Races Start With Brunch

On Derby Day, Linda and Curtis Green host an all-day party. Guests gather at Bel-Mar Farm near Lexington early on the first Saturday in May for a pre-Derby brunch.

Eggs Bel-Mar
Vegetable crudités
Baked Spinach Tomatoes
Cheese Loaf
Biscuits With Country Ham
French Toast With
Grand Marnier Fruit Sauce
Miniature Carrot Cakes
Special Derby Brownies

EGGS BEL-MAR

¼ cup butter or margarine
¼ cup all-purpose flour
2 cups milk
1 teaspoon salt
½ teaspoon pepper
1 (6-ounce) package Canadian
   bacon, chopped
¼ cup chopped green pepper
¼ cup sliced green onions
½ pound fresh mushrooms, sliced
3 tablespoons butter or
   margarine, melted
1 tablespoon butter or margarine
18 eggs, slightly beaten
1 cup soft breadcrumbs
2 tablespoons butter or
   margarine, melted

Melt ¼ cup butter in a heavy saucepan over low heat; add flour, stirring until smooth. Cook 1 minute, stirring constantly. Gradually add milk; cook over medium heat, stirring constantly, until thickened and bubbly. Stir in salt and pepper. Set aside.

Sauté Canadian bacon and next 3 ingredients in 3 tablespoons butter in a skillet until vegetables are crisp-tender; drain.

Melt 1 tablespoon butter in skillet, tilting to coat bottom; add eggs. Cook without stirring until mixture begins to set on bottom. Draw a spatula across bottom of pan to form large curds. Continue until eggs are thickened but still moist; do not stir constantly. Remove from heat. Gently stir in Canadian bacon mixture and white sauce. Spoon egg mixture into a greased 13- x 9- x 2-inch baking dish.

Combine breadcrumbs and 2 tablespoons melted butter, stirring well; sprinkle evenly over egg mixture.

Bake, uncovered, at 350° for 20 to 25 minutes or until thoroughly heated. Yield: 12 servings.

To make ahead: Prepare casserole as directed, but do not bake. Cover and refrigerate up to 24 hours. Remove from refrigerator; let stand 30 minutes. Bake as directed.

BAKED SPINACH TOMATOES

12 medium tomatoes
1½ teaspoons salt
1½ teaspoons sugar
3 (10-ounce) packages frozen
   chopped spinach
1 medium onion, chopped
⅓ cup butter or margarine,
   melted
3 tablespoons all-purpose flour
1½ cups milk
¾ teaspoon salt
½ teaspoon white pepper

Cut top quarter off each tomato. Scoop out pulp, leaving shells intact;

reserve pulp for other uses. Sprinkle inside of each tomato shell with ⅛ teaspoon salt and ⅛ teaspoon sugar, and invert on paper towels to drain.

Cook spinach according to package directions. Drain well by pressing out excess liquid with back of a spoon.

Sauté onion in butter in a heavy saucepan until tender. Add flour, stirring until blended. Cook 1 minute, stirring constantly. Gradually add milk; cook over medium heat, stirring constantly, until mixture is thickened and bubbly. Stir in spinach, ¾ teaspoon salt, and pepper.

Spoon mixture into tomato shells, and place in a greased 13- x 9- x 2-inch baking dish. Bake at 350° for 20 minutes or until thoroughly heated. Yield: 12 servings.

To make ahead: Prepare tomatoes as directed, but do not bake. Cover and chill up to 24 hours. Remove from refrigerator; let stand 30 minutes. Bake as directed.

CHEESE LOAF

1¼ cups cracker crumbs
1 cup milk
¼ cup white vinegar
3 eggs, beaten
¼ cup sugar
1 teaspoon salt
2 cups (8 ounces) shredded sharp
   Cheddar cheese
2 cups (8 ounces) shredded
   American cheese
1 (2-ounce) jar diced pimiento,
   drained

Combine first 6 ingredients in top of a double boiler. Place over boiling water, and cook, stirring constantly, 13 to 15 minutes or until thickened. Remove from heat; stir in Cheddar and American cheeses and pimiento.

Line a 9- x 5- x 3-inch loafpan with aluminum foil; grease aluminum foil.

Spoon mixture evenly into pan. Bake at 350° for 55 to 60 minutes, covering with foil the last 15 minutes to prevent overbrowning.

Let stand in pan until cool. Remove from pan; carefully peel off foil. Cut into ½-inch slices. Yield: 16 servings.

BISCUITS WITH COUNTRY HAM

2 cups self-rising flour
⅓ cup shortening
¾ cup milk
3 tablespoons butter or
   margarine, melted
1 pound thinly sliced country
   ham, cut into 1½-inch
   squares

Place flour in a large bowl; cut in shortening with a pastry blender until mixture resembles coarse meal. Add milk to mixture, stirring until dry ingredients are moistened. Turn dough out onto a lightly floured surface, and knead 5 times.

Roll dough to ½-inch thickness; cut with a fluted or regular 1½-inch biscuit cutter. Place on a lightly greased baking sheet. Bake at 450° for 12 to 14 minutes or until biscuits are lightly browned. Remove biscuits from oven; brush tops with melted butter. Split biscuits in half. Place a ham slice in each, and replace tops. Serve biscuits warm or at room temperature. Yield: 3½ dozen.

To make ahead: Biscuits may be frozen after they are cut in half. Wrap securely in aluminum foil; freeze up to 2 weeks. Remove from freezer; let thaw at room temperature. Bake at 350° in foil 15 to 20 minutes or until thoroughly heated. Fill with ham.

FRENCH TOAST WITH GRAND MARNIER FRUIT SAUCE

12 (1½-inch-thick) slices French
   bread
1 (8-ounce) package cream
   cheese, softened
2 tablespoons sugar
½ teaspoon ground nutmeg
½ teaspoon ground cinnamon
6 eggs
1 cup half-and-half
½ cup milk
Grand Marnier Fruit Sauce

Make a horizontal pocket in each bread slice; set aside.

Combine cream cheese and next 3 ingredients, stirring well. Spoon about 1½ tablespoons mixture into each bread slice, spreading evenly. Place 8 slices in a buttered 12- x 8- x 2-inch baking dish and 4 slices in a buttered 8-inch square baking dish.

Combine eggs, half-and-half, and milk; beat well. Pour over bread, turning slices to coat evenly. Bake at 350° for 35 minutes or until golden. Serve immediately with Grand Marnier Fruit Sauce. Yield: 12 servings.

Grand Marnier Fruit Sauce

1 cup sifted powdered sugar
2 tablespoons cornstarch
½ cup butter or margarine,
   melted
⅓ cup Grand Marnier
3 cups sliced fresh strawberries

Combine sugar and cornstarch in a saucepan; add butter, stirring until smooth. Add Grand Marnier, and cook over medium heat, stirring constantly, until mixture comes to a boil. Boil 1 minute, stirring constantly. Add strawberries; cook 1 minute. Yield: 3 cups.

To make ahead: Prepare, but do not bake. Cover up to 24 hours. Let stand 30 minutes; bake.

MINIATURE CARROT CAKES

1½ cups all-purpose flour
1 teaspoon baking powder
1 teaspoon baking soda
½ teaspoon salt
1 teaspoon ground cinnamon
1 cup sugar
1¼ cups grated carrots
⅔ cup vegetable oil
2 eggs
1 (8¼-ounce) can crushed
   pineapple, drained
1 teaspoon vanilla extract
1 (3-ounce) package cream
   cheese, softened
¼ cup butter or margarine,
   softened
½ teaspoon vanilla extract
2 to 2½ cups sifted powdered
   sugar

Combine first 6 ingredients in a large bowl. Combine carrots and next 4 ingredients, mixing well. Add to dry ingredients, and beat at medium speed of an electric mixer 2 minutes. Pour into a greased and floured 13- x 9- x 2-inch pan. Bake at 350° for 35 minutes or until a wooden pick inserted in center comes out clean. Cool in pan. Turn cake out onto a cutting board. Cut cake into individual servings, using a 1¾-inch round cutter.
   Combine cream cheese and butter, mixing well. Add vanilla and enough powdered sugar to reach desired consistency. Spoon into a decorating bag. Using a star tip, pipe a rosette on top of each cake. Yield: 35 cakes.

Note: Cakes may be baked in lightly greased miniature (1¾-inch) muffin pans. Bake at 350° for 13 minutes. Yield: 4½ dozen.

Tip: *Use a clean toothbrush to remove bits of rind from a grater.*

SPECIAL DERBY BROWNIES

½ cup butter or margarine,
   softened
1 cup sugar
4 eggs
1 cup all-purpose flour
¼ teaspoon salt
1 (16-ounce) can chocolate syrup
1 cup chopped pecans
½ teaspoon almond extract
¼ cup butter or margarine,
   softened
2 cups sifted powdered sugar
2½ tablespoons green crème de
   menthe
1 (6-ounce) package semisweet
   chocolate morsels
¼ cup butter or margarine

Cream ½ cup butter; gradually add sugar, beating well at medium speed of an electric mixer. Add eggs, one at a time, beating after each addition.
   Combine flour and salt; add to creamed mixture alternately with chocolate syrup, beginning and ending with flour mixture. Stir in pecans and almond extract. Spoon batter into a greased and floured 13- x 9- x 2-inch pan. Bake at 350° for 25 minutes or until a wooden pick inserted in center comes out clean; let brownies cool in pan.
   Combine ¼ cup butter, powdered sugar, and crème de menthe; beat at medium speed of an electric mixer until mixture is smooth. Spread over brownie layer.
   Combine chocolate morsels and ¼ cup butter in top of a double boiler; bring water to a boil. Reduce heat to low; cook until chocolate melts. Spread over frosting. Cover and chill at least 1 hour. Cut into 1½-inch squares. Yield: 4 dozen.

Kids Kindle The Derby Spirit

Don't forget the children when it's time for Derby parties. Prepare a kid-pleasing menu, and invite them to tag along to an adult party, or plan a separate event for them another day. Either way, the children will enjoy the special attention and will gain early appreciation for the excitement of the occasion.

Wide-Eyed Pizzas
Carrot and celery sticks
Buckin' Bronco Cookies
Kid's Cooler

WIDE-EYED PIZZAS

½ cup tomato sauce
½ teaspoon dried whole oregano
4 English muffins, split
1 (6-ounce) package mozzarella
   cheese slices
1 cup (4 ounces) shredded
   Cheddar cheese
4 pitted ripe olives, sliced
Pimiento strips

Combine tomato sauce and oregano; spread 1 tablespoon mixture on cut surface of each muffin half. Place on an ungreased baking sheet.
   Using a 3¼-inch round cutter, cut 8 circles of mozzarella cheese; place on top of tomato sauce mixture for the face. Arrange shredded Cheddar cheese around edge for hair. Position olive slices for eyes and pimiento strips for noses and mouths. Bake at 425° for 5 minutes or until cheese melts. Yield: 8 servings.
Erma Jackson
Huntsville, Alabama

Horsin' Around

Create a playful Derby party atmosphere simply and inexpensively by starting with the basics: a child's dining set, paper plates, construction paper, and plastic derby hats.

Brightly colored paper plates and contrasting cups make the party setting festive. A centerpiece can be made from a plastic derby hat with a "Finish Line" flag inserted in the top to give height to the tablescape.

For contrast and interest, glue a colorful construction paper band and a paper horse to each of the hats. Use one hat for the centerpiece and give the others to the guests as party favors.

Complete the theme by decorating with stuffed rocking horses and colorful paper chains.

BUCKIN' BRONCO COOKIES

1 cup butter or margarine, softened
2 cups sugar
3 eggs
1 teaspoon vanilla extract
4½ cups all-purpose flour
1 teaspoon baking soda
1 teaspoon cream of tartar
¼ teaspoon salt
Powdered Sugar Glaze
Currants
Chocolate sprinkles

Position knife blade in food processor bowl. Add butter and sugar; top with cover, and process 1 minute or until creamed, stopping once to scrape sides of bowl. Add eggs and vanilla; process 30 seconds or until blended.

Combine flour and next 3 ingredients. Add to creamed mixture; process just until blended. Remove dough from processor bowl, and divide into fourths. Place each portion on a large piece of plastic wrap or aluminum foil. Press dough to ½-inch thickness. Fold dough in half, and seal securely in plastic wrap. Chill 3 to 4 hours.

Work with one portion of dough at a time, leaving remainder chilled. Roll dough on a floured surface to ⅛-inch thickness; cut with a 3-inch horse-shaped cutter. Place 1 inch apart on ungreased cookie sheets; bake at 375° for 5 to 6 minutes or until done. Remove immediately from cookie sheets; cool on wire racks. Brush Powdered Sugar Glaze over cookies, using a pastry brush; decorate with currants and chocolate sprinkles. Yield: about 6½ dozen.

Powdered Sugar Glaze

⅔ to ¾ cup milk
6 cups sifted powdered sugar
Brown paste food coloring

Gradually stir enough milk into powdered sugar to reach glazing consistency. Add food coloring to make desired color; stir until blended. Yield: 2 cups.
Gayle H. Agnew
Roswell, Georgia

KID'S COOLER

1 (0.18-ounce) package punch-flavored unsweetened drink mix
1 (46-ounce) can pineapple juice
1 (33.8-ounce) bottle ginger ale
1 cup water
¼ cup sugar

Combine all ingredients, stirring well. Chill. Yield: 11 cups.
Mrs. David Miller
Stuarts Draft, Virginia

Reach For The Granola

Nutty Granola is easy to prepare and can be eaten as a snack or breakfast cereal. In addition to tasting good, granola is nutritious, as well as a good source of fiber. Try adding it to fruited yogurt for a snack, or put a bag in your lunchbox. Granola is also a great topping for ice cream.

NUTTY GRANOLA

3 cups regular oats, uncooked
1 cup pecan halves
1 (2¼-ounce) package sliced almonds
½ cup flaked coconut
¼ cup sunflower kernels
¼ cup plus 2 tablespoons honey
¼ cup vegetable oil
2 tablespoons water
¾ teaspoon vanilla extract
¼ teaspoon salt
1 (8-ounce) container diced dried fruit mix

Combine first 5 ingredients in a large bowl; stir well, and set aside.

Combine honey and next 4 ingredients; pour over oats mixture, and stir well. Spread mixture evenly in a 15- x 10- x 1-inch jellyroll pan. Bake at 350° for 25 minutes or until golden brown, stirring every 5 minutes. Cool. Stir in dried fruit. Store in an airtight container in a cool, dry place. Yield: 8 cups.
Gail Tourtellotte
Birmingham, Alabama

Medaillons Make A Showy Entrée

You don't have to dine in a fine restaurant to enjoy a spectacular presentation of meat medaillons, recently popularized by professional chefs with a flair for food styling. With these recipes you can artfully spoon on your own sauce and arrange garnishes to make these entrées take center stage. The four stunning dishes featured on pages 78 and 79 are sure to inspire you.

For these entrées, lobster tails and tenderloin cuts of meat give near-perfect rounds when sliced. Other entrées, such as turkey or chicken breasts, can be flattened, stuffed, formed into a round shape, and sliced into meat medaillons.

MEDAILLONS OF BEEF WITH HORSERADISH CREAM
(pictured on page 79)

2 tablespoons vegetable oil
¼ cup red wine vinegar
¼ teaspoon salt
¼ teaspoon dried whole thyme
¼ teaspoon pepper
4 beef tenderloin steaks (1-inch thick and about 4 ounces each)
½ pound carrots, scraped and cut into julienne strips
2 tablespoons butter or margarine
¼ teaspoon ground nutmeg
¼ teaspoon salt
⅛ teaspoon white pepper
Horseradish Cream
Garnish: diced carrot

Combine first 5 ingredients in a shallow dish. Add steaks, turning to coat other side. Cover and marinate in refrigerator 4 hours, turning once.

Cook julienned carrots in water to cover 4 minutes or until crisp-tender; drain. Stir butter, nutmeg, salt, and white pepper into carrots. Set aside, and keep warm.

Remove steaks from marinade. Broil or grill steaks 3 inches from heat 3 to 4 minutes on each side or to desired degree of doneness, basting with marinade just before turning.

Place each steak in center of individual dinner plates. Spoon 3 to 4 tablespoons Horseradish Cream on plate on one side of steak; place carrots on plate on other side. Garnish, if desired. Yield: 4 servings.

Horseradish Cream

1¼ cups whipping cream
2½ tablespoons prepared horseradish
⅛ teaspoon salt
⅛ teaspoon pepper
Pinch of ground nutmeg

Heat whipping cream in a heavy saucepan until reduced to about ¾ cup (do not boil). Add remaining ingredients. Cook over low heat just until mixture is thoroughly heated. Yield: ¾ cup.

LOBSTER MEDAILLONS IN GARLIC-CHIVE BUTTER SAUCE
(pictured on page 78)

2 quarts water
2 (10-ounce) lobster tails
Garlic-Chive Butter Sauce
Garnish: fresh chives

Bring water to a boil; add lobster tails. Cover, reduce heat, and simmer 12 minutes. Drain. Rinse with cold water. Split and clean tails. Cut lobster meat into ½-inch slices; cover and chill.

To serve, arrange lobster medaillons on individual serving plates, and spoon Garlic-Chive Butter Sauce around medaillons. Garnish, if desired. Serve immediately. Yield: 2 entrée or 4 appetizer servings.

Garlic-Chive Butter Sauce

½ cup butter
2 tablespoons whipping cream
2 tablespoons lemon juice
1 tablespoon sliced fresh or frozen chives
1 clove garlic, finely minced

Melt butter in a heavy saucepan. Add whipping cream, and cook over low heat 1 minute. Add lemon juice and remaining ingredients, and remove from heat. Serve immediately. Stir sauce if butter starts to settle. Yield: ⅔ cup.

PORK MEDAILLONS IN MUSTARD SAUCE
(pictured on page 78)

3 tablespoons vegetable oil
1 tablespoon coarse-grained mustard
½ teaspoon salt
½ teaspoon pepper
2 (¾-pound) pork tenderloins
¼ cup dry white wine
Mustard Sauce
Garnish: fresh basil sprigs

Combine first 4 ingredients, stirring well. Rub mixture over pork. Place in a plastic bag; refrigerate 8 hours.

Place tenderloins on rack in a shallow roasting pan. Insert meat thermometer into thickest part of meat. Bake at 375° for 25 minutes or until meat thermometer registers 160°, basting every 10 minutes with wine.

Slice tenderloins into ¾-inch slices, and arrange 4 slices on each dinner plate. Spoon Mustard Sauce around pork on each plate. Garnish, if desired. Yield: 4 servings.

Mustard Sauce

1¾ cups whipping cream
¼ cup coarse-grained mustard
¼ teaspoon salt
⅛ teaspoon white pepper

Heat whipping cream in a heavy saucepan until reduced to 1¼ cups (about 15 minutes). Do not boil. Stir in remaining ingredients, and heat 1 minute. Yield: 1¼ cups.

CHICKEN-RICE MEDAILLONS IN PEPPER PESTO
(pictured on page 79)

½ cup uncooked brown rice
¼ cup minced onion
¼ cup minced celery
1 clove garlic, minced
2 tablespoons butter or margarine, melted
¼ cup pine nuts or almonds, toasted and chopped
½ teaspoon salt
¼ teaspoon white pepper
1 egg, beaten
6 large chicken breast halves, skinned and boned (about 1½ pounds)
Pepper Pesto
3 tablespoons pine nuts or slivered almonds, toasted

Cook rice according to package directions, omitting salt. Set aside.

Sauté onion, celery, and garlic in butter in a small skillet over medium heat until vegetables are tender. Remove from heat. Add rice, chopped pine nuts, salt, and pepper. Gradually stir about one-fourth of hot mixture into egg; add to remaining rice mixture. Set aside.

Place each chicken breast half between 2 sheets of plastic wrap; flatten to ¼-inch thickness, using a meat mallet or rolling pin.

Spread about ⅓ cup rice mixture over each breast; roll up chicken, starting with a short side. Place seam side down in a 12- x 8- x 2-inch baking dish; cover and bake at 350° for 45 minutes or until done.

To serve, slice chicken rolls crosswise into ¾-inch slices. Arrange slices on individual dinner plates. Spoon Pepper Pesto onto plate and medaillons as desired; sprinkle 3 tablespoons pine nuts on top. Yield: 6 servings.

Pepper Pesto

2 large sweet red or yellow peppers
½ cup grated Parmesan cheese
¼ cup pine nuts or almonds
2 small cloves garlic, cut in half
¼ teaspoon salt
¼ teaspoon white pepper
½ cup olive oil
½ to ¾ cup chicken broth

Place whole peppers on their sides on a large baking sheet. Bake at 500° for 20 minutes or until skin is blackened and charred. Transfer peppers immediately to a paper bag, and seal. Refrigerate 10 minutes or until peppers cool to touch. Peel and seed peppers, discarding seeds and charred skin.

Position knife blade in food processor bowl; add peppers, cheese, pine nuts, garlic, salt, and white pepper. Cover processor bowl with top. Process until mixture is smooth. With processor running, pour oil through food chute in a slow, steady stream until combined. Add chicken broth, and pour into a saucepan; heat thoroughly. Yield: 2 cups.

Something Different With Steak

If you are looking for a new way to enhance your favorite cookout menu, try these side dishes. Each promises good flavor and has a natural affinity with juicy steak. And each colorful combination is easy to make.

FETTUCCINE WITH BROCCOLI

1 (10-ounce) package frozen broccoli spears, thawed
8 ounces uncooked fettuccine
1 small onion, chopped
1 clove garlic, minced
2 tablespoons olive oil
½ cup chicken broth
1 (8-ounce) carton sour cream
1 teaspoon dried whole basil
1 teaspoon dried parsley flakes
⅛ teaspoon salt
¼ teaspoon pepper
¼ cup (1 ounce) shredded Cheddar cheese

Drain broccoli, and cut into ½-inch pieces. Set aside.

Cook fettuccine according to package directions. Drain well; place in serving bowl, and keep warm.

Sauté onion and garlic in oil in a large skillet over medium heat. Add broccoli, and cook 5 minutes. Stir in chicken broth and next 5 ingredients; cook until thoroughly heated. Pour mixture over fettuccine, and toss. Sprinkle with cheese. Yield: 4 to 6 servings.

Patricia Palmer
Irving, Texas

ROMANO ONION BAKE

4 cups sliced onion
2 tablespoons butter or
    margarine, melted
2 eggs, well beaten
1 cup whipping cream
¼ teaspoon salt
¼ teaspoon pepper
¼ cup grated Romano cheese

Sauté onion in butter until crisp-tender. Arrange in a lightly greased 8-inch square baking dish.

Combine eggs and next 3 ingredients; mix well. Pour over onion. Bake at 375° for 20 minutes. Sprinkle with Romano cheese; bake an additional 5 minutes. Serve immediately. Yield: 6 servings.

Elizabeth M. Haney
Dublin, Virginia

ARTICHOKE HEARTS WITH LEMON

½ cup minced onion
1 clove garlic, crushed
1 tablespoon butter or margarine,
    melted
2 (14-ounce) cans artichoke
    hearts, drained and halved
1 cup chicken broth
3 tablespoons lemon juice
1 teaspoon dried whole oregano
1 teaspoon salt

Sauté onion and garlic in butter in a saucepan until onion is tender but not browned. Add artichoke hearts and remaining ingredients. Simmer about 10 minutes or until heated, stirring gently. Yield: 4 to 6 servings.

Mrs. Donald MacMillan
Cartersville, Georgia

PEPPER-MUSHROOM MEDLEY

1 tablespoon butter or margarine
1 tablespoon olive oil
3 cups (1-inch pieces) green
    pepper
1½ cups sliced fresh mushrooms
1 clove garlic, minced
⅓ cup dry white wine
1 (2-ounce) jar diced pimiento,
    drained
½ teaspoon salt
⅛ teaspoon pepper
⅛ teaspoon dried whole oregano
⅛ teaspoon celery seeds
    (optional)

Heat butter and oil in a large skillet; add green pepper, mushrooms, and garlic, and sauté 3 minutes.

Add wine; bring to a boil. Reduce heat, and simmer 5 minutes. Stir in pimiento, salt, pepper, oregano, and, if desired, celery seeds; simmer 1 minute or until thoroughly heated. Yield: 4 to 6 servings.

Yvonne M. Greer
Greenville, South Carolina

MICROWAVE COOKERY

The Microwave Is A Natural For Vegetables

The microwave oven, a relatively modern appliance, may seem an ironic choice, but it offers the least fuss when it comes to cooking vegetables. Less water and seasoning are needed, and cooking time is shorter, so more nutrients are left in the food, not the discarded liquid. Your favorite produce is naturally flavorful and usually crisp-tender—not overcooked. Preparing and serving in the same dish is an added advantage.

ORANGE-GLAZED CARROTS

2 tablespoons butter or margarine
3 tablespoons brown sugar
3 tablespoons orange juice
1 teaspoon grated lemon rind
⅛ teaspoon salt
1 pound carrots, scraped and
    thinly sliced

Place butter in a 1-quart casserole; microwave at HIGH 50 seconds or until melted. Add brown sugar and next 3 ingredients, stirring well. Add sliced carrots; cover with lid, and microwave at HIGH 6 to 8 minutes or until tender, stirring after 3 minutes. Use a slotted spoon to serve. Yield: 4 servings.

Belinda Fornea
Mendenhall, Mississippi

LEEKS IN DILLED LEMON-BUTTER

6 medium leeks (3 to 4 pounds)
¼ cup chicken broth
¼ cup butter or margarine
1½ tablespoons lemon juice
1 tablespoon chopped fresh
    dillweed or 1 teaspoon dried
    whole dillweed
Dash of white pepper

Remove roots, tough outer leaves, and tops from leeks, leaving 4 inches of dark leaves. Split leeks in half lengthwise; wash well.

Combine leeks and broth in a 12- x 8- x 2-inch baking dish. Cover tightly with heavy-duty plastic wrap; fold back a small corner of wrap to allow steam to escape. Microwave at HIGH 8 to 10 minutes or until tender, rearranging after 4 minutes. Drain and set aside.

Place butter in a 2-cup glass measure; microwave at HIGH 55 seconds or until melted. Stir in lemon juice, dillweed, and pepper. Pour over leeks, and toss gently. Cover and microwave at HIGH 1 to 2 minutes or until thoroughly heated. Serve immediately. Yield: 6 to 8 servings.

MINTED PEAS AND PEPPERS

½ pound fresh snow pea pods
1 tablespoon butter or margarine
1 large sweet red pepper, cut
  into ¼-inch strips
2 tablespoons chopped onion
1 teaspoon chopped fresh mint
¼ teaspoon salt

Wash snow peas; trim ends, and remove any tough strings. Set aside.

Place butter in a shallow 1½-quart casserole; microwave at HIGH 35 seconds or until melted. Add snow peas, red pepper, and remaining ingredients, stirring gently.

Cover tightly with heavy-duty plastic wrap; fold back a small corner of wrap to allow steam to escape. Microwave at HIGH 4 minutes or until crisp-tender, stirring after 2 minutes. Serve immediately. Yield: 4 servings.

Outstanding Standbys

Southern gardens are springing to life with their annual colorful bounty of offerings, and our ideas for tasty, innovative ways to enjoy these vegetables are as fresh as the season itself.

MEDITERRANEAN SALAD

1 head romaine lettuce, torn into
  bite-size pieces
1 (4-ounce) package feta cheese,
  crumbled
½ cup seedless green grape
  halves
½ cup pine nuts, toasted
½ cup olive oil
¼ cup white wine vinegar
¼ teaspoon pepper
Dash of salt

Combine lettuce, feta cheese, grape halves, and toasted pine nuts in a large bowl; set aside.

Combine olive oil, vinegar, and seasonings in a jar; cover tightly, and shake vigorously. Pour over salad, and toss gently. Yield: 6 to 8 servings.
Betty Joyce Mills
Birmingham, Alabama

LAYERED TOMATO ASPIC

2 envelopes unflavored gelatin
4 cups tomato juice, divided
2 bay leaves
2 tablespoons chopped onion
¾ teaspoon celery salt
⅛ teaspoon red pepper
1 tablespoon lemon juice
1 teaspoon Worcestershire sauce
1 envelope unflavored gelatin
¼ cup cold water
¾ cup boiling water
½ teaspoon salt
1 tablespoon lemon juice
1 sweet red pepper
1 green pepper
1 (8-ounce) carton cream-style
  cottage cheese
Lettuce leaves

Sprinkle 2 envelopes gelatin over ½ cup tomato juice; let stand 1 minute.

Combine remaining 3½ cups tomato juice, bay leaves, and next 3 ingredients in a heavy saucepan; bring to a boil. Reduce heat, and simmer 15 minutes. Remove bay leaves. Add gelatin mixture; stir until dissolved. Stir in 1 tablespoon lemon juice and Worcestershire sauce; cool and set aside.

Combine 1 envelope gelatin and ¼ cup cold water. Add ¾ cup boiling water and salt; stir until gelatin dissolves. Add 1 tablespoon lemon juice. Pour 3 tablespoons mixture into a lightly oiled 6-cup ring mold; reserve remainder. Chill mold until gelatin mixture is firm.

Cut desired flat designs, such as circles, diamonds, or strips, from red and green peppers; arrange over congealed layer. Spoon 3 tablespoons reserved gelatin mixture over peppers, setting remainder aside; chill mold until firm.

Combine remaining gelatin mixture and cottage cheese; pour over congealed layer. Chill until almost set. Pour tomato mixture into mold; cover and chill until firm. Unmold onto lettuce leaves. Yield: 8 to 10 servings.
Twila Gardner
Durham, North Carolina

EGGPLANT SALAD

1 large eggplant
1 large tomato, peeled and
  chopped
1 garlic clove, crushed
½ cup finely chopped onion
1 tablespoon chopped fresh
  parsley
1 tablespoon olive oil
1 teaspoon dried whole marjoram
1 teaspoon fines herbes
¼ teaspoon salt
¼ teaspoon pepper
6 small tomatoes, cored
Lettuce leaves
18 pitted ripe olives

Pierce eggplant with a fork several times, and bake at 350° for 1 hour. Let cool to touch; peel and chop eggplant into ½-inch cubes. Add chopped tomato and next 8 ingredients, stirring well. Chill.

Cut each tomato into 4 wedges, cutting only halfway through tomato. Gently spread wedges, and place a spoonful of eggplant mixture into tomatoes. Place on lettuce leaves, and garnish with olives. Yield: 6 servings.

Note: To make a dip, place eggplant mixture in food processor, and process until coarsely chopped (not pureed). Serve with crackers.
Libby Winstead
Nashville, Tennessee

Toss A Healthy Stir-Fry

Stir-fry dishes feature fresh vegetables, rice, noodles, and small to moderate amounts of lean red meat, fish, or poultry. Stir-frying allows these fresh ingredients to cook quickly in very little oil so that vitamins and minerals are preserved and calories and fat are kept low.

Although the wok is the favored cooking utensil for stir-frying, a large, heavy skillet or an electric skillet works very well. The wok's advantage is its gradually sloping sides that allow the even distribution of heat and quick cooking. Nonstick woks and skillets provide an extra bonus because little or no fat is needed for cooking.

The amount of fat in the recipes below has been kept to a minimum. All use only vegetable cooking spray for stir-frying, but in some cases a little oil is added to prevent sticking. Make sure the wok or skillet is cool before coating with vegetable cooking spray; never spray a hot wok or skillet with the spray.

BEEF WITH ASPARAGUS

1 pound fresh asparagus
1 pound lean top sirloin, trimmed
2 teaspoons cornstarch
2 tablespoons dry sherry
2 tablespoons reduced-sodium soy sauce
Vegetable cooking spray
3 tablespoons water

Snap off tough ends of asparagus. Remove scales from stalk with a knife or vegetable peeler, if desired. Cut asparagus into 1½-inch pieces, and set aside.

Partially freeze steak; slice diagonally across grain into ¼-inch strips; set aside. Combine cornstarch, sherry, and soy sauce in a medium bowl; add steak strips. Let stand 10 minutes.

Coat a wok or heavy skillet with cooking spray; heat to medium high (325°) for 2 minutes. Add steak, and stir-fry until browned; remove meat from skillet. Add asparagus and water; cook about 2 minutes, stirring often. Return meat to skillet; cook until thoroughly heated. Yield: 4 servings (192 calories per ¾-cup serving).

☐ *27.9 grams protein, 6.1 grams fat, 6.5 grams carbohydrate, 69 milligrams cholesterol, 310 milligrams sodium, and 35 milligrams calcium.*
Marge Killmon
Annandale, Virginia

STEAK LO MEIN

1 pound lean boneless top round steak, trimmed
Vegetable cooking spray
2 cups shredded cabbage
1 cup diagonally sliced carrots
1 medium onion, sliced into rings
½ cup sliced fresh mushrooms
⅓ cup sliced green onions
½ cup diagonally sliced celery
15 fresh snow pea pods, trimmed
1 (8-ounce) can sliced water chestnuts, drained
1 teaspoon beef-flavored bouillon granules
¾ cup water
¼ cup reduced-sodium soy sauce
4 ounces thin spaghetti (cooked without salt or fat)

Partially freeze top round steak; slice diagonally across the grain into ¼-inch strips. Set steak aside.

Coat a wok or heavy skillet with cooking spray; heat to medium high (325°) for 2 minutes. Add meat, and stir-fry 5 minutes. Push meat to sides of wok; add cabbage and next 7 ingredients. Stir-fry about 3 minutes. Stir meat into vegetables.

Combine bouillon granules, water, and soy sauce; stir into meat mixture. Cover and cook 3 minutes. Add spaghetti; toss gently, and cook until thoroughly heated. Yield: 6 servings (219 calories per 1⅓-cup serving).

☐ *21.7 grams protein, 3.7 grams fat, 24.4 grams carbohydrate, 43 milligrams cholesterol, 558 milligrams sodium, and 42 milligrams calcium.*
Mrs. Garwood Briggs
Moultrie, Georgia

CHINESE CHICKEN STIR-FRY

1 egg white
1 tablespoon dry sherry
1 teaspoon cornstarch
4 (3-ounce) skinned, boned chicken breast halves
3 tablespoons reduced-sodium soy sauce
2 tablespoons water
1 tablespoon rice wine
1½ teaspoons cornstarch
¼ teaspoon salt
2 teaspoons sesame oil
Vegetable cooking spray
2 tablespoons vegetable oil
1 (16-ounce) package frozen broccoli, green beans, pearl onions, and red peppers
1 (8-ounce) can bamboo shoots, drained
1 (6-ounce) package frozen snow pea pods
3 cups hot cooked rice (cooked without salt or fat)

Combine first 3 ingredients; beat with a wire whisk until frothy. Add chicken; cover and let stand at least 15 minutes.

Combine soy sauce and next 5 ingredients; beat with wire whisk. Set mixture aside.

Coat a wok or heavy skillet with cooking spray; add vegetable oil, and heat to medium high (325°) for 2 minutes. Add chicken; stir-fry 2 to 3 minutes. Remove chicken from wok.

Add mixed vegetables, bamboo shoots, and snow peas to wok; stir-fry 3 to 4 minutes. Add chicken and soy sauce mixture; stir-fry until vegetables are crisp-tender. Serve over rice. Yield: 4 servings (432 calories per 1½ cups stir-fry and ¾ cup rice).

□ *29.1 grams protein, 10.7 grams fat, 55.9 grams carbohydrate, 49 milligrams cholesterol, 645 milligrams sodium, and 69 milligrams calcium.*

PORK CHOW MEIN

1 pound lean pork loin, trimmed
1 cup no-salt-added chicken broth
¼ cup reduced-sodium soy sauce
1 tablespoon cornstarch
1 teaspoon ground ginger
Vegetable cooking spray
1 clove garlic, minced
1 cup thinly sliced carrot
1 cup thinly sliced celery
1 cup chopped onion
1 cup coarsely chopped cabbage
1 cup coarsely chopped fresh
    spinach

Partially freeze pork loin; slice diagonally across grain into ¼-inch-thick strips. Set aside.

Combine chicken broth and next 3 ingredients; set aside.

Coat a wok or heavy skillet with cooking spray; heat to medium high (325°) for 2 minutes. Add garlic and pork; stir-fry 5 minutes or until slightly browned. Add carrot and remaining vegetables; stir-fry 3 minutes. Add broth mixture; cover and cook 3 minutes. Yield: 4 servings (240 calories per 1¼-cup serving).

□ *26 grams protein, 9 grams fat, 12.4 grams carbohydrate, 68 milligrams cholesterol, 608 milligrams sodium, and 64 milligrams calcium.*
        Lana W. Fuller
    Martinsville, Virginia

Serve A Hearty Supper

Flank steak filled with a spinach-and-artichoke mixture and served on a bed of fettuccine makes an enticing entrée for this light and healthy menu. Crisp-tender Snow Peas With Red Pepper and Lemon Curd With Berries complete this menu that's less than 25% fat.

**Stuffed Flank Steak
With Noodles
Snow Peas With Red Pepper
Lemon Curd With Berries**

STUFFED FLANK STEAK WITH NOODLES

1 cup chopped fresh spinach
1 cup sliced green onions
⅓ cup freshly grated Parmesan
    cheese
½ cup frozen artichoke hearts,
    thawed, drained, and chopped
¼ cup soft breadcrumbs
½ teaspoon freshly ground pepper
¼ teaspoon salt
1½ pounds lean cubed flank steak
2 cloves garlic, crushed
2 tablespoons low-sodium
    Worcestershire sauce
Vegetable cooking spray
¼ pound fresh mushrooms, sliced
1 small onion, thinly sliced
1 teaspoon chicken-flavored
    bouillon granules
½ cup water
2 fresh sprigs parsley
1 bay leaf
1 tablespoon cornstarch
2 tablespoons water
1½ pounds cooked fettuccine
    (cooked without salt or fat)

Combine spinach, green onions, Parmesan cheese, artichoke hearts, and breadcrumbs; set mixture aside.

Sprinkle pepper and salt over flank steak; spread spinach mixture in center of meat within 1 inch of sides. Roll up jellyroll fashion, starting with long side. Secure at 2-inch intervals with string. Rub crushed garlic over meat roll, and drizzle with Worcestershire sauce.

Coat a nonstick skillet with cooking spray; place over medium-high heat until hot. Brown steak roll on all sides; transfer to a 13- x 9- x 2-inch pan. Combine mushrooms and onion; place around steak.

Dissolve bouillon granules in ½ cup water; add to pan. Add parsley sprigs and bay leaf. Cover and bake at 300° for 50 minutes or until meat is tender.

Transfer steak to a serving platter. Let stand 15 minutes; remove string and slice steak. Arrange cooked noodles around steak slices on platter. Keep warm.

Place pan drippings, mushrooms, and onion in a medium saucepan. Remove and discard parsley sprigs and bay leaf. Combine cornstarch and 2 tablespoons water; stir into pan drippings. Bring mixture to a boil; boil 1 minute, stirring constantly. Yield: 6 servings (434 calories per 2 slices steak, ½ cup cooked noodles, and 3 tablespoons gravy).

Note: To cube flank steak, ask butcher to run steak through meat tenderizer twice.

□ *32.3 grams protein, 13.2 grams fat, 45.1 grams carbohydrate, 60 milligrams cholesterol, 493 milligrams sodium, and 119 milligrams calcium.*

Tip: *Grills or pans with a nonstick finish may become scratched or lose their finish. They can still be used. Just spray the damaged surface with a nonstick vegetable spray to prevent food from sticking.*

SNOW PEAS
WITH RED PEPPER

Olive oil-flavored vegetable
  cooking spray
3 cups snow pea pods, trimmed
1 cup diced sweet red pepper
1 small clove garlic, minced
2 teaspoons sesame seeds
½ teaspoon lemon-pepper
  seasoning
¼ teaspoon Chinese 5-spice
  powder

Coat a large, nonstick skillet with
cooking spray; place over medium-
high heat until hot. Add snow peas
and sweet red pepper; cook 5 minutes, stirring constantly.

Add garlic, sesame seeds, and seasonings; cook 2 to 3 minutes or until
vegetables are crisp-tender, stirring
constantly. Yield: 6 servings (45 calories per ½-cup serving).

☐ 2.4 grams protein, 0.9 gram fat,
7.3 grams carbohydrate, 0 milligrams
cholesterol, 32 milligrams sodium,
and 35 milligrams calcium.

Jan Gilbert
Carrboro, North Carolina

LEMON CURD WITH BERRIES

½ cup sugar
¼ cup cornstarch
¼ teaspoon salt
2 cups skim milk
¼ cup egg substitute
1½ teaspoons grated lemon rind
¼ cup lemon juice
1½ cups fresh or frozen
  raspberries, thawed
1½ cups fresh or frozen
  blueberries, thawed
Garnish: fresh mint sprigs

Combine sugar, cornstarch, and salt
in a heavy saucepan; gradually add
milk, stirring well. Cook over medium heat, stirring constantly, until
mixture thickens. Remove from heat;
gradually add egg substitute to hot
mixture, stirring constantly with a

wire whisk. Cook over medium-low
heat 2 minutes; remove from heat,
and let cool slightly. Stir in lemon
rind and juice; let cool.

Alternate layers of berries and
lemon curd into 6 parfait glasses.
Chill until ready to serve. Garnish
with mint, if desired. Yield: 6 servings (155 calories per serving).

☐ 4.4 grams protein, 0.4 gram fat,
35 grams carbohydrate, 2 milligrams
cholesterol, 158 milligrams sodium,
and 115 milligrams calcium.

LIGHT FAVORITE

Trimmed-Down
Cheese Grits

We've lightened up Cheese Grits, a
favorite side dish, so that it can be
included in health-conscious menus.

CHEESE GRITS

3 cups water
¾ cup uncooked regular grits
¼ teaspoon salt
⅛ teaspoon garlic powder
1½ cups (6 ounces) shredded
  sharp 40% less-fat Cheddar
  cheese
⅛ teaspoon hot sauce
⅓ cup egg substitute
Vegetable cooking spray

Bring water to a boil in medium
saucepan; add grits. Cover, reduce
heat, and simmer 10 minutes. Add
salt, garlic powder, Cheddar cheese,
and hot sauce, stirring until cheese
melts. Stir a small amount of hot
grits into egg substitute; add to remaining grits, stirring constantly.

Pour mixture into a 1-quart baking
dish coated with cooking spray. Bake
at 350° for 40 minutes or until mixture is set. Yield: 6 servings (128
calories per ¾-cup serving).

☐ 10.1 grams protein, 5.1 grams fat,
7.9 grams carbohydrate, 20 milligrams cholesterol, 460 milligrams sodium, and 258 milligrams calcium.

COMPARE THE NUTRIENTS (per serving)		
	Traditional	Light
Calories	276	128
Fat	22.1g	5.1g
Cholesterol	152mg	20mg

Sit Down To Some
Crawfish

Folks all over the South are now familiar with crawfish and are cooking
the tender, white tail meat at home.
Aquaculture (fish farming) has made
the supply of crawfish more predict-
able and has somewhat stabilized
prices, although the best buys on
crawfish come in April and May when
production peaks. This is right before
the crawfish burrow for the summer.

Crawfish are available in a variety
of forms: whole live, whole cooked
(fresh and frozen), peeled and deveined raw or cooked tail meats
(fresh and frozen, with or without
fat), and in the softshell (the stage
the crawfish, like a crab, goes
through right after it sheds its hard
shell). Softshell crawfish are usually
battered and fried.

The most commonly found form of
crawfish outside Louisiana is usually

frozen, especially in nonpeak months. For the best results, ask your grocer for vacuum-packed crawfish that have just come into the store, fresh from the packager. Crawfish meat is tender and therefore requires only a short cooking time. Fresh or frozen (thawed) meat requires only about 10 minutes to cook, and is added near the end.

Fresh crawfish fat is a flavor enhancer, a secret addition to many South Louisiana recipes. You may wonder where the "fat" comes from in such a crustacean. Actually, it's a yellow secretion from the hepatopancreas gland. If you peel your own crawfish, you'll notice it on the tail meat and on your hands. It's a desirable flavoring in cooked dishes, yet crawfish will go rancid much sooner if frozen with the fat on. Rancid crawfish will smell "fishy" and have an "off" taste.

LOUISIANA CRAWFISH DRESSING

6 cups sliced squash (about 2 pounds)
2 cups water
1 large onion, chopped
1 green pepper, chopped
1 cup chopped celery
1 clove garlic, minced
½ cup butter or margarine, melted
1 egg, slightly beaten
1 cup Italian-seasoned breadcrumbs
⅓ cup grated Parmesan cheese
1 teaspoon Beau Monde seasoning
½ teaspoon salt
¼ to ½ teaspoon pepper
¼ teaspoon dried whole thyme
⅛ teaspoon red pepper
⅛ teaspoon hot sauce
2 cups peeled crawfish tails

Combine squash and water in a Dutch oven; cook until tender. Drain well. Sauté onion and next 3 ingredients in butter until tender.

Add vegetables and egg to squash; stir in breadcrumbs and remaining ingredients. Spoon mixture into a greased 12- x 8- x 2-inch baking dish. Bake at 350° for 30 minutes. Yield: 8 servings.   *Betty Starnes*
Baton Rouge, Louisiana

CRAWFISH ÉTOUFFÉE

½ cup chopped onion
½ cup chopped celery
½ cup chopped green pepper
2 cloves garlic, minced
⅓ cup butter or margarine, melted
¼ teaspoon dried whole thyme
¼ teaspoon chili powder
½ teaspoon dried whole basil
2 tablespoons all-purpose flour
1 teaspoon tomato paste
½ cup fish or seafood stock
½ cup Chablis or other dry white wine
1 (10¾-ounce) can cream of mushroom soup, undiluted
2½ cups peeled crawfish tails
½ cup chopped green onions
¼ cup chopped parsley
¼ teaspoon Creole seasoning
¼ to ½ teaspoon hot sauce
Garnish: chopped green onions

Sauté first 4 ingredients in butter until tender. Add thyme and next 4 ingredients; stir well, and cook 15 minutes, stirring often. Add fish stock and Chablis; cook 10 minutes. Stir in mushroom soup and crawfish tails; cover and simmer 15 to 20 minutes. Stir in ½ cup chopped green onions, parsley, Creole seasoning, and hot sauce; cover and cook 3 to 5 minutes. Remove from heat, and let stand 15 minutes before serving. Garnish, if desired. Yield: 4 servings.

Note: Fish or seafood stock may be made from fish-flavored bouillon cubes or granules. *Yolanda Trahan*
Houma, Louisiana

Crawfish Yields

1 pound unpeeled whole crawfish = 3 to 4 ounces peeled tail meat

1 pound unpeeled crawfish tails = 10 ounces (just over 1 cup) peeled tail meat

1 pound peeled crawfish tails = 1 to 2 cups meat

Hats Off To Spring Beverages

Like a hat completes a stunning outfit, innovative fruit garnishes put the finishing touches on these refreshing beverages. Cool and slushy, these spring drinks can be made in a hurry and are as enticing to look at as they are to drink.

For garnishing, choose ingredients used in the recipe or that complement the drink's color and flavor. Use your imagination, and wedge fruits on the glass rim or place them on wooden or festive skewers.

YELLOW BIRDS

1 (6-ounce) can frozen orange juice concentrate, thawed and undiluted
2¼ cups water
1½ cups pineapple juice
1 to 1½ cups light rum
¾ cup crème de bananes

Combine all ingredients; stir well, and serve over ice. Yield: 6½ cups.
Mrs. Harland J. Stone
Ocala, Florida

BLUSHING PINK SODA

1 (8-ounce) can crushed
    unsweetened pineapple, drained
½ cup mashed fresh strawberries
1 quart strawberry soda, chilled
    and divided
1 quart vanilla ice cream, divided
Garnish: strawberry fans

Combine pineapple, strawberries, 1
cup strawberry soda, and ½ cup vanilla ice cream in container of an
electric blender; process until mixture is smooth.
    Divide mixture evenly into 6
glasses. Add one scoop of ice cream
and ½ cup soda to each glass. Garnish, if desired. Serve immediately.
Yield: 6 servings.

Pam Wondolowski
Corpus Christi, Texas

PEACH PETALS

1 (16-ounce) package frozen
    sliced peaches, partially
    thawed
1 (6-ounce) can frozen lemonade
    concentrate, undiluted
⅔ cup light rum
½ cup water
Ice cubes
Garnishes: lemon slices and fresh
    mint sprigs

Combine first 4 ingredients in container of an electric blender; process
until smooth. Add enough ice cubes
to bring mixture to the 5-cup level.
Process until smooth. Garnish, if desired, and serve immediately. Yield:
5 cups.

Kristy LeFevre
Arlington, Virginia

FROSTY LIME FIZZ

1½ cups pineapple juice, chilled
⅓ cup lime juice
⅓ cup sugar
1 quart lime sherbet, divided
3½ cups lemon-lime carbonated
    beverage, chilled
Garnishes: fresh mint sprigs, lime
    slices, lemon slices, and
    maraschino cherries

Combine first 3 ingredients in container of an electric blender, and process until blended. Add 2 cups lime
sherbet to pineapple juice mixture;
process until smooth.
    Pour ½ cup pineapple-lime mixture
into each of 7 (12-ounce) glasses.
Add one scoop of sherbet and ½ cup
lemon-lime carbonated beverage to
each glass. Garnish, if desired. Serve
immediately. Yield: 7 servings.

Mrs. P. J. Davis
Pineville, North Carolina

BANANA-BLUEBERRY
SMOOTHIE

2 bananas, sliced and frozen
1 cup frozen blueberries
1 (8-ounce) carton plain low-fat
    yogurt
½ cup milk
Ice cubes

Combine first 4 ingredients in container of an electric blender. Add
enough ice cubes to bring mixture to
4-cup level. Blend until mixture is
smooth, and serve immediately.
Yield: about 4 cups.

Note: Fresh fruit may be substituted, but frozen fruit will yield a
thicker consistency. *Cathy Schroeder*
Taylor, Texas

Tip: *Create a tempting nonalcoholic
bubbly beverage by adding sparkling
mineral water to nutritious fruit
juice concentrates.*

Not Such A Tough Nut To Crack

You can enjoy coconut's taste of the
islands all year, either fresh or commercially processed. Packaged flaked
coconut from the grocer is good for 6
to 12 months unopened in your pantry. After opening, keep it in the refrigerator a month or in the freezer
for a year.
    Fresh coconuts should feel heavy,
and the three soft spots or "eyes" on
the end should be free from mold.
Shake the coconut to be sure you
hear plenty of liquid inside.

UNFORGETTABLE
COCONUT CAKE

2½ cups sifted cake flour
2½ teaspoons baking powder
½ teaspoon salt
1 cup milk
¼ cup water
1½ teaspoons vanilla extract
4 egg whites
¼ cup sugar
½ cup shortening
¼ cup butter, softened
1¼ cups sugar
Lemon-Apricot Filling
Fluffy White Frosting
3 to 4 cups grated coconut
Garnishes: apricot roses, lemon
    rind curls

Combine first 3 ingredients, and set
aside. Combine milk, water, and vanilla; set aside.
    Beat egg whites (at room tempera-
ture) until foamy; gradually add ¼
cup sugar, 1 tablespoon at a time,
beating until soft peaks form. Set
beaten egg whites aside.
    Combine shortening, butter, and
1¼ cups sugar in a large mixing
bowl; beat at medium speed of an
electric mixer 3 minutes. Add flour
mixture alternately with milk mixture, beginning and ending with flour
mixture. Mix after each addition.
Fold in beaten egg whites.

Pour batter into 3 greased and floured 9-inch round cakepans. Bake at 350° for 15 to 20 minutes or until a wooden pick inserted in center comes out clean. Cool in pans 10 minutes; remove from pans, and let cool completely on wire racks.

Spread Lemon-Apricot Filling between layers and Fluffy White Frosting on top and sides of cake. Sprinkle with grated coconut. Garnish, if desired. Yield: one 3-layer cake.

Lemon-Apricot Filling

2 cups dried apricots, diced
⅔ cup sugar
1 tablespoon cornstarch
⅛ teaspoon salt
¾ cup water
⅓ cup lemon juice
1 tablespoon butter
2 egg yolks, beaten
1 tablespoon grated lemon rind

Combine first 7 ingredients in a medium saucepan; stir well. Bring to a boil over medium heat, stirring constantly; boil 3 to 4 minutes or until thickened. Reduce heat, and cook 1 minute, stirring constantly.

Gradually stir about one-fourth of hot mixture into egg yolks; add to remaining hot mixture, stirring constantly. Remove from heat; stir in lemon rind. Let cool; cover and chill 1 hour. Yield: 2½ cups.

Fluffy White Frosting

1 cup sugar
¼ cup cold water
2 egg whites
⅛ teaspoon cream of tartar
⅛ teaspoon salt
1½ teaspoons vanilla extract

Combine all ingredients except vanilla in top of a double boiler. Beat at low speed of an electric mixer 30 seconds or just until blended. Place over boiling water; beat constantly at high speed 7 minutes or until stiff peaks form. Remove from heat. Add vanilla; beat 2 minutes or until thick enough to spread. Yield: 4¼ cups.

Clairiece Gilbert Humphrey
Charlottesville, Virginia

TOASTED COCONUT PIE

¾ cup sugar
¾ cup light corn syrup
3 eggs, beaten
⅛ teaspoon salt
1 teaspoon vanilla extract
2 cups flaked coconut, toasted
1 unbaked 9-inch pastry shell

Combine first 5 ingredients; stir in coconut. Pour mixture into pastry shell. Bake at 425° for 10 minutes. Reduce heat to 350°, and bake 30 minutes, shielding pie with aluminum foil the last 10 minutes. Yield: one 9-inch pie.

Pauline Lyons
Mena, Arkansas

HAWAIIAN BANANA CREAM PIE

2 egg whites
1 cup chopped cashews or macadamia nuts
1 (3½-ounce) can flaked coconut
2 tablespoons brown sugar
¾ cup sugar
3 tablespoons cornstarch
3 egg yolks, beaten
1½ cups milk
1 tablespoon butter or margarine, melted
1 teaspoon vanilla extract
½ cup whipping cream, whipped
2 bananas, divided
½ cup finely chopped cashews or macadamia nuts

Beat egg whites (at room temperature) until stiff peaks form. Combine 1 cup cashews, coconut, and brown sugar; fold into egg whites. Spread mixture in bottom and on sides of a 9-inch pieplate, forming a shell. Bake at 375° for 7 to 10 minutes or until lightly browned. Cool on a wire rack.

Combine sugar and cornstarch in a saucepan. Combine egg yolks and milk; slowly add to sugar mixture, stirring constantly until smooth. Add butter. Cook over medium heat until mixture comes to a boil, stirring constantly. Boil 1 minute. Remove from heat; stir in vanilla. Cool. Fold whipped cream into custard.

Slice one banana, and line meringue shell with slices. Spoon custard over bananas. Cover with plastic wrap, and chill 2 hours.

Sprinkle ½ cup cashews around outer edge of pie. Slice remaining banana, and place slices around outer edge on nuts. Yield: one 9-inch pie.

Mrs. Stanley Pichon, Jr.
Slidell, Louisiana

COCONUT CRUNCH PIE

1 cup graham cracker crumbs
½ cup flaked coconut
½ cup finely chopped walnuts
4 egg whites
¼ teaspoon salt
1 cup sugar
1 teaspoon vanilla extract
Vanilla ice cream (optional)

Combine first 3 ingredients in a small bowl, mixing well. Set aside.

Beat egg whites (at room temperature) and salt at high speed of an electric mixer until foamy. Gradually add sugar, 1 tablespoon at a time, beating until stiff peaks form. Fold in vanilla and crumb mixture. Spread in a well-greased 9-inch pieplate.

Bake at 350° for 25 minutes or until lightly browned. Cool at least 3 hours at room temperature. Serve with ice cream, if desired. Yield: one 9-inch pie.

Mrs. James W. Strayer
Hilton Head, South Carolina

Tip: *Tinted coconut makes a child's cake more festive. Fill a pint jar one-third to one-half full of coconut. Add a few drops of food coloring to 1 to 2 tablespoons water, and add to coconut; cover jar, and shake well.*

COCONUT KISSES

2 egg whites
⅔ cup sugar
½ teaspoon vanilla extract
2 cups corn flakes cereal
1 (3½-ounce) can flaked coconut
½ cup chopped pecans

Preheat oven to 350°. Beat egg whites (at room temperature) at high speed of an electric mixer until foamy. Gradually add sugar, 1 tablespoon at a time, beating until stiff peaks form. Fold in vanilla, corn flakes, coconut, and chopped pecans.

Drop by teaspoonfuls onto cookie sheets lined with aluminum foil. Place in oven, and immediately turn off heat. Do not open oven door for at least 8 hours. Carefully peel cookies from foil. Yield: 3 dozen.

Christie Dawson
Newport, Arkansas

Desserts Tailored For Passover

As a part of Passover each year, families and individuals gather at homes and temples for the Seder, a special meal that combines food, storytelling, and religious ceremony. The Seder has a number of parts, one being a lavish meal.

During Passover no leavening or *hametz* (leavened products) can be used, therefore restricting the use of baking powder and baking soda. The prohibition of these substances commemorates the Jews leaving Egypt so quickly that they didn't have time to let bread rise. *Hametz* also includes fermented grain products. Rice, millet, and beans are also foods that are not eaten by some Jews because they undergo a process similar to fermentation.

■ "Pareve" margarine is made from water, oil, and flavorings (not dairy products); the pareve margarine or butter is used in **Passover Linzer Torte**. Matzo or matzos (plural) are unleavened bread made from special Passover flour and water.

PASSOVER LINZER TORTE

½ cup matzo cake meal
½ cup potato starch
1 cup pareve margarine or butter, cut into 1-inch pieces
1 cup ground unpeeled almonds
½ cup sugar
½ teaspoon ground cinnamon
2 eggs, separated
½ cup red raspberry jam

Position knife blade in food processor bowl; add cake meal and potato starch. Top with cover, and pulse 3 or 4 times or until blended. Add margarine to cake meal mixture. Pulse 7 or 8 times or until blended. Add almonds, sugar, cinnamon, and egg yolks; process until smooth. Remove two-thirds of dough (1¾ cups), and spread on bottom and 1 inch up sides of an ungreased 9-inch springform pan; top with jam.

Divide remaining dough into six equal portions. Shape each portion with fingers into a ropelike cylinder; arrange on top of jam in lattice fashion, pressing each end into dough at edge of pan.

Slightly beat egg whites (at room temperature), and brush evenly over dough. Bake at 325° for 45 minutes. Let cool slightly before removing sides of springform pan. Yield: 8 servings.

Tina Wasserman
Dallas, Texas

■ For **Passover Sponge Cake**, potato starch is substituted for flour. Vanilla flavoring, a typical ingredient in sponge cake, may not be used during Passover.

PASSOVER SPONGE CAKE

2 eggs
7 egg yolks
1¼ cups sugar
1 teaspoon grated lemon rind
3 tablespoons lemon juice
1 cup potato starch
7 egg whites
Fresh strawberries and blueberries

Combine eggs and egg yolks; beat at high speed of an electric mixer until well blended. Gradually add sugar, 1 tablespoon at a time, beating at medium speed. Add lemon rind and lemon juice, and beat well. Fold in potato starch.

Beat egg whites (at room temperature) at high speed until stiff peaks form; fold into batter.

Pour batter into an ungreased 10-inch tube pan with removable bottom. Bake at 350° for 45 minutes. Invert pan; let cool 1 hour. Loosen cake from sides of pan, using a narrow metal spatula; remove from pan. Serve with fresh berries. Yield: one 10-inch cake.

Fancy Cakes From Basic Layers

You can make spectacular cakes in record time with these recipes and a little advance planning. While the desserts look very different, each starts with the same tender layers. Just make one or two recipes of Basic Light Cake; then wrap the layers separately, and freeze.

The unfrosted cake layers should hold their freshness in the freezer up to five months if properly wrapped. Let them cool completely on wire racks; then wrap separately in aluminum foil, and seal in a heavy-duty plastic bag.

When you're ready to make a cake, let the layers thaw at room temperature in their wrappers. Then fill and frost as desired. Don't re-freeze the cakes after they are frosted, as the layers will not freeze well more than once.

BASIC LIGHT CAKE

1 cup shortening
2 cups sugar
4 eggs
3 cups sifted cake flour
2½ teaspoons baking powder
½ teaspoon salt
1 cup milk
1½ teaspoons vanilla extract

Cream shortening; gradually add sugar, beating well at medium speed of an electric mixer. Add eggs to creamed mixture, one at a time, beating well after each addition.

Combine flour, baking powder, and salt; add to creamed mixture alternately with milk, beginning and ending with flour mixture. Mix after each addition. Stir in vanilla.

Pour batter into 3 greased and floured 9-inch round cakepans. Bake at 350° for 25 to 30 minutes or until a wooden pick inserted in center comes out clean. Cool in pans 10 minutes; remove from pans, and let cool completely on wire racks. Assemble and frost as desired. Yield: 3 cake layers.

APRICOT-FILLED CHOCOLATE TORTE

1 layer Basic Light Cake
⅔ cup apricot preserves
¼ cup cocoa
3 tablespoons water
2 tablespoons vegetable oil
2 tablespoons light corn syrup
2 cups sifted powdered sugar
Garnish: apricot rose

Carefully split cake layer in half horizontally to make 2 layers. Heat apricot preserves in a small saucepan until of thinner consistency; press preserves through a sieve. Cool slightly, and spread preserves between layers and on top of cake. Let stand 20 minutes.

Combine cocoa, water, oil, and corn syrup in a small saucepan; cook over low heat, stirring constantly, until mixture is smooth. Remove from heat; stir in powdered sugar. Pour warm chocolate glaze over cake, spreading evenly over top and sides. Garnish cake, if desired. Yield: one 2-layer torte.

Note: To make apricot rose, roll about 7 dried apricots to ⅛-inch thickness, using a rolling pin. (One side of apricots will be sticky.) Roll 1 apricot, jellyroll fashion, sticky side in, into a bud. Roll remaining apricots around bud, pressing sticky side inward and curling upper edges outward to achieve a petal effect. Pinch rose at bottom to make stem end.

PEACHY ALMOND-BUTTER CAKE

2 layers Basic Light Cake
Peach Filling
½ cup butter or margarine, softened
½ cup shortening
2 (16-ounce) packages powdered sugar, sifted and divided
1 egg white
¼ teaspoon salt
½ teaspoon almond extract
⅓ to ½ cup whipping cream

Carefully split each cake layer in half horizontally to make 4 layers. Stack layers, spreading Peach Filling between layers.

Cream butter and shortening in a large mixing bowl at medium speed of an electric mixer; gradually add about one-third of sugar, beating until light and fluffy.

Add egg white, salt, and almond extract; mix well. Gradually add remaining sugar and ⅓ cup whipping cream alternately, beginning and ending with sugar; add more whipping cream, if necessary, to make frosting a good piping consistency. Mix well after each addition. Continue beating until mixture is fluffy and creamy.

Spread frosting on sides and top of cake, spreading it smoothly with the back of a long metal spatula. Spoon remaining frosting into a decorating bag fitted with large tip No. 2110. Pipe a shell border around top and bottom edges of cake. Yield: one 4-layer cake.

Peach Filling

1 (8¾-ounce) can sliced peaches, drained
¼ cup amaretto

Combine peach slices and amaretto in container of an electric blender. Process until blended and smooth. Yield: ¾ cup.

COCOA CROWN CAKE

3 egg whites
¾ cup sugar
⅓ cup light corn syrup
⅛ teaspoon cream of tartar
Dash of salt
3 layers Basic Light Cake
About 1 tablespoon cocoa
About 1 tablespoon powdered sugar

Combine first 5 ingredients in top of a double boiler. Beat at low speed of an electric mixer 30 seconds or just until blended. Place mixture over boiling water; beat constantly at high speed 7 minutes or until stiff peaks form. Remove from heat.

Arrange strips of wax paper around edges of a cake plate. Stack layers on top of wax paper, spreading frosting between layers. Spread frosting into swirls on sides of cake and smoothly on top of cake.

Lightly, but thoroughly, sift cocoa over top of cake. Carefully place a paper doily over cake, and sift powdered sugar over cocoa. Gently remove doily and wax paper strips. Yield: one 3-layer cake.

CHOCOLATE BUTTERCREAM CAKE

1 (6-ounce) package semisweet
   chocolate morsels
½ cup half-and-half
1 cup butter or margarine
2½ cups sifted powdered sugar
2 layers Basic Light Cake
1 cup chopped almonds, toasted

Combine chocolate morsels, half-and-half, and butter in a saucepan; cook over medium heat, stirring until melted and smooth. Remove from heat; blend in powdered sugar. Set saucepan in a bowl of ice water; beat at medium speed of an electric mixer until frosting holds its shape.

Spread frosting between layers and on top and sides of cake. Comb frosting on top of cake, using a metal icing comb, if desired. Gently pat chopped almonds onto sides of cake. Yield: one 2-layer cake.

Note: Metal icing combs are available in kitchen specialty shops. Or you may use the tines of a fork or a regular wide-toothed hair comb bought just for cake decorating.

From Our Kitchen To Yours

Adding decorative touches to food can be simple using a decorating bag and a variety of metal tips. With practice you can garnish desserts and canapés or decorate cookies. Begin by following these basic food decorating guidelines and instructions.

Before actually decorating, practice piping designs on wax paper, using decorator frosting or whipped cream. No matter which one you use, the key is the consistency. It must be firm enough to hold a design, yet pliable enough to mold. The uniformity of the design is determined by the amount of pressure and the steadiness with which it is applied. You want to maintain a steady, even flow as you move the bag across the surface, stopping the pressure completely and breaking off cleanly. If the frosting breaks, you are moving the bag too quickly, relaxing the pressure, or using frosting that's too thick. If the frosting builds up or ripples, you are squeezing the decorating bag too hard.

The metal decorating tips come in five basic groups—drop flower, star, round, leaf, and rose—determined by the size and shape of the tips' openings. **Drop flower** tips make flowers of all sizes and shapes. **Star** tips produce stars, rosettes, shells, drop flowers, and zigzag borders. The **round** tips are used for dots, outlines, figure piping, beads, stringwork, and writing.

To create drop flowers, hold the bag at a 90-degree angle with tip almost touching surface; steadily squeeze out frosting, lifting the bag slightly as frosting forms the desired design. To finish, push the tip down slightly, release pressure, and lift.

For decorating with straight lines and writing, hold the bag at a 45-degree angle, touching tip to surface. For best results, use your arm, not wrist, to form the desired design. To finish, touch surface with the tip, release pressure, and lift.

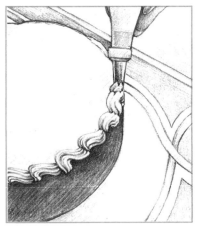

For a shell border, hold the bag at a 45-degree angle, touching tip to surface. Squeeze bag, hesitating to let design build up and fan out, while slightly lifting tip. To finish, gradually release pressure as the tip is lowered to surface, bringing design to a point.

MAY

Now is the perfect time to gather friends and entertain outdoors. On a sunny day or a balmy evening, treat guests to a light, healthy menu, served Southern style or with Southwestern flavor and flair. For a more casual gathering, fire up the grill and try your hand at cooking a regional specialty, barbecued ribs, along with all the trimmings.

ON THE LIGHT SIDE

Host A Healthy Springtime Get-Together

From the first warm breeze of spring to the last glow of Indian summer, Southerners seize the chance to entertain outdoors. And warm weather and healthy eating go hand-in-hand, so we put together a light menu that not only reflects the freshness of the season but also lends itself to outdoor entertaining.

This menu is low in fat—only 16% of total calories come from fat—and high in complex carbohydrates. And the amount of cholesterol for the whole meal is only 85 milligrams.

Another benefit is that almost everything can be made ahead of time so the host and hostess can enjoy visiting with their guests.

Bellini Spritzers
Quick Fruit Dip
Marinated Chicken Strips and
Vegetables
Whole Wheat Rolls
Chocolate Angel Food Cake

BELLINI SPRITZERS

6 medium to large ripe peaches,
   peeled and halved (2 pounds)
1 (750-milliliter) bottle
   champagne, chilled
1 (23-ounce) bottle sparkling
   mineral water

Place peaches in container of an electric blender or food processor. Top with cover; process until smooth.

Combine 3 cups peach puree, champagne, and mineral water in a large pitcher. Pour into chilled wine glasses; serve immediately. Yield: 9 cups (74 calories per ¾-cup serving).

☐ *0.6 gram protein, 0.1 gram fat, 7.7 grams carbohydrate, 0 milligrams cholesterol, 3 milligrams sodium, and 13 milligrams calcium.*

QUICK FRUIT DIP

1⅓ cups plain low-fat yogurt
¼ cup low-sugar orange
   marmalade
¼ teaspoon ground cinnamon
6 cups assorted fresh fruit

Combine first 3 ingredients; cover and chill. Serve with assorted fresh fruit. Yield: 1½ cups (55 calories per 2 tablespoons dip and ½ cup fruit).

☐ *1.8 grams protein, 0.7 gram fat, 11.8 grams carbohydrate, 2 milligrams cholesterol, 21 milligrams sodium, and 55 milligrams calcium.*
Lillie Bellamy
Shallotte, North Carolina

MARINATED CHICKEN STRIPS AND VEGETABLES

¾ cup reduced-sodium soy sauce
⅔ cup honey
⅓ cup sherry
½ teaspoon garlic powder
¼ teaspoon ground ginger
12 (4-ounce) chicken breast
   halves, skinned, boned, and
   cut into ¼-inch strips
3 pounds asparagus spears
¼ cup coarse-grained mustard
¼ cup sesame seeds
7 cups torn Bibb lettuce
7 cups torn romaine lettuce
4 cups torn iceberg lettuce
6 tomatoes, cut into 6 wedges
   each
Honey-Mustard Dressing

Combine soy sauce, honey, sherry, garlic powder, and ginger in a 13- x 9- x 2-inch baking dish. Add chicken; cover and chill at least 2 hours.

Snap off tough ends of asparagus. Remove scales from stalks with a knife or vegetable peeler, if desired. Arrange asparagus in steaming rack, and place over boiling water. Cover and steam 8 to 12 minutes or until asparagus is crisp-tender; drain. Cover and chill 1 hour.

Drain chicken, reserving ½ cup marinade; return chicken to baking dish. Combine coarse-grained mustard, sesame seeds, and reserved marinade; pour mixture over chicken. Bake at 350° for 30 minutes or until chicken is done, turning once. Remove chicken from marinade; drain on paper towels.

Combine lettuces; place 1½ cups on each of 12 serving plates. Arrange tomato wedges and asparagus spears evenly on lettuce; arrange chicken strips on top. Serve with Honey-Mustard Dressing. Yield: 12 main-dish servings (335 calories per 1½ cups lettuce, ½ medium tomato, 3 ounces chicken strips, 4 ounces asparagus, and 2 tablespoons Honey-Mustard Dressing).

☐ *33.2 grams protein, 7.4 grams fat, 34.6 grams carbohydrate, 73 milligrams cholesterol, 846 milligrams sodium, and 92 milligrams calcium.*

Honey-Mustard Dressing

¾ cup plain nonfat yogurt
¼ cup reduced-calorie
  mayonnaise
¼ cup honey
2 tablespoons Dijon mustard
2 tablespoons coarse-grained
  mustard
1 tablespoon rice vinegar

Combine all ingredients in a small bowl; cover and chill dressing thoroughly. Yield: 1½ cups (25 calories per tablespoon).

☐ *0.5 gram protein, 0.9 gram fat, 3.8 grams carbohydrate, 1 milligram cholesterol, 68 milligrams sodium, and 13 milligrams calcium.*

WHOLE WHEAT ROLLS

2 packages dry yeast
1¾ cups warm water (105° to
  115°)
⅓ cup sugar
1 teaspoon salt
¼ cup vegetable oil
1 egg, slightly beaten
2¼ cups whole wheat flour
2¼ to 2¾ cups all-purpose flour
Butter-flavored vegetable cooking
  spray

Dissolve yeast in warm water in a large mixing bowl; add sugar and next 4 ingredients. Beat at medium speed of an electric mixer 2 minutes. Gradually stir in enough all-purpose flour to make a soft dough.

Turn dough out onto a well-floured surface, and knead until smooth and elastic (about 5 minutes). Place dough in a bowl coated with cooking spray, turning to grease top. Cover and let rise in a warm place (85°), free from drafts, 1 hour or until dough is doubled in bulk.

Punch dough down; cover and let rise in a warm place, free from drafts, until doubled in bulk.

Punch dough down, and divide in half; roll each portion to a 14- x 9-inch rectangle. Cut dough in half crosswise; cut each half into 9 (1-inch-wide) strips. Roll each strip, jellyroll fashion, into a spiral, and place in muffin pans coated with cooking spray. Spray tops of rolls with cooking spray. Let rise, uncovered, in a warm place, free from drafts, 40 minutes or until doubled in bulk. Bake at 400° for 12 to 15 minutes; spray with cooking spray. Yield: 3 dozen (91 calories per roll).

☐ *2.4 grams protein, 2.4 grams fat, 15 grams carbohydrate, 8 milligrams cholesterol, 67 milligrams sodium, and 4 milligrams calcium.*

CHOCOLATE ANGEL FOOD CAKE

1 (14.5-ounce) angel food cake
  mix
¼ cup unsweetened cocoa, sifted
¼ teaspoon chocolate flavoring
1 tablespoon sifted powdered
  sugar
Garnish: strawberry fans

Combine flour packet from cake mix and cocoa. Prepare cake according to package directions; fold chocolate flavoring into batter. Bake according to package directions.

Sprinkle cooled cake with powdered sugar. Garnish cake, if desired. Yield: 32 (½-inch) servings (54 calories per serving).

☐ *1.2 grams protein, 0.1 gram fat, 12.2 grams carbohydrate, 0 milligrams cholesterol, 24 milligrams sodium, and 17 milligrams calcium.*

Blue-Ribbon Cookies

Louise Bodziony of Gladstone, Missouri, won a blue ribbon at the 1987 Missouri State Fair for her Raspberry Swirl Cookies.

RASPBERRY SWIRL COOKIES

½ cup butter or margarine,
  softened
1 cup sugar
1 egg
1 teaspoon vanilla extract
2 cups all-purpose flour
1 teaspoon baking powder
¼ teaspoon salt
Raspberry Filling

Cream butter; gradually add sugar, beating well at medium speed of an electric mixer. Add egg and vanilla; beat well. Combine flour, baking powder, and salt; add to creamed mixture, beating well. Shape dough into a ball; wrap in plastic wrap, and chill 2 hours.

On floured wax paper, roll dough to a 12- x 9-inch rectangle. Spread Raspberry Filling evenly to within ½ inch of edges. Carefully roll dough, jellyroll fashion, starting at long end and peeling wax paper from dough as you roll. Pinch side seam to seal (leave ends open). Wrap dough in plastic wrap. Chill 1 hour or until dough is firm.

Unwrap roll, and cut into ¼-inch slices. Place 2 inches apart on greased cookie sheets. Bake at 375° for 8 to 10 minutes or just until cookies begin to brown around edges. Cool on wire racks. Yield: 3½ dozen.

Raspberry Filling

½ cup raspberry jam
½ cup flaked coconut
¼ cup finely chopped walnuts

Combine all ingredients; stir well. Yield: 1 cup.

Shellfish: Fast And Flavorful

When you're cooking shellfish, you can count on the microwave to make the meal fast and flavorful.

For Mussels Linguine, the microwave makes quick work of opening mussel shells—the process occurs naturally as the dish cooks. As soon as the shells open, the mussels are done. Don't cook them any longer, as the mussels will toughen.

While this shell-opening process works well with mussels, it's not as effective for oysters; by the time the shells open, the oysters inside are already overcooked.

SPEEDY CRABMEAT IMPERIAL

2 tablespoons butter or margarine
¼ cup chopped onion
¼ cup chopped green pepper
1 (2-ounce) jar diced pimiento, drained
3 tablespoons all-purpose flour
2 teaspoons dry mustard
¼ teaspoon salt
¼ teaspoon white pepper
Dash of hot sauce
1 cup milk
3 tablespoons Chablis or other dry white wine
1 pound fresh lump crabmeat, drained
Garnish: pimiento strips

Combine butter, onion, and green pepper in a 1½-quart casserole. Microwave at HIGH, uncovered, 2 minutes. Stir in diced pimiento and next 5 ingredients, stirring until smooth. Gradually add milk and Chablis, stirring well. Microwave at HIGH, uncovered, 3 to 4 minutes or until mixture is bubbly, stirring after 2 minutes. Stir in crabmeat.

Spoon mixture evenly into 6 baking shells. Arrange shells on a 12-inch glass pizza plate. Cover with wax paper, and microwave at HIGH 3 to 4 minutes or until thoroughly heated. Garnish, if desired. Yield: 6 servings.

SWEET-AND-SOUR SHRIMP

1½ pounds unpeeled medium-size fresh shrimp
1 tablespoon vegetable oil
¼ cup chopped sweet red pepper
¼ cup sliced green onions
1 clove garlic, minced
⅓ cup red plum jam
2 tablespoons dry white wine
2 tablespoons white vinegar
2 tablespoons cocktail sauce
2 tablespoons chutney
½ teaspoon salt
¼ teaspoon crushed red pepper
¼ pound fresh snow pea pods
Hot cooked rice

Peel and devein shrimp; set aside. Combine oil, sweet red pepper, green onions, and garlic in a 1½-quart baking dish. Microwave at HIGH, uncovered, 2 to 3 minutes or until tender; stir mixture at 1-minute intervals.

Add shrimp, and cover with heavy-duty plastic wrap; fold back a small edge of wrap to allow steam to escape. Microwave at MEDIUM (50% power) 8 to 10 minutes or until shrimp are opaque and firm, stirring at 3-minute intervals. Drain.

Combine jam and next 6 ingredients; stir well. Pour over shrimp, and stir gently. Cover and microwave at HIGH 1 to 1½ minutes or until sauce is heated. Add snow peas, and stir gently. Cover and microwave at HIGH 2 to 2½ minutes or until snow peas are crisp-tender. Let stand, covered, 1 to 2 minutes. Serve over cooked rice. Yield: 4 servings.

MUSSELS LINGUINE

2 pounds raw mussels in shells
3 tablespoons olive oil
½ cup chopped fresh parsley
5 cloves garlic, minced
2 tablespoons dry white wine
1 (15½-ounce) jar spaghetti sauce
½ teaspoon dried whole oregano
⅛ teaspoon freshly ground pepper
8 ounces linguine

Remove beards on mussels, and scrub mussel shells well with a brush. Discard opened, cracked, or heavy mussels.

Combine oil, parsley, and garlic in a 12- x 8- x 2-inch baking dish; microwave at HIGH, uncovered, 3 to 5 minutes. Stir in wine, spaghetti sauce, oregano, and pepper. Arrange mussels over sauce in a single layer. Cover tightly with heavy-duty plastic wrap; fold back a corner of wrap to allow steam to escape. Microwave at HIGH 6 to 7 minutes or until mussels open.

Cook linguine according to package directions; drain. Place cooked linguine on a platter; top with mussels and sauce. Yield: 4 servings.

Carol Y. Chastain
San Antonio, Texas

Right: *Serve a heart-healthy menu. Start out with (clockwise from top) Watermelon-Berry Slush and Ranch-Style Dip with fresh vegetables. Then offer Asparagus Vinaigrette, Grilled Flank Steak With Sweet Peppers, Roasted New Potatoes, and Quick Crouton Bread. Top the meal off with Frozen Fresh Peach Yogurt. (Recipes begin on page 137.)*

Page 116: *Quick Chicken, served with Rainbow Pepper Topping, puts bright colors and festive flavors on your dinner table in a hurry. (Recipes, page 117.)*

Above: *Broccoli-Chicken Salad (page 129) provides a quick, chilled main dish using only five ingredients.*

Left: *Fresh herbs impart a savory flavor to Onion-Herb Bread (page 165) and Italian Green Beans (page 164).*

QUICK!

Team Chicken And Sauces

For a single career woman on the go, a home-cooked meal is sometimes hard to come by. "It's a little bit difficult," says Carolyn Rahn of Lewisville, North Carolina. "I work, so everything I cook has to be quick." Knowing that lots of people are in the same situation, she enjoys creating and sharing recipes with friends to dispel the myth that food for single people must come from a package in the freezer or a fast food drive-through window.

QUICK CHICKEN
(pictured, left)

Vegetable cooking spray
4 chicken breast halves, skinned and boned
½ cup water

Coat a nonstick skillet with vegetable cooking spray; place over medium heat until hot. Add chicken, and cook 10 minutes, turning once.

Add ½ cup water; cover, and simmer 15 minutes. Drain chicken, and serve with one of the following sauces or toppings. Yield: 4 servings.

GREEN PEPPERCORN BUTTER

½ cup butter or margarine, melted
2 tablespoons whole green peppercorns, drained
2 teaspoons lemon juice
2 teaspoons Worcestershire sauce
1 teaspoon Dijon mustard

Combine all ingredients in a small saucepan. Cook over low heat, stirring gently; do not boil. Spoon sauce over chicken, and serve immediately. Yield: ½ cup.

RAINBOW PEPPER TOPPING
(pictured, left)

1 small onion, sliced and separated into rings
1 clove garlic, minced
2 tablespoons olive oil
1 small sweet red pepper, cut into strips
1 small green pepper, cut into strips
1 small yellow pepper, cut into strips
½ cup dry sherry
1 tablespoon chopped fresh parsley
⅛ teaspoon salt
⅛ teaspoon pepper
Hot cooked pasta
Garnish: fresh parsley sprigs

Sauté onion and garlic in olive oil in a skillet over medium heat 1 minute. Add peppers, and sauté 2 minutes. Add sherry, parsley, salt, and pepper; simmer 2 minutes. Spoon pepper mixture over chicken and pasta; garnish, if desired. Serve immediately. Yield: 4 servings.

CHICKEN CURRY SAUCE

½ cup finely chopped onion
2 tablespoons butter or margarine, melted
1 (10¾-ounce) can cream of chicken soup
½ cup half-and-half
1 tablespoon lemon juice
1 teaspoon curry powder
½ teaspoon ground ginger
Hot cooked rice
Assorted condiments

Sauté onion in butter in a saucepan. Stir in soup and next 4 ingredients; cook over medium heat until thoroughly heated, stirring occasionally. Spoon cooked rice onto a serving plate. Place chicken on rice, and spoon sauce over chicken. Serve with several of the following condiments: chutney, toasted coconut, raisins, sliced green onions, or peanuts. Yield: about 2 cups.

COUNTRY HAM SAUCE

½ cup diced cooked country ham
1 clove garlic, minced
1 teaspoon butter or margarine, melted
1 teaspoon white wine Worcestershire sauce
½ teaspoon lemon juice
¼ teaspoon paprika
⅛ teaspoon white pepper
½ cup sour cream

Sauté ham and garlic in butter 2 to 3 minutes. Stir in Worcestershire sauce and next 3 ingredients. Fold in sour cream, and cook over low heat until thoroughly heated (do not boil). Spoon over chicken; serve immediately. Yield: about ¾ cup.

CHERVIL-AND-SAVORY SAUCE

¼ cup chopped onion
1½ teaspoons butter or margarine, melted
¼ cup dry white wine
½ teaspoon dried whole chervil
⅛ teaspoon salt
⅛ teaspoon dried whole savory
⅛ teaspoon pepper
½ cup plain yogurt

Sauté onion in butter until crisp-tender. Add wine, and simmer over low heat until wine almost evaporates (about 5 minutes). Add seasonings; stir in yogurt (at room temperature). Cook over low heat, stirring constantly, until thoroughly heated (do not boil). Spoon sauce over chicken, and serve immediately. Yield: ⅔ cup.

BASIL AND CREAM SAUCE

2 tablespoons chopped shallots
¼ cup chopped green onions
1 tablespoon butter or margarine,
   melted
1 cup half-and-half
⅛ teaspoon pepper
2 teaspoons dried whole basil or
   2 tablespoons chopped fresh
   basil
2 slices bacon, cooked and
   chopped

Sauté shallots and green onions in
butter in a skillet until crisp-tender.
Add half-and-half; simmer 5 minutes
or until cream is reduced and slightly
thickened. Stir in pepper and remaining
ingredients. Spoon sauce over
chicken, and serve immediately.
Yield: ½ cup.

Make A Meal
Of Tex-Mex
Appetizers

If you're planning a gathering that's
festive and casual, a menu of Tex-
Mex appetizers is ideal. Chiles, guacamole, spicy sausage, tortillas, cilantro, picante sauce, and more give
these recipes a Southwestern flavor.

But don't wait until it's time for a
large party to enjoy these recipes.
They're tasty for serving to the family or just as a prelude to a meal with
a couple of friends. In fact, some of
the recipes are hearty enough to
serve as an entrée. Two-Cheese
Tortilla Snack is a good example.
Provide all the typical accompaniments, such as sour cream, picante
sauce or salsa, and chopped chiles;
then let guests assemble their own
combinations. Round out the menu
with a serving of spicy rice or refried
beans and a fresh fruit salad.

TURKEY NACHOS

¼ cup chopped onion
2 tablespoons butter or
   margarine, melted
½ cup chopped cooked turkey or
   chicken
1 tablespoon chopped pickled
   jalapeños
Dash of ground oregano
Dash of ground cumin
½ cup sour cream
½ (10-ounce) package plain
   tortilla chips
½ cup (2 ounces) shredded
   Monterey Jack cheese
½ cup (2 ounces) shredded
   mozzarella or provolone cheese
Freshly grated pepper

Sauté onion in butter until tender.
Add turkey and next 4 ingredients;
stir well, and cook over medium heat
until thoroughly heated.

Arrange chips on an ovenproof
platter. Dollop or spread turkey mixture over chips; sprinkle with
cheeses. Bake at 425° for 8 minutes
or until cheese melts. Sprinkle with
pepper, and serve immediately.
Yield: 4 to 6 servings.

Carol E. Velek
Friendswood, Texas

SAUSAGE QUESADILLAS

1 pound chorizo sausage, sliced
3 cups (12 ounces) shredded
   Cheddar cheese
3 cups (12 ounces) shredded
   Monterey Jack cheese
10 jalapeño peppers, seeded and
   thinly sliced
24 (6-inch) flour tortillas
Commercial guacamole, sour
   cream, and salsa

Cook chorizo in a skillet over medium heat until browned. Drain and
set aside.

Divide chorizo, cheeses, and peppers evenly over 12 tortillas; moisten
tortilla edges with water. Moisten
edges of remaining 12 tortillas; place

over sausage mixture. Press tortilla
edges together with a fork; place on
ungreased baking sheets. Bake at
400° for 7 to 10 minutes or until
lightly browned.

Cut quesadillas into quarters.
Serve hot with guacamole, sour
cream, and salsa. Yield: 12 appetizer
servings.

Note: A mixture of 1 pound bulk
pork sausage, 1 tablespoon chopped
cilantro, 2 tablespoons vinegar, and 2
teaspoons chili powder may be substituted for chorizo, if desired.

R. Patricia Saylor
Crofton, Maryland

FIERY FRIED STUFFED
JALAPEÑOS

1 (10-ounce) can whole jalapeños,
   drained
1 (6-ounce) can crabmeat, drained
¼ cup all-purpose flour
2 tablespoons regular cornmeal
¼ teaspoon salt
¼ teaspoon pepper
1 cup buttermilk
½ cup all-purpose flour
¼ cup regular cornmeal
Vegetable oil

Cut stems from jalapeños. Scoop out
seeds, using a small, sharp knife (do
not cut jalapeños). Stuff each pepper
with crabmeat; set aside.

Combine ¼ cup flour and next 4
ingredients; stir until smooth, and set
aside. Combine ½ cup flour and ¼
cup cornmeal; set aside. Dip stuffed
jalapeños in batter; dredge in flour
mixture. Pour oil to a depth of 2 to 3
inches in a Dutch oven; heat to 375°.
Fry jalapeños, a few at a time, 1 to 2
minutes on each side or until golden
brown. Drain on paper towels. Yield:
about 20 appetizer servings.

Sunny Hueholtz
Argyle, Texas

BURRITO ROLLUPS

2 (8-ounce) packages cream
    cheese, softened
1 (6-ounce) can pitted black
    olives, drained and chopped
1 (4-ounce) can diced green
    chiles, undrained
½ cup chopped onion
1 (18-ounce) package 10-inch
    flour tortillas
Commercial jalapeño salsa

Combine first 4 ingredients, mixing
well. Spread about 1 heaping tablespoon of cream cheese mixture on
each tortilla. Tightly roll tortillas, and
wrap in wax paper; chill 8 hours.

Slice each tortilla into seven 1-inch
slices, and serve with jalapeño salsa.
Yield: 7 dozen appetizer servings.
Marilyn Campbell
Orlando, Florida

TWO-CHEESE TORTILLA
SNACK

3 ripe avocados, peeled and
    mashed
¼ cup grated onion
1 tablespoon lemon juice
2 teaspoons chopped jalapeño or
    canned jalapeño juice
2 cups (8 ounces) shredded
    mozzarella cheese
2 cups (8 ounces) shredded
    Monterey Jack cheese
1 medium-size green pepper,
    chopped
1 medium onion, chopped
12 (6-inch) flour tortillas
Commercial picante sauce, sour
    cream, or chopped chiles

Combine first 4 ingredients, stirring
until blended. Set aside.

Combine cheeses, green pepper,
and chopped onion in top of a double
boiler; bring water to a boil. Reduce
heat to medium; cook, stirring constantly, until blended. Set aside, and
keep warm.

Wrap tortillas in aluminum foil, and
bake at 325° for 15 minutes.

To serve, place a small amount of
cheese mixture in center of tortillas.
Spread avocado mixture over cheese,
and top with picante sauce, sour
cream, or chiles. Fold tortillas in
thirds. Serve immediately. Yield: 12
appetizer servings. *Betty Manning*
El Dorado, Arkansas

MEXICAN CHEESE SPREAD

2 cups (8 ounces) shredded sharp
    Cheddar cheese
½ cup sour cream
¼ cup butter or margarine,
    softened
2 tablespoons chopped green
    chiles
2 tablespoons chopped pimiento
2 green onions, chopped
    (optional)

Combine cheese (at room temperature), sour cream, and butter; beat
at medium speed of an electric mixer
until smooth. Stir in chiles, pimiento,
and, if desired, green onions. Serve
with fresh fruit or crackers. Yield:
about 2 cups. *Linda Vaughn*
Dallas, Texas

HOMEMADE TEXAS CHIPS
WITH GUACAMOLE SPREAD

2 cups biscuit mix
½ cup water
Regular cornmeal
Vegetable oil
Guacamole Spread

Combine biscuit mix and water; stir
just until blended. Turn dough out
onto a lightly floured surface, and
knead lightly 3 or 4 times. Divide
dough into 16 pieces, and shape each
piece into a ball.

Sprinkle surface with cornmeal;
roll each ball to a 5-inch circle. Pour
oil to a depth of 2 to 3 inches into a
Dutch oven; heat to 375°. Drop

rolled dough, two pieces at a time,
into hot oil, and cook 15 seconds on
each side or until puffed and golden.
Drain on paper towels. Serve warm
with Guacamole Spread. Yield: 16 appetizer servings.

Guacamole Spread

1 ripe avocado, peeled and
    mashed
1½ tablespoons lime juice
1½ tablespoons mayonnaise or
    salad dressing
1½ tablespoons chopped green
    chiles
1 tablespoon chopped onion
½ teaspoon Worcestershire sauce
⅛ teaspoon ground cumin
⅛ teaspoon hot sauce
1 tomato, peeled and chopped
1 clove garlic, crushed
2 slices bacon, cooked and
    crumbled

Combine all ingredients, stirring until
blended. Yield: 1½ cups.
Margaret G. Quaadman
Roswell, Georgia

Onion Tips

■ For a small amount of grated
onion, place in a garlic press.

■ Always store onions in a cool,
dark place with air circulation to
prevent sprouting.

■ When selecting onions, consider all of the flavor possibili-
ties. The large Spanish or
Bermuda onion and the small
white onion are usually mild
in flavor; on the other hand,
Globe types, such as red,
brown, and small yellow onions,
are stronger flavored.

Enjoy Barbecue, Memphis Style

Memphians will tell you that good " 'cue" means pork—especially ribs. A few Memphis restaurant personalities were willing to share their recipes so that you can try these ribs and traditional side dishes at home. We've scaled them down to make them manageable in your kitchen.

■ **Leonard's** delicious onion rings boast a batter of cornmeal sweetened with a little sugar, according to general manager Dan Brown.

LEONARD'S-STYLE ONION RINGS

2 extra-large Spanish onions
1¾ cups all-purpose flour
½ cup self-rising cornmeal
1 tablespoon onion powder
1½ teaspoons salt
¾ teaspoon sugar
2 cups milk
1 egg, beaten
Vegetable oil

Peel onions; cut into ½-inch slices, and separate into rings. Set aside.

Combine flour and next 6 ingredients; beat with a wire whisk until mixture is smooth.

Pour oil to a depth of 2 to 3 inches into a Dutch oven or heavy saucepan; heat to 375°. Dip onion rings in batter; fry, turning once, until golden brown (about 2 minutes). Drain on paper towels, and serve immediately. Yield: 12 servings.

■ At the **Germantown Commissary Co.,** owned by Walker Taylor, Jr., the baked beans feature chopped barbecued pork, a little barbecue sauce, and brown sugar.

COMMISSARY BARBECUE BEANS

1 (28-ounce) can fancy pork and beans
½ pound cooked, chopped barbecued pork shoulder
½ cup chopped purple onion
½ cup commercial barbecue sauce
¼ to ½ cup Worcestershire sauce
1½ tablespoons dark brown sugar
2 teaspoons chili powder
1 teaspoon prepared mustard

Combine all ingredients in a lightly greased 2-quart casserole. Cover and bake at 350° for 40 minutes or until beans are hot and bubbly. Yield: 6 to 8 servings.

■ John Wills met his wife, Patrice, during preparation for the Memphis in May World Barbecue Cooking Contest held annually the second weekend in May. He won the contest and has since opened **John Wills Bar-B-Que Pit** and **John Wills Bar-B-Que Bar and Grill.**

JOHN WILLS'S BABY LOIN BACK RIBS

2 slabs baby loin back ribs (about 4 pounds)
3 tablespoons Dry Spices
1 cup Basting Sauce
1 cup Sweet Sauce

Place ribs in a large, shallow pan. Rub Dry Spices all over ribs. Cover and refrigerate ribs 3 hours prior to cooking.

Heat one side of a charcoal or gas grill. Place ribs on cool side of grill throughout cooking time. Cook over 300° to 350° coals for 1½ to 2 hours, basting sparingly with Basting Sauce (about once every 30 minutes) and turning ribs occasionally. Brush ribs with Sweet Sauce during last 30 minutes of cooking time. Yield: 3 to 4 servings.

Dry Spices

3 tablespoons paprika
2 teaspoons seasoned salt
2 teaspoons black pepper
2 teaspoons garlic powder
1 teaspoon red pepper
1 teaspoon ground oregano
1 teaspoon dry mustard
½ teaspoon chili powder

Combine all ingredients; stir well. Yield: 6½ tablespoons.

Basting Sauce

¼ cup firmly packed brown sugar
1½ tablespoons Dry Spices
2 cups red wine vinegar
2 cups water
¼ cup Worcestershire sauce
½ teaspoon hot sauce
1 small bay leaf

Combine all ingredients; cover and let stand 8 hours. (This may not taste pleasant when sampled by itself.) Yield: 4½ cups.

Sweet Sauce

1 (8-ounce) can tomato sauce
½ cup spicy honey mustard
1 cup catsup
1 cup red wine vinegar
¼ cup hickory-smoked Worcestershire sauce
¼ cup Worcestershire sauce
¼ cup butter or margarine
2 tablespoons hot sauce
1 tablespoon lemon juice
2 tablespoons brown sugar
1 tablespoon paprika
1 tablespoon seasoned salt
1½ teaspoons garlic powder
⅛ teaspoon chili powder
⅛ teaspoon red pepper
⅛ teaspoon black pepper

Combine all ingredients in a Dutch oven. Bring to a boil; reduce heat, and simmer 30 minutes, stirring occasionally. Yield: 1 quart.

Celebrate Cinco De Mayo

Cinco de Mayo (May 5) marks the anniversary of the 1862 battle of Puebla, in which Mexican forces against overwhelming odds defeated French invaders. In the Southwest every year folks celebrate *Cinco de Mayo* with a variety of festivities. Authentic Mexican foods are served at the celebrations.

Green Chile Quesadillas
Chicken Enchiladas
Southwestern Rice
Jicama-Orange Salad

GREEN CHILE QUESADILLAS

1 (4-ounce) can chopped green
  chiles
8 (6-inch) corn tortillas
Vegetable cooking spray
1 cup (4 ounces) shredded
  part-skim mozzarella cheese
½ cup (2 ounces) low-fat process
  American cheese
⅛ to ¼ teaspoon red pepper

Drain chiles on paper towels. Place 4 tortillas on a baking sheet coated with cooking spray. Divide cheeses and chiles evenly among 4 tortillas; spread to within ½ inch of edge. Sprinkle evenly with red pepper, and top with remaining tortillas. Bake at 375° for 5 minutes or until cheese melts. Cut each into 8 wedges. Yield: 8 appetizer servings (124 calories per 4 wedges).

☐ *7 grams protein, 4.4 grams fat, 14.1 grams carbohydrate, 12 milligrams cholesterol, 234 milligrams sodium, and 183 milligrams calcium.*

CHICKEN ENCHILADAS

5 (4-ounce) skinned, boned
  chicken breast halves
Vegetable cooking spray
1½ tablespoons chopped onion
1½ tablespoons chopped cilantro
1 jalapeño pepper, seeded and
  chopped
3 (10-ounce) cans enchilada
  sauce, divided
8 (6-inch) corn tortillas
1½ cups (6 ounces) ⅓-less-fat
  mild Cheddar cheese
½ cup diced tomato
⅓ cup sliced ripe olives
4 cups shredded lettuce

Combine chicken and enough water to cover in a medium saucepan. Cook over medium heat 15 minutes or until tender; drain and cool slightly. Shred chicken, and set aside.

Coat a nonstick skillet with cooking spray; place over medium-high heat until hot. Add onion, cilantro, and jalapeño pepper; sauté until tender. Add 1 can enchilada sauce and chicken. Cook 5 minutes.

To soften tortillas, wrap in aluminum foil and bake at 350° for 1 minute. Fill each tortilla with chicken mixture; roll up, and place seam side down in a 13- x 9- x 2-inch baking dish. Heat remaining 2 cans enchilada sauce; pour over enchiladas. Top with cheese, tomato, and olives. Bake at 350° for 10 minutes or until cheese melts and enchiladas are thoroughly heated. Serve over shredded lettuce. Yield: 8 servings (281 calories per enchilada and ½ cup shredded lettuce).

☐ *26.5 grams protein, 7.8 grams fat, 25.3 grams carbohydrate, 59 milligrams cholesterol, 323 milligrams sodium, and 304 milligrams calcium.*

Tip: *Did you know that scallions are the same as green onions? The only differences are that green onions are more mature, and each onion has a tiny bulb at its base.*

SOUTHWESTERN RICE

3 (10½-ounce) cans no-salt-added
  chicken broth
2 teaspoons ground cumin
1½ cups uncooked long-grain rice
½ cup thinly sliced green onions

Bring chicken broth to a boil in a Dutch oven. Add cumin and rice; cover, reduce heat, and simmer 20 minutes or until rice is tender and liquid is absorbed. Add green onions; toss gently. Yield: 8 servings (140 calories per ½ cup).

☐ *2.7 grams protein, 0.3 gram fat, 29.4 grams carbohydrate, 0 milligrams cholesterol, 5 milligrams sodium, and 17 milligrams calcium.*

Identifying Chiles

■ Anaheim or California green chile: Slender green chile about 6 to 8 inches long with rounded tip; mild flavored. Substitute: Canned green chiles.

■ Ancho chile: Dried form of poblano chile. Substitute: ½ teaspoon chili powder for each ancho chile.

■ Jalapeño pepper: Small green or red cigar-shaped chile about 2½ inches long; very hot. Substitute: Pickled jalapeños.

■ Poblano chile: Large dark green chile that resembles an elongated bell pepper; difficult to find outside of Texas and Southwestern states; ranges from mild to hot. Substitute: Sweet green pepper.

■ Serrano chile: Dark green to red chile 1 to 1½ inches long; hot to very hot. Substitute: Jalapeño pepper.

JICAMA-ORANGE SALAD

4 large oranges, peeled and
  sectioned
2 sweet red peppers, cut into
  strips
2 cups julienne-cut jicama
¼ cup white vinegar
2 tablespoons vegetable oil
½ teaspoon sugar
¼ teaspoon white pepper
¼ teaspoon chili powder

Combine orange sections, red pepper strips, and julienne-cut jicama in a medium bowl; cover and chill.

Combine vinegar and remaining ingredients in a jar; cover tightly, and shake vigorously. Chill thoroughly.

If necessary, drain orange mixture; add dressing, and toss gently. Yield: 8 servings (81 calories per ¾-cup serving).

□ *1.2 grams protein, 3.7 grams fat, 12.3 grams carbohydrate, 0 milligrams cholesterol, 3 milligrams sodium, and 32 milligrams calcium.*

LIGHT FAVORITE

Better-Than-Ever Potato Salad

Potato Salad has long been a summer tradition in the South. In the past, nutritionists cringed over the amount of mayonnaise and eggs used in most recipes. But now Patricia Wenzel of Hurst, Texas, has successfully lightened up this fat-laden favorite. She worked on her Potato Salad recipe for a long time to get the right amount of flavor and creaminess without all the fat and calories. We think you'll agree it's a success.

POTATO SALAD

¾ pound red potatoes, unpeeled
½ cup diced onion
½ cup diced celery
¼ cup chopped sweet red pepper
¼ cup chopped green pepper
¼ cup grated carrot
¼ cup diced dill pickle
¼ cup sweet pickle relish
1 (2-ounce) jar diced pimiento,
  drained
¼ cup plain nonfat yogurt
¼ cup reduced-calorie
  mayonnaise
2 tablespoons spicy brown
  mustard
⅛ teaspoon pepper
⅛ teaspoon red pepper

Wash potatoes, and cut into ½-inch cubes; cook in boiling water to cover 8 to 10 minutes or until tender. Drain and let cool.

Combine potatoes and next 8 ingredients; toss gently. Set aside.

Combine yogurt, mayonnaise, mustard, pepper, and red pepper; stir well, and pour over potato mixture. Toss gently; cover and chill. Yield: 9 servings (72 calories per ½-cup serving).

□ *1.8 grams protein, 2.2 grams fat, 11.9 grams carbohydrate, 2 milligrams cholesterol, 238 milligrams sodium, and 32 milligrams calcium.*

COMPARE THE NUTRIENTS (per serving)		
	Traditional	Light
Calories	260	72
Fat	10.8g	2.2g
Cholesterol	141mg	2mg

Embellish Pasta For An Entrée

Because they provide both the meat and side dish, these pasta entrées make meal preparation easier and quicker. A salad and bread are all you'll need to add to make the meal complete. Along with a classic pasta, Saucy Meatballs, we've included two delicious fish selections.

SAUCY MEATBALLS

½ cup chopped onion
2 tablespoons butter or
  margarine, melted
1 pound ground beef
1 pound ground pork
3 slices bread, crumbled
¼ cup milk
1 egg, beaten
1 teaspoon salt
½ teaspoon pepper
½ teaspoon ground nutmeg
1 clove garlic, crushed
3 tablespoons butter or
  margarine, melted
¼ cup all-purpose flour
2 cups beef broth
1 teaspoon tomato paste
1 teaspoon dried whole basil
1 (8-ounce) carton sour cream
Hot cooked noodles

Sauté onion in 2 tablespoons butter until tender. Combine onion, ground beef, and next 7 ingredients, mixing well; shape into 1½-inch meatballs. Place on lightly greased rack of a broiler pan; bake at 350° for 25 minutes or until done.

Sauté garlic in 3 tablespoons butter; add flour, stirring well. Cook 1 minute. Gradually add broth, stirring until smooth; stir in tomato paste and basil. Remove from heat. Add sour cream and meatballs; cook over medium heat, stirring constantly, just until heated. Serve over noodles. Yield: 6 to 8 servings. *Mig Sturr*
Kingsville, Maryland

PASTA WITH CATFISH AND ARTICHOKES

½ pound catfish fillets
8 ounces uncooked angel hair pasta
1 sweet red pepper, cut into julienne strips
1 carrot, cut into julienne strips
1 zucchini, cut into julienne strips
3 tablespoons butter or margarine, melted
1 (14-ounce) can artichoke hearts, drained and cut into quarters
⅔ cup whipping cream
½ cup grated Parmesan cheese
¼ teaspoon ground nutmeg

Cut catfish fillets into 2-inch strips, and set aside.

Cook pasta according to package directions; drain and set aside.

Sauté red pepper, carrot, and zucchini in butter in a skillet until crisp-tender (about 10 minutes). Remove vegetables from skillet. Add catfish, and sauté until tender.

Return vegetables to skillet, and add artichokes and whipping cream. Cook over low heat just until heated. Add pasta and cheese, and toss gently. Sprinkle with nutmeg, and serve immediately. Yield: about 4 servings.

SALMON FETTUCCINE

8 ounces uncooked fettuccine
1½ tablespoons butter or margarine
1½ tablespoons all-purpose flour
2 cups half-and-half
1 cup freshly grated Parmesan cheese
1½ teaspoons dry sherry
¼ teaspoon salt
¼ teaspoon white pepper
1 clove garlic, minced
2 tablespoons butter or margarine, melted
½ pound salmon fillet, cut into 2-inch pieces

Cook fettuccine according to package directions; drain and set aside.

Melt 1½ tablespoons butter in a heavy saucepan over low heat; add flour, stirring until smooth. Cook 1 minute, stirring constantly. Gradually add half-and-half; cook over medium heat, stirring constantly, until mixture is thickened and bubbly. Stir in cheese, sherry, salt, and pepper. Keep warm.

Sauté garlic in 2 tablespoons butter in a large skillet. Add salmon; cook until fish begins to flake. Add sauce and fettuccine, tossing gently. Cook over low heat just until thoroughly heated. Serve immediately. Yield: 4 servings.
Dina Walker
Garland, Texas

Mold A Salad Ahead Of Time

Whether you want to put fruit, vegetables, or meat on the menu, gelatin salads offer handy options from which to choose. You can make them ahead of time and store in the refrigerator. As with any dish that contains cooked chicken, use the Chicken Salad Ring within two or three days.

Flavored gelatin must be dissolved in boiling liquid, while unflavored gelatin must first be softened in cold liquid before dissolving it by cooking or by adding boiling liquid. Be sure to use only the type gelatin the recipe calls for, and follow the dissolving directions exactly.

BEET ASPIC

1 (16-ounce) can sliced beets
¾ cup white wine vinegar
2 teaspoons grated onion
2 (3-ounce) packages lemon-flavored gelatin
¾ cup sugar
1 tablespoon prepared horseradish

Drain beets, reserving liquid. Place beets in container of a food processor or electric blender; process until pureed. Set aside.

Combine reserved beet liquid, vinegar, and onion in a medium saucepan; bring to a boil. Dissolve gelatin and sugar in boiling liquid. Remove from heat. Stir in beet puree and horseradish. Pour mixture into a lightly greased 8-inch square dish. Cover and chill until firm. Cut into squares to serve. Yield: 9 servings.
Iva J. Adams
Camilla, Georgia

CHICKEN SALAD RING

2 envelopes unflavored gelatin
1 cup cold water
1 (10¾-ounce) can cream of celery soup, undiluted
1 cup mayonnaise or salad dressing
2 tablespoons lemon juice
2 tablespoons grated onion
½ teaspoon salt
2 cups chopped cooked chicken
1 cup chopped celery
½ cup sweet pickle relish
1 (2-ounce) jar diced pimiento, drained
Lettuce leaves
Garnishes: lettuce leaves, lemon slices

Sprinkle gelatin over cold water in a large saucepan; let stand 1 minute. Cook over low heat, stirring until gelatin dissolves; remove from heat.

Stir soup and next 4 ingredients into gelatin mixture. Chill until mixture is the consistency of unbeaten egg white. Fold in chicken, celery, pickle relish, and pimiento. Spoon into a lightly oiled 6-cup mold; cover and chill until firm. Unmold onto a lettuce-lined plate, and garnish, if desired. Cut into slices to serve. Yield: 8 servings. *Mrs. Arthur L. Barton*
Marion, Alabama

SHERRIED FRUIT MOLD

1 (8½-ounce) can pear halves,
  undrained
1 (8-ounce) can pineapple tidbits,
  undrained
1 cup seedless green grapes,
  halved
2 (3-ounce) packages
  orange-flavored gelatin
2 cups boiling water
⅓ cup cream sherry
¼ cup water
⅓ cup slivered almonds, toasted
Lettuce leaves (optional)

Drain pear halves and pineapple tidbits, reserving juices. Combine pear
halves, pineapple, and grapes; set
aside. Combine reserved juices; add
enough water to juices to equal 1
cup. Set aside.

Dissolve gelatin in boiling water;
stir in cream sherry, ¼ cup water,
and fruit juice mixture. Chill until
mixture is the consistency of unbeaten egg white.

Fold fruit and almonds into gelatin
mixture. Pour into a lightly oiled 6-
cup mold; cover and chill until firm.
Unmold onto lettuce leaves, if desired. Yield: 10 to 12 servings.

Janet M. Filer
Arlington, Virginia

CONGEALED CRANBERRY SALAD

1 (8-ounce) can crushed
  pineapple, undrained
1 (6-ounce) package red raspberry
  gelatin
1 (8-ounce) package cream
  cheese, softened
2 tablespoons mayonnaise or
  salad dressing
1 (16-ounce) can whole-berry
  cranberry sauce
1 small apple, unpeeled and
  chopped
½ cup chopped walnuts
1 (1.25-ounce) envelope whipped
  topping mix
Lettuce leaves

Drain pineapple, reserving juice. Add
enough water to juice to measure 1
cup. Set fruit aside. Bring reserved
juice to a boil in a saucepan. Dissolve
gelatin in boiling juice.

Beat cream cheese and mayonnaise in a large mixing bowl at low
speed of an electric mixer until
blended. Gradually add gelatin mixture, beating well. Stir in pineapple,
cranberry sauce, apple, and chopped
walnuts.

Prepare whipped topping according
to package directions; fold into gelatin mixture. Spoon mixture into a
lightly oiled 8-cup mold. Cover and
chill until firm. Unmold onto lettuce
leaves. Yield: 12 to 14 servings.

Anne Fowler Newell
Johnsonville, South Carolina

Serve Fruit
On The Side

Don't forget about fruit when deciding what side dish to put on the
menu. These concoctions are as satisfying as vegetable dishes and can
be served at any meal of the day.

BAY LAUREL PEACHES

1 (29-ounce) can peach halves,
  undrained
1 bay leaf
2 tablespoons butter or margarine
½ teaspoon paprika
½ teaspoon onion salt
1 teaspoon honey
¼ cup tarragon vinegar

Drain peaches, reserving liquid. Arrange peach halves, cut side up, in
an 8-inch square baking dish. Set
peaches aside.

Combine reserved peach liquid,
bay leaf, and butter in a saucepan;
bring to a boil, and boil 1 minute.
Add paprika and remaining ingredients to mixture in saucepan, stirring well; pour over peaches. Bake,
uncovered, at 325° for 20 to 25 minutes or until thoroughly heated. Remove bay leaf. Yield: 8 servings.

Microwave Directions: Drain
peaches, reserving liquid. Arrange
peach halves, cut side up, in an 8-
inch square baking dish. Set aside.
Combine reserved peach liquid and
remaining ingredients; pour over
peaches. Cover tightly with heavy-
duty plastic wrap; fold back a small
corner of wrap to allow steam to escape. Microwave at HIGH 8 minutes
or until thoroughly heated, giving
dish a half-turn after 4 minutes. Remove bay leaf.   *George Darling*
Grafton, West Virginia

HOT FRUIT COMPOTE

1 (12-ounce) package pitted
  prunes
1 (6-ounce) package dried apricots
1 (20-ounce) can pineapple
  chunks, undrained
1 (11-ounce) can mandarin
  oranges, undrained
1 (21-ounce) can cherry pie filling
½ cup cooking sherry

Place prunes and apricots in a 12- x
8- x 2-inch baking dish. Combine remaining ingredients; spoon over dried
fruit. Bake, uncovered, at 350° for 1
hour. Yield: 12 servings.

Microwave Directions: Place
prunes and apricots in a 12- x 8- x
2-inch baking dish. Combine remaining ingredients; spoon over dried
fruit. Cover tightly with heavy-duty
plastic wrap; fold back a small corner
of wrap to allow steam to escape.
Microwave at HIGH 11 to 12 minutes; stir after 6 minutes.

Note: Substitute dry sherry for cooking sherry by flaming it before baking the fruit to prevent possible ignition in oven. Place in a small, long-handled saucepan; heat just until warm (do not boil). Remove from heat. Ignite with a long match; stir into fruit after flames die down.

Mrs. Robert W. Meyer
Seminole, Florida

HONEY-GLAZED APPLES

5 medium-size cooking apples
   (about 2 pounds)
2 tablespoons water
¼ cup honey
⅓ cup firmly packed brown sugar
1 tablespoon butter or margarine,
   melted
½ teaspoon vanilla extract
⅛ teaspoon ground cinnamon
Dash of ground nutmeg

Cut apples in half lengthwise; core. Place apples, cut side up, in a lightly greased 12- x 8- x 2-inch baking dish. Add water to dish. Combine remaining ingredients; spoon into apple cavities. Cover dish with aluminum foil; bake at 375° for 25 minutes or until apples are tender. Yield: 10 servings.

Microwave Directions: Cut apples in half lengthwise; core. Place apples, cut side up, in a lightly greased 12- x 8- x 2-inch baking dish. Add water to dish. Combine remaining ingredients; spoon into apple cavities. Cover tightly with heavy-duty plastic wrap; fold back a small corner of wrap to allow steam to escape. Microwave at HIGH 8 to 10 minutes, giving dish a half-turn after 5 minutes. *Gayle Wallace*
Memphis, Tennessee

Feast On Fresh Strawberries

Now is the time to enjoy fresh strawberries. For the next couple of months, the ruby red fruit is at its peak of flavor; the prices are most reasonable now, too.

For the best flavor and texture, pick strawberries of medium size with a uniform red color and fresh-looking green leaves. They'll keep for several days loosely covered in the refrigerator, but don't wash them until you're ready to use them. Always rinse them before hulling; if you take the little plug of leaves out first, water will get inside the berry and dilute the fresh flavor.

OLD-FASHIONED ROCK CREAM WITH STRAWBERRIES

1 envelope unflavored gelatin
¼ cup cold water
2 eggs, separated
⅓ cup sugar
2 cups milk, divided
2 tablespoons powdered sugar
¾ teaspoon vanilla extract
¼ teaspoon almond extract
2 cups fresh strawberries, sliced

Sprinkle gelatin over cold water in a medium saucepan; let mixture stand 1 minute.

Beat egg yolks well; add yolks, ⅓ cup sugar, and 1 cup milk to gelatin mixture, stirring until blended. Cook over low heat until mixture is hot (do not boil). Stir in remaining 1 cup milk, and cook until mixture begins to simmer. Simmer 1 minute, stirring constantly; cool. Chill until the consistency of unbeaten egg white.

Beat egg whites (at room temperature) at high speed of an electric mixer until foamy. Gradually add powdered sugar, beating until soft peaks form.

Fold egg whites and flavorings into yolk mixture. Spoon into a lightly greased 4-cup mold. Cover mixture and let chill.

Unmold onto a serving platter; arrange strawberries around mold. Yield: 8 servings.

Maureen Thomas Jones
Augusta, Georgia

STRAWBERRY DAIQUIRIS

1 (6-ounce) can frozen lemonade
   concentrate, thawed and
   undiluted
⅔ to 1 cup light rum
2 tablespoons powdered sugar
2 cups sliced fresh strawberries
1 cup frozen whipped topping
Ice cubes
Garnish: fresh mint leaves

Combine half each of the first 5 ingredients in container of an electric blender. Blend mixture 30 seconds. Gradually add enough ice cubes to bring mixture to 4-cup level. Blend until smooth. Repeat procedure with remaining half of ingredients. Garnish each serving, if desired. Yield: about 2 quarts.

Note: Strawberry Daiquiris may be prepared ahead of time and frozen. Let thaw until mixture becomes slushy (about 20 minutes). Blend 15 seconds, and serve immediately.

Anne Fowler Newell
Johnsonville, South Carolina

Tip: *It is best to store most fruit in the refrigerator. Allow melons, avocados, and pears to ripen at room temperature; then refrigerate. Berries should be sorted to remove imperfect fruit before refrigerating; then wash and hull just before serving.*

FRESH FRUIT SALAD WITH ORANGE CREAM

2 apples, cored and cut into
  wedges
2 bananas, cut into 1-inch slices
1 tablespoon lemon juice
2 cups fresh strawberries
1 fresh pineapple, peeled, cored,
  and cut into spears
1 pound seedless green grapes
Orange Cream

Sprinkle apple wedges and banana slices with lemon juice. Arrange fruit on a serving platter. Serve with Orange Cream. Yield: 12 servings.

Orange Cream

1 cup whipping cream
1 (6-ounce) can frozen orange
  juice concentrate, thawed and
  undiluted
2 tablespoons chopped pecans,
  toasted

Beat whipping cream at medium speed of an electric mixer until soft peaks form. Slowly add orange juice concentrate, and beat until firm peaks form. Spoon into a serving dish; sprinkle with pecans. Use as a dressing for fruit salad or as a fruit dip. Yield: about 2½ cups.

Kathy Ramsey
Nashville, Tennessee

Tip: *When squeezing fresh lemons, limes, or oranges for juice, first grate the rind by rubbing the washed fruit against surface of grater, taking care to remove only the outer colored portion of the rind. Wrap the rind in plastic in teaspoon portions, and freeze for future use.*

From Our Kitchen To Yours

Selecting thoughtful gifts for occasions such as Mother's Day, bridal showers, or birthdays can be baffling. But it doesn't need to be a difficult decision if you choose from the wide array of kitchen gadgets now on the market. Choose one for a fun, economical surprise, or decoratively wrap an assortment of gadgets to delight the novice as well as the gourmet cook. (You'll want to add to your own collection, too.)

In our Test Kitchens many gadgets are stored in a central location; however, each home economist keeps favorites in her work area. The versatile gadgets shown here and others, such as an egg slicer and cheese plane, are useful tools that you'll enjoy using and giving.

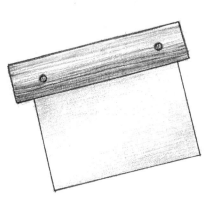

The metal scraper aids in the first steps of kneading dough and helps to lift pastry. The sharp, straight edge can cut fudge and bar cookies.

Pastry forms a shell when pressed into miniature tart pans with a tart tamper. The tool is also handy for flattening balls of cookie dough.

The pounder quickly flattens chicken breasts and other meats. The stainless-steel base can also crack ice and crush garlic.

A pastry wheel cuts smooth or fluted edges of pastry and cookie dough. The fluted wheel seals and crimps edges of turnovers.

JUNE

Summertime—long synonymous with light, healthy food—is the perfect time to establish a healthy lifestyle. That's why we present a special section entitled "On the Light Side: A Guide for Heart-Healthy Living." The recipes are low in cholesterol and fat yet high in flavor, including even pizza and Mexican food made light. And because summer cooking should be as simple as it is light, we offer menu ideas and recipes that are easy on the cook, starting with Easy Entrées.

Relax! The Entrées Are Easy

Summer cooking means simple cooking—a few ingredients, a little imagination, and lots of flavor, awakening the taste buds and evoking a sense of real living.

If you have plans for a backyard cookout, a weekend at the lake, or a beach trip with friends, these selections provide easy meals for lazy summer days.

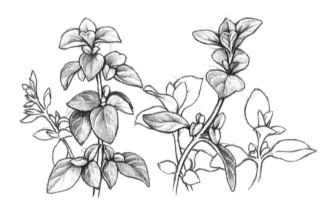

GRILLED PORK WITH SALSA

⅓ cup fresh lime juice
¼ cup soy sauce
1 teaspoon dried whole oregano
½ teaspoon dried whole thyme
1 (1-pound) pork tenderloin
Commercial salsa
Garnish: lime wedges

Combine fresh lime juice, soy sauce, oregano, and thyme in a shallow container or zip-top plastic bag. Add tenderloin, turning to coat evenly. Cover or seal, and refrigerate at least 4 hours.

Remove tenderloin from marinade. Grill, covered, 6 inches from hot coals (450°) for 25 minutes or until done, turning and basting once. (Meat in center will be light pink). To serve, thinly slice tenderloin, and arrange slices on a serving platter. Serve with salsa, and, if desired, garnish. Yield: 4 servings.

HAM-AND-PASTA SALAD

4 ounces uncooked corkscrew macaroni
2 cups cooked chopped ham
4 hard-cooked eggs, diced
¼ cup chopped celery
¼ cup chopped onion
⅓ cup commercial French dressing
6 tomatoes
Lettuce leaves

Cook macaroni according to package directions; drain. Rinse with cold water; drain.

Combine macaroni and next 5 ingredients, tossing well; chill.

Core tomatoes; cut each into 6 wedges, cutting to but not through base of tomato. Spread wedges slightly apart. Spoon pasta mixture into tomatoes. Serve on a lettuce-lined plate. Yield: 6 servings.

Diane Boysen
Martinez, Georgia

SWEET-AND-SOUR BURGERS

1 (8-ounce) can shredded sauerkraut, drained
½ cup whole-berry cranberry sauce
¼ cup chili sauce
¼ cup water
3 tablespoons brown sugar
1 egg, slightly beaten
1 (1.35-ounce) envelope dried onion soup mix
¼ cup water
1½ pounds ground beef
6 onion rolls, lightly toasted

Combine first 5 ingredients in a saucepan; bring to a boil. Reduce heat, and simmer 20 minutes, stirring occasionally.

Combine egg, soup mix, and water in a small bowl; let stand 5 minutes. Add ground beef, mixing well; shape into 6 patties. Grill patties over medium coals (425°) for 5 minutes on each side or to desired degree of doneness.

Place hamburger patties on toasted onion rolls; serve with sauce. Yield: 6 servings.

Edna H. Clyburn
Kershaw, South Carolina

SMOKED TURKEY MEDLEY

1 (15-ounce) can black beans
8 ounces smoked turkey, cut into julienne strips
1 (3-ounce) jar cocktail onions, undrained
⅓ cup chopped purple onion
2 tablespoons chopped fresh parsley
2 tablespoons olive oil
¼ teaspoon pepper

Drain beans; rinse and drain well. Combine beans and remaining ingredients, stirring gently to coat well. Cover and refrigerate 2 hours. Yield: 4 servings.

Note: Smoked turkey is available prepackaged at the meat counter.

Edith Askins
Greenville, Texas

BROCCOLI-CHICKEN SALAD

(pictured on page 115)

4 cups chopped cooked chicken
  (4 breast halves)
¼ cup sliced pimiento-stuffed
  olives
1 pound fresh broccoli, broken
  into flowerets
⅔ cup mayonnaise or salad
  dressing
¼ teaspoon curry powder
Lettuce leaves (optional)

Combine chicken, olives, and broccoli. Combine mayonnaise and curry powder, stirring well; add to chicken mixture, and toss well. Cover and chill. Serve in a lettuce-lined bowl, if desired. Yield: 6 to 8 servings.

Note: To **microwave** chicken, arrange breasts in a shallow casserole. Add 2 tablespoons water. Cover and microwave at HIGH 12 to 15 minutes or until chicken is tender, giving dish a quarter-turn at 5-minute intervals.
Mary Ruth Mason
Pearsall, Texas

GRILLED CATFISH
CAJUN-STYLE

1 teaspoon lemon-pepper
  seasoning
1 teaspoon white pepper
1 teaspoon Creole seasoning
1 teaspoon blackened fish
  seasoning
2 tablespoons lemon juice
4 catfish fillets (1⅓ pounds)
Vegetable cooking spray
Garnishes: lemon wedges, celery
  tops

Combine first 4 ingredients in a small bowl. Sprinkle lemon juice and seasoning mixture on both sides of fish.
Spray a wire fish basket with cooking spray; place fish in basket. Grill fish, covered, over medium coals (400°) for 7 to 10 minutes on each side or until fish flakes easily when tested with a fork.

Remove fish from basket; place on a serving platter. Garnish, if desired. Yield: 4 servings. *Chuck Behnke*
Peachtree City, Georgia

GRILLED TUNA STEAKS

4 (¾-inch-thick) tuna steaks
1 cup commercial Italian salad
  dressing
2 teaspoons freshly ground pepper
1 lemon, quartered

Place tuna steaks in a 12- x 8- x 2-inch dish; pour salad dressing over tuna. Cover and refrigerate 1 hour, turning once. Remove steaks from marinade; reserve marinade. Sprinkle pepper on both sides of steaks.
Grill, covered, over medium coals (425°) for 5 minutes on each side or until fish flakes easily when tested with a fork, basting occasionally with marinade. Place on a serving plate; squeeze a lemon wedge over each steak. Serve with assorted vegetables, if desired. Yield: 4 servings.

SCALLOPS AND WILD RICE

1 (6-ounce) package long-grain
  and wild rice mix
¼ cup butter or margarine,
  melted
¼ cup fresh lemon juice
½ teaspoon celery salt
1 pound fresh sea scallops,
  drained

Cook rice according to package directions. Set aside.
Combine butter, lemon juice, and celery salt in a large skillet; bring mixture to a boil. Add scallops, and cook over high heat, stirring constantly, 6 to 8 minutes, until scallops are done. Serve over cooked wild rice. Yield: 3 to 4 servings.
Nancy Clark
Columbia, South Carolina

Shortcuts to Great Meals

■ Take advantage of fresh vegetables as side dishes. Brush yellow squash, zucchini, or onion with olive oil, and grill alongside meat for 3 to 5 minutes on each side or until vegetables are tender.

■ Use herbed or flavored vinegars, such as tarragon or raspberry, and oil-and-vinegar salad dressings as quick marinades for meats and vegetables.

■ Keep sliced carrots, celery, peppers, and other vegetables on hand for snacks, salads, or side dishes. They'll keep in the refrigerator in zip-top plastic bags for two to three days.

■ Cut vegetables such as zucchini and yellow squash into fans and steam about 10 minutes.

■ Purchase deli pasta salads—or make your own—to keep on hand as a handy side dish.

■ Serve appetizers that are easy on the cook—a block of cream cheese with commercial chutney, salsa and chips, or toasted bagel chips or pita bread rounds.

■ To speed up salad making, wash, trim, and dry all ingredients as soon as you buy them; then tie all of them together in a plastic bag and refrigerate. At mealtime, just pull out the bag and make the salad.

■ For dessert, offer a medley of fruit in a cantaloupe shell or tangy frozen yogurt topped with slices of kiwifruit. Don't forget icy sorbets that you can make with your ice-cream freezer or buy commercially.

From Our Kitchen To Yours

When purchasing fish, select fresh fish with firm, elastic flesh; a moist fresh-cut appearance; and a fresh, mild aroma. Shop at a reliable store that has a good turnover of seafood. Get to know the seafood market manager, and before purchasing, ask where the fish was caught and when it came in. If you're not planning to cook it that same day, you'll want to know when it came in and if the fish was previously frozen.

Some fish sold in the unfrozen state has been flash frozen or blast frozen to maintain quality. (Within hours of being caught, the fish is flash frozen in blast freezers that circulate frigid air or blast frozen in cryogenic freezers using liquid nitrogen or carbon dioxide.)

If undecided about what kind of fish to buy, tell the manager how you plan to prepare the fish and ask for suggestions. When making your choice, pick the freshest and the best buy for the week.

When a particular fresh fish is unavailable, purchase another with similar characteristics. Substitute one of comparable oil content and with a similar texture and firmness. Lean fish has mild-flavored light flesh; however, its low percentage of fat causes the flesh to dry out easily during cooking.

You can interchange any lean light fish, but there will be subtle differences in color, flavor, and texture. The fat or oil content makes the flesh of a fat fish species darker, richer, and stronger flavored. Because the fat moistens the flesh during cooking, fat fish is particularly suitable for broiling and grilling. The textures of both fish categories can be either firm or soft and delicate. For grilling, it is easier to handle a firm-textured fish, such as grouper, swordfish, snapper, salmon, or tuna.

If you're not going directly home after purchasing fish, have the package placed in a plastic bag filled with ice. Ideally, fresh fish tastes best when promptly used. If you cannot cook it on the day of purchase, proper handling and storage are crucial. When you arrive home, remove fish from its wrapper, rinse in cold water, and pat dry with paper towels. Then repackage in wax paper and an airtight plastic bag. Place bag directly on ice in a colander set in a larger bowl.

The fish can be refrigerated overnight and cooked the following day. Some fish is shipped in a flash-frozen state; ask if it can be purchased in this condition (when planning to prepare it within two days). Place the original leakproof wrapper in the refrigerator, and the fish will thaw overnight. Once flash-frozen fish has thawed, do not refreeze.

What Is Seafood Mix?

This is low-cost fish transformed into a flavorful paste, which is then formed into the shape and texture of higher quality or higher priced seafood. Also called surimi, it is low in price and rich in protein, yet it is not the perfect substitute for fresh seafood. During processing some nutritional value is lost, and the sodium content often increases 6 to 10 times that of fresh seafood.

The advantages to surimi are that it is generally low in fat and cholesterol, fully cooked, and ready to eat. Look in the supermarket for fresh or frozen imitation crab-flavored chunk and flake seafood. Shrimp-, scallop-, and lobster-flavored surimi seafood are also available.

Fish Substitution Suggestions

(Fish from Southeastern salt waters boldfaced)

- Light-flesh, delicate-flavor lean fish: **sea bass, tilefish, grouper,** halibut, orange roughy, **redfish, flounder**
- Light-flesh, moderate-flavor lean fish: **red snapper, swordfish,** mahimahi, **shark, sea trout** (speckled trout)
- Light-flesh, firm-texture fat fish: **croaker, mullet, pompano,** and **amberjack**
- Dark-flesh, firm-texture fat fish: **king mackerel, Spanish mackerel, bluefish,** tuna

General Grilling Guidelines

- Grill fish over medium-hot coals approximately 10 minutes per inch of thickness or until the fish turns opaque and starts to flake easily when you test it with a fork.
- Cook fish steaks and fillets that are at least ¾-inch thick directly on the grill; fragile pieces can be supported by using a hinged, wire fish basket.
- Spray the grid and fish basket with vegetable cooking spray before placing it over the fire; this procedure prevents the flesh of the fish from sticking.
- Keep fish tender by marinating it 1 hour in the refrigerator before grilling or by frequently basting with melted butter or basting sauce while grilling.
- Steam fish on the grill. Place the fillets in heavy-duty aluminum foil; add your favorite seasonings, herbs, or vegetables; and cook on the grill 4 to 5 inches above the heat, approximately 15 minutes per inch of thickness.
- Pay close attention to the grill. Don't leave fish unattended and risk overcooking. Begin checking for doneness halfway through cooking time; the time will vary according to the thickness and size of the fish, the humidity, the wind, the temperature of the coals, and whether or not the grill is covered.

Do Your Heart A Favor; Adopt A Healthy Lifestyle

The Southern lifestyle, which reflects our tastes and attitudes, has evolved to include healthy living. Why? Because most of us realize that a healthy lifestyle can help prevent one of the major causes of death in America—heart disease.

We've put together a special section that focuses on cholesterol—one of the risk factors of heart disease—to help you better understand what it is, where it comes from, and how to lower it in your blood. The recipes in this section were selected for their taste appeal and low-cholesterol, low-fat content. So sit back and get ready to see how healthy living can fit into your lifestyle.

Cholesterol—What Is It?

Cholesterol is a waxy fatlike substance produced by the liver that's essential in the body. It's needed to make strong cell membranes, transmit nerve impulses, and synthesize hormones. But an excess in the blood is a culprit in the development of heart disease.

Most heart disease can be traced to atherosclerosis—the narrowing of arteries. The coronary arteries are the only way blood has to reach the heart. They are very small—about the size of an uncooked macaroni noodle. Even if only a little bit of cholesterol circulating in the blood sticks to the artery walls each day, over the years enough can build up

to cut off the flow of blood and cause a heart attack.

The Fats of Life

The liver wraps cholesterol in one of three lipoproteins—high-density lipoprotein (HDL), low-density lipoprotein (LDL), or very-low-density lipoprotein (VLDL)—so it can travel easily through the bloodstream. HDL, the "good" cholesterol, seems to protect against heart disease by removing cholesterol from artery walls and returning it to the liver where excess can be excreted.

LDL and VLDL are villains in the cholesterol/heart disease story. They keep cholesterol circulating in the blood, where excess can be deposited in the arteries. The higher the level of LDLs and VLDLs, the higher the total cholesterol and the risk of heart disease.

Say "So Long!" to Saturated Fat

Saturated fat has the greatest effect on blood-cholesterol levels; it's much more potent than dietary cholesterol. Saturated fats are generally solid at room temperature, and most come from animal foods, such as beef, lamb, pork, butter, and products made from butterfat (cheese, sour cream, and ice cream). Tropical oils (coconut oil, palm oil, and palm kernel oil) are the exception because they are highly saturated fats that come from plants.

Vegetable-oil margarine and vegetable shortening are special cases. They are cholesterol free, but the hydrogenation process that makes these products firm also makes them more saturated.

It's just about impossible to eliminate saturated fat from the diet, but it is feasible to limit it. Making changes in eating habits *gradually* instead of going cold turkey works best for most people. Choose three or four of the suggestions below to get started.

—Choose fish, poultry without skin, lean meats, and low-fat or nonfat dairy products instead of fatty meats and whole milk dairy products.

—Go a step further than drinking 2% fat milk; try 1%, ½%, or skim.

—Reduce all kinds of fat in the diet, particularly saturated fats, such as butter, lard, bacon grease, cream, shortening, and tropical oils.

—Bake, broil, boil, grill, poach, or steam foods instead of frying.

—Keep fat and oil to a minimum in cooking by using nonstick pans and vegetable cooking spray.

—Limit cholesterol-rich foods, such as egg yolks and organ meats.

—Increase vegetables, fruits, beans, and whole grains in the diet.

Meet the Monos and Polys

The American Heart Association recommends that 30% of total calories in the diet come from fat with only 10% from saturated fat. The remaining 20% of daily calories should come from monounsaturated fat and polyunsaturated fat.

The latest evidence indicates that monounsaturated fats decrease the risk of heart disease. They do this by lowering the artery-clogging, low-density lipoproteins (LDL) without affecting the high-density lipoproteins (HDL). Sources of monounsaturated fats are olive oil, olives, canola oil, peanut oil, peanuts, peanut butter, and avocados.

Not too long ago polyunsaturated fat was the favored fat for lowering cholesterol levels. But now it is playing "second fiddle" to monounsaturated fat. Although polyunsaturated fat is effective in lowering total cholesterol and LDLs, it may lower beneficial HDLs. Replacing saturated fat in the diet with polyunsaturated fat is a step in the right direction. Corn oil, safflower oil, soybean oil, and cottonseed oil are all sources of polyunsaturated fat.

The Fiber Factor

There's been a lot of interest in the role water-soluble fiber plays in lowering blood-cholesterol levels. Research has shown that people who follow a low-fat, low-cholesterol, high-fiber diet can lower blood cholesterol levels even further by eating foods high in water-soluble fiber. Oat bran is the best known water-soluble fiber but other foods, such as beans, fruits, and some vegetables, also contain water-soluble fiber. A recent study suggests that the reason cholesterol levels decrease when oat bran is added to the diet is because it takes the place of fatty foods. Whether it's the oat bran or the fact that it replaces fatty foods that lowers cholesterol, eating foods that contain water-soluble fiber isn't going to hurt, and it may help.

Eating Healthy Isn't Enough

Next to following a heart-healthy diet, regular aerobic exercise—the kind that makes your heart beat fast—is one of the best ways to lower cholesterol levels. Plus, it is a way to help reduce fatigue, keep weight down, lower blood pressure, and reduce stress levels.

Aerobic exercise improves cholesterol levels by building up protective HDLs and lowering LDLs. And it

lowers triglyceride levels (see "Triglycerides: Why Are They Important?" on page 134).

The word "exercise" conjures up pictures of marathon runners, professional football and basketball players, or Olympic hopefuls. Few of us think

in terms of taking brisk walks, weeding a garden, working around the house, dancing, or climbing stairs, yet these are all examples of moderate aerobic exercise.

How much exercise is needed to lessen the risk of heart disease? It

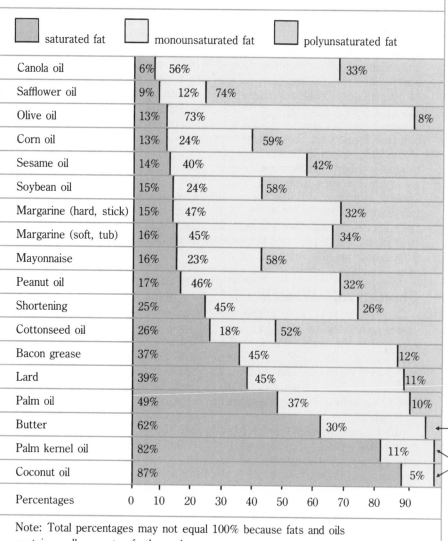

depends on age, health, and other circumstances, but most experts agree that moderate exercise done 25 to 40 minutes three to five times a week is enough to improve cholesterol levels and overall fitness.

What Else Is Important?

Smoking is more deadly than all the other risks of heart disease combined. The nicotine in cigarettes constricts the arteries, increases the heart rate, and raises the blood pressure. With all of this happening at once, the heart has no choice but to work harder and beat faster.

Even a few cigarettes a day are a threat. But there's evidence that the damage caused by smoking is not necessarily permanent. The risk of heart disease can decrease to that of a nonsmoker only a few years after a person has quit smoking.

Stress, though it's difficult to measure, is thought to be another factor contributing to heart disease. It's a part of modern life that may never go away but it *can* be managed successfully, no doubt. Simply "stopping to smell the roses along the way" isn't always enough; an organized stress-management program can be helpful, especially for people with chronic stress.

Some risk factors of heart disease, such as age, sex, and heredity, cannot be changed. A healthy lifestyle, though, is a matter of choice. Choosing to eat a low-fat, low-cholesterol, high-fiber diet; to exercise regularly; to quit smoking; and to deal positively with stress can increase the chances of living a longer, happier, healthier life.

A Fiesta Of Mexican Food

Just as Mexican food is not all tacos and beans, neither does it have to be laden with fat and calories. Many of the staples of Mexican cooking—rice, beans, corn, and other fresh vegetables—have little fat and are nutrient dense. So preparing low-fat, low-calorie Mexican recipes is a challenge that can be met by using the varied flavors and textures from south-of-the-border in unique ways. The results are delicious.

TACORITOS
(pictured on page 4)

1 cup skim milk
¼ teaspoon salt
⅛ teaspoon white pepper
1½ teaspoons chili powder
½ clove garlic, minced
2 tablespoons uncooked cream of rice cereal
¼ teaspoon ground sage
¼ teaspoon dried whole oregano
¼ teaspoon cumin
1 tablespoon minced green chile
½ pound ground chuck
½ cup diced onion
1 cup chopped tomato
1½ cups chopped lettuce
1 cup (4 ounces) shredded 40%-less-fat Cheddar cheese
6 (6-inch) flour tortillas
Vegetable cooking spray

Combine first 5 ingredients in a saucepan; bring to a boil over medium-high heat. Add cereal; cook 1 minute, stirring constantly. Pour into container of an electric blender; process until smooth. Stir in sage and next 3 ingredients; set aside.

Cook ground chuck in a small skillet over medium heat until browned, stirring to crumble meat. Drain meat in a colander, and pat dry with a paper towel.

Combine meat, onion, tomato, and lettuce in a large bowl. Add half each of shredded cheese and sauce mixture; toss gently. Spoon ½ cup meat mixture onto each tortilla; roll and place seam side up in a 13- x 9- x 2-inch baking dish coated with cooking spray. Top tortillas evenly with remaining sauce; cover with aluminum foil. Bake at 350° for 10 minutes. Uncover tortillas; sprinkle with remaining cheese, and bake an additional 5 minutes. Yield: 6 servings (259 calories each).

☐ *16.9 grams protein, 8.6 grams fat, 31 grams carbohydrate, 24 milligrams cholesterol, 440 milligrams sodium, and 225 milligrams calcium.*

VEGETABLE BURRITOS

Vegetable cooking spray
1 cup sliced onion
1 cup sliced fresh mushrooms
2 cloves garlic, minced
4 cups sliced zucchini
1½ cups thinly sliced carrots
1 cup sliced green pepper
2 cups chopped tomato
¼ cup chopped ripe olives
1 tablespoon seeded minced
  jalapeño pepper
2 (4-ounce) cans chopped green
  chiles, drained
1 teaspoon chili powder
¼ teaspoon salt
½ teaspoon dried whole oregano
½ teaspoon ground cumin
1 cup (4 ounces) shredded
  Monterey Jack cheese
1½ cups (6 ounces) shredded
  40%-less-fat Cheddar cheese
15 (6-inch) warm flour tortillas

Coat a large Dutch oven with cooking spray; place over medium-high heat until hot. Add onion, mushrooms, and garlic. Sauté until vegetables are tender and all liquid is absorbed. Add zucchini, carrot, green pepper, tomato, olives, and jalapeño pepper; sauté, stirring constantly, about 10 minutes or until vegetables are crisp-tender. Drain vegetables; add green chiles and next 6 ingredients; stir mixture well.

Spoon ⅓ cup vegetable mixture onto each tortilla, and fold edges over. Serve immediately. Yield: 15 servings (187 calories each).

Note: Tortillas may be warmed by wrapping tightly in aluminum foil; bake at 350° for about 15 minutes.

☐ *8.1 grams protein, 6.1 grams fat, 27.7 grams carbohydrate, 6 milligrams cholesterol, 306 milligrams sodium, and 180 milligrams calcium.*

Triglycerides: Why Are They Important?

One of the keys to developing a heart-healthy lifestyle is understanding what causes heart disease. It seems that where this disease is concerned, the layman's knowledge of triglycerides has generally taken a back seat to cholesterol. Triglycerides are responsible for providing the body with fuel by releasing fatty acids into the bloodstream and storing excess calories. A high triglyceride level generally goes along with the high LDL (low-density lipoprotein) and low HDL (high-density lipoprotein) levels that increase the risk of heart disease.

Blood triglyceride levels vary from hour to hour depending on the kind and amount of food eaten; therefore, blood tests should only be done after an overnight fast to assure accuracy. A normal triglyceride level ranges from 50 to 250 mg/dl (milligrams per deciliter), depending on age and sex. Levels tend to increase with age, along with cholesterol levels, and women tend to have higher levels than men.

People who have levels between 250 and 500 mg/dl are twice as likely to be at risk for heart disease as those whose levels fall within the normal range. This is especially true if they have other risk factors, including cigarette smoking, a family history of heart disease, or high blood pressure.

If your triglyceride level is above normal, check with your physician. Then make some lifestyle changes. Some of the same changes for lowering cholesterol, beginning on page 131, also help lower triglyceride levels. In many cases, achieving an ideal body weight will dramatically decrease triglyceride levels.

Because exercise burns triglycerides for energy, regular exercise helps lower triglyceride levels while increasing the "good" HDL cholesterol. Alcohol should be avoided with high triglyceride levels because it stimulates the liver's production of VLDL (very-low-density lipoproteins), the fat that transports triglycerides in the bloodstream.

Fiber For Your Arteries

Did you get caught up in the oat craze? A lot of folks did. What advertisers didn't tell us is that oat products aren't the only foods that contain the water-soluble fiber responsible for lowering cholesterol levels. Beans, peas, brown rice, barley, carrots, corn, sweet potatoes, apples, and citrus fruits are also good sources of water-soluble fiber.

Kidney beans and black-eyed peas top the list of vegetables that are high in water-soluble fiber. Whether dried, frozen, or canned, they're equally beneficial. They are also good sources of protein and minerals and are low-fat meat substitutes.

There are other benefits of oat bran besides the cholesterol-fighting properties (about which there has been some dispute). It provides some insoluble fiber, the kind that helps prevent cancer, and contains minerals, B vitamins, and complex carbohydrates. To ensure that you are getting the variety of fiber needed for a balanced diet, alternate oats with other grains, such as barley, wheat, bulgur, and rice.

CINNAMON-OAT BREAD

1⅔ cups bread flour
1 cup regular oats, uncooked
½ cup unprocessed oat bran
1½ teaspoons salt
3 packages dry yeast
1¾ cups water
½ cup honey
½ cup vegetable oil
½ cup egg substitute
2½ cups whole wheat flour
1¾ cups bread flour, divided
Butter-flavored vegetable cooking
  spray
1 tablespoon sugar
2 teaspoons ground cinnamon

Combine first 5 ingredients in a large mixing bowl. Combine water, honey, and oil in a medium saucepan; heat to 120° to 130°.

Gradually add liquid mixture and egg substitute to flour mixture; beat at low speed of an electric mixer until blended. Beat an additional 3 minutes at medium speed. Gradually stir in wheat flour and ¼ cup bread flour to form a soft dough.

Turn dough out onto a lightly floured surface. Knead until smooth and elastic (about 10 minutes); add enough of remaining 1½ cups bread flour to prevent dough from sticking to hands. Place dough in a large bowl coated with cooking spray, turning to coat top. Cover and let rise in a warm place (85°), free from drafts, 1 hour or until doubled in bulk.

Punch dough down; let rest 15 minutes. Divide dough in half. Roll each portion to a 15- x 7-inch rectangle on a lightly floured surface. Coat dough with butter-flavored cooking spray. Combine sugar and cinnamon; sprinkle half of spice mixture over each rectangle.

Roll up dough, jellyroll fashion, starting with narrow end. Place seam side down in a 9- x 5- x 3-inch loaf-pan coated with cooking spray. Let dough rise in a warm place, free from drafts, 30 minutes or until loaves are doubled in bulk.

Bake at 375° for 35 minutes or until loaves sound hollow when tapped. (Cover loaves loosely with aluminum foil for the last 20 minutes of baking to prevent overbrowning, if necessary.) Remove from pans immediately; cool. Yield: 2 loaves (134 calories per ½-inch slice).

☐ *3.8 grams protein, 3.6 grams fat, 21.8 grams carbohydrate, 0 milligrams cholesterol, 104 milligrams sodium, and 9 milligrams calcium.*

BARLEY-BROCCOLI SALAD

1 cup water
⅛ teaspoon salt
½ cup barley
1 cup coarsely chopped fresh
  broccoli
⅓ cup commercial oil-free Italian
  salad dressing
1¼ cups chopped tomato
¼ cup shredded carrot
2 tablespoons diced onion
2 tablespoons diced green pepper
1 (2-ounce) jar diced pimiento,
  drained
2 cups shredded lettuce

Bring water and salt to a boil in a medium saucepan; add barley. Cover, reduce heat, and simmer 15 minutes or until barley is tender and water is absorbed.

Combine broccoli and dressing. Add barley, tomato, and next 4 ingredients; toss gently. Cover and chill at least 30 minutes. Serve on lettuce. Yield: 4 servings (128 calories per ¾ cup salad with ½ cup lettuce).

☐ *3.8 grams protein, 0.6 gram fat, 28.4 grams carbohydrate, 0 milligrams cholesterol, 308 milligrams sodium, and 31 milligrams calcium.*

SPICY-HOT
BLACK-EYED PEAS

Vegetable cooking spray
½ cup chopped onion
½ cup chopped green pepper
1 (15.8-ounce) can black-eyed
  peas, undrained
1 (14.5-ounce) can no-salt-added
  stewed tomatoes, undrained
1 teaspoon dry mustard
½ teaspoon chili powder
⅛ teaspoon red pepper
½ teaspoon pepper
1 tablespoon low-sodium soy
  sauce
1 teaspoon liquid smoke
1 tablespoon minced fresh parsley

Coat a large, nonstick skillet with cooking spray; place skillet over medium heat until hot. Add onion and green pepper; sauté until vegetables are crisp-tender. Add black-eyed peas and next 7 ingredients; bring to a boil. Reduce heat; simmer 20 minutes, stirring often. Transfer to a serving dish; sprinkle with parsley. Yield: 5 servings (108 calories per ½-cup serving).

☐ *5.6 grams protein, 0.9 gram fat, 20.1 grams carbohydrate, 0 milligrams cholesterol, 364 milligrams sodium, and 51 milligrams calcium.*
Rublelene Singleton
Scotts Hill, Tennessee

Tip: *When grains, such as rice, are served together with dried beans or peas, the two dishes complement each other, providing a good source of high quality protein.*

KIDNEY BEAN CASSEROLE

Vegetable cooking spray
½ cup chopped onion
¼ cup chopped green pepper
¼ cup chopped celery
2 large cloves garlic, minced
1 (15.5-ounce) can kidney beans,
  drained and rinsed
1 cup peeled and chopped tomato
¼ cup water
½ teaspoon chili powder
¼ teaspoon pepper
3 dashes of hot sauce
2 cups hot cooked rice (cooked
  without salt or fat)
¼ cup (1 ounce) shredded
  40%-less-fat sharp Cheddar
  cheese

Coat a large, nonstick skillet with cooking spray; place over medium-high heat until hot. Add onion, green pepper, celery, and garlic; sauté until tender. Stir in beans and next 5 ingredients. Cover and cook 8 to 10 minutes, stirring often.

Place hot rice in a 1-quart casserole; spoon bean mixture over rice. Sprinkle with cheese; cover and let stand 5 minutes. Yield: 4 servings (183 calories per ½-cup serving).

□ *6.4 grams protein, 0.7 gram fat, 38 grams carbohydrate, 0 milligrams cholesterol, 256 milligrams sodium, and 42 milligrams calcium.*

BROWN RICE PILAF

1 chicken-flavored bouillon cube
1¼ cups boiling water
½ cup uncooked brown rice
½ cup chopped onion
1 (2.5-ounce) jar sliced
  mushrooms, drained
¼ teaspoon salt
¼ teaspoon pepper
⅛ teaspoon dried whole thyme
½ cup thinly sliced celery

Combine bouillon cube and water in a 1-quart casserole; stir until bouillon dissolves. Add remaining ingredients except celery; stir well. Cover and bake at 350° for 1 hour and 10 minutes. Stir in sliced celery; cover and bake an additional 10 minutes. Yield: 5 servings (79 calories per ½-cup serving).

□ *1.9 grams protein, 0.6 gram fat, 16.8 grams carbohydrate, 0 milligrams cholesterol, 312 milligrams sodium, and 17 milligrams calcium.*
Eleanor K. Brandt
Arlington, Texas

Homegrown Sprouts

Every bean, pea, and seed has a rich store of nutrients that is released when it sprouts. Protein and vitamins actually increase in the sprouting process, while carbohydrates and fats from the original food are used up. The amount of fiber and minerals in sprouts remains the same as the original bean, pea, or seed. Yet sprouts are lower in calories and easier to digest than their originator.

Besides being nutritious, sprouts are also versatile. In fact, you can add a new dimension to menus with homegrown sprouts. Different sprouts have different flavors and textures and add flavor, crunch, and nutrition to salads, sandwiches, stir-fries, and casseroles. The three different types of sprouts used in Sprout Salad make it a tasty and unique combination. All three types of sprouts—alfalfa, mung bean, and lentil—can be grown at home.

STIR-FRIED VEGETABLES

2 teaspoons cornstarch
½ teaspoon chicken-flavored
  bouillon granules
½ cup water
2 tablespoons dry sherry
1 tablespoon reduced-sodium
  soy sauce
1 teaspoon sesame oil
1 clove garlic, minced
¼ teaspoon crushed red
  pepper
1 teaspoon peeled, grated
  gingerroot
2½ cups sliced squash
1 cup sliced green onions
1 cup sweet red pepper
  strips
1 cup bean sprouts
1 (6-ounce) package frozen
  snow pea pods, thawed

Combine cornstarch, bouillon granules, water, sherry, and soy sauce in a small bowl. Add oil to wok, and heat at medium high (325°) for 1 minute. Add garlic, red pepper, and ginger; stir-fry 1 minute. Add squash, green onions, and red pepper strips. Stir-fry 3 minutes or until crisp-tender. Add bean sprouts and snow peas; stir-fry 2 minutes.

Pour cornstarch mixture over vegetables; stir-fry until thickened. Serve immediately. Yield: 8 servings (38 calories per ½-cup serving).

□ *2 grams protein, 0.9 gram fat, 6.8 grams carbohydrate, 0 milligrams cholesterol, 124 milligrams sodium, and 29 milligrams calcium.*

SPROUT SALAD

1 cup cherry tomatoes,
  halved
¾ cup unpeeled, diced
  cucumber
¼ cup sliced green onions
¼ cup diced celery
¼ cup reduced-calorie Italian
  dressing
½ cup alfalfa sprouts
½ cup lentil sprouts
½ cup bean sprouts

Combine tomatoes, cucumber, green onions, and celery in a medium bowl; drizzle with dressing, and toss to coat. Cover and chill 15 minutes.

Line individual serving plates with equal portions of alfalfa, lentil, and bean sprouts. Spoon ½ cup vegetable mixture on each serving of sprouts. Yield: 4 servings (30 calories per ½ cup vegetable mixture and 2 tablespoons of each sprout).

☐ *2 grams protein, 0.3 gram fat, 6.1 grams carbohydrate, 0 milligrams cholesterol, 203 milligrams sodium, and 18 milligrams calcium.*

Betty S. Wyatt
Pembroke Pines, Florida

Growing Your Own Sprouts

A small amount of beans, peas, or seeds will greatly expand when they are sprouted. Depending on how large they are grown, sprouts may increase in volume 2 to 10 times. The amount of time it takes to grow sprouts can range from a day to a week. In general, figure on three to five days for sprouting to take place. Follow these steps for sprouting.

■ Measure out about ¼ cup beans, peas, or seeds (alfalfa, barley, for example); rinse thoroughly in a strainer. For small seeds, start with 2 tablespoons; for larger beans, use ½ cup.

■ Place rinsed beans in a clean quart-size jar. Cover opening with cheesecloth or a nylon stocking, and secure with a string, rubberband, or metal ring of a canning jar. Keep cover on jar throughout sprouting process.

Fill jar with lukewarm water, and let beans soak at room temperature overnight.

■ The next day, pour off the water; then rinse, and drain sprouts again.

■ Place the jar of sprouts, tilted, in a warm, dark place. This lets moisture out and oxygen in.

■ During this period, rinse and drain the sprouts several times each day.

■ When sprouts have reached their desired length (at least as long as the original bean, pea, or seed), place the jar in a sunny spot so that the sprouts will turn green.

■ Give sprouts a final rinsing and draining before storing them in the refrigerator. Sprouts will keep up to two weeks in the refrigerator if tightly sealed in a plastic bag or jar.

A Heart-Healthy Feast For Guests

Whether it's a backyard cookout or an elegant dinner party, heart-healthy eating can fit your entertaining style.

**Watermelon-Berry Slush
Ranch-Style Dip
with fresh vegetables
Grilled Flank Steak
With Sweet Peppers
Roasted New Potatoes
Asparagus Vinaigrette
Quick Crouton Bread
Frozen Fresh Peach Yogurt**

WATERMELON-BERRY SLUSH
(pictured on page 113)

4 cups cubed, seeded watermelon
1 (10-ounce) package frozen
  raspberries, unthawed
1 (12-ounce) bottle sparkling
  mineral water

Place a single layer of watermelon in a shallow pan; freeze until firm. Remove watermelon from freezer, and let stand 5 minutes. Drop watermelon through food chute of a food processor or blender with the motor running. Add frozen chunks of raspberries alternately with mineral water, processing until smooth. Yield: 5½ cups (31 calories per ½-cup serving).

☐ *0.6 gram protein, 0.4 gram fat, 7.1 grams carbohydrate, 0 milligrams cholesterol, 1 milligram sodium, and 15 milligrams calcium.*

Eileen Wehling
Austin, Texas

ON THE
LIGHT SIDE

RANCH-STYLE DIP
(pictured on page 113)

1 cup low-fat cottage cheese
2 tablespoons skim milk
½ cup plain low-fat yogurt
1 tablespoon lemon juice
½ tablespoon chopped fresh
   parsley
⅛ teaspoon onion powder
⅛ teaspoon garlic powder

Position knife blade in food processor bowl; add cottage cheese and milk. Process about 45 seconds or until smooth. Fold in yogurt and remaining ingredients. Cover and chill thoroughly. Serve with assorted fresh vegetables. Yield: 1½ cups (10 calories per tablespoon).

☐ *1.5 grams protein, 0.2 gram fat, 0.7 gram carbohydrate, 1 milligram cholesterol, 42 milligrams sodium, and 16 milligrams calcium.*
Patsy Bell Hobson
Liberty, Missouri

GRILLED FLANK STEAK WITH SWEET PEPPERS
(pictured on page 113)

2 (1-pound) flank steaks
2 tablespoons dry red wine
1 tablespoon low-sodium
   Worcestershire sauce
1 tablespoon red wine vinegar
1 tablespoon prepared horseradish
1 tablespoon tomato paste
½ teaspoon freshly ground pepper
2 teaspoons fresh thyme or ½
   teaspoon dried whole thyme
2 cloves garlic, minced
2 large yellow or red peppers,
   seeded and sliced

Trim all visible fat from steaks; score on both sides in 1½-inch squares, and place in a shallow dish. Combine red wine and next 7 ingredients; pour over steaks, and turn to coat. Cover; marinate in refrigerator at least 8 hours, turning occasionally.

Remove steaks from marinade. Grill, covered, over hot coals 7 minutes on each side or to desired degree of doneness. Add peppers to grill during last 7 minutes of cooking. To serve, cut steaks diagonally across grain into thin slices. Yield: 8 servings (231 calories per 3 ounces steak with ⅓ pepper).

☐ *22.7 grams protein, 13.3 grams fat, 4.1 grams carbohydrate, 61 milligrams cholesterol, 85 milligrams sodium, and 14 milligrams calcium.*
Jackie Broome
Greenville, South Carolina

ROASTED NEW POTATOES
(pictured on page 113)

24 small new potatoes (about 2⅔
   pounds)
Olive oil-flavored vegetable
   cooking spray
¼ cup Italian-seasoned
   breadcrumbs
¼ cup freshly grated Parmesan
   cheese
¾ teaspoon paprika

Cook unpeeled potatoes in boiling water 15 minutes; drain and cool slightly. Quarter potatoes; coat cut sides with cooking spray. Combine breadcrumbs and remaining ingredients; dredge cut sides of potatoes in breadcrumb mixture. Arrange in a single layer on a baking sheet coated with cooking spray. Bake at 450° for 15 minutes. Yield: 8 servings. (143 calories per 12 potato quarters).

☐ *4.9 grams protein, 1.7 grams fat, 27.8 grams carbohydrate, 2 milligrams cholesterol, 157 milligrams sodium, and 58 milligrams calcium.*

ASPARAGUS VINAIGRETTE
(pictured on page 113)

48 fresh asparagus spears (about
   22 ounces)
¼ cup rice vinegar
2 tablespoons water
2 tablespoons lemon juice
2 tablespoons olive oil
½ teaspoon dry mustard
½ teaspoon grated lemon rind
1 (2-ounce) jar diced pimiento,
   drained
¼ teaspoon white pepper
1 head Boston lettuce

Snap off tough ends of asparagus. Remove scales with vegetable peeler or knife, if desired. Cook asparagus, covered, in a small amount of boiling water 6 to 8 minutes or until crisp-tender; drain. Place asparagus in a shallow dish.

Combine vinegar and next 7 ingredients in a jar; cover tightly, and shake vigorously. Pour over asparagus; cover and chill. Serve on lettuce leaves. Yield: 8 servings (54 calories per serving).

☐ *2.7 grams protein, 3.7 grams fat, 4.6 grams carbohydrate, 0 milligrams cholesterol, 4 milligrams sodium, and 19 milligrams calcium.*
Sandra G. Behrens
La Grange, Texas

QUICK CROUTON BREAD
(pictured on page 113)

½ (1-pound) loaf French bread
Butter-flavored vegetable cooking
   spray
½ teaspoon Italian herb blend
½ teaspoon garlic powder

Slice bread into 4 equal pieces; half each piece. Coat cut sides with cooking spray. Combine Italian herb blend and garlic powder; sprinkle evenly over bread. Bake at 250° for 30 minutes. Yield: 8 servings (85 calories per serving).

☐ *2.6 grams protein, 0.8 gram fat, 15.9 grams carbohydrate, 1 milligram cholesterol, 165 milligrams sodium, and 15 milligrams calcium.*

Bonnie Dockery
Cedar Hill, Texas

FROZEN FRESH PEACH YOGURT
(pictured on page 113)

¼ cup sugar
2 cups mashed ripe peaches (about 4)
1 cup sugar
2 envelopes unflavored gelatin
Dash of salt
2 cups skim milk
5 cups plain low-fat yogurt
1 tablespoon vanilla extract

Sprinkle ¼ cup sugar over peaches; let stand 15 minutes. Combine 1 cup sugar, gelatin, and salt in a saucepan; add milk, and let stand 1 minute. Cook over low heat, stirring constantly, 5 minutes or until gelatin and sugar dissolve; cool. Stir in yogurt, peaches, and vanilla; chill.

Pour mixture into freezer can of a 1-gallon hand-turned or electric freezer; freeze according to manufacturer's instructions. Serve immediately, or ripen 1 hour. Yield: 12½ cups (84 calories per ½ cup).

☐ *3.6 grams protein, 0.7 gram fat, 15.9 grams carbohydrate, 3 milligrams cholesterol, 54 milligrams sodium, and 108 milligrams calcium.*

Pizza Goes Light

Turkey-Vegetable Pizza boasts much less fat and fewer calories than regular pizza but still has an authentic Italian flavor. It's made with ground turkey, which is lower in fat, sodium, and calories than many other commonly used toppings. Ground turkey can be found in the frozen foods section of the grocery store.

Because the crust recipe makes enough for two pizzas, there's one to freeze to give you a headstart on making this delicious family pleaser at another time.

TURKEY-VEGETABLE PIZZA
(pictured on page 149)

1 (4-ounce) can no-salt-added tomato sauce
1 (6-ounce) can tomato paste
2 tablespoons grated Parmesan cheese
¾ teaspoon dried whole Italian seasoning
½ teaspoon dried whole basil
¼ teaspoon garlic powder
1 teaspoon sugar
⅛ teaspoon ground pepper
½ pound raw ground turkey
Dash of red pepper
¼ teaspoon fennel seeds, crushed
Special Pizza Crust
1 (4-ounce) can sliced mushrooms, drained
¼ cup thinly sliced onion
1 green pepper, cut into strips
1 cup thinly sliced fresh broccoli
1 cup (4 ounces) shredded part-skim mozzarella cheese

Combine first 8 ingredients in a bowl; stir well. Let stand 1 hour.

Sauté ground turkey, red pepper, and fennel seeds in a nonstick skillet, stirring to crumble meat; drain.

Spread sauce over Special Pizza Crust. Sprinkle turkey mixture over sauce. Top with mushrooms, onion, green pepper, and broccoli.

Bake at 425° for 15 minutes. Top with cheese; bake 5 minutes. Yield: 8 slices (249 calories per slice).

☐ *14.9 grams protein, 7.2 grams fat, 32.3 grams carbohydrate, 9 milligrams cholesterol, 208 milligrams sodium, and 153 milligrams calcium.*

Special Pizza Crust

1 package dry yeast
¼ cup warm water
1 cup whole wheat flour
1 cup all-purpose flour
¼ teaspoon salt
1 tablespoon olive oil
½ to ⅔ cup warm water
Vegetable cooking spray

Dissolve yeast in ¼ cup warm water in a small bowl; let stand 5 minutes. Combine flours and salt in a large bowl; stir in yeast mixture and oil. Add enough warm water to make a moderately stiff dough; stir well. Cover and let stand 15 minutes.

Turn dough out onto a lightly floured surface. Knead 5 to 8 times; divide dough in half.

Roll each half to a 12-inch circle; place each on a 12-inch pizza pan coated with vegetable cooking spray. Bake at 425° for 5 minutes. Freeze 1 crust for later use. Yield: 2 (12-inch) pizza crusts.

QUICK!

These Eggs Can't Be Beat

Need a speedy breakfast before scurrying out the door for a busy day? It doesn't take long to scramble or fry an egg, but you'll be surprised that you can do even more with eggs in less than 30 minutes.

CHEESY BREAKFAST SANDWICHES

6 slices Canadian bacon
1 (11-ounce) can Cheddar cheese soup, undiluted
2 tablespoons milk
3 tablespoons dry sherry
6 eggs
3 English muffins, split and toasted
Paprika

Cook bacon over medium heat 3 minutes on each side. Set aside.

Combine soup and milk in a small saucepan; cook over medium heat, stirring until blended. Stir in sherry; reduce heat to low.

Lightly grease a deep skillet. Pour water to a depth of 2 inches in skillet. Bring water to a boil; reduce heat, and maintain at a light simmer. Break eggs, one at a time, into a saucer. Slip eggs, one at a time, into water, holding saucer as close as possible to surface of water. Simmer 3 to 5 minutes or to desired degree of doneness. Remove eggs with a slotted spoon. Trim edges of eggs, if desired.

Place a slice of Canadian bacon on each toasted muffin half; top with a poached egg, and cover with cheese sauce. Sprinkle with paprika. Yield: 6 servings. *Eileen R. MaCutchan Largo, Florida*

BREAKFAST PIZZA

1 (8-ounce) can refrigerated crescent dinner rolls
6 eggs, beaten
½ pound bacon, cooked and crumbled
1 cup (4 ounces) shredded Cheddar cheese
1 (4-ounce) can sliced mushrooms, drained

Spread rolls into a lightly greased 12-inch pizza pan; firmly press perforations to seal.

Combine eggs, bacon, cheese, and mushrooms in a medium bowl; pour over prepared crust. Bake at 375° for 12 to 15 minutes. Yield: 6 servings. *Mrs. C. L. Goldsmith Crewe, Virginia*

SPICY EGG ROLL-UPS

1 pound chorizo or bulk pork sausage
6 eggs, lightly beaten
⅓ cup milk
1 tablespoon butter or margarine
1 (12-ounce) package flour tortillas
2 cups (8 ounces) shredded Cheddar cheese
Picante sauce, sour cream, and guacamole

Cook sausage until browned, stirring to crumble; drain. Set aside.

Combine eggs and milk; mix well. Melt butter in a large nonstick skillet over medium heat. Pour in egg mixture, and cook, without stirring, until mixture begins to set on bottom. Draw a spatula across bottom of pan to form large curds. Continue until eggs are thickened, but still moist; do not stir constantly. Remove skillet from heat.

Divide tortillas into 2 stacks. Place stacks side by side between 2 slightly dampened paper towels. Microwave at HIGH 30 to 45 seconds or until tortillas are warm.

Layer sausage, scrambled eggs, and shredded Cheddar cheese on each tortilla; roll up. Serve immediately with picante sauce, sour cream, and guacamole. Yield: 6 servings. *Bridget Shinn Cypress, Texas*

Burstin' With Blueberries

Fresh blueberries, sweetened whipped cream, tender cake—these foods team up to make Blueberry-Sour Cream Cake, a summer dessert too tempting to resist. Its unique presentation makes it a showstopper.

BLUEBERRY-SOUR CREAM CAKE

½ cup butter or margarine, softened
½ cup sugar
1 egg
1½ cups all-purpose flour
1½ teaspoons baking powder
1 teaspoon vanilla extract
4 cups fresh blueberries
2 (8-ounce) cartons sour cream
2 egg yolks
½ cup sugar
1 teaspoon vanilla extract
1½ cups whipping cream
¼ cup sifted powdered sugar
Garnish: fresh blueberries

Cream butter; gradually add ½ cup sugar, beating well at medium speed of an electric mixer. Add egg, beating well. Combine flour and baking powder; add to creamed mixture, and mix just until blended. Stir in 1 teaspoon vanilla. Spread into a greased 9-inch springform pan. Sprinkle with 4 cups blueberries.

Combine sour cream and next 3 ingredients; pour over blueberries.

Bake at 350° for 1 hour or until edges are lightly browned. Cool on a wire rack; cover and chill.

To serve remove cake from pan, and place on a serving plate. Beat whipping cream until foamy; gradually add powdered sugar, beating until soft peaks form. Spoon half of whipped cream over top of cake. Spoon remaining cream into a decorating bag with metal tip No. 2110. Pipe a border around top. Garnish, if desired. Yield: 8 servings.

Margaret Ajac
Raleigh, North Carolina

MICROWAVE COOKERY

Poaching Imparts Flavor

Poaching fruit in flavorful liquids enhances its naturally good taste. Plums poached in apple juice, port, and lime juice fare well as an accompaniment for chicken and pork. Or you can serve plums and potent juices over ice cream for dessert. Poaching in the microwave is a natural because it preserves nutrients and maintains moisture.

It's important to use ripened fruit. Unripened fruit may soften during cooking but will lack the nice, rich fruit flavor. Let fruit ripen at room temperature.

Test the ripeness of pears by pressing at stem ends; they should yield to gentle pressure. Pears ripen from the inside out, so don't wait until the surface is completely soft; by that time, the center may be brown and mealy.

Serve whole poached pears and apples standing upright in individual dessert dishes for a regal presentation. But if the fruit is mistakenly overcooked, it will not hold its shape. In this case, stand the fruit in a mound of yogurt or whipped cream.

POACHED PEARS WITH DARK CHOCOLATE SAUCE

½ cup water
¼ cup brandy
¼ cup sugar
1 tablespoon grated orange rind
2 tablespoons grated fresh gingerroot
4 whole black peppercorns
4 firm ripe pears
⅓ cup lemon juice
2 (1-ounce) squares semisweet chocolate
2 tablespoons whipping cream
1 tablespoon light corn syrup
1 tablespoon Grand Marnier or brandy
½ teaspoon vanilla extract

Combine first 6 ingredients in a 2-quart casserole. Microwave at HIGH 1 to 2 minutes or until sugar dissolves. Peel pears, and core just from the bottom, cutting to, but not through, the stem end. Baste pears with lemon juice.

Place pears on their sides in brandy mixture in casserole. Cover tightly with heavy-duty plastic wrap; fold back a small edge of wrap to allow steam to escape. Microwave at HIGH 4 minutes. Uncover, baste pears with brandy mixture, and turn them over. Cover and microwave at HIGH 3 to 5 minutes or until tender. (A sharp knife should pierce the fruit as it would room-temperature butter, yet fruit should retain its shape.) Let pears cool in liquid, turning and basting once. Place pears in individual serving dishes.

Place chocolate in a 1-quart glass bowl. Microwave at MEDIUM (50% power) 2 to 3 minutes or until melted, stirring every minute. Cool slightly. Add whipping cream, corn syrup, Grand Marnier, and vanilla; stir until smooth. Spoon chocolate sauce over pears. Yield: 4 servings.

POACHED PLUMS

½ cup sugar
¼ cup apple juice
¼ cup port
2 teaspoons lime juice
1½ pounds ripe plums, pitted and quartered
Freshly grated nutmeg (optional)

Combine first 4 ingredients in a 2-quart baking dish; stir well. Add plums. Cover tightly with heavy-duty plastic wrap; fold back a small edge of wrap to allow steam to escape. Microwave at HIGH 2 to 3 minutes or just until tender, stirring once. (Do not overcook or plums will lose their shape.)

Serve plums warm with roasted meat, or let cool in liquid, stirring once, and serve over ice cream or yogurt. Sprinkle with freshly grated nutmeg, if desired. Yield: 6 servings.

SPICY POACHED APPLES

4 large cooking apples
1 orange, quartered
1 cup cranberry juice cocktail
¼ cup sugar
2 (3-inch) sticks cinnamon
8 whole cloves

Cut a ¼-inch slice from the bottom of each apple. Peel apples, leaving a 1-inch border of peel at stem end. Core apples just from the bottom, cutting to, but not through, the stem end. Set aside.

Combine orange quarters and remaining ingredients in a shallow 2-quart casserole; stir well. Place apples in juice mixture. Cover tightly with heavy-duty plastic wrap; fold back a small edge of wrap to allow steam to escape. Microwave at HIGH 3 minutes. Uncover and turn apples over; cover and microwave at HIGH an additional 4½ to 5 minutes or until apples are tender but still hold their shape. Turn apples again; let cool in liquid. Place apples in individual serving dishes; spoon liquid over each. Yield: 4 servings.

Picture Perfect, From Garden To Table

A consummate hostess, Chip Schwab enjoys herself most when she's entertaining friends, sharing the secret of a really good recipe, or tending the vegetable and flower gardens around her refurbished Valle Crucis, North Carolina, homestead and inn.

Try Chip's brunch menu, served one course at a time. It's delicious, easy, and sure to bring compliments. The menu serves eight.

No-Crust Spinach Quiche
Sour Cream Pancakes
With Fruit Topping
Brunch Pears
With Blue Cheese Sauce
Tea Punch

NO-CRUST SPINACH QUICHE

¾ cup chopped green pepper
¾ cup chopped onion
1½ cups sliced mushrooms
1½ cups sliced zucchini
1½ teaspoons minced garlic
3 tablespoons vegetable oil
5 eggs
1 (16-ounce) carton ricotta cheese
¾ teaspoon salt
¼ teaspoon freshly ground pepper
1½ teaspoons chopped fresh
   thyme
1 tablespoon chopped fresh
   parsley
1 (10-ounce) package frozen
   chopped spinach, thawed and
   well drained
1 (7-ounce) package feta cheese
Garnishes: hard-cooked egg
   slices, paprika, yellow cherry
   tomatoes

Sauté first 5 ingredients in vegetable oil until crisp-tender. Drain and cool.

Combine eggs and ricotta cheese; beat until blended. Add sautéed vegetables, salt, and next 5 ingredients, stirring until blended.

Pour mixture into a lightly greased 10-inch deep-dish quiche pan with removable bottom or a 10-inch springform pan. Bake at 350° for 1 hour or until set. Let stand 10 minutes before cutting. Garnish, if desired. Yield: one 10-inch quiche.

Note: For best results, drain cooked spinach, cover with paper towels, and squeeze out additional moisture.

SOUR CREAM PANCAKES WITH FRUIT TOPPING

3 eggs, separated
¾ cup skim milk
¾ cup sour cream
1 cup plus 2 tablespoons
   all-purpose flour
1½ teaspoons baking powder
1½ tablespoons sugar
Dash of salt
¾ cup butter, melted
Strawberry Topping
Garnishes: sour cream, fresh mint
   sprigs

Combine egg yolks, milk, and sour cream; stir well. Set mixture aside. Combine flour, baking powder, sugar, and salt; gradually add to sour cream mixture, stirring until smooth. Stir in melted butter.

Beat egg whites (at room temperature) at high speed of an electric mixer until stiff peaks form. Gently fold egg whites into batter.

For each pancake pour about ¼ cup batter onto a hot, lightly greased griddle. Turn pancakes when tops are covered with bubbles and edges look cooked. Serve with warm Strawberry Topping. Garnish, if desired. Yield: 18 pancakes.

Strawberry Topping

2 cups sliced fresh strawberries
¼ cup red currant jelly

Combine strawberries and jelly in a medium saucepan; cook over low heat about 5 minutes, stirring often. Yield: 1¾ cups.

BRUNCH PEARS WITH BLUE CHEESE SAUCE

4 pears
4 cups water
1 tablespoon sugar
1 tablespoon lemon juice
¼ cup white wine
1½ tablespoons butter, softened
8 slices thin white bread
Blue Cheese Sauce
Garnishes: edible flowers, fresh
   chive stems

Peel and core pears; cut in half lengthwise. Place in a Dutch oven, and cover with 4 cups water. Add sugar, lemon juice, and wine; bring mixture to a boil. Cover, reduce heat, and simmer 12 to 15 minutes or until pears are tender. Drain pear halves, and refrigerate until cool.

Spread butter on both sides of bread; cook on a hot griddle 2 to 3 minutes on each side or until bread is golden brown. Place one slice of grilled bread on each plate. Arrange pear half, cut side down, on each slice of bread. Pour Blue Cheese Sauce over pears. Garnish, making floral pattern, if desired. Yield: 8 servings.

Blue Cheese Sauce

2 tablespoons butter or margarine
2 tablespoons all-purpose flour
1⅓ cups half-and-half
1 (4-ounce) package blue cheese,
   crumbled

Melt butter in a heavy saucepan over low heat; add flour, stirring until smooth. Cook 1 minute, stirring constantly. Gradually add half-and-half; cook over medium heat, stirring constantly, until thickened and bubbly. Add blue cheese, and continue cooking over low heat, stirring constantly, until cheese melts. Yield: 1⅔ cups.

TEA PUNCH

2 cups apple juice
6 regular-size tea bags
4 cups apple juice, chilled
3 cups unsweetened pineapple
  juice, chilled
Garnishes: orange slices, lemon
  slices, fresh mint sprigs

Bring 2 cups apple juice to a boil; pour over tea bags, and let stand 5 minutes. Remove tea bags. Stir in 4 cups apple juice and pineapple juice; chill. Garnish with orange, lemon, and mint, if desired. Yield: 9 cups.

A Taste Of English Peas In A Salad

If you usually savor the delicate sweetness of fresh English peas in a hot side dish, try something different. These recipes feature peas in chilled salads.

When selecting fresh English peas to be used in side dishes or salads, choose large, bright green pods that are plump and snap easily. Use the peas as soon as possible. If storage is necessary, place the unshelled peas in the refrigerator.

ENGLISH PEA SALAD

1½ pounds fresh English peas
  (1½ cups shelled)
1 cup (4 ounces) sharp Cheddar
  cheese, cut into cubes
¼ cup chopped onion
2 hard-cooked eggs, chopped
1 (4-ounce) jar diced pimiento,
  drained
6 small gherkins, chopped
3 tablespoons mayonnaise
¼ teaspoon prepared mustard
⅛ teaspoon pepper
Tomato slices

Shell and wash peas; cover with water in a medium saucepan. Bring to a boil; cover, reduce heat, and simmer 8 to 12 minutes or until tender. Drain.

Combine peas and next 8 ingredients; mix well. Chill. Serve with tomato slices. Yield: 6 servings.
Mrs. Homer Baxter
Charleston, West Virginia

CHILLED DILLY PEAS

2 pounds fresh English peas
  (2 cups shelled)
½ cup sour cream
2 tablespoons chopped fresh
  chives
2 tablespoons chopped fresh
  dillweed
¼ teaspoon curry powder

Shell and wash peas; cover with water in a medium saucepan. Bring to a boil; cover, reduce heat, and simmer 8 to 12 minutes or until tender. Drain, cool, and set aside.

Combine remaining ingredients; stir well. Add peas; toss gently. Cover and chill 2 to 3 hours. Yield: 4 servings.
Dorothy Nieman
Dunnellon, Florida

CRUNCHY PEA SALAD

3 pounds fresh English peas (3
  cups shelled)
1 cup sliced celery
½ cup sliced radishes (about ¼
  pound)
½ cup sliced green onions
1 (8-ounce) carton sour cream
2 tablespoons lemon juice
½ teaspoon Dijon mustard
¼ teaspoon salt
½ teaspoon freshly ground pepper
Garnishes: green onions, whole
  radishes

Shell and wash peas; cover with water in a medium saucepan. Bring

to a boil; cover, reduce heat, and simmer 8 to 12 minutes or until tender. Drain well.

Combine peas, celery, sliced radishes, and sliced green onions, mixing well. Cover and chill.

Combine sour cream, lemon juice, mustard, salt, and pepper. Serve dressing with salad. Garnish salad, if desired. Yield: 8 servings.
Gwen Louer
Roswell, Georgia

The Time Is Ripe For Cucumbers

Even though fresh cucumbers are available all year, when summer rolls around, we seem to crave their deliciously cool taste.

EASY PICKLED CUCUMBER ROUNDS

1½ cups sugar
1½ cups white vinegar
1½ teaspoons salt
1½ teaspoons mustard seeds
1½ teaspoons celery seeds
1½ teaspoons ground turmeric
6 cups thinly sliced cucumber
2 medium onions, thinly sliced
1 small sweet red pepper, thinly
  sliced
1 small green pepper, thinly
  sliced

Combine first 6 ingredients in a medium saucepan; bring mixture to a boil, stirring until sugar dissolves. Set aside to cool.

Layer vegetables in a 13- x 9- x 2-inch dish; set aside. Pour vinegar mixture over vegetables. Cover and refrigerate at least 24 hours. Mixture may be stored in an airtight container in refrigerator up to 1 month. Yield: 8 cups.
Cathy Darling
Grafton, West Virginia

CUCUMBER-TOMATO SALAD

3 tablespoons olive oil
1½ tablespoons lemon juice
1 teaspoon Dijon mustard
⅛ teaspoon salt
⅛ teaspoon pepper
2 tomatoes, cut into wedges
1 cucumber, sliced
⅓ cup sliced, pitted ripe olives
Lettuce leaves

Combine first 5 ingredients in a jar; cover tightly, and shake vigorously. Pour mixture over tomatoes, cucumber, and olives, tossing to coat. To serve, arrange on lettuce leaves on individual plates. Yield: 4 servings.
Lula Bell Hawks
Newport, Arkansas

CUCUMBER DRESSING

1 small cucumber
¼ cup mayonnaise or salad
  dressing
¼ cup whipping cream, whipped
1 tablespoon finely chopped onion
1 tablespoon catsup
1 teaspoon lemon juice
Dash of hot sauce

Peel cucumber, and cut in half lengthwise; scoop out and discard seeds. Finely chop cucumber, and measure to make ½ cup. Drain on paper towels.
Combine cucumber and remaining ingredients; chill thoroughly. Serve dressing on salad or sliced tomatoes. Yield: 1 cup.
Maybelle Pinkston
Corryton, Tennessee

VEGETABLE SPREAD

2 medium cucumbers
1 green pepper, quartered
2 carrots, scraped and cut into
  1-inch pieces
¼ cup finely chopped onion
1 envelope unflavored gelatin
1 cup mayonnaise or salad
  dressing
⅛ teaspoon salt

Peel cucumber, and cut in half lengthwise; scoop out and discard seeds. Place cucumber in container of a food processor or electric blender, and process until finely chopped. Place cucumber in a sieve, reserving liquid.
Place green pepper, carrot, and onion in food processor, and process until finely chopped. Place in sieve with cucumbers; drain, combining liquid with reserved cucumber liquid.
Measure 3 tablespoons reserved liquid, discarding remainder. Sprinkle gelatin over reserved liquid in a small saucepan; let stand 1 minute. Cook over medium heat, stirring until gelatin dissolves.
Combine vegetables, mayonnaise, salt, and gelatin mixture, stirring well. Cover and chill until firm. Serve with crackers. Yield: 3½ cups.
Omega C. Hood
Charlotte, North Carolina

A Hero, Any Way You Stack It

The same old sandwich ingredients get boring after a while. To make sure those who gather around your table never have that complaint, try one of these hero sandwiches.
They take their name from their "heroic" size—they're made from whole loaves of crusty bread that are sliced horizontally and filled with meats, cheeses, and/or vegetables.

BACON, PIMIENTO, AND CHEESE HOAGIES

2 cups (8 ounces) shredded
  Cheddar cheese
12 slices bacon, cooked and
  crumbled
1 (4-ounce) jar diced pimiento,
  drained
3 green onions, thinly sliced
¼ cup mayonnaise or salad
  dressing
6 (6-inch) French rolls, split
  horizontally

Combine first 4 ingredients; stir well. Spread mayonnaise on cut side of each split roll. Spread about ⅓ cup cheese mixture on bottom half of roll; cover each with roll top. Wrap sandwiches individually in aluminum foil. Bake at 350° for 15 minutes or until thoroughly heated. Yield: 6 servings.
Mary Quesenberry
Dugspur, Virginia

OPEN-FACED JALAPEÑO HEROES

1 pound ground beef
1 jalapeño pepper, seeded and
  chopped
1 (15-ounce) can tomato sauce,
  divided
1½ teaspoons dried whole
  oregano
⅛ teaspoon garlic powder
1 (16-ounce) loaf French bread
1 (8-ounce) jar process cheese
  spread with jalapeños
1 (4-ounce) can mushroom stems
  and pieces, drained and
  chopped
½ cup chopped onion
1 cup (4 ounces) shredded
  mozzarella cheese

Cook ground beef until browned, stirring to crumble; drain and return to skillet. Add chopped jalapeño pepper and half of tomato sauce. Bring to a boil; reduce heat and simmer, uncovered, 5 minutes, stirring often.

Add oregano and garlic powder; simmer mixture 2 minutes, stirring often. Remove from heat.

Slice bread in half horizontally. Place both slices, cut side up, on a baking sheet. Spread cut surfaces evenly with cheese spread. Top bread slices evenly with meat mixture, mushrooms, and chopped onion. Drizzle each slice evenly with remaining tomato sauce.

Bake, uncovered, at 325° for 15 minutes. Sprinkle with mozzarella cheese; bake an additional 5 minutes or until cheese melts. Cut into slices, and serve immediately. Yield: 4 to 6 servings.
Carol Barclay
Portland, Texas

Meaty Ways
With Rice

These one-dish meat-and-rice combinations may be just what you need to simplify meal preparation and cleanup. Recipes that include fruit or vegetables in the dish can make a complete meal, but you might like to toss a few greens for a salad for recipes without the added fiber of fruit and vegetables.

When the recipe calls for cooked rice, take advantage of partially cooked rice packaged in bags for boiling. The quality is good, and it's an excellent timesaver.

CREAMY SHRIMP CURRY

6 cups water
1 tablespoon salt
2 pounds unpeeled medium-size
   fresh shrimp
½ cup minced onion
⅓ cup butter or margarine,
   melted
⅓ cup all-purpose flour
1 tablespoon curry powder
1 (14½-ounce) can ready-to-serve
   chicken broth
1½ cups milk
½ teaspoon salt
1½ teaspoons sugar
¼ teaspoon ground ginger
1 teaspoon lemon juice
Hot cooked rice
Assorted condiments

Combine water and 1 tablespoon salt in a Dutch oven; bring to a boil. Add shrimp, and cook 3 to 5 minutes. Drain well; rinse with cold water. Peel and devein shrimp. Set aside.

Sauté onion in butter until crisp-tender. Add flour and curry powder, stirring until smooth. Cook 1 minute, stirring constantly. Gradually add chicken broth and milk; cook over medium heat, stirring constantly, until thickened and bubbly. Stir in ½ teaspoon salt, sugar, ginger, and lemon juice. Add shrimp, and cook

over medium heat until thoroughly heated. Serve over rice with several of the following condiments: peanuts, sliced green onions, raisins, toasted coconut, and bacon pieces. Yield: 6 servings.
De Lea Lonadier
Montgomery, Louisiana

MEATBALLS WITH
PINEAPPLE AND PEPPERS

1 egg, slightly beaten
1 tablespoon cornstarch
2 tablespoons chopped onion
1 teaspoon salt
¼ teaspoon pepper
1 pound ground beef
Vegetable cooking spray
1 cup pineapple juice
2 green peppers, cut into strips
¼ cup sugar
3 tablespoons cornstarch
⅓ cup water
3 tablespoons white vinegar
1 tablespoon soy sauce
1 (8-ounce) can unsweetened
   pineapple chunks, drained
Hot cooked rice

Combine first 6 ingredients, and shape into 1½-inch meatballs; set aside. Coat a large nonstick skillet with cooking spray; place skillet over medium-high heat until hot. Add meatballs, and cook until brown; drain. Discard drippings. Return meatballs to skillet; add pineapple juice and green pepper. Bring to a boil over medium heat; cook 3 minutes, stirring often.

Combine sugar and next 4 ingredients; add to skillet, and bring mixture to a boil, stirring constantly. Cook 1 minute, stirring constantly. Stir in pineapple chunks; cook until thoroughly heated. Serve meatballs over rice. Yield: 4 servings.
Clairiece Gilbert Humphrey
Charlottesville, Virginia

TURKEY HERO
WITH GARLIC SAUCE

¼ cup mayonnaise or salad
   dressing
2 cloves garlic, minced
2 tablespoons vegetable oil
1 tablespoon minced fresh chives
1 tablespoon Dijon mustard
1 teaspoon sugar
2 teaspoons lemon juice
1 (16-ounce) loaf French bread
Lettuce leaves
12 ounces sliced cooked turkey
2 tomatoes, sliced
1¾ cups loosely packed alfalfa
   sprouts
1 small purple onion, sliced
Garnish: lettuce leaves

Combine first 7 ingredients in container of an electric blender; blend well. Slice bread in half horizontally, and spread mayonnaise mixture on cut surfaces. Layer lettuce leaves, turkey, tomato, alfalfa sprouts, and onion on cut surface of bottom slice of bread; cover with bread top. Secure sandwich with wooden picks, garnishing wooden picks with lettuce, if desired; cut into 6 slices. Yield: 6 servings.
Erma Jackson
Huntsville, Alabama

CHICKEN CREOLE

¼ cup all-purpose flour
2 teaspoons salt
½ teaspoon pepper
1 tablespoon chili powder
3 pounds chicken pieces, skinned
2 tablespoons vegetable oil
1 cup chopped onion
½ cup chopped green pepper
1 large clove garlic, crushed
1 (16-ounce) can tomatoes,
   undrained and chopped
1 cup chicken broth
¾ cup uncooked long-grain rice
1 (10-ounce) package sliced or
   whole okra

Combine first 4 ingredients in a shallow dish, mixing well. Dredge chicken in flour mixture, shaking off excess flour.

Cook chicken in hot oil in a Dutch oven over medium heat about 4 minutes on each side or until golden brown. Remove chicken.

Add onion, green pepper, and garlic to Dutch oven; sauté 3 to 5 minutes or until vegetables are crisp-tender. Add chicken, tomatoes, chicken broth, and rice, stirring well. Cover and simmer 40 minutes or until most of liquid is absorbed, stirring occasionally. Add okra; cover and simmer an additional 10 minutes. Yield: 4 servings.   *Jean Voan*
Shepherd, Texas

Chicken Salad, Better Than Ever

Chicken salad has long since seen the days of simple combinations, such as mayonnaise, chopped eggs, and celery. Today, such flavors as ginger, soy sauce, lemon, and Beau Monde seasoning find splendid partnership with chicken, especially in salads.

CHICKEN SALAD ORIENTAL

½ cup uncooked macaroni
2 cups chopped cooked chicken
½ cup sliced green onions
1 (8-ounce) can sliced water
   chestnuts, drained
½ cup mayonnaise or salad
   dressing
2 teaspoons soy sauce
¼ teaspoon ground ginger
⅛ teaspoon pepper
2 cups (¾-pound) fresh snow pea
   pods, blanched
½ cup slivered almonds, toasted

Cook macaroni according to package directions; drain. Combine macaroni, chicken, green onions, and water chestnuts; toss well. Combine mayonnaise and next 3 ingredients, stirring well; fold into chicken mixture. Cover and chill 2 hours.

To serve, divide snow peas among 4 serving dishes. Top with chicken salad, and sprinkle with toasted almonds. Yield: 4 servings.
Sandra Byer
Sterling, Virginia

MICROWAVE CHEF SALAD

2 slices pumpernickel bread
Vegetable cooking spray
¼ teaspoon garlic powder
1 egg
2 chicken breast halves, skinned
1 tablespoon water
1 teaspoon onion flakes
3 cups torn mixed salad greens
1 small yellow squash, sliced
1 carrot, sliced
½ cup sliced cucumber
¼ cup (1 ounce) shredded Swiss
   cheese
Honey-Mustard Dressing

Spray both sides of bread with cooking spray; sprinkle with garlic powder, and cut into ½-inch cubes. Place bread cubes in an 8-inch square baking dish. Microwave at HIGH 2 to 2½ minutes or until dry. Set aside.

Gently break egg into a lightly greased 6-ounce custard cup; pierce yolk with a wooden pick. Cover cup with heavy-duty plastic wrap; fold back a small edge of wrap to allow steam to escape. Microwave at MEDIUM (50% power) 1 to 2 minutes or until white is set. Let stand 5 minutes. Chop and set aside.

Place chicken in an 8-inch square baking dish; add water and onion flakes. Cover with heavy-duty plastic wrap; fold back a small corner of wrap to allow steam to escape. Microwave at HIGH 7 to 8 minutes, turning chicken over halfway through cooking time. Cool. Remove chicken from bone, and chop.

Combine chicken, egg, salad greens, squash, carrot, cucumber, and cheese; toss gently. Sprinkle bread cubes on top; serve with Honey-Mustard Dressing. Yield: 2 servings.

Honey-Mustard Dressing

¼ cup honey
1½ tablespoons Dijon mustard
2 to 3 tablespoons lemon juice

Combine all ingredients; stir well. Yield: about ¼ cup.

CHICKEN-SPAGHETTI SALAD

8 ounces uncooked spaghetti,
   broken in half
2 cups chopped cooked chicken
2 cups fresh broccoli flowerets
1½ cups sliced fresh mushrooms
10 cherry tomatoes, halved
¼ cup chopped purple onion
½ cup commercial Italian salad
   dressing
1 tablespoon lemon juice
1 teaspoon dried whole basil
½ teaspoon seasoned salt
½ teaspoon Beau Monde
   seasoning

Cook spaghetti according to package directions; drain.

Combine spaghetti and next 5 ingredients in a large bowl. Combine salad dressing, lemon juice, basil, seasoned salt, and Beau Monde seasoning; pour over spaghetti mixture, tossing to coat. Cover and chill. Toss salad before serving. Yield: 4 to 6 servings.

Note: Beau Monde seasoning, a blend of 5 ingredients, is available at the spice counter of supermarkets.

Yvonne M. Greer
Greenville, South Carolina

Appetizers From The Vegetable Patch

Now is the perfect time to savor a juicy tomato in Bacon-and-Tomato Dip. Tomato, green pepper, and onion are the primary ingredients for Vegetable Relish. Both of these appetizers are best with crispy crackers or bread. For variety, try serving them with toasted pita bread pieces, bagel chips, or seasoned breadsticks.

ZUCCHINI FRIES

½ cup all-purpose flour
1 teaspoon onion salt
½ teaspoon ground oregano
¼ teaspoon garlic powder
1 egg, slightly beaten
⅓ cup milk
1 tablespoon olive oil
3 medium zucchini
1 cup crushed corn flakes
Vegetable oil

Combine first 4 ingredients; add egg, milk, and olive oil, stirring until blended. Set aside.

Cut zucchini in half crosswise. Cut each half into 8 strips. Dip zucchini in batter; shake off excess, and dredge in crushed corn flakes. Pour oil to a depth of 2 to 3 inches into a Dutch oven or heavy saucepan; heat to 350°. Fry zucchini in oil until golden brown. Drain on paper towels, and serve immediately. Yield: about 6 appetizer servings.

Mary Eaby
Smithfield, Virginia

BACON-AND-TOMATO DIP

8 slices bacon, cooked and crumbled
1 tomato, peeled and chopped
1 (8-ounce) package cream cheese, cubed
¼ cup mayonnaise or salad dressing
¼ teaspoon salt
¼ teaspoon pepper
¼ teaspoon dried whole basil
1 (1-pound) round loaf bread (optional)
Garnishes: tomato rose and fresh parsley sprigs

Combine first 7 ingredients in container of an electric blender; process on high speed 1 minute or until smooth. Cover and chill at least 1 hour. Serve with assorted crackers or toasted bread cubes. If desired, hollow out a round loaf of bread, and place dip inside. Garnish, if desired. Yield: 1¾ cups.

Ray Jackson
Birmingham, Alabama

SQUASH NOSH

1 cup large-curd cottage cheese, drained
2 tablespoons mayonnaise or salad dressing
¼ cup finely chopped celery
¼ cup shredded carrot
¼ cup finely chopped green onions
2 tablespoons finely chopped green pepper
1 tablespoon chopped pimiento
½ teaspoon seasoned salt
¼ teaspoon pepper
2 large yellow squash, sliced
Spinach leaves (optional)

Combine first 9 ingredients in a small bowl; stir well. Place bowl in center of a round tray. Arrange squash slices on a bed of spinach leaves on tray, if desired. Yield: 1½ cups.

Violet Moore
Montezuma, Georgia

VEGETABLE RELISH

2 tomatoes, peeled and diced
1 green pepper, diced
1 medium onion, chopped
3 tablespoons minced fresh parsley
¼ teaspoon pepper
3 tablespoons olive oil
2 tablespoons tarragon wine vinegar
2 tablespoons pine nuts or chopped walnuts, toasted (optional)

Combine first 7 ingredients; stir well. Stir in pine nuts, if desired. Cover and chill. Serve with crackers or bagel chips. Yield: 3½ cups.

Geraldine A. Murphy
Holmes Beach, Florida

Tip: *Marinate leftover vegetables in pourable salad dressing for relishes and salads.*

Fired Up About Grilled Entrées

On a summer evening, chances are you'll catch a whiff of aromatic smoke from a neighbor's grill. Our readers have come up with some great ideas for grilling meat. Whether you choose beef or pork, you're sure to be pleased with the results.

HONEY-AND-HERB GRILLED PORK

1 cup beer or ginger ale
½ cup honey
½ cup Dijon mustard
¼ cup vegetable oil
2 tablespoons onion powder
1½ teaspoons dried whole
   rosemary
1 teaspoon garlic powder
1 teaspoon salt
¼ teaspoon pepper
1 (3-pound) rolled and tied
   boneless pork loin roast

Combine first 9 ingredients; stir well. Pierce roast on all sides with a fork; place in a large shallow dish. Pour marinade over pork, and cover tightly. Refrigerate 4 hours, turning roast occasionally. Remove pork from marinade, reserving marinade. Insert meat thermometer into thickest part of roast, being careful not to touch fat. Grill roast, covered, over indirect heat 2½ hours or until thermometer registers 160°, turning occasionally and basting with reserved marinade. Yield: 10 servings.
Lula Bell Hawks
Newport, Arkansas

BARBECUED SHORT RIBS

5½ to 6 pounds beef short ribs
½ teaspoon salt
½ teaspoon pepper
½ cup water
1 cup pineapple preserves
½ cup canned whole-berry
   cranberry sauce
½ cup chili sauce
⅓ cup white vinegar

Trim excess fat from ribs; sprinkle with salt and pepper. Place ribs in a Dutch oven; add water. Bring water to a boil. Cover, reduce heat, and simmer 2 hours or until meat is tender. Drain.

Combine pineapple preserves and remaining ingredients. Grill ribs over slow coals, 5 inches from heat, 15 to 20 minutes, brushing with sauce and turning ribs frequently. Heat remaining sauce, and serve with ribs. Yield: 4 to 6 servings.
Velma P. Kestner
Berwind, West Virginia

BEEF KABOBS WITH VEGETABLES

¾ cup soy sauce
¾ cup water
4 cloves garlic, minced
1 teaspoon coarsely ground black
   pepper
1½ teaspoons brandy
2 pounds lean boneless sirloin
   steak, cut into 1½-inch cubes
6 small onions
2 large green peppers, cut into
   1½-inch pieces
2 medium zucchini, cut into
   1-inch slices
6 cherry tomatoes
½ pound medium-size fresh
   mushrooms

Combine first 5 ingredients in a shallow container. Add meat; cover and marinate 1 hour, stirring occasionally.

Parboil onions 10 minutes; drain well, and set aside.

Remove meat from marinade, reserving marinade. Alternate meat and vegetables on skewers. Grill kabobs over medium-hot coals 7 to 8 minutes on each side or to desired degree of doneness, turning and basting frequently with reserved marinade. Yield: 6 servings.
Betty J. Casey
Montgomery, Alabama

BOURBON STEAK

1 (1¼-pound) flank steak
1 teaspoon sugar
¼ cup bourbon
2 tablespoons soy sauce
2 tablespoons water
1 small clove garlic, crushed

Place steak in a large shallow dish. Combine remaining ingredients, stirring well. Pour over steak; cover and marinate in refrigerator 4 hours, turning steak occasionally.

Drain steak, reserving marinade. Grill steak over hot coals 7 to 10 minutes on each side or to desired degree of doneness, basting often with marinade. To serve, slice steak across grain into thin slices. Yield: 4 servings.
Mrs. Doug Campbell
Gainesville, Florida

Right: *You'll be tempted to open your own pizza parlor once you make Turkey-Vegetable Pizza (page 139).*

Page 152: *Tea cakes and lemonade bring back memories of summers past. This tea table presents (from front) Grandma's Tea Cakes and Dropped Tea Cakes, served with Front Porch Lemonade. (Recipes, page 156.)*

Tomatoes, ready to slice, along with crisp Deep-Fried Okra (page 154) and Parslied Corn (page 155), grilled in its husk, will make any mouth water.

JULY

It's prime time to enjoy some of summer's most eagerly awaited vegetables, cooked in traditional ways but often with new twists. And because it's also time for family reunions, we've devoted the entire "Summer Suppers" special section to that subject, spotlighting four families. We've included their ideas on reunions and their favorite family recipes. While you read about these reunions and maybe even plan your own, treat yourself to a pitcher of fresh-squeezed lemonade and a batch of old-fashioned tea cakes, part of "Summer's Sweet Traditions."

Vegetables That Signal The Season

Baskets of fire engine-red tomatoes, bushels of corn with bright-green husks so fresh they feel silky and damp, and mounds of tiny, tapering pods of okra that "snap" when broken. When this medley of vegetables appears at produce markets and roadside stands, you know it's summer. So get ready to savor some traditional favorites, such as Deep-Fried Okra or Seafood Gumbo.

Or maybe you'd like a fresh new way to serve this popular trio. For a classy combination of okra, corn, and tomatoes, try Limping Susan, a summer rendition of Hopping John.

Cooking corn in the husk has been done for years. For Parslied Corn, the husks trap the flavored butter that seeps down between each kernel as the corn cooks.

SEAFOOD GUMBO

1 pound okra, sliced
¼ cup plus 2 tablespoons butter or margarine, melted and divided
¼ cup all-purpose flour
1 bunch green onions, sliced
½ cup chopped celery
2 cloves garlic, minced
1 (16-ounce) can tomatoes, undrained
1 bay leaf
1 tablespoon chopped fresh parsley
1 fresh thyme sprig
1½ teaspoons salt
½ to 1 teaspoon red pepper
2 quarts water
1 pound unpeeled medium-size fresh shrimp
½ pound fresh crabmeat
Hot cooked rice
Gumbo filé (optional)

Sauté okra in 2 tablespoons butter in a large skillet until okra is lightly browned. Set aside.

Combine remaining ¼ cup butter and flour in a large iron skillet; cook over medium heat, stirring constantly, until roux is the color of chocolate (20 to 25 minutes). Stir in green onions, celery, and garlic; cook until vegetables are tender.

Combine roux, sautéed okra, tomatoes, bay leaf, chopped parsley, fresh thyme, salt, red pepper, and water in a large Dutch oven. Bring mixture to a boil; reduce heat, and simmer, uncovered, 2 hours, stirring occasionally.

Peel and devein shrimp; add shrimp and crabmeat to okra mixture. Simmer an additional 10 minutes. Remove bay leaf. Serve gumbo over rice. Add gumbo filé, if desired. Yield: 2½ quarts.

Danella Neely
Freeport, Florida

DEEP-FRIED OKRA
(pictured on pages 150 and 151)

1 pound fresh okra
1 cup all-purpose flour
1 cup cracker meal
1½ teaspoons salt, divided
½ teaspoon pepper
1 egg
1 cup buttermilk
Vegetable oil

Wash okra; drain. Cut off tips and stem ends; cut okra crosswise into ½-inch slices.

Combine flour, cracker meal, 1 teaspoon salt, and pepper in a shallow dish. Combine egg, buttermilk, and remaining ½ teaspoon salt in a dish, mixing well. Add about one-third of okra to egg mixture; remove okra with a slotted spoon, and place in flour mixture, stirring gently to coat okra. Pour oil to a depth of 2 inches into a Dutch oven; heat to 375°. Fry okra until golden brown. Drain well on paper towels. Repeat procedure twice. Serve hot. Yield: 4 servings.

Valerie Stutsman
Norfolk, Virginia

OKRA SALAD

½ cup vegetable oil
3 tablespoons white or balsamic
  vinegar
½ teaspoon salt
¼ teaspoon pepper
½ teaspoon hot sauce
1 pound small okra pods
1 small onion, thinly sliced and
  separated into rings
1 large clove garlic, minced
Tomato slices (optional)

Combine first 5 ingredients in a small bowl, and stir well.

Blanch okra in boiling water 3 minutes. Drain. Combine warm okra, onion, and garlic in a 12- x 8- x 2-inch dish. Pour vinaigrette over okra mixture; toss gently to coat. Marinate at least 2 hours; drain. Arrange on a serving plate with tomato slices, if desired. Yield: 6 servings.
Susan Murphy
New Orleans, Louisiana

PARSLIED CORN
(pictured on pages 150 and 151)

4 ears fresh corn
¼ cup butter or margarine,
  melted
2 tablespoons chopped fresh
  parsley
2 tablespoons minced fresh chives
⅛ teaspoon garlic powder
Pinch of salt
Pinch of pepper

Pull back husks from corn, leaving husks attached at base of cob; remove silks. Rinse corn, and soak in water 20 minutes. Drain well.

Combine butter and remaining ingredients; brush over kernels of corn. Pull husks up over corn; wrap in foil, and twist wrap at each end. Place corn on rack of grill; cover and grill over medium-hot coals 30 minutes, or bake at 400° for 25 minutes. Remove husks or pull husks back, and tie in knot. Yield: 4 servings.

Microwave Directions: Prepare corn according to above directions, wrapping in heavy-duty plastic wrap. Arrange corn, spoke-fashion, on paper towels; microwave at HIGH 12 to 15 minutes or until corn is done, rearranging ears every 4 minutes. Let stand 5 minutes.

Note: Cooking time varies depending on size of ears.
Julie Earhart
St. Louis, Missouri

LIMPING SUSAN

4 slices thick bacon
⅔ cup finely chopped onion
½ cup finely chopped celery
⅓ cup diced carrot
2½ cups thickly sliced okra
1 cup corn cut from cob (about 2
  ears)
½ cup water
6 fresh thyme sprigs
1 clove garlic, crushed
1 bay leaf
¼ teaspoon red pepper
Hot cooked rice
1 medium tomato, chopped
2 green onions, chopped
1 cup (4 ounces) shredded sharp
  Cheddar cheese

Cook bacon in a large skillet until crisp; remove bacon, reserving drippings in skillet. Crumble bacon, and set aside. Sauté onion, celery, and carrot in bacon drippings until tender. Add okra and next 6 ingredients; cover and cook over medium heat 10 to 12 minutes or until tender. Remove from heat; stir in bacon. Remove bay leaf. Serve over rice; sprinkle with tomato, green onions, and cheese. Yield: 6 servings.
Claudia McCalla
Norman, Oklahoma

ICY-SPICY MEXICAN TOMATO SOUP

2 pounds ripe tomatoes, peeled
½ cup chopped onion
1 teaspoon minced garlic
2 tablespoons olive oil
2 tablespoons all-purpose flour
3 cups chicken broth
1 (4-ounce) can chopped green
  chiles
1 chicken-flavored bouillon cube
1 teaspoon sugar
¼ teaspoon ground coriander
¼ teaspoon ground cumin
¼ teaspoon ground pepper
½ cup sour cream (optional)

Quarter tomatoes, and remove seeds. Place tomatoes in container of a food processor or electric blender; process until smooth. Set aside.

Sauté onion and garlic in oil in a large saucepan. Add flour, and cook 1 minute, stirring constantly. Gradually add pureed tomato and chicken broth, stirring constantly. Add green chiles and next 5 ingredients; bring to a boil over medium heat. Reduce heat, and simmer 20 minutes. Cool. Cover and refrigerate at least 3 hours. Serve with sour cream, if desired. Yield: 7 cups. *Judy R. Falls*
Grapevine, Texas

Corn Tips

■ If it is necessary to store fresh corn, buy it in the husks and store in the refrigerator. This prevents sugar in the corn from turning to starch.

■ To select fresh corn, look for fresh green husks, dry silks, and even rows of plump kernels.

■ To test the freshness of corn at the market, pop a kernel with your fingernail. If the milk is watery, then the corn is immature. If it is thick and starchy, the corn is old.

Summer's Sweet Traditions

On hot summer afternoons and with simple ingredients Louise Ellis makes pitcher after pitcher of old-fashioned lemonade the way Grandma used to do it.

Take your own trip down memory lane and a break from the heat with the simple goodness of timeless tea cakes and fresh-squeezed lemonade. They're still as good as you remember them. When Dorothy Burgess thinks of her childhood home in Texas, it's the tea cakes that stand out. And that's the reason she still makes Grandma's Tea Cakes.

GRANDMA'S TEA CAKES
(pictured on page 152)

1 cup shortening
1½ cups sugar
3 eggs
4 cups all-purpose flour
2 teaspoons baking powder
1 teaspoon baking soda
½ teaspoon salt
¼ cup buttermilk
1 to 1¼ teaspoons almond
  extract
Sugar (optional)

Cream shortening in a large bowl; gradually add 1½ cups sugar, beating well at medium speed of an electric mixer. Add eggs, one at a time, beating after each addition.

Combine flour and next 3 ingredients; add to creamed mixture alternately with buttermilk. Mix well. Stir in extract. Cover; chill 1 hour.

Roll dough to ¼-inch thickness on a floured surface. Cut with a 2¾-inch round cookie cutter; place on greased cookie sheets. Bake at 350° for 15 minutes or until edges begin to brown. Sprinkle with sugar, if desired. Cool. Yield: 4 dozen.
Dorothy Burgess
Huntsville, Texas

DECORATIVE TEA CAKES

¼ cup butter, softened
1½ cups sugar
2 eggs
1 teaspoon vanilla extract
1 teaspoon lemon extract
1 teaspoon orange extract
4 cups all-purpose flour
2½ teaspoons baking powder
½ cup milk
Sugar or colored sugar crystals
  (optional)

Cream butter; gradually add 1½ cups sugar, beating well at medium speed of an electric mixer. Add eggs, one at a time, beating well after each addition. Add flavorings, and beat until blended.

Combine flour and baking powder; add to creamed mixture alternately with milk. Mix just until blended after each addition. Divide dough into 4 equal portions; wrap each portion in plastic wrap. Chill at least 2 hours.

Work with one portion of dough at a time, and store remainder in refrigerator. Roll dough to ⅛-inch thickness on a well-floured surface. Cut with a 2½-inch shaped cookie cutter, and place on greased cookie sheets. Decorate with sugar, if desired. Bake at 375° for 5 to 6 minutes or until edges brown. Cool. Yield: 5 dozen.
Mrs. Curtis H. Ward
Auburn, Alabama

DROPPED TEA CAKES
(pictured on page 152)

1 cup butter, softened
2¼ cups sugar
4 eggs
4½ cups all-purpose flour
1 teaspoon baking powder
1 teaspoon baking soda
½ teaspoon ground nutmeg
¼ cup buttermilk
1 teaspoon vanilla extract

Cream butter; gradually add sugar, beating well at medium speed of an electric mixer. Add eggs, beating well. Combine flour, baking powder, soda, and nutmeg; add to creamed mixture alternately with buttermilk, mixing well. Stir in vanilla.

Drop dough by tablespoonfuls onto greased cookie sheets. Bake at 375° for 8 to 10 minutes or until lightly browned. Cool. Yield: 6 dozen.
Margaret Kennard
Starkville, Mississippi

BACK-HOME TEA CAKES

½ cup shortening
1 cup sugar
1 egg
2 teaspoons vanilla extract
2 cups all-purpose flour
1 tablespoon baking powder
¼ cup milk
Sugar

Cream shortening; gradually add 1 cup sugar, beating well at medium speed of an electric mixer. Add egg and vanilla; beat well. Combine flour and baking powder; add to creamed mixture alternately with milk, mixing well. Divide dough in half; wrap each half in plastic wrap. Chill 2 hours.

Work with half of dough at a time, and store remainder in refrigerator. Roll dough to ¼-inch thickness on a lightly floured surface. Cut with a 2-inch cookie cutter; place on greased cookie sheets. Bake at 375° for 6 to 8 minutes or until edges begin to brown. Sprinkle with sugar. Cool. Yield: 3 dozen.
Mary Lou Adkins
Sulphur, Louisiana

FRONT PORCH LEMONADE
(pictured on page 152)

1¼ cups sugar
½ cup boiling water
1½ cups fresh lemon juice
4½ cups cold water
Garnish: lemon slices

Combine sugar and boiling water, stirring until sugar dissolves. Add lemon juice and cold water; mix well. Chill and serve over ice. Garnish with lemon slices, if desired. Yield: 7¼ cups.
Louise Ellis
Baker, Florida

summer Suppers.

Treasured Reunion Recipes

Each year during August, relatives invade the James Baethge Ranch outside Doss, Texas, for three days. James and his wife, Edna, have designated a grove of pecan trees near a stream for the Owen-Handley family reunion.

"All family members know that the reunion is always the first weekend in August," explains Louise Lightsey. "They plan their vacations for then, and they *don't* plan weddings that weekend. Since we've gotten so spread out, the annual reunion is the only way we can keep up with each other."

First impressions tend to be memorable; that's why the Owen-Handley family reunion places so much emphasis on fun for future generations. "We old folks are happy just to get together and reminisce," says Lovena Owen, "but the kids need to have fun. If they don't, they won't bring their children to the reunion after they are grown."

Children's activities include balloon relays, face painting, and a kite-flying contest. There are also water sports, such as stone skipping, dam building, and catching minnows and water snakes. The most highly anticipated event is the annual softball game between the Owen and Handley families. And with interest sparked by viewing photo albums, members of the younger generation also enjoy hearing family stories.

Throughout the weekend, two of the most important activities are cooking and eating.

After years of swapping recipes at their reunion, the Owens and Handleys put together a cookbook entitled *Kinfolk Cookin'*. Here are a few favorite recipes out of that publication.

ITALIAN CRÊPES

2 pounds lean ground beef
¼ cup diced onion
6 stalks celery, thinly sliced
½ teaspoon garlic powder
¼ teaspoon salt
½ teaspoon pepper
1 (16-ounce) can whole tomatoes, undrained and chopped
3 (8-ounce) cans tomato sauce
1 cup water
1 (16-ounce) carton cottage cheese
3 to 4 cups (12 to 16 ounces) shredded Cheddar cheese
1 cup grated Parmesan cheese
Crêpes (recipe follows)

Cook ground beef, onion, and celery in a Dutch oven until meat is browned, stirring to crumble meat; drain. Stir in garlic powder and next 5 ingredients; cover, reduce heat, and simmer 3 hours, stirring often.

Combine cottage cheese, Cheddar cheese, and Parmesan cheese; set mixture aside.

Spoon half of meat sauce into a lightly greased 13- x 9- x 2-inch baking dish. Layer 6 crêpes over meat mixture, and spread with half of cheese mixture. Place 6 crêpes on

cheese mixture, and layer with remaining meat mixture, crêpes, and cheese mixture. Bake at 350° for 30 minutes. Remove from oven, and let stand about 5 minutes. Yield: 8 to 10 servings.

Crêpes

1 cup all-purpose flour
¼ teaspoon salt
1¼ cups milk
¼ cup water
3 eggs
2 tablespoons butter or margarine, melted
Vegetable oil

Combine first 6 ingredients in container of an electric blender or food processor; process about 20 seconds or until blended. Refrigerate batter at least 2 hours. (This allows flour particles to swell and soften so that crêpes will be light in texture.)

Brush the bottom of a 6-inch crêpe pan or heavy skillet with oil; place over medium heat just until hot, not smoking. Pour 2 tablespoons batter into pan; quickly tilt pan in all directions so that batter covers pan in a thin film. Cook 1 minute or until lightly browned.

Lift edge of crêpe to test for doneness. Crêpe is ready for flipping when it can be shaken loose from pan. Flip crêpe, and cook about 30 seconds on other side. (This side is usually spotty brown.)

Place crêpes on a towel to cool. Stack between layers of wax paper to prevent sticking. Repeat until all batter is used. Yield: 18 crêpes.

Marilyn Russell Vandeveer
Sinton, Texas

GAZEBO CHEESE SOUP

3 stalks celery, chopped
3 green onions, chopped
¼ cup butter or margarine,
    melted
2 (10¾-ounce) cans condensed
    chicken broth, undiluted
3 cups water
2 carrots, scraped and grated
2 (10¾-ounce) cans cream of
    potato soup, undiluted
2 cups (8 ounces) shredded
    American cheese
½ teaspoon dried parsley flakes
⅛ teaspoon pepper
Dash of hot sauce
1 (8-ounce) carton sour cream
3 tablespoons sherry

Sauté celery and green onions in butter in a large Dutch oven until vegetables are tender. Add chicken broth, water, and carrot, stirring well. Bring to a boil. Cover, reduce heat, and simmer 30 minutes. Add potato soup and next 4 ingredients, stirring well. Simmer 15 minutes. Add sour cream and sherry, and heat thoroughly. Yield: 2½ quarts.

Lennah Baethge Hooper
San Antonio, Texas

SNOWFLAKE BISCUITS

1 package dry yeast
¼ cup warm water (105° to 115°)
2 cups buttermilk
5 cups all-purpose flour
1 tablespoon baking powder
1 teaspoon baking soda
2 teaspoons salt
3 tablespoons sugar
¾ cup shortening

Combine yeast and warm water; let stand 5 minutes. Add buttermilk to yeast mixture, and set aside.

Combine flour and next 4 ingredients in a large bowl; cut in shortening with a pastry blender until mixture resembles coarse meal. Add buttermilk mixture, stirring with a fork until dry ingredients are moistened. Turn dough out onto a floured surface, and knead 4 or 5 times.

Roll dough to ½-inch thickness; cut with a 2½-inch biscuit cutter. Place on lightly greased baking sheets. Cover and let rise in a warm place (85°), free from drafts, 1 hour. Bake at 425° for 10 minutes or until browned. Yield: 2 dozen.

Reva Handley McNeill
Amarillo, Texas

Gather Around The Porter Table

Preston S. and Mary Ann Porter would be pleased to know that their descendants gather for a weeklong reunion each year at White Lake, North Carolina, 18 miles from the original homeplace in Kelly. The reunion that they fondly call The Porter Houseparty has been a tradition for more than 40 years.

To prevent confusion and to make advance vacation plans, the Porter reunion always begins on the third Sunday in July. Two relatives who live nearby are appointed to supervise the annual first night's feast, a covered-dish dinner called "Sunday Supper."

The rooming committee takes care of cabin assignments and groups family members by age. Married couples from the second generation and their little ones bunk together. The cabin with the largest kitchen and dining room is designated as the main house. It's the gathering place for meals and where check-in lists, guest cards, workday and room assignments, and activity announcements are posted.

Cooking for more than a hundred people may seem like an overwhelming task, but the Porters have a system to make this responsibility easier as well as more meaningful. The workday committee designates a head cook and 20 co-workers (including children and teenagers) for each day of the week. "Spending a whole day working together," Aunt Bunny Porter says, "is when we really get to know each other."

There are many activities—a hayride, a golf tournament, a talent show, to name a few—but one of the most popular is an auction from which proceeds are used to defray reunion costs and maintain the family graveyard. "What makes the auction unique is that most items are made by family," Marianne Porter says. "You can buy one of Dick's dulcimers, one of Mother's cross-stitch pieces, or a jar of Aunt Julia's watermelon rind pickles."

Since the reunion is held at the end of July, vegetable gardens are at their peak. And to go with that wonderful handpicked produce, the Porters have cooked up lots of special dishes that keep their folks coming back every year.

TURKEY BARBECUE

1 tablespoon all-purpose flour
1 (10- to 12-pound) turkey,
    skinned and cut up
2 (18-ounce) bottles barbecue
    sauce, divided

Shake flour in a large oven-cooking bag; place in a large roasting pan at least 2 inches deep. Place turkey pieces in bag; pour 1 bottle barbecue sauce over turkey. Close bag and seal; make 6 half-inch slits in top of bag. Bake at 350° for 2½ to 3 hours or until turkey is very tender.

Remove bag from oven; carefully cut a large slit in top of bag. Remove turkey pieces, discarding bag and drippings; let turkey cool to touch. Bone and chop turkey, and return to roasting pan; stir in remaining bottle of barbecue sauce. Cover and bake at 350° for 20 to 25 minutes or until thoroughly heated. Yield: 12 to 13 cups or 3½ to 4 pounds.

Dick Porter
Hartsville, South Carolina

CHICKEN CORNBREAD DRESSING

½ pound chicken gizzards
3 cups water
½ pound chicken livers
1 large onion, chopped
½ cup chopped celery
½ cup butter or margarine, melted
½ pound bulk pork sausage
4 cups cornbread crumbs
1 cup corn flakes cereal
4 slices white bread, torn
1 (10¾-ounce) can cream of chicken soup, undiluted
1 (14½-ounce) can ready-to-serve chicken broth
¼ teaspoon rubbed sage
¼ teaspoon pepper
Dash of thyme
Paprika

Combine chicken gizzards and water in a medium saucepan. Bring to a boil, and cook 10 minutes. Add chicken livers, and cook an additional 5 minutes; drain. Let cool slightly, and chop.

Sauté onion and celery in butter until tender. Set aside. Brown sausage in a heavy skillet; drain. Combine giblets, onion mixture, sausage, cornbread crumbs, and remaining ingredients except paprika. Spoon mixture into a lightly greased 12- x 8- x 2-inch baking dish. Sprinkle with paprika. Bake at 350° for 30 minutes or until lightly browned. Yield: 8 servings.

Mary Catherine Porter
Kelly, North Carolina

PEAR HONEY

8 ripe pears, peeled, quartered, and cored
4 cups sugar
1 (15¼-ounce) can crushed pineapple, drained

Position knife blade in food processor bowl. Add pears, and cover with lid. Process until finely chopped, not pureed. Measure pears to equal 4 cups. Combine pears and sugar in a heavy saucepan; bring mixture slowly to a boil, and cook, stirring frequently, until sugar dissolves. Reduce heat, and simmer 45 minutes, stirring frequently. Add pineapple; cook an additional 5 minutes.

Spoon hot mixture into hot sterilized jars, leaving ¼-inch headspace; wipe jar rims. Cover at once with metal lids, and screw on bands. Process jars in boiling-water bath 10 minutes. Yield: 6 half pints.

Bunny Ard
Macon, Georgia

CRANBERRY COFFEE CAKE

1 cup butter or margarine, softened
1 cup sugar
2 eggs
2 cups self-rising flour
1 (8-ounce) carton sour cream
½ teaspoon almond extract
1 cup whole-berry cranberry sauce
½ cup chopped almonds
Glaze (recipe follows)

Cream butter; gradually add sugar, beating well at medium speed of an electric mixer. Add eggs, one at a time, beating after each addition. Add flour alternately with sour cream, beginning and ending with flour. Stir in almond extract.

Pour batter into a greased 13- x 9- x 2-inch pan. Spread cranberry sauce evenly over batter, and sprinkle with almonds. Bake at 350° for 35 to 40 minutes or until a wooden pick inserted in center comes out clean. Drizzle coffee cake with glaze. Yield: 15 servings.

Glaze

1 cup sifted powdered sugar
2 tablespoons milk
½ teaspoon vanilla extract

Combine all ingredients, stirring until smooth. Yield: ⅓ cup.

Marianne Absher
Raleigh, North Carolina

Tip: *Sifting flour, with the exception of cake flour, is no longer necessary. Simply stir the flour, gently spoon it into a dry measure, and level the top. Powdered sugar, however, should be sifted to remove the lumps.*

Reunion Samplings

Clouds fill the early-morning sky outside Fincastle, Virginia, near Roanoke. Judy Barnett never looks up; she has too much to do—last-minute arrangements, name tags, food. Besides, rain won't dampen these spirits. The Barnett-Girty family is coming home. This year, almost 150 family members and a few friends will strengthen family ties, eat, celebrate, and hug.

The celebration begins with hymn singing. Then after the blessing, the family lines up for food. Three tables are crowded with bowls of fried chicken, fresh green beans, casseroles, slaw, corn on the cob, roast turkey, rolls, and mouth-watering desserts.

The family photo session starts the afternoon activities. Clipboard in hand, Judy makes a final head count for photographer Eugene Journiette, who has photographed the Barnett-Girty family for years.

Later in the afternoon, children and adults play games, win door prizes, and share skills, poems, and songs at family talent time.

The next day is Rally Day—or homecoming—at Lily of the Valley Baptist Church outside Fincastle. For this family, reunion means worship, too. The grandfather of reunion committee member Betty Smith helped build the church; the membership roster bulges with relatives' names.

After church, the family's thoughts turn to dinner on the grounds. Edward Barnett of Washington, D.C., bashfully admits that the food is his favorite part of the Barnett-Girty Reunion. "I like seeing everybody and all, but there are some wonderful cooks in this family!" he says.

Such enthusiasm led the reunion planning committee to compile a cookbook of their kin's favorite recipes, embellished with bits of family history and nostalgia. The recipes presented here are just a few selections from the cookbook entitled *Family Reunion.*

APPLE-BARBECUE SPARERIBS

3½ pounds spareribs
¾ cup soy sauce
¼ cup applesauce
4 cloves garlic, minced
1 tablespoon sugar
1 teaspoon salt

Cut ribs into serving-size pieces; place meaty side down in a large shallow pan. Combine remaining ingredients, and pour over ribs. Cover and marinate in refrigerator 2 hours.

Cover and bake at 350° for 1 hour. Uncover, turn ribs over, and bake, uncovered, an additional 30 minutes, basting frequently. Yield: 3 to 4 servings.
Betty Barnett Smith
Roanoke, Virginia

ALMOND-CHICKEN SALAD SHANGHAI

2½ pounds boned and skinned
  chicken breast
2 tablespoons soy sauce
1 teaspoon dry minced garlic
2 tablespoons vegetable oil
5 cups sliced celery
2 pounds tomatoes, diced
½ cup chopped parsley
1 cup slivered almonds, toasted
  and divided
Ginger Dressing, divided
Lettuce leaves

Cut chicken into 1-inch pieces. Combine chicken, soy sauce, and garlic. Sauté chicken mixture in hot oil in a wok or large skillet 10 minutes or until chicken is tender and liquid is absorbed. Remove chicken to a large bowl; cover and chill. Combine chicken, celery, tomato, parsley, and ¾ cup almonds. Stir in 1⅓ cups Ginger Dressing, and toss gently. Cover and chill.

To serve, line a large serving platter with lettuce leaves. Spoon chicken salad onto lettuce. Sprinkle remaining ¼ cup almonds over salad. Serve with remaining Ginger Dressing. Yield: 10 servings.

Ginger Dressing

⅔ cup sugar
2½ teaspoons ground ginger
1½ teaspoons salt
½ cup white vinegar
1 cup vegetable oil
3 tablespoons sesame seeds,
  toasted

Combine first 4 ingredients in container of an electric blender or food processor. Cover and blend at high speed about 5 seconds. With blender on high, gradually add oil. Blend about 30 seconds or until mixture is thickened. Stir in sesame seeds. Yield: about 2 cups.
Gloria Lee Smith
Tucson, Arizona

PATIO POTATO SALAD

7 medium-size red potatoes (3
  pounds)
3 hard-cooked eggs, chopped
Salad Dressing
Paprika

Cook potatoes in boiling water to cover 30 minutes or until tender. Drain and cool slightly. Peel potatoes; cut into ½-inch cubes.

Combine potatoes, eggs, and Salad Dressing; toss gently. Cover and chill. Sprinkle with paprika before serving. Yield: 8 to 10 servings.

Salad Dressing

¼ to ⅓ cup sugar
1 tablespoon cornstarch
1 teaspoon salt
¾ teaspoon celery seeds
¼ teaspoon dry mustard
¼ cup white vinegar
½ cup milk
1 egg, slightly beaten
¼ cup butter or margarine
¼ cup diced onion
¼ cup mayonnaise or salad
   dressing

Combine first 8 ingredients in a medium saucepan. Add butter; cook over medium heat until mixture thickens and butter melts, stirring constantly. Remove from heat; stir in onion and mayonnaise; cool. Yield: 1½ cups.   *Judith C. Barnett*
Fincastle, Virginia

A Taste Of Tennessee

Virginia Walters Cheek opens the front door, graciously welcoming guests on this Fourth of July eve. For the 14th year, "branches" of the Walters family tree are gathering for their reunion from as near as down the road and as far as Florida and California.

Sometimes the Walters family gathers in other states at transplanted relatives' homes, but usually the clan returns here to Brentwood, Tennessee, to home ground. This afternoon Virginia and her husband, Jim, are enjoying the merry gathering of about 50 kinfolks in their home. After catching up on the last year spent apart, the group joins hands,

and blesses the feast Jim and Virginia have prepared.

Though tempted to eat to capacity by this delicious spread, everyone saves room for the dessert buffet. A short drive away, a smorgasbord of sweets awaits at the home of Jim and Virginia's daughter, Laurie Staggs.

Backyard volleyball and croquet follow dessert on the deck. After hours of fun and conversation, the evening closes in anticipation of the big day ahead—an old-fashioned Fourth of July picnic at a family farm.

This special reunion holiday will be a full day of fun, with activities and conversations—and, most of all, opportunities to form bonds with relatives. By noon another feast is underway as tables quickly fill with tasty offerings.

Good food and fellowship are part of any Southern family reunion, and everyone looks forward to favorite dishes *and* relatives year after year. We succeeded in getting these cooks to share their secret family recipes with you.

SWEET-AND-SOUR CHICKEN

½ cup sugar
¼ cup white vinegar
2 tablespoons soy sauce
2 tablespoons catsup
2 pounds chicken legs and wings

Combine all ingredients except chicken in a 12- x 8- x 2-inch baking dish. Remove skin from chicken legs. Place chicken in baking dish with marinade, turning to coat. Cover and refrigerate 2 hours, turning chicken occasionally.

Bake, uncovered, at 350° for 45 minutes, basting occasionally with marinade. Yield: 4 servings.
Virginia Cheek
Brentwood, Tennessee

SQUASH CASSEROLE

2 pounds yellow squash, sliced
½ cup chopped onion
¾ cup water
¾ cup (3 ounces) shredded
   Cheddar cheese
½ cup chopped pecans
½ cup mayonnaise or salad
   dressing
¼ cup finely chopped green
   pepper
1 egg, slightly beaten
2 teaspoons sugar
¼ teaspoon salt
¼ teaspoon pepper
½ cup round buttery cracker
   crumbs
1 tablespoon butter or margarine,
   melted

Combine squash, onion, and water in a saucepan. Bring to a boil; reduce heat, and simmer 5 to 10 minutes or until squash is tender. Drain and mash. Combine squash, cheese, and next 7 ingredients, stirring well. Spoon into a lightly greased 2-quart casserole. Combine cracker crumbs and butter, stirring well. Sprinkle over casserole. Bake at 350° for 40 minutes or until thoroughly heated. Yield: 6 to 8 servings.
Lucille Thurman
Mount Juliet, Tennessee

TANGY SAUCE FOR FRUIT

⅓ cup frozen lemonade
   concentrate, thawed
⅓ cup vegetable oil
⅓ cup honey
1 teaspoon celery seeds

Combine all ingredients in container of an electric blender; blend 1 minute. Serve sauce with fresh fruit. Yield: 1 cup.   *Virginia Cheek*
Brentwood, Tennessee

FRUIT-GLAZED CHEESECAKE

1 cup all-purpose flour
⅓ cup sugar
⅓ cup butter or margarine
2 egg yolks
1 teaspoon grated lemon rind
5 (8-ounce) packages cream
  cheese, softened
1¾ cups sugar
¼ cup whipping cream
1 tablespoon grated orange rind
1 tablespoon grated lemon rind
1 teaspoon vanilla extract
6 eggs
⅓ cup red currant jelly
1 teaspoon water
1 cup halved fresh strawberries
1 kiwifruit, peeled and sliced

Combine flour and ⅓ cup sugar in a small bowl; cut in butter with a pastry blender until mixture resembles coarse meal. Add egg yolks and lemon rind; stir with a fork just until dry ingredients are moistened. Divide dough in half, and shape each half into a ball.

Press half of pastry onto bottom of a lightly greased 9-inch springform pan without ring attached. Bake at 400° for 8 minutes or until golden brown. Remove from oven, and let cool slightly. Attach ring of pan onto bottom; press remaining pastry up sides to top edge of pan. Set aside.

Beat cream cheese at high speed of an electric mixer until light and fluffy; gradually add 1¾ cups sugar, beating well. Add whipping cream, orange rind, lemon rind, and vanilla, beating well. Add 6 eggs; beat just until blended. Pour into pastry crust.

Bake at 300° for 1½ hours; turn oven off, and partially open door. Leave cheesecake in oven 2 hours. Remove from oven, and let cool on a wire rack. Cover cheesecake, and chill at least 8 hours.

Combine jelly and water in a small saucepan. Cook over low heat until jelly melts; let cool slightly. Spoon half of mixture over center of cheesecake. Arrange strawberries and kiwifruit over glaze. Drizzle remaining glaze over fruit. Yield: one 9-inch cheesecake. *Laurie Staggs*
Nashville, Tennessee

FRENCH COCONUT PIE

1½ cups sugar
2 tablespoons all-purpose flour
¼ teaspoon salt
¼ cup plus 2 tablespoons butter
  or margarine, melted
3 eggs, beaten
1 teaspoon white vinegar
1 teaspoon vanilla extract
½ to 1 teaspoon coconut extract
¼ teaspoon almond extract
1 (3½-ounce) can flaked coconut
1 unbaked 9-inch pastry shell

Combine sugar, flour, and salt in a medium bowl. Add butter, mixing well. Add eggs, and beat until blended. Add vinegar, flavorings, and coconut; mix well. Pour filling into pastry shell. Bake at 350° for 45 minutes or until set, shielding with aluminum foil after 25 minutes. Yield: one 9-inch pie. *Dolores Walters*
Pulaski, Tennessee

Stop Talking And Start Planning!

When letters and long-distance telephone calls don't satisfy desires to visit with extended family, maybe it's time to plan a reunion. Gathering the whole family in one place isn't difficult if you're a good planner.

Start with a Chairman

The chairmanship of your reunion may rotate among family members; each chairman should maintain precise files and pass them on each year. Set the date months ahead. (Rather than a different date each year, some families keep the same one, pinpointing perhaps "the third weekend in June" for the annual event.) About five months before the reunion the chairman sends a snappy letter to relatives to generate excitement and request confirmation of who will attend, their arrival and departure times, and perhaps to solicit a set dollar amount per family unit. Once responses are gathered, the chairman sends out a work detail.

Pick the Place

Whether the reunion site is the same each year or different, make plans for all out-of-towners to have a place to sleep. Mail relatives a form letter about accommodations, requesting responses much like a multiple choice test. Include listings of local hotels and accommodations with relatives in the area. Since many families choose state parks for their reunion site, some relatives bring campers or RVs.

Put Cooks in the Kitchen

For one-day events where most folks live nearby, the simplest way to feed the crowd is with a covered-dish arrangement. However, the longer the reunion, the more involved the task of feeding everyone. Those who stay for several days in cabins or hotels with cooking facilities usually share meal preparation responsibilities. They are grouped by immediate family, relative classification (cousins or uncles), or as mixed groups drawn by lot.

Leave Time to Play

You probably won't need to plan activities for reunions that last just a few hours—relatives enjoy chatting, as well as the spontaneity of a game of pitch. Some families go all out for activities during a longer reunion. Appoint committees for games that include adults and children.

Making Cents of It All

Lengthy reunions can be costly. Printing cookbooks and T-shirts can run expenses even higher. Some groups require a certain amount of money per family in advance. Some families conduct an auction instead of taking up money to help defray costs. Items to be auctioned off may range from pecans to handmade quilts to baked goods.

From Generation to Generation

Many families have found joy in compiling reunion albums or memory books. Black-and-white, color, and even Polaroid photographs may be reproduced on a copy machine to make a memory book. Some family members bring copies of their family albums to successive gatherings to get photos autographed. Relatives also fill in pages with family tales and history.

Personalizing a memory book or family history makes it even more endearing. For example, include the menu and any handouts and programs from your reunion.

Create a family calendar, a printed rendition complete with photos of family members and the important dates printed on the appropriate months' spaces.

T-shirts can be worn and enjoyed long after a reunion has ended. The T-shirts may name each family member and delineate duties for the reunion. Or the color of the T-shirt may determine the relative's primary responsibility at the reunion. For example, blue may indicate meal preparation; green may mean talking with everyone, a privilege of being a senior citizen.

Other memorabilia and mementos could include buttons, corsages, sun visors, cross-stitch Christmas ornaments, needlepoint, or plaques painted with family crests. Several families work together to make quilts with each square representing a part of their heritage or roots. Some families choose "award spies" to keep an eye out for potential recipients of awards such as "Most Colorful Lobster" (sunburn award) or "King of the Naps."

Many people use video cameras to record talent shows, funny moments, speeches, bits of family history, and remembrances. Also, a slide show of old family photos set to period music will evoke smiles, laughter, and maybe even a tear or two.

Publish Your Family Recipes

The task of publishing a family cookbook will be easier if you get a good committee to share the load. Put a different relative in charge of each section of the book or each task to be performed; appoint a dependable person to be in charge and keep things flowing smoothly. Here is a guide to follow.

Collect the Recipes—Send a form letter to relatives asking for what you want. Suggest that each relative submit at least five recipes, each from a different food category and each typed on a separate piece of paper. Provide a form on which to submit the recipe (list of ingredients first, yield at the end). Ask that the contributor's name and telephone number be on each recipe.

Categorize the Recipes—Check your favorite cookbook for a suggested list of subjects or chapters, and group the recipes accordingly. Organize the recipes within each category alphabetically or by type. Number each recipe in the order it will appear in the cookbook.

Check for Details—Make sure each recipe has a title, contributor's name, list of ingredients, and cooking instructions. Check can and package sizes, pan sizes, baking temperatures, baking times, yields, and other pertinent information.

Write the Recipes—You'll need to transfer the recipes to pages for photocopying or for sending to a professional printer. Check to see if a family member has a home computer to simplify the process. Proofread carefully, especially the numbers!

Print the Book—Determine how to put the book together. Photocopied pages bound with wire ring clips or placed in a soft-cover folder are cheapest to produce. The price goes up and can vary greatly with a professional printer, but the quality improves as well.

Herbs—Nature's Own Seasonings

Fresh herbs transform the simplest foods into gourmet delights. Their aromatic leaves permeate cooked dishes and add flavor and dimension to fruits, vegetables, and salad dressings. These revered plants work another kind of magic—they lessen the need for fat and salt to flavor food. And herbs have minimal calories compared to breadings, batters, butter, gravies, and sauces.

They can be grown outdoors in the summer or indoors in window pots year-round. It's best to snip garden herbs frequently because they respond with bushy new growth. So use them often, and freeze or dry excesses.

LAMB CHOPS WITH HERBS

4 (4-ounce) lean lamb chops
¼ teaspoon freshly ground pepper
2 tablespoons minced fresh chives
2 tablespoons minced fresh parsley
2 tablespoons fresh rosemary, chopped
Vegetable cooking spray

Trim fat from lamb chops; sprinkle with pepper. Combine chives, parsley, and rosemary; press herb mixture on each side of chops.

Coat a nonstick skillet with cooking spray; place over medium-high heat until hot. Add lamb chops, and cook 10 minutes on each side or to desired degree of doneness. Yield: 2 servings (231 calories per serving).

Note: Lamb chops may be grilled, if desired. Grill over medium-hot coals 10 minutes on each side or to desired degree of doneness.

☐ *33.5 grams protein, 9.4 grams fat, 1.2 grams carbohydrate, 118 milligrams cholesterol, 85 milligrams sodium, and 37 milligrams calcium.*
Martha T. Leoni
New Bern, North Carolina

ITALIAN GREEN BEANS
(pictured on pages 114 and 115)

7½ cups fresh green beans (about 2¼ pounds)
2 cups chopped, peeled tomato
2 cloves garlic, minced
¼ cup chopped fresh oregano
½ teaspoon pepper
¾ cup canned ready-to-serve, no-salt-added chicken broth

Wash beans, and remove strings; cut beans into 1½-inch pieces. Place in a Dutch oven; add remaining ingredients, and bring mixture to a boil. Cover, reduce heat, and simmer 15 minutes or until beans are tender. Yield: 10 servings (38 calories per ¾-cup serving).

☐ *2 grams protein, 0.2 gram fat, 8.3 grams carbohydrate, 0 milligrams cholesterol, 7 milligrams sodium, and 46 milligrams calcium.*   *Peggy Parsons*
Athens, Georgia

PESTO POTATO SALAD

2½ pounds tiny new potatoes (about 24)
1 clove garlic
⅓ cup freshly grated Parmesan cheese
1 cup packed fresh basil leaves
2 tablespoons pine nuts
½ teaspoon salt
2 tablespoons water
3 tablespoons olive oil

Cook potatoes in boiling water to cover 15 minutes or until tender. Drain and cool 15 minutes. Leaving the skins intact, cut potatoes into ¼-inch slices.

Position knife blade in food processor bowl; top with cover. Drop garlic through food chute with processor running; process 3 to 5 seconds or until garlic is minced. Add Parmesan cheese and next 4 ingredients; top with cover, and process until smooth. With processor running, pour oil through food chute in a slow, steady stream until combined.

Combine basil mixture and potatoes in a large bowl, and toss gently, being careful not to break slices. Serve potato salad warm or at room temperature. Yield: 7 cups (109 calories per ½-cup serving).

☐ *3 grams protein, 4.8 grams fat, 14.7 grams carbohydrate, 2 milligrams cholesterol, 127 milligrams sodium, and 64 milligrams calcium.*

ONION-HERB BREAD

(pictured on pages 114 and 115)

3 packages dry yeast
4 cups warm water (105° to 115°)
½ cup nonfat dried milk powder
⅓ cup sugar
1½ tablespoons fresh dillweed
1 tablespoon fresh rosemary
1½ teaspoons salt
¼ cup vegetable oil
1 cup diced onion
4 cups whole wheat flour
6 to 6½ cups all-purpose flour
Butter-flavored vegetable cooking
  spray

Dissolve yeast in warm water in a mixing bowl; let stand 5 minutes.

Add dried milk powder and next 7 ingredients. Gradually stir in enough all-purpose flour to make a soft dough. Beat at medium speed of an electric mixer 2 minutes or until smooth.

Turn dough out onto a floured surface; knead until smooth and elastic (about 10 minutes). Place in a bowl coated with cooking spray, turning to coat top. Cover and let rise in a warm place (85°), free from drafts, 35 minutes or until doubled in bulk.

Punch dough down, and divide into thirds; shape each portion into a loaf. Place in three 9- x 5- x 3-inch loafpans coated with cooking spray. Cover and let rise in a warm place, free from drafts, 30 minutes or until

doubled in bulk. Bake at 350° for 40 to 45 minutes or until golden brown. Spray tops with cooking spray. Remove from pans, and let cool on wire racks. Yield: 3 loaves (104 calories per ½-inch slice).

Note: Baked loaves may be frozen up to 3 months.

☐ *3.2 grams protein, 1.4 grams fat, 19.9 grams carbohydrate, 0 milligrams cholesterol, 70 milligrams sodium, and 15 milligrams calcium.*

Herb Suggestions

Instead of seasoning with fat or using the saltshaker, sprinkle food with herbs. Start with the suggestions below.

Beef, Pork, Lamb	Oregano Rosemary Basil	Tarragon Thyme Marjoram
Poultry	Parsley Dillweed Oregano Rosemary Sage Chervil	Savory Marjoram Tarragon Thyme Basil
Fish, Seafood	Parsley Basil Tarragon Rosemary Marjoram	Thyme Dillweed Chervil Oregano
Green and Yellow Vegetables	Basil Oregano Rosemary Tarragon Chives	Thyme Dillweed Marjoram Mint
Potatoes, Rice, Pasta	Basil Marjoram Oregano Parsley	Tarragon Thyme Dillweed Chives
Salads	Basil Dillweed Mint Oregano Tarragon	Chervil Chives Marjoram Parsley Thyme
Fruits	Mint Tarragon	Parsley

APRICOT MINT COOLER

6 fresh mint sprigs, chopped
1⅓ cups boiling water
3 tablespoons sugar
2 (12-ounce) cans apricot
  nectar
½ cup lemon juice
¼ cup lime juice

Combine chopped fresh mint, boiling water, and sugar in a large bowl; stir until sugar dissolves. Cover and let stand 1 hour; strain, discarding mint. Add apricot nectar, lemon juice, and lime juice; chill thoroughly. Yield: 5⅓ cups (72 calories per ⅔-cup serving).

☐ *0.4 gram protein, 0.1 gram fat, 18.9 grams carbohydrate, 0 milligrams cholesterol, 3 milligrams sodium, and 8 milligrams calcium.*
                              Evelyn Weisman
                              Corpus Christi, Texas

Tip: *Crush dried herbs gently with a mortar and pestle to enhance their flavor. Slightly bruising fresh plants will increase their effectiveness.*

Invite Friends For A Healthy Cookout

Summer and grilling go hand-in-hand. For those concerned with eating right, grilling heightens foods' natural flavors without all the fat.

A 1-ounce slice of French bread, tossed green salad, and a 1½-pound slice (including rind) of ice-cold watermelon were figured into this lean menu, all for only 592 calories.

Tossed green salad
Grilled Marinated Grouper
Grilled Corn-on-the-Cob
Pretty Pepper Kabobs
French bread
Watermelon

GRILLED MARINATED GROUPER

⅓ cup lemon juice
1 teaspoon lemon rind
2 teaspoons prepared horseradish
1 clove garlic, halved
½ teaspoon dried whole oregano
½ teaspoon dried whole basil
½ teaspoon salt
¼ teaspoon pepper
⅓ cup olive oil
8 (4-ounce) grouper fillets or other lean white fish
Vegetable cooking spray

Combine first 8 ingredients in container of an electric blender or food processor. Process 20 seconds. With motor running, gradually add olive oil in a slow, steady stream. Set aside.

Arrange fish in a 13- x 9- x 2-inch baking dish. Pour marinade over fish, turning to coat both sides. Cover and refrigerate 8 hours.

Arrange fish in a fish basket coated with cooking spray. Grill, covered, over medium-hot coals 7 to 8 minutes on each side or until fish flakes easily when tested with a fork, basting fish frequently with marinade. Yield: 8 servings (189 calories per serving).

□ 22.1 grams protein, 10.3 grams fat, 1.3 grams carbohydrate, 42 milligrams cholesterol, 195 milligrams sodium, and 25 milligrams calcium.

Dan Gillis
Alabaster, Alabama

GRILLED CORN-ON-THE-COB

8 ears fresh corn
Butter-flavored vegetable cooking spray
1 teaspoon chopped fresh dillweed

Remove husks and silks from corn just before grilling. Spray each ear with cooking spray, and sprinkle with dillweed. Place each ear on a piece of heavy-duty aluminum foil, and roll up; twist foil at each end. Grill, covered, over medium-hot coals 20 minutes, turning occasionally. Yield: 8 servings (108 calories per serving).

□ 3.9 grams protein, 1.8 grams fat, 23 grams carbohydrate, 0 milligrams cholesterol, 19 milligrams sodium, and 5 milligrams calcium.

PRETTY PEPPER KABOBS

12 (6-inch) wooden skewers
1 large onion, cut into wedges
1 large sweet yellow pepper, cubed
1 large sweet red pepper, cubed
1 large green pepper, cubed
Olive oil-flavored vegetable cooking spray

Soak wooden skewers in water at least 30 minutes.

Alternate vegetables on skewers; spray each kabob with vegetable cooking spray. Grill, covered, over medium-hot coals 8 to 10 minutes or until vegetables are done, turning frequently. Yield: 8 servings (43 calories per serving).

□ 1.3 grams protein, 1 gram fat, 8.4 grams carbohydrate, 0 milligrams cholesterol, 4 milligrams sodium, and 17 milligrams calcium.

Lean Butterbeans

Ham hock, fat back, or bacon have traditionally seasoned vegetables in the South. Nutrition-conscious folks have learned that cooking vegetables, such as butterbeans, with lean ham can give flavor without all the fat.

BUTTERBEANS

2 cups water
1 ounce chopped lean ham
2 cups shelled fresh butterbeans or lima beans (about 1¾ pounds)
¼ teaspoon salt
⅛ teaspoon pepper

Combine water and ham in a saucepan; bring to a boil, and cook 5 to 10 minutes. Add beans, salt, and pepper; bring to a boil. Cover, reduce heat, and simmer 45 minutes or until beans are tender. Yield: 4 servings (140 calories per ½-cup serving).

□ *8.7 grams protein, 1.3 grams fat, 23.6 grams carbohydrate, 7 milligrams cholesterol, 406 milligrams sodium, and 28 milligrams calcium.*

COMPARE THE NUTRIENTS (per serving)		
	Traditional	Light
Calories	203	140
Fat	8.7g	1.3g
Cholesterol	9mg	7mg

MICROWAVE COOKERY

Play It Cool With Soup

Just because it's summertime doesn't mean you can't enjoy a variety of flavorful soups. Garden-fresh vegetables promise good taste and great ideas for entertaining. With a microwave oven, you can cook the vegetables quickly and have these soups on the table without ever heating up the kitchen.

Two of these soups are perfect for serving as appetizers or with light entrées. Serve Chilled Carrot-Mint Soup as a prelude to a grilled pork tenderloin and a variety of sautéed vegetables. Dilled Cucumber Soup complements fish nicely. Italian Garden Harvest Soup, a hot summer soup, is a meal in itself with chopped chicken or ham.

EASY MICROWAVE CHICKEN BROTH

3 pounds chicken pieces
5 cups water
2 onions, sliced
1 celery stalk with leaves
1 carrot, sliced
2 bay leaves
4 peppercorns, crushed
¼ teaspoon dried whole thyme
¾ teaspoon salt

Combine all ingredients in a 4-quart casserole. Cover and microwave at HIGH 15 to 20 minutes or until mixture boils; stir. Microwave, covered, at MEDIUM (50% power) 1 hour, stirring after 30 minutes. Let stand 10 minutes. Remove chicken, reserving for other uses.

Strain broth; let stand until cool. Cover and chill at least 8 hours. Remove and discard fat layer on surface before serving. Yield: 4½ cups.

DILLED CUCUMBER SOUP

3 tablespoons butter or margarine
1 small onion, chopped
½ teaspoon garlic powder
3 medium cucumbers, peeled and sliced (about 2 pounds)
1½ tablespoons cornstarch
2 cups chicken broth
1 tablespoon chopped fresh dillweed
¼ teaspoon white pepper
1 cup milk
1 (8-ounce) carton plain yogurt
Garnish: cucumber slices

Place butter in a 3-quart casserole. Microwave at HIGH 50 seconds or until melted. Add chopped onion; microwave at HIGH 2 to 2½ minutes or until transparent. Stir in garlic powder and peeled, sliced cucumber. Cover with heavy-duty plastic wrap; microwave at HIGH 7 to 8 minutes, stirring at 3-minute intervals.

Stir cornstarch into broth; add to cucumber mixture. Cover and microwave at HIGH 5½ to 6 minutes or until slightly thickened.

Pour into container of an electric blender; process until smooth. Pour into a large bowl; stir in dillweed, and cool. Cover and chill 3 to 4 hours. Just before serving, stir in white pepper, milk, and yogurt. Ladle into serving bowls; garnish, if desired. Yield: 6 cups.

ITALIAN GARDEN HARVEST SOUP

2 medium-size tomatoes, peeled and cut into wedges
1 small eggplant, peeled and diced
1 sweet red pepper, chopped
1 green pepper, chopped
2 cups chicken broth
1 to 2 teaspoons minced fresh basil
1 teaspoon minced fresh thyme
1 teaspoon minced fresh oregano
1 bay leaf
3 tablespoons tomato paste
2 cups chopped cooked chicken or ham

Combine tomato wedges, diced eggplant, chopped red pepper, and chopped green pepper in a 3-quart casserole; cover and microwave at HIGH 5 to 7 minutes or until vegetables are crisp-tender, stirring after 3 minutes. Stir in chicken broth and remaining ingredients; cover and microwave at HIGH 12 to 14 minutes, stirring at 4-minute intervals. Let stand 5 minutes. Remove bay leaf. Yield: 7½ cups.

Note: If desired, you can use this broth and add the reserved cooked chicken from Easy Microwave Chicken Broth.

CHILLED CARROT-MINT SOUP

2 cups sliced carrots
2 tablespoons water
½ teaspoon onion powder
2 cups chicken broth
1 tablespoon sugar
¼ to ½ teaspoon salt
2 tablespoons minced fresh mint
1 cup milk
Garnishes: sour cream, fresh mint
    sprigs

Combine first 3 ingredients in a 1-quart bowl; cover with heavy-duty plastic wrap. Fold back a small edge of wrap to allow steam to escape. Microwave at HIGH 6 to 8 minutes or until carrots are tender. Spoon mixture into container of an electric blender. Add broth and next 3 ingredients; process at high speed until mixture is smooth. Pour into a bowl; cover and chill. Stir milk into chilled soup. Spoon into serving bowls. Garnish, if desired. Yield: 4 cups.

QUICK!

Sauces Take The Lead

When you want an entrée with a home-cooked touch, pair convenience products and a little imagination for tasty results. In these recipes, commercial sauces set the stage, and after you've served them, you can take a bow.

COCKTAIL SMOKY LINKS

1 (12-ounce) bottle chili sauce
1 (10-ounce) jar grape jelly
1 (16-ounce) package cocktail-size
    smoked link sausages

Combine chili sauce and grape jelly in a large saucepan; cook over medium heat, stirring constantly, 3 minutes or until mixture begins to boil. Add sausage; cook an additional 3 minutes or until thoroughly heated, stirring often. Serve with wooden picks. Yield: 3½ dozen.
Janet Bain
Ohatchee, Alabama

EASY POCKET PIZZAS

4 (7-inch) pita bread rounds
1 cup commercial pizza sauce
1 (3½-ounce) package sliced
    pepperoni
1½ cups (6 ounces) shredded
    mozzarella cheese
2 tablespoons grated Parmesan
    cheese

Cut each pita bread round in half crosswise to form 2 pockets. Spread 2 tablespoons pizza sauce inside each pita half. Arrange about 6 pepperoni slices inside each half. Divide mozzarella and Parmesan cheeses evenly among pockets. Place on a baking sheet, and bake at 400° for 8 to 10 minutes. Serve immediately. Yield: 4 servings.
Mary K. Gex
Eufaula, Alabama

SWEET-AND-SOUR CHICKEN NUGGETS

1 (12-ounce) package frozen
    breaded chicken nuggets
1 cup water
1 cup uncooked instant rice
1 (16-ounce) can apricot halves,
    drained
1 (6-ounce) package frozen snow
    pea pods
¾ cup commercial sweet-and-sour
    sauce

Cook chicken according to package directions. Set aside.

Bring water to a boil in a small saucepan; add rice. Cover and remove from heat. Let rice stand 5 minutes.

Combine apricot halves, snow peas, and sweet-and-sour sauce in a medium saucepan; cook over medium heat until thoroughly heated. Stir in chicken nuggets. Spoon rice onto a serving plate, and arrange chicken mixture evenly over rice. Yield: 4 servings.
Marge Killmon
Annandale, Virginia

QUICK NACHO DIP

1 pound ground beef
1 small onion, chopped
1 small green pepper, chopped
1 (16-ounce) can refried beans
1 (8-ounce) jar picante sauce
1 (1¼-ounce) envelope taco
    seasoning mix
1 cup (4 ounces) shredded
    Cheddar cheese

Combine first 3 ingredients in a large skillet, and cook until meat is browned, stirring to crumble meat; drain. Add beans, picante sauce, and taco seasoning mix, stirring well. Cook over medium heat until thoroughly heated. Spoon into a 12- x 8- x 2-inch baking dish; sprinkle with shredded cheese. Bake at 400° for 5 minutes or until cheese melts. Serve dip with tortilla chips. Yield: 4 cups.
Jackie Barnard
Keller, Texas

CRANBERRY-ORANGE DELIGHT

1 (8-ounce) carton sour cream
¼ cup sifted powdered sugar
1 (12-ounce) jar cranberry-orange
    sauce
1 (8-ounce) can unsweetened
    crushed pineapple, drained
½ cup chopped pecans, toasted

Combine sour cream and powdered sugar, mixing well; stir in remaining ingredients. Pour mixture into a lightly greased 3-cup mold; cover and freeze until firm. Unmold onto a platter. Yield: 6 servings.

Patty McCoy Horton
Demopolis, Alabama

Drinks With A Taste Of The Tropics

South Florida's sun and soil provide just the right elements for producing fruits that were originally from the tropics. That's why markets all across the South abound with fruits that look unfamiliar—all with prices that seem to be more affordable every year.

PASSION FRUIT PUNCH

1 cup pineapple juice
⅓ cup passion fruit juice
2 tablespoons lime juice
2 cups ginger ale

Combine first 3 ingredients in a pitcher; stir well. Slowly stir in ginger ale just before serving. Serve immediately. Yield: 3½ cups.

TROPICAL SMOOTHIE

2 cups peeled, seeded, and chopped mango or papaya
1 cup orange juice
½ cup milk
2 tablespoons honey

Combine all ingredients in container of an electric blender. Process until smooth. Yield: 3 cups.

TROPICAL FRUIT PUNCH

3 cups pineapple juice
1 cup light rum
½ cup lime juice
2 cups carbonated grapefruit juice beverage, chilled
Garnishes: pineapple chunks, lime slices, maraschino cherries

Combine first 3 ingredients; chill. Add carbonated beverage just before serving; stir gently. Serve immediately over crushed ice. Garnish, if desired, threading fruit alternately onto skewers. Yield: 6½ cups.

Mary Hammack
Dothan, Alabama

PAPAYA SHAKE

1 ripe papaya, peeled, seeded, and cut into chunks
1 teaspoon vanilla extract
3 tablespoons sugar
⅛ to ¼ teaspoon ground cinnamon
1 cup milk
12 ice cubes
Garnish: fresh mint leaves

Combine first 5 ingredients in container of an electric blender; process until smooth. Add ice cubes; process until frothy. Garnish, if desired. Serve immediately. Yield: 3 cups.

Yvonne M. Greer
Greenville, South Carolina

CARAMBOLA-YOGURT CALYPSO

2 medium carambola, sliced and seeded
1 (8-ounce) carton vanilla yogurt
½ cup orange juice
2 tablespoons honey
Garnish: carambola slices

Combine first 4 ingredients in container of an electric blender. Process until smooth. Garnish each glass, if desired. Yield: 2 cups.

Pick a Tropical Fruit

Papaya—Yellow speckling is a sign of ripeness; the interior pulp ranges from light orange to deep yellow and is perfect for blending into shakes or slicing into salads. Papaya is available in markets year-round.

Carambola—Also known as starfruit, carambola has a beautiful golden-yellow color and a tender, edible skin when ripe. Slice it crosswise to make thin stars to blend into beverages or to use as accents for salads. It is available from mid-summer to February.

Pineapple—Look for a yellow blush on pineapples as a sign of maturity. Juicy, fresh pineapples are available year-round, as is canned pineapple.

Mango—A ripe mango gives off a delicate floral aroma and yields slightly to the touch; the interior is bright yellow. Available from November through August, mangoes can be blended into beverages, or they can be sliced for salads.

Passion fruit—Select passion fruit that is firm to the touch and free from brown spots; color can range from yellow to red to purple. Wrinkling is a sign of maturity, not deterioration. Strain the interior pulp to get juice for use in beverages and in sherbets. Passion fruit is in season from June through September; you will also find juice commercially bottled.

Lime—Grown year-round, the juice of this tart, seedless fruit is popular for beverages and desserts. Bottled juice is also available.

The Best Berries Of The Season

Does your July calendar include hosting a party? A bridal or baby shower or a birthday is a great occasion to celebrate and a good excuse to indulge in some of the natural sweets of the season.

MINIATURE CHEESECAKES

¼ cup butter or margarine
1 cup graham cracker crumbs
2 (8-ounce) packages cream cheese, softened
¾ cup sugar
3 eggs, separated
1 teaspoon grated lemon rind
¾ cup sour cream
1 tablespoon sugar
1 teaspoon vanilla extract
⅓ cup black currant jelly
1 cup fresh blueberries

Grease miniature (1¾-inch) muffin pans with butter. Sprinkle each muffin cup with 1 teaspoon graham cracker crumbs. Turn pans upside down, and discard excess crumbs.

Beat cream cheese at high speed of an electric mixer until light and fluffy; gradually add ¾ cup sugar, and mix well. Add egg yolks and lemon rind, mixing well.

Beat egg whites (at room temperature) until stiff peaks form. Gently fold into cream cheese mixture; spoon into prepared pans. Bake at 350° for 15 minutes.

Combine sour cream, 1 tablespoon sugar, and vanilla. Spoon 1 teaspoon mixture on each cheesecake; bake at 350° for 5 minutes.

Cook jelly in a saucepan over low heat until melted; stir in blueberries. Spoon about 1 teaspoon topping on each cheesecake. Chill thoroughly. Yield: 4 dozen. *Winona Hancock La Grange, Georgia*

STRAWBERRIES WITH LEMON CREAM

1 (8-ounce) package cream cheese, softened
½ cup sifted powdered sugar
1½ teaspoons grated lemon rind
1 tablespoon lemon juice
2 quarts fresh strawberries

Combine first 4 ingredients in a small mixing bowl; beat at medium speed of an electric mixer until blended. Cover and chill.

Wash strawberries; cap, if desired. Make two perpendicular slices down pointed end of each strawberry, cutting to within ½ inch of stem end. Carefully spread out quarter sections of each strawberry to form a "cup." Using a pastry bag, fill each strawberry with cream mixture. Refrigerate until ready to serve. Yield: about 3½ dozen. *Cathy Schroeder Taylor, Texas*

RASPBERRY PARTY PUFFS

2¼ cups all-purpose flour
1 cup butter or margarine
½ cup sour cream
1 egg yolk
Cream Cheese Filling
⅓ cup red currant jelly
Fresh raspberries

Position knife blade in food processor bowl; add flour and butter. Process, pulsing 4 or 5 times or until mixture resembles coarse meal. Add sour cream and egg yolk; process until dough forms a ball, leaving sides of bowl. Divide in half; cover and chill at least 8 hours.

Roll pastry to ⅛-inch thickness on a lightly floured surface; cut into 2½-inch squares. Gently press squares into miniature (1¾-inch) muffin pans, leaving corners extending beyond circles' edges. Spoon 1 rounded teaspoonful of Cream Cheese Filling into each pastry. Chill 30 minutes.

Bake at 375° for 20 minutes or until golden brown. Remove from pan, and cool on wire racks.

Cook currant jelly over low heat until melted. Spoon about ¼ teaspoon jelly into center of each pastry; top with a whole raspberry. Yield: 4 dozen.

Cream Cheese Filling

1 (8-ounce) package cream cheese, softened
1 egg
½ cup sugar
1 tablespoon Grand Marnier or other orange-flavored liqueur
1 teaspoon grated orange rind

Combine all ingredients; beat at medium speed of an electric mixer until smooth and fluffy. Yield: 1½ cups.

Berry and Fruit Tips

■ When you select blueberries at the market, look for those that are plump, firm, clean, and deep blue in color. A reddish tinge indicates immature berries.

■ Remember to hull strawberries after washing so that they won't become mushy.

■ When you use fresh lemons for cooking, remember that one medium lemon will yield 2 to 4 tablespoons juice and 1 tablespoon grated rind.

■ Whenever a recipe calls for both the rind and the juice of citrus fruit, wash and grate before juicing.

■ Store lemon, orange, and grapefruit rinds in the freezer; grate as needed for pies, cakes, and cookies. Or use the rinds candied for the holidays.

AUGUST

Looking for a new lunch or brunch idea? Try cheesecake as the main dish. Yes, cheesecake! Without the sugar, it makes a perfect base for meat and vegetables. Or look for other new combinations and cooking techniques to update traditional favorites. Start with the mouth-watering recipes featured in "Contemporary Cuisine With a Southern Accent." And while you're updating recipes, consider the lighter versions of sandwiches featured in "Healthy Sandwiches That Satisfy."

Contemporary Cuisine
With A Southern Accent

The food we Southerners ate as children nourished our souls as well as our bodies. And it still evokes fond memories—waking up to the aroma of bacon, eggs, and grits; feasting on grandmother's lunches, which included enough creamed corn, fried okra, and black-eyed peas to feed an army; inviting the whole family for fried catfish with all the trimmings.

While we still enjoy the same basic foods today, menus and styles of cooking have evolved to accommodate busy lifestyles, new cooking techniques, and increased interest in nutrition.

For example, instead of frying the catfish, try grilling it and serving with a zippy salsa. Rather than overcooking the vegetables, blanch them and toss with a vinaigrette; then serve on a bed of leafy greens. And in addition to serving grits at breakfast, keep in mind that they can be flavored with herbs, shaped like timbales, and highlighted on the dinner menu.

Popularized by some of the region's finest restaurants, these intrinsically Southern foods being used in new ways have captured the hearts of cooks at home, too. When cooks understand basic techniques, they can put peaches in a fancy tart instead of a cobbler and create other new combinations as shown in the recipes that follow.

GRILLED CATFISH WITH RED SALSA

8 catfish fillets (about 3 pounds)
⅓ cup lime juice
¼ cup olive oil
⅛ teaspoon salt
Red Salsa

Place catfish fillets in a large shallow dish. Combine lime juice, olive oil, and salt; pour marinade over fish. Cover and marinate 15 minutes in refrigerator.

Drain fish fillets, reserving marinade; place fillets in a lightly greased wire fish basket. Grill fish, covered, over medium-hot coals 7 to 8 minutes on each side or until fish flakes easily when tested with a fork, basting often with marinade. Serve with Red Salsa. Yield: 8 servings.

Red Salsa

4 large tomatoes, peeled, seeded, and chopped
⅓ cup diced purple onion
1 serrano pepper, seeded and diced
½ cup chopped fresh cilantro
2 tablespoons lime juice
½ teaspoon ground cumin
¼ teaspoon salt
¼ teaspoon freshly ground pepper

Combine all ingredients, stirring well; cover and chill. Yield: 4 cups.

GARLIC GRILLED PORK TENDERLOIN
(pictured on pages 186 and 187)

3 tablespoons olive oil
1 tablespoon white wine vinegar
2 teaspoons chopped fresh rosemary
½ teaspoon salt
¼ teaspoon pepper
2 cloves garlic, crushed
2 (¾-pound) pork tenderloins

Combine first 6 ingredients; stir well. Place tenderloins in a 12- x 8- x 2-inch dish; brush oil mixture over tenderloins. Cover and chill 3 hours.

Insert meat thermometer into tenderloin, being careful not to touch fat. Grill tenderloins, covered, over hot coals 12 to 15 minutes or until a meat thermometer registers 160°, turning once. Cut into slices to serve. Yield: 6 servings.

CHIVES-GRITS TIMBALES
(pictured on pages 186 and 187)

3 cups water
¾ cup uncooked regular grits
1 teaspoon salt
2 cloves garlic, minced
¾ cup (3 ounces) shredded sharp Cheddar cheese
1½ tablespoons chopped fresh chives
1 egg yolk

Bring water to a boil; add grits and salt. Cook according to package directions. Remove from heat. Stir in garlic, cheese, and chives. Beat egg yolk until thick and lemon colored. Stir about one-fourth of hot mixture into yolk; add to remaining hot mixture, stirring constantly.

Spoon mixture into 6 greased 4-ounce ramekins. Place ramekins in a large pan; pour hot water to a depth of 1 inch in pan. Cover with aluminum foil; bake at 350° for 30 minutes. Cool. Invert timbales onto a greased baking sheet; remove ramekins. Bake at 300° for 5 minutes or until thoroughly heated. Yield: 6 servings.

BLACK-EYED PEA SALAD
(pictured on pages 186 and 187)

½ pound dried black-eyed peas
2 slices bacon
1 medium onion
2 cloves garlic
½ teaspoon salt
4 cups water
1 (6-ounce) jar marinated
  artichoke hearts, undrained
1 tablespoon Dijon mustard
1 tablespoon Worcestershire
  sauce
½ pound spinach leaves
4 slices bacon, cooked and
  crumbled

Sort and wash peas; place in a Dutch oven. Add 2 slices bacon and next 4 ingredients. Bring to a boil; cover, reduce heat, and simmer 40 minutes or until peas are tender. Drain. Remove and discard bacon slices, onion, and garlic. Keep peas warm.

Drain artichoke hearts, reserving marinade. Chop artichoke hearts, and add to black-eyed peas. Combine reserved marinade, Dijon mustard, and Worcestershire sauce; pour over peas, and toss gently.

Arrange spinach leaves on salad plates; spoon salad onto spinach. Sprinkle with crumbled bacon; serve warm. Yield: 6 servings.

OKRA-CORN-AND-TOMATO VINAIGRETTE
(pictured on page 186)

½ pound fresh okra
3 ears fresh corn
Vinaigrette Dressing, divided
2 large tomatoes, peeled and
  chopped
Boston lettuce leaves

Wash okra; blanch in 2 cups boiling water 1 minute or until crisp-tender. Drain; rinse with cold water. Cool. Remove and discard ends; cut okra into ½-inch slices. Set aside.

Cook corn in 5 cups boiling water 10 minutes. Drain and cool. Slice corn from cob, and set aside.

Stir ½ cup Vinaigrette Dressing into okra, ½ cup dressing into corn, and ½ cup dressing into chopped tomato. Cover each tightly, and chill at least 3 hours.

Line individual serving plates with lettuce. Drain vegetables, and spoon even amounts of each into 3 separate groupings onto lettuce leaves. Yield: 6 servings.

Vinaigrette Dressing

1 cup olive oil
½ cup white wine vinegar
½ cup chopped fresh basil
1 teaspoon salt
¼ teaspoon pepper

Combine all ingredients in a jar. Cover tightly, and shake vigorously. Yield: 1½ cups.

HERBED EGGPLANT SOUP

1 medium eggplant (about 1¼
  pounds)
1 large onion, chopped
1 large clove garlic, crushed
2 tablespoons butter or
  margarine, melted
2 cups water, divided
2 cups beef broth
¾ teaspoon salt
½ teaspoon pepper
½ teaspoon dried whole rosemary
¼ teaspoon dried whole basil
1 (8-ounce) can tomato sauce
Grated Parmesan cheese

Peel eggplant; cut into 1-inch cubes. Sauté onion and garlic in butter in a Dutch oven over medium heat until tender. Add eggplant, 1 cup water, and next 5 ingredients. Bring to a boil; reduce heat, and simmer 5 minutes or until eggplant is tender. Add tomato sauce and remaining 1 cup water. Simmer 10 minutes. Sprinkle Parmesan cheese on each serving. Yield: 5 cups.
Georgie O'Neill
Welaka, Florida

PEACH CREAM TART

¾ cup sugar
¼ cup all-purpose flour
⅓ cup sour cream
3 egg yolks
6 medium peaches, peeled and
  sliced (about 2 pounds)
Butter Crust
Whipped cream (optional)

Combine sugar, flour, sour cream, and egg yolks in a medium mixing bowl; beat at medium speed of an electric mixer until blended. Set mixture aside.

Arrange peach slices, overlapping, in concentric circles in Butter Crust. Pour sour cream mixture over peach slices. Bake at 350° for 1 hour or until set. If surface browns too quickly, cover with aluminum foil. Let tart cool on a wire rack. Serve tart warm or at room temperature. Top with whipped cream, if desired. Yield: one 9-inch tart.

Butter Crust

1¼ cups all-purpose flour
½ cup butter
2 tablespoons sour cream

Combine flour and butter in a medium bowl; cut in butter with a pastry blender until mixture resembles coarse meal. Add sour cream, stirring with a fork until dry ingredients are moistened and dough forms a ball.

Press dough in bottom and halfway up sides of a 9-inch springform pan. Prick bottom of pastry with a fork. Bake at 375° for 10 minutes; remove from oven, and gently prick again with a fork. Bake an additional 10 minutes. (Pastry should be set but not browned.) Let pastry cool to room temperature. Yield: one 9-inch tart shell.
Margaret Ajac
Raleigh, North Carolina

New Choices For Cheesecake

Thoughts could easily turn to chocolate and cherries at the mention of cheesecake, but keep your options open in regard to this versatile treat. Have you ever considered serving cheesecake as the main dish? To do this, all you need is a change in some of the ingredients.

The ongoing popularity of quiche, a similar entrée made with eggs, cheese, and cream and flavored with such foods as meat and vegetables, suggests the appropriateness of a savory cheesecake. So consider this unique dish the next time you're looking for a new brunch or lunch idea. Choose a fruit or vegetable salad to accompany it.

The crumb crusts that accompany these cheesecakes were developed specifically to enhance the fillings. In addition to breadcrumbs, the crust for Spinach Pesto Cheesecake includes ground pine nuts and grated Parmesan cheese. The crust for Reuben Cheesecake is fashioned from rye cracker crumbs.

For best results when making a cheesecake, always use the pan size specified in the recipe. If you use a different size, you'll need to adjust the baking time accordingly. A springform pan is ideal for baking cheesecake because it has a removable bottom and a spring lock on the side to aid removal.

Most of these recipes specify leaving the cheesecake in the oven with the door cracked for a while after baking. This helps the cheesecake cool gradually, which can help prevent cracks from forming. They sometimes form anyway, but they don't affect the flavor of the dish. You may cover the cracks with a sauce or a garnish.

If you plan to chill the cheesecake, as most recipes specify, loosen it from the sides of the pan beforehand; then cover, and chill it in the pan. Remove the pan when you are ready to serve it.

CURRIED CHICKEN CHEESECAKE

1⅓ cups round buttery cracker crumbs
¼ cup butter or margarine, melted
1½ teaspoons chicken-flavored bouillon granules
1 tablespoon boiling water
3 (8-ounce) packages cream cheese, softened
3 eggs
1 (8-ounce) carton sour cream
3 tablespoons grated onion
3 tablespoons minced celery
1 tablespoon all-purpose flour
1 tablespoon curry powder
¼ teaspoon salt
1½ cups chopped cooked chicken
½ cup chopped almonds, toasted
⅓ cup raisins
Lettuce leaves
Garnishes: chopped sweet red pepper, flaked coconut, chopped green pepper
Assorted condiments
Curried Sour Cream Sauce

Combine crumbs and butter; press on bottom and 1 inch up sides of a 9-inch springform pan. Set aside.

Combine bouillon and boiling water; stir until granules dissolve.

Beat cream cheese at high speed of an electric mixer until light and fluffy; add eggs, one at a time, beating well after each addition. Add bouillon mixture, sour cream, and next 5 ingredients; beat at low speed until blended. Stir in chicken, almonds, and raisins.

Pour mixture into prepared pan. Bake at 300° for 45 minutes or until set. Turn oven off, and partially open oven door; leave cheesecake in oven 1 hour. Remove from oven, and let cool completely on a wire rack. Cover and chill.

Unmold cheesecake onto a lettuce-lined platter; garnish, if desired. Serve cheesecake with several of the following condiments: flaked coconut, toasted slivered almonds, chutney, chopped green or sweet red pepper, raisins, and crumbled cooked bacon. Serve with Curried Sour Cream Sauce. Yield: 8 servings.

Curried Sour Cream Sauce

1 (8-ounce) carton sour cream
1½ teaspoons curry powder
⅛ teaspoon ground ginger

Combine all ingredients, stirring well; cover and chill. Yield: 1 cup.

HAM-AND-ASPARAGUS CHEESECAKE

1⅓ cups whole grain rye cracker crumbs
¼ cup plus 2 tablespoons butter or margarine, melted
1 (10-ounce) package frozen asparagus
2 (8-ounce) packages cream cheese, softened
3 eggs
¼ cup all-purpose flour
1 (8-ounce) carton sour cream
¼ teaspoon white pepper
2 cups (8 ounces) shredded Swiss cheese
1¼ cups diced cooked ham

Combine cracker crumbs and butter; gently press on bottom of a 9-inch springform pan. Set aside.

Cook asparagus according to package directions; drain well, and set aside to cool. Cut asparagus into bite-size pieces.

Beat cream cheese at high speed of an electric mixer until light and fluffy; add eggs, one at a time, beating well after each addition. Add flour, sour cream, and pepper. Beat at low speed of an electric mixer until blended and smooth. Stir in Swiss cheese.

Pour about one-third of cream cheese mixture into prepared pan; sprinkle with ham. Top with about half of remaining cream cheese mixture; sprinkle with asparagus. Top with remaining cream cheese mixture. Bake at 300° for 1 hour or until set. Turn oven off, and partially open oven door; leave cheesecake in oven 1 hour. Serve immediately, or let cool completely. Cover and chill. Yield: 8 servings.

SPINACH PESTO CHEESECAKE

¾ cup fine, dry breadcrumbs
⅓ cup ground pine nuts or
  walnuts
¼ cup grated Parmesan cheese
⅓ cup butter or margarine,
  melted
1 cup coarsely chopped fresh
  spinach
⅓ cup grated Parmesan cheese
¼ cup pine nuts or walnut pieces
1 large clove garlic, cut in half
¼ teaspoon salt
¼ teaspoon freshly ground pepper
⅓ cup olive oil
3 (8-ounce) packages cream
  cheese, softened
3 eggs
¼ cup milk
Garnish: pine nuts or walnut
  halves

Combine breadcrumbs, ground pine nuts, ¼ cup Parmesan cheese, and butter; press on bottom and 1 inch up sides of an 8-inch springform pan. Set aside.

Position knife blade in food processor bowl; add spinach and next 5 ingredients. Top with cover; process until smooth. With processor running, pour oil through food chute in a steady stream until mixture is blended.

Beat cream cheese at high speed of an electric mixer until light and fluffy; add eggs, one at a time, beating well after each addition. Add milk and spinach mixture, mixing well.

Pour mixture into prepared pan. Bake at 300° for 1 hour or until cheesecake is almost set. Turn oven off, and partially open oven door; leave cheesecake in oven 1 hour. Garnish, if desired, and serve immediately, or let cheesecake cool completely on a wire rack. Cover and chill. Yield: 6 to 8 servings.

Tip: *When buying spinach, remember that 1 pound fresh spinach yields about 1½ cups cooked.*

REUBEN CHEESECAKE

1⅓ cups whole grain rye cracker
  crumbs
¼ cup plus 2 tablespoons butter
  or margarine, melted
2 (8-ounce) packages cream
  cheese, softened
4 eggs
¼ cup all-purpose flour
1 (8-ounce) bottle Thousand
  Island salad dressing
1¼ cups (5 ounces) shredded
  Swiss cheese
1 (8-ounce) can sauerkraut, well
  drained and chopped
½ pound sliced corned beef,
  shredded

Combine cracker crumbs and butter; press on bottom and 1 inch up sides of a 9-inch springform pan. Set aside.

Beat cream cheese at high speed of an electric mixer until light and fluffy; add eggs, one at a time, beating well after each addition. Add flour and salad dressing, mixing at low speed until blended. Fold in Swiss cheese and remaining ingredients.

Pour mixture into prepared pan. Bake at 300° for 1 hour or until set. Turn oven off, and partially open oven door; leave cheesecake in oven 1 hour. Remove from oven, and let cool completely on a wire rack. Cover and chill. Yield: 10 servings.

QUICK!

Olé, It's Mexican

Enjoy the aroma and flavor of some *really* Southern cooking (south of the border, that is). With Mexican convenience products so widely available, you can stock your pantry and satisfy your friends' and family's cravings for spicy-hot foods in 30 minutes or less.

For recipes using tortillas, the "bread" of Mexico, warm refrigerated tortillas to make them supple and tender so that they won't crack when rolled or folded. The package or the recipe will give directions for using the microwave, conventional oven, or skillet for heating.

Many Mexican dishes feature salsa. For a chunkier, less watery product, drain commercial salsa in a strainer or sieve before serving.

OVEN-FRIED CHICKEN CHIMICHANGAS

3 (5-ounce) cans white chicken,
  drained and flaked
1 (4-ounce) can chopped green
  chiles, drained
1 cup (4 ounces) shredded
  Monterey Jack cheese
½ cup sliced green onions
8 (9-inch) flour tortillas
Vegetable oil
Shredded lettuce, salsa or picante
  sauce, sour cream

Combine first 4 ingredients; set aside. Wrap tortillas in damp paper towels; microwave at HIGH 15 seconds or until hot. Brush both sides of tortillas, one at a time, with vegetable oil (keep remaining tortillas warm). Place a scant ½ cup chicken mixture just below center of each tortilla. Fold in left and right sides of tortilla to partially enclose filling. Fold up bottom edge of tortilla; fold into a rectangle, and secure with a wooden pick. Repeat with remaining tortillas and chicken mixture.

Place filled tortillas on a lightly greased baking sheet. Bake at 425° for 10 minutes or until crisp and lightly browned. Serve with shredded lettuce, salsa, and sour cream. Yield: 4 servings. *Mrs. Fred Armstrong Whitesboro, Texas*

CHILI CASSEROLE

1 (6½-ounce) package tortilla
  chips, coarsely broken
1 (11-ounce) can Cheddar soup,
  undiluted
1 (15-ounce) can chunky chili
  with beans

Place 2 cups broken chips in a lightly greased 1-quart baking dish; spread half of soup over chips. Spread chili over soup, and top with remaining soup. Bake, uncovered, at 350° for 15 minutes; sprinkle with remaining chips, and bake 5 minutes longer. Yield: 4 servings.   *Linda Parker*
Huntsville, Alabama

MEXICAN BEEF ROLL-UPS

10 (8-inch) flour tortillas
½ cup sour cream
¼ cup mayonnaise or salad
  dressing
3 tablespoons hot salsa
1 pound thinly sliced roast beef
10 large lettuce leaves
Additional salsa

Heat tortillas according to package directions. Combine sour cream, mayonnaise, and 3 tablespoons salsa, stirring to blend; spread on tortillas. Arrange roast beef and a leaf of lettuce over sauce. Roll tortillas, jellyroll fashion; secure with a wooden pick. Slice each tortilla roll in half. Serve roll-ups with additional salsa. Yield: 10 servings.   *Lisa Curry*
Bagdad, Kentucky

JIFFY SPANISH RICE

1 pound lean ground beef
1 (28-ounce) can whole tomatoes,
  undrained and chopped
1 tablespoon instant minced onion
2 tablespoons chili powder
½ teaspoon salt
½ teaspoon pepper
1 cup instant rice, uncooked

Brown ground beef in a large skillet, stirring to crumble. Drain and return to skillet. Add remaining ingredients except rice, stirring to mix; bring to a boil. Add rice; cover, remove from heat, and let stand 5 minutes. Yield: 4 servings.

Microwave Directions: Crumble ground beef in a 2½-quart casserole. Cover with heavy-duty plastic wrap; fold back a small edge of wrap to allow steam to escape. Microwave at HIGH 5 to 6 minutes; stir and drain. Add remaining ingredients. Cover and microwave at HIGH 11 to 12 minutes; stir. Let stand 5 to 10 minutes.   *Pam Ernst*
Owasso, Oklahoma

ON THE LIGHT SIDE

Healthy Sandwiches That Satisfy

Sandwiches have evolved from a simple piece of meat between two slices of bread to include a wide variety of breads, fillings, and condiments. Making sandwiches a part of healthy eating calls for choosing these basic ingredients skillfully.

Mayonnaise is perhaps the biggest culprit in turning an otherwise healthful sandwich into one that is fat laden. At about 100 calories per tablespoon, slathering it on both pieces of sandwich bread is asking for trouble. Try spreading the bread with mustard (only 12 calories per tablespoon) instead of mayonnaise, or use reduced-calorie mayonnaise when mayonnaise is a must.

Choosing lean meat and poultry, low-fat or part-skim cheese, whole

wheat bread, and lots of fresh vegetables also goes a long way toward keeping calories and fat to a minimum in favorite sandwiches.

Most of these sandwiches contain less than 300 calories with only 30% of those calories from fat. Serve them with fresh fruit and/or raw vegetables for a meal that meets the American Heart Association's and the American Dietetic Association's guidelines for healthful eating.

LASAGNA IN A BUN

6 (3-ounce) French-style rolls
½ pound ground round
½ cup diced onion
1 (8-ounce) can no-salt-added
  tomato sauce
1 teaspoon dried Italian
  seasoning
½ teaspoon salt
1 egg white
¾ cup (3 ounces) shredded
  part-skim mozzarella cheese,
  divided
⅓ cup part-skim ricotta cheese
3 tablespoons grated Parmesan
  cheese
½ teaspoon dried Italian
  seasoning

Cut thin slices off tops of rolls. Hollow out centers, leaving ½-inch-thick shells; set aside. (Reserve breadcrumbs for other uses.)

Cook ground round in a nonstick skillet over medium heat until browned, stirring to crumble. Drain; pat dry with paper towels. Wipe pan drippings from skillet. Return meat to skillet; add onion and next 3 ingredients; cover and cook over low heat 5 minutes. Uncover and cook 5 minutes, stirring frequently.

Combine egg white, half of mozzarella cheese, and remaining ingredients. Spoon ¼ cup meat mixture into bottom of each roll; top with 2 tablespoons cheese mixture, and sprinkle with remaining mozzarella cheese. Replace tops, and wrap each sandwich in aluminum foil. Bake at 400° for 20 to 25 minutes or until hot. Yield: 6 sandwiches (349 calories per sandwich).

Note: Sandwiches may be frozen after assembling and before baking. Thaw and bake at 400° for 20 to 25 minutes or until hot.

☐ *21 grams protein, 10.3 grams fat, 41 grams carbohydrate, 41 milligrams cholesterol, 727 milligrams sodium, and 209 milligrams calcium.*

FAJITA IN A PITA

⅓ cup commercial oil-free Italian salad dressing
⅓ cup low-sodium soy sauce
4 (4-ounce) skinned, boned chicken breast halves
Vegetable cooking spray
1 medium-size sweet red pepper
1 medium-size sweet yellow pepper
1 medium onion, sliced into rings
2 (7-inch) pita rounds, halved
¼ cup plain low-fat yogurt
½ cup picante sauce

Combine salad dressing and soy sauce in a 1-quart casserole; add chicken. Cover and chill at least 8 hours. Remove chicken from marinade, reserving marinade. Grill chicken, covered, over medium-hot coals 5 minutes on each side. Cut chicken into strips, and keep warm.

Coat a nonstick skillet with cooking spray. Place over medium-high heat until hot. Add peppers and onion; sauté 3 minutes. Add 3 tablespoons marinade; cook until vegetables are crisp-tender and liquid is absorbed.

Fill pita halves with chicken strips and vegetables. Serve with yogurt and picante sauce. Yield: 4 sandwiches (297 calories per sandwich).

☐ *29.6 grams protein, 4.5 grams fat, 29.5 grams carbohydrate, 71 milligrams cholesterol, 809 milligrams sodium, and 88 milligrams calcium.*

TURKEY-IN-THE-SLAW SANDWICH

1 cup shredded green cabbage
1 cup shredded red cabbage
½ cup shredded carrot
¼ cup reduced-calorie mayonnaise
¼ cup plain nonfat yogurt
1½ teaspoons sugar
¼ teaspoon white pepper
8 slices whole wheat bread
1 tablespoon commercial reduced-calorie Thousand Island salad dressing
¾ pound thinly sliced cooked turkey

Combine first 7 ingredients in a large bowl; cover and chill.

Spread 4 slices of bread equally with dressing. Place 3 ounces sliced turkey and one-fourth of slaw on each slice of bread; top with remaining bread slices. Cut each sandwich in half, and secure with wooden picks. Yield: 4 servings (272 calories per 3 ounces turkey, ½ cup slaw, and 2 slices bread).

☐ *32.3 grams protein, 2.7 grams fat, 30.6 grams carbohydrate, 73 milligrams cholesterol, 368 milligrams sodium, and 110 milligrams calcium.*
Mrs. Richard D. Conn
Kansas City, Missouri

HEALTHY HEROES

¾ cup thinly sliced fresh mushrooms
½ cup seeded and chopped cucumber
1 tablespoon sliced green onions
1 clove garlic, minced
2 tablespoons balsamic vinegar
⅛ teaspoon freshly ground pepper
1 (2-ounce) hoagie bun
2 lettuce leaves
2 ounces thinly sliced lean ham
2 ounces thinly sliced turkey breast
4 slices tomato
¼ cup (1 ounce) shredded part-skim mozzarella cheese

Combine first 6 ingredients; let stand 30 minutes.

Slice bun in half lengthwise; pull out soft inside of top and bottom, leaving a shell (reserve crumbs for other uses).

Spoon mushroom mixture into each half of bun; cover with a lettuce leaf. Top with ham, turkey, tomato slices, and cheese. Cut in half to serve. Yield: 2 servings (195 calories per sandwich).

☐ *18.2 grams protein, 4.7 grams fat, 19.9 grams carbohydrate, 36 milligrams cholesterol, 838 milligrams sodium, and 122 milligrams calcium.*

ACADIAN STUFFED PITAS

2 (4-ounce) skinned, boned chicken breast halves, cooked
2 cups shredded lettuce
1 medium apple, peeled and shredded
¼ cup reduced-calorie whipped salad dressing
¾ teaspoon ground cinnamon
½ teaspoon poultry seasoning
Dash of hot sauce
1 medium carrot, scraped and grated
½ cup alfalfa sprouts
2 (6-inch) whole wheat pita bread rounds, halved

Position knife blade in food processor bowl; add chicken, and process until finely chopped. Combine chicken, lettuce, and next 5 ingredients, stirring well. Set aside.

Combine carrot and sprouts, and divide evenly among pita bread halves; fill with chicken mixture. Yield: 4 sandwiches (207 calories per sandwich).

☐ *14.7 grams protein, 6.7 grams fat, 20.7 grams carbohydrate, 40 milligrams cholesterol, 138 milligrams sodium, and 47 milligrams calcium.*
Karen Ann Jenkins
Scott, Louisiana

SHRIMP SALAD SANDWICHES

1 (4¼-ounce) can tiny shrimp,
   drained
2 tablespoons chopped celery
1 tablespoon minced fresh chives
2 tablespoons reduced-calorie
   mayonnaise
1½ tablespoons lemon juice
1 teaspoon Worcestershire sauce
½ teaspoon Dijon mustard
¼ teaspoon caraway seeds
16 thin slices cucumber
8 slices whole wheat bread,
   toasted
4 slices tomato
1 cup alfalfa sprouts

Rinse shrimp, and drain thoroughly.
Combine shrimp and next 7 ingredients; stir well. Cover mixture, and
chill 1 hour.

Arrange 4 slices cucumber on each
of 4 slices toasted bread. Top each
with one-fourth of shrimp mixture,
one tomato slice, and one-fourth of
alfalfa sprouts. Top with remaining
toasted bread slices. Serve immediately. Yield: 4 sandwiches (184 calories per sandwich).

☐ *12.9 grams protein, 4.2 grams fat,
25.6 grams carbohydrate, 60 milligrams cholesterol, 376 milligrams sodium, and 78 milligrams calcium.*
                        Mrs. Wesley Hull
                        Dallas, Texas

LIGHT MENU

A Breakfast
For Kids

School starts this month for many,
and what better way to begin the
year than with a nutritious breakfast
for your children, grandchildren, or

the neighborhood kids. Here is a
menu that features foods from the
four basic food groups and keeps fat
and cholesterol to a minimum. Children will be surprised to find out that
this tasty pizza breakfast is also
healthy.

Begin with Orange Juicy, a frothy
beverage that gives plain orange juice
a flavor boost.

Orange Juicy
Breakfast Pizza
Fruit-on-a-Pick

ORANGE JUICY

1 (6-ounce) can frozen orange
   juice concentrate, thawed and
   undiluted
1 cup water
1 cup skim milk
¼ cup sugar
1 teaspoon vanilla extract
Ice cubes

Combine orange juice concentrate,
water, skim milk, sugar, and vanilla
in container of an electric blender;
blend until mixture is smooth. Add
enough ice cubes to blender container to bring mixture to 6-cup
level; blend until smooth. Serve beverage immediately. Yield: 6 cups (70
calories per ¾-cup serving).

☐ *1.5 grams protein, 0.1 gram fat,
16 grams carbohydrate, 1 milligram
cholesterol, 17 milligrams sodium,
and 44 milligrams calcium.*
                        Judy P. Wood
                        Savannah, Tennessee

Tip: *When using an electric blender,
fill the container of the blender three-
fourths full for liquids and just one-
fourth full for solids. The result will
be even blending of ingredients.*

BREAKFAST PIZZA

¾ cup regular oats, uncooked
1 teaspoon sugar
¼ teaspoon salt
1 package dry yeast
1 tablespoon vegetable oil
½ cup warm water (120° to 130°)
⅓ cup whole wheat flour
⅓ cup all-purpose flour
Vegetable cooking spray
8 ounces Italian turkey sausage
1 cup (4 ounces) 40%-less-fat
   sharp Cheddar cheese
1 cup (4 ounces) part-skim
   mozzarella cheese
1½ cups egg substitute
½ cup skim milk
¼ teaspoon dried whole oregano
⅛ to ¼ teaspoon freshly ground
   pepper

Place oats in container of an electric
blender or food processor; cover and
process until oats resemble flour.

Combine oat flour, sugar, salt, and
yeast; add oil and water, mixing well.
Add remaining flours; stir until
blended.

Turn dough out onto a lightly
floured surface, and knead until
smooth and elastic (about 5 minutes).
Place dough in a large bowl coated
with cooking spray, turning to coat
top. Cover and let rise in a warm
place (85°), free from drafts, 1 hour
or until doubled in bulk. Punch dough
down, and turn out onto a lightly
floured surface. Roll dough to a 14-
inch circle; place on a 12-inch pizza
pan coated with cooking spray. Turn
dough under to form a ½-inch-high
rim. Bake at 425° for 15 minutes.

Cook sausage in a nonstick skillet
over medium heat until browned,
stirring to crumble. Drain; pat dry
with paper towels. Spread meat over
crust; sprinkle with cheeses. Combine egg substitute, milk, oregano,
and pepper; pour over sausage mixture. Bake at 350° for 30 to 35 minutes. Yield: 8 servings (235 calories
per serving).

☐ *21 grams protein, 9.6 grams fat,
16 grams carbohydrate, 32 milligrams
cholesterol, 639 milligrams sodium,
and 238 milligrams calcium.*

FRUIT-ON-A-PICK

2 small bananas
1 tablespoon unsweetened
  pineapple juice
16 unsweetened pineapple chunks
1 kiwifruit, cut into 8 wedges
8 large fresh strawberries

Cut bananas into eight 1-inch pieces; add pineapple juice, and toss gently. Drain. Alternate fruit on 8 wooden skewers. Yield: 8 servings (43 calories per serving).

☐ 0.6 gram protein, 0.3 gram fat, 10.3 grams carbohydrate, 0 milligrams cholesterol, 1 milligram sodium, and 10 milligrams calcium.

Combine all ingredients in container of an electric blender or food processor. Top with cover, and process until peaches are finely chopped. Pour into an 8-inch square pan, and freeze until almost firm. Break mixture into large pieces, and place in blender container; process several seconds or until fluffy but not thawed. Return mixture to pan; freeze until firm. Let stand at room temperature 10 minutes before serving. Yield: 6 servings (115 calories per ½-cup serving).

☐ 2.6 grams protein, 0.6 gram fat, 26.7 grams carbohydrate, 2 milligrams cholesterol, 28 milligrams sodium, and 75 milligrams calcium.

BANANA MILKSHAKE

1½ cups milk
2 medium bananas, peeled, sliced, and frozen
2 teaspoons honey
½ teaspoon vanilla extract

Combine all ingredients in container of an electric blender; blend until smooth. Serve immediately. Yield: 3½ cups.
June Lipscomb
Foley, Alabama

LIGHT FAVORITE

A Peach Of A Sherbet

It's hard to beat peach ice cream on a hot summer's day, but its high fat and cholesterol content is a concern for many folks. Virginia Stalder of Nokesville, Virginia, has shared her recipe for a healthier version of a frozen peach dessert.

PEACH SHERBET

1 (8-ounce) carton plain low-fat
  yogurt
½ cup orange juice
⅓ cup honey
2 cups peeled, sliced ripe peaches
  or 2 cups frozen peaches,
  partially thawed

COMPARE THE NUTRIENTS (per serving)		
	Traditional	Light
Calories	210	115
Fat	6.3g	0.6g
Cholesterol	72mg	2mg

In The Mood For A Soda?

Time-honored soda fountain beverages are just a few shakes away with this collection of recipes. Full of ice cream, fruit, and milk or carbonated beverages, these concoctions will satisfy a craving for smooth shakes and sodas.

Milkshakes contain milk, fruit, and flavoring ingredients that are whipped in a blender until thickened and frothy. The sodas usually include fruit and milk as well, but they also contain ice cream that makes a thicker texture and carbonated beverages that give the drinks their characteristic "fizz."

ROSY RASPBERRY FIZZ

1 (10-ounce) package frozen
  raspberries, partially thawed
2 cups pineapple juice, chilled
1 pint vanilla ice cream, softened
1 pint raspberry sherbet, softened
2 cups cream soda, chilled
Garnish: fresh mint sprigs

Mash raspberries with a fork in a large bowl until raspberries are blended with their juice. Add pineapple juice, ice cream, and sherbet; stir well. Slowly pour cream soda into ice cream mixture; stir well. Pour into glasses, and garnish, if desired. Serve immediately. Yield: 2 quarts.
Mrs. Harland J. Stone
Ocala, Florida

PINEAPPLE SODA

1 (8-ounce) can unsweetened
  crushed pineapple, undrained
2 tablespoons milk
1 pint vanilla ice cream
1 cup club soda

Combine first 3 ingredients in container of an electric blender; blend until smooth. Stir in club soda. Serve immediately. Yield: 3½ cups.
Sarah Watson
Knoxville, Tennessee

Celebrating The Fruits Of Summer

There is no substitute for fresh fruit in season. Juicy melon, succulent cantaloupe, ripe strawberries, and tangy kiwifruit enhance menus and delight guests.

When fruit is fresh and ripe, arranged trays and salads need only a few additional ingredients to make them truly special.

FRESH FRUIT WITH HONEY-SOUR CREAM DIP

1 (8-ounce) carton sour cream
¼ cup honey
¼ teaspoon ground cinnamon
Assorted fresh fruit

Combine sour cream, honey, and cinnamon in a small serving bowl, and stir well. Serve as a dip or salad dressing with assorted fresh fruit. Yield: 1¼ cups.   *Frances Bowles*
Mableton, Georgia

Put a Stop to Browning

Fresh fruits, such as apples, apricots, avocados, bananas, nectarines, papayas, peaches, and pears, often turn brown after being bruised, sliced, or exposed to air. Enzymes in the fruit react with oxygen and natural tannins that are present in the cells of the fruit, causing the product to change colors.

This process is easy to stop. Simply dip the fruit in pineapple juice, which offers a more appealing taste than salt water or lemon juice, both of which slow or stop browning. A quick dip of the fruit will work—soaking isn't necessary.

WATERMELON-CHERRY COMPOTE

6 cups cubed, seeded watermelon
2 cups pitted fresh sweet cherries (about 1 pound)
1 cup fresh blueberries
1 (10-ounce) package frozen strawberries, thawed
2 tablespoons lime juice
¾ cup club soda, chilled

Combine first 3 ingredients in a large bowl; chill 3 hours. Combine strawberries and lime juice in container of an electric blender; process until smooth. Chill.

Combine strawberry mixture and club soda; drizzle over chilled fruit. Serve immediately. Yield: 8 to 10 servings.   *Janie Wallace*
Seguin, Texas

PEACH-AND-KIWI SALAD

2 medium peaches, sliced
2 bananas, diagonally sliced
Lemon or pineapple juice
2 cups cubed fresh pineapple
2 to 3 kiwifruit, peeled and sliced
2 large strawberries (optional)
Lettuce leaves
Peach Dressing

Sprinkle sliced peaches and bananas with lemon or pineapple juice. Arrange all fruits on a lettuce-lined plate. Serve salad with chilled Peach Dressing. Yield: 6 servings.

Peach Dressing

2 medium peaches, unpeeled
¼ cup vegetable oil
2 tablespoons orange juice
2 tablespoons flaked coconut
1½ teaspoons lime juice
1 teaspoon grated fresh ginger

Combine all ingredients in container of an electric blender; process until smooth. Chill. Yield: 1¼ cups.
Mrs. H. D. Baxter
Charleston, West Virginia

MELON-BERRY SALAD

1 cup cubed cantaloupe or honeydew melon
1 cup blueberries
1 cup pineapple chunks
¼ cup honey
3 tablespoons frozen orange juice concentrate, thawed
1 tablespoon vinegar
½ teaspoon dry mustard
⅛ teaspoon salt
⅓ cup vegetable oil
Lettuce leaves

Combine fruits; toss gently. Chill at least 1 hour.

Combine honey and next 4 ingredients in a small mixing bowl. Add oil in a slow, steady stream while beating at high speed of an electric mixer. Chill 1 hour.

Line 6 salad plates with lettuce leaves; arrange fruit on top. Drizzle with dressing. Yield: 6 servings.
Charlotte Pierce
Greensburg, Kentucky

Toss Around New Ideas For Salads

If you think salads only say "summer," think again. Many ingredients that are timely candidates for fall salads will set your imagination off and running. Fran Ginn's Robust Salad is a prime example; if fresh produce is unavailable, it's no obstacle to her. She starts with canned asparagus and olives atop a bed of salad greens, and her creativity takes over from there.

"I don't ever do the same thing twice," Fran says. "This recipe is a good base." She suggests using more vegetables to make her salad a side dish, and adding chicken, shrimp, or other meats for an entrée salad.

An outdoor evening symphony concert inspired Heather Riggins to concoct Marinated Mushroom Salad, and the compliments she gets on it are music to her ears. A fairly elegant dish, it is easily packed for just such a picnic. When she travels with her husband, Heather gets many new recipe ideas and experiments with them upon returning to her Nashville kitchen.

MARINATED MUSHROOM SALAD

1 pound mushrooms, sliced
1 medium-size purple onion, thinly sliced and separated into rings
½ cup finely chopped celery
1 cup tarragon wine vinegar
½ cup olive oil
½ cup vegetable oil
1 teaspoon dried whole oregano
1 teaspoon dried whole basil
1 teaspoon dry mustard
⅛ teaspoon salt
⅛ teaspoon pepper
Lettuce leaves

Combine sliced mushrooms, onion rings, and chopped celery in a bowl.

Combine vinegar and next 7 ingredients in a jar; cover tightly, and shake vigorously. Pour over vegetables, stirring well. Cover and refrigerate 8 hours.

To serve, drain mushrooms, and place on lettuce leaves. Yield: 6 to 8 servings. *Heather Riggins Nashville, Tennessee*

ROBUST SALAD

5 to 6 cups mixed salad greens
1 (15-ounce) can asparagus spears, chilled and drained
½ cup sliced ripe olives
⅓ cup grated Parmesan cheese
Commercial vinaigrette dressing

Line a serving plate with mixed salad greens; arrange asparagus spears and sliced olives on greens. Sprinkle salad with Parmesan cheese, and serve with vinaigrette dressing. Yield: 6 servings. *Fran Ginn Columbia, Mississippi*

CORN-AND-PEA SALAD

⅓ cup vegetable oil
⅓ cup white vinegar
¼ cup sugar
⅛ teaspoon salt
1 (10½-ounce) can shoepeg whole kernel corn, drained
1 (8½-ounce) can English peas, drained
1 (4-ounce) jar chopped pimiento
1 cup chopped celery
1 cup chopped green pepper
1 cup chopped green onions

Combine oil, vinegar, sugar, and salt in a saucepan; bring to a boil, stirring to dissolve sugar. Cool 5 minutes.

Combine corn and remaining ingredients in a bowl; stir in vinegar mixture. Cover and chill at least 8 hours, stirring occasionally. To serve, use a slotted spoon. Yield: 8 servings. *Lena Christopher Paris, Texas*

TURKEY-APPLE SALAD

1 cup diced cooked turkey
¾ cup chopped, unpeeled apple
½ cup sliced celery
2 tablespoons raisins
⅓ cup commercial Italian salad dressing
1 tablespoon brown sugar
Shredded lettuce or cabbage
Garnish: apple slices

Combine first 4 ingredients, and set mixture aside.

Combine salad dressing and brown sugar; add to turkey mixture, and

toss. Cover and chill. Serve on a bed of shredded lettuce or cabbage. Garnish, if desired. Yield: 2 to 3 servings. *Jackie Bridges Leeds, Alabama*

Pastries Are Her Cup Of Tea

There's just no shortage of occasions for Apricot Crescents. Serve these goodies fresh from the oven, or make them the day before an entertaining event.

APRICOT CRESCENTS

1 cup butter or margarine
2 cups all-purpose flour
1 egg yolk, beaten
½ cup sour cream
½ cup apricot preserves
½ cup flaked coconut
¼ cup finely chopped pecans
Sugar

Cut butter into flour with a pastry blender until mixture resembles coarse meal. Combine egg yolk and sour cream; stir into flour mixture. Divide and shape dough into 4 balls; wrap each portion of dough in wax paper, and chill 4 hours.

Roll out one portion of dough on a floured surface to a 10-inch circle. (Keep remaining portions chilled until needed.) Spread 2 tablespoons apricot preserves on each circle, and sprinkle with 2 tablespoons coconut and 1 tablespoon pecans. Cut each circle into 12 wedges; roll up wedges, beginning at wide end, and place point side down on ungreased baking sheets. Sprinkle lightly with sugar. Repeat procedure with remaining dough.

Bake at 350° for 20 to 22 minutes or until lightly browned. Remove from baking sheets; cool on wire racks. Yield: 4 dozen. *Betty Rabe Plano, Texas*

From Our Kitchen To Yours

When entertaining guests in your dining area, follow this diagram as a guide to setting the table. Color and warmth can be added with a linen place mat; or the charger, or service plate, can rest on a wooden table. A simply folded napkin is placed on the left. If food is served family style or filled plates are brought from the kitchen after guests are seated, the napkin can be placed in the center of the service plate or place mat when setting the table.

The charger and flatware are arranged one inch from the edge of the table; the flatware pieces begin at the outside edge according to their order of use. The knife, with the blade turned toward the plate, is on the right beside the plate, and spoons are placed to the right of the knife. Forks are set on the plate's left, beginning at the outside edge according to their logical sequence. The dessert fork or spoon can be brought in with the dessert; however, it's easier to use the European-style placement of putting the fork or spoon at the top of the plate, parallel to the edge of the table.

The water glass or goblet is placed to the right, above the knife. If iced tea or wine is served, this glass is set to the right of the water glass above the spoon. If soup or salad is served as a separate course, place the individual dish on the charger. However, salad may be served with the meal, in which case, the salad plate or bowl is positioned on the left side by the fork.

If the entrée is served with a sauce or gravy, you may prefer using a separate, small plate for bread and butter. When using an individual butter spreader, it rests at the top of the bread plate parallel to the edge of the table, with the handle to the right. When coffee or hot tea is served with the meal, the cup and saucer go to the right of the spoons, but if it is served only with dessert, the cup and saucer can be brought in when dessert is served.

Because of busy lifestyles, it has become necessary to simplify setting the family table. Follow the same guidelines for a casual table setting, putting only the necessary dishes and utensils at each place. Usually only a dinner plate, a dessert plate, one glass, and flatware are essential for the meal. A salad plate, soup bowl, and salad fork are optional items. When setting your table, follow the illustration below, eliminating pieces that won't be needed.

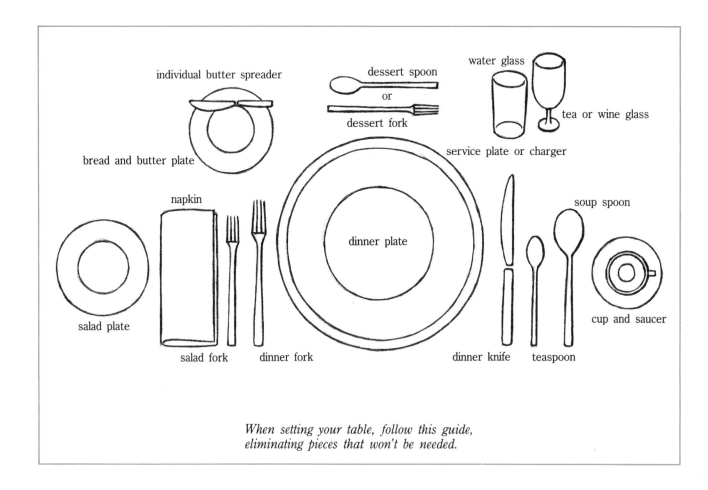

When setting your table, follow this guide, eliminating pieces that won't be needed.

Around The World With Rice

There's no denying the Southernness of rice; fields producing this crop span from Texas to the East Coast. But Southerners sometimes look abroad for new ways to flavor the dish to fit their moods or the rest of the menu.

CURRIED RICE

2½ cups water
½ teaspoon salt
1 cup uncooked long-grain rice
½ cup boiling water
⅓ cup raisins
2 tablespoons butter or
    margarine, melted
2 teaspoons curry powder
⅓ cup chopped walnuts, toasted

Combine 2½ cups water and salt in a medium saucepan; bring to a boil, and add rice. Cover, reduce heat, and simmer 20 minutes or until rice is tender and water is absorbed.

Pour ½ cup boiling water over raisins; let stand 1 minute. Drain raisins; set aside. Combine butter and curry powder, stirring to blend; stir curry mixture, raisins, and walnuts into cooked rice. Yield: 4 servings.

SPANISH RICE

4 slices bacon
1 cup chopped onion
½ cup chopped green pepper
1 (16-ounce) can whole tomatoes,
    undrained
1 (8-ounce) can tomato sauce
2 teaspoons sugar
1 teaspoon salt
1⅓ cups uncooked long-grain rice
½ cup (2 ounces) shredded
    Cheddar cheese

Cook bacon in a large skillet until crisp; remove bacon, reserving 2 tablespoons drippings in skillet. Crumble bacon, and set aside. Sauté onion and green pepper in drippings until crisp-tender.

Drain tomatoes, reserving liquid. Add enough water to liquid to measure 1¾ cups. Chop tomatoes; add tomatoes, tomato liquid, tomato sauce, and next 3 ingredients to onion mixture. Bring to a boil, stirring constantly. Spoon mixture into a lightly greased 2-quart baking dish. Cover and bake at 350° for 35 to 40 minutes or until rice is tender. Stir rice; sprinkle with cheese, and bake an additional 5 minutes. Sprinkle with bacon. Yield: 6 servings.

Dawn Lolley
Double Springs, Alabama

ORIENTAL SHRIMP AND RICE

1 pound unpeeled medium-size
    fresh shrimp
3¾ cups water
½ cup soy sauce
2 cups uncooked long-grain
    rice
1 cup chopped onion
½ cup chopped green pepper
¼ cup butter or margarine,
    divided
4 eggs, beaten
⅛ teaspoon pepper
Garnish: green onion fan

Peel and devein shrimp; set aside.

Combine water and soy sauce in a large Dutch oven; bring mixture to a boil. Add rice; cover, reduce heat, and simmer 20 minutes or until rice is tender and liquid is absorbed.

Sauté onion and green pepper in 2 tablespoons melted butter until vegetables are crisp-tender. Add shrimp, and sauté over medium heat 3 minutes or until shrimp is done. Stir shrimp mixture into rice.

Melt remaining 2 tablespoons butter in a large skillet. Add eggs; cook, without stirring, until eggs begin to set on bottom. Draw a spatula across bottom of pan to form large curds. Continue until eggs are thickened, but still moist; do not stir constantly. Stir eggs and pepper into rice mixture; toss gently. Garnish, if desired. Yield: 6 servings.

Audrey M. Canavan
Altamonte Springs, Florida

CREOLE RICE

2 (10-ounce) cans tomatoes with
    green chiles, undrained
1½ cups water
2 tablespoons butter or
    margarine
1 teaspoon garlic powder
½ teaspoon dried parsley flakes
½ teaspoon dried whole
    oregano
¼ teaspoon salt
½ cup chopped green pepper
½ cup chopped green onions
1 cup uncooked long-grain rice

Drain tomatoes, reserving 1 cup liquid. Combine tomato liquid, water, butter, garlic powder, parsley flakes, oregano, and salt in a large saucepan. Bring mixture to a boil. Add tomatoes, green pepper, green onions, and rice. Cover, reduce heat, and simmer 20 minutes or until rice is tender and liquid is absorbed. Yield: 4 to 6 servings. *Lynne Teal Weeks*
Columbus, Georgia

Tip: *Reheat cooked rice in a metal strainer or colander over a pan of steaming water. Cover the strainer with aluminum foil, and steam the rice for 15 minutes.*

Pecans Make The Pie

True lovers of pecan pies, gooey sweets, and crunchy cookies all rate pecans as the quintessential Southern delicacy. And most Southern cooks treat them as if they were gold. That's understandable since pecans are a little expensive when compared to the cost of flour, sugar, or other pantry staples; you don't use them in just anything.

Some folks still shell them by hand either on the back porch or sitting around the dinner table, chatting all the while. Busy suburbanites often buy them in packages, containing chopped, uniform pieces or shapely halves. Something about them remains special, however, and most would agree—they shouldn't be wasted.

The ladies who contributed these recipes must feel that way about pecans, too. These pies are all mighty good, and you won't be sorry if you use a little of your stash to make them.

TEXAS STAR PECAN PIE

4 egg whites
⅛ teaspoon salt
½ teaspoon vanilla extract
½ cup sugar
¼ cup firmly packed brown sugar
1 cup chopped pecans
1 (9-inch) graham cracker crust
Vanilla ice cream
Commercial caramel sauce

Beat egg whites (at room temperature) in a small bowl at high speed of an electric mixer until foamy; add salt and vanilla, beating until soft peaks form. Gradually add sugar and brown sugar, 1 tablespoon at a time, beating until stiff peaks form. Stir in chopped pecans.

Spoon mixture into crust. Bake at 350° for 25 to 27 minutes or until pie is done. Cool on a wire rack. Serve pie with vanilla ice cream and caramel sauce. Yield: one 9-inch pie.

LaJuan Coward
Jasper, Texas

HONEY-PECAN FINGER PIES

1¼ cups all-purpose flour
⅓ cup sugar
½ cup butter, softened
⅔ cup sugar
½ cup honey
3 tablespoons all-purpose flour
¼ teaspoon salt
2 eggs, lightly beaten
2 tablespoons butter, melted
1½ teaspoons vanilla extract
1 cup chopped pecans

Combine 1¼ cups flour and ⅓ cup sugar in a medium bowl; cut ½ cup softened butter into flour mixture with a pastry blender until mixture resembles coarse meal. Press flour mixture firmly and evenly into an ungreased 9-inch square baking pan. Bake at 375° for 10 to 15 minutes or until edges of crust are lightly browned.

Combine ⅔ cup sugar and remaining ingredients in a medium bowl, and stir well. Pour honey mixture over prepared crust. Bake at 375° for 20 to 25 minutes, shielding with aluminum foil the last 5 minutes, if necessary. Let cool on a wire rack. Cut into 1½- x 1-inch bars. Yield: 4½ dozen.

Louise W. Mayer
Richmond, Virginia

CHOCOLATE PECAN PIE

1½ cups pecan halves
1 unbaked 9-inch pastry shell
3 (1-ounce) squares semisweet chocolate
¼ cup butter or margarine
1 cup light corn syrup
½ cup sugar
1 teaspoon vanilla extract
¼ teaspoon salt
3 eggs, lightly beaten

Place pecan halves in unbaked pastry shell; set aside.

Combine semisweet chocolate and butter in a medium saucepan; cook over low heat until chocolate and butter melt, stirring until mixture is smooth. Remove from heat.

Add corn syrup, sugar, vanilla, salt, and beaten eggs to chocolate mixture, mixing well. Pour mixture over pecans in pastry shell.

Bake at 350° for 1 hour or until knife inserted 1 inch from edge comes out clean. Serve pie warm, or let cool completely on a wire rack. Yield: one 9-inch pie.

Right: In time you'll want to bake them all, but it'll be tough to decide whether to first try (from front) Glazed Orange Rolls, Coconut-Pecan Coils, or Cheese-Apricot Sweet Rolls. (Recipes begin on page 194.)

Page 188: These regional favorites offer as much appeal today as they did generations ago: (from front) Bourbon Yams, Turnip Greens, Zesty Deviled Chicken, and Old-Fashioned Corn Sticks. (Recipes, page 232.)

The flavor and color of the vegetables stay fresh in Okra-Corn-and-Tomato Vinaigrette (page 173), making it perfect for summer menus.

Serve Garlic Grilled Pork Tenderloin with Chive-Grits Timbales and Black-Eyed Pea Salad. (Recipes begin on page 172.)

SEPTEMBER

Cool mornings and evenings usher in the autumn season. With it comes a taste for warm, nourishing food. Steaming hot soups, all prepared quickly and easily, fit the bill. Side dishes for the season include squash in new combinations and flavors. And for the health-conscious, "On the Light Side" throws the spotlight on legumes—those low-fat, low-cholesterol, high-fiber sources of protein—served as colorful side dishes or attractive alternatives to meats. As for sweets, there's nothing as warm and satisfying in the morning as freshly baked cinnamon rolls, orange rolls, or other sweet rolls.

Meet Our Cooks Across The South

Up to 4,000 recipes pour into our office each month from readers like you. They're all reviewed, and many are used in the magazine.

Through the years, many of the contributors' names have become familiar to the foods staff. So to celebrate the 25th anniversary of our magazine, it seemed natural to honor a group of longtime recipe contributors. Thus was born "Cooks Across the South"—a plan to bring in 12 special cooks for a trip to Birmingham as guests of *Southern Living*.

Narrowing down thousands of recipe contributors to 12 was not easy. We compiled a list of those who had consistently submitted outstanding recipes. Each received questionnaires, and the honorees were chosen by their responses.

Across the South from Texas to Virginia, these cooks flew in for a busy three days. Introductions showed that they represent a broad cross section of our readers and our region. All have children. Half of them work full time or part-time, three enjoy retirement, two are full-time homemakers, and one has returned to college. All regard food preparation with pleasure.

From the start, it seemed more like a reunion of old friends than a first-time meeting. We knew we felt close to our readers, and now we know why. They're real people, just like all of us, who share a love of good food and fellowship. We're appreciative that they take the time to share their recipes with us.

For this cookbook, we've arranged their recipes (along with an introduction to each cook) as we do all recipes, starting with soups and appetizers and ending with desserts. Now meet these special ladies, and sample their favorite dishes.

Slice one-third of fresh mushrooms; finely chop remaining mushrooms, and set aside.

Melt butter in a Dutch oven; add onion and brown sugar. Cook over medium heat, stirring constantly, 15 minutes or until onion is caramel colored. Add all of mushrooms, and sauté 5 minutes. Add flour, stirring until smooth. Cook 1 minute, stirring constantly. Gradually add water, chicken broth, and vermouth; cook over medium heat until mixture is slightly thickened. Reduce heat, and simmer 10 minutes. Stir in salt and pepper. Yield: 6 cups.

■ **Pat Rush Benigno** has loved to cook since she won a cookie-baking contest in junior high school. Her collection of over 200 cookbooks reaffirms her fondness for cooking. Hailing from **Gulfport, Mississippi,** she frankly declares that "everyday suppers are boring," and describes herself as a creative cook.

■ **Lynne Weeks** of **Columbus, Georgia,** recalls her mother encouraging her as a child to cook for her young friends. She has enjoyed cooking and entertaining ever since and frequently experiments with and develops new recipes. This creative cook says she developed her recipe for Fresh Mushroom Soup, presented here, from a French onion soup recipe; because her family particularly likes mushrooms, Lynne just substituted the fresh mushrooms for the onions.

FRESH MUSHROOM SOUP

1 pound fresh mushrooms
¼ cup plus 2 tablespoons butter or margarine
2 cups chopped onion
1 tablespoon brown sugar
¼ cup all-purpose flour
1 cup water
1¾ cups chicken broth
¾ cup dry vermouth
1 teaspoon salt
¼ teaspoon coarsely ground pepper

CRABMEAT MOUSSE

2 envelopes unflavored gelatin
½ cup cold water
1 (8-ounce) package cream cheese, cubed
1 (10¾-ounce) can cream of celery soup
2 tablespoons Worcestershire sauce
1 cup mayonnaise or salad dressing
1½ cups lump white crabmeat
¼ cup diced onion
¼ cup diced celery
¼ teaspoon salt
¼ teaspoon red pepper

Sprinkle gelatin over cold water in a medium saucepan; let stand 1 minute. Cook over low heat, stirring until gelatin dissolves. Add cream cheese, soup, and Worcestershire sauce; cook over low heat, stirring until cream cheese melts and mixture is smooth. Remove from heat; stir in mayonnaise and remaining ingredients. Pour into a lightly oiled 5-cup mold. Cover and chill until firm. Serve with crackers. Yield: 4½ cups.

■ In **Winston-Salem, North Carolina, Linda Sutton** can be found in her kitchen, using her microwave and preparing salads. For 10 years, she and her husband, Jim, owned a catering business. She baked wedding cakes, and he decorated them. When they celebrated their 25th wedding anniversary in July, they catered their own party. Try Linda's newest offering, Luncheon Pasta Salad.

LUNCHEON PASTA SALAD

1 (8-ounce) package elbow
  macaroni
2 cups chopped cooked chicken
  or ham
1 (11-ounce) can mandarin
  oranges, drained
½ cup chopped celery
¼ teaspoon salt
¼ teaspoon pepper
½ cup mayonnaise or salad
  dressing
¼ cup commercial creamy blue
  cheese salad dressing
Lettuce leaves

Cook macaroni according to package directions; drain. Rinse with cold water; drain.

Combine macaroni, chicken, mandarin oranges, chopped celery, salt, pepper, mayonnaise, and salad dressing, tossing lightly; chill thoroughly. Serve salad on lettuce leaves. Yield: 4 to 6 servings.

■ If you could see the list of ribbons **Mary Kay Menees** of **White Pine, Tennessee,** has won at the county fair for her baking, you'd think she'd been cooking all her life. Actually, she didn't cook much until after she married, but she's made up for lost time since then! Mary Kay prepares Lasagna Maria once a week for her husband, Robert; it seems his favorite meal is "anything Italian," and he's especially fond of this recipe.

LASAGNA MARIA

1 (8-ounce) package lasagna
  noodles
1 pound mild bulk pork sausage
1 (32-ounce) jar commercial
  spaghetti sauce
1 egg, slightly beaten
1 (12-ounce) carton ricotta
  cheese
1 tablespoon dried parsley flakes
½ teaspoon dried whole oregano
¼ teaspoon pepper
¼ cup grated Parmesan cheese
2 cups (8 ounces) shredded
  mozzarella cheese, divided
1 (4½-ounce) jar sliced
  mushrooms, drained
1 (3½-ounce) package sliced
  pepperoni

Cook lasagna noodles according to package directions, omitting salt, and drain well.

Cook sausage in a large skillet until browned, stirring to crumble; drain. Stir spaghetti sauce into sausage; set aside. Combine egg and next 5 ingredients, stirring well.

Spread about ½ cup meat sauce in a lightly greased 13- x 9- x 2-inch baking dish. Layer half of the noodles, half of the ricotta cheese mixture, one-third of mozzarella cheese, and one-third of remaining meat sauce; repeat layers, using equal amounts. Arrange mushrooms and pepperoni slices on top. Spoon remaining meat sauce on top. Bake at 375° for 20 minutes. Sprinkle with remaining cheese, and bake an additional 5 minutes. Yield: 6 servings.

■ **Rublelene Singleton** reads cookbooks like novels but rarely actually goes by a recipe. "I just get ideas from them and combine two or three recipes that sound good into one," explains this native of **Scotts Hill, Tennessee.** She developed Cornish Hens With Fruited Stuffing one year for Christmas, but she cooks it throughout the year as well, sometimes grilling the hens instead of baking them.

CORNISH HENS WITH FRUITED STUFFING

1½ cups herb-seasoned croutons
1 (8¾-ounce) can apricot halves,
  drained and chopped
½ cup seedless green grapes,
  halved
⅓ cup chopped pecans
2 tablespoons apricot nectar
2 tablespoons butter or
  margarine, melted
1 tablespoon capers
1 tablespoon chopped fresh
  parsley
¼ teaspoon salt
¼ teaspoon pepper
4 (1- to 1½-pound) Cornish hens
⅓ cup apricot nectar
2 tablespoons butter or
  margarine, melted
2 teaspoons soy sauce

Combine first 10 ingredients; stir gently, and set aside.

Remove giblets from hens; reserve for other uses, if desired. Rinse hens with cold water, and pat dry. Stuff hens with crouton mixture, and close cavities. Secure with wooden picks; truss.

Place hens, breast side up, on rack in a shallow roasting pan. Combine ⅓ cup apricot nectar, 2 tablespoons butter, and soy sauce; brush on hens. Bake at 350° for 1½ hours, basting occasionally with apricot mixture. Yield: 4 servings.

"I have a theory: If you can read, you can cook," **Sue-Sue Hartstern** of **Louisville, Kentucky,** says. Sue-Sue is a spontaneous cook. She plans her menus after work with a cookbook in her lap in the parking lot outside the grocery store. She didn't start cooking until she married. Then it was a different recipe every night for an entire year.

BREAKFAST BURRITOS

8 (8-inch) flour tortillas
½ pound bulk pork sausage
2 large potatoes, peeled and grated
1 medium-size green pepper, chopped
½ cup chopped onion
2 tablespoons butter or margarine
8 eggs, beaten
½ teaspoon salt
¼ teaspoon pepper
2 cups (8 ounces) shredded Cheddar cheese
Taco sauce

Wrap tortillas securely in aluminum foil; bake at 350° for 15 minutes or until thoroughly heated.

Brown sausage in a large nonstick skillet; drain. Remove sausage, and set aside. Add potatoes, green pepper, and onion to skillet; cook over medium heat until potatoes are browned, stirring occasionally. Add butter, eggs, salt, and pepper. Cook over medium heat, stirring gently, until eggs are set. Stir in sausage.

Fill each tortilla evenly with egg-sausage mixture. Roll up tortillas, and place seam side down in a lightly greased 13- x 9- x 2-inch baking dish. Cover with foil, and bake at 375° for 10 minutes; sprinkle with Cheddar cheese. Cover and bake an additional 5 minutes. Serve with taco sauce. Yield: 6 to 8 servings.

■ **Eileen Wehling** of **Austin, Texas,** is a woman of many talents, including restoring old Mustangs and cooking healthy. "Good texture and taste, plus good for you—that is the epitome of a good recipe," she says knowingly. Cooking with herbs and grilling are ways she trims calories. Her recipe for Oven-Baked French Toast omits some of the butter used in cooking a skillet version of French toast and offers great flavor at the same time.

OVEN-BAKED FRENCH TOAST

¼ cup butter or margarine
3 egg yolks
3 tablespoons sugar
½ teaspoon salt
⅔ cup milk
2 tablespoons amaretto
3 egg whites, stiffly beaten
16 (¾-inch-thick) slices French bread

Place 2 tablespoons butter in each of two 13- x 9- x 2-inch pans, and heat at 425° until hot.

Combine egg yolks, sugar, and salt; beat at high speed of an electric mixer until thick and lemon colored. Gradually add milk and amaretto; fold in egg whites. Dip bread slices into egg mixture; place in hot pans. Bake at 425° for 10 minutes; turn and bake an additional 5 minutes or until golden brown. Serve immediately. Yield: 6 to 8 servings.

■ A former home economics teacher, **Marie Allison Davis** of **Charlotte, North Carolina,** recalls cooking her first meal at age 10, but she had to pester her mother and grandmother for years before they let her try. Marie especially enjoys baking homemade yeast bread. "It's a great release of tension," she explains with a laugh. Every Christmas she bakes Glazed Sweet Bread Wreath.

GLAZED SWEET BREAD WREATH

5¼ cups all-purpose flour
¼ cup sugar
1 teaspoon salt
2 packages dry yeast
1 cup milk
1 cup butter or margarine
½ cup water
2 eggs, beaten
½ teaspoon grated lemon rind
½ teaspoon grated orange rind
½ cup raisins
½ cup chopped candied cherries
½ cup chopped pecans
½ cup pitted dates, chopped
3 tablespoons butter or margarine, softened
½ cup sugar
1 tablespoon ground cinnamon
1 cup sifted powdered sugar
¼ teaspoon vanilla extract
2 to 3 tablespoons milk
Garnish: candied cherry halves

Combine first 4 ingredients in a large bowl; stir and set aside.

Combine 1 cup milk, 1 cup butter, and water in a medium saucepan; cook over low heat, stirring constantly, until mixture reaches 120° to 130°. Stir milk mixture into flour mixture. Add eggs, stirring until blended. Stir in lemon rind and next 5 ingredients. Cover and refrigerate at least 8 hours.

Turn dough out onto a floured surface, and roll to an 18- x 12-inch rectangle. Spread with 3 tablespoons butter. Combine ½ cup sugar and cinnamon; sprinkle over butter.

Roll up dough, jellyroll fashion, starting at one long side; pinch seam to seal. Place roll on a large greased baking sheet, seam side down; shape into a ring, and pinch ends together to seal.

Using kitchen shears, make cuts in dough at 1-inch intervals around ring, cutting two-thirds of the way through roll with each cut. Gently turn each piece of dough on its side, slightly overlapping slices.

Cover dough, and let rise in a warm place (85°), free from drafts, 1 hour or until doubled in bulk. Uncover and bake at 350° for 25 to 30 minutes or until golden brown. Transfer to a wire rack.

Combine powdered sugar, vanilla, and enough milk to make a glaze consistency. Drizzle glaze over warm coffee cake. Garnish, if desired. Yield: 1 coffee cake.

■ "I cook just like my mother," says **Mary Pappas** of **Richmond, Virginia,** her dark Greek eyes flashing proudly. "I cook with olive oil and butter, and lots of garlic, too." Folks often call Mary, asking her questions or requesting recipes. The bread recipe here, Koulourakia, is a Greek butter twist.

KOULOURAKIA

¾ cup butter, softened
¼ cup shortening
1 cup sugar
3 eggs
1 teaspoon vanilla extract
4 cups all-purpose flour
1 tablespoon baking powder
¼ teaspoon baking soda
1 egg yolk, beaten
1 tablespoon water
2 to 3 teaspoons ground
    cinnamon
2 to 3 teaspoons sesame seeds

Cream butter and shortening in a large mixing bowl; gradually add sugar, beating well at medium speed of an electric mixer. Add eggs, one at a time, beating well after each addition. Add vanilla; beat until blended.

Combine flour, baking powder, and soda; gradually add to creamed mixture, mixing after each addition. Chill dough 1 to 2 hours.

Divide dough into fourths. Divide each fourth into 16 portions. Roll each portion into a 4-inch rope; fold each rope in half, and twist. Place twists 2 inches apart on greased baking sheets.

Combine egg yolk and water; brush over twists. Sprinkle lightly with cinnamon and sesame seeds. Bake at 325° for 20 to 25 minutes or until light golden brown. Immediately transfer to wire racks to cool. Yield: 5⅓ dozen.

■ "I'm a messy cook; my family stays out of my way when I'm in the kitchen, but they do help me clean up," laughs **Linda Camp Keith** of **Carrollton, Texas.** Having returned to college, Linda usually prepares quick, vegetarian-style meals during the week, but she admits that's mostly so she doesn't feel guilty about splurging and trying new, more extravagant recipes on the weekend—especially desserts.

SPUMONI CHARLOTTE

20 ladyfingers, split
¼ cup amaretto
⅔ cup chocolate wafer crumbs
1 quart vanilla ice cream,
    softened
1 tablespoon rum
1 (6-ounce) jar maraschino
    cherries, drained
1 quart pistachio ice cream,
    softened
1 cup whipping cream
½ cup sifted powdered sugar
1 tablespoon rum
Garnish: maraschino cherries

Brush cut side of ladyfingers with amaretto; roll lightly in wafer crumbs. Line bottom and sides of a 9-inch springform pan with crumb-coated ladyfingers.

Combine vanilla ice cream and 1 tablespoon rum; spoon into pan, spreading to sides. Place maraschino cherries over ice cream; press cherries gently.

Spoon pistachio ice cream over cherries; spread to sides. Freeze until firm.

Combine whipping cream, sugar, and rum in a mixing bowl; beat at high speed of an electric mixer until soft peaks form. Spoon whipped cream into a decorating bag fitted with large metal tip No. 2110. Remove dessert from pan. Pipe rosettes over top and around bottom edge. Garnish, if desired. Return to freezer until ready to serve. Yield: 10 to 12 servings.

■ **Jodie McCoy** of **Tulsa, Oklahoma,** actually began cooking 25 years ago when she made after-school treats for her son and two daughters. She finds even more time to cook now and enjoys sharing Chocolate Chip Cookies with her grandchildren and husband, Bill, "who loves sweets."

CHOCOLATE CHIP COOKIES

1 cup butter or margarine,
    softened
1 cup vegetable oil
1 cup sugar
1 cup firmly packed brown sugar
1 egg
2 teaspoons vanilla extract
3½ cups all-purpose flour
1 teaspoon baking soda
1 teaspoon salt
1 teaspoon cream of tartar
1 cup regular oats, uncooked
1 cup crisp rice cereal
1 (12-ounce) package semisweet
    chocolate morsels
¾ cup chopped pecans

Cream butter and oil; gradually add sugars, beating at medium speed of an electric mixer. Add egg and vanilla, mixing well.

Combine flour, soda, salt, and cream of tartar; gradually add to creamed mixture, mixing well. Stir in oats and remaining ingredients.

Drop dough by teaspoonfuls onto greased cookie sheets. Bake at 375° for 10 to 12 minutes. Cool on wire racks. Yield: 10 dozen.

■ **Sandra Haynes Pichon of Slidell, Louisiana,** changed gears in the kitchen when she married her Louisiana husband, Stanley. Sandra, who was used to meat-and-potatoes-style cooking suddenly found herself fixing fresh seafood and the French and Creole cuisines indigenous to Louisiana. A savvy cook, she quickly adapted and still makes many of her favorite recipes, such as Frosted Chocolate Snack Cake.

FROSTED CHOCOLATE SNACK CAKE

2 cups all-purpose flour
2 cups sugar
1 cup water
½ cup butter or margarine
½ cup shortening
¼ cup cocoa
½ cup buttermilk
2 eggs, beaten
1 teaspoon baking soda
1 teaspoon vanilla extract
Chocolate Frosting
Vanilla ice cream (optional)

Combine flour and sugar in a large bowl; mix well, and set aside.

Combine water, butter, shortening, and cocoa in a heavy saucepan; bring mixture to a boil, stirring constantly. Gradually stir butter mixture into flour mixture. Stir in buttermilk, eggs, soda, and vanilla.

Pour batter into a greased and floured 15- x 10- x 1-inch jellyroll pan. Bake at 375° for 20 minutes or until a wooden pick inserted in center of cake comes out clean. Spread with Chocolate Frosting while cake is warm. Top frosted cake with vanilla ice cream, if desired. Yield: 15 to 18 servings.

Chocolate Frosting

½ cup butter or margarine
¼ cup plus 2 tablespoons milk
¼ cup cocoa
1 (16-ounce) package powdered sugar, sifted
1 cup chopped pecans
1 teaspoon vanilla extract

Combine butter, milk, and cocoa in a large heavy saucepan; bring to a boil, stirring constantly. Remove from heat. Stir in sugar, mixing until smooth. Stir in pecans and vanilla. Yield: enough for one 15- x 10- x 1-inch cake.

Sweet Rolls On The Rise

If by nature you're an early riser in a household of weekend late sleepers, take advantage of the time alone to do some baking just for fun.

For those mornings when you're inspired to serve sweet rolls but not to race the sun up, you can look to our quicker versions using convenience products, such as frozen bread dough, biscuit mix, and refrigerated rolls.

GLAZED ORANGE ROLLS
(pictured on page 185)

1 package dry yeast
¾ cup warm water (105° to 115°)
3 to 3¼ cups all-purpose flour, divided
2 tablespoons sugar
1½ teaspoons salt
1 egg
2 tablespoons butter or margarine, melted
1 tablespoon grated orange rind
¼ cup orange juice
1 orange, peeled, sectioned, and chopped
1 tablespoon sugar
Orange Butter Glaze

Dissolve yeast in warm water in a large bowl; let stand 5 minutes. Add

1 cup flour, 2 tablespoons sugar, and next 5 ingredients; beat at medium speed of an electric mixer until blended. Gradually stir in enough remaining flour to make a soft dough.

Turn dough out onto a well-floured surface, and knead until smooth and elastic (about 5 minutes). Place in a well-greased bowl, turning to grease top. Cover and let rise in a warm place (85°), free from drafts, 1 hour or until doubled in bulk.

Punch dough down; turn out onto a lightly floured surface, and knead lightly 4 or 5 times. Roll dough to ¼-inch thickness; cut with a 2½-inch biscuit cutter. Cover with a towel, and let stand 10 minutes.

Combine chopped orange and 1 tablespoon sugar; let stand 5 minutes. Drain and pat dry between paper towels; set aside.

Make a crease across each circle, and place an orange piece in center. Fold over; gently press edges to seal. Place rolls in a lightly greased 13- x 9- x 2-inch baking pan. Cover and let rise in a warm place, free from drafts, 30 minutes. Bake at 425° for 15 minutes. Spread with glaze. Yield: 2 dozen.

Orange Butter Glaze

1 tablespoon butter or margarine, softened
1 teaspoon grated orange rind
1 cup sifted powdered sugar
1½ tablespoons orange juice
1½ teaspoons lemon juice

Cream butter and orange rind at medium speed of an electric mixer; add powdered sugar alternately with juices, beating until blended. Yield: ⅓ cup.
Sandra Russell
Gainesville, Florida

CHEESE-APRICOT
SWEET ROLLS
(pictured on page 185)

⅓ cup sugar
1 teaspoon ground cinnamon
1 (16-ounce) loaf frozen bread
    dough, thawed
2 tablespoons sugar
2 teaspoons all-purpose flour
1 (3-ounce) package cream
    cheese, softened
1 egg yolk
½ teaspoon vanilla extract
2 tablespoons apricot preserves

Combine ⅓ cup sugar and cinnamon in a large shallow dish; stir well. Set dish aside.

Divide dough into 12 pieces, and shape each piece of dough into a 12-inch rope. Roll ropes of dough in sugar-cinnamon mixture. Shape each rope into a loose coil, tucking ends under roll; place rolls on a lightly greased baking sheet.

Combine 2 tablespoons sugar and flour. Add cream cheese, and stir until smooth. Add egg yolk and vanilla, stirring well. Spoon about 1 teaspoon cheese mixture into center of each coil, and top with ½ teaspoon apricot preserves.

Let rise, uncovered, in a warm place (85°), free from drafts, 30 minutes or until doubled in bulk. Bake at 375° for 15 minutes or until golden brown. Remove immediately from baking sheet, and cool on wire rack. Yield: 1 dozen. *Mrs. E. W. Hanley*
Palm Harbor, Florida

EASY CARAMEL ROLLS

2 cups biscuit mix
½ cup milk
2 tablespoons butter or margarine
½ cup firmly packed brown sugar,
    divided
1 teaspoon ground cinnamon
¼ cup butter or margarine,
    melted
½ cup chopped pecans

Combine biscuit mix and milk, stirring with a fork until blended. Turn dough out onto a lightly floured surface, and knead 4 or 5 times. Roll dough to a 15- x 9-inch rectangle; spread with 2 tablespoons butter.

Combine ¼ cup brown sugar and cinnamon; sprinkle mixture over dough. Starting with long side, roll up dough, jellyroll fashion. Pinch seam to seal (do not seal ends). Cut into 12 slices.

Combine remaining ¼ cup brown sugar, melted butter, and pecans; divide mixture equally into well-greased muffin pans. Place slices, cut side down, in muffin pans. Bake at 350° for 20 to 22 minutes or until lightly browned. Remove from pans immediately. Yield: 1 dozen.
Naomi Reed
Knoxville, Tennessee

PRALINE BUNS

1 package dry yeast
½ cup warm water (105° to 115°)
½ cup boiling water
¼ cup shortening
¼ cup butter or margarine
⅓ cup sugar
1 egg
1 egg yolk
1½ teaspoons salt
3½ to 4 cups bread flour, divided
¼ cup butter or margarine,
    melted
1 cup chopped pralines
Glaze

Dissolve yeast in ½ cup warm water in a large bowl. Combine ½ cup boiling water and next 3 ingredients; stir until shortening melts. Cool to 105° to 115°; stir into yeast mixture. Add egg, egg yolk, and salt, mixing well. Gradually add 2 cups flour, beating at medium speed of an electric mixer until smooth. Stir in enough remaining flour to form a soft dough.

Turn dough out onto a lightly floured surface, and knead until smooth and elastic (5 to 7 minutes). Place in a greased bowl, turning to grease top. Cover and let rise in a warm place, free from drafts, 1 hour or until doubled in bulk.

Punch dough down, and divide in half; roll each half to a 15- x 9-inch rectangle. Spread each with 2 tablespoons melted butter, and sprinkle evenly with pralines. Starting with long side, roll up jellyroll fashion. Pinch seam to seal (do not seal ends). Cut each roll into 9 slices; place slices, cut side down, in 2 greased 9-inch square pans. Cover and let rise in a warm place, free from drafts, 1 hour.

Bake at 350° for 20 to 25 minutes or until golden brown. Drizzle glaze over warm rolls. Yield: 1½ dozen.

Glaze

1½ cups sifted powdered sugar
3 to 4 tablespoons milk
½ teaspoon vanilla extract

Combine all ingredients; mix well. Yield: ½ cup.

Note: To make ahead, bake rolls at 350° for 15 minutes; cool. Wrap in aluminum foil; freeze. To serve, thaw and bake at 350° for 5 to 10 minutes or until golden brown; glaze while warm.

QUICK BREAKFAST
SWEET ROLLS

1 tablespoon orange-flavored
    breakfast drink mix
2 tablespoons flaked coconut
2 tablespoons orange marmalade
¼ cup chopped pecans
1 (8-ounce) can refrigerated
    crescent dinner rolls

Combine first 4 ingredients; set aside. Remove rolls from package, leaving in rectangular shape; seal perforations. Spread pecan mixture over dough. Starting with long side, roll up jellyroll fashion. Pinch seam to seal (do not seal ends). Cut roll into 12 slices; place in greased muffin pans. Bake at 350° for 12 minutes or until golden brown. Remove from pans immediately. Yield: 1 dozen.
Erma Jackson
Huntsville, Alabama

OLD-FASHIONED CINNAMON ROLLS

½ cup milk
⅓ cup shortening
¼ cup firmly packed brown sugar
1 teaspoon salt
1 package dry yeast
½ cup warm water (105° to 115°)
2 eggs
3 to 3½ cups bread flour, divided
¾ cup quick-cooking oats, uncooked
2 tablespoons butter or margarine, softened
1 cup firmly packed brown sugar
⅓ cup butter or margarine, softened
¼ cup raisins
2 teaspoons ground cinnamon
2 cups sifted powdered sugar
3 to 4 tablespoons water

Combine milk, shortening, ¼ cup brown sugar, and salt in a medium saucepan; heat until shortening melts, stirring occasionally. Cool mixture to 105° to 115°.

Dissolve yeast in ½ cup warm water in a large mixing bowl; let stand 5 minutes. Stir in milk mixture, eggs, 1 cup flour, and oats, mixing well. Gradually stir in enough remaining flour to make a soft dough.

Turn dough out onto a lightly floured surface, and knead until smooth and elastic (about 8 minutes). Place in a well-greased bowl, turning to grease top. Cover and let rise in a warm place (85°), free from drafts, 1 hour or until doubled in bulk.

Punch dough down; cover and let rest 10 minutes. Divide dough in half, and roll each half to a 12-inch square. Spread each square with 1 tablespoon butter. Combine 1 cup brown sugar, ⅓ cup butter, raisins, and cinnamon; sprinkle brown sugar mixture evenly over dough. Roll up each square of dough, jellyroll fashion; pinch seams to seal (do not seal ends). Cut each roll into 1-inch slices, and place slices, cut side down, in two greased 8-inch square baking pans.

Cover and let rise in a warm place, free from drafts, about 45 minutes or until almost doubled in bulk. Bake at 375° for 15 to 20 minutes or until rolls are golden brown. Combine powdered sugar and water; drizzle glaze over warm rolls. Yield: 2 dozen.
Carolyn Rosen
Nashville, Tennessee

COCONUT-PECAN COILS
(pictured on page 185)

2 packages dry yeast
½ cup warm water (105° to 115°)
2 tablespoons butter or margarine, softened
⅓ cup sugar
1 teaspoon salt
2 eggs
1 (8-ounce) carton sour cream
1 cup flaked coconut
3¾ to 4¼ cups all-purpose flour, divided
1 cup finely chopped pecans
¾ cup firmly packed light brown sugar
½ cup butter or margarine, melted

Dissolve yeast in warm water in a large bowl; let stand 5 minutes. Add 2 tablespoons butter, sugar, salt, eggs, sour cream, coconut, and 2 cups flour; beat at medium speed of an electric mixer until well blended. Gradually stir in enough remaining flour to make a stiff dough.

Turn dough out onto a floured surface, and knead until smooth and elastic (8 to 10 minutes). Divide dough into 24 pieces; shape each piece into a 9-inch rope. Combine pecans and brown sugar. Dip each rope in melted butter, and coat with pecan mixture. Coil ropes into lightly greased muffin pans, tucking ends into centers.

Cover and let rise in a warm place (85°), free from drafts, 30 minutes. (Rolls will not be doubled in bulk.) Bake at 375° for 15 to 18 minutes or until golden. Immediately remove rolls from pan; serve warm, or let cool on wire racks. Yield: 2 dozen.
Mary Dishon
Stanford, Kentucky

Microwave Cheesecake

This Luscious Lemon Cheesecake can be made in the microwave in less than 30 minutes, and then chilled and served. The springform pan, one of the newer pieces of microwave cooking equipment available on the market, can also be used when you're microwaving other cakes.

LUSCIOUS LEMON CHEESECAKE

3 tablespoons butter or margarine
1½ cups graham cracker crumbs
2 tablespoons sugar
3 (8-ounce) packages cream cheese
¾ cup sugar
1 teaspoon grated lemon rind
2 tablespoons lemon juice
1½ teaspoons vanilla extract
3 eggs
1½ cups sour cream
2 tablespoons sugar
½ teaspoon grated lemon rind
1 teaspoon lemon juice
Garnishes: kiwifruit slices, lemon twist

Place butter in a medium bowl. Microwave, uncovered, at HIGH 50 seconds or until melted. Add graham cracker crumbs and 2 tablespoons sugar, stirring well. Press mixture into a lightly greased 10-inch microwave springform pan. Microwave, uncovered, at HIGH 2 to 2½ minutes or until firm, rotating a half-turn after 1 minute. Let cool; set aside.

Place cream cheese in a 3-quart mixing bowl; microwave, uncovered, at MEDIUM (50% power) 2½ to 3 minutes or until cream cheese is softened. Add ¾ cup sugar and next 3 ingredients; beat at medium speed of an electric mixer until blended. Add eggs, one at a time, beating after each addition; spoon into prepared crust. Microwave, uncovered, at MEDIUM 12 to 14 minutes or until cheesecake is almost set in center, rotating pan a quarter-turn every 3 minutes.

Combine sour cream and next 3 ingredients; spoon evenly over cheesecake. Microwave, uncovered, at MEDIUM 3 minutes, giving pan a quarter-turn every minute. Refrigerate for several hours before serving. Garnish, if desired. Yield: one 10-inch cheesecake.

ON THE LIGHT SIDE

Spilling The Beans About Legumes

After years of being called "poor man's meat," legumes are finally gaining respect. The fact that they're low-fat, low-cholesterol, high-fiber sources of protein is only enhanced by their nutrient density. A ½-cup serving of kidney beans provides as much soluble fiber (the cholesterol-lowering kind) as ¼ cup oat bran and more protein than most fruits and vegetables.

And the protein in legumes is naturally low in fat and devoid of cholesterol. Those same kidney beans also boast B vitamins—thiamin, niacin, folacin, and B₆—as well as magnesium, phosphorus, iron, zinc, calcium, and potassium.

Just exactly what are legumes? They're plants that produce pods with edible seeds. There are thousands of species, but only a few make it to our supermarkets. Black beans, black-eyed peas, chick-peas (garbanzo beans), kidney beans, lentils, lima beans, peanuts, peas (split and whole, yellow and green), pinto beans, soybeans, and white beans are the best known legumes.

Although peanuts are technically legumes, they're usually eaten like nuts. Nutritionists refer to peanuts as "a protein source with a price" because of their considerable fat content.

All dried legumes—except lentils, split peas, and black-eyed peas—must be soaked in water before cooking. Soak them in enough water to cover 2 inches for 6 to 8 hours or overnight. For a quick soak, boil beans for 2 minutes, cover the pot, and let stand 1 hour.

Soaking softens legumes and leaches out oligosaccharides, the sugars that cause digestive discomfort in some people. Changing the water several times during soaking reduces oligosaccharides even more.

To cook legumes, discard soaking water and cover with fresh water. Cooking times depend on the size and age of the beans. Adding an acidic ingredient, such as tomatoes or vinegar, before cooking can lengthen the cooking time and may prevent the beans from softening.

For those who have never eaten legumes, starting off slowly is probably a good idea. Lentils, black-eyed peas, lima beans, chick-peas, and white beans tend to be easier to digest than other legumes, although the effect is highly individual. The more often legumes are included in the diet the easier it is for the body to digest them.

MARINATED LEGUMES

1 (12-ounce) package 13-bean
    soup mix
8 cups water
⅔ cup oil-free Italian salad
    dressing
1 tablespoon red wine vinegar
½ teaspoon dried whole Italian
    seasoning
⅛ teaspoon crushed red pepper
2 tomatoes, chopped
½ cup sliced green onions
Lettuce leaves

Sort and wash beans; place in a Dutch oven. Add water, and bring to a boil; reduce heat, and simmer 1 hour and 20 minutes or until beans are tender. Drain.

Combine salad dressing and next 3 ingredients; pour over beans, and toss gently. Cover and chill at least 8 hours, stirring occasionally.

Add tomato and green onions; toss gently. Serve on lettuce leaves. Yield: 12 servings (110 calories per ½-cup serving).

☐ *7.2 grams protein, 0.3 gram fat, 20.4 grams carbohydrate, 0 milligrams cholesterol, 154 milligrams sodium, and 53 milligrams calcium.*

LENTILS-AND-RICE SALAD

⅓ cup dried lentils
1⅔ cups water
1 cup cooked long-grain rice
    (cooked without salt or fat)
⅓ cup diced green pepper
⅓ cup diced green onions
⅓ cup diced celery
1 (2-ounce) jar diced pimiento,
    drained
⅓ cup oil-free Italian salad
    dressing
5 lettuce leaves

Combine lentils and water; bring to a boil. Cover, reduce heat, and simmer 30 minutes or until lentils are tender. Drain well.

Combine lentils, rice, and next 5 ingredients; toss gently. Cover and chill 3 to 4 hours, stirring occasionally. Serve on lettuce leaves. Yield: 5 servings (104 calories per ⅔-cup serving).

☐ *4.9 grams protein, 0.3 gram fat, 20.6 grams carbohydrate, 0 milligrams cholesterol, 186 milligrams sodium, and 23 milligrams calcium.*

                Kathy Smith
            Callahan, Florida

TEXAS RANCH BEANS

1 (16-ounce) package dried pinto
   beans
6 cups water
¾ cup (4 ounces) chopped cooked
   lean ham
¾ cup chopped onion
1½ tablespoons chili powder
1½ teaspoons salt-free
   herb-and-spice blend
½ teaspoon pepper
½ teaspoon red pepper
¼ teaspoon salt
1 (10-ounce) can tomatoes and
   green chiles, undrained and
   chopped

Sort and wash beans; place in a
Dutch oven. Cover with water 2
inches above beans; let soak 8 hours.
   Drain beans, and return to Dutch
oven. Add 6 cups water and next 7
ingredients to beans. Bring to a boil;
reduce heat, and simmer 1½ hours
or until beans are tender, stirring occasionally. Add tomatoes, and simmer an additional 30 minutes. Yield:
6½ cups (152 calories per ½-cup
serving).

☐ *10.3 grams protein, 1.5 grams fat,
25.2 grams carbohydrate, 8 milligrams cholesterol, 152 milligrams sodium, and 55 milligrams calcium.*
            Patricia Wenzel
              Hurst, Texas

SPLIT PEA SOUP

1 (16-ounce) package dried green
   split peas
8 cups water
2 bay leaves
1½ teaspoons salt
1 teaspoon dried whole thyme
3 cloves garlic, minced
¼ cup Chablis or other dry white
   wine
2 cups sliced carrots
1½ cups diced potato
1 cup chopped celery
¾ cup chopped onion
2 tablespoons dried parsley flakes
2 tablespoons lemon juice

Combine split peas, water, bay
leaves, salt, thyme, and minced garlic in a Dutch oven. Bring mixture to
a boil; reduce heat, and simmer, uncovered, 1 hour.
   Add wine and remaining ingredients to mixture in Dutch oven;
cook 30 minutes or until peas are
tender. Remove bay leaves.
   Spoon mixture into container of an
electric blender or food processor,
and process until mixture is smooth.
Yield: 11 servings (178 calories per
1-cup serving).

☐ *11.2 grams protein, 0.6 gram fat,
33.4 grams carbohydrate, 0 milligrams cholesterol, 347 milligrams sodium, and 47 milligrams calcium.*

LENTIL SPAGHETTI SAUCE

Vegetable cooking spray
¾ cup chopped onion
2 cloves garlic, minced
4 cups water
1½ cups dried lentils, uncooked
1 teaspoon crushed red pepper
¾ teaspoon salt
½ teaspoon pepper
1 (14½-ounce) can no-salt-added
   whole tomatoes, undrained and
   chopped
1 (6-ounce) can no-salt-added
   tomato paste
1 tablespoon white vinegar
2 beef-flavored bouillon cubes
½ teaspoon dried whole basil
½ teaspoon dried whole oregano
8 cups hot cooked spaghetti
   (cooked without salt or fat)

Coat a Dutch oven with cooking
spray. Add onion and garlic; sauté
until tender. Add water and next 4
ingredients. Bring to a boil; cover,
reduce heat, and simmer 30 minutes.
   Add tomatoes and next 5 ingredients. Bring to a boil; reduce heat,
and simmer 45 minutes to 1 hour or
to desired thickness, stirring often.
Serve over hot cooked spaghetti.

Yield: 8 servings (351 calories per 1
cup sauce and 1 cup spaghetti).

☐ *18.2 grams protein, 1.2 grams fat,
67.8 grams carbohydrate, 0 milligrams cholesterol, 263 milligrams sodium, and 67 milligrams calcium.*
            Marsha Canning
         Tallahassee, Florida

LIGHT MENU

A Healthy Salute
To Summer

In the South, September days can be
as hot as those in July or August.
Keeping those steamy days in mind,
we pulled together a healthy menu
(containing less than 30% fat) in
which most of the preparation can be
done in advance. Only a minimum of
stove-top cooking is required, avoid-
ing extra heat.

      Scarlet Sipper
Tarragon Chicken Salad
    Sourdough Wedges
     Angel Food Cake
With Amaretto-Almond Sauce

SCARLET SIPPER

2 cups cranberry-apple juice,
   chilled
½ cup orange juice, chilled
2 tablespoons lemon juice
1 (11-ounce) bottle sparkling
   mineral water, chilled

Combine all ingredients; stir gently, and serve immediately. Yield: 4 cups (98 calories per 1-cup serving).

☐ *0.2 gram protein, 0 grams fat, 23.5 grams carbohydrate, 0 milligrams cholesterol, 1 milligram sodium, and 14 milligrams calcium.*

Cecylle Powell
Knoxville, Tennessee

TARRAGON CHICKEN SALAD

4 (4-ounce) skinned, boned
  chicken breast halves
1 medium onion, halved
1 stalk celery, halved
1 carrot, halved
1 bay leaf
1 egg white
1 teaspoon chopped fresh
  tarragon
¼ teaspoon salt
⅛ teaspoon garlic powder
⅛ teaspoon white pepper
1 teaspoon lemon juice
2 tablespoons olive oil
2 tablespoons plain nonfat yogurt
Lettuce leaves
4 cups shredded lettuce
16 tomato slices
16 cucumber slices

Combine first 5 ingredients in a Dutch oven; add water to cover. Bring to a boil; cover, reduce heat, and simmer 15 minutes or until chicken is tender. Remove chicken, and chop into bite-size pieces. Set chicken aside. Discard cooked vegetables and water.

Combine egg white and next 5 ingredients in container of an electric blender or food processor; process until smooth. With motor running, gradually add olive oil in a slow, steady stream, mixing just until well blended; fold in yogurt (at room temperature). Pour over chicken; stir well. Cover and chill 4 hours.

Line a serving plate with lettuce leaves. Serve chopped chicken over shredded lettuce with tomato and cucumber slices. Yield: 4 servings (226 calories per ⅓ cup chicken salad, ½ cup lettuce, 4 tomato slices, and 4 cucumber slices).

☐ *28.1 grams protein, 9.9 grams fat, 5.2 grams carbohydrate, 70 milligrams cholesterol, 236 milligrams sodium, and 49 milligrams calcium.*

SOURDOUGH WEDGES

4 (2-ounce) sourdough rolls
Butter-flavored vegetable cooking
  spray
1 tablespoon grated Parmesan
  cheese
¼ teaspoon paprika

Quarter each roll, and coat cut surfaces with cooking spray. Combine Parmesan cheese and paprika; sprinkle on cut surfaces. Place bread on a baking sheet, and broil 6 inches from heat 2 to 3 minutes or until golden brown. Yield: 4 servings (117 calories per 4 wedges).

☐ *4.6 grams protein, 1.8 grams fat, 23.1 grams carbohydrate, 1 milligram cholesterol, 233 milligrams sodium, and 37 milligrams calcium.*

Edith Askins
Greenville, Texas

ANGEL FOOD CAKE WITH AMARETTO-ALMOND SAUCE

⅓ cup water
2 tablespoons sugar
1½ teaspoons cornstarch
2 tablespoons amaretto or other
  almond-flavored liqueur
½ teaspoon lemon juice
1½ tablespoons sliced almonds
¼ teaspoon almond extract
4 (1-ounce) slices commercial
  angel food cake

Combine first 3 ingredients in a small saucepan; stir well. Cook over medium heat, stirring constantly, until mixture begins to boil; boil 1 minute, stirring constantly, until mixture is thickened and bubbly. Stir in amaretto and lemon juice; cook until thoroughly heated (do not boil).

Remove from heat; stir in almonds and extract. Serve warm over angel food cake. Yield: 6 tablespoons (140 calories per 1-ounce slice of cake and 1½ tablespoons sauce).

☐ *2.2 grams protein, 1.4 grams fat, 30.2 grams carbohydrate, 0 milligrams cholesterol, 29 milligrams sodium, and 8 milligrams calcium.*

Sauce Tips

■ Never add cornstarch to hot liquid because it will lump. Dilute cornstarch in twice as much cold liquid and stir until smooth. Then stir the cornstarch mixture into a hot mixture.

■ When substituting cornstarch for flour in a sauce, remember that 1 tablespoon of cornstarch has the same thickening power as 2 tablespoons of flour.

■ Tapioca is a thickener suited for sauces that are to be frozen. They reheat well without separating. For freezing, use 1 to 2½ tablespoons tapioca to 1 cup liquid.

■ Press plastic wrap directly on the surface of custards, puddings, or white sauce immediately after cooking to prevent a skin from forming.

■ When a sauce curdles, remove pan from heat and plunge into a pan of cold water to stop the cooking process. Beat sauce vigorously, or pour it into a blender and blend until smooth.

Serve This Bread With A Spoon

Spoonbread dates back to early Colonial days. It's a soufflé-like bread that can be served with the same foods as cornbread or as a replacement for grits at breakfast.

We've used evaporated skimmed milk and egg substitute to get the same delicate flavor and texture as traditional spoonbread but without all the fat and calories.

SPOONBREAD

2 cups evaporated skimmed milk
1 cup water
1 cup white cornmeal
2 tablespoons reduced-calorie
   margarine
½ teaspoon salt
2 egg whites
½ cup egg substitute
Vegetable cooking spray

Combine first 5 ingredients; cook over medium heat 5 minutes or until thickened, stirring constantly. Remove from heat.

Beat egg whites (at room temperature) at medium speed of an electric mixer until stiff. With mixer running, slowly add egg substitute. Gradually stir about one-third of hot mixture into egg mixture; add to remaining hot mixture, stirring constantly. Pour into a 1½-quart casserole coated with vegetable cooking spray.

Bake at 350° for 35 minutes or until a knife inserted in center comes out clean. Yield: 9 servings (119 calories per ½-cup serving).

□ 7.6 grams protein, 2 grams fat, 17.3 grams carbohydrate, 2 milligrams cholesterol, 251 milligrams sodium, and 172 milligrams calcium.

COMPARE THE NUTRIENTS (per serving)		
	Traditional	Light
Calories	196	119
Fat	9.4g	2g
Cholesterol	125mg	2mg

Squash Side Dishes To Savor

Whether green, yellow, or white, squash lends itself to new combinations and flavors. If you've been looking for ways to serve squash, try these recipes that offer some tasty options for side dishes.

STUFFED SQUASH MEXICAN

3 medium-size yellow squash
   (1 pound)
2 cloves garlic, chopped
¼ cup chopped onion
¼ cup chopped green pepper
½ to 1 jalapeño, seeded and
   chopped
1 tablespoon olive oil
1 teaspoon chili powder
¼ teaspoon salt
¼ teaspoon pepper
¾ cup (3 ounces) shredded
   Monterey Jack cheese
3 tablespoons sour cream
2 tablespoons picante sauce
2 tablespoons shredded Cheddar
   cheese
1 tablespoon sliced ripe olives

Cook squash in boiling water to cover 7 minutes or until tender but still firm. Drain and cool slightly. Remove and discard stems. Cut each squash in half lengthwise; scoop out pulp, leaving a ¼-inch shell. Reserve squash pulp.

Sauté garlic, onion, green pepper, and jalapeño in olive oil until crisp-tender. Stir in squash pulp, and cook, stirring often, until liquid has been absorbed. Add chili powder, salt, and pepper; remove from heat. Add Monterey Jack cheese and sour cream; stir well.

Place squash shells in a lightly greased 12- x 8- x 2-inch baking dish. Spoon squash mixture evenly into shells. Bake at 350° for 25 minutes. Divide picante sauce, Cheddar cheese, and ripe olives evenly among squash; bake an additional 5 minutes. Yield: 6 servings.

Microwave Directions: Place squash in a 12- x 8- x 2-inch baking dish. Cover with heavy-duty plastic wrap; fold back a small corner of wrap to let steam escape. Microwave at HIGH 4 to 6 minutes, rearranging after 2 minutes. Let stand 5 minutes. Cut each squash in half lengthwise; scoop out pulp, leaving a ¼-inch shell. Reserve pulp.

Combine reserved pulp, garlic, and next 4 ingredients in a 1-quart dish. Microwave at HIGH 4 minutes or until liquid has been absorbed, stirring after 2 minutes. Stir in chili powder, salt, and pepper. Add Monterey Jack cheese and sour cream. Spoon squash mixture evenly into shells.

Place in 12- x 8- x 2-inch baking dish; microwave at HIGH 1 minute or until thoroughly heated. Divide picante sauce, shredded Cheddar cheese, and ripe olives evenly among squash; microwave at HIGH 30 seconds. Yield: 6 servings.

Sheila Davis
Johnson City, Tennessee

HERB BUTTER ZUCCHINI FANS

⅓ cup butter or margarine, softened
2 tablespoons minced fresh parsley
½ teaspoon dried whole tarragon
⅛ teaspoon salt
⅛ teaspoon pepper
4 small zucchini
¼ cup water
2 tablespoons freshly grated Parmesan cheese
1 tablespoon soft breadcrumbs

Combine first 5 ingredients in a small bowl, and set aside.

Cut each zucchini into lengthwise slices, leaving slices attached at stem end. Fan slices out, and spread evenly with butter mixture. Place in a 15- x 10- x 1-inch jellyroll pan; add water. Bake at 400° for 20 minutes or until crisp-tender.

Combine cheese and breadcrumbs; sprinkle on zucchini, and broil 4 inches from heat 2 minutes or until cheese melts. Yield: 4 servings.
Edith Askins
Greenville, Texas

STUFFED WHITE SQUASH

2 medium pattypan squash (about 1¼ pounds)
2 tablespoons water
3 tablespoons butter or margarine
1 small onion, chopped
2 tablespoons chopped green pepper
1 egg, beaten
½ cup herb-seasoned stuffing mix
½ cup (2 ounces) shredded sharp Cheddar cheese
½ cup (2 ounces) shredded Swiss cheese
Grated Parmesan cheese

Place squash in a pieplate; add water. Cover with heavy-duty plastic wrap; fold back a small edge of wrap to allow steam to escape. Microwave at HIGH 7 to 8 minutes, rearranging

after 2 minutes; remove from dish, and set aside.

Place butter in pieplate, and microwave at HIGH 50 seconds. Stir in onion and green pepper; microwave at HIGH 2 minutes. Combine sautéed vegetables, egg, and next 3 ingredients. Set aside.

Remove a slice from stem end of each squash. Scoop out and discard pulp, leaving ¼-inch shells. Spoon stuffing mixture into shells; sprinkle with Parmesan cheese. Place squash in pieplate, and microwave, uncovered, at HIGH 2 minutes or until thoroughly heated. Yield: 2 to 4 servings.
Bessie M. Lamb
Winchester, Virginia

QUICK!

Ladle Up Some Soup

With today's busy schedules, shortcuts in soupmaking are sure to be appreciated, so these soups take advantage of convenience products. And to keep them from being too salty, we've called for no-salt-added soup or broth, when possible.

WHITE BEAN SOUP

1 (16-ounce) can navy beans, undrained
1 (15.8-ounce) can Great Northern beans, undrained
1 cup water
¼ cup chopped onion
1 carrot, diced
¼ cup butter or margarine, melted
1 (6¾-ounce) can chunk ham, drained and flaked

Combine beans in a large saucepan; mash slightly with a potato masher. Stir in water, and cook over low heat until thoroughly heated.

Sauté onion and carrot in butter until onion is tender. Add sautéed vegetables and ham to bean mixture. Cook over low heat 10 minutes, stirring occasionally. Yield: 1 quart.
Betty P. Givan
Richmond, Kentucky

TORTILLA SOUP

2 (10½-ounce) cans reduced-sodium chicken with rice soup, undiluted
1 (10-ounce) can tomatoes with green chiles
Tortilla chips, broken
Shredded Cheddar cheese

Combine soup and tomatoes with green chiles in a saucepan. Cook over medium heat until thoroughly heated, stirring occasionally. Sprinkle each serving with chips and cheese. Yield: 1 quart.
Nina Holloway
Converse, Texas

EASY TEXAS CHILI

1 pound lean ground beef
1 small onion, chopped
1 (15½-ounce) can pinto beans, drained
1 (6-ounce) can tomato paste
1½ cups water
1½ teaspoons chili powder
½ teaspoon garlic salt

Combine beef and onion in a Dutch oven; cook until beef is browned, stirring to crumble. Drain. Add pinto beans and remaining ingredients; cover, reduce heat, and simmer 15 minutes, stirring occasionally. Yield: about 5 cups.
Lynn Barber
Siler City, North Carolina

BROCCOLI-AND-CHICKEN SOUP

¾ cup water
1 (10-ounce) package frozen
chopped broccoli
1 (10¾-ounce) can cream of
chicken soup, undiluted
½ cup milk
⅛ teaspoon red pepper
½ cup grated Parmesan cheese

Bring water to a boil in a large saucepan; add broccoli. Cover, reduce heat, and simmer 5 minutes or until broccoli is tender. Stir in soup and milk. Cook over medium heat, stirring constantly, until thoroughly heated. Stir in pepper. Pour into serving bowls. Top each serving with 2 tablespoons Parmesan cheese. Yield: 1 quart. *Tracy Liles*
Hattiesburg, Mississippi

CLAM CHOWDER

1 tablespoon minced garlic
1 small onion, chopped
2 tablespoons butter or
margarine, melted
2 (10½-ounce) cans
ready-to-serve, no-salt-added
chicken broth
1 (6½-ounce) can clams,
undrained
2 (10¾-ounce) cans cream of
potato soup, undiluted
1 to 2 teaspoons pepper
½ cup half-and-half

Sauté garlic and onion in butter until tender. Add broth and next 3 ingredients, stirring well. Bring to a boil; reduce heat, and simmer 15 minutes. Add half-and-half, stirring well. Cook over medium heat until thoroughly heated. Yield: about 1½ quarts.
Dan McNeely
Bradenton, Florida

CORN CHOWDER

1 (10¾-ounce) can cream of
potato soup, undiluted
1 (17-ounce) can reduced-sodium
whole kernel corn, drained
1⅓ cups milk
1 tablespoon butter or margarine
½ teaspoon pepper
4 slices bacon, cooked and
crumbled
2 small green onions, sliced

Combine first 5 ingredients in a saucepan. Cook over medium heat until thoroughly heated, stirring occasionally. Sprinkle each serving with crumbled bacon and green onions. Yield: 1 quart. *Vicki Sledge*
Plano, Texas

Dried Tomatoes Burst With Flavor

Before tomatoes were available year-round, and even before canning and refrigeration, the fruit was dried to preserve it. But the distinctive flavor these tomatoes possess is reason enough to dry them. Their taste and texture differ greatly from the plump, juicy form in which they grow.

In the drying process, tomatoes shrink to about 1/17 their original size. They become brittle and develop an intense, concentrated flavor that's richer and sweeter than the fruit just plucked from the vine. Shriveled and with dense flavor, dried tomatoes offer a bold new identity to such mild foods as pasta, chicken, cream soups, and cheese spreads. And upscale pizza establishments frequently adorn their rounds of dough with nuggets of dried tomato in addition to, or even instead of, the familiar spiced tomato sauce.

Gourmet shops and supermarkets offer dried tomatoes in several forms. They come in packages of minced dried tomatoes (one heaping teaspoon of the minced replaces one large fresh tomato), as well as in dried halves or pieces. There's no need to pre-soften the minced ones, but large pieces need blanching prior to using in recipes. Dried tomatoes are also available packed in flavored or unflavored olive oil; they're blanched before being packed in oil. Always refrigerate oil-packed tomatoes after opening.

As common as dried tomatoes have become, one question still looms in the minds of many people confused by different brands on the market: What's the difference between dried tomatoes and sun-dried tomatoes? Those labeled "sun-dried" are indeed dried in the sun. This original method of drying is a process that requires the tomatoes be salted to protect them against mold and insects. Some companies, especially Italian-based firms, still preserve them in this manner. Other companies now dry them in dehydrators, a method that allows salt-free production. Check the package label to determine whether or not the tomatoes have been salted if you're on a salt-restricted diet or to guide you in seasoning dishes that include dried tomatoes.

DRIED TOMATO SPAGHETTI SAUCE

1 (7-ounce) jar oil-packed dried
tomatoes, undrained
1 cup chopped onion
1 cup chopped celery
1 cup diced carrot
3 cloves garlic, minced
2 (28-ounce) cans whole
tomatoes, undrained
⅔ cup Chablis or other dry white
wine
1 teaspoon dried fennel seeds
½ teaspoon pepper

Drain dried tomatoes, reserving ¼ cup oil. Chop tomatoes; set aside.
Heat reserved oil in a Dutch oven; sauté onion, celery, carrot, and garlic

in hot oil 15 minutes, stirring occasionally. Stir in dried and canned tomatoes, wine, fennel seeds, and pepper; cook, uncovered, over medium heat 1 hour or to desired consistency, stirring occasionally.

Position knife blade in food processor bowl; add half of sauce mixture. Pulse 4 or 5 times or until mixture is chopped but not smooth. Repeat procedure with remaining half of sauce mixture. Serve over hot pasta. Yield: 6 cups.
Mike Singleton
Memphis, Tennessee

Place tomatoes in a small saucepan, and add water to cover. Bring to a boil; reduce heat, and simmer 8 to 10 minutes. Drain tomatoes, and set aside.

Combine cheeses and butter in a small mixing bowl; beat at medium speed of an electric mixer 1 minute or until light and fluffy. Add eggs, one at a time, beating well after each addition. Add tomatoes, 2 tablespoons flour, pepper, and basil; beat just until blended.

Pour into prepared pastry shell; bake at 350° for 30 to 35 minutes or until set. Remove from oven; serve hot or at room temperature. Yield: one 10-inch tart.

DRIED TOMATO-CREAM SOUP

¾ cup dried tomatoes
2 cups water
2 cups whipping cream
½ teaspoon salt
¼ teaspoon freshly ground pepper

Combine tomatoes and water in a large saucepan; bring to a boil, and let boil 2 minutes. Remove from heat, and let cool in pan 30 minutes. Pour mixture into an electric blender; blend until smooth. Return to saucepan, and stir in whipping cream, salt, and pepper. Cook over low heat until thoroughly heated. Do not boil. Yield: 3½ cups.

DRIED TOMATO-CHEESE TART

1⅓ cups all-purpose flour
½ teaspoon salt
⅛ teaspoon garlic salt
½ cup shortening
3 to 4 tablespoons cold water
½ cup minced dried tomatoes
1 (8-ounce) package cream cheese, softened
⅓ cup ricotta cheese
¼ cup butter or margarine, softened
2 eggs
2 tablespoons all-purpose flour
¼ teaspoon pepper
2 tablespoons chopped fresh basil

Combine 1⅓ cups flour, salt, and garlic salt in a medium bowl; cut in shortening with a pastry blender until mixture resembles coarse meal. Sprinkle cold water (1 tablespoon at a time) evenly over surface; stir with a fork until dry ingredients are moistened. Shape dough into a ball; chill.

Roll dough to ⅛-inch thickness on a lightly floured surface. Trim dough to a 12-inch circle, and place in a 10-inch round tart pan. Prick bottom and sides of pastry generously with a fork. Cover and chill 30 minutes. Uncover pastry, and bake at 450° for 10 to 12 minutes or until pastry is golden brown.

Have a Tomato Surplus? Dry Your Own

If you have extra tomatoes from a garden, you can dry them at home to produce a product similar to those commercially dried. Some sources suggest drying them in a conventional oven, but this is a tricky process. We had better results drying them in a food dehydrator; they tasted better and had a brighter, prettier color.

The ideal drying temperature for tomatoes is 140°, but the lowest available temperature on the dial of most conventional ovens is 200°. When drying temperatures exceed 140°, the natural sugar in the tomatoes caramelizes and can leave the product with a burned flavor. We dried some tomatoes at 200°, and even though they were not as dark as most commercially dried tomatoes, they tasted burned.

Some people who oven-dry tomatoes leave the oven door open slightly and set up fans outside the door to circulate the air and help maintain a lower temperature. While this method produces better results, it is not precise and wastes energy.

To dry tomatoes in a food dehydrator, first wash them well. If you want to peel them, dip the tomatoes in boiling water 30 seconds; then peel away the skins. Slice tomatoes ⅛-inch thick, and arrange them on the dehydrator rack. Drying will take from 5 to 7 hours for ovens that dry at 140°. Drying times can vary, however, depending on the thickness of the tomato slices and the efficiency of the dryer.

When properly dried, tomatoes should be crisp and tough, but still pliable. Examine each batch carefully to determine exact dryness, and remove slices as they dry. Let dried tomato slices cool after removal from the oven; store in an airtight container in a cool, dry place. Refrigerate or freeze the dried tomatoes to lengthen their freshness.

DRIED TOMATO PESTO

1 cup dried tomatoes
¾ cup grated Parmesan cheese
½ cup walnut pieces
2 large cloves garlic, cut in half
¼ teaspoon salt
¼ teaspoon freshly ground pepper
⅔ cup warm olive oil

Place tomatoes in a small saucepan; add water to cover. Bring to a boil; reduce heat, and simmer 8 to 10 minutes. Drain tomatoes.

Position knife blade in food processor bowl; add tomatoes, and pulse 2 or 3 times or until tomatoes are chopped. Add Parmesan cheese and next 4 ingredients. Top with cover, and process until smooth. With processor running, pour warm olive oil through food chute in a slow, steady stream, processing until combined. Use pesto immediately, or place in an airtight container, and refrigerate up to 1 week. Serve over hot pasta. Yield: 2 cups.

Using Leftover Pesto

Pesto has more uses than the one it's most known for—tossing with pasta. You might consider using leftover pesto in the following ways:

■ Stir ¼ cup pesto into one 8-ounce carton of sour cream for an instant dip for vegetables.

■ Try pesto as an omelet filling. Spoon about 2 tablespoons of the sauce over half of a three-egg omelet; fold omelet over, and serve.

■ Stir 3 tablespoons pesto into ½ cup softened unsalted butter. Serve the pesto butter as a bread spread, or toss it with hot vegetables.

CHICKEN-AND-TOMATOES OVER FETTUCCINE

1 (7-ounce) jar oil-packed dried
    tomatoes, undrained
½ cup chopped onion
2 cloves garlic, minced
4 chicken breast halves, skinned,
    boned, and cut into strips
3 tablespoons chopped fresh basil
    or 1 tablespoon dried whole
    basil
¼ teaspoon salt
¼ teaspoon pepper
6 ounces fettuccine, uncooked

Drain tomatoes, reserving oil. Coarsely chop tomatoes; set aside.

Heat 1 tablespoon reserved oil in a large skillet. Set remaining oil aside. Sauté onion and garlic in hot oil until tender. Add chicken, and sauté 8 minutes or until tender. Add basil and reserved tomatoes; sauté an additional 2 minutes. Add salt, pepper, and 2 tablespoons reserved oil.

Cook fettuccine according to package directions, omitting salt. Drain well; place on a large platter. Spoon chicken mixture over fettuccine, and toss well. Yield: 4 servings.

Lula Bell Hawks
Newport, Arkansas

DRIED TOMATO-CHEESE SPREAD

1 (8-ounce) package cream
    cheese, softened
½ cup unsalted butter, softened
½ cup grated Parmesan cheese
¼ cup drained, oil-packed dried
    tomatoes
2 tablespoons oil from oil-packed
    dried tomatoes
1 tablespoon chopped fresh basil
    or 1 teaspoon dried whole basil
Garnishes: fresh basil sprig, dried
    tomato slice

Position knife blade in food processor bowl. Combine first 6 ingredients in processor bowl, and pulse several times or until smooth. Spoon mixture

into a cheese crock or small bowl. Cover and chill until ready to serve. Let spread come to room temperature before serving. Garnish, if desired. Serve with pita toast triangles. Yield: 2 cups.

A Banker Lends His Culinary Talents

In his Albany, Georgia, kitchen, Doug Wren sautés onion marinated in soy sauce and Italian salad dressing. On the grill outside, chicken sizzles over hot coals, and a pot of Mexican Kidney Beans bubbles contentedly on the cook top beside the sautéed onion. He pauses a moment to spoon up fresh, creamy Guacamole and place it on the buffet. Pint jars of Homemade Picante Sauce line the counter beside him. The aroma of the sizzling onion fills the air, and Doug remembers why he enjoys cooking so much.

An executive vice president at a local bank, Doug turns to the kitchen during his off time to socialize, have fun, and most importantly—cook.

CHICKEN FAJITAS

⅔ cup commercial zesty Italian
    salad dressing
⅔ cup soy sauce
8 chicken breast halves, skinned
    and boned
2 medium onions, cut into strips
8 (8½-inch) flour tortillas
Garnish: fresh cilantro or parsley
    sprigs

Combine salad dressing and soy sauce in an 8-inch square dish; set aside ¼ cup marinade. Add chicken to dish, and stir to coat. Cover and chill 1 hour.

Sauté onion in reserved ¼ cup marinade over medium-high heat 3 to 5 minutes; set aside.

Drain chicken, reserving marinade. Grill chicken over hot coals 5 minutes on each side, basting twice with marinade. Cut chicken into ¼-inch-wide strips; set aside.

Wrap tortillas in aluminum foil; heat according to package directions.

To serve, spoon chicken onto tortillas; top with onion. Garnish, if desired. Serve with Homemade Picante Sauce, Guacamole, and sour cream. Yield: 8 fajitas.

MEXICAN KIDNEY BEANS

1 cup chopped onion
1½ teaspoons vegetable oil
1 (14½-ounce) can stewed
　tomatoes, undrained
2 (15½-ounce) cans kidney beans,
　undrained
Garnish: fresh cilantro or parsley
　sprigs

Sauté onion in oil until crisp-tender. Stir in tomatoes and kidney beans; cook, uncovered, over low heat 25 to 30 minutes, stirring occasionally. Garnish, if desired. Yield: 6 to 8 servings.

HOMEMADE PICANTE SAUCE

8 (29-ounce) cans whole
　tomatoes, undrained
11 green onions
4 fresh jalapeño peppers
4 canned jalapeño peppers
½ cup red wine vinegar
¼ cup chili powder
2 tablespoons garlic powder
1 tablespoon vegetable oil
2 teaspoons red pepper
1 teaspoon salt

Position knife blade in food processor bowl, and add one-third each of tomatoes, green onions, and peppers. Pulse 2 to 3 times until coarsely chopped. Repeat procedure two more times with remaining tomatoes, green onions, and peppers.

Combine tomato mixture, vinegar, and remaining ingredients in a large Dutch oven or kettle; bring mixture to a boil over medium heat. Reduce heat to low; simmer, uncovered, 30 minutes.

Pour hot mixture into hot sterilized jars, leaving ½ inch of headspace. Remove air bubbles; wipe jar rims. Cover at once with metal lids, and screw on bands. Process sauce in boiling-water bath 10 minutes. Yield: 16 pints.

Note: To make both a hot and mild sauce, use only the fresh jalapeños in the hot sauce and only the canned in the mild sauce.

GUACAMOLE

1 medium avocado, peeled
1 small tomato, quartered
2 tablespoons lime or lemon juice
2 tablespoons mayonnaise or
　salad dressing
2 tablespoons sour cream
¼ teaspoon salt
¼ to ½ teaspoon red pepper
¼ to ½ teaspoon garlic powder
⅓ cup chopped onion

Position knife blade in food processor bowl; add all ingredients except onion. Process 1 minute or until lumpy. Stir in onion. Yield: 2 cups.

Tip: *You can hurry the ripening process of avocados by placing them in a brown paper bag at room temperature. This facilitates softening by confining and concentrating the gases the fruit gives off. When the fruit is soft, you can store it in the refrigerator up to 10 days.*

From Our Kitchen To Yours

Create innovative table arrangements using snippings from your garden's bedding plants and greenery with fruits and vegetables. These centerpieces use inexpensive items and are simpler than arranged flowers.

A casserole dish may provide the base for a simple yet attractive arrangement. Fill the dish with bright, shiny lemons, and let additional fruit spill onto the table. Draw interest by placing the top of the casserole to the side. To complete the arrangement, tuck the cut ends of several ivy sprigs into the stacked lemons.

A wooden bowl, a basket, or a favorite inherited piece also works well as a container. Apples, oranges, or other fruits, mixed with smilax or other vines, can be substituted easily in the arrangement.

For another appealing arrangement combine thistle-like artichoke and a vivid-pink geranium. To assemble, wrap a florist water pick with Spanish moss, and secure it with raffia; fill the pick with water, and insert the pointed end into the artichoke. (The water pick ensures fresh flowers for at least 1 day.) Fill a 6-inch terra-cotta saucer with Spanish moss, and place the artichoke in the center. Insert the flower's stem into the pick, and arrange three geranium leaves around the top of the pick.

A fruit, such as an apple, can replace the artichoke; a marigold, gerbera daisy, or another flower and clippings from ferns and other greenery can be substituted for the geranium and its leaves. Florist water picks, raffia, and moss can be purchased in florist and craft shops.

Appetizers To Cheer For

Whether folks gather to watch football on television or go to the stadium to cheer their favorite team, there's bound to be an opportunity to serve appetizers. Be ready with these tasty treats, and you're sure to score points.

SWEET-AND-SOUR CHICKEN WINGS

3 pounds chicken wings
1 cup cornstarch
2 eggs, beaten
Vegetable oil
½ cup red currant jelly
½ cup white vinegar
½ cup sugar
¼ cup soy sauce
3 tablespoons catsup
2 tablespoons lemon juice

Cut chicken wings in half at joint; cut off tips of wings, and discard.

Dredge chicken in cornstarch, coating well; dip in egg. Pour oil to a depth of 2 to 3 inches into a Dutch oven; heat to 375°. Fry chicken until golden brown; drain on paper towels. Place chicken in a 13- x 9- x 2-inch baking dish; set aside.

Combine jelly and remaining ingredients in a small saucepan. Bring mixture to a boil over medium heat; reduce heat, and simmer, uncovered, 10 minutes. Pour over chicken. Bake at 350° for 30 minutes, basting once. Yield: about 3 dozen appetizers.

Jean Voan
Shepherd, Texas

HOT NUT CRACKERS

2 cups all-purpose flour
½ teaspoon red pepper
¼ teaspoon salt
½ cup butter or margarine
2 cups (8 ounces) shredded Cheddar cheese
Dash of hot sauce
4 to 6 tablespoons cold water
1 cup pecan halves

Combine first 3 ingredients; cut in butter and cheese with a pastry blender until mixture resembles coarse meal. Add hot sauce. Sprinkle cold water (1 tablespoon at a time) evenly over surface; stir with a fork until dry ingredients are moistened. Shape into a ball.

Roll dough to ⅛-inch thickness on a lightly floured surface; cut with a 2½-inch round cutter. Press a pecan half to right of center of each circle. Moisten edges of circle with water; fold in half, and press edges together with a fork.

Place on a lightly greased baking sheet. Bake at 350° for 15 minutes or until lightly browned. Cool.

To freeze, place baked crackers on baking sheet, and freeze. Store in airtight container. Thaw to serve. Yield: 4½ dozen. *Jeannie R. Atwell*
Durham, North Carolina

ONION CRESCENT CRUNCH STICKS

2 eggs, beaten
2 tablespoons butter or margarine, melted
1 teaspoon all-purpose flour
1 teaspoon dried parsley flakes
½ teaspoon garlic salt
¼ teaspoon onion salt
1 (8-ounce) can crescent dinner rolls
2 (2.8-ounce) cans fried onion rings, crushed

Combine first 6 ingredients in a small bowl. Set aside.

Unroll crescent rolls; separate dough into 4 rectangles, pressing perforations to seal. Cut each rectangle crosswise into 8 strips. Dip each strip into egg mixture, and coat with crushed onions. Place on ungreased baking sheets; bake at 375° for 12 to 15 minutes. Yield: 32 appetizers.
Mrs. Vincent J. Colimore
Cockeysville, Maryland

CHUNKY SALSA

1 (4¼-ounce) can chopped ripe olives, drained
1 (4-ounce) can chopped green chiles, drained
1 large tomato, chopped
1 bunch green onions, chopped
⅔ cup white vinegar
⅓ cup vegetable oil
1 tablespoon sugar
½ teaspoon garlic powder
½ teaspoon coarsely ground pepper
Tortilla chips

Combine olives, chiles, tomato, and green onions in a medium bowl. Combine vinegar and next 4 ingredients in a jar; cover tightly, and shake vigorously. Pour vinegar mixture over vegetables. Cover and refrigerate at least 3 hours. Drain salsa, and serve with tortilla chips. Yield: 2 cups. *Bonnie J. Sellers*
Ruston, Louisiana

Here's To The Game

As the gridiron action heats up this season, you'll want to cool down with these easy-to-tackle beverages. Some are as spirited as your favorite team and will be popular with adult fans, while others are nonalcoholic and will draw cheers from the entire family.

MIXED FRUIT PUNCH

1 quart grape juice
2 cups white grape juice
2⅔ cups fresh orange juice
 (about 12 oranges)
1½ cups fresh lemon juice (about
 10 lemons)
½ cup sugar
2 (33.8-ounce) bottles ginger ale,
 chilled
2 cups sparkling mineral water,
 chilled

Combine first 5 ingredients; chill. To
serve, pour juice over crushed ice in
a large punch bowl. Gently stir in
ginger ale and sparkling water. Yield:
5 quarts. *Betty Czebotar*
Baltimore, Maryland

TROPICAL PUNCH

5 cups pineapple juice, chilled
3 cups guava nectar, chilled
1 (6-ounce) can frozen limeade
 concentrate, thawed and
 undiluted
1 (12-ounce) can lemon-lime
 carbonated beverage
Garnish: lime wedges

Combine pineapple juice, guava nectar, and limeade concentrate in a
large pitcher; stir well. Add carbonated beverage; stir gently. Serve
over ice, and garnish, if desired.
Yield: approximately 2½ quarts.
Elizabeth M. Haney
Dublin, Virginia

PINEAPPLE COOLER

1 (12-ounce) can frozen
 unsweetened pineapple juice
 concentrate, thawed and
 undiluted
1½ cups cold water
3 (16-ounce) bottles lemon-lime
 carbonated beverage, chilled
1½ teaspoons almond extract

Combine all ingredients in a large
pitcher; stir well. Serve over ice.
Yield: 2 quarts. *Joann M. Conaway*
Guyton, Georgia

TEA PUNCH

1 quart water
7 regular-size tea bags
¾ to 1 cup sugar
1 (6-ounce) can frozen orange
 juice concentrate, thawed and
 undiluted
1 (12-ounce) can frozen lemonade
 concentrate, thawed and
 undiluted
9½ cups water

Bring 1 quart water to a boil. Remove from heat; add tea bags. Cover
and steep 5 minutes.
 Remove tea bags. Combine tea
and remaining ingredients; chill.
Serve punch over ice. Yield: 1
gallon. *Virginia Cheek*
Brentwood, Tennessee

SOUTHERN LONG ISLAND ICED TEA

1 cup cola-flavored beverage
½ cup sweet-and-sour mix
2 tablespoons gin
2 tablespoons vodka
2 tablespoons light rum
2 tablespoons tequila
2 tablespoons Triple Sec
2 tablespoons lemon juice
2 tablespoons lime juice
3 cups crushed ice

Combine all ingredients in a pitcher.
Serve over additional crushed ice.
Yield: 2½ cups. *Jo Ann Cotton*
Prosperity, South Carolina

SPICY BLOODY MARYS

1 (46-ounce) can cocktail
 vegetable juice
3 tablespoons lemon juice
2 tablespoons Worcestershire
 sauce
1 tablespoon prepared horseradish
⅛ teaspoon hot sauce
Dash of freshly ground pepper
¾ cup vodka

Combine all ingredients except
vodka; stir well, and refrigerate until
ready to serve. Stir in vodka just
before serving beverage over ice.
Yield: about 7 cups. *Jan Thompson*
Highland, Maryland

Speedy Vegetables

Canned vegetables make cooking
easier by eliminating the time spent
washing, peeling, and cooking fresh
vegetables. Most of the items for
these casseroles come from the pantry. You may want to keep these
ingredients on hand so that you can
fix a quick meal.

CREAMY CORN

3 tablespoons all-purpose flour
¼ cup butter or margarine,
 melted
2 (11-ounce) cans white corn,
 undrained
1 cup whipping cream

Stir flour into butter in a medium
bowl. Stir in corn and whipping
cream. Pour into a lightly greased
1½-quart casserole; bake at 350° for
30 minutes. Stir; bake an additional
15 minutes. Yield: 4 to 6 servings.
Delma Ford Marshall
De Ridder, Louisiana

PORK CHOP-VEGETABLE CASSEROLE

6 (½-inch-thick) pork chops
2 tablespoons vegetable oil
1 (10¾-ounce) can cream of
  mushroom soup, undiluted
½ teaspoon garlic salt
½ teaspoon dried whole thyme
½ teaspoon Worcestershire sauce
1 (4-ounce) can mushroom stems
  and pieces, drained
1 (16-ounce) can whole potatoes,
  drained
1 (10-ounce) package frozen
  English peas, thawed
1 tablespoon pimiento, chopped

Brown chops in oil 3 to 5 minutes on each side; arrange chops in a 13- x 9- x 2-inch dish. Combine soup and remaining ingredients; spoon over chops. Cover and bake at 350° for 30 minutes or until bubbly. Yield: 6 servings.
Charlotte Pierce
Greensburg, Kentucky

FRENCH GREEN BEANS

2 (16-ounce) cans French-style
  green beans, drained
1 (4-ounce) can sliced
  mushrooms, drained
2 tablespoons butter or
  margarine, melted
1 teaspoon sugar (optional)
½ to 1 teaspoon dried whole
  tarragon
⅛ teaspoon salt
¼ teaspoon pepper

Combine all ingredients in a saucepan, and bring to a boil over medium heat. Reduce heat, and simmer 10 minutes or until thoroughly heated. Yield: 6 servings.
Microwave Directions: Combine all ingredients in a 1½-quart casserole. Cover with heavy-duty plastic wrap, and turn back a small corner for steam to escape. Microwave at HIGH 5 to 6 minutes or until thoroughly heated, stirring once.
Susie Lavenue
Alamo, Tennessee

CORN-AND-BEAN CASSEROLE

2 (11-ounce) cans white corn,
  drained
1 (16-ounce) can French-style
  green beans, drained
¼ cup chopped green pepper
⅓ cup chopped onion
1 (10¾-ounce) can cream of
  celery soup, undiluted
½ cup sour cream
½ cup (2 ounces) shredded
  Cheddar cheese
¼ teaspoon pepper
2 tablespoons sliced almonds,
  toasted

Combine all ingredients except almonds; spoon into a lightly greased 2-quart baking dish. Bake, uncovered, at 350° for 45 minutes. Sprinkle with almonds. Yield: 8 servings.

Note: Casserole may be refrigerated 8 hours; let stand at room temperature 30 minutes, and bake as directed.

Microwave Directions: Combine all ingredients except almonds; spoon into a lightly greased 2-quart baking dish. Cover with heavy-duty plastic wrap, and turn back a small corner for steam to escape. Microwave at HIGH 8 to 10 minutes or until thoroughly heated, turning once. Sprinkle with almonds.
Jan Downs
Shreveport, Louisiana

BLACK-EYED PEAS WITH RICE

1 pound bulk Italian sausage
½ cup chopped onion
¼ teaspoon garlic powder
⅛ teaspoon pepper
2 (15.8-ounce) cans black-eyed
  peas, undrained
1⅔ cups water
2 tablespoons cornstarch
¼ cup water
Hot cooked rice

Cook sausage in a small Dutch oven until browned, stirring to crumble; drain well. Return sausage to pan; add onion, garlic powder, and pepper, and cook until onion is tender. Stir in peas and 1⅔ cups water; bring to a boil. Reduce heat, and simmer 20 minutes. Combine cornstarch and ¼ cup water; stir into peas, and bring to a boil. Cook 1 minute, stirring constantly. Serve over rice. Yield: 6 servings.
Harry L. Kincaid, Jr.
Albany, Georgia

Cooking Tips

■ A special topping for cooked vegetables or casseroles can be made by crushing ½ cup herb-seasoned stuffing mix and combining it with 2 tablespoons melted butter or margarine; top the dish with this mixture, and then sprinkle with 1 cup shredded cheese.

■ Use leftover liquid from canned or cooked fruit and vegetables in frozen desserts, gelatin molds, soups, stews, sauces, or casseroles.

■ Cooking such vegetables as green peppers and cucumbers briefly in boiling water will make them more digestible than when they are raw.

■ Wash or chop vegetables and open cans before you begin preparing any recipe. It is also a good idea to have most ingredients measured before beginning to cook.

■ When browning food in a skillet, be sure to dry the food first on paper towels.

OCTOBER

When the tantalizing aroma of chicken pot pie fills the air,

Southerners know they are about to be served one of the

region's classic dishes. Other traditional favorites—sweet

potato pie, corn pudding, bread pudding, and peach

cobbler—are also among our collection of Southern recipes

updated to fit in with busy schedules. This month's light

fare, too, features trimmed-down versions of Cajun food, as

well as other popular dishes of the South. And to make the

most of the region's fall harvest, our recipes for cream

soups offer a rich variety of smooth, delicate concoctions to

serve as appetizers or main dishes.

Ladle Up The Cream Of The Crop

The thought of homemade soup usually conjures up images of a huge stockpot planted on the back burner simmering a hearty concoction of meats, seasonings, and every conceivable vegetable. It sounds great if a robust flavor fits the bill and you have a lot of time. But too often you're in a hurry, and the occasion calls for a more subtle taste. That's where cream soups come in. And we've taken our pick of favorite fall vegetables and made the best of the best—smooth, delicate cream soups.

Because vegetables are versatile, simple preparation sometimes highlights them best. Instead of a myriad of ingredients, each of these recipes features one vegetable and can be ready in less than an hour. Their rich, refined textures result from pureeing the mixture in a blender, and then adding cream, half-and-half, or milk to the pot.

These soups are perfect as appetizers when you entertain, and some could be served as a complete meal with salad and bread on the side.

until smooth. Repeat procedure with remaining mixture, returning pureed mixture to Dutch oven.

Remove skin from Brie; add Brie, milk, and remaining ingredients to Dutch oven. Cook over medium heat, stirring constantly, until cheese melts and soup is thoroughly heated. Yield: 5 cups.
Georgie O'Neill
Welaka, Florida

CARROT CREAM SOUP
(pictured on page 222)

3 cups sliced carrots
1 cup chopped onion
3 cups chicken broth
¼ teaspoon white pepper
1 cup whipping cream
Ground nutmeg (optional)
Garnishes: carrot curl, fresh
   chives

Combine first 3 ingredients in a Dutch oven; cover and cook over medium heat 25 minutes or until tender. Spoon half of mixture into a food processor or electric blender; process until smooth. Repeat procedure with remaining mixture. Stir in white pepper; cover and chill thoroughly. Stir in cream; ladle into individual soup bowls. If desired, sprinkle with nutmeg, and garnish. Yield: 5 cups.
Mrs. J. A. Allard
San Antonio, Texas

CREAM OF CELERY SOUP

¼ cup sliced green onions
¼ cup chopped onion
1½ cups chopped celery with
   leaves
1½ tablespoons butter or
   margarine, melted
1½ cups water
1 cup chicken broth
1 medium potato, peeled and
   diced (1 cup)
4½ ounces Brie cheese
1 cup milk
½ teaspoon salt
½ teaspoon white pepper
Pinch of dried whole marjoram

Sauté onions and celery in butter in a Dutch oven until tender. Add water, broth, and potato; cover and cook over low heat 15 minutes or until potato is tender.

Pour half of soup mixture into container of an electric blender; process

CREAM OF CORN SOUP

4 shallots, coarsely chopped
2 cloves garlic, minced
2 tablespoons butter or
   margarine, melted
3 cups fresh corn (about 6 ears),
   divided
3 cups chicken broth
1 bay leaf
1 tablespoon cornstarch
1 cup half-and-half
¼ cup chopped sweet red pepper
¼ teaspoon white pepper

Sauté shallots and garlic in butter in a Dutch oven until tender. Add 2 cups corn, and cook over medium heat 3 minutes, stirring often. Gradually stir in broth, and add bay leaf. Bring to a boil; cover, reduce heat, and simmer 10 minutes, stirring often. Remove and discard bay leaf.

Pour half of corn mixture into container of an electric blender; process until smooth. Repeat process with remaining mixture, returning pureed mixture to Dutch oven. Add remaining 1 cup corn, and bring to a boil. Cover, reduce heat, and simmer 10 minutes. Combine cornstarch and half-and-half; stir into soup. Heat 1 minute. Add chopped red pepper and white pepper, and cook just until thoroughly heated. Serve immediately. Yield: 5 cups.

CAULIFLOWER SOUP

1 cup chopped cauliflower
2 teaspoons minced shallot
3 cups chicken broth
¼ cup butter or margarine
¼ cup all-purpose flour
½ cup half-and-half
1 tablespoon minced fresh parsley
⅛ teaspoon dried whole tarragon
⅛ teaspoon pepper

Combine first 3 ingredients in a large saucepan; bring to a boil. Cover, reduce heat, and simmer 15 minutes. Remove from heat, and drain vegetables, reserving liquid. Set both aside.

Melt butter in a heavy saucepan over low heat; add flour, stirring until smooth. Cook 1 minute, stirring constantly. Gradually stir in reserved liquid; cook over medium heat, stirring constantly, until thickened and bubbly. Stir in reserved vegetables, half-and-half, and remaining ingredients; cook until thoroughly heated. Yield: 1 quart.
Margaret Ellen Holmes
Jackson, Tennessee

CREAM PEA SOUP
(pictured on page 222)

4 cups shredded lettuce
1 medium onion, chopped
¼ cup butter or margarine, melted
1 tablespoon all-purpose flour
¼ teaspoon ground coriander
2 (10-ounce) packages frozen peas, thawed and divided
3 (14½-ounce) cans chicken broth
1 cup milk
Cream sherry (optional)
Garnish: fresh mint sprigs

Sauté lettuce and onion in butter in a Dutch oven until onion is tender. Add flour and coriander, and cook 1 minute, stirring constantly. Set aside ¼ cup peas; gradually add remaining peas and broth to Dutch oven. Cover and cook 15 minutes, stirring often.

Place one-fourth of soup mixture in container of an electric blender; process until smooth. Repeat procedure with remaining mixture, returning pureed mixture to Dutch oven. Stir in milk and reserved ¼ cup peas, and cook until thoroughly heated. If desired, add sherry to individual servings, and garnish with fresh mint sprigs. Yield: 9 cups.
Dan Tuck
Alabaster, Alabama

CREAMY ONION SOUP

2 large onions, thinly sliced and quartered (about 1¾ pounds)
¼ cup butter or margarine, melted
3 tablespoons all-purpose flour
4 cups chicken broth
1 cup half-and-half
1 cup (4 ounces) shredded Cheddar cheese
1 tablespoon diced green pepper
¼ teaspoon white pepper

Sauté onion in butter in a Dutch oven until tender; add flour, stirring until smooth. Cook 1 minute, stirring constantly. Gradually add chicken broth; simmer, uncovered, 30 minutes, stirring often. Add half-and-half and remaining ingredients; cook until cheese melts and soup is heated. Yield: 7 cups.
Marian Parsons
Hurricane, West Virginia

CREAM OF SPINACH SOUP

1 (10-ounce) package frozen chopped spinach, thawed
½ cup chopped onion
2 tablespoons butter or margarine, melted
3 tablespoons all-purpose flour
1 quart milk
½ teaspoon salt
⅛ to ¼ teaspoon pepper

Drain spinach thoroughly; set aside. Sauté onion in butter in a large saucepan until tender; add flour, stirring until smooth. Cook 1 minute, stirring constantly.

Gradually add milk; stir in spinach, salt, and pepper. Cook over medium heat, stirring constantly, until mixture is thickened and bubbly. Yield: 1 quart.
Sandra Russell
Gainesville, Florida

Fruit Makes It Fancy

The slight nip in the air this time of year whets our appetites for heartier foods. Everyone loves a good pot roast or meat loaf, but how about a new approach to these old favorites? Traditional dishes of the season take on exciting flavors and colors with the addition of fresh fall produce as well as dried and canned fruits.

FRUITED POT ROAST

1 (4-pound) boneless chuck roast
2 tablespoons vegetable oil
1½ teaspoons salt
⅛ teaspoon pepper
1 cup apple juice
1 cup water
2 (3-inch) sticks cinnamon
1 (6-ounce) package dried apricots
1 cup pitted prunes
1 large cooking apple, peeled and sliced

Brown roast on all sides in hot oil in a Dutch oven; pour off drippings. Sprinkle meat with salt and pepper; add apple juice, water, and cinnamon sticks. Bring to a boil; cover, reduce heat, and simmer 1 hour. Add apricots, prunes, and apple; simmer, covered, 30 minutes. Yield: 8 to 10 servings.
Mrs. L. W. Mayer
Richmond, Virginia

PEACHY CHICKEN

½ cup all-purpose flour
½ teaspoon salt
1 teaspoon paprika
4 chicken breast halves, skinned
   and boned
2 tablespoons vegetable oil
½ cup dry sherry
2 tablespoons brown sugar
1 tablespoon soy sauce
½ teaspoon ground ginger
2 teaspoons sesame seeds
1 (16-ounce) can peach halves,
   drained

Combine flour, salt, and paprika; dredge chicken in flour mixture. Brown chicken on both sides in hot oil. Drain chicken, and place in a 12- x 8- x 2-inch baking dish. Combine sherry and next 3 ingredients; pour over chicken. Sprinkle sesame seeds on chicken. Cover and bake at 350° for 15 minutes; add peach halves, and bake an additional 15 minutes or until chicken is tender. Yield: 4 servings.
Millie Givens
Savannah, Georgia

ORIENTAL PORK CHOPS

1 cup pureed persimmon
¼ cup sugar
¼ teaspoon grated lemon rind
1 teaspoon lemon juice
2 tablespoons vegetable oil
6 (1-inch-thick) boneless,
   center-cut pork chops
2 green onions, cut into ¼-inch
   slices
1 tablespoon minced gingerroot
⅓ cup rice vinegar
¾ cup chicken broth
3 tablespoons soy sauce
1 teaspoon julienne-sliced
   gingerroot
1 tablespoon julienne-sliced green
   onion tops

Combine first 4 ingredients in a small mixing bowl; stir well. Set aside.

Heat oil in a large skillet. Add pork chops; cook over medium heat 12 to 15 minutes or until browned, turning once. Remove pork chops from skillet, and keep warm.

Add sliced green onions and minced gingerroot to skillet; sauté 1 minute. Add vinegar; cook 1 minute, stirring to scrape particles from skillet. Add broth, soy sauce, and persimmon mixture; stir until smooth. Add pork chops; cover and simmer 30 minutes.

Arrange pork chops on a platter; spoon about 1 tablespoon sauce over each. Sprinkle with remaining gingerroot and green onions; serve with remaining sauce, if desired. Yield: 6 servings.
Carrie Byrne Bartlett
Gallatin, Tennessee

GLAZED HAM LOAF

1 pound ground cooked ham
1 pound bulk pork sausage
1 egg, slightly beaten
⅓ cup soft breadcrumbs
2 tablespoons minced celery
2 tablespoons minced onion
2 tablespoons minced fresh
   parsley
½ teaspoon salt
¼ teaspoon ground nutmeg
¼ teaspoon ground thyme
¼ teaspoon pepper
4 medium-size sweet potatoes
1 (16-ounce) can whole-berry
   cranberry sauce
¼ cup dark corn syrup
⅛ teaspoon ground cloves
Garnish: celery leaves

Combine first 11 ingredients, mixing well. Shape into a loaf, and place on a lightly greased rack of broiler pan. Bake at 350° for 50 minutes.

Cook sweet potatoes in boiling water to cover 45 minutes or until tender. Let cool to touch; peel and cut into ⅓-inch slices.

Combine cranberry sauce, corn syrup, and cloves in a saucepan; cook over low heat, stirring until cranberry sauce melts.

Place ham loaf on an ovenproof platter; arrange potatoes around loaf. Spoon sauce on top, and bake an additional 5 to 10 minutes. Garnish, if desired. Yield: 8 servings.
Ellie Wells
Lakeland, Florida

It's Apple Season

Crisp fall air signals more than brilliant foliage and cooler days; it's time to harvest apples. In backyards and orchards across the South, apples of all shapes and varieties hang ready for the picking.

APPLE-DATE-NUT RING

2 packages dry yeast
½ cup warm water (105° to 115°)
¾ cup milk
½ cup sugar
½ teaspoon salt
½ cup butter or margarine
1 egg, slightly beaten
4¼ to 4¾ cups all-purpose flour,
   divided
2 tablespoons butter or
   margarine, melted
2 cups peeled, finely chopped
   apple
1 (8-ounce) package pitted dates,
   chopped
½ cup chopped walnuts
¼ cup sugar
2 teaspoons ground cinnamon
2 cups sifted powdered sugar
3 tablespoons milk
¼ teaspoon vanilla extract

Dissolve yeast in warm water in a large bowl; let stand 5 minutes. Combine ¾ cup milk and next 3 ingredients in a saucepan; heat until butter melts. Stir occasionally. Cool to 105° to 115°.

Add milk mixture, egg, and 2 cups flour to yeast mixture; beat at medium speed of an electric mixer just until blended. Stir in enough remaining flour to make a soft dough. Turn dough out onto a floured surface, and knead until smooth and elastic. Place in a well-greased bowl, turning to grease top. Cover and chill 8 hours.

Punch dough down, and divide in half; roll each half to a 14- x 9-inch rectangle, and brush each with 1 tablespoon butter. Combine apple and next 4 ingredients. Spoon half of mixture over each rectangle of dough to within ½ inch of edges.

Roll up each rectangle, jellyroll fashion, starting at long side; moisten edges with water, and pinch to seal. Place each on a greased 12-inch pizza pan, seam side down; shape into a ring. Pinch ends together to seal.

Using kitchen shears, make cuts in dough in 1-inch intervals around rings, cutting two-thirds of the way through rolls. Gently turn each piece of dough on its side, slightly overlapping slices. Cover and let rise in a warm place (85°), free from drafts, 45 minutes or until doubled in bulk. Bake at 350° for 20 to 25 minutes or until golden. Cool.

Combine powdered sugar, 3 tablespoons milk, and vanilla; stir until smooth. Drizzle half over each ring. Yield: 2 rings. *Sheryl Shenk*
Victoria, Virginia

HONEY-BAKED APPLE DESSERT

3 large unpeeled cooking apples
¼ cup firmly packed light brown
  sugar
1 tablespoon chopped pecans
3 tablespoons honey
1 tablespoon brandy
1 teaspoon ground cinnamon
1 teaspoon ground nutmeg
Dash of ground cloves
Vanilla ice cream or whipped
  topping

Cut a ¼-inch slice from top of apples; core each apple to within ⅛ inch of bottom. Place each apple in a 10-ounce custard cup; set aside.

Combine brown sugar and next 6 ingredients; stir well. Spoon into apple cavities, drizzling excess over apples. Cover each cup tightly with heavy-duty plastic wrap; fold back an edge of wrap to allow steam to escape. Arrange cups in a triangle in microwave. Microwave at HIGH 4 to 7 minutes or until almost tender, rotating triangle at 2-minute intervals. Top with vanilla ice cream or whipped topping. Yield: 3 servings.
Thomas E. Cole
Pasadena, Texas

WHOLE WHEAT-APPLE CRUMBLE

Butter or margarine
1½ cups whole wheat
  breadcrumbs, divided
1¼ pounds cooking apples, cut
  into ⅛-inch slices
¾ cup firmly packed brown sugar
3 tablespoons butter or margarine
1 egg, beaten
⅓ cup milk
1 tablespoon lemon juice
½ teaspoon ground cinnamon
½ teaspoon vanilla extract
Sweetened whipped cream
  (optional)

Lightly butter bottom of a 9-inch, deep-dish pieplate; sprinkle with 3 tablespoons breadcrumbs. Layer one-third each of apple slices, remaining breadcrumbs, and brown sugar in pieplate; dot with 1 tablespoon butter. Repeat procedure twice.

Combine egg and next 4 ingredients, mixing well; pour over apple mixture. Cover with wax paper, and microwave at HIGH 5 minutes. Rotate dish one-third turn. Microwave at MEDIUM (50% power) 8 minutes or until apples are tender, rotating after 6 minutes. Let stand 5 minutes. Serve dessert with sweetened whipped cream, if desired. Yield: 6 to 8 servings.

Classic Creations With Cornmeal

Give your dinner table a down-home touch with a real Southern classic—savory, hot cornbread. Once a mainstay of the Southern farm family's diet simply due to a plentiful crop, today cornmeal dishes are still a favorite for city and country folks simply due to their great taste! You get a lot of flavor for just a little effort with these recipes.

Herbed Cornbread offers a shortcut: both the flour and cornmeal used are self-rising. That means the leavening agents and salt have already been added to these ingredients, cutting out preparation steps and ensuring accuracy for a better product. Marjoram, thyme, and celery seeds blend for a new twist in this version of an old standard.

PAPRIKA CORNBREAD

1⅓ cups white cornmeal
⅔ cup biscuit mix
1 tablespoon plus 1 teaspoon
  sugar
1½ teaspoons baking powder
½ teaspoon baking soda
1 teaspoon salt
¼ teaspoon pepper
1½ teaspoons paprika
2 eggs, beaten
1½ cups buttermilk
2 tablespoons bacon drippings or
  margarine, melted

Combine first 8 ingredients in a large bowl; add eggs, buttermilk, and bacon drippings, stirring just until dry ingredients are moistened. Pour batter into a well-greased 8-inch square pan. Bake at 450° for 25 to 30 minutes or until golden brown. Yield: 9 servings.
Doris T. Ramsey
Martinsville, Virginia

MEXICAN HUSH PUPPIES

2 cups self-rising cornmeal
1 cup self-rising flour
½ teaspoon salt
3 tablespoons sugar
3 eggs, beaten
½ cup milk
1 (17-ounce) can cream-style corn
1½ cups (6 ounces) shredded
    Cheddar cheese
1 large onion, chopped
2 jalapeño peppers, seeded and
    chopped
Vegetable oil

Combine first 4 ingredients in a large bowl. Combine eggs and milk; add to dry ingredients, stirring just until moistened. Stir in corn, shredded cheese, chopped onion, and chopped pepper. (Do not overmix batter.)

Pour oil to a depth of 2 inches into a small Dutch oven; heat to 375°. Carefully drop batter by rounded tablespoonfuls into oil; fry a few at a time 3 minutes or until golden brown, turning once. Drain on paper towels. Yield: 3½ dozen.

Nell H. Amador
Guntersville, Alabama

HERBED CORNBREAD

1¼ cups self-rising cornmeal
¾ cup self-rising flour
1 teaspoon sugar
½ teaspoon dried whole marjoram
½ teaspoon dried whole thyme
¼ teaspoon celery seeds
2 eggs, beaten
1¼ cups milk
¼ cup plus 2 tablespoons butter
    or margarine, melted

Combine first 6 ingredients in a large bowl. Combine eggs, milk, and butter; add to dry ingredients, stirring just until moistened. Pour batter into a lightly greased 9-inch square pan. Bake at 425° for 25 minutes or until golden brown. Yield: 9 servings.

DeLea Lonadier
Montgomery, Louisiana

CORN STICKS

3 cups water
1 teaspoon salt
1½ cups cornmeal
1½ cups (6 ounces) shredded
    sharp Cheddar cheese
1½ cups vegetable oil

Combine water and salt in a saucepan; bring to a boil. Gradually stir in cornmeal; cook 2 minutes, stirring constantly, until smooth and thickened. Remove from heat; add shredded cheese, stirring until cheese melts. Cool.

Shape mixture into 3- x 1-inch logs, using 2 tablespoons for each corn stick. Heat oil in a large, heavy skillet to 375°. Fry corn sticks, a few at a time, 3 to 5 minutes on each side or until golden brown. Drain on paper towels. Yield: about 2 dozen.

M. K. Quesenberry
Dugspur, Virginia

Usher In Autumn With Breads

Freshly baked loaves of bread laced with nuts and spices lend the perfect warming touch to chilly fall days. Soon one of our quick breads served with a cup of tea in front of the fireplace will be a welcome treat.

IRISH SODA BREAD

2 cups all-purpose flour
¾ teaspoon baking soda
1 teaspoon salt
⅓ cup sugar
½ cup raisins or currants
1 egg, beaten
1 cup buttermilk
¼ cup butter or margarine,
    melted

Combine first 4 ingredients; stir in raisins. Set aside. Combine egg, buttermilk, and butter; add to flour mixture, stirring just until dry ingredients are moistened.

Spoon batter into a greased 8½- x 4½- x 3-inch loafpan. Bake at 350° for 40 to 45 minutes or until a wooden pick inserted in center comes out clean. Cool in pan 10 minutes; remove from pan, and let bread cool completely on a wire rack. Yield: 1 loaf.

Note: Top of loaf has a characteristic rough texture. *Lounora Gordon*
Dublin, Georgia

EASY MONKEY BREAD

2 teaspoons dried whole basil,
    divided
3 to 3½ cups bread flour, divided
1 package dry yeast
1 egg
1 cup warm water (120° to 130°)
2 tablespoons butter or
    margarine, softened
1 tablespoon sugar
½ teaspoon salt
¼ cup butter or margarine,
    melted and divided

Grease a 10-inch Bundt pan; sprinkle with 1 teaspoon basil. Set aside.

Position knife blade in food processor bowl; add 1½ cups flour and next 6 ingredients to processor bowl. Process 2 minutes. Add enough remaining flour through food chute with processor running until dough begins to form a ball.

Turn dough out onto a lightly floured surface, and knead 1 minute. Roll dough to a 15- x 12-inch rectangle; brush with one-third of melted butter. Cut into 1½-inch diamond-shaped pieces; layer half of pieces, buttered side down, in prepared pan. Brush top with half of remaining butter, and sprinkle with ½ teaspoon basil. Repeat procedure with remaining dough, butter, and basil.

Cover and let rise in a warm place (85°), free from drafts, about 45 minutes or until doubled in bulk. Bake at 400° for 20 to 25 minutes or until done. Cool in pan 2 minutes; invert onto a wire rack to cool completely. Yield: 1 loaf.   *Merle R. Downs*
Tryon, North Carolina

HARVEST PUMPKIN BREAD

½ cup chopped pecans
1 tablespoon graham cracker crumbs
½ cup butter or margarine, softened
1 cup firmly packed brown sugar
2 eggs
2 cups all-purpose flour
2 teaspoons baking powder
¼ teaspoon baking soda
½ teaspoon salt
1¼ teaspoons ground cinnamon
½ teaspoon ground nutmeg
¼ teaspoon ground cloves
¼ teaspoon ground ginger
1 cup mashed, cooked pumpkin
1 teaspoon vanilla extract
1 tablespoon graham cracker crumbs
Peachy Cream Cheese Spread

Spread pecans in a single layer in a glass pieplate; microwave at HIGH 1 minute; set aside.

Grease a 1½-quart soufflé dish; sprinkle bottom and sides with 1 tablespoon graham cracker crumbs, and set aside.

Cream butter; gradually add sugar, beating well at medium speed of an electric mixer. Add eggs, one at a time, beating well after each addition.

Combine flour and next 7 ingredients; add to creamed mixture alternately with pumpkin, beginning and ending with flour mixture. Mix after each addition just until dry ingredients are moistened. Stir in vanilla.

Spoon batter into prepared dish; sprinkle 1 tablespoon graham cracker crumbs over batter. Place dish on top of an inverted microwave-safe bowl in the center of oven. Microwave at MEDIUM (50% power) 12 minutes, giving dish a quarter-turn every 4 minutes. Microwave at HIGH 1 to 4 minutes or until a wooden pick inserted in center of bread comes out clean. (Top will appear moist but not wet.) Remove from oven, and let stand 10 minutes. Remove bread from dish, and serve with Peachy Cream Cheese Spread. Yield: 1 loaf.

Peachy Cream Cheese Spread

1 (8-ounce) package cream cheese
⅓ cup peach preserves
¼ teaspoon ground ginger

Microwave cream cheese in a small glass bowl at LOW (10% power) 1½ to 2 minutes or until softened. Add preserves and ginger; stir well. Yield: 1⅓ cups.

Yogurt Adds Culture To These Dishes

Every time you've heard about Little Miss Muffet sitting on her tuffet, you've probably wondered why anyone would want to eat something called "curds and whey." Surprisingly, she was likely enjoying one of today's most popular snacks—yogurt, which is a blend of coagulated milk (curds) and the liquid that separates from it (whey).

The packaging and variety of flavors have changed since antiquity, but the versatility is still there and waiting to be discovered by modern cooks. The next time you spoon up some yogurt for a meal or snack, consider stirring it into a favorite recipe as an ingredient. You can give up fat and calories, but not flavor, by substituting plain yogurt for all or part of the sour cream or mayonnaise in salads, sauces, soups, casseroles, and even baked goods.

YOGURT-MUESLI MUFFINS

1½ cups biscuit mix
1 cup muesli
¼ cup firmly packed brown sugar
2 eggs, beaten
1 (8-ounce) carton strawberry-banana yogurt or strawberry yogurt
2 tablespoons vegetable oil

Combine first 3 ingredients in a large bowl; make a well in center of mixture. Combine eggs, yogurt, and oil; add to dry ingredients, stirring just until moistened. Spoon into greased muffin pans, filling three-fourths full. Bake at 400° for 16 to 18 minutes or until golden brown. Remove from pans immediately. Yield: 1 dozen.
Mrs. Earl L. Faulkenberry
Lancaster, South Carolina

BLUE CHEESE SPREAD

½ (8-ounce) package cream cheese, softened
⅓ cup crumbled blue cheese
⅓ cup plain low-fat yogurt
¼ cup chopped pecans, toasted
2 tablespoons minced chives

Combine all ingredients; stir well. Serve on crackers or bread. Yield: 1⅓ cups.   *Mrs. E. W. Hanley*
Palm Harbor, Florida

SHRIMP DEE-LISH

1 pound unpeeled medium-size
   fresh shrimp
Vegetable cooking spray
1 cup sliced green onions
½ cup chopped celery
½ cup sliced fresh mushrooms
4 cloves garlic, minced
1 (10¾-ounce) can cream of
   mushroom soup, undiluted
¼ teaspoon Creole seasoning
1 (8-ounce) carton plain yogurt
Hot cooked noodles
Garnish: green onion fan

Peel and devein shrimp; set aside.
Coat a large nonstick skillet with
cooking spray; place over medium
heat until hot. Add green onions and
next 3 ingredients; sauté until vegetables are tender. Add shrimp; cook
5 minutes, stirring constantly. Stir in
soup and seasoning; bring to a boil.
Remove from heat; stir in yogurt (at
room temperature), and serve immediately over noodles. Garnish, if desired. Yield: 4 servings.

Ellen Aman
Baton Rouge, Louisiana

YOGURT-SESAME CHICKEN

1¼ cups crushed corn flakes
   cereal
¼ cup sesame seeds
¾ teaspoon paprika
½ teaspoon salt
¼ teaspoon ground ginger
Dash of red pepper
1 (8-ounce) carton plain yogurt
2 tablespoons honey
1 (2½- to 3-pound) broiler-fryer,
   cut up and skinned
2 tablespoons butter or
   margarine, melted

Combine first 6 ingredients in a medium bowl; set aside. Combine yogurt and honey. Dip each piece of
chicken in yogurt mixture; dredge in
corn flakes mixture.

Place chicken in a greased 13- x 9-
x 2-inch pan; drizzle with butter.
Bake, uncovered, at 350° for 1 hour
or until chicken is tender and golden
brown. Yield: 4 servings.

Joanna H. Latham
Huntsville, Alabama

CHICKEN-APPLE SALAD

4 chicken breast halves, skinned
6 cups water
1 teaspoon salt
2 cups chopped Red Delicious
   apple
1 cup chopped celery
1 (2.25-ounce) package sliced
   almonds, toasted
⅓ cup plain yogurt
3 tablespoons mayonnaise or
   salad dressing
1½ tablespoons honey
1 tablespoon lemon juice
¼ teaspoon salt
¼ teaspoon white pepper
Lettuce leaves

Combine first 3 ingredients in a large
saucepan. Bring to a boil; cover, reduce heat, and simmer 45 minutes.
Drain, reserving broth for other
uses. Bone chicken, and cut into
bite-size pieces.

Combine chicken, apple, celery,
and almonds in a large bowl. Combine yogurt and next 5 ingredients in
a small bowl; stir well. Add to
chicken mixture, and toss well.
Cover and chill.

Serve on lettuce leaves. Yield: 4
to 6 servings.

Bettye Cortner
Cerulean, Kentucky

Yogurt Tips

■ Use lemon or vanilla yogurt in
fruit dishes and some salad
dressings or as toppings for desserts. Fruited and flavored yo-
gurts add a rich texture to
shakes and snacks with less fat
and cholesterol.

■ When cooking with yogurt,
remember to use low temperatures. Cooking at high temperatures may result in separation,
evaporation of liquid, and cur-
dling, but the flavor of the product will not be affected.

■ When mashing potatoes, use
plain yogurt instead of milk for a
hearty side dish.

■ When a recipe such as beef
stroganoff or Swedish meatballs
calls for sour cream, substitute
plain yogurt. Stir 2 tablespoons
of all-purpose flour or 1 tablespoon of cornstarch into each
cup of yogurt needed before
adding it to the recipe.

■ For a flavor boost to hot cereal, stir a tablespoonful of vanilla yogurt into each serving.

■ Combine plain yogurt with
cut-up fresh fruit, raisins, quick
oats, finely ground nuts, and
grated lemon peel for a quick
breakfast muesli.

■ Stir together plain yogurt, a
crushed garlic clove, salt, pepper, and dillweed, cumin, curry,
or tarragon and use to marinade
mushrooms, artichoke hearts, or
cooked green beans.

■ Stir vanilla yogurt into
strained fruit, such as applesauce, for added nutrition.

Introducing Mirlitons

You may see mirlitons in your supermarket and wonder what they are. They're known by many names. Louisiana Cooperative Extension Specialist Mike Cannon says the French pronounce them "millie-taa." Mirlitons are also called vegetable pears, chayote squash, or mango squash. Whatever name they're given, the vegetable grows on a vine which is often routed onto a trellis. They taste similar to squash and are often cooked like squash. Select small, firm, unblemished mirlitons.

STUFFED MIRLITONS

6 large mirlitons
½ cup chopped celery
½ cup chopped onion
½ cup chopped green pepper
½ teaspoon minced garlic
¼ cup butter or margarine, melted
1½ cups Italian-seasoned breadcrumbs
1 tablespoon chopped fresh chives
1 tablespoon chopped fresh parsley
½ teaspoon sugar
⅛ teaspoon Worcestershire sauce
⅛ teaspoon hot sauce
1 egg yolk, slightly beaten
¾ teaspoon salt
⅛ teaspoon white pepper
¼ cup Italian-seasoned breadcrumbs
2 tablespoons butter or margarine, melted
Garnishes: paprika, fresh parsley

Wash mirlitons; place in a Dutch oven. Cover with water, and bring to a boil. Cover, reduce heat, and simmer 35 minutes or until tender. Drain and cool slightly. Cut in half lengthwise. Discard seeds; scoop out pulp, leaving 1¼-inch shell. Place pulp in container of a food processor; process 30 seconds or until smooth. Set aside.

Sauté celery and next 3 ingredients in ¼ cup melted butter until vegetables are crisp-tender. Add pulp, 1½ cups breadcrumbs, and next 8 ingredients, mixing well.

Fill mirliton shells with stuffing mixture. Combine ¼ cup breadcrumbs and 2 tablespoons melted butter in a small bowl, mixing well; sprinkle breadcrumb mixture on top of stuffing. Bake at 350° for 20 minutes or until thoroughly heated. Garnish, if desired. Yield: 12 servings.

Susie Pharr
New Iberia, Louisiana

MIRLITON BALLS

4 medium mirlitons
½ cup chopped onion
⅓ cup chopped green pepper
1 tablespoon vegetable oil
1 egg, slightly beaten
½ cup (2 ounces) shredded Cheddar cheese
1 teaspoon garlic powder
¾ teaspoon ground cumin
¾ teaspoon dried whole rosemary
1 tablespoon lemon juice
½ cup Italian-seasoned breadcrumbs
½ cup all-purpose flour
¼ teaspoon salt
⅛ teaspoon pepper
Vegetable oil

Place mirlitons in a large saucepan; cover with water, and bring to a boil. Cover, reduce heat, and simmer 30 minutes or until tender; drain. Peel, if desired. Seed and dice mirlitons; let stand in strainer.

Sauté onion and green pepper in 1 tablespoon oil until tender; remove from heat. Combine sautéed vegetables, egg, and next 6 ingredients in a large bowl. Mash mirlitons, using a potato masher; add to onion mixture. Shape mixture into balls, using ¼ cup mixture per ball.

Combine flour, salt, and pepper; dredge balls in flour mixture. Pour oil to a depth of 2 to 3 inches into a Dutch oven or heavy saucepan; heat to 375°. Fry balls in hot oil until browned; drain on paper towels. Yield: 1 dozen.

Note: For appetizer servings, shape into balls using 2 tablespoons mixture per ball. Yield: 2 dozen.

Bessie Stewart
Harvey, Louisiana

Sweet Send-Offs

A break from the three R's is fun for any young scholar, and discovering what lunchbox treats Mom packed is often the best part. Prepackaged convenience products make lunch preparation easy on busy days, but homemade goodies can't be beat for showing kids you care.

A bowl of hot oatmeal may be greeted by turned-up noses at the breakfast table, but later in the day your kids won't turn down our cookie selections that include the grain. Leslie Stacks grinds oats to a powder and stirs it into the cookie batter for her Oatmeal-Chocolate Chippers. "Most people don't detect the oats, so it's an easy way of adding fiber for folks who say they don't like it," she comments.

OATMEAL-CHOCOLATE CHIPPERS

1 cup quick-cooking oats, uncooked
½ cup butter or margarine, softened
⅓ cup sugar
⅓ cup firmly packed brown sugar
1 egg
½ teaspoon vanilla extract
1 cup all-purpose flour
½ teaspoon baking soda
1 (6-ounce) package semisweet chocolate morsels

Place oats in food processor bowl or container of electric blender, and process until finely ground. Set ground oats aside.

Cream butter; gradually add sugars, beating well at medium speed of an electric mixer. Add egg and vanilla, beating well. Combine ground oats, flour, and soda; add to creamed mixture, and mix well. Stir in semisweet chocolate morsels.

Drop dough by tablespoonfuls onto lightly greased cookie sheets. Bake at 375° for 10 to 12 minutes. Cool slightly on cookie sheets; remove cookies to wire racks to cool completely. Yield: about 3 dozen.
Leslie R. Stacks
Bethesda, Maryland

CRISPY-CHEWY MOLASSES COOKIES

1 cup butter or margarine
2½ cups sugar
1 teaspoon ground cinnamon
1 teaspoon ground nutmeg
¼ teaspoon salt
1 egg
¼ cup plus 1 tablespoon water
1 teaspoon baking soda
¼ cup molasses
3½ cups all-purpose flour

Melt butter; cool to room temperature. Combine butter, sugar, cinnamon, nutmeg, salt, and egg in a large mixing bowl; beat well at medium speed of an electric mixer.

Combine water and soda in a small bowl, stirring until soda dissolves; add soda mixture to creamed mixture, beating well. Stir in molasses and flour.

Drop dough by teaspoonfuls, 3 inches apart, onto greased cookie sheets. Bake at 350° for 7 to 9 minutes. Cool cookies completely on wire racks. Yield: 8 dozen.
Lynette Walther
East Palatka, Florida

APPLE-OATMEAL COOKIES

1 cup all-purpose flour
1 teaspoon baking soda
½ teaspoon salt
1 cup quick-cooking oats, uncooked
½ cup firmly packed brown sugar
1 teaspoon ground cinnamon
¼ teaspoon ground nutmeg
1 egg
½ cup vegetable oil
1 teaspoon vanilla extract
1 cup peeled, shredded apple (1 medium)
½ cup raisins
⅓ cup chopped pecans

Combine first 7 ingredients in a large bowl, mixing well. Combine egg, oil, and vanilla; stir into dry ingredients. Stir in apple, raisins, and pecans. Drop dough by rounded teaspoonfuls onto greased cookie sheets. Bake at 350° for 10 to 12 minutes or until lightly browned. Carefully transfer cookies to wire racks to cool. Yield: 4 dozen.
Mrs. Paul Raper
Burgaw, North Carolina

Quick Southern Classics

Today's busy schedules demand food that's fast, easy to fix, and good tasting. And what better place to turn than to our traditional heritage for recipes and inspiration.

Our readers handily adapted today's convenience products to the food they grew up with, creating dishes that are speedier and easier to make than those their mothers prepared. Granted, a few of these recipes still take a little time to bake, but the time saved allows you to make a salad, fix the bread, or better yet, relax on the sofa.

■ Because canned sweet potatoes are substituted for fresh ones in **Speedy Sweet Potato Pie,** there's no time spent cooking, cooling, peeling, and slicing.

SPEEDY SWEET POTATO PIE

1 (16-ounce) can cut sweet
   potatoes, drained and mashed
1 (14-ounce) can sweetened
   condensed milk
2 eggs
1 teaspoon vanilla extract
½ teaspoon ground nutmeg
1 unbaked 9-inch pastry shell

Combine first 5 ingredients in a bowl; beat at medium speed of an electric mixer until blended. Pour filling into pastry shell. Bake at 425° for 15 minutes; reduce heat to 350°, and bake 35 minutes or until a knife inserted in center of pie comes out clean. Cool. Yield: one 9-inch pie.

Erma Jackson
Huntsville, Alabama

■ Cinnamon-raisin bread provides spicy flavor and bread in one product to use for **Bread Pudding.**

BREAD PUDDING

1 (1-pound) loaf cinnamon-raisin
   bread
1 quart milk
3 eggs, slightly beaten
1 cup sugar
2 tablespoons vanilla extract
Pinch of ground nutmeg
3 tablespoons butter or
   margarine, melted

Break bread into small chunks; place in a large bowl. Add milk, and let soak 10 minutes. Work mixture with hands until milk is absorbed.
   Combine eggs and remaining ingredients. Stir into bread mixture; pour

into a 13- x 9- x 2-inch baking dish. Bake at 350° for 50 minutes or until a knife inserted in center comes out clean. Yield: 12 servings.

Edith Michel
Upper Marlboro, Maryland

■ Using a cake mix shortens the mixing time for **Quick Upside Down Cake.**

QUICK UPSIDE DOWN CAKE
(pictured on page 224)

3 tablespoons butter or margarine
½ cup firmly packed brown sugar
¼ teaspoon ground cinnamon
1 (15¼-ounce) can unsweetened
   pineapple slices, drained
7 maraschino cherries
¼ cup chopped pecans
1 (18.25-ounce) package yellow
   cake mix without pudding

Melt butter in a 10½- x 2-inch cast-iron skillet. Combine brown sugar and cinnamon; sprinkle over butter. Arrange 7 pineapple slices over brown sugar, reserving remaining slice for other uses. Place a cherry in the center of each pineapple slice; sprinkle with pecans. Set aside.
   Prepare cake mix according to package directions. Pour batter over pineapple. Bake at 350° for 50 minutes or until a wooden pick inserted in center comes out clean. Remove cake from oven; immediately invert onto plate. Yield: one 10½-inch cake.

■ Using frozen sliced peaches eliminates the time spent washing and peeling peaches for **Peach Cobbler.** Thaw the peaches in the microwave to further shorten preparation time.

PEACH COBBLER

½ cup butter or margarine
¾ cup self-rising flour
¾ cup sugar
¾ cup milk
⅛ teaspoon almond extract
1 (16-ounce) package frozen
   sliced peaches, thawed and
   drained

Melt butter in an 8-inch square baking dish. Combine flour and next 3 ingredients; pour over butter. Do not stir. Arrange peaches on top. Bake at 350° for 55 minutes or until browned. Yield: 6 servings.

Robin Harbuck
Stone Mountain, Georgia

■ Canned corn and a commercial cornbead mix make **Corn Pudding** light work for the cook.

CORN PUDDING

3 eggs, slightly beaten
¼ cup butter or margarine,
   melted
1 small onion, chopped
1 green pepper, chopped
1 (17-ounce) can cream-style corn
1 (17-ounce) can whole-kernel
   corn, undrained
1 (8½-ounce) package cornbread
   mix
Garnishes: fresh parsley, pimiento
   strips

Combine first 7 ingredients; stir well. Spoon into 6 well-greased 10-ounce custard cups. Place on a baking sheet, and bake at 350° for 40 to 45 minutes or until set. To serve, loosen edges with a spatula; invert onto plate, and garnish, if desired. Yield: 6 servings.

Note: Pudding may be baked in a shallow 2-quart casserole at 350° for 1 hour or until set.

Martha Limbaugh
Birmingham, Alabama

■ **Easy Red Beans and Rice** substitutes canned beans for dried beans, which may soak or cook for hours. This method also omits the roux, a cooked mixture of butter or oil and flour.

EASY RED BEANS AND RICE
(pictured on page 221)

1 pound smoked link sausage, cut into ½-inch slices
1 medium onion, chopped
1 green pepper, chopped
1 clove garlic, minced
2 (15-ounce) cans kidney beans, drained
1 (16-ounce) can tomatoes, undrained and chopped
½ teaspoon dried whole oregano
½ teaspoon pepper
Hot cooked rice

Cook sausage over low heat 5 to 8 minutes. Add onion, green pepper, and garlic; sauté until tender. Drain, if necessary. Add beans, tomatoes, and seasonings; simmer, uncovered, 20 minutes. Serve over rice. Yield: 4 to 6 servings.   *Linda Keller*
Jonesboro, Arkansas

■ In **Shortcut Chicken and Rice,** a commercial long-grain and wild rice mix provides seasonings and rice for this entrée.

SHORTCUT
CHICKEN AND RICE

Vegetable cooking spray
4 chicken breast halves, skinned and boned
1 (10¾-ounce) can cream of chicken soup, undiluted
⅔ cup dry white wine
1 cup water
1 (6-ounce) package long-grain and wild rice mix

Coat a large skillet with cooking spray; place over medium heat until hot. Brown chicken on both sides. Remove chicken, and set aside.

Combine soup, wine, and water; stir in rice mix. Pour mixture into skillet, and bring to a boil. Arrange chicken over rice; cover, reduce heat, and simmer 25 minutes or until rice is tender. Let stand 10 minutes. Yield: 4 servings.
Laura Greene Knapp
Elkin, North Carolina

■ Refrigerated piecrusts will fool friends into thinking you slaved over pastry for **Double-Crust Chicken Pot Pie.** Canned vegetables and chicken make the recipe even simpler.

DOUBLE-CRUST
CHICKEN POT PIE
(pictured on page 224)

2 (9-inch) refrigerated piecrusts
1 (6¾-ounce) can boneless chicken in broth, undrained and chopped
1 (16-ounce) can mixed vegetables, drained
1 (10¾-ounce) can cream of chicken soup, undiluted
½ teaspoon celery flakes
¼ teaspoon pepper
¼ teaspoon poultry seasoning

Fit 1 refrigerated piecrust into a 9-inch pieplate, according to package directions (do not bake).

Combine chicken and remaining ingredients except piecrust; spoon mixture into prepared pieplate. Moisten edges of pastry with water; place remaining crust on top. Fold edges under, and flute. Cut slits in top to allow steam to escape.

Bake at 400° for 45 to 50 minutes. Let stand 10 minutes before serving. Yield: one 9-inch pie.   *Kay Kutz*
Jackson, Tennessee

■ To avoid peeling fresh shrimp, use frozen shrimp for **Shrimp Creole.** This shortcut makes this seafood favorite an easy dish to prepare.

SHRIMP CREOLE

½ cup chopped green pepper
¼ cup chopped celery
4 green onions, thinly sliced
1 clove garlic, minced
2 tablespoons butter or margarine
1 (16-ounce) can whole tomatoes
1 (6-ounce) can tomato paste
2 teaspoons dried parsley flakes
½ teaspoon salt
¼ teaspoon red pepper
1 (12-ounce) package frozen peeled and deveined shrimp, thawed
Hot cooked rice

Combine green pepper, celery, green onions, garlic, and butter in a shallow 2-quart baking dish. Cover with heavy-duty plastic wrap; fold back a corner of wrap to allow steam to escape. Microwave at HIGH 3 minutes.

Drain tomatoes, reserving ½ cup liquid; chop tomatoes. Add tomatoes, ½ cup reserved liquid, tomato paste, parsley flakes, salt, red pepper, and shrimp to vegetable mixture. Cover and microwave at MEDIUM HIGH (70% power) 11 to 13 minutes or until shrimp are done, stirring at 5-minute intervals. Let stand 5 minutes. Serve over hot cooked rice. Yield: about 4 servings.
Koenia Pereira
Newark, Texas

Right: *Serve Easy Red Beans and Rice with cornbread muffins for a complete meal. (Recipe, this page.)*

Whet a variety of appetites with Cream Pea Soup (page 211), sparked with the warmth of sherry, or chilled Carrot Cream Soup (page 210); both are elegant first courses.

You'll be proud to serve your heartiest eaters this light version of Beef Stew (page 230).

Double-Crust Chicken Pot Pie (page 220) and Quick Upside Down Cake (page 219) rely on convenience products to shorten cooking time.

From Our Kitchen To Yours

Having dinner together is important in our families. Besides learning how a table is properly set, our children gain mastery of table manners and conversational skills. Knowing the simple rules of etiquette prepares them to feel confident and at ease when dining away from home. Here are some tips:

- Lean slightly against the back of the chair; keep hands in your lap, or your hands and wrists (not the entire forearm) on the table's edge when you're eating. Remember to keep elbows off the table.
- For dinner at home, women seat themselves. On special occasions, the mother and grandmother may appreciate assistance with their chairs from the men. At dinners outside the home, a man seats the woman on his right. It is always courteous for the men and boys to remain standing at the table until all females are seated.
- As soon as you are seated, place the napkin in your lap even though you may not be eating right away. Never tuck it in a collar or a belt. When dining out, you may find the napkin in a coffee cup or goblet to your right or in the center of the place setting. Remove the napkin from your lap only to pat your lips or to cover a cough or sneeze. Upon leaving the table, lay the napkin in loose folds on the left side of your plate, or if the plate has been removed, lay it in the center of your place. Don't refold it.
- Before eating, wait until everyone has been served and the hostess picks up a piece of silverware. If the group is large, or small children are present, it is not always necessary to wait. After several guests have been served, the hostess often requests that you begin.
- When you are ready to eat, begin with the piece of each type of silverware that is farthest from your plate; just remember "from the outside in."

If you are unsure, follow the hostess's lead.
- Pass serving dishes, bread baskets, and served plates to your right. If an item is out of reach, quietly request it.
- When not in use, silverware has designated places. A soup spoon is placed on the saucer underneath the soup cup or left in the soup bowl. After the main course, the knife and fork should be placed side by side on the dinner plate diagonally from upper left to lower right, with the handles extending over the plate's edge. The dessert fork or spoon is left in this same position. But if dessert is served in a stemmed bowl on a plate, the spoon is placed on the plate unless the bowl is shallow and wide. Then the spoon is left in it.

The knife is for cutting, buttering, and guiding food onto the fork when bread is not available. After using the knife, rest it horizontally on the top edge of the plate with the cutting edge facing the plate's center.
- Table conversation should be about pleasant subjects, and voices should be kept at a moderate level. Everyone needs to contribute to the conversation, remembering to say "excuse me" when interrupting.
- Remember to say "please," "thank you," "you're welcome," "excuse me," "I enjoyed it," and to ask "may I be excused?"
- Practice drinking quietly, taking small bites, and chewing with your mouth closed. Do not drink or talk with food in your mouth.

No Trick To Treats For Teens

Halloween is on its way, and if you have young teens too old for trick or treating in the neighborhood, you're probably haunted by the question of what to do with them instead. Don't

be spooked; we have the answer you need. We've planned party foods for 16 that won't be a frightening experience for you. These simple treats are easy to make, and your shopping list will be short; each recipe has five or fewer ingredients.

You can prepare Chocolate-Peanut Butter Snacks and Marshmallow Popcorn Balls the day before the party for a head start. Wrap the popcorn balls in orange cellophane, and tie with black curling ribbon for take-home party favors. You may want to arrange them in a small black cauldron or bowl as a centerpiece, and let kids help themselves when the party's over.

HOT APPLE CIDER

¾ to 1 cup firmly packed brown sugar
1 gallon apple juice
2 (3-inch) sticks cinnamon
1 orange, sliced
1 lemon, sliced

Combine all ingredients in a Dutch oven. Bring to a boil; reduce heat, and simmer 10 minutes. Strain, discarding fruit and cinnamon sticks. Serve hot. Yield: 1 gallon.

Polly Tillotson
Reidsville, North Carolina

CHILI-CHEESE DIP

2 (15-ounce) cans hot chili without beans
1 (10-ounce) can diced tomatoes with chiles, undrained
1 (16-ounce) loaf process cheese spread, cubed

Combine all ingredients in a saucepan; cook over medium heat until cheese melts, stirring often.

To serve, transfer dip to a chafing dish; serve warm with tortilla chips. Yield: 5¾ cups. *Lou Baughman*
Fort Walton Beach, Florida

SALAMI ROLLUPS

1 (8-ounce) package cream
cheese, softened
1 (3-ounce) package cream
cheese, softened
2 to 3 tablespoons prepared
horseradish
3 (12-ounce) packages sliced
salami
Green onion tops (optional)

Combine first 3 ingredients. Spread
1½ teaspoons of mixture on each salami slice; roll up, and secure with a
wooden pick. If desired, cut green
onion tops into long strips, and tie
around rolled salami slices; remove
wooden picks. Yield: 36 appetizers.
Jeanne S. Hotaling
Augusta, Georgia

ALMOND DELIGHT DIP

2 (8-ounce) cartons vanilla low-fat
yogurt
⅛ teaspoon almond extract
2 tablespoons chopped almonds,
toasted

Combine yogurt and almond extract
in a small bowl; chill at least 1 hour.
Sprinkle with chopped almonds, and
serve with red and green apple
slices. Yield: about 2 cups.

Note: To prevent darkening, toss
apple slices with lemon juice or pineapple juice.
Becky Griffin
Marietta, Georgia

CHOCOLATE-PEANUT BUTTER
SNACKS

¾ cup creamy peanut butter
80 round buttery crackers
16 (1-ounce) squares
chocolate-flavored candy
coating
2 (1-ounce) squares
vanilla-flavored candy coating
Orange paste food coloring

Spread 1 teaspoon peanut butter on
half of crackers; top with remaining
crackers. Set aside.
Melt chocolate-flavored candy
coating in top of a double boiler; dip
sandwich crackers in melted coating,
allowing excess to drain. Place on
wax paper to cool.
Melt vanilla-flavored candy coating
in top of double boiler; add orange
food coloring, stirring well. Place
mixture in a heavy-duty zip-top plastic bag; seal. Using scissors, snip a
tiny hole in corner of bag; drizzle
mixture in a zigzag pattern on top of
crackers. Yield: 40 snacks.

MARSHMALLOW
POPCORN BALLS

50 large marshmallows
⅓ cup butter or margarine
6 quarts popped corn
Vegetable cooking spray

Combine marshmallows and butter in
a Dutch oven; cook over low heat
until marshmallows melt, stirring
mixture occasionally.
Place popped corn in a large pan.
Pour hot mixture over popped corn,
tossing to coat.
Coat hands with vegetable cooking
spray; shape mixture into balls. Place
on wax paper to cool. Wrap popcorn
balls individually in colored cellophane
or plastic wrap; store in a cool, dry
place. Yield: 16 balls.
Sue Hines
Hobart, Oklahoma

Appetizer and Dessert
Preparation Tips

■ When preparing finger sandwiches in advance, keep them
from drying out by placing the
sandwiches in a shallow container lined with a damp towel
and wax paper. Separate sandwich layers with wax paper, and
cover with another layer of wax
paper and a damp towel; then
refrigerate the sandwiches until
you're ready to use them.

■ To keep appetizers appealingly
hot—and you out of the
kitchen—use your chafing dish
and warming trays for serving.

■ Make spice cupcakes from a
white or yellow cake mix by
adding ground spices, such as
nutmeg, cinnamon, and cloves,
to the batter.

■ Cupcake pans should be
greased well on the bottom and
very lightly on the sides to
allow for easy removal of the
cupcakes.

■ Let cookies cool completely
before storing. To keep cookies
fresh, store soft and chewy
ones in an airtight container and
crisp cookies in a jar with a
loose-fitting lid.

■ Make homemade candy from
leftover cake frosting by mixing
it with shredded coconut or
chopped nuts. Shape into balls
and place on wax paper to
harden.

■ Avoid doubling a candy recipe.
It is always better to make a
second batch.

Crazy About Caramel

It's hard to beat the creamy dessert called flan that's served in so many restaurants these days. This baked custard is served in a dainty pool of caramelized sugar syrup that drenches the top of the shapely dessert as it's inverted onto the plate. We took this sinfully rich dessert one step further and crowned it with additional caramelized sugar that forms a crunchy nest.

Despite its spectacular appearance, Caramel-Crowned Flans is actually pretty simple to make. You can prepare all but the final drizzling of sugar up to three days early. And if you run short of time, just omit the crunch topping. Follow this step-by-step guide to help you make this special dessert.

CARAMEL-CROWNED FLANS

¾ cup sugar
1 (14-ounce) can sweetened
   condensed milk
⅔ cup milk
2 eggs
2 egg yolks
1 teaspoon vanilla extract
1 cup sugar
4 to 6 drops of hot water

Place ¾ cup sugar in a heavy saucepan; cook over medium heat until sugar melts and turns a light golden brown, stirring constantly. Remove from heat; pour hot caramelized sugar evenly into four 10-ounce custard cups. Let cool.

Combine sweetened condensed milk and next 4 ingredients in container of an electric blender; process at high speed 15 seconds. Pour evenly into custard cups. Place custard cups in a 13- x 9- x 2-inch pan; pour hot water to a depth of 1 inch into pan, and cover pan with aluminum foil. Bake at 350° for 30 minutes or until a knife inserted near center comes out clean. Remove cups from water; let cool. Cover and chill at least 8 hours.

To serve, loosen edge of custard with a spatula; invert onto individual plates, letting caramel drizzle over top. Set aside.

Place 1 cup sugar in a heavy saucepan; cook over medium heat until sugar melts and syrup is light golden brown, stirring constantly. Stir in drops of water; let stand 1 minute or until syrup spins a thread when drizzled from a spoon. Drizzle syrup, quickly wrapping threads around and over flans until a delicate web is formed. (If sugar hardens before webs are formed, place saucepan over medium heat until mixture softens.) Chill flans (uncovered) up to 45 minutes before serving. Yield: 4 servings.

Note: If spiced flans are desired, add ¼ teaspoon ground cinnamon, ⅛ teaspoon ground ginger, and ⅛ teaspoon ground nutmeg to egg mixture in blender. Spices will float to the top as mixture bakes.

Plump And Delicious

Prune sales have increased almost 50% in the last five years, paralleling an increased desire of people to add fiber to their diets. This dramatic increase is not surprising when you consider that prunes are one of the richest sources of fiber available. And they're convenient for cooking as well as for snacking.

Prunes are actually sun-ripened plums. Many people eat them right from the package, while others like to plump them beforehand to make them wonderfully juicy. To plump prunes, simply bring them to a boil with an equal amount of water. Then cover them, and reduce the heat; let pitted prunes simmer 3 to 4 minutes, and whole prunes, 10 minutes. Drain them, and let cool.

CHICKEN BREASTS WITH CURRIED PEPPERS

2 tablespoons butter or margarine
1 clove garlic, crushed
1 teaspoon curry powder
4 chicken breast halves, skinned
   and boned
½ cup dry white wine
½ cup pitted prunes
½ teaspoon salt
⅛ teaspoon pepper
1 medium-size sweet red pepper,
   cut into strips
1 medium-size green pepper, cut
   into strips

Melt butter in a large skillet over medium heat; stir in garlic and curry powder. Add chicken, and cook 5 minutes on each side. Add wine, prunes, salt, and pepper; cover and simmer over low heat 15 to 20 minutes. Remove chicken to a serving platter; keep warm.

Add peppers to skillet; cook 3 to 4 minutes or until crisp-tender, stirring occasionally. Spoon over chicken. Yield: 4 servings.

PEPPY PRUNE RELISH

1 cup chopped pitted prunes
   (about 8 ounces)
1 (4-ounce) can chopped green
   chiles, drained
⅓ cup sliced green onions
¼ cup chopped pecans, toasted
¼ cup balsamic vinegar
2 tablespoons diced pimiento
⅛ teaspoon hot sauce

Combine all ingredients. Serve with cream cheese and assorted crackers. Yield: about 2 cups.

ON THE LIGHT SIDE

Fight Cancer
With Your Fork

One of the latest weapons in the fight against cancer is food rich in beta carotene. Research has shown that people who regularly eat foods containing beta carotene have a lower risk of cancer (particularly lung and mouth cancers).

The fruits and vegetables that are good sources of beta carotene are also storehouses for other substances. In fact, it may be one of the other substances that is responsible for the protection against cancer; researchers aren't sure yet.

How can you make sure you're getting enough beta carotene? The National Academy of Sciences recommends eating at least five servings of fruits and vegetables each day.

Food Sources of Beta Carotene

Acorn squash, apricots, broccoli, brussels sprouts, butternut squash, cabbage, cantaloupe, carrots, kale, mango, papaya, pumpkin, red pepper, spinach, sweet potatoes, turnip greens

---

CURRIED CARROTS AND PINEAPPLE

1 (8-ounce) can pineapple tidbits in juice, undrained
1 pound carrots, scraped and cut into julienne sticks
½ teaspoon curry powder
¼ teaspoon salt
Dash of white pepper

Drain pineapple, reserving juice. Add enough water to pineapple juice to measure 1 cup liquid. Combine pineapple juice mixture, carrot, and remaining ingredients in a medium saucepan. Bring to a boil; cover, reduce heat, and simmer 8 minutes. Add pineapple, and cook 2 minutes or until carrots are crisp-tender. Yield: 6 servings (57 calories per ½-cup serving).

☐ *0.8 gram protein, 0.2 gram fat, 13.6 grams carbohydrate, 0 milligrams cholesterol, 125 milligrams sodium, and 26 milligrams calcium.*

SWEET POTATOES-AND-APPLE CASSEROLE

4 small sweet potatoes (1½ pounds), peeled and sliced
2 cooking apples (1 pound), cored and sliced
Vegetable cooking spray
3 tablespoons sugar
½ teaspoon ground cinnamon
Dash of white pepper
2 tablespoons reduced-calorie margarine, melted

Layer half each of sweet potatoes and apples in an 8-inch square baking dish coated with cooking spray. Combine sugar, cinnamon, and white pepper; sprinkle half of mixture over potatoes and apples. Drizzle with half of margarine. Repeat procedure with remaining ingredients.

Cover casserole, and bake at 350° for 1 hour. Yield: 8 servings (120 calories per ½-cup serving).

☐ *1 gram protein, 2.2 grams fat, 25.6 grams carbohydrate, 0 milligrams cholesterol, 35 milligrams sodium, and 17 milligrams calcium.*
Mrs. Grant Adkins
Wichita Falls, Texas

FRUITED ACORN SQUASH

2 medium acorn squash (about 1 pound each)
Vegetable cooking spray
⅓ cup canned pineapple tidbits in juice, drained
⅓ cup chopped orange
3 tablespoons brown sugar
2 tablespoons chopped pecans

Cut squash in half, and remove seeds. Place squash, cut side down, in a 15- x 10- x 1-inch jellyroll pan coated with cooking spray. Bake at 350° for 35 minutes. Cut each squash half into 2 pieces.

Combine pineapple and remaining ingredients; spoon evenly into squash. Bake an additional 10 to 15 minutes. Yield: 8 servings (60 calories per serving).

☐ *0.8 gram protein, 1.4 grams fat, 12.5 grams carbohydrate, 0 milligrams cholesterol, 3 milligrams sodium, and 27 milligrams calcium.*
Joy Garcia
Bartlett, Tennessee

BRUSSELS SPROUTS IN MUSTARD SAUCE

2 pounds brussels sprouts
1½ cups water
1 tablespoon reduced-calorie margarine
1 tablespoon all-purpose flour
⅔ cup ready-to-serve, no-salt-added chicken broth
⅓ cup skim milk
2 tablespoons Dijon mustard
½ teaspoon lemon juice
⅛ teaspoon white pepper

Wash brussels sprouts thoroughly, and remove discolored leaves. Cut off stem ends, and slash bottom of each sprout with a shallow x.

Combine brussels sprouts and water in a saucepan; bring to a boil. Cover, reduce heat, and simmer 12 to 15 minutes or until tender; drain.

Melt margarine in a heavy saucepan over low heat; add flour, stirring until smooth. Cook 1 minute, stirring constantly. Gradually add broth and milk; cook over medium heat 5 minutes, stirring constantly. Remove from heat, and stir in mustard, lemon juice, and pepper; pour over brussels sprouts, tossing to coat. Yield: 7 servings (56 calories per 4 brussels sprouts).

☐ *3.9 grams protein, 1.5 grams fat, 8 grams carbohydrate, 0 milligrams cholesterol, 176 milligrams sodium, and 73 milligrams calcium.*

Lorraine Stalecki
Fort Lauderdale, Florida

A Healthy Meal With A Cajun Flair

Folks everywhere are singing the praises of Cajun and Creole cuisines. Their unique flavors reflect the French, Spanish, Italian, African, and American Indian influences in South Louisiana.

This light and healthy meal centers around Shrimp Étouffée, which is a favorite Cajun recipe that's chock-full of flavor. And this version of the recipe contains only 12% fat. Just add Mixed Green Salad, commercial French bread, and Bread Pudding With Whiskey Sauce to complete this tasty menu, which has only 565 calories per serving.

SKILLET CABBAGE

Vegetable cooking spray
7 cups coarsely shredded cabbage
1½ cups sliced tomatoes
½ cup sliced onion
½ cup green pepper strips
½ cup chopped celery
2 tablespoons water
1 tablespoon reduced-calorie margarine
1½ teaspoons sugar
½ teaspoon salt
¼ teaspoon pepper

Coat a large Dutch oven with cooking spray; add cabbage and remaining ingredients. Bring mixture to a boil; cover, reduce heat, and simmer 20 minutes or until crisp-tender, stirring occasionally. Yield: 6 servings (54 calories per 1-cup serving).

☐ *1.8 grams protein, 1.7 grams fat, 9.8 grams carbohydrate, 0 milligrams cholesterol, 243 milligrams sodium, and 51 milligrams calcium.*

Willie Morgan
Alabaster, Alabama

Shrimp Étouffée
Mixed Green Salad
Commercial French bread
Bread Pudding With Whiskey Sauce

SHRIMP ÉTOUFFÉE

2 pounds unpeeled medium-size fresh shrimp
3 cups water
Vegetable cooking spray
2 tablespoons reduced-calorie margarine
2 cups chopped onion
4 cloves garlic, minced
1 cup sliced green onions
3 tablespoons cornstarch
⅓ cup chopped fresh parsley
¾ teaspoon salt
¼ teaspoon white pepper
6 cups hot cooked rice (cooked without salt or fat)

Peel and devein shrimp, reserving shells and tails; chop shrimp, and set aside. Place shells and tails in medium saucepan; add water, and bring to a boil. Cover, reduce heat, and simmer 30 minutes. Drain stock from shells, and set aside; discard shells and tails.

Coat a large, nonstick skillet with cooking spray; place over medium-high heat until hot. Add margarine, chopped onion, and garlic; sauté until tender. Add 2 cups reserved stock, and bring mixture to a boil. Add sliced green onions and chopped shrimp. Cook over low heat 5 to 7 minutes, stirring occasionally.

Combine cornstarch and ½ cup reserved stock; stir into shrimp mixture. Bring mixture to a boil; boil 1 minute, stirring constantly. Add parsley, salt, and pepper; stir well. Serve over rice. Yield: 8 servings (296 calories per ⅔-cup serving shrimp with ¾ cup rice).

☐ *21.6 grams protein, 3.7 grams fat, 42 grams carbohydrate, 135 milligrams cholesterol, 382 milligrams sodium, and 82 milligrams calcium.*

MIXED GREEN SALAD

3 cups torn romaine lettuce
3 cups torn Bibb lettuce
3 cups torn red leaf lettuce
3 cups torn endive
18 cherry tomatoes, halved
1 (8-ounce) bottle oil-free Italian
   dressing

Combine all ingredients, and toss gently. Yield: 8 servings (31 calories per 1½-cup serving).

☐ *1.5 grams protein, 0.3 gram fat, 6.6 grams carbohydrate, 0 milligrams cholesterol, 267 milligrams sodium, and 36 milligrams calcium.*

BREAD PUDDING WITH WHISKEY SAUCE

⅓ cup firmly packed brown sugar
½ cup egg substitute
2 cups skim milk
1 teaspoon ground nutmeg
1¼ teaspoons ground cinnamon
1½ teaspoons vanilla extract
5 cups (1-inch) French bread
   cubes
⅓ cup raisins
Butter-flavored vegetable cooking
   spray
Whiskey Sauce

Combine first 6 ingredients, beating with a wire whisk. Add bread and raisins; stir well. Spoon mixture into eight 6-ounce custard cups coated with cooking spray. Place cups in a large shallow pan; add hot water to a depth of ¾ inch to pan.
   Bake at 350° for 25 minutes or until a knife inserted in center of pudding comes out clean. Spoon Whiskey Sauce over pudding. Yield: 8 servings (165 calories per serving with 2 tablespoons sauce).

☐ *6.2 grams protein, 1.1 grams fat, 32.1 grams carbohydrate, 2 milligrams cholesterol, 208 milligrams sodium, and 107 milligrams calcium.*

Whiskey Sauce

2 tablespoons sugar
1 tablespoon cornstarch
1 tablespoon reduced-calorie
   margarine
¾ cup water
¼ cup whiskey or bourbon

Combine all ingredients in a small saucepan. Cook over medium heat, stirring constantly, until mixture begins to boil; boil 1 minute, stirring constantly. Serve warm. Yield: 1 cup (13 calories per tablespoon).

☐ *0 grams protein, 0.5 gram fat, 2.3 grams carbohydrate, 0 milligrams cholesterol, 7 milligrams sodium, and 0 milligrams calcium.*

Tips for the Calorie Conscious

■ Satisfy your craving for sweets by choosing low-fat foods. For example, have a slice of low-fat angel food cake for dessert rather than a slice of cheesecake. Or opt for plain low-fat gingersnaps for a snack instead of a fat-laden doughnut.

■ Reduce calories in meat dishes by trimming away visible fat before cooking the meat.

■ Try a little calorie-free club soda in grape or apple juice to add a bubbly sparkle and to make the fruit juice calories go further.

■ Lighten cream soups by replacing heavy cream with evaporated skimmed milk. The soup will have the rich texture with almost no fat.

LIGHT FAVORITE

Beef Stew Minus All The Fat

Beef Stew, a favorite comfort food, has been successfully lightened in calories and fat by JoAnn Maupin of Fort Payne, Alabama. Her recipe uses lean top round beef and only 1 tablespoon vegetable oil, yet it has the same rich flavor of traditional beef stew.

BEEF STEW
(pictured on page 223)

1 pound top boneless round steak
¼ cup all-purpose flour
¼ teaspoon pepper
¾ cup chopped onion
1 tablespoon vegetable oil
3 cups water
½ cup finely chopped carrot
¼ cup finely chopped celery
2 tablespoons minced fresh
   parsley
½ teaspoon salt
⅛ teaspoon dried whole thyme
2 cups cubed potato
1 cup sliced carrot
1 cup chopped onion
1 cup frozen green peas, thawed

Trim fat from steak; cut into 1-inch cubes. Combine flour and pepper; dredge meat in flour mixture, reserving excess.
   Cook meat, ¾ cup onion, and reserved flour mixture in oil in a Dutch oven over low heat until meat is lightly browned. Add water and next 5 ingredients. Cover, reduce heat, and simmer 1½ hours.
   Stir in potato, 1 cup carrot, and 1 cup onion; cover and simmer 20 minutes. Add green peas, and cook an

additional 10 minutes. Yield: 6 cups (349 calories per 1½-cup serving).

☐ *31.1 grams protein, 8.3 grams fat, 36 grams carbohydrate, 63 milligrams cholesterol, 424 milligrams sodium, and 58 milligrams calcium.*

COMPARE THE NUTRIENTS (per serving)		
	Traditional	Light
Calories	533	349
Fat	24.1g	8.3g
Cholesterol	68mg	63mg

Tastefully Tossed Salad

A truly eye-catching first course, Tropical Spinach Salad is just the dish to start off your next dinner party. Guests will marvel at this work of art with its interesting mix of colors, shapes, and textures.

TROPICAL SPINACH SALAD

5 cups torn fresh spinach
3 cups torn romaine lettuce
2 cups torn leaf lettuce
1 (11-ounce) can mandarin
   oranges, drained
1 small purple onion, sliced and
   separated into rings
Cooked Salad Dressing
¼ cup sliced almonds, toasted

Place first 5 ingredients in a large bowl. Toss with Cooked Salad Dressing. Sprinkle almonds over top. Serve immediately. Yield: 8 servings.

Cooked Salad Dressing

¼ cup sugar
¼ cup white vinegar
¼ teaspoon salt
¼ teaspoon dry mustard
¼ teaspoon instant minced onion
Dash of paprika
1 egg, slightly beaten
¼ cup vegetable oil

Combine first 7 ingredients in a small saucepan; bring to a boil. Boil 1 minute. Gradually stir in oil. Chill. Yield: ¾ cup.
Billie Nichols
Charlotte, North Carolina

Fiesta Supper In A Snap

This Microwave Mexican Casserole is a snap to cook. You can get supper on the table in less than 30 minutes. While the ground beef is cooking, you can shred the cheese. During the last 15 to 17 minutes that the casserole cooks, you'll have time to shred lettuce, chop tomatoes, and set the table.

MICROWAVE MEXICAN CASSEROLE

1 pound ground beef
1 medium onion, chopped
1 clove garlic, minced
1 (10¾-ounce) can cream of
   mushroom soup, undiluted
1 (10-ounce) can enchilada sauce
¾ cup evaporated milk
3 cups tortilla chips, divided
1 (4-ounce) can chopped green
   chiles, drained
1½ cups (6 ounces) shredded
   Cheddar cheese, divided
Shredded lettuce
Chopped tomato
Garnish: jalapeño pepper slices

Combine ground beef, chopped onion, and minced garlic in a 2-quart casserole. Cover tightly with heavy-duty plastic wrap; fold back a small edge of wrap to allow steam to escape. Microwave at HIGH 6 to 7 minutes or until meat is browned, stirring once. Drain. Add mushroom soup, enchilada sauce, and evaporated milk to ground beef mixture; stir well.

Place 2 cups tortilla chips in a 2-quart shallow casserole. Spoon half of ground beef mixture over chips; layer with chiles and half of shredded Cheddar cheese. Top with remaining ground beef mixture. Cover tightly with heavy-duty plastic wrap; fold back a small edge of wrap to allow steam to escape.

Microwave at HIGH 10 to 12 minutes or until casserole is thoroughly heated, giving dish a quarter-turn after 5 minutes. Sprinkle top of casserole with remaining cheese, and let stand 5 minutes. Serve with shredded lettuce and chopped tomato. Garnish with remaining chips and, if desired, jalapeño slices. Yield: 4 to 6 servings.
Paula Patterson
Round Rock, Texas

Tip: *Most cheeses should be wrapped in moisture-proof airtight wrappers. (One exception is "moldy" cheeses, such as blue cheese, which need to breathe and should be kept in covered containers with the tops loosened a bit.) Remember, too, that all cheeses keep best on the bottom shelf of the refrigerator.*

A Southern Menu With A Few Surprises

Fried chicken, sweet potatoes, turnip greens, and corn sticks—you won't find a menu more Southern than this one by Willa Govoro of Bossier City, Louisiana. We liked that she grouped together these favorite regional foods, but it was the surprise ingredients that caught our eye. For example, Willa adds lemon juice to Turnip Greens for extra punch.

Zesty Deviled Chicken
Bourbon Yams
Turnip Greens
Old-Fashioned Corn Sticks

ZESTY DEVILED CHICKEN
(pictured on page 188)

3 tablespoons butter or margarine
1 cup dry breadcrumbs
1 teaspoon sugar
1 teaspoon paprika
¼ teaspoon onion powder
1 egg, beaten
¼ cup prepared mustard
1 (2½- to 3-pound) broiler-fryer, cut up and skinned

Melt butter in a 12- x 8- x 2-inch baking dish. Set aside.

Combine breadcrumbs, sugar, paprika, and onion powder in a shallow dish. Combine egg and mustard; brush evenly on chicken. Coat chicken with breadcrumb mixture, and place in prepared dish. Bake at 400° for 25 minutes; turn chicken in baking dish. Bake an additional 20 minutes. Yield: 4 servings.

BOURBON YAMS
(pictured on page 188)

1 (29-ounce) can whole sweet potatoes, drained and cut into ½-inch slices
3 tablespoons butter or margarine, melted
3 tablespoons brown sugar
3 tablespoons orange juice
3 tablespoons bourbon
¼ teaspoon ground cinnamon
⅛ teaspoon ground cloves
⅛ teaspoon ground nutmeg
¼ teaspoon chopped pecans, toasted

Place sliced potatoes in a lightly greased 8-inch square dish. Combine butter and next 6 ingredients; pour over potatoes. Sprinkle with pecans. Bake at 350° for 25 minutes or until thoroughly heated. Yield: 4 servings.

Note: You can substitute 3 medium-size fresh sweet potatoes (about 1½ pounds) for canned sweet potatoes. Cook potatoes in boiling water to cover 30 to 45 minutes or until tender. Let potatoes cool to touch; peel and slice.

TURNIP GREENS
(pictured on page 188)

6 slices bacon, chopped
¼ cup chopped onion
1 bunch fresh turnip greens (about 4 pounds)
½ cup water
¼ cup lemon juice
1 tablespoon sugar
¼ teaspoon salt

Cook chopped bacon and onion in a large Dutch oven until bacon is crisp and onion is tender; drain well, and set aside.

Remove stems from greens; wash greens thoroughly, and tear into bite-size pieces. Combine greens and water in Dutch oven; bring to a boil over medium heat. Cover, reduce heat, and simmer 30 minutes or until tender, adding additional water, if necessary. Stir in bacon mixture, lemon juice, sugar, and salt; cook an additional 5 minutes. Yield: 4 to 6 servings.

OLD-FASHIONED CORN STICKS
(pictured on page 188)

1½ cups cornmeal
½ cup all-purpose flour
2 teaspoons baking powder
½ teaspoon baking soda
1 teaspoon salt
1 teaspoon sugar
2 eggs, lightly beaten
1½ cups buttermilk
¼ cup vegetable oil or bacon drippings

Combine first 6 ingredients in a large bowl. Combine eggs, buttermilk, and oil; add to dry ingredients, stirring just until moistened.

Place a well-greased cast-iron corn stick pan in a 450° oven 3 minutes or until pan is hot. Remove pan from oven; spoon batter into pan, filling three-fourths full. Bake at 450° for 15 minutes or until lightly browned. Yield: 1½ dozen.

Note: To make muffins, grease and heat muffin pans as directed. Spoon batter into pans, filling two-thirds full. Bake as directed.

QUICK!

Supper From The Sea

When you want an entrée that cooks fast, think seafood. Because it has little or no connective tissue, seafood requires a relatively short cooking time. Be careful not to overcook it as overcooking toughens it and destroys the delicate flavor.

Enjoy the high-priced flavor of crabmeat at a much lower cost by substituting seafood mix for crabmeat in Seafood and Pasta. Seafood mix can be found in the freezer section or at the fish counter at your local supermarket.

QUICK CLAM LINGUINE

8 ounces linguine, uncooked
3 to 5 cloves garlic, minced
¼ cup plus 1 tablespoon butter or margarine, melted
2 (6½-ounce) cans minced clams, undrained
1 cup (4 ounces) shredded Monterey Jack cheese
¼ cup chopped fresh parsley

Cook linguine according to package directions, omitting salt. Drain linguine, and set it aside.

Sauté garlic in butter in a large skillet. Drain clams, and add liquid to garlic and butter in skillet; bring mixture to a boil. Cook over medium-high heat 7 minutes. Add clams and cheese; cook over low heat, stirring constantly, until cheese melts. Pour sauce over linquine; add parsley, and toss gently. Yield: 4 servings.

Carol Chastain
San Antonio, Texas

GROUPER WITH SAUTÉED VEGETABLES

1 small onion, thinly sliced
1 small green pepper, cut into strips
1 tablespoon olive oil
1 teaspoon garlic salt, divided
¾ teaspoon dried whole thyme, divided
1 medium tomato, peeled, seeded, and chopped
1 (1-pound) grouper fillet
3 tablespoons lemon juice
¼ teaspoon hot sauce
Garnishes: leaf lettuce, lemon wedges

Combine onion, green pepper, and olive oil in a 9-inch pieplate; sprinkle with ½ teaspoon garlic salt and ¼ teaspoon thyme. Microwave, uncovered, at HIGH 2 to 3 minutes. Stir in chopped tomato; microwave at HIGH 1 minute.

Cut fillet into 4 equal portions, and arrange in an 8-inch square baking dish, with thickest portions of fish toward outside of dish. Combine lemon juice, hot sauce, remaining ½ teaspoon garlic salt, and ½ teaspoon thyme in a small bowl; pour over fish. Cover with wax paper, and microwave at HIGH 6 to 7 minutes or until fish flakes easily when tested with a fork. Drain.

Spoon vegetable mixture over fish; microwave at MEDIUM HIGH (70% power) 1 minute. Garnish each serving with leaf lettuce and lemon wedges, if desired. Yield: 4 servings.

SHRIMP VERSAILLES

2 tablespoons sliced green onions
3 tablespoons butter or margarine, melted
2 (12-ounce) packages frozen uncooked shrimp, thawed
1 (8-ounce) package cream cheese, cubed
3 tablespoons milk
½ cup (2 ounces) shredded Swiss cheese
2 tablespoons dry white wine
Dash of red pepper
¼ cup fine dry breadcrumbs
2 tablespoons butter or margarine, melted
Hot cooked rice

Sauté green onions in 3 tablespoons butter in a large skillet until tender. Add shrimp; cook over medium heat about 5 minutes, stirring occasionally. Remove shrimp with a slotted spoon; set aside.

Add cream cheese and milk to skillet; cook over low heat, stirring constantly, until cheese melts. Stir in Swiss cheese and wine. Add shrimp and red pepper; cook just until heated, stirring constantly. Pour into a lightly greased 1½-quart casserole. Combine breadcrumbs and 2 tablespoons butter; sprinkle over casserole. Broil 6 inches from heat 1 to 2 minutes or until golden. Serve over rice. Yield: 4 to 6 servings.

Carrie T. Finley
Crowley, Louisiana

Tip: *To use a griddle or frying pan, preheat to medium or medium-high heat before adding the food. The pan is properly preheated when a few drops of water spatter when they hit the surface. Add food to the pan, and reduce heat to cook without spattering and smoking.*

SEAFOOD AND PASTA

2 cups sliced fresh mushrooms
¾ cup chopped onion
¼ cup butter or margarine, melted
1 (10¾-ounce) can cream of mushroom soup, undiluted
1 cup half-and-half
2 tablespoons grated Parmesan cheese
¼ teaspoon garlic salt
½ teaspoon dried parsley flakes
1 (16-ounce) package seafood mix, chopped
Hot cooked shell macaroni

Sauté mushrooms and onion in butter in a large skillet until tender. Add mushroom soup and next 5 ingredients. Cook over medium heat, stirring constantly, until thoroughly heated. Serve over shell macaroni. Yield: 4 to 6 servings.

Dawn F. Ellen
Bishopville, South Carolina

Pick An Entrée For Two

One of the frustrations of cooking for two is having so many leftovers. With these entrées, however, you won't have a problem. Each is sized with two appetites in mind.

CHICKEN-FRUIT SALAD

1 small head Bibb lettuce
1 avocado
2 chicken breast halves, cooked and cubed
1 small apple, diced
1 small banana, sliced
1 (8-ounce) can pineapple chunks, drained
½ cup chopped pecans
⅓ to ½ cup mayonnaise or salad dressing

Remove 6 outer leaves of lettuce; wash and set aside. Chop remaining lettuce; set aside.

Peel and seed avocado. Slice half of avocado, and set slices aside; chop remaining avocado.

Combine chopped lettuce, chopped avocado, chicken, and remaining ingredients; toss gently. Serve on reserved lettuce leaves, and garnish with avocado slices. Yield: 2 servings.

Paula Patterson
Round Rock, Texas

CREAM CHEESE CHICKEN BREASTS

2 chicken breast halves, skinned and boned
Paprika
Pepper
2 tablespoons butter or margarine, melted
2 tablespoons brandy
¼ cup water
¼ teaspoon dry mustard
¼ teaspoon dried whole basil
¼ teaspoon celery seeds
¼ teaspoon ground ginger
¼ teaspoon dried parsley flakes
¼ teaspoon garlic powder
1 (3-ounce) package cream cheese, cubed
1 tablespoon slivered almonds, toasted

Sprinkle chicken breasts lightly with paprika and pepper; cook chicken in butter in a heavy skillet 12 minutes or until done, turning once. Remove chicken, and keep warm.

Add brandy to drippings in skillet; cook on high heat, stirring constantly, until liquid is reduced to 1 tablespoon. Add water and next 7 ingredients. Cook over low heat, stirring constantly with a wire whisk, until mixture is smooth. Pour sauce over chicken breasts. Sprinkle with almonds. Yield: 2 servings.

Mrs. Robert L. Fetzer
Jacksonville, Florida

SIMPLE BEEF BURGUNDY

¼ cup all-purpose flour
¼ teaspoon salt
¼ teaspoon pepper
¾ pound sirloin steak, cut into thin strips
2 tablespoons olive oil
1 medium onion, cut into strips
1 small clove garlic, minced
⅔ cup beef broth
⅔ cup Burgundy
½ teaspoon dried whole basil
Hot cooked rice

Combine first 3 ingredients; dredge steak in flour mixture. Brown steak in hot oil in a large skillet. Remove steak from skillet; set aside.

Add onion and garlic to skillet; cook until tender. Add steak, broth, Burgundy, and basil; cover and simmer 20 minutes or until steak is tender. Serve over rice. Yield: 2 servings.

Carolyn Shelbourne
Paducah, Kentucky

TEX-MEX MEAT LOAF FOR TWO

1 (4-ounce) can chopped green chiles, drained and divided
¼ cup regular oats, uncooked
1 egg
2 tablespoons catsup
1 teaspoon chopped onion
¼ teaspoon chili powder
¼ teaspoon salt
½ pound ground beef
⅓ cup catsup
1 teaspoon minced onion
Dash of garlic powder
¼ cup (1 ounce) shredded Cheddar cheese

Combine 2 tablespoons chopped chiles and next 6 ingredients; stir well. Add ground beef, and stir just until blended. Shape mixture into two 4- x 2-inch loaves; place in an 8-inch square baking dish. Bake at 375° for 20 to 25 minutes.

Combine ⅓ cup catsup, remaining chopped chiles, 1 teaspoon onion,

and garlic powder in a small saucepan. Cook over low heat 3 to 5 minutes or until thoroughly heated. Spoon sauce over cooked loaves, and sprinkle with cheese. Yield: 2 servings.   *Kathleen Stone*
Houston, Texas

Ham With New Appeal

Ham is a favorite breakfast and brunch meat, and our readers present it with style and lots of flavors.

Mustard complements ham nicely, especially in Spicy Ham Patties. The mustard, along with applesauce, seasons and binds ham and sausage. Brown sugar, mustard, and vinegar give the sauce an appealing sweet-and-sour flavor.

HAM PINWHEELS

2½ cups ground ham
¼ cup chopped onion
1 tablespoon prepared horseradish
2 tablespoons chopped fresh
  parsley
2 teaspoons prepared mustard
⅛ teaspoon red pepper
1 egg, slightly beaten
2 cups all-purpose flour
3½ teaspoons baking powder
½ teaspoon salt
2 teaspoons sugar
2 teaspoons caraway seeds
½ cup shortening
1 egg, slightly beaten
½ cup milk
Cheese Sauce

Combine first 7 ingredients in a medium bowl; mix well. Set aside.

Combine flour and next 4 ingredients; cut in shortening with a pastry blender until mixture resembles coarse meal. Combine egg and milk; add to dry ingredients, stirring until dry ingredients are moistened. Turn dough out onto a lightly floured surface, and knead lightly 4 or 5 times. Roll dough to a 12- x 10-inch rectangle (about ½-inch thick).

Spread ham mixture over dough. Starting on short side, roll up jellyroll fashion, pinching edges to seal. Cut into ¾-inch slices. Place 2 inches apart on a lightly greased baking sheet. Bake at 450° for 20 minutes or until lightly browned. Serve with Cheese Sauce. Yield: 14 biscuits.

Cheese Sauce

3 tablespoons butter or margarine
3 tablespoons all-purpose flour
2 cups milk
¼ teaspoon salt
Dash of white pepper
1 cup (4 ounces) shredded
  Cheddar cheese
2 teaspoons white wine
  Worcestershire sauce

Melt butter in a heavy saucepan over low heat; add flour, stirring until smooth. Cook 1 minute, stirring constantly. Gradually add milk; cook over medium heat, stirring constantly, until thickened and bubbly. Stir in salt, white pepper, cheese, and Worcestershire sauce; cook until cheese melts. Yield: 2 cups.
BariLynn Mitchell
St. Peters, Missouri

HAM LOAVES

1¼ pounds ground smoked ham
¾ pound ground pork
¾ cup cracker crumbs
2 eggs, slightly beaten
½ cup milk
⅛ teaspoon pepper
¾ cup firmly packed brown sugar
1½ teaspoons prepared mustard
¼ cup water
¼ cup white vinegar

Combine first 6 ingredients in a large bowl; stir well. Divide mixture into 8 equal portions; shape into loaves. Arrange loaves in a 13- x 9- x 2-inch baking dish.

Combine brown sugar and remaining ingredients in a small saucepan; stir well. Bring to a boil over medium heat; simmer 10 minutes, stirring occasionally. Pour sauce over ham loaves. Bake, uncovered, at 350° for 45 minutes, basting ham loaves occasionally with sauce.

Note: Ham loaves may be frozen up to one month after baking. To reheat, bake frozen loaves at 350° for 30 minutes or until loaves are thoroughly heated. Yield: 8 servings.
Elinor Zollinger
Louisville, Kentucky

SPICY HAM PATTIES

2 eggs, beaten
½ cup applesauce
1½ cups herb-seasoned stuffing
  mix
⅓ cup nonfat dry milk powder
¼ cup chopped onion
½ teaspoon dry mustard
¾ pound ground cooked ham
½ pound bulk pork sausage
6 crabapple rings, drained
1 teaspoon cornstarch
2 tablespoons white vinegar
1 tablespoon brown sugar
¼ teaspoon dry mustard
Dash of ground cloves
¾ cup applesauce

Combine first 6 ingredients, mixing well. Add ham and sausage; mix well. Shape into 6 patties. Place on a broiler pan; bake at 350° for 40 minutes. Top each patty with a crabapple ring. Bake an additional 5 minutes.

Combine cornstarch and vinegar in a saucepan; add brown sugar and remaining ingredients, stirring well. Cook over medium heat, stirring constantly, until mixture boils; boil 1 minute. Serve with ham patties. Yield: 6 servings.   *Margot Foster*
Hubbard, Texas

Side Dishes That Satisfy

When planning menus for the holidays, the entrée is usually the easy part. Most folks know from the start whether they'll bake a traditional turkey, ham, or perhaps beef tenderloin. And while they're just as persnickety about side dishes, there's usually a little more room for variety. Here are several recipe options from which to choose.

SQUASH DELIGHT

2½ cups herb-seasoned stuffing mix
3 tablespoons butter or margarine, melted
1 pound yellow squash, sliced
1 pound zucchini, sliced
2 carrots, scraped and shredded
½ cup chopped onion
1 (2-ounce) jar diced pimiento, drained
1 (10¾-ounce) can cream of chicken soup, undiluted
1 (8-ounce) carton sour cream
¼ teaspoon salt
¼ teaspoon pepper

Combine stuffing mix and melted butter in a medium bowl, stirring well. Spoon 2 cups stuffing mixture into a lightly greased 13- x 9- x 2-inch baking dish. Set baking dish and remaining stuffing mixture aside.

Cook yellow squash and zucchini together in a small amount of boiling water 6 to 8 minutes or until tender; drain and mash. Drain again. Add carrot and remaining ingredients except stuffing mixture, stirring well. Spoon into prepared baking dish. Sprinkle with remaining stuffing mixture. Bake casserole at 350° for 30 minutes. Yield: 8 servings.

Mildred Sherrer
Bay City, Texas

EGGPLANT DRESSING

4 cups peeled, cubed eggplant
⅓ cup milk
1 (10¾-ounce) can cream of mushroom soup, undiluted
1 egg, slightly beaten
½ cup chopped onion
1¼ cups herb-seasoned stuffing mix, divided
¼ teaspoon salt
1 tablespoon butter or margarine, melted

Cook eggplant in boiling salted water 6 to 8 minutes or until tender; drain well. Combine eggplant, milk, soup, egg, onion, ¾ cup stuffing mix, and salt, stirring well. Spoon into a lightly greased 1-quart casserole. Combine remaining ½ cup stuffing mix and butter; sprinkle over eggplant mixture. Bake at 350° for 20 to 25 minutes. Yield: 6 servings.

Mrs. H. G. Drawdy
Spindale, North Carolina

RICE À L'ORANGE

1 (8-ounce) can pineapple slices
⅓ cup chopped green pepper
⅓ cup chopped sweet red pepper
⅓ cup chopped onion
¼ cup butter or margarine, divided
1¾ cups orange juice
2 cups instant rice, uncooked
Dash of salt
⅛ teaspoon curry powder
Garnishes: green and sweet red pepper strips

Drain pineapple slices, reserving juice for other uses. Chop pineapple, and set aside.

Sauté chopped peppers and onion in 1 tablespoon melted butter until tender. Add orange juice, and bring to a boil. Add rice, remaining 3 tablespoons butter, chopped pineapple, salt, and curry powder. Remove from heat; cover and let stand 10 minutes, stirring once. Garnish, if desired. Yield: 6 servings.

Ann G. Gullett
St. Petersburg, Florida

Artichokes Fill This Strata

One of the easiest ways to entertain at home is with a brunch. Lighter, less formal menus with dishes that can be made in advance make serving easy.

ARTICHOKE-CHEESE STRATA

½ cup sliced fresh mushrooms
½ cup chopped green onions
1 tablespoon butter or margarine, melted
3 slices white bread, cubed
¾ cup (3 ounces) shredded sharp Cheddar cheese
1 (14-ounce) can artichoke hearts, drained and quartered
1 (4-ounce) jar diced pimiento, drained
4 eggs, beaten
1½ cups milk
½ teaspoon dry mustard
¼ teaspoon salt
⅛ teaspoon white pepper

Sauté mushrooms and green onions in butter until tender; drain, if necessary, and set aside.

Layer half each of bread cubes, sautéed vegetables, shredded cheese, artichokes, and diced pimiento in a lightly greased 9-inch quiche dish; repeat layers.

Combine eggs and remaining ingredients; stir well. Pour mixture into quiche dish; cover and chill 3 hours.

Remove from refrigerator; let stand 30 minutes. Bake, uncovered, at 350° for 50 to 55 minutes or until set. Let stand 10 minutes. Yield: 6 servings.

NOVEMBER

Capture the spirit of the season and share it with family and friends. One of the best ways is to host a gathering in your home. To make it easy for you, our "Holiday Dinners" special section offers a complete party guide, including a wide range of recipes, menus, and ideas for entertaining. There are three open house menus featuring recipes that you can mix or match. Dinner offerings include impressive main-dish casseroles, perfect for holiday buffets.

Company's Coming For Casseroles

SAUSAGE-CHEESE GRITS

4 cups water
1 cup quick-cooking yellow or
  white grits, uncooked
2 cups (8 ounces) shredded sharp
  Cheddar cheese
¼ cup milk
2 tablespoons butter or margarine
2 teaspoons Worcestershire sauce
1½ teaspoons garlic salt
1 egg, beaten
1 pound hot bulk pork sausage,
  cooked and drained
1 cup (4 ounces) shredded sharp
  Cheddar cheese

It's a priority during the busy holiday season to spend time with special people. But how many times have you bid farewell to dinner guests or out-of-town company and realized you served fabulous food but somehow missed the visit?

These casseroles are just what you need. All can be assembled a day ahead and chilled overnight, and some can even be made a couple of months before an event and frozen. When you team one of these casseroles with commercial rolls or bread and an easy make-ahead salad and dessert, all that's left to do before company arrives is set the table while heating the main dish. Friends and family will enjoy both your attention *and* a great meal.

Bring water to a boil in a large saucepan; stir in grits. Return to a boil; cover, reduce heat, and cook 5 minutes, stirring occasionally. Remove from heat, and add 2 cups Cheddar cheese and next 4 ingredients, stirring until cheese melts. Stir a small amount of grits mixture into beaten egg; add to remaining grits mixture, stirring constantly.

Spoon half of grits mixture into a lightly greased 8-inch square baking dish; top with sausage. Spoon remaining grits mixture over sausage. Cover and chill 8 hours.

To bake, remove from refrigerator, and let stand at room temperature 30 minutes. Bake, uncovered, at 350° for 40 minutes. Sprinkle with 1 cup cheese, and bake an additional 5 minutes. Yield: 8 servings.

Microwave Heating: Prepare casserole as directed; cover and chill 8 hours. Remove from refrigerator, and let stand at room temperature 30 minutes. Cover loosely with wax paper, and microwave at HIGH 20 minutes, giving dish a half-turn after 10 minutes. Uncover and microwave at HIGH an additional 5 minutes or until heated. Sprinkle with 1 cup cheese, and let stand 5 minutes.

Jane Gray Suggs
Anderson, South Carolina

ITALIAN CASSEROLE
(pictured on pages 258 and 259)

1 (8-ounce) package spaghetti,
  uncooked
1 (10-ounce) package frozen
  chopped spinach, thawed and
  well drained
1 (10¾-ounce) can cream of
  mushroom soup, undiluted
1 clove garlic, minced
½ teaspoon dried whole marjoram
¼ to ½ teaspoon dried whole
  tarragon
¼ teaspoon salt
¼ teaspoon pepper
1 pound Italian sausage
1 large onion, chopped
1 egg, slightly beaten
1 (16-ounce) carton ricotta
  cheese
1 tomato, chopped
⅓ cup chopped fresh parsley

Cook spaghetti according to package directions; drain. Spoon into a lightly greased 13- x 9- x 2-inch baking dish; set aside.

Combine spinach and next 6 ingredients; spoon over spaghetti.

Remove casing from sausage. Cook sausage and onion in a large skillet over medium-high heat until meat is browned, stirring to crumble. Drain well. Sprinkle sausage mixture over spinach mixture.

Combine egg and ricotta cheese; spread over sausage mixture. Cover and chill 8 hours.

To bake, remove casserole from refrigerator, and let stand at room temperature 30 minutes. Bake, covered, at 375° for 35 to 40 minutes or until thoroughly heated. Sprinkle top with tomato and parsley. Yield: 6 to 8 servings.

Note: Unbaked casserole may be frozen. To bake, thaw in refrigerator 24 hours. Remove from refrigerator, and let stand at room temperature 30 minutes. Bake, covered, at 375° for 50 minutes or until thoroughly heated. Sprinkle with tomato and parsley. *Mrs. Harland J. Stone*
Ocala, Florida

BROCCOLI-HAM AU GRATIN
(pictured on pages 258 and 259)

1 medium onion, chopped
1 tablespoon butter or margarine, melted
1 (11-ounce) can Cheddar cheese soup, undiluted
1 (6-ounce) package sharp process cheese roll, sliced
½ teaspoon garlic powder
1 (8-ounce) can sliced mushrooms, drained
1 (10-ounce) package frozen chopped broccoli, thawed and drained
3 cups cooked rice
2 cups diced cooked ham
1 (2-ounce) jar diced pimiento, drained
1 (2.8-ounce) can fried onion rings

Sauté onion in butter in a Dutch oven until tender. Add soup, cheese, and garlic powder; stir until cheese melts. Add mushrooms and next 3 ingredients. Gently stir in pimiento, and spoon into a lightly greased 12- x 8- x 2-inch baking dish. Cover and chill 8 hours.

To bake, remove from refrigerator, and let stand at room temperature 30 minutes. Bake, covered, at 350° for 40 minutes. Sprinkle onion rings over casserole, and bake an additional 5 to 8 minutes. Yield: 6 to 8 servings.

Note: Unbaked casserole may be frozen. To bake, thaw in refrigerator 24 hours. Remove from refrigerator, and let stand at room temperature 30 minutes. Bake, covered, at 350° for 40 minutes. Sprinkle onion rings over casserole, and bake an additional 5 to 8 minutes.

Microwave Heating: Prepare casserole as directed; cover and chill 8 hours. Remove from refrigerator, and let stand at room temperature 30 minutes. Shield corners of casserole with aluminum foil. Cover dish tightly with heavy-duty plastic wrap; fold back a small corner of wrap to allow steam to escape. Microwave at MEDIUM (50% power) 5 minutes; stir and microwave at HIGH 10 minutes, stirring after 5 minutes. Uncover, remove shields, and sprinkle onion rings over casserole; microwave at HIGH, uncovered, 3 to 5 minutes.

To microwave **frozen** casserole, remove from freezer, and shield corners with aluminum foil. Cover tightly with heavy-duty plastic wrap; fold back a small corner of wrap to allow steam to escape. Microwave at MEDIUM (50% power) 30 minutes, stirring after 15 minutes. Microwave at HIGH 10 to 12 minutes, stirring after 5 minutes. Uncover, remove shields, and sprinkle onion rings over casserole; microwave at HIGH 3 to 5 minutes.

Eleanor K. Brandt
Arlington, Texas

TURKEY-NOODLE-POPPYSEED CASSEROLE
(pictured on page 259)

1 (8-ounce) package medium-size egg noodles, uncooked
½ cup chopped onion
¼ cup chopped green pepper
¼ cup butter or margarine, melted
3 tablespoons all-purpose flour
3 cups milk
¼ cup grated Parmesan cheese
1 tablespoon poppyseeds
1 teaspoon salt
⅛ teaspoon red pepper
3 cups diced cooked turkey
1 (4-ounce) jar diced pimiento, drained
2 tablespoons grated Parmesan cheese

Cook noodles according to package directions. Drain well, and set aside.

Sauté onion and green pepper in butter in a Dutch oven until tender; add flour, stirring until smooth. Cook 1 minute, stirring constantly. Gradually add milk; cook over medium heat, stirring constantly, until thickened and bubbly. Stir in noodles, ¼ cup Parmesan cheese, poppyseeds, salt, red pepper, and turkey; add pimiento, and stir gently.

Spoon mixture into a lightly greased 12- x 8- x 2-inch baking dish. Cover and chill 8 hours. To bake, remove from refrigerator, and let stand at room temperature 30 minutes. Bake, covered, at 350° for 45 minutes. Uncover and sprinkle with 2 tablespoons Parmesan cheese. Bake, uncovered, an additional 10 minutes or until thoroughly heated. Yield: 6 to 8 servings.

Note: Unbaked casserole may be frozen. To bake, thaw in refrigerator 24 hours. Remove from refrigerator, and let stand at room temperature 30 minutes. Bake, covered, at 350° for 45 minutes. Uncover, and sprinkle with 2 tablespoons cheese. Bake, uncovered, an additional 10 minutes or until thoroughly heated.

Microwave Heating: Prepare casserole as directed; cover and chill 8 hours. Remove from refrigerator, and let stand at room temperature 30 minutes.

Shield corners of casserole with aluminum foil. Cover dish tightly with heavy-duty plastic wrap; fold back a small corner of wrap to allow steam to escape. Microwave at MEDIUM (50% power) 10 minutes, stirring after 5 minutes. Microwave at HIGH 20 minutes, stirring after 10 minutes. Uncover and remove shield; sprinkle with 2 tablespoons cheese, and microwave at HIGH 3 minutes.

To microwave **frozen** casserole, remove from freezer, and shield corners with aluminum foil. Cover tightly with heavy-duty plastic wrap; fold back a small corner of wrap to allow steam to escape. Microwave at MEDIUM (50% power) 30 minutes, stirring after 15 minutes. Microwave at HIGH 10 to 12 minutes, stirring after 5 minutes. Uncover and remove shield; sprinkle with 2 tablespoons cheese, and microwave at HIGH 3 minutes.

Jeanne S. Hotaling
Augusta, Georgia

CRAB, SHRIMP, AND ARTICHOKE AU GRATIN

4 cups water
1 pound unpeeled medium-size
    fresh shrimp
1 (9-ounce) package frozen
    artichoke hearts
2 (6-ounce) cans lump crabmeat,
    rinsed and drained
2 cups (8 ounces) shredded sharp
    Cheddar cheese, divided
1 clove garlic, minced
2 tablespoons sliced green onions
½ pound fresh mushrooms, sliced
¼ cup plus 2 tablespoons butter
    or margarine, divided
¼ cup all-purpose flour
¾ cup half-and-half
1 tablespoon chopped fresh
    dillweed or 1 teaspoon dried
    whole dillweed
½ teaspoon pepper
⅔ cup dry white wine
2 tablespoons crushed corn flakes
    cereal
1½ teaspoons butter or
    margarine, melted

Bring water to a boil; add shrimp, and cook 3 to 5 minutes. Drain well; rinse with cold water. Peel and devein shrimp; set aside.

Cook artichoke hearts according to package directions; drain. Combine artichokes, shrimp, crabmeat, and 1 cup shredded Cheddar cheese in a large bowl; set mixture aside.

Sauté garlic, green onions, and mushrooms in 2 tablespoons butter until tender; drain. Stir sautéed vegetables into shrimp mixture.

Melt ¼ cup butter in a large heavy skillet over low heat; add flour, stirring until smooth. Cook 1 minute, stirring constantly. Gradually add half-and-half; cook over medium heat, stirring constantly, until thickened and bubbly. Remove from heat; stir in dillweed, pepper, and remaining 1 cup shredded Cheddar cheese, stirring until cheese melts.

Gradually stir in wine. Cook sauce over medium heat, stirring constantly, until thickened. Add shrimp mixture, stirring well. Spoon into a lightly greased shallow 2-quart baking dish; cover and chill 8 hours.

To bake, remove from refrigerator, and let stand at room temperature 30 minutes. Combine crushed corn flakes and 1½ teaspoons butter; sprinkle over casserole. Bake, uncovered, at 350° for 45 minutes. Yield: 6 to 8 servings.

Microwave Heating: Prepare casserole as directed; cover and chill 8 hours. Remove from refrigerator, and let stand at room temperature 30 minutes. Cover tightly with heavy-duty plastic wrap; fold back a corner of wrap to allow steam to escape. Microwave at MEDIUM (50% power) 5 to 6 minutes. Stir and microwave, covered, at HIGH 8 to 10 minutes, stirring after 5 minutes. Uncover, sprinkle with crumb topping, and microwave at HIGH 1 minute.

Carol Barclay
Portland, Texas

SHRIMP-AND-NOODLE CASSEROLE

(pictured on pages 258 and 259)

6 cups water
2 pounds unpeeled large fresh
    shrimp
1 (8-ounce) package medium-size
    egg noodles, uncooked
½ cup sliced green onions
¼ cup chopped green pepper
2 tablespoons butter or
    margarine, melted
2 (10¾-ounce) cans cream of
    mushroom soup, undiluted
1 (8-ounce) carton plain yogurt
½ cup (2 ounces) shredded
    Cheddar cheese
1½ teaspoons chopped fresh
    dillweed or ½ teaspoon dried
    whole dillweed
½ teaspoon white pepper
¼ teaspoon salt
Garnish: fresh dillweed

Bring water to a boil; add shrimp, and cook 3 to 5 minutes. Drain well; rinse shrimp with cold water. Peel and devein shrimp. Chop half of shrimp, leaving the remainder whole. Set shrimp aside.

Cook noodles according to package directions; drain well, and set aside.

Sauté green onions and green pepper in butter in a Dutch oven. Add soup and next 5 ingredients. Gently stir in chopped shrimp and noodles. Spoon mixture into a lightly greased shallow 2½-quart casserole. Arrange whole shrimp on noodles; cover and chill 8 hours.

To bake, remove from refrigerator, and let stand at room temperature 30 minutes. Bake, covered, at 350° for 35 to 40 minutes or until thoroughly heated. Garnish, if desired. Yield: 6 servings.

Ginny Munsterman
Garland, Texas

REUBEN CASSEROLE

1 (32-ounce) jar sauerkraut,
    drained
1¼ cups sour cream
1 medium onion, grated
¼ teaspoon garlic powder
4 (2.5-ounce) packages thinly
    sliced corned beef, diced
2½ cups (10 ounces) shredded
    Swiss cheese
9 slices rye bread
2 tablespoons butter or
    margarine, melted

Combine first 4 ingredients; spoon into a lightly greased 8-inch square baking dish. Arrange corned beef over sauerkraut mixture; sprinkle with cheese. Remove crust from bread to make 2½-inch squares. Halve each square diagonally into triangles; arrange bread over cheese completely covering top of casserole. Brush with melted butter. Cover and refrigerate 8 hours.

To bake, remove from refrigerator, and let stand at room temperature 30 minutes. Bake, uncovered, at 350° for 35 minutes or until bread is lightly browned. Yield: 6 to 8 servings.

Mrs. Grant Adkins
Wichita Falls, Texas

Holiday Dinners

Holiday Entertaining At Its Best

This year our "Holiday Dinners" special section takes a new twist. We're offering a complete party guide planned and tested by our foods staff. You'll find an assortment of recipes, menus, and tips for holiday entertaining.

The section starts with an open house featuring easy yet scrumptious recipes in three basic menus that you can mix and match to suit your needs. We offer suggestions on everything from entertaining a crowd to lighting your home for that special evening.

Of course, great entertaining isn't limited to one gathering of friends. We've loaded this section with additional ideas, such as a Louisiana gumbo menu, a dessert party, and the traditional foods that signal the holidays—such as sweet potatoes, a golden turkey, and mouth-watering dressing.

Feast on the recipes and ideas in this special section. We hope you'll relish each bite just as we did in planning and testing it. It's our special holiday gift to you—a complete plan for the most festive entertaining ever. Cheers!

An Open House They Won't Forget

What better way to start the holidays than with a stunning open house. This one will thrill guests but won't exhaust the host or hostess. It's achievable; to be sure it worked, one of our home economists tested the day-by-day plan for the week prior to the party. It is easier on the hostess to invite a friend to help out and then return the favor, but if that's not an option, this party is definitely one you can do by yourself. Just follow the step-by-step plan beginning on page 244.

The recipes are grouped into three menus, so that you can prepare one menu or serve all three. Put food in three different areas of the house to keep people moving. Most recipes yield enough to serve 25 guests. If you're serving 50, double recipes or see the notes added after the recipe. Check "From Our Kitchen to Yours" on page 276 for information on quantities of biscuits, crackers, wine, and coffee to buy and serve.

Sampler of Holiday Flavors

Boiled shrimp
Cocktail Sauce
Pesto-and-Cream Cheese Round
Crackers
Yule Street Truffles
Coffee

■ To lessen the time you spend in the kitchen, purchase 4 pounds of medium-size unpeeled, cooked shrimp from a seafood market or supermarket. If you're too busy to make Cocktail Sauce, substitute a commercial one.
■ Flavored coffees are in good supply during the holidays. Don't forget to count cups and saucers, and add cream and sugar cubes to the grocery list. In our Test Kitchens, we've decorated sugar cubes with tiny holly leaves and berries that are made from cake decorating icing.

Holiday Dinners

COCKTAIL SAUCE

2 cups catsup
½ cup finely chopped celery
½ cup chopped fresh parsley
¼ cup Worcestershire sauce
¼ cup lemon juice
¼ cup prepared horseradish
¼ teaspoon sugar
2 drops of hot sauce
Garnishes: lemon rind,
    lemon slices, fresh parsley
    sprigs

Combine first 8 ingredients in a medium bowl; cover and chill. Garnish, if desired. Serve with shrimp. Yield: 3 cups, enough for 4 pounds cooked medium shrimp, peeled.
Sharon Leftwich
Glade Valley, North Carolina

PESTO-AND-CREAM CHEESE ROUND

2 (8-ounce) packages cream
    cheese, softened
1 cup chopped fresh parsley
¾ cup grated Parmesan cheese
¼ cup chopped pine nuts
2 cloves garlic, crushed
1 tablespoon dried whole basil
¼ teaspoon salt
⅛ teaspoon pepper
⅓ cup olive oil
2 tablespoons butter or
    margarine, melted
2 tablespoons boiling water
Garnish: pimiento strips

Shape cream cheese into a 5½-inch circle on a serving dish; set aside. Combine parsley and next 9 ingredients; stir well. Spoon onto cream cheese round; garnish, if desired. Cover and chill at least 2 hours. Serve with crackers or toasted pita

triangles. Yield: 3 cups, enough for 25 appetizer servings.

Note: For 50 servings, make two cheese rounds; keep one refrigerated until time to replenish the table.
Patricia Cairns
Elmore, Alabama

YULE STREET TRUFFLES

1 (6-ounce) package semisweet
    chocolate morsels
2 tablespoons butter or margarine
1 tablespoon brandy
1⅓ cups almonds, toasted,
    chopped, and divided
¼ cup sifted powdered sugar
½ cup flaked coconut
½ cup whole pitted dates,
    chopped
¼ cup red candied cherries,
    chopped

Combine chocolate morsels and butter in a microwave-safe, 1-quart casserole. Microwave, uncovered, at HIGH 1 to 2 minutes or until melted. Add brandy, stirring well. Add ½ cup almonds and remaining ingredients, stirring well. Shape mixture into ¾-inch balls, and roll in remaining almonds. Store truffles in refrigerator. Yield: 3 dozen.

Note: For 50 servings, make two batches rather than double the recipe.
Doris Ruth Craigo
Austin, Texas

Fireside Appetizers

Marinated Vegetables Italian
Horseradish Spread
Burgundy Eye-of-Round
Commercial biscuits
Wine

■ A Chardonnay or blush wine is a good choice to serve with varying flavors and would complement the menus on pages 241 and 243, too. Wine buffs might enjoy serving a different wine at every table. Let guests pour their own wine from bottles chilled in a large punch bowl.
■ Eye-of-round is a less-expensive meat selection than tenderloin. Ask your butcher to thinly slice the roast after you have cooked it.

MARINATED VEGETABLES ITALIAN

½ cauliflower, broken into
    flowerets
4 carrots, sliced
2 stalks celery, cut into 2-inch
    pieces
1 green pepper, cut into ¾-inch
    square pieces
½ pound medium-size fresh
    mushrooms
1 (3-ounce) jar pimiento-stuffed
    olives, drained
1 cup pitted ripe olives
¾ cup white wine vinegar
½ cup olive oil
¼ cup water
2 tablespoons sugar
1 teaspoon salt
½ teaspoon dried whole oregano

Place first 7 ingredients in a 13- x 9- x 2-inch dish; set aside.

Combine vinegar and remaining ingredients in a small saucepan; cook over medium heat, stirring constantly, until mixture boils. Remove from heat, and pour over vegetables. Toss gently to coat. Cover tightly, and chill at least 8 hours, stirring vegetables several times.

Drain vegetables, and serve in a glass dish or on a lettuce-lined platter with wooden picks. Yield: 15 to 17 appetizer servings.

Note: To make ahead, marinate all vegetables except mushrooms. Add mushrooms 2 hours before serving. **For 50 servings,** triple the recipe.

Betty Beske
Arlington, Virginia

HORSERADISH SPREAD

1 envelope unflavored gelatin
¼ cup cold water
1 (3-ounce) package
    lemon-flavored gelatin
½ cup boiling water
1 (8-ounce) carton sour cream
1 (5-ounce) jar prepared
    horseradish
¾ cup mayonnaise
Purple kale or lettuce

Sprinkle unflavored gelatin over ¼ cup cold water; let stand 1 minute.

Dissolve lemon-flavored gelatin in ½ cup boiling water; add unflavored gelatin mixture, stirring until dissolved. Add sour cream, horseradish, and mayonnaise, stirring until blended. Pour mixture into a lightly oiled 4-cup mold; cover and chill until firm. Unmold onto purple kale. Serve spread with beef or ham biscuits. Yield: 25 appetizer servings.

Jane Maloy
Wilmington, North Carolina

BURGUNDY EYE-OF-ROUND

1 tablespoon all-purpose flour
1 oven cooking bag
1 (3½- to 4-pound) eye-of-round
    roast, trimmed
¼ teaspoon seasoned salt
⅛ teaspoon garlic powder
⅛ teaspoon freshly ground pepper
¾ cup Burgundy wine

Shake flour into oven cooking bag; leave flour in bag to prevent bursting. Set aside.

Sprinkle roast with seasoned salt, garlic powder, and pepper. Place roast in oven cooking bag, and pour Burgundy over roast. Tie bag securely. Place bag in a shallow dish, and refrigerate overnight.

Cut six ½-inch slits in top of bag. Place on a roasting pan, and insert meat thermometer into thickest part of roast. Bake at 325° for 50 to 60 minutes or until thermometer registers 140°. Cool and slice. Serve with biscuits. Yield: about 25 appetizer servings.

Mary F. Clark
Burkburnett, Texas

A Spread for The Dining Room

Commercial baked ham
Commercial wheat rolls
and spicy mustard
Buttery Brown Sugar Dip
With Fruit
Marinated Cheese and crackers
Strawberry Punch (page 273)

■ Shorten the time spent in the kitchen by purchasing a commercially baked and sliced ham. A whole ham (12 to 16 pounds) yields 36 to 48 buffet servings. Half of a ham (6 to 10 pounds) yields 10 to 30 buffet servings.

■ A variety of commercial sweet-and-spicy mustards are available to complement the flavor of ham.

BUTTERY BROWN SUGAR DIP WITH FRUIT

1¾ cups firmly packed brown
    sugar
1 cup butter
1 cup whipping cream
1 cup pecans, toasted
3 pounds pears, cored and sliced
3 pounds apples, cored and sliced

Combine first 4 ingredients in a heavy saucepan; cook over medium heat until butter melts, stirring occasionally. Reduce heat, and simmer 12 to 15 minutes, stirring occasionally. Serve with pear and apple slices. Yield: 25 appetizer servings.

Wanda Sanders
Tuscaloosa, Alabama

Tip: *Silver serving pieces lend elegance to the party. Serving pieces such as wooden trays, pewter, contemporary glass, or lacquer selections set a more casual mood. Adapt your serving pieces to your own style of entertaining. Whatever you choose, be sure the pieces are complementary, such as a silver punch bowl and crystal tray.*

MARINATED CHEESE

1 (0.7-ounce) envelope Italian
  salad dressing mix
½ cup vegetable oil
¼ cup white vinegar
2 tablespoons water
2 tablespoons minced green
  onions
1½ teaspoons sugar
1 (8-ounce) package Monterey
  Jack cheese
1 (8-ounce) package sharp
  Cheddar cheese
1 (8-ounce) package cream cheese
1 (4-ounce) jar diced pimiento,
  drained
Garnish: fresh parsley sprigs

Combine first 6 ingredients in a small
jar; cover tightly, and shake vigorously to blend. Set aside.

Cut Monterey Jack cheese crosswise into ¼-inch strips. Cut each
strip in half to form 2 squares. Set
aside. Repeat cutting procedure with
Cheddar cheese and cream cheese.

Assemble cheese slices like domi-
noes in two rows in a 2-quart dish,
alternating Monterey Jack cheese,
cream cheese, and Cheddar cheese
side by side. Pour marinade over
cheese. Cover and refrigerate overnight. Drain and arrange cheese on a
platter in rows. Top each row with
diced pimiento. Garnish, if desired.
Serve with crackers. Yield: 25 appetizer servings.

Open House
Planning Guide

Planning goes hand in hand with a
successful party. Although this
list is tailored to the open house
beginning on page 241, you can
adapt it to other gatherings—just
make any necessary adjustments
on the steps for food preparation.

Many of the recipes in the
open house menus from the pre-
vious pages can be made ahead.

Also by doing a little party planning and food preparation every
day, the job becomes less overwhelming, and you may even
have fun checking items off your
list as you complete them. Adjust
whatever plans you have to fit
your schedule and your needs.
You may come up with another
calendar that works just as well.

Party Planning Checklist

Six Weeks Before the Party:
If invitations are going to be
printed, get estimates from print-
ers. Choose a printer, and submit
information to be typeset. Determine when you'll need to proofread the invitations, select the
paper, and make any other deci-
sions concerning the invitations.

**Four Weeks Before
The Party:**
■ Assemble guest list with cor-
rect addresses. Buy postage

stamps. Pick up printed invitations, or photocopy invitations, if
they are not printed.
■ Ask your spouse or a friend to
help you with arrangements and
with food preparation.
■ Arrange for a sitter for young
children, if needed. See the suggestions for a children's party,
which begins on page 269, if children are on the guest list.
■ Arrange for "helpers" to pick
up dirty glasses and dishes and
wash them during the party. A

local youth organization might be a good source of energetic volunteers who will work for a donation to their group.

Three Weeks Before The Party:

■ Address and mail all invitations. Keep an RSVP list close by the telephone.

■ Plan table coverings (if desired). Take cloths to cleaners if needed.

■ Plan serving pieces for each recipe you plan to serve. Do you need to borrow or rent silver or a punch bowl?

■ Check on rentals—tables, glassware, plates, coffeepots, and other items. Check the Yellow Pages for a listing of rental stores, and visit them to see what is available.

■ Order wine.

Two Weeks Before the Party:

■ Polish silver.

■ Order centerpieces from a florist, or plan what materials you will need if you decide to arrange the centerpieces yourself. See page 280 for an easy step-by-step door decoration.

■ Make a grocery list. Don't forget garnishes, napkins, wooden picks, oven cooking bags, and other supplies. Make a note of any cookware needed to make a recipe. Be sure to think through the items on every serving table. Include a snack or take-out food for your family on the busy day of the party.

■ Order bread, ham, and shrimp from local stores or deli.

■ Plan refrigerator space. Do you need to ask a neighbor if you may borrow space in her refrigerator the day before the party? Do you have a chest for ice?

Four Days Before the Party:

■ Make Yule Street Truffles and Cocktail Sauce. (Preparation time: about one hour.)

Three Days Before the Party:

■ Make Pesto-and-Cream Cheese Round, but don't put pesto on cheese until the day of the party; store separately in refrigerator. Cut up pimiento for garnish. Shortcuts: soften cream cheese in the microwave oven; chop fresh parsley in a food processor. (Preparation time: about one hour.)

■ Let strawberries thaw overnight in the refrigerator to use in Strawberry Punch.

■ Put up greenery and any additional decorations.

Two Days Before the Party:

■ Cut up vegetables (except mushrooms) for Marinated Vegetables Italian. Place each type of vegetable in a separate zip-top heavy-duty plastic bag that you have filled with cold water, and chill in refrigerator.

■ Marinate Burgundy Eye-of-Round; store in refrigerator.

■ Make Strawberry Punch, but don't add the carbonated beverage to the punch until right before guests arrive. (Preparation time for the vegetables, meat, and punch: about one hour.)

One Day Before the Party:

■ Cook Burgundy Eye-of-Round. Make Horseradish Spread, Buttery Brown Sugar Dip, and Marinated Cheese. Mix up the marinade and combine all of the vegetables except mushrooms for Marinated Vegetables Italian. Prepare all garnishes and refrigerate. Tip: kale and parsley may be washed, wrapped in damp paper towels, and stored in plastic bags in the refrigerator. (Total preparation time: about two and a half hours.)

■ Pick up ham, bread, and all rental items.

■ Set up serving tables, and cover with cloths. Set out all serving pieces, napkins, cups, glasses, plates, and other necessary party tableware.

■ Refrigerate wine.

Day of the Party:

■ Have meat sliced at the butcher shop or supermarket. Pick up shrimp and ice.

■ Peel shrimp; refrigerate in airtight container.

■ Slice rolls and biscuits for ham and beef sandwiches; store in an airtight container.

■ Cut up the apples and pears to use in Buttery Brown Sugar Dip With Fruit; soak the fruit in pineapple juice to prevent discoloration. (Preparation for fruit, shrimp, and rolls: about two hours.)

■ Place pesto on cheese; garnish with pimiento.

■ Call the florist to have the floral arrangements delivered during the day.

A Few Hours Before the Party:

■ Give instructions to helpers.

■ Stir mushrooms into Marinated Vegetables Italian. Reheat Buttery Brown Sugar Dip. Assemble food on serving trays, making sure garnishes are in place, 30 minutes before guests arrive.

■ Make coffee. Add carbonated beverage to Strawberry Punch, and pour into punch bowl just before guests arrive.

■ Change clothes, welcome guests, and have fun!

It's Easy
To Host A Buffet

Buffet entertaining, where guests serve themselves from a sideboard or table, has increased in popularity for good reason. A buffet can offer the graciousness of a formally served meal without a host, hostess, or hired help having to serve it! Party planners are free to mingle with guests and replenish food as needed.

This style of serving a meal also offers a way to invite more guests than can be seated at the dining table. Equally effective for informal entertaining, a buffet can carry out a theme, whether it is served indoors or out. While this type of meal service usually looks effortless at the party, it requires careful planning ahead of time, and there are lots of options to consider.

Plan a Workable Menu

Make sure all food is simple to serve and eat. If guests will be seated at a table while eating, food that requires a knife and fork will work fine. Guests who'll be seated in a chair with a plate of food on their lap will appreciate food they can eat with only a fork. If there is not a place to seat everyone, however, plan a menu of finger food.

Because guests will serve themselves, make sure the food is easy to handle. Choose dishes that are easy to serve in average-size portions. They should require a single serving spoon or fork and should not need to be cut with a knife.

One main dish is sufficient for a buffet menu, although several may be served. If more than one is offered, be sure to have plenty on hand because guests will take a little of each. In addition, they are more likely to go back for seconds when food is

presented buffet-style, so don't be caught with an empty dish too soon.

When the guest list is large and some of the food is served hot, it's a good idea to make two or three pans of each recipe rather than one very large pan; this way, a fresh, hot one can be brought out after the first one is emptied. To entertain without using chafing dishes or replacing empty dishes with hot ones, consider a menu that's served cold—it can be equally inviting and easier to serve.

Setting Up the Buffet

Sideboards and dining room tables tend to be popular locations for setting up buffets, although tables, counters, and almost any large piece of furniture of similar height in a kitchen, den, or on a terrace will work well for buffet service. Be sure to pick an area with close proximity to the kitchen.

Arrange plates, food, and utensils on the buffet in logical order for guests to serve themselves without backtracking. Plates go at the beginning, then the entrée, vegetables, salad, and bread. Many sources suggest placing napkins and utensils beside the plates, but it makes more sense to place these items at the end of the line so that guests won't have to fumble with them as they serve themselves. It is also important to set salad dressings, sauces, and other condiments beside the food they complement.

Place the dessert at the end of the buffet, or better yet, on a separate cart for guests to serve themselves after they complete the main meal. Offer beverages from a separate area as well, or serve them from a tray after guests are seated.

When there's a large crowd and the food is arranged on a freestanding table, the line will flow twice as fast with twin serving lines set up on either side of the table.

Where Will Guests Go?

If seating area is limited, just encourage guests to scatter throughout the main part of the house after they serve themselves. It's nice to provide trays for those who find a seat on a sofa or chair.

There might be enough room for everyone to sit at a table if guests are directed to each one available—in the dining room, kitchen, den, and on the terrace. If there is enough table space for everyone, either let guests determine their own seating arrangement or set out place cards beforehand. If a large crowd requires the use of multiple china patterns, use place cards to discreetly make sure that each table ends up with the same pattern of dishes. To do this, set the tables with place cards and plates before guests arrive rather than stacking plates on the buffet table. Ask guests to locate their seats before serving themselves. Then each guest will pick up the plate, go through the buffet line, and return to the assigned seat.

Holiday Dinners

Set The Mood
For A Party

Entertaining involves more than simply preparing a meal for guests. Rivaling the food in importance is the setting where everyone will gather, and the mood of the party.

The setting refers to how the house is decorated and prepared for company and has nothing to do with the size of the house or the quality of furnishings. Special effects, such as an interesting table setting or the aroma of spices simmering on the cooktop, comfort and charm visitors.

The mood of the party, on the other hand, involves the fun, laughter, and spontaneity of the group. The mood is set, in part, as soon as guests walk through the door and receive their first greeting. If made to feel at home, guests will be warm and responsive.

Party planners can't totally control the setting or mood of a party any more than they can make sure the tenderloin is the right temperature at precisely 8 p.m., but they can make advance preparations that help give the party the character they desire. Here are some ideas.

Welcome and Introductions

As guests arrive, greet them with a pretty bow or bright balloons on the mailbox or streetlight. Such a special welcome signals to all that "this is the place" and gets guests in the spirit as soon as they spot it.

If the party is held after dark, turn on outdoor lights to help guests see their way to the front door. If the walk from the parking area is dark, set up luminaries along the way.

Plan to be dressed and ready to greet guests 30 minutes early. This helps ensure a relaxed welcome. If guests are greeted with a frenzied look, the mood might be contagious.

The first few moments of a party can be awkward, so look guests in the eye when greeting them, and make an extra effort to welcome and relax everyone. Provide a place for coats and purses, either designating an area and letting guests handle it themselves or assigning the task to a person who wants to help.

If the crowd is large and not already acquainted, set name tags and pens in a handy spot, and guide guests there first. Have a small wastebasket handy to eliminate clutter if the name tags have peel-off backings.

When making introductions, include something about each person's profession, background, or hobbies to stimulate conversation.

Around the House

Having a party provides a great excuse to put things in order around the house and to decorate with flair. Get the date on the calendar early so that there's time to paint the flaking windowsills. When everything sparkles, flank the fireplace with pretty poinsettias or fresh cut pine, and hang mistletoe above a doorway. Special touches scattered throughout the house will impress guests and make them appreciative of the extra time spent on details.

Don't overlook sprucing up one room folks inevitably visit—the bathroom. Set out fresh fingertip towels, and spray a little cologne in the air. Tuck a few flowers leftover from the centerpiece in a little vase to dress the vanity. Folks will probably peek into adjacent rooms on the way to the bathroom, so make them look inviting. Turn on bedside lamps, and place a small arrangement of flowers on the bedside table, as well.

When preparing for the party, don't forget about the room temperature. If more than six or eight guests will attend, set the thermostat at a lower-than-normal setting.

If planning to host more than one event during the holidays, line them up during the same week if your schedule for food preparation makes that possible. This way fresh greenery and flower arrangements can serve double duty, and food preparation and housecleaning can also be completed at the same time.

Scents of the Season

Look for other ways to give the house a wonderful aroma if the Christmas tree or greenery doesn't do the job. Decorative candles are scented like spices, pine, or flowers. Used wisely, they add a nice touch; however, don't use too many in one small area because the aroma may overpower the room.

Potpourri is available in similar choices of aroma. Purchase containers especially made to hold this decorative blend, or place it in pretty bowls or tureens that are already part of the decor. Scatter the potpourri throughout the house for continuity of aroma.

Large cinnamon sticks are available to decorate and scent the house. Tie them together with a red bow, and add a little greenery to make a simple but attractive arrangement. With this decoration you will also have a nice adornment for the kitchen door.

For a more potent aroma of spices, toss broken cinnamon sticks, whole cloves, crushed nutmeg, and strips of citrus rind into a pot of cider, and let them simmer over low heat during a party. With this technique, the aroma drifts throughout the entire house.

A Touch of Greenery

Don't worry if the food budget leaves little room for a florist. It's not necessary to hire a professional or even to have flowers, but you can supplement garden greenery with a few store-bought blooms. Pretty greenery and red berries from the garden offer even a novice enough decorating options to span from the mantel to the tabletop. Magnolia leaves, pine sprigs and pine cones, boxwood, ivy, and holly leaves and berries are traditionally used for holiday decorating, but many other evergreens are available, too.

If there are only one or two types of greenery in the garden, and a friend or neighbor has a couple of other types, consider setting up a trade. This will add interest and variety to your holiday arrangements.

Set the Mood With Lighting

Scatter lamps in nooks and crannies to create a dramatic effect. Even if the light of a decorative lamp set on a secretary is not needed, turn it on anyway to spotlight family photos or decorations beside it.

Candles also provide lighting as well as' decoration when teamed with imaginative holders. For an inexpensive and colorful holder, carve a little hole in an apple, and insert a candle, wedging in a little fresh greenery at the same time. The moisture from the apple will make long-lasting boxwood stay fresh and pretty for up to five days. Just be sure to replace the burned candles with new ones before they burn close enough to the greenery to become a fire hazard.

Don't underestimate the dramatic effect a dimmer switch can have on

overhead lights in a living room or dining room. Lowering the lighting gradually over the evening creates a warm and cozy feeling. For these and other ideas on special lighting for the holidays, see "Accent With Light" on page 282.

Put a Song in the Air

Music can set a playful mood for a party if the right type is played at the proper volume. Soft music tends to be relaxing and offers a nice background for conversation, while louder music can create a tense, rushed feeling. Pick the music based on the guests who'll enjoy it, sorting the selections ahead and arranging them by the stereo.

Consider having live music for large parties. A single strolling musician or a string quartet can add a special quality to a party.

Setting the Table

Round tables are good for entertaining because everyone can more easily participate in a conversation. Tables with leaves that expand or reduce the table size to match the guest list aid conversation, too. Chatting is encouraged when diners are shoulder to shoulder rather than when there's a lot of extra room between them.

Arrange a centerpiece to spark conversation, as well. Either make it low enough that guests can see each other over it, or make a taller arrangement that everyone can see through with the aid of decorations like candelabras.

Pay special attention to the table setting for holiday gatherings. Expensive red and green place mats that aren't used any other time of the year aren't necessary. Rely on simple features—such as holly leaves tucked between the napkin ring and napkin—to add a nice touch.

Set the table a day early so that there will be enough time to carefully

and thoughtfully arrange each appointment. Some party givers set the table several days in advance when the table is not routinely used. That way, the family can enjoy the pretty setting in anticipation of the event.

Always tell guests exactly where to sit, whether orally as they enter the dining room or with place cards at each seat. Inviting folks to sit wherever they like usually causes more confusion and apprehension than assigning seats.

Always wait until the last person has finished eating before removing dinner plates; then remove them yourself or with the help of one appointed helper. There's too much confusion when everyone gets up and discards his own plate. Don't try to clean the dishes between courses, and never clean the kitchen until guests have gone.

Plan a Party Favor

Send guests home with a favor to help them remember the evening. A decorative jar of Champagne Jelly or a bag of Party Nibbles will be a thoughtful memento that they can enjoy in their own homes. Either set the favors out above each dinner plate, or arrange them in a basket on a table near the door for guests to pick up as they leave your home.

CHAMPAGNE JELLY

3 cups sugar
2 cups pink champagne
1 (3-ounce) package liquid pectin

Combine sugar and champagne in a large Dutch oven. Cook over medium heat, stirring until sugar dissolves (do not boil). Remove from heat; stir in liquid pectin. Skim off foam with a metal spoon.

Quickly pour hot jelly into hot sterilized jars, leaving ¼ inch of headspace; wipe jar rims. Cover at once with metal lids, and screw on bands. Process in boiling-water bath 5 minutes. Let stand 8 hours for jelly to set up. Yield: 5 half pints.

PARTY NIBBLES

1 (6-ounce) package seasoned croutons
1 (6-ounce) package fish-shaped crackers
1 (6.5-ounce) package pretzel twists
1 (12-ounce) can mixed nuts
¾ cup butter or margarine, melted
1 teaspoon hickory-flavored salt
¼ teaspoon garlic powder

Combine first 4 ingredients in a large roasting pan; stir well.

Combine last 3 ingredients; stir well. Drizzle over nut mixture; stir well. Bake at 250° for 1 hour, stirring every 15 minutes. Yield: about 3 quarts.
Tracie Vann
Birmingham, Alabama

Dishes That Make Holiday Tradition

Turkey, dressing, sweet potatoes, cranberry sauce, ambrosia, pecan pie, fruitcake—the foods we eat during the holiday season are steeped in tradition. Most families have favorite dishes they serve for holiday dinners, yet there's always room for additions. Why not add one or two new recipes to your menu this year?

In some parts of the South, Smoked Turkey rivals baked turkey as a holiday entrée. Stuff the cavity with apple, celery, carrots, and onion for flavor and moisture. Whether it's smoked with mesquite, hickory, or another fragrant wood, the result will be mouth-watering.

Amaretto-Hot Fruit Compote blends a variety of canned fruits, bananas, crumbled macaroons, and amaretto for a side dish that's rich as well as flavorful. Once you've served it during the holidays, it's sure to be requested year after year.

Sweet potatoes are a must on most Southern holiday menus, and Glazed Sweet Potato Casserole is as attractive as it is delicious. This dish can be made the day before it's to be served, so you'll have more time to spend with guests.

SMOKED TURKEY

1 (10- to 15-pound) turkey
1 clove garlic, cut
½ lemon
¼ teaspoon salt
¼ teaspoon pepper
1 cooking apple, cored and quartered
2 stalks celery, cut into thirds
2 carrots, cut into thirds
1 small onion, quartered
2 tablespoons butter or margarine, melted

Remove giblets and neck from turkey; reserve for other uses, if desired. Rinse turkey with cold water; pat dry. Rub cavity with garlic and lemon; sprinkle with salt and pepper. Place apple, celery, carrot, and onion in cavity of turkey; close cavity with skewers. Tie ends of legs to tail with cord; lift wingtips up and over back so that they are tucked under bird. Baste turkey with butter.

Prepare charcoal fire in smoker, and let burn 15 to 20 minutes. Soak mesquite chunks in water at least 15 minutes. Place mesquite chunks on coals. Place water pan in smoker, and fill with water.

Place turkey on food rack. Cover with smoker lid; cook turkey 8 to 12 hours or until meat thermometer reaches 180° to 185° when inserted in breast or meaty part of thigh. (Make sure thermometer does not touch bone.) Refill the water pan, and add charcoal as needed.

Remove turkey from food rack; cover and refrigerate. To serve, remove vegetables, and discard; thinly slice turkey. Yield: 14 to 18 servings.
Jan Sutton
Gadsden, Alabama

SCALLOPED OYSTERS

4½ cups crushed saltine crackers
½ cup butter or margarine, melted
2 (12-ounce) containers fresh Standard oysters, undrained
⅛ teaspoon salt
⅛ teaspoon pepper
1 tablespoon chopped fresh parsley
1¼ cups half-and-half
Paprika

Brown cracker crumbs in butter, and set aside.

Drain oysters, reserving ½ cup liquid. Place half of crumbs in a lightly greased 12- x 8- x 2-inch baking dish; add oysters, salt, pepper, and parsley. Cover with remaining cracker crumbs.

Combine half-and-half and reserved oyster liquid; pour over cracker crumbs. Sprinkle with paprika. Bake at 350° for 35 to 40 minutes. Yield: 8 to 10 servings.
Jane Feagin
Louisville, Kentucky

HOLIDAY HAM SLICE WITH CINNAMON APPLE RINGS

1 (1-inch-thick) fully cooked ham
  slice (about 2 pounds)
¼ teaspoon hot sauce
Cinnamon Apple Rings

Slash fat along edges of ham to pre-vent curling. Spread hot sauce over surface of ham, and place in a lightly greased 13- x 9- x 2-inch baking dish. Bake at 325° for 25 minutes or until meat thermometer registers 140°. Transfer to a serving platter; serve with Cinnamon Apple Rings. Yield: 6 to 8 servings.

Cinnamon Apple Rings

24 whole cloves
3 medium cooking apples,
  unpeeled, cored, and cut into
  ½-inch rings
2 cups water
1 cup red cinnamon candies
½ cup sugar

Stick cloves into apple rings. Com-bine water and candies in a large skil-let; bring to a boil, stirring until candies dissolve. Add apple rings; re-duce heat, and simmer 5 minutes or just until apple rings are tender, turning several times.

Remove apple rings from skillet. Add sugar to skillet, and bring to a boil; boil 3 minutes. Pour syrup over apple rings, turning to glaze both sides. Cool slightly. Yield: 8 servings. *Karen Ann Jenkins*
Scott, Louisiana

SOUTHERN RICE

Vegetable cooking spray
1 cup sliced celery
¾ cup sliced green onions
¾ cup chopped green pepper
2¾ cups chicken broth
1 teaspoon poultry seasoning
½ teaspoon salt
⅛ teaspoon pepper
1½ cups long-grain rice,
  uncooked
¼ cup chopped pecans, toasted

Coat a large nonstick skillet with cooking spray; place over medium-high heat until hot. Add celery, green onions, and green pepper; sauté until crisp-tender. Stir in broth and next 3 ingredients; bring to a boil.

Spoon rice into a shallow 2-quart baking dish; add hot broth mixture. Cover and bake at 350° for 30 min-utes or until rice is tender and liquid is absorbed. Sprinkle with pecans. Yield: 6 to 8 servings. *Marion Hall*
Knoxville, Tennessee

GLAZED SWEET POTATO CASSEROLE

6 medium-size sweet potatoes
  (about 3½ pounds)
¼ cup firmly packed brown sugar
¼ cup honey
1 tablespoon cornstarch
½ teaspoon ground cinnamon
¼ teaspoon ground nutmeg
2 teaspoons grated orange rind
2 tablespoons butter or margarine
½ cup pineapple juice
¼ cup chopped walnuts

Cook sweet potatoes in boiling water to cover 20 to 25 minutes or until fork-tender. Let cool to touch; peel and cut into ½-inch slices. Arrange slices in a lightly greased 12- x 8- x 2-inch baking dish; set aside.

Combine brown sugar and next 7 ingredients in a saucepan. Cook over medium heat, stirring constantly, until mixture begins to boil; boil 1 minute, stirring constantly, until mix-ture is thickened and bubbly. Pour over sweet potatoes; sprinkle with chopped walnuts. Cover and refriger-ate 8 hours.

Remove dish from refrigerator; let stand 30 minutes. Uncover and bake at 350° for 30 minutes or until thor-oughly heated. Yield: 8 servings.

AMARETTO-HOT FRUIT COMPOTE

1 (16-ounce) can peach halves
1 (16-ounce) can pear halves
1 (15¼-ounce) can pineapple
  chunks
1 (17-ounce) can apricot halves
1 (16½-ounce) can pitted dark
  sweet cherries
2 bananas, sliced
1 teaspoon lemon juice
12 soft coconut macaroons,
  crumbled
1 (2¼-ounce) package sliced
  almonds, toasted and divided
¼ cup butter or margarine
⅓ cup amaretto or other
  almond-flavored liqueur

Drain fruits, reserving syrup for other uses. Combine canned fruits in a large bowl; set aside. Combine ba-nanas and lemon juice, and toss gently. Add to fruit mixture.

Layer half each of fruit mixture and macaroon crumbs in a 2½-quart baking dish; sprinkle with 3 table-spoons sliced almonds, and dot with 2 tablespoons butter. Repeat proce-dure. Pour amaretto evenly over fruit mixture.

Bake at 350° for 30 minutes; sprinkle with remaining almonds. Stir before serving. Yield: 12 to 14 servings.
Linda Kay Downing
Columbus, Mississippi

FREEZER DINNER ROLLS

5½ to 6 cups all-purpose flour, divided
½ cup sugar
1 teaspoon salt
2 packages dry yeast
1¼ cups water
½ cup milk
⅓ cup butter or margarine
2 eggs

Combine 2 cups flour, sugar, salt, and yeast in a large mixing bowl; stir mixture, and set aside.

Combine water, milk, and butter in a saucepan; heat until butter melts. Cool to 120° to 130°. Stir into flour mixture, and beat at medium speed of an electric mixer 2 minutes. Add ½ cup flour and eggs; beat at high speed 2 minutes. Gradually stir in enough remaining flour to make a soft dough.

Place dough in a well-greased bowl, turning to grease top. Cover and let rise in a warm place (85°), free from drafts, 30 minutes or until doubled in bulk.

Punch dough down; turn out onto a lightly floured surface, and knead 4 or 5 times. Lightly grease muffin pans. Shape dough into 1-inch balls; place 3 balls in each muffin cup. Cover and let rise in a warm place, free from drafts, 30 minutes or until doubled in bulk. Bake at 350° for 15 minutes or until golden brown. Yield: 3 dozen.

To freeze: Shape dough into 1-inch balls, and place on a wax paper-lined baking sheet. Freeze. Place frozen dough balls in a plastic bag, and freeze up to 1 month.

To bake: Lightly grease muffin pans. Remove desired amount of dough from freezer, and place 3 balls in each muffin cup. Cover and let rise in a warm place, free from drafts, 1 hour or until doubled in bulk. Bake at 350° for 15 minutes or until golden brown.
Missy Wilson
Birmingham, Alabama

Taste
A Sentimental
Journey

When it comes to holidays, we all know that how the food tastes isn't as important as who prepared it or how long it has been a tradition. We want the same things year after year so that we can reminisce. We bait youngsters with a bite of Aunt Martha's pie, waiting for them to ask, "Now, what's this called?" and "So who was she?" Then they're hooked into a line of "remember when" stories they'll find themselves telling years from now.

We hope you'll enjoy this collection of holiday recipes from our readers. Each came to us with a note explaining its place in the family.

■ The dish that stands out in Dana Adkins Campbell's memory is Mom's Creamy Holiday Fruit Salad. She fondly recalls, "There were three givens on Thanksgiving Day for me as a child—watching the Macy's parade in my pajamas, going to church, and most important, nabbing the seat at the dining room table within closest reach of the colorful salad. Of course, I had to be quicker than my father—from whom I inherited my insatiable sweet tooth—but if I wasn't fast enough, it was all right. I knew I had another chance coming on Christmas Day, and I'd be ready."

CREAMY HOLIDAY
FRUIT SALAD

1 (20-ounce) can pineapple tidbits, undrained
3 egg yolks
2 tablespoons sugar
⅛ teaspoon salt
2 tablespoons white vinegar
1 tablespoon butter or margarine, melted
1 (16½-ounce) can pitted light sweet cherries, drained
1 cup red maraschino cherries, drained
1 cup green maraschino cherries, drained
2 cups miniature marshmallows
1 cup whipping cream, whipped

Drain pineapple, reserving 2 tablespoons juice. Set aside.

Combine egg yolks, sugar, and salt in a heavy saucepan. Gradually add reserved pineapple juice, vinegar, and butter. Cook over medium heat until thickened, stirring constantly. Remove from heat; cool.

Combine pineapple, cherries, and miniature marshmallows in a bowl.

Fold egg mixture into whipped cream; pour over fruit, stirring gently to coat. Cover and chill 8 hours. Yield: 10 to 12 servings.
Mary Lou Adkins
Sulphur, Louisiana

■ Diane Haft loves to serve a rich, three-layer chocolate cake and watch raised eyebrows when she announces that this is her family's favorite, One-Foot-in-the-Fire Fudge Cake. Now there's a tale just waiting to be told. The dessert is a long-standing Christmas tradition but had no official name until recently. A relative tasting it for the first time was instantly enamored and exclaimed, "Well, I don't care what it's called; it's good enough to eat with one foot in the fire!" We thought so, too.

ONE-FOOT-IN-THE-FIRE FUDGE CAKE

⅓ cup water
2 (1-ounce) squares unsweetened chocolate
⅔ cup shortening
1¾ cups sugar
2 eggs
2½ cups all-purpose flour
1¾ teaspoons baking soda
½ teaspoon salt
1 cup buttermilk
1 teaspoon vanilla extract
Fluffy White Filling
Chocolate Frosting

Combine water and chocolate in a small heavy saucepan. Cook over low heat, stirring constantly, until chocolate melts. Remove from heat; cool.

Cream shortening in a large bowl; gradually add sugar, beating well at medium speed of an electric mixer. Add eggs, one at a time, beating well after each addition.

Combine flour, soda, and salt; add to creamed mixture alternately with buttermilk, beginning and ending with flour mixture. Add cooled chocolate and vanilla; mix just until blended.

Pour batter into 3 greased and floured 9-inch round cakepans. Bake at 350° for 17 to 19 minutes or until a wooden pick inserted in center comes out clean. Cool in pans 10 minutes; remove from pans, and cool completely on wire racks.

Spread Fluffy White Filling between layers. Spread Chocolate Frosting on top and sides of cake. Yield: one 3-layer cake.

Fluffy White Filling

¼ cup all-purpose flour
1 cup milk
½ cup butter or margarine, softened
½ cup shortening
1 cup sugar
¼ teaspoon salt
1 tablespoon vanilla extract

Place flour in a small saucepan; gradually stir in milk. Cook over low heat, stirring constantly, until thickened. Remove from heat; cool, stirring occasionally.

Cream butter and shortening; gradually add sugar, beating until light and fluffy. Add salt, vanilla, and flour mixture; beat until smooth. Yield: about 4 cups.

Chocolate Frosting

2 cups sugar
2 (1-ounce) squares unsweetened chocolate
½ cup milk
½ cup butter or margarine
½ teaspoon vanilla extract

Combine first 4 ingredients in a heavy saucepan; cook over low heat until chocolate and butter melt, stirring constantly. Cook over medium heat, stirring constantly, until mixture boils. Boil 1 minute, stirring constantly. Remove from heat; stir in vanilla. Beat at high speed of an electric mixer until frosting is of spreading consistency. Immediately spread on cake. Yield: enough for one 3-layer cake.
Diane S. Haft
Jacksonville Beach, Florida

■ The taste of Japanese Fruitcake takes Susan Houston back to her childhood home where her father sat at the kitchen table cracking pecans and her mother stood mixing the batter for this traditional holiday treat every year. When this baking ritual began, Susan didn't need to consult the calendar for Santa's arrival. "It was the signal that Christmas really was coming when this heavenly smell filled the kitchen," she remembers with a smile.

JAPANESE FRUITCAKE
(pictured on page 298)

1 cup butter or margarine, softened
2 cups sugar
4 eggs
3¼ cups all-purpose flour
2 teaspoons baking powder
1 cup milk
1 teaspoon vanilla extract
1 teaspoon ground cinnamon
1 teaspoon ground allspice
½ teaspoon ground cloves
1 cup raisins
Lemon-Coconut Frosting
Garnish: pecan halves

Cream butter; gradually add sugar, beating well at medium speed of an electric mixer. Add eggs, one at a time, beating well after each addition.

Combine flour and baking powder; add to creamed mixture alternately with milk, beginning and ending with flour mixture. Mix after each addition. Stir in vanilla.

Pour one-third of batter into a greased and floured 9-inch round cakepan. Stir cinnamon and next 3 ingredients into remaining batter; pour into 2 greased and floured 9-inch round cakepans. Bake at 350° for 20 to 25 minutes or until a wooden pick inserted in center comes out clean. Cool in pans 10 minutes; remove from pans, and cool completely on wire racks.

Spread Lemon-Coconut Frosting between layers and on top and sides of cake, stacking white layer between spiced layers. Garnish, if desired. Yield: one 3-layer cake.

Lemon-Coconut Frosting

2 tablespoons cornstarch
1½ cups water, divided
2 cups sugar
1 tablespoon grated lemon rind
3½ tablespoons lemon juice
1 medium coconut, grated (3½ cups)

Dissolve cornstarch in ½ cup water; set aside.

Bring remaining 1 cup water to a boil in a medium saucepan. Stir in sugar, lemon rind, and lemon juice. Return to a boil, and cook to soft ball stage (236°), stirring often.

Gradually stir in cornstarch mixture; cook over medium heat, stirring constantly, until mixture is thickened and bubbly. Remove from heat; stir in coconut. Cool. Stir frosting just before spreading on cake. Yield: enough for one 3-layer cake.

Susan A. Houston
Tucker, Georgia

■ For years, holiday baking brought a little tension to Frances Crum's grandparents' kitchen. Her grandfather insisted on a traditional fruitcake kept moist with alcohol. Her grandmother wanted no candied fruit and declared alcohol was out of the question. Wanting to keep peace in the family, they talked the situation over and created The Compromise Cake. Four generations now know the secret to the recipe as well as to a good marriage.

THE COMPROMISE CAKE
(pictured on page 302)

1½ cups applesauce
1½ teaspoons baking soda
1 cup raisins
1 cup chopped dates
1 cup chopped pecans
½ cup shortening
1⅓ cups sugar
2 eggs
2 cups sifted cake flour
2 tablespoons unsweetened cocoa
½ teaspoon salt
½ teaspoon ground cinnamon
½ teaspoon ground cloves
½ teaspoon ground nutmeg
1 teaspoon vanilla extract

Grease bottom of a 10-inch tube pan; line bottom of pan with wax paper. Grease and flour lining and pan; set aside. Combine applesauce and soda; set aside. Combine raisins, dates, and pecans; set aside.

Cream shortening in a large bowl; gradually add sugar, beating well at medium speed of an electric mixer. Add eggs, one at a time, beating well after each addition.

Combine flour and next 5 ingredients. Add ½ cup flour mixture to raisin mixture; toss gently, and set aside. Gradually add remaining flour mixture to creamed mixture, mixing well. Add applesauce mixture and raisin mixture. Stir in vanilla.

Spoon batter into prepared pan. Bake at 350° for 30 minutes. Reduce temperature to 325°, and bake 20 minutes or until a wooden pick inserted in center of cake comes out clean. Cool in pan 10 to 15 minutes; remove from pan, and cool completely on a wire rack. Yield: one 10-inch cake.

Frances Crum
Searcy, Arkansas

■ "A pound cake resting on the cake stand in my kitchen is part of the feeling of home, according to my children," says Estelle Geno, "and it began with my mother's kitchen. There was always a plain pound cake and usually some sugar cookies under the dome there." Estelle keeps this sweet tradition of home alive with her holiday rendition, Eggnog Pound Cake.

EGGNOG POUND CAKE

1 cup butter or margarine, softened
½ cup shortening
3 cups sugar
6 eggs
3 cups all-purpose flour
1 cup commercial dairy eggnog
1 cup flaked coconut
1 teaspoon lemon extract
1 teaspoon vanilla extract
½ teaspoon coconut extract

Cream butter and shortening; gradually add sugar, beating well at medium speed of an electric mixer. Add eggs, one at a time, beating well after each addition.

Add flour to creamed mixture alternately with eggnog, beginning and ending with flour. Mix just until blended after each addition. Stir in coconut and flavorings.

Pour batter into a greased and floured 10-inch tube pan. Bake at 325° for 1 hour and 30 minutes or until a wooden pick inserted in center of cake comes out clean. Cool in pan 10 minutes; remove from pan, and cool completely on a wire rack. Yield: one 10-inch cake.

Estelle K. Geno
Waco, Texas

■ When Dot Moore's grandmother took her cut-glass bowl from the cabinet, good things were sure to follow. "That bowl always meant ambrosia," says Dot. "We had it for all holidays, state occasions, and when the minister ate with us. It was a handsome bowl with a beautiful scalloped edge, and today, it is my bowl, in trust for my daughter." Dot's ambrosia recipe is simple to follow, and she concludes, "By all means, serve it in a cut-glass bowl!"

GRANDMA'S AMBROSIA

8 oranges, peeled
¼ cup sugar
2 cups flaked coconut
1 cup coarsely chopped pecans
Garnishes: sweetened whipped
    cream, orange sections, flaked
    coconut

Section oranges over small bowl to catch juice; cut orange sections in half. Set juice aside.

Place half of oranges in a serving bowl. Sprinkle with 2 tablespoons sugar, and top with 1 cup coconut; repeat layers. Sprinkle with pecans, and pour ¼ cup reserved juice over fruit. Cover and chill. Garnish, if desired. Yield: 8 servings. *Dot Moore*
Birmingham, Alabama

Tasty, Timeless Hanukkah Treats

Year after year, the rituals remain the same, but the meanings can change. A few decades of Hanukkah

celebrations behind him, Rabbi Paul Caplan of Baton Rouge, Louisiana, finds that instead of being routine for him as an adult, the Jewish holiday still holds childlike discoveries.

He remembers the eight-day Festival of Lights simply being fun as a youngster. It wasn't until college that Caplan realized Hanukkah was more than child's play. Being educated about the world around him, he and his friends recognized the holiday's symbolism of political and religious freedom and its application to modern global events. For him, the Festival of Lights became a time of compassion and observance.

"Today, my wife, Linda, and I find a blend of both worlds," Caplan comments. "We celebrate Hanukkah with our daughter as our parents did with us. Sharing it with a child adds joy, significance, and depth to the holiday that we hadn't previously experienced. Perhaps a child at Hanukkah makes you realize the beauty and mystery of God's world more than anything else."

Paul and Linda pull out their recipes for Latkes (potato pancakes), Applesauce, and Sufganiyot (jelly-filled doughnuts) every year for the Festival of Lights. The custom of deep-fried foods is reminiscent of the eight-day oil.

LATKES

6 medium potatoes, peeled and
    shredded (about 2 pounds)
1 small onion, grated
2 eggs, beaten
2 tablespoons all-purpose flour
¼ teaspoon baking powder
1 teaspoon salt
Vegetable oil
Applesauce (optional)
Garnish: fresh parsley sprigs

Place shredded potatoes in a colander; rinse with cold water. Squeeze potatoes between paper towels to remove excess moisture. Combine potatoes and next 5 ingredients.

Pour oil to a depth of ¼ inch into a large heavy skillet. Drop ¼ cup potato mixture at a time into hot oil; press into 3-inch rounds with the back of a fork. Fry over high heat until golden brown, turning once. Drain on paper towels. Serve with applesauce, and garnish, if desired. Yield: 10 latkes.

SWEET KUGEL

1 (12-ounce) package wide egg
    noodles
3 eggs, slightly beaten
1 (16-ounce) carton cream-style
    cottage cheese
1 (8-ounce) carton sour cream
¼ cup sugar
¼ cup butter or margarine,
    melted
1 teaspoon all-purpose flour
½ teaspoon salt
1 teaspoon vanilla extract
½ cup corn flakes cereal

Cook noodles according to package directions, omitting salt and fat. Drain well, and set aside.

Combine eggs and next 7 ingredients; stir half of cottage cheese mixture into noodles. Spoon noodles into a lightly greased 13- x 9- x 2-inch baking dish. Pour remaining cottage cheese mixture over casserole; bake at 325° for 1 hour. Sprinkle with corn flakes, and serve. Yield: 10 to 12 servings.

APPLESAUCE

6 large cooking apples
1 cup water
1 (2½-inch) stick cinnamon
¼ teaspoon ground nutmeg

Peel, core, and thinly slice apples. Combine apples and water in a Dutch oven; bring to a boil. Cover, reduce heat, and simmer 45 minutes, stirring occasionally. Add cinnamon stick and nutmeg; cook, uncovered, over medium heat, stirring constantly, 15 minutes or until liquid is evaporated. Remove from heat; cool at least 30 minutes, and remove cinnamon stick.

Position knife blade in food processor bowl; add half of apple mixture. Process 1½ minutes or until smooth, scraping sides of processor bowl once. Repeat procedure with remaining apple mixture. Yield: 3¼ cups.

SUFGANIYOT
(Jelly-Filled Doughnuts)

1 package dry yeast
1¼ cups warm milk (105° to
    115°), divided
4½ to 5 cups all-purpose flour,
    divided
4 egg yolks
⅔ cup sugar
1 teaspoon vanilla extract
1 teaspoon grated lemon rind
½ cup butter, softened
½ cup raspberry or strawberry
    preserves
Vegetable oil
Powdered sugar

Dissolve yeast in ¼ cup warm milk; let stand 5 minutes. Combine 1 cup flour and remaining 1 cup warm milk in a large mixing bowl, mixing well at medium speed of an electric mixer. Add yeast mixture; mix well. Cover and let rise in a warm place (85°), free from drafts, 30 minutes.

Combine egg yolks and next 3 ingredients in a small bowl, mixing well; add to yeast mixture. Stir in butter and enough remaining flour to make a soft dough. Place in a well-greased bowl, turning to grease top. Cover and let rise in a warm place, free from drafts, 45 minutes or until doubled in bulk.

Punch dough down; turn out onto a lightly floured surface, and knead several times. Divide dough in half. Roll one portion to ¼-inch thickness, leaving other portion covered; cut 24 circles with a 2½-inch cutter.

Place 12 circles on a lightly greased baking sheet. Place ½ teaspoon preserves in center of each circle. Brush edges of each jelly-topped circle with water. Place remaining 12 circles over jelly-filled circles; pinch edges to seal. Repeat procedure with remaining dough and preserves. Cover and let rise in a warm place, free from drafts, 45 minutes or until doubled in bulk.

Pour oil to a depth of 2 to 3 inches in a Dutch oven; heat to 375°. Fry 2 or 3 doughnuts at a time 1 minute on each side or until golden brown. Drain well on paper towels. Sprinkle with powdered sugar, and serve immediately. Yield: 2 dozen.

Longing For Louisiana Flavor

The next time you are in the mood for some Cajun food, try Chicken-and-Sausage Gumbo introduced by Shrimp Rémoulade and topped off with Pecan Tart With Praline Cream.

Making a roux for the gumbo is an easy process, but it is one not to be interrupted. Stir over medium heat for a half hour or so without stopping, to get a rich, deep brown roux without any burned mishaps. Don't be afraid to get the roux darker than you're used to seeing in a finished gumbo. When you add what Louisiana natives call the "holy trinity"—celery, green pepper, and onion—the roux will get even darker. Stirring in the water will lighten it, and you're on your way to a true gumbo.

SHRIMP RÉMOULADE

4½ cups water
1½ teaspoons liquid
    shrimp-and-crab boil seasoning
1 tablespoon salt
1½ pounds unpeeled fresh shrimp
¼ cup mayonnaise or salad
    dressing
¼ cup vegetable oil
3 tablespoons Dijon mustard
1 to 2 tablespoons prepared
    horseradish
1 tablespoon lemon juice
2 teaspoons chopped fresh parsley
1 teaspoon red wine vinegar
½ teaspoon paprika
2 cloves garlic, crushed
6 cups shredded lettuce
Garnishes: lettuce leaves, lemon
    wedges, fresh parsley sprigs

Combine first 3 ingredients in a Dutch oven; bring to a boil. Add shrimp, and cook 3 to 5 minutes. Drain well; rinse with cold water. Chill. Peel and devein shrimp.

Combine mayonnaise and next 8 ingredients in container of an electric blender. Process at high speed until blended; chill.

Toss shrimp and shredded lettuce with dressing to coat. Serve on lettuce leaves, and garnish, if desired. Yield: 8 appetizer servings.

CHICKEN-AND-SAUSAGE GUMBO
(pictured on page 257)

1 pound hot smoked sausage, cut
　　into ¼-inch slices
4 chicken breast halves, skinned
¼ to ⅓ cup vegetable oil
¾ cup all-purpose flour
1 cup chopped onion
½ cup chopped green pepper
½ cup sliced celery
2 quarts hot water
3 cloves garlic, minced
2 bay leaves
2 teaspoons Creole seasoning
½ teaspoon dried whole thyme
1 tablespoon Worcestershire
　　sauce
½ to 1 teaspoon hot sauce
½ cup sliced green onions
¼ teaspoon salt (optional)
Hot cooked rice
Gumbo filé (optional)

Brown sausage in a Dutch oven over medium heat. Remove to paper towels, leaving drippings in Dutch oven. Brown chicken in drippings; remove to paper towels, reserving drippings.

Measure drippings, adding enough vegetable oil to measure ½ cup. Heat in Dutch oven over medium heat until hot. Add flour to hot oil; cook, stirring constantly, until roux is the color of chocolate (about 30 minutes). Add onion, green pepper, and celery; cook until vegetables are tender, stirring often. Gradually stir in water; bring to a boil. Return chicken breasts to Dutch oven; add garlic and next 5 ingredients. Reduce heat; simmer, uncovered, 1 hour.

Remove chicken; let cool. Return sausage to Dutch oven; cook gumbo, uncovered, 30 minutes. Stir in green onions; cook, uncovered, an additional 30 minutes. Add salt, if desired. Bone chicken breasts, and cut into strips. Add to gumbo, and cook until thoroughly heated. Remove bay leaves; serve gumbo over rice. Sprinkle with gumbo filé, if desired. Yield: 8 servings.

Making the Most Of Vegetables

■ Remember that leftover vegetables go nicely in a salad. Or make a chef's salad with leftover meats, cheeses, and cold cuts cut in strips and tossed with leftover vegetables, greens, and salad dressing.

■ Be sure to save your celery leaves. The outer leaves can serve as seasonings in soups, stuffings, and other cooked dishes. The inner leaves of the celery add a nice flavor to tossed salads.

PECAN TART WITH PRALINE CREAM
(pictured on page 264)

Pastry for 9-inch pie
⅓ cup butter or margarine,
　　melted
1 cup sugar
1 cup light corn syrup
4 eggs, beaten
1 teaspoon vanilla extract
¼ teaspoon salt
1 cup pecan halves
¼ cup semisweet chocolate
　　morsels
½ cup whipping cream
½ teaspoon vanilla extract
1 teaspoon praline liqueur
2 tablespoons powdered sugar

Press pie pastry into a 9-inch tart pan with removable bottom; set pastry aside.

Combine butter, 1 cup sugar, and corn syrup in a medium saucepan; cook over low heat, stirring constantly, until all sugar dissolves. Let mixture cool slightly.

Add beaten eggs, 1 teaspoon vanilla, and salt; stir well. Pour filling into prepared pastry shell, and top with pecan halves. Bake at 325° for 50 to 55 minutes.

Place chocolate morsels in a heavy-duty zip-top plastic bag; seal. Submerge bag in boiling water until chocolate morsels melt. Snip a tiny hole in end of bag with scissors; drizzle melted chocolate thinly over top of pecan pie.

Combine whipping cream, ½ teaspoon vanilla, and praline liqueur in mixing bowl; beat at medium speed of an electric mixer until mixture is foamy. Gradually add powdered sugar to whipped cream mixture, beating until soft peaks form.

Serve on individual dessert plates. Spoon about 2 tablespoons whipped cream mixture onto each dessert plate. Place a slice of pie on top of cream mixture, and serve immediately. Yield: one 9-inch pie.

Right: *The aroma of Chicken-and-Sausage Gumbo slowly simmering makes guests eager for the moment when they can finally ladle servings into their bowls. (Recipe, this page.)*

Above: *Turkey-Noodle-Poppyseed Casserole (page 239) turns leftover holiday turkey into an exciting new dish to serve your family or guests.*

Left: *Garnishes lend festive touches to (from left) Broccoli-Ham au Gratin, Italian Casserole, and Shrimp-and-Noodle Casserole. (Recipes begin on page 238.)*

Individual Chicken Bake, New Potato Medley, and Mixed Greens With Blue Cheese Vinaigrette confirm that eating right and good food go hand in hand. (Recipes begin on page 279.)

Chock-full of vegetables and catfish, a bowl of Catfish Gumbo (page 278) makes a filling lunch or dinner.

Delight your guests by serving Chocolate-Mint Whipped Cream Cake (page 265). Marbled chocolate curls dress the cake and hint at the flavor.

Make the holidays special; build a dessert party around Caramel Brie With Fresh Fruit, Amaretto-Irish Cream Cheesecake, and Roulage. (Recipes begin on page 266.)

Chocolate, a favorite dessert ingredient, is drizzled over Pecan Tart With Praline Cream (page 256).

A Grand Finale

Lynette Granade, of Mobile, Alabama, won grand prize in a local cooking contest with Chocolate-Mint Whipped Cream Cake.

To make curls, you'll need to buy both vanilla- and chocolate-flavored candy coating, available in squares, wafers, or morsels. You'll also need green-paste food coloring to tint the vanilla-flavored coating pale green. You can make the curls a day or two ahead of time, and store them in a cool, dry place. For longer storage, freeze up to three months.

CHOCOLATE-MINT WHIPPED CREAM CAKE
(pictured on page 262)

½ cup cocoa
1 cup hot water
½ cup butter or margarine, softened
1¼ cups sugar
2 eggs
1⅓ cups all-purpose flour
1 teaspoon baking soda
¼ teaspoon baking powder
½ teaspoon salt
Whipped Cream Filling
Chocolate Frosting
Garnish: marbled chocolate curls

Combine cocoa and hot water, stirring until smooth.

Cream butter; gradually add sugar, beating well at medium speed of an electric mixer. Add eggs, one at a time, beating well.

Combine flour and next 3 ingredients; add to creamed mixture alternately with cocoa mixture, beginning and ending with flour mixture. Mix after each addition.

Pour batter into 3 greased and floured 8-inch round cakepans. Bake at 350° for 15 minutes. Cool in pans 10 minutes; remove cakes from pans, and let cool completely on wire racks. Spread Whipped Cream Filling between layers; spread Chocolate Frosting on top and sides of cake. Garnish, if desired, placing curls around outside of cake first, and working to the center. Yield: one 3-layer cake.

Whipped Cream Filling

1½ cups whipping cream
1 tablespoon powdered sugar
2 teaspoons peppermint extract
Green paste food coloring

Combine first 3 ingredients in a medium mixing bowl; add a small amount of food coloring to mixture, and beat until soft peaks form. Yield: 3 cups.

Chocolate Frosting

2 (1-ounce) squares unsweetened chocolate, melted
2 cups sifted powdered sugar
2 tablespoons hot water
1 egg white
⅓ cup butter or margarine, softened
½ teaspoon vanilla extract

Combine first 3 ingredients in a mixing bowl; beat at medium speed of an electric mixer until mixture is smooth. Add egg white, butter, and vanilla; beat until smooth. Set bowl in a pan of ice water, and beat until frosting is thick enough to spread. Yield: 1¾ cups.

Note: To make marbled chocolate curls, melt 12 ounces chocolate-flavored candy coating (squares, wafers, or morsels) in a double boiler placed over hot water. Pour onto a smooth surface, such as marble or an aluminum foil-lined baking sheet. Then melt 12 ounces vanilla-flavored candy coating. Stir a small amount of green-paste food coloring into vanilla coating; pour over chocolate layer. Using a spatula, swirl the two colors to create a marbled effect, covering about a 12- x 9-inch area. Let stand at room temperature until coating cools and feels slightly tacky but is not firm. (If coating is too hard, curls will break; if too soft, coating will not curl.) Pull a cheese plane across coating until curl forms.

Drop By For Dessert

The Nutcracker ballet provides a great backdrop for a holiday "Nutcracker Sweet" party. Invite guests to drop by after a live performance, or rent a videotape of the ballet to play during the party.

AMARETTO-IRISH CREAM CHEESECAKE
(pictured on page 263)

1½ cups vanilla wafer crumbs
½ cup blanched whole almonds, toasted and finely chopped
¼ cup butter or margarine, melted
1 tablespoon amaretto
3 (8-ounce) packages cream cheese, softened
1 cup sugar
4 eggs
⅓ cup whipping cream
⅓ cup blanched whole almonds, toasted and ground
¼ cup Irish Cream liqueur
¼ cup amaretto
1½ cups sour cream
1 tablespoon sugar
½ teaspoon vanilla extract
¼ cup sliced almonds

Combine first 4 ingredients; firmly press mixture evenly on bottom of a lightly greased 10-inch springform pan. Bake at 350° for 10 minutes. Set aside to cool.

Beat softened cream cheese at high speed of an electric mixer until light and fluffy; gradually add 1 cup sugar, beating well. Add eggs, one at a time, beating after each addition. Stir in whipping cream and next 3 ingredients; pour into pan. Bake at 350° for 50 minutes; turn oven off, and leave in oven 30 minutes.

Combine sour cream, 1 tablespoon sugar, and vanilla; stir, and spoon over cake. Sprinkle ¼ cup almonds around edge. Bake at 500° for 5 minutes. Cool; chill. Yield: 12 servings.
Betty L. Beske
Arlington, Virginia

ROULAGE
(pictured on page 263)

5 eggs, separated
1 cup sugar
3 tablespoons cocoa
1 tablespoon cocoa
1 teaspoon unflavored gelatin
2 tablespoons cold water
1¼ cups whipping cream
2 tablespoons powdered sugar
Garnish: chocolate-dipped strawberries

Grease bottom and sides of a 15- x 10- x 1-inch jellyroll pan with vegetable oil; line pan with wax paper, and grease and flour wax paper. Set pan aside.

Beat egg yolks in a large bowl at high speed of an electric mixer until foamy. Gradually add 1 cup sugar, beating until mixture is thick and lemon colored. Gradually stir 3 tablespoons cocoa into yolk mixture.

Beat egg whites (at room temperature) until stiff peaks form; fold into chocolate mixture. Spread batter evenly in prepared pan. Bake at 375° for 12 to 15 minutes.

Sift 1 tablespoon cocoa in a 15- x 10-inch rectangle on a towel. When cake is done, loosen from sides of pan, and turn cake out onto towel. Peel off wax paper. Trim edges; discard. Starting at narrow end, roll up cake and towel. Place seam side down on a wire rack; cool.

Sprinkle gelatin over cold water in a small saucepan; let stand 1 minute. Cook over low heat, stirring until gelatin dissolves.

Beat whipping cream at low speed of an electric mixer, gradually adding dissolved gelatin. Increase mixer speed to medium; beat until mixture begins to thicken. Add powdered sugar, and beat at high speed until soft peaks form.

Unroll cake, and remove towel. Spread whipped cream on cake, leaving 1-inch margin around edges; reroll cake. Place on a serving plate, seam side down. Garnish, if desired. Yield: 8 servings.   *Jane Maloy*
Wilmington, North Carolina

CARAMEL BRIE WITH FRESH FRUIT
(pictured on page 263)

1 (15-ounce) mini-Brie
2 tablespoons butter or margarine
¾ cup firmly packed brown sugar
¼ cup light corn syrup
1½ tablespoons all-purpose flour
¼ cup milk
½ cup coarsely chopped pecans, toasted
1 tablespoon lemon juice
¼ cup water
Pear wedges
Apple wedges
Grapes

Place Brie on a large serving plate.

Melt butter in a saucepan; add brown sugar, corn syrup, and flour, stirring well. Bring mixture to a boil; reduce heat, and simmer 5 minutes, stirring constantly. Remove from heat; cool to lukewarm. Gradually stir in milk. Pour caramel over Brie, allowing excess to drip down sides; sprinkle with pecans.

Combine lemon juice and water; toss with wedges. Drain. Arrange fruit around Brie. Serve immediately. Yield: 14 appetizer servings.

Theresa Burst
Birmingham, Alabama

Gifts Say "Thank You"

Finding something a little different—whether it's a recipe or a purchased item—is often the fun part of holiday planning and gift giving. We chose these recipes and ideas because they offer a personal touch. For example, Chocolate Chip-Banana Bread departs sweetly from the ones we usually make. Full of chocolate mini-morsels, it's a delightful treat, perfect for the holiday season. Perhaps you'll find something that's just right for your grocery or shopping list.

Host or hostess gifts are often some of the most challenging to select. Clothing or other old standbys just don't fit the bill when saying "thank you" to someone who has invited you to a party or dinner. A gift related to the home, entertaining, decorating, or the host's or hostess's own personal background makes the best choice.

Take a practical, lighthearted approach to such selections. When you give something, think about what kinds of things you would like to get. Several suggestions are pearl garlands for Christmas trees or holiday arrangements, antique perfume bottles, or antique serving spoons.

Fruited Rice Mix is a quick addition to menus during this busy season, and the party-givers can cook it at their convenience. Clever packaging, such as tins, colorful bags, or decorative boxes, and a snappy recipe card make giving this food gift as much fun as getting it.

CHOCOLATE CHIP-BANANA BREAD

½ cup butter or margarine,
  softened
1 cup sugar
2 eggs
2 ripe bananas, mashed
2 cups all-purpose flour
1 teaspoon baking powder
½ teaspoon baking soda
½ teaspoon salt
¾ cup semisweet chocolate
  mini-morsels
½ cup chopped walnuts

Cream butter; gradually add sugar, beating well at medium speed of an electric mixer. Add eggs, one at a time, beating after each addition. Stir in bananas.

Combine flour and next 3 ingredients; gradually add to creamed mixture, beating until blended. Stir in mini-morsels and walnuts.

Spoon batter into a greased 9- x 5- x 3-inch loafpan. Bake at 350° for 1 hour and 10 minutes or until a wooden pick inserted in center comes out clean, shielding with aluminum foil after 1 hour. Cool in pan 10 minutes; remove from pan, and cool completely on a wire rack. Yield: 1 loaf.
Connie Burgess
Knoxville, Tennessee

FRUITED RICE MIX

1 cup long-grain rice, uncooked
½ cup finely chopped dried
  apricots
¼ cup raisins or currants
1 (2-ounce) package slivered
  almonds
1 tablespoon chicken-flavored
  bouillon granules
2 teaspoons dried parsley flakes
1½ teaspoons dried orange rind
½ teaspoon onion powder

Combine all ingredients; store in an airtight container or plastic bag. Yield: 1¾ cups.

Directions for recipe gift card: Combine rice mix, 2½ cups water, and 2 tablespoons butter in a medium saucepan; bring to a boil. Cover, reduce heat, and simmer 20 to 25 minutes or until rice is tender and water is absorbed. Yield: 4 to 6 servings.

Too Busy to Cook? Select from this List

Many of these ideas will work for the discriminating host or hostess. Bringing along a thoughtful gift is an expressive way to say, "Thanks for the invitation."

■ Flavored coffees or coffee beans given with a Christmas mug or storage canister
■ After-dinner liqueurs and beverages, such as amaretto, Irish cream, port, or Kahlúa
■ Champagne or wine stopper
■ Corkscrew, party napkins, cocktail glasses, swizzle sticks, or martini shaker
■ Fresh flowers
■ Chocolates, biscotti, or a flask of virgin olive oil
■ A serving spoon, fork, or knife from a local antique shop
■ Handmade tree ornaments or holiday photo frames
■ Candlesticks or figurines appropriate to the season
■ A guest registry book, seasonal note cards, or gift tags
■ A fine copy of *The Velveteen Rabbit*, *A Christmas Carol*, or other seasonal classics

Entertain Young Adults With A Festive Menu

For children home for Christmas vacation the promise of home-cooked food and an evening spent with old friends offers a special holiday treat. You can welcome your children and their friends with this small dinner party. They'll enjoy reminiscing and catching up.

Serving this simple menu won't keep you in the kitchen all day long. It features make-ahead recipes, such as Cold Spiced Fruit and Ice Cream Bombe. It also offers an excellent opportunity for visiting and reminding your children how to set a table properly and create a simple centerpiece. Sharing these entertaining tips helps the next generation establish holiday traditions of their own.

The keys to successful entertaining are planning and presentation. The combination of Easy Beef Tenderloin with carefully selected accompaniments offers a harmonious blend of foods that will please all guests. The colorful fruit and vivid green beans complement the muted tones of the potatoes and beef; the contrasting shapes of potato wedges, green beans, and oval meat slices lend interest to the plate.

With some advance preparation, this menu can be ready to serve in about one hour.

Easy Beef Tenderloin
Special Green Beans
Lemon-Buttered New Potatoes
Cold Spiced Fruit
Commercial rolls
Ice Cream Bombe

SPECIAL GREEN BEANS

2½ pounds fresh green beans
3 cups water
1 cup sliced fresh mushrooms
⅓ cup chopped onion
3 cloves garlic, crushed
1 (8-ounce) can sliced water chestnuts, drained
½ teaspoon salt
½ teaspoon freshly ground black pepper
½ teaspoon dried whole basil
1 teaspoon dried Italian seasoning
⅓ cup olive oil
¼ cup grated Parmesan cheese

Wash beans; trim ends, and remove strings. Combine beans and water in a Dutch oven. Bring to a boil; cover, reduce heat, and simmer 6 to 8 minutes or until crisp-tender. Drain. Plunge beans into ice water to stop the cooking process. Drain beans, and set aside.

Sauté mushrooms and next 7 ingredients in oil in a Dutch oven. Stir in beans, and cook until thoroughly heated. Sprinkle with Parmesan cheese. Yield: 8 to 10 servings.
Lauren Salter
Marietta, Georgia

EASY BEEF TENDERLOIN

6 green onions, chopped
½ cup butter or margarine, melted
3 beef-flavored bouillon cubes
2 tablespoons red wine vinegar
1 (5- to 6-pound) beef tenderloin, trimmed

Sauté green onions in butter in a small saucepan until tender; add beef-flavored bouillon cubes, stirring until dissolved. Remove from heat, and stir in vinegar.

Place tenderloin in a large shallow dish. Spoon butter mixture over top of tenderloin; cover with aluminum foil, and let stand at room temperature 15 minutes.

Place tenderloin on a rack in a roasting pan; insert meat thermometer into thickest portion of tenderloin. Bake at 425° for 30 to 45 minutes or until meat thermometer registers 140° (rare) or 160° (medium). Let stand 10 minutes before slicing. Yield: 8 to 10 servings.
Lynn Casey
Birmingham, Alabama

LEMON-BUTTERED NEW POTATOES

2 pounds small new potatoes, unpeeled and quartered
¼ cup butter or margarine
2 tablespoons chopped fresh parsley
2 tablespoons lemon juice
1 teaspoon grated lemon rind
½ teaspoon salt
¼ teaspoon pepper
⅛ teaspoon ground nutmeg
Garnish: fresh parsley sprigs

Cook potatoes, covered, in boiling water to cover 10 minutes or until tender; drain carefully, leaving skins intact. Combine butter and next 6 ingredients in a small saucepan; cook over medium heat, stirring until butter melts. Pour butter mixture over potatoes, tossing gently to coat. Garnish, if desired. Serve immediately. Yield: 8 servings.

Dolly G. Northcott
Fairfield, Alabama

COLD SPICED FRUIT

2 oranges, unpeeled and thinly sliced
1 teaspoon salt
1 (15¼-ounce) can pineapple chunks, undrained
1 (16-ounce) can sliced peaches, undrained
1 (16-ounce) can pear halves, undrained
1 (16-ounce) can apricot halves, undrained
1 cup sugar
½ cup white vinegar
3 (3-inch) sticks cinnamon
7 whole cloves
1 (3-ounce) package cherry-flavored gelatin

Cut orange slices in half. Combine oranges and salt in a large saucepan; add water to cover. Bring to a boil, and cook 5 minutes; drain well, and set aside.

Drain canned fruits, combining and reserving enough juice to measure 2½ cups, adding water, if necessary. Set fruit aside. Combine reserved juice, sugar, and remaining ingredients in a medium saucepan. Bring mixture to a boil, stirring until gelatin dissolves; reduce heat, and simmer 15 minutes.

Layer canned fruits and orange slices in a large bowl. Pour gelatin mixture over fruit; cover and refrigerate 8 hours. Stir and serve with a slotted spoon. Yield: 8 to 10 servings.

Jane Maloy
Wilmington, North Carolina

ICE CREAM BOMBE

1 quart vanilla ice cream, softened
1 (6-ounce) package semisweet chocolate morsels
1 tablespoon sugar
3 egg whites
2 teaspoons vanilla extract
½ cup whipping cream, whipped
Garnishes: semisweet chocolate shavings, red maraschino cherries, fresh mint sprigs

Line a 5-cup mold with plastic wrap; spread ice cream evenly on bottom and sides of mold, and freeze 1 hour.

Combine chocolate morsels and sugar in a 1-quart mixing bowl; microwave at MEDIUM (50% power) 3 to 3½ minutes or until chocolate melts, stirring once.

Beat egg whites (at room temperature) and vanilla until stiff peaks form. Gradually stir about one-fourth of chocolate mixture into egg whites; fold into remaining chocolate mixture. Fold in whipped cream. Spoon mixture into center of mold; cover and freeze until firm.

To serve, let mold stand at room temperature about 10 minutes; invert onto a chilled serving plate. Remove plastic wrap; garnish with chocolate shavings, if desired. Return bombe to freezer until ready to serve. Garnish, if desired. Yield: 8 servings.

Linda Tompkins
Birmingham, Alabama

Invite Kids To The Party

Children are all smiles when they hear that they've been included in party plans for the holidays. To make the occasion fun for all, however, the host or hostess must have a special strategy. It's not much of a party for adults when children continually race through the room shouting at the top of their lungs. But kids can only sit still and smile for a limited time. So what's the solution?

Smart party planners have a scheme in mind when they invite children to come along. The plan may vary with the size of the party and the number and age of the children. Just be sure to start the party early enough in the evening so that the children won't be out much past their bedtime to help keep them happy and satisfied.

Get Your Child to Help

Let children age 4 or older assist with the party plans, from start to finish. By this age, they can actually speed you up rather than slow you down when they help. Let them assist in putting together the menu and selecting disposable place settings. They can also help decorate, as well as prepare some of the food. Getting children involved is a great way to teach them how to entertain.

Set Up a "Kids' Room"

Most parents will want their friends at the party to see how their children have grown, especially when the little ones are all decked out in their holiday finery. The children would enjoy an opportunity to mingle with the adults for a short while, as well. But for the majority of the time, you *and* the children will appreciate having a separate room set up just for the children in another part of the house. A playroom or den works well for this, as does a child's bedroom if it's large enough.

The adult party area will, no doubt, be adorned with holiday greenery and decorations, and you won't want to forget about the children's area. Decorations as simple as red and green helium balloons and streamers are all it takes to set the mood and make them feel special. A children's Christmas tree full of playful ornaments would go over well, too. You can decorate the tree before the party, or save the tree trimming as an activity for the children.

Who's in Charge?

You'll need someone to coordinate activities and food for the children at all times because you'll have your hands full with the adult festivities. If most of the children are at the infant and toddler stage, all you really need is a babysitter. Hire an older sitter with experience caring for this age child, and set up a "nursery." Put up available portable cribs or playpens in case they need naps. If you have access to crank or battery-powered swings for babies, these will assist the sitter, especially when there are several guests in this age group. Make sure the room has a door that can be closed or a portable gate to help keep toddlers from wandering.

If most of the children are age 4 and above, enlist a young but dependable neighborhood teenager to help supervise them. Little children like someone who'll get on the floor and really play with them, and these age groups usually get along well together.

Depending on the children attending the party and the helpers you hire, you'll probably need one sitter for every four or five children. The host or hostess should pay the sitter a prearranged hourly fee after all guests depart. Most sitters charge

an hourly fee and add a small amount per extra child when keeping more than one or two children.

Keep the Kids Busy

If most of the children are infants and toddlers, you won't need to plan any special activities. Just provide plenty of toys, and let them make up their own games. But by age 4, you'll need organized games or activities to keep the children occupied.

Kids of all ages enjoy watching videos, and movies with a holiday theme would be fun at this time of year. Keep the average age of the child in mind, as well as how long you'd like to occupy them with this activity when you select a movie, which can last anywhere from 25 minutes to 2 hours.

One activity is making gumdrop trees. You can use the trees as a decoration for the party as well as individual favors for the children to take home. Be sure to have plenty of gumdrops on hand; children tend to eat as many as they place on the tree. It's a good idea to make two or three trees before the children arrive to use as decorations and as samples for the children to look at as they assemble their own. To make the gumdrop trees, buy large gumdrops, round wooden picks, and as many plastic foam cones as you desire. Break the wooden picks in half; insert the pointed ends of the picks in the cones, and attach gumdrops to the broken ends. (Be sure to supervise the use of wooden picks when young children participate.) Cones that are 3 to 6 inches work well for the children, while cones from 6 to 9 inches can be grouped together as a centerpiece.

Another craft that children of all ages enjoy is making Christmas cards. Provide plenty of glue, glitter, construction paper, and colored markers, and then let them design their own cards. They might also

enjoy cutting up old Christmas cards to adorn the new ones they make.

Games usually go over well, and you can restructure familiar games to reflect a holiday theme, such as Pin the Nose on Rudolf and Musical Chairs (using Christmas carols).

As a special feature, children and adults would enjoy a visit from Santa.

Plan Special Party Food

Let's face it—children and adults don't have the same food in mind when they think of a party, so consider planning a few special recipes just for the kids. Concentrate on quick things that you can make ahead of time and things that are easy to serve. Here's a simple menu, most of which you can make a day or two ahead. The children will appreciate the extra time you've taken to make the party fun for them, too.

Elf Gorp
Ham-and-Cheese Pita Pockets
Thick-and-Creamy Dip
Cut vegetables
Kid-Pleasin' Chocolate Mousse
Santa's Slush

ELF GORP

8 cups popped corn
2 cups round crispy oat cereal
2 cups goldfish cracker pretzels
2 cups bite-size crispy rice cereal
1 cup peanuts
½ cup butter or margarine, melted
½ teaspoon seasoned salt
½ teaspoon garlic powder
1 tablespoon Worcestershire sauce

Combine first 5 ingredients in a large bowl. Combine butter and remaining ingredients in a small bowl; stir well. Pour over popcorn mixture; toss gently to coat, and pour into a large roasting pan. Bake at 250° for 1 hour, stirring at 15-minute intervals. Cool completely; store in an airtight container. Yield: 2½ quarts.

Delana Smith
Birmingham, Alabama

HAM-AND-CHEESE PITA POCKETS

4 (7-inch) whole pita bread
   rounds
¼ cup mayonnaise or salad
   dressing
1 (6-ounce) package sliced cooked
   ham
1 (6-ounce) package sliced Swiss
   or American cheese

Cut pita bread in half, using kitchen shears. Lay pita pockets on a baking sheet. Spread 1½ teaspoons mayonnaise inside each pita pocket, on bottom side. Place a slice of ham and a slice of cheese on top of mayonnaise, folding them to fit inside pita. Cover; chill up to 2 days, if desired.

Bake, uncovered, at 400° for 8 minutes or until cheese melts. Serve immediately. Yield: 8 servings.

THICK-AND-CREAMY DIP

½ cup sour cream
½ cup mayonnaise or salad
   dressing
1 tablespoon grated onion
1½ teaspoons Worcestershire
   sauce
½ teaspoon seasoned salt

Combine all ingredients, stirring well. Chill at least 3 hours. Serve with cut broccoli spears, cauliflower flowerets, cherry tomatoes, and celery and carrot sticks. Yield: 1 cup.

Note: To make a simple vegetable wreath, cover a plastic foam wreath (approximately 10 inches in diameter) with leaf lettuce, securing lettuce with wooden picks. Attach cut vegetables to wreath, using wooden picks. (Supervise the use of wooden picks if young children participate.)

KID-PLEASIN' CHOCOLATE MOUSSE

1 (6-ounce) package chocolate
   instant pudding mix
3 cups cold milk
1 cup frozen whipped topping,
   thawed and divided
12 cream-filled chocolate
   sandwich cookies, crumbled
8 whole cream-filled chocolate
   sandwich cookies

Combine pudding mix and milk in a small mixing bowl; beat at low speed of an electric mixer until blended. Beat at low speed an additional 2 minutes. Fold in ½ cup whipped topping and cookie crumbs. Spoon mousse into eight 6-ounce dessert dishes. Cover and chill.

Garnish each serving with a dollop of remaining whipped topping and a cookie just before serving. Yield: 8 servings.

Gale Rigby Kennedy
Columbia, South Carolina

SANTA'S SLUSH

2 (6-ounce) cans frozen limeade
   concentrate, thawed and
   undiluted
1 (12-ounce) can frozen lemonade
   concentrate, thawed and
   undiluted
1 cup sifted powdered sugar
7 cups crushed ice
4 drops green food coloring
   (optional)
1 (33.8-ounce) bottle club soda,
   chilled

Combine half each of first 4 ingredients in container of an electric blender; add 2 drops of food coloring, if desired. Blend at high speed until slushy. Pour into an 8-inch square dish. Repeat procedure with remaining half of ingredients, pouring mixture into same dish. Cover and freeze until mixture is firm.

Remove from freezer 30 minutes before serving. Break mixture into chunks with a spoon; transfer to punch bowl. Add club soda; stir until slushy. Yield: about 3 quarts.

Freezing Tips

■ Select containers for freezing that will hold only enough of a fruit or vegetable for one meal.

■ For the quickest freezing, leave a little space between containers so that air can circulate freely. Place containers closer together after they are frozen.

■ To easily remove wax paper or aluminum foil from frozen food, place frozen package in 300° oven for 5 minutes.

Beverages Brewed For The Season

This holiday season be prepared for drop-in guests with one of these tasty beverages that can be served on a minute's notice.

Rich hot chocolate topped with sweetened whipped cream and chocolate shavings makes Hot Chocolate Deluxe an extra-special treat.

Chances are, you have most of the ingredients in your pantry.

Cranapple Wine blends spices, Burgundy, and cranapple juice for a refreshing drink that can be made ahead. Keep the beverage in the refrigerator throughout the season for family and guests.

HOLIDAY BREW

1 quart unsweetened apple juice
1½ cups unsweetened pineapple
  juice
2 tablespoons honey
2 tablespoons lemon juice
3 (4-inch) sticks cinnamon

Combine all ingredients in a Dutch oven; bring to a boil. Remove from heat, and discard cinnamon sticks. Serve hot. Yield: about 1½ quarts.

Note: Beverage may be stored in the refrigerator and reheated.
Jackie Helen Bergenheier
Wichita Falls, Texas

CRANAPPLE WINE

¾ cup water
¾ cup sugar
2 (4-inch) sticks cinnamon
1 teaspoon whole cloves
Pinch of salt
3¼ cups Burgundy, chilled
3 cups cranapple juice, chilled

Combine first 5 ingredients in a saucepan; bring to a boil. Remove from heat, and chill 8 hours. Strain and discard cinnamon and cloves. Combine syrup mixture, Burgundy, and cranapple juice. Yield: 7½ cups.
Deborah Hudson Tyson
Birmingham, Alabama

HOT CHOCOLATE DELUXE
(pictured on page 299)

¼ cup boiling water
⅓ cup chocolate syrup
4 cups milk
⅓ cup Kahlúa or other
  coffee-flavored liqueur
Garnishes: whipped cream,
  chocolate shavings

Combine boiling water and chocolate syrup in a medium saucepan; add milk, stirring until blended. Cook over medium heat until hot (do not boil). Stir in Kahlúa. Garnish, if desired. Yield: 5 cups. *Libby Idom*
Houston, Texas

AMARETTO

1 lemon
3 cups sugar
2 cups water
3 cups vodka
3 tablespoons brandy
2 tablespoons almond extract
2 teaspoons vanilla extract
1 teaspoon chocolate extract

Peel lemon, leaving inner white skin on fruit. Cut rind into 2- x ¼-inch strips. Reserve fruit for other uses.

Combine lemon rind strips, sugar, and water in a saucepan. Bring to a boil; cover, reduce heat, and simmer 30 minutes. Remove from heat; remove lemon rind, and discard. Refrigerate liquid. Stir in vodka and remaining ingredients. Store in an airtight container. Yield: 1½ quarts.
Dorothy C. Taylor
Palm City, Florida

SPARKLING GIN COOLER

3 cups orange juice, chilled
¾ cup gin
1 cup ginger ale, chilled
Garnishes: lime slices,
  maraschino cherries

Combine orange juice and gin. Add ginger ale, and stir gently. Pour over ice cubes, and garnish each glass with a lime slice and a maraschino cherry. Yield: about 5 cups.

Jennifer O. Rosti
Salem, Virginia

Beverages For All Ages

If you need a party beverage for both kids and adults, Strawberry Punch and Peppermint-Eggnog Punch offer tasty solutions. The base for Strawberry Punch can be made ahead of time and frozen. That's one of the reasons we selected it as the punch for the open house menu on page 243. Peppermint-Eggnog Punch mixes up quickly, and chances are, it won't last long.

For the coffee enthusiast, offer a cup of steaming Holiday Coffee. You may wish to mail-order your favorite blend of coffee to use in this brew.

PEPPERMINT-EGGNOG PUNCH

1 quart peppermint ice cream, softened
1 quart commercial dairy eggnog
4 (12-ounce) bottles ginger ale, chilled
Peppermint sticks

Combine first 3 ingredients in a punch bowl, stirring until blended. Serve immediately with peppermint sticks. Yield: 4½ quarts.

WASSAIL

2 quarts apple cider
½ cup sugar
¼ cup firmly packed brown sugar
2 (3-inch) sticks cinnamon
12 whole cloves
4 cups grapefruit juice
4 cups orange juice
1 cup pineapple juice

Combine first 5 ingredients in a Dutch oven; bring to a boil, and cook until sugar dissolves. Reduce heat, and simmer 5 minutes.

Add juices, and heat just until hot (do not boil). Strain and discard spices. Serve hot. Yield: about 4½ quarts.

Dorothy Burgess
Huntsville, Texas

HOLIDAY COFFEE

¾ cup ground coffee
4 cups water
½ cup sweetened condensed milk
Whipped cream
4 (3-inch) sticks cinnamon
4 maraschino cherries with stems

Prepare coffee according to manufacturer's directions using ¾ cup ground coffee and 4 cups water.

Stir sweetened condensed milk into coffee, and serve immediately with a dollop of whipped cream, a stick of cinnamon, and a maraschino cherry. Yield: 4½ cups.

Heather Riggins
Nashville, Tennessee

LIME SLUSH PUNCH

½ cup sugar
1 (3-ounce) package lime-flavored gelatin
2 cups boiling water
3 cups unsweetened pineapple juice
⅓ cup lemon juice
1 cup cold water
1 (64-ounce) bottle ginger ale, chilled

Dissolve sugar and gelatin in boiling water in a large bowl; stir in juices and cold water. Cover and freeze at least 8 hours.

Remove from freezer 1 hour before serving. Place in a punch bowl, and break into chunks. Add ginger ale; stir until slushy. Yield: 1 gallon.

Mrs. Bob Nester
Charleston, West Virginia

STRAWBERRY PUNCH

2 cups sugar
6 cups boiling water
2½ cups orange juice
½ cup lemon juice
4 cups unsweetened pineapple juice
2 (10-ounce) packages frozen strawberries with juice, thawed
1 (64-ounce) bottle lemon-lime carbonated beverage

Dissolve sugar in boiling water in a Dutch oven; stir in orange juice and next 3 ingredients. Pour mixture into a large plastic container, and freeze until firm.

Remove from freezer 1 hour before serving. Place in a punch bowl, and break into chunks. Add lemon-lime beverage; stir until slushy. Yield: about 6 quarts.

Lou Baughman
Fort Walton Beach, Florida

A Clear Look At Glassware

With over 60 shapes and sizes of drinking glasses on the market, it's no wonder selecting drinkware for entertaining can be confusing. The Europeans started the involved custom of using different glasses for various wines, and if you're familiar and comfortable with that practice, then by all means, go right ahead. But today's entertaining—whether formal or informal—is usually simpler than that, and you shouldn't feel as though you need an instruction manual and a substantial investment in crystal just to serve beverages.

The key is to learn the basic use for each type of glassware, and then evaluate your needs and entertaining style. Collecting an elaborate set of crystal in one pattern may suit you, or you might find it fun to pick up interesting pieces along the way for an eclectic approach.

What Are Some Options?

Balloon or bubble—This is a good all-purpose glass suitable for a variety of beverages, including wine, beer, cocktails, or brandy if you aren't planning to purchase a wide variety of stemware.

Wine—Eight ounces is a good size; fill the glass about two-thirds full because five ounces is a standard serving of wine.

Water—This is the same shape as the wine glass, but a little larger—usually 10 ounces.

Iced tea/beverage—This has a shorter stem and larger bowl than water and wine glasses and is suitable for drinks served over ice with a seated meal.

Cocktail—It's readily recognized as a martini glass, but manhattans, stingers, and even daiquiris are commonly served this way.

Fluted champagne—The tall, narrow bowl is good for champagne and sparkling wines because it decreases the surface exposed to air, retaining the drink's effervescence longer.

Tulip champagne—This is an attractive variation of the fluted champagne and serves the same function.

Champagne saucer or champagne/sherbet—Although it is thought to be the classic champagne vessel, its wide-mouthed bowl allows champagne bubbles to escape too quickly. But it makes a spectacular presentation for chilled soups, fruit compotes, and desserts.

Brandy snifter—The shape of this glass is thought to enhance the liquor's aroma.

Pilsner—Serving beer is the most popular use for this piece.

Hurricane—This is used for coolers and colorful fruit and frozen drinks.

Liqueur or cordial—Sipping after-dinner liqueurs from this tiny glassware is a wonderful way to end an evening.

Highball or tumbler—This tall, straight-sided piece is used for larger iced beverages.

Coupette—If you're serving a spirited ice cream dessert, try this one. Put the scoop of ice cream in first; then add the liquid ingredients.

On-the-rocks or old-fashioned—This straight-sided, heavy-bottomed glass is used for beverages served at a cocktail party rather than at a seated meal.

How Do I Care for It?

—Put heavier, everyday pieces in the dishwasher for cleaning, but wash fine crystal by hand in a sink lined with a towel or rubber mat to prevent breakage. Remove your rings and bracelets to avoid scratching the glasses, and wash and rinse one piece at a time. Never place ice-cold glasses in hot dishwater because the drastic temperature change may cause the glassware to crack.

—If you have cabinets with glass doors, store your crystal there and show it off. Stand stemmed glasses with the bowl up; storing glasses upside down puts too much pressure on the rim, which is the most delicate part of the piece. Leave enough space between glasses to avoid scratches or chips from their touching one another. For extra protection, line shelves with a soft cloth.

—If crystal is slightly chipped on the rim, use an emery board to lightly and carefully smooth the damaged area. Otherwise, take the crystal to a professional to repair it.

—Purchase quilted, compartmentalized storage cases made for crystal at fine department stores or china shops. These portable cases can be put away in a closet if cabinet space is limited.

—Don't pack crystal in newspaper, excelsior, or other materials that tend to hold moisture. This can cause a cloudy appearance called "hazing." If this happens to your glassware, clean it with lemon juice or vinegar.

wine

pilsner

liqueur or cordial

brandy snifter

iced tea/beverage

balloon or bubble

fluted champagne

champagne saucer or
champagne/sherbet

highball or tumbler

old-fashioned or on-the-rocks

From Our Kitchen To Yours

Entertaining 50 or more people doesn't have to be intimidating. You can host a party with confidence and pleasure using "Holiday Entertaining at Its Best" on page 241 as a guide, plus these additional tips shared by Fran Ginn, a caterer in the Columbia, Mississippi, area.

When planning your menu, consider a balance of color, texture, and temperature. If you are preparing the food, select make-ahead hors d'oeuvres to avoid last-minute cooking, and arrange food so that the trays do not need constant replenishing. To keep the traffic flow moving, Ginn suggests a balance of "pickups," such as vegetables, and "stops," such as spreads. Prepare the recipes you do best; if you need help, fill in with prepared food from a caterer or

a delicatessen. Your guests will be unaware there was another cook if you transfer prepared food, such as smoked salmon, pâté, or sliced roast beef, to your serving pieces.

Ginn suggests at least seven heavy hors d'oeuvres and two sweets. Two or three of these items should be meat and seafood, which are the most popular foods no matter how large the crowd; however, experience has taught her that people tend to eat more at smaller parties. To offset the more expensive meat and seafood items, serve one vegetable and other substantial fillers, such as cheese, dips, and spreads.

Select miniature desserts, including one chocolate, that are not crumbly or messy. "Always have extra hors d'oeuvres in the pantry," Ginn advises. "If you run out of a particular food, a wedge of cheese or a package of cream cheese and a jar of pepper jelly with crackers can easily fill the empty tray, and your guests will think you planned something new

for the last hour." She suggests serving a less expensive appetizer the last hour of the party, replacing a high-priced food such as shrimp or crabmeat.

Guidelines for behind-the-scene activities are just as important as planning the menu. Select the trays you'll use, choosing separate containers for crackers and rolls to prevent the possibility of their becoming soggy; label and arrange the positions on your table. Placement of food sometimes determines what guests eat the most, so you'll want to separate the meat and seafood items, putting at least one near the end of the buffet. Set trays that most often need replenishing close to the kitchen. Label the table to remember the position of the trays; this helps when you are in a rush or when someone else assists you.

"Then be a guest at your own party," states Ginn. Begin outside the front door objectively walking through your house. Think about

How Much to Buy?

Stumped by how much to purchase for your party? Below are approximate amounts based on average servings for 50 people. For guidance in purchasing liquor, see page 277.

Beef—12½ pounds or 4 ounces uncooked meat per person

Ham (bone in)—12 to 16 pounds

Whole turkey—12 to 16 pounds or 2 (5-pound) turkey breasts

Shrimp—12½ to 16½ pounds, unpeeled

Cheese—3 pounds

Dip—2 to 3 quarts

Cream cheese mold—2 to 3 pounds

Vegetable tray—1 cauliflower, 1 large broccoli, 1 pound carrots, 1 pound mushrooms

Mayonnaise for beef or ham—2 cups

Miniature sweets—9 dozen

Party rolls—9 dozen

Biscuits—9 dozen

Crackers—1 to 1½ pounds

Pear and apple wedges—12 pounds

Coffee—1 to 1½ pounds

Punch—2 gallons

Napkins—150 to 200

coat storage and the traffic flow from the bar to the food table. Avoid placing the bar next to the food; it is awkward for guests to hold a glass while filling their plates. Walk around the table, and serve an imaginary plate to be sure the trays are correctly positioned with necessary spreaders and serving pieces.

If possible, consider hiring someone to help wash glasses, replenish ice and food, pick up dirty plates and glasses, and clean up after the party. It will be money well spent so that you can enjoy the party.

Setting Up a Bar

When planning a basic bar, you'll need to include liquor and mixers for what your guests prefer. Scotch, vodka, bourbon, gin, and rum are the most often requested. Fruit juices, carbonated beverages, sparkling water, wine, and beer should also be available to your visitors.

To calculate how much to buy, consider the number of guests, how long the party will last, and what other available beverages there will be, such as punch and coffee. For each guest, estimate one drink, one beer, or two glasses of wine per hour; for each guest who doesn't drink alcoholic beverages, have three to four cans of cola or sparkling water available during the evening. Plan 10 ounces of mixer, two to three glasses, and ¾ to 1 pound of ice per person.

Even with these guidelines, it is difficult to determine in advance how much liquor, beer, or wine you'll actually need. It's better to have more than you estimate; therefore, when purchasing liquor for the party, ask if the store gives refunds for returned unopened bottles.

If the bar is unsupervised, some guests might overindulge and leave your home intoxicated. So if you cannot hire a bartender, take the responsibility of designating one. Or ask several friends to help out at 30-minute intervals; hopefully, this suggestion will keep you from running out of liquor and will help your guests return home safely.

Use this guide to help estimate what you'll need.
1 (750-milliliter) bottle liquor = 17 (1½-ounce) jiggers.
1 (33.8-ounce) bottle liquor = 22 (1½-ounce) jiggers.
1 (750-milliliter) bottle wine or champagne = 6 (4-ounce) servings.

Innovative Invitations

During the holiday season there are many parties, but this year make yours stand out from the array of festivities by designing your own invitations. An original invitation will instantly create excitement for your guests prior to the event and will also help reduce your party expenses. Making them is a fun holiday project for the entire family.

Set aside an evening when you and your family or friends will be able to make the invitations. Have all the materials on hand, along with some holiday goodies, such as eggnog, spiced tea, and a variety of Christmas cookies. Creative minds work better on a full stomach. Christmas carols playing in the background will put everyone in the holiday spirit.

Try one of the ideas below, or design your own invitation to welcome guests in a unique way.

When sending invitations, give guests two weeks' notice of the event (longer during the holidays).

Allow adequate time for mail delivery. Include an RSVP so that you will be able to plan accordingly.

Hand-Tinted Invitations

Materials: old Christmas cards, postcards, pastels, colored pencils, markers, colored paper, rubber cement, envelopes.

Start with old Christmas cards, or purchase antique Christmas postcards from an antique/junk store. Next, have the cards copied on colored paper, using different colors of ink for variety. (All paper must be able to go through a copy machine.) Reduce or enlarge the image to desired size. Then use pastels, colored pencils, or markers to add color to the card. Mount the image on a contrasting color of paper, leaving a ¼- to ½-inch border on all sides. Fill in party details on the back of the invitation. This is an easy way to update an old card with little expense. For fun, use a Christmas card from one of your guests a few years back. See if he/she recognizes your updated version.

Children's Puzzle Invitations

Materials: gift wrapping paper, colored paper, rubber cement, envelopes, felt-tip pen, scissors.

First, unroll wrapping paper, and choose a section that you think will make a nice puzzle. For best results, choose wrapping paper with a large design because the design will determine the size of the invitation. Next, cut out desired portion, and glue it to the colored paper, leaving a ¼- to ½-inch border on all sides. It will be much easier to read if you write all the party details in an area on the paper that has little design. Cut invitations into six to eight puzzle-shaped pieces, place in an envelope, and mail. Make sure all pieces are in the envelope; it could be crucial to guests' arrivals.

ON THE LIGHT SIDE

Simmer A Pot Of Soup

On a cold, wintry day nothing satisfies like a hot bowl of soup or stew. And both are excellent investments in healthful eating. When served as a first course, soup can blunt your appetite so that you won't overeat. As a main dish, stews and heartier soups offer a whole meal in a bowl at minimal calorie and fat costs.

To make soups and stews virtually free of fat, start with a fat-free broth or stock. Using lots of vegetables and only lean meats, poultry, or fish also keeps fat low. When the soup is ready, chill it thoroughly so that fat will congeal on top; then remove the hardened fat, and discard. You'll save about 100 calories for each tablespoon removed.

Simmering is one of the most important words in making soup because simmering develops a rich flavor. A simmer is the languid movement of heated liquid just before bubbles break to the surface. It extracts flavors from ingredients while cooking without allowing them to be broken in pieces.

Here we offer a variety of soups and stews for the holidays. Most are built on ready-to-serve, no-salt-added canned chicken broth. However, homemade stock may be substituted for canned broth if you're lucky enough to have it available. It will add extra flavor without additional calories or fat.

For Mexican taste in a soup try Mex-Tex Soup. Topped with Light Tortilla Chips, this recipe is sure to become a favorite.

MEX-TEX SOUP

1 cup chopped onion
1 cup chopped green pepper
1 cup chopped tomato
½ cup chopped fresh parsley
2 (10½-ounce) cans
    ready-to-serve, no-salt-added
    chicken broth
1 teaspoon dried whole oregano
1 teaspoon chili powder
¾ teaspoon ground cumin
¼ teaspoon salt
¼ teaspoon pepper
1 bay leaf
1 cup diced cooked chicken
    breast (skinned before cooking
    and cooked without salt)
2 tablespoons (½ ounce) shredded
    sharp 40%-less-fat Cheddar
    cheese
Light Tortilla Chips

Combine first 11 ingredients in a Dutch oven. Bring to a boil; cover, reduce heat, and simmer 30 minutes. Remove bay leaf, and stir in diced chicken; cook until soup is thoroughly heated.

Pour soup into individual serving bowls. Top each serving with shredded cheese and Light Tortilla Chips. Yield: 4 servings (144 calories per 1¼ cups soup, 2 tortilla chips, and ½ tablespoon cheese).

☐ *15.9 grams protein, 2.6 grams fat, 13.1 grams carbohydrate, 35 milligrams cholesterol, 264 milligrams sodium, and 82 milligrams calcium.*

Light Tortilla Chips

1 (6-inch) corn tortilla
Cold water

Dip tortilla in water; drain on paper towels. Using a pizza cutter or kitchen shears, cut tortilla into 8 triangles. Place triangles in a single layer on an ungreased baking sheet. Bake at 350° for 15 minutes or until chips are crisp and begin to brown. Remove from oven, and let cool. Yield: 4 servings (17 calories per triangle).

☐ *0.5 gram protein, 0.3 gram fat, 3.2 grams carbohydrate, 0 milligrams cholesterol, 13 milligrams sodium, and 11 milligrams calcium.*

CATFISH GUMBO
(pictured on page 261)

Vegetable cooking spray
1 cup chopped celery
1 cup chopped onion
1 cup chopped green pepper
2 cloves garlic, minced
3 (10½-ounce) cans
    ready-to-serve, no-salt-added
    chicken broth
2 (14½-ounce) cans no-salt-added
    tomatoes, undrained and
    chopped
1 (6-ounce) can low-sodium
    cocktail vegetable juice
2 bay leaves
1½ teaspoons salt
½ teaspoon pepper
½ teaspoon dried whole thyme
½ teaspoon hot sauce
1½ pounds farm-raised catfish
    fillets, cut into 1½-inch pieces
2 (10-ounce) packages frozen
    sliced okra, thawed
4 cups hot cooked rice (cooked
    without salt or fat)

Coat a Dutch oven with cooking spray; place over medium-high heat until hot. Add chopped celery, onion, green pepper, and minced garlic; sauté until crisp-tender.

Add chicken broth and next 7 ingredients. Bring mixture to a boil; cover, reduce heat, and simmer 30 minutes. Stir in fish and okra; cover and simmer 15 minutes.

Remove and discard bay leaves. Serve gumbo over hot cooked rice. Yield: 8 servings (304 calories per 1⅓-cup serving and ½ cup rice).

☐ *21.3 grams protein, 4.4 grams fat, 43.3 grams carbohydrate, 49 milligrams cholesterol, 534 milligrams sodium, 160 milligrams calcium.*

Terri L. Farmer
West, Mississippi

TURKEY-TOMATO STEW

2 (10½-ounce) cans
   ready-to-serve, no-salt-added
   chicken broth
1 (14½-ounce) can no-salt-added
   tomatoes, undrained and
   chopped
1 cup sliced carrots
1 cup sliced celery
½ cup chopped onion
1 clove garlic, minced
2 tablespoons no-salt-added
   tomato paste
1 teaspoon dried whole basil
½ teaspoon salt
¼ teaspoon pepper
3½ cups chopped, cooked turkey
   breast (skinned before cooking
   and cooked without salt)
1 (10-ounce) package frozen green
   peas

Combine first 10 ingredients in a Dutch oven. Bring to a boil; reduce heat, and simmer, uncovered, 30 minutes. Stir in turkey and peas; simmer an additional 15 minutes. Yield: 4 servings (252 calories per 1⅓-cup serving).

☐ *40 grams protein, 1.3 grams fat, 23.4 grams carbohydrate, 94 milligrams cholesterol, 489 milligrams sodium, and 102 milligrams calcium.*

Louise E. Ellis
Talbott, Tennessee

LIGHT MENU

Dinner For The Health-Conscious

Flavors reminiscent of the holidays abound in Individual Chicken Bake, the entrée for this health-minded menu. Make it with chicken breasts or leftover holiday turkey breast; they are both low in calories, fat, and cholesterol.

Individual Chicken Bake
New Potato Medley
Mixed Greens With
Blue Cheese Vinaigrette
Baked Apples à l'Orange

INDIVIDUAL CHICKEN BAKE
(pictured on page 260)

2 cups diced cooked chicken
   breast (skinned before cooking
   and cooked without salt)
¾ cup diced celery
¼ cup diced onion
1 (4-ounce) can sliced
   mushrooms, drained
1 cup evaporated skimmed milk
¼ cup egg substitute
1 tablespoon reduced-sodium
   Worcestershire sauce
½ teaspoon salt
¼ teaspoon white pepper
Vegetable cooking spray
⅓ cup whole-berry cranberry
   sauce

Combine first 9 ingredients; divide equally into six 6-ounce custard cups coated with cooking spray. Cover loosely with aluminum foil; bake at 350° for 50 minutes or until a knife inserted in center comes out clean. Uncover and let stand 5 minutes. Remove chicken from custard cups; top each serving with cranberry sauce. Yield: 6 servings (160 calories per serving).

☐ *20.9 grams protein, 2.3 grams fat, 13.4 grams carbohydrate, 46 milligrams cholesterol, 325 milligrams sodium, and 145 milligrams calcium.*

NEW POTATO MEDLEY
(pictured on page 260)

1 tablespoon reduced-calorie
   margarine
3 cups cubed new potatoes
1½ cups diagonally sliced carrots
1 cup chopped onion
¼ teaspoon salt
¼ teaspoon pepper

Melt reduced-calorie margarine in a large saucepan over medium heat. Add potatoes and remaining ingredients; toss gently. Cover, reduce heat, and cook 20 minutes, stirring once. Yield: 6 servings (105 calories per ¾-cup serving).

☐ *2.8 grams protein, 1.4 grams fat, 21.3 grams carbohydrate, 0 milligrams cholesterol, 135 milligrams sodium, and 30 milligrams calcium.*

Cathy Buetow Schroeder
Taylor, Texas

MIXED GREENS WITH BLUE CHEESE VINAIGRETTE

(pictured on page 260)

3 cups torn iceberg lettuce
3 cups torn romaine lettuce
2 cups torn Bibb lettuce
Blue Cheese Vinaigrette

Combine salad greens in a large bowl; divide evenly among 6 serving plates. Drizzle Blue Cheese Vinaigrette over greens. Yield: 6 servings (87 calories per 1½ cups lettuce and 2 tablespoons dressing).

☐ *2.7 grams protein, 7.5 grams fat, 3.1 grams carbohydrate, 5 milligrams cholesterol, 143 milligrams sodium, and 58 milligrams calcium.*

Blue Cheese Vinaigrette

¼ cup water
3 tablespoons vegetable oil
2 tablespoons white vinegar
2 tablespoons lemon juice
2 teaspoons Dijon mustard
1 teaspoon dried whole oregano
½ teaspoon sugar
½ teaspoon freshly ground black pepper
⅓ cup (2 ounces) crumbled blue cheese

Combine all ingredients in a jar; cover tightly, and shake vigorously. Chill thoroughly. Yield: 1 cup (38 calories per tablespoon).

☐ *0.8 gram protein, 3.7 grams fat, 0.6 gram carbohydrate, 3 milligrams cholesterol, 68 milligrams sodium, and 21 milligrams calcium.*

BAKED APPLES À L'ORANGE

6 medium-size cooking apples
¼ cup unsweetened apple juice
¼ cup water
1 tablespoon lemon juice
2 whole cloves
1 (4-inch) stick cinnamon, broken in half
⅓ cup reduced-calorie orange marmalade
6 small gingersnap cookies, crushed

Core apples to within ½ inch from bottom; peel top third of each apple. Place apples in a 12- x 8- x 2-inch baking dish; add apple juice and next 4 ingredients. Bake, uncovered, at 350° for 30 minutes, basting often with cooking liquid. Remove apples from oven; spoon equal amounts of marmalade into center of each apple, and sprinkle with gingersnap crumbs. Bake an additional 5 minutes or until apples are done. Yield: 6 servings (127 calories per serving).

☐ *0.9 gram protein, 1.9 grams fat, 29 grams carbohydrate, 3 milligrams cholesterol, 14 milligrams sodium, and 36 milligrams calcium.*

Decorate The Door Naturally

Dried seed pods, a dead tree limb, trimmings of shrubbery. That may sound like the start of a rubbish pile, but this collection of garden "debris" can be transformed into a stunning holiday arrangement for your table or your door. As Maloy Love, a Mountain Brook, Alabama, floral designer

says, "With a little imagination, you can use just about anything you gather from the garden and turn it into an arrangement."

The example illustrated here is for a door spray. And what better way to welcome guests into your home during the holiday season. Using a combination of fresh-cut and dried materials, Love demonstrates that making your own arrangement may not be as hard as it seems.

Gathering materials is the first step. A walk through your garden or neighboring woods should yield all the materials you will need. Keep an eye open for greenery, berries, pine cones, moss, interesting limbs, and seed pods. Let your imagination guide you, keeping in mind that what may seem mundane and unappealing on the garden floor can be striking as a focal point in an arrangement. For this door spray, Love chose Burford holly, white pine, magnolia, mahonia, cypress, pine cones, okra pods, and a lichen-covered tree branch.

To start, he used what is called a "cage." Available in many sizes and shapes, this is simply a block of florist foam that is held in an open-grid, plastic frame. It has a strip extending from the frame that allows you to hang the completed arrangement. Before you actually start arranging, be sure to soak the foam in water for several hours. Once the arrangement is complete, it will be difficult to wet the foam.

Love used stems of holly, magnolia, white pine, and mahonia to establish the basic form of the arrangement. "I used these for the 'bones' of the design to determine the length and width," Love says. "Nothing else extends beyond these branches." (Don't forget that most front doors are 36 inches wide, so scale the width of the arrangement accordingly.) The length you choose is largely a matter of taste. The door decoration shown here is about twice

as long as it is wide, but a more rounded or longer shape might suit your taste better.

With a basic triangular outline in place, Love used pieces of moss to help mask the cage and to form a solid background. (If you can't find moss in your garden, it is usually available from florists.) In this case, cypress was used to fill in the background and hold the moss in place.

"The next thing I wanted to do was add some interest with textures and colors," Love says. "I used a simple and loose X-shape of okra pods and pine cones." These items were wired to floral picks and then stuck into the cage. If you are a novice at this, experiment with different arrangements of materials until you come up with a look you like. With most of these items in place, Love then wired the lichen-covered branch to the center of the arrangement. The pale yellow shade of the lichens

To establish the basic outline of the arrangement, stems of evergreens are stuck into florist foam covered with a plastic frame.

Moss is used to cover the cage and to help fill in the background of the arrangement. Cypress is used to hold the moss in place.

Dried okra pods, pine cones, and a lichen-covered tree branch are placed on top of the evergreens to add interest with colors and texture.

serves as a striking accent against the rich evergreen foliage.

To dress up the arrangement even further, and to give it a more festive, holiday appearance, Love also added dried cockscomb and the bright-red berries of Japanese ardisia. Nandina, holly, or other berries will do as well. You may even consider visiting a florist for one or two special accents to add to the arrangement if your garden doesn't offer all the colors and textures you desire. Love added lotus seed pods to this arrangement as a finishing touch.

The completed holiday arrangement was wired to a doorknocker, but it could have been hung on a nail using the plastic strip that is part of the cage. The arrangement stands out about 8 inches from the face of the door, which is something to keep in mind as you make your door spray. "You need to keep door decorations pretty flat," Love notes, "That way people won't be bumping into it as they come and go."

Accent With Light

Add the special sparkle of the holidays to your home with lighting. A few small lights, carefully placed, can bring drama and depth to any room. Here are some tips on how to let lighting help set the holiday mood.

- The most important thing to remember is to balance the light throughout the room so that no area is too bright and glaring or too dark and uninviting. By adding several other light sources, you can make the room seem larger and more inviting.
- Control the light level of ceiling fixtures with rheostats or dimmer switches. These replace the standard wall switch and allow you to easily raise or lower the light level of the room. Dimmers are available at hardware and home center stores for under $10. Special dimmers are needed for three-way switches and for fluorescent lights. Small, plug-in dimmers are also available for use with floor or table lamps.
- Another way to lower the light from too-bright fixtures is by under-lamping. This simply means substituting lower wattage bulbs

in lamps and fixtures. For infrequently used lamps, this is a much less expensive option than adding a dimmer. Incandescent bulbs to fit standard medium-screw sockets are available in wattages as low as 7½.

- Add other light sources around the room to accent artwork or collections and to bring life to dark corners. Table or floor lamps can be used, as can inexpensive, clip-on picture lights. Miniature table lamps, sized to fit on shelves, can brighten bookcases or built-ins. Floor-mounted uplights can be hidden behind furniture or houseplants to dramatically accent a corner.
- Use small, clip-on shades to cut the glare of chandeliers and other fixtures with exposed bulbs. The shades are available in opaque paper, as well as in translucent paper or cloth that will let some of the light through.
- Candles are an excellent way to add accent lights for special occasions. Votive candles in glass cups are especially handy, since there is no danger of wax dripping onto tabletops. For safety,

never leave candles burning unattended, and always place them far enough from greenery, ribbons, curtains, or other flammables to prevent a fire hazard.

- In the dining room, add a pair of tall table lamps on the sideboard for extra light and easier serving. Make sure that the chandelier is hung at the correct height. For a room with an 8-foot-high ceiling, the bottom of the chandelier should be 30 inches above the table top. For a 9-foot ceiling, the distance should be 33 inches, and for a 10-foot ceiling, 36 inches.
- If your home has built-in lighting, such as recessed downlights or track lights that use reflector bulbs, consider trying the new tungsten-halogen bulbs. Available at electrical and lighting stores, these offer brighter, more focused light and reduced energy consumption. For example, you could use one of these bulbs to spotlight a painting or to provide a dramatic accent of light on a table. Some manufacturers offer these bulbs in spot as well as flood versions.

QUICK!

No-Fret Breads

If time is the only thing holding you back from serving freshly baked bread, try these recipes that can be made in a jiffy. Most start with biscuit mix, self-rising flour, or commercial bread to keep preparation time to a minimum. Family members will never guess you've scrimped on time, because there's no compromise in flavor.

ALMOND CRESCENT ROLLS

2 tablespoons butter or margarine, softened
¼ cup sifted powdered sugar
2 tablespoons fine, dry breadcrumbs
½ teaspoon almond extract
1 (8-ounce) package refrigerated crescent dinner rolls
Milk
2 tablespoons sliced almonds

Cream butter and powdered sugar; stir in breadcrumbs and almond extract. Set aside.

Separate crescent dough into 8 triangles. Spoon ½ tablespoon breadcrumb mixture on shortest side of triangle; roll according to package directions. Place rolls, point side down, on a lightly greased baking sheet. Brush with milk, and sprinkle with almonds. Bake at 375° for 11 to 13 minutes or until rolls are golden brown. Yield: 8 servings.
Eleanor K. Brandt
Arlington, Texas

MAYONNAISE ROLLS

1 cup self-rising flour
3 tablespoons mayonnaise or salad dressing
½ cup milk
¾ teaspoon sugar

Combine all ingredients, stirring just until dry ingredients are moistened. Spoon batter into greased muffin pans, filling three-fourths full. Bake at 425° for 15 minutes. Yield: ½ dozen.
Bettye Lewis
Morrison, Tennessee

QUICK GARLIC BREAD

1 (16-ounce) loaf unsliced French bread
½ cup butter or margarine, softened
1 tablespoon mayonnaise or salad dressing
2 tablespoons grated Parmesan cheese
¼ teaspoon garlic powder
¼ teaspoon paprika

Cut French bread in half lengthwise. Combine butter and remaining ingredients; spread on cut sides of bread. Broil 4 inches from heat 4 to 5 minutes. Yield: 1 loaf.
Fredee Carr
New Braunfels, Texas

LIGHTNIN' CHEESE BISCUITS

2 cups biscuit mix
⅔ cup (2.6 ounces) finely shredded Cheddar cheese
½ cup water

Combine all ingredients in a medium bowl, stirring just until dry ingredients are moistened. Turn dough out onto a well-floured surface, and knead 15 to 20 times. Pat dough to ½-inch thickness; cut with a 2½-inch biscuit cutter. Place biscuits on a lightly greased baking sheet. Bake at 450° for 8 to 10 minutes or until lightly browned. Yield: ½ dozen.
Gerry Spradlin
Russellville, Arkansas

EASY HERB BISCUITS

2 cups biscuit mix
1 tablespoon freeze-dried chives
1 teaspoon dried parsley flakes
¾ cup plain yogurt

Combine all ingredients in a medium bowl, stirring just until dry ingredients are moistened. Turn dough out onto a floured surface, and knead lightly 4 or 5 times.

Roll dough to ½-inch thickness; cut with a 2-inch biscuit cutter. Place biscuits on a lightly greased baking sheet. Bake at 450° for 8 minutes or until biscuits are lightly browned. Yield: 1 dozen. *Patsy Bell Hobson*
Liberty, Missouri

SOUR CREAM MUFFINS

½ cup butter, softened
1 (8-ounce) carton sour cream
2 cups biscuit mix

Cream butter; stir in sour cream. Gradually add biscuit mix, stirring just until dry ingredients are moistened. Spoon into lightly greased miniature (1¾-inch) muffin pans, filling two-thirds full. Bake at 350° for 15 minutes or until lightly browned. Yield: 3 dozen.

Note: Muffins can be made in regular muffin pans. Bake at 350° for 20 minutes. Yield: 1 dozen. *Sue Rives*
Cleveland, Mississippi

A Passion For Pound Cake

Many of us stake our prowess in the kitchen on the golden favorite, the pound cake. If you're hungry for pound cake, try these outstanding recipes from three of our readers. They passed the strictest tests in our kitchens, and our home economists and foods editors have given them their stamp of approval. For more information and tips on how to make the perfect pound cake, please see page 285.

WHIPPING CREAM POUND CAKE

1 cup butter or margarine, softened
3 cups sugar
6 eggs
3 cups sifted cake flour
1 cup whipping cream
1 teaspoon vanilla extract
½ teaspoon orange extract

Cream butter; gradually add sugar, beating well at medium speed of an electric mixer. Add eggs, one at a time, beating after each addition.

Add flour to creamed mixture, alternately with whipping cream, beginning and ending with flour. Mix just until blended after each addition. Stir in flavorings.

Pour batter into 2 greased and floured 9- x 5- x 3-inch loafpans. Bake at 325° for 1 hour or until a wooden pick inserted in center comes out clean. Cool cakes in pans 10 to 15 minutes; remove from pans, and cool on a wire rack. Yield: 2 loaves.

Note: Cake may be baked in a greased and floured 10-inch tube pan. Bake at 325° for 1 hour and 30 minutes or until a wooden pick inserted near center comes out clean. Cool as directed above. *Pauletta McKenzie Blountville, Tennessee*

CHOCOLATE POUND CAKE WITH FROSTING

1 cup shortening
3 cups sugar
6 eggs
2⅔ cups all-purpose flour
½ teaspoon baking powder
¼ teaspoon salt
⅓ cup cocoa
1 cup milk
1 teaspoon vanilla extract
Chocolate Frosting (optional)

Cream shortening; gradually add sugar, beating well at medium speed of an electric mixer. Add eggs, one at a time, beating after each addition.

Combine flour and next 3 ingredients; add to mixture alternately with milk, beginning and ending with flour mixture. Mix just until blended after each addition. Stir in vanilla.

Pour batter into a greased and floured 10-inch tube pan. Bake at 325° for 1 hour and 25 to 30 minutes or until a wooden pick inserted near center comes out clean. Cool in pan 10 minutes; remove from pan, and let cool completely on a wire rack. Spread with Chocolate Frosting, if desired. Yield: one 10-inch cake.

Chocolate Frosting

1 cup sugar
¼ cup butter or margarine
⅓ cup evaporated milk
½ cup semisweet chocolate morsels
½ teaspoon vanilla extract

Combine first 3 ingredients in a small saucepan; bring to a boil, and boil 1 minute, stirring occasionally. Stir in chocolate morsels and vanilla. Beat with a wooden spoon about 3 minutes or to desired spreading consistency. Yield: 1¼ cups.

Helen Dosier Sparta, North Carolina

GOLDEN POUND CAKE

½ cup butter or margarine, softened
½ cup shortening
3 cups sugar
5 eggs
2¾ cups all-purpose flour
½ teaspoon baking powder
½ teaspoon salt
1 cup milk
1 teaspoon vanilla extract
½ teaspoon lemon extract

Cream butter and shortening; gradually add sugar, beating well at medium speed of an electric mixer. Add eggs, one at a time, beating after each addition.

Combine flour, baking powder, and salt; add to creamed mixture alternately with milk, beginning and ending with flour mixture. Mix just until blended. Stir in flavorings.

Pour batter into a greased and floured 12-cup Bundt pan. Bake at 325° for 1 hour and 15 minutes or until a wooden pick inserted near center comes out clean. Cool in pan 10 to 15 minutes; remove from pan, and let cool completely on a wire rack. Yield: one 10-inch cake.

Note: To determine the size of a Bundt pan, measure the amount of water it holds. *Ann M. Johnston Spartanburg, South Carolina*

Tip: *To measure shortening, use the easy water-displacement method if the water that clings to the shortening will not affect the product. (Keep in mind this important point: Do not use this method for measuring shortening for frying.) To measure ¼ cup shortening using this method, put ¾ cup water in a measuring cup; then add shortening until the water reaches the 1-cup level. Just be sure that the shortening is completely covered with water. Drain off the water before using the shortening.*

Making The Best Pound Cakes

Around the Test Kitchens, we know that some of our home economists have a special touch with pound cakes. Follow their tips to ensure that your cake is as delicious as those on page 284.

Cream That Butter; Add Eggs

The most important step in pound cake-making is creaming the butter or shortening with an electric mixer. The air whipped into a cake during creaming makes the cake rise during baking.

Beat the butter until soft and creamy, about 2 minutes. Gradually add the sugar, beating at medium speed. The amount of time we cream the butter and sugar is approximately 5 to 10 minutes. Use the upper end of the time range with a hand mixer, the middle of the range with a stand mixer, and 5 minutes with a heavy-duty mixer.

Add eggs, one at a time, and blend just until the yellow disappears (about 30 seconds). We use large eggs for our recipe testing. Overmixing during this stage incorporates too much air, causing the cake to overflow and fall.

Different Flours For Different Recipes

Two kinds of flour are used in these pound cake recipes—cake flour and all-purpose flour. Cake flour is milled from soft wheat and yields a soft, fine texture.

All-purpose flour is milled from both hard wheat and soft wheat and yields a taller, firmer cake. Some all-purpose flours milled in the South are from soft wheat, which makes them comparable to cake flour. If a recipe calls for all-purpose flour, we use national brands.

The bonus of using all-purpose flour is that it doesn't need to be sifted; cake flour does need sifting. If you find yourself out of flour, don't attempt to substitute self-rising flour for all-purpose flour. To substitute all-purpose flour for cake flour, use 1 cup minus 2 tablespoons of all-purpose flour for the equivalent 1 cup of cake flour.

Whatever flour is used, add the flour mixture alternately with the liquid, beating at low speed of an electric mixer. Be sure to begin and end with the flour mixture, beating only until each addition is blended into the batter.

Preparing the Pan

Greasing and flouring the pan prevents the cake from sticking. Use solid shortening for greasing rather than butter, margarine, or vegetable cooking spray.

On a wire rack, cool pound cake, right side up, in the pan 10 to 15 minutes. Remove the cake from pan, and cool completely on a wire rack. Keep the cake away from drafts so that it won't fall.

A Guide to Solving Pound Cake Dilemmas

Problem	Possible Cause
Batter overflows	-Too much batter in pan -Overmixing
Sticky crust	-Too much sugar -Underbaking
Damp cake	-Cooled too long in pan -Underbaking
Tough crust	-Overmixing -Not enough sugar, fat or leavening
Sinking in center	-Underbaking -Removed from pan too soon -Exposed to draft during baking or cooling -Too much liquid, leavening, or sugar
Heavy texture	-Not enough leavening -Old baking powder or baking soda -Overmixing -Wrong baking temperature -Too much fat, sugar, or liquid
Crust too brown on bottom	-Use of dark baking pan -Pan placed too low in oven
Cake falls	-Insufficient baking -Oven temperature too low (check oven temperature with oven thermometer) -Removed from pan too soon

Choose A Better Salad

It's easy to fall into the habit of making the same kind of salad every time—iceberg lettuce, sliced tomatoes, and croutons, for example. But with a little imagination and variation, salad can play a significant role on the menu, and it can even be a meal in itself. Refer to our chart below about options, and design a different salad every time.

Iceberg lettuce is often chosen for salads because it keeps well and has a pleasing texture. But it's nice to team other salad greens with this familiar one to offer variation in color and texture. Two or three different types of salad greens make a nice combination.

Fruits and vegetables add color, texture, nutrients, and fiber to a salad. Combine two or three fruits or two or three vegetables with salad greens. Be careful to choose fruits and vegetables that go together well—for example, pineapple and green pepper or orange slices and green onions.

Pick one or two of the foods listed in the protein category to turn the salad into a main dish. Adding just two ounces of protein per person will make the salad a meal. And don't forget one or two toppings; they add color and texture.

BLUE CHEESE DRESSING

1 (3-ounce) package cream
  cheese, softened
1½ ounces crumbled blue cheese
1 (8-ounce) carton sour cream
1 teaspoon lemon juice
½ teaspoon onion salt
2 tablespoons milk

Combine cream cheese and blue cheese; stir in sour cream and remaining ingredients. Cover and chill at least 2 hours. Yield: 1½ cups.

Jeanne S. Hotaling
Augusta, Georgia

CREAMY FRENCH DRESSING

⅔ cup catsup
½ cup white vinegar
¼ cup sugar
2½ teaspoons dry mustard
1 teaspoon salt
¾ teaspoon pepper
1 teaspoon Worcestershire sauce
1 cup vegetable oil

Combine all ingredients except oil in container of an electric blender; process until smooth. Add oil, ¼ cup at a time, processing after each addition. Cover and chill at least 2 hours. Yield: 2 cups. *Nina L. Andrews*
Tappahannock, Virginia

GREEK SALAD DRESSING

1½ cups olive oil
¼ cup white vinegar
¼ cup fresh lemon juice
¼ teaspoon salt
½ teaspoon pepper
1 tablespoon dried whole
  oregano
2 small cloves garlic, minced

Combine all ingredients in a jar; cover tightly, and shake vigorously. Chill salad dressing at least 2 hours. Shake dressing again just before serving. Yield: 2 cups.

Betty Watts
Panama City, Florida

The Makings of a Good Green Salad

Take your choice of foods from several categories of salad ingredients to personalize a salad. The options are almost endless with a little imagination.

Greens	Vegetables	Fruits	Protein	Toppings
Bibb	Artichoke hearts	Apple	Beef	Bacon bits
Boston	Beans	Avocado	Cheese	Bean sprouts
Cabbage	Beets	Banana	Chicken	Chinese noodles
Endive	Broccoli	Blueberries	Crabmeat	Chopped chives
Escarole	Carrot	Grapefruit	Egg	Croutons
Iceberg	Cauliflower	Grapes	Ham	Mushrooms
Kale	Celery	Kiwifruit	Shrimp	Olives
Oakleaf	Cucumber	Melon	Tuna	Raisins
Radicchio	Onion	Orange		Sesame seeds
Romaine	Radishes	Peach		Sieved egg yolk
Sorrel	Snow pea pods	Pear		Sunflower kernels
Spinach	Sweet pepper	Pineapple		Toasted coconut
Swiss chard	Tomato	Raspberries		Toasted nuts
Watercress	Zucchini	Strawberries		Trail mix

Tasty Turkey Soup

When you come in from a nippy day outdoors, few foods are as inviting as a steaming bowl of soup. And this recipe takes advantage of leftover holiday turkey. Serve creamy Williamsburg Turkey Soup with cornbread or French bread for a tasty meal that's sure to satisfy big appetites. And it makes enough to feed a crowd.

WILLIAMSBURG TURKEY SOUP

1 turkey carcass
4 quarts water
1 cup butter or margarine
1 cup all-purpose flour
3 onions, chopped
2 large carrots, diced
2 stalks celery, diced
1 cup long-grain rice, uncooked
2 teaspoons salt
¾ teaspoon pepper
2 cups half-and-half

Place turkey carcass and water in a large Dutch oven; bring to a boil. Cover, reduce heat, and simmer 1 hour. Remove carcass from broth, and pick meat from bones. Set broth and meat aside. Measure broth; add water to broth, if necessary, to measure 3 quarts.

Heat butter in Dutch oven; add flour, and cook over medium heat, stirring constantly, 5 minutes. (Roux will be a very light color.)

Stir chopped onion, diced carrot, and celery into roux; cook over medium heat 10 minutes, stirring often. Add reserved 3 quarts broth, turkey, rice, salt, and pepper; bring mixture to a boil. Cover, reduce heat, and simmer 20 minutes or until rice is tender. Add half-and-half, and cook until soup is thoroughly heated. Yield: 4½ quarts. *Rhea Hatch*
Birmingham, Alabama

Crimson Cranberries

You can't judge a book by its cover, but you can tell a good cranberry by its bounce. That's the theory a long-ago schoolteacher was testing when he tossed cranberries down a flight of stairs and watched the firm ones reach the bottom while the undesirable, soft ones failed to make the steep grade. Processors still use the scholar's idea today, sorting the native North American fruit on small, sanitary, wooden barriers and passing on an assortment of cranberry products to you.

Here we suggest hot, baked casseroles and sweet, chilled salads as holiday side dishes, but don't let that limit your imagination. These ruby-red treasures are great for breads, pies, sauces, and beverages, to name a few. They also come in handy for garnishing. For festive color on your holiday table, place roasted turkey or pork on a serving platter lined with greens or lettuce. Dip fresh cranberries in egg white and then in sugar for a frosted look, and arrange in clusters on the greens.

CRANBERRY-MUSTARD FRUIT BAKE

1 (16-ounce) can pear halves
1 (16-ounce) can peach halves
1 (17-ounce) can apricot halves
1 (20-ounce) can pineapple slices
¼ cup butter or margarine
⅔ cup firmly packed brown sugar
3 to 4 tablespoons Dijon mustard
1 (16-ounce) can whole-berry cranberry sauce

Drain fruit; cut pear, peach, and apricot halves in half, and pineapple slices into quarters. Combine fruit in a 12- x 8- x 2-inch baking dish; set dish aside.

Melt butter in a small saucepan; add brown sugar and mustard. Cook over low heat until sugar dissolves. Add cranberry sauce, and simmer, uncovered, 5 minutes. Spoon cranberry mixture over fruit. Bake, uncovered, at 325° for 30 minutes or until thoroughly heated. Yield: 12 servings.

Microwave Directions: Drain fruit; cut pear, peach, and apricot halves in half, and pineapple slices into quarters. Combine fruit in a 12- x 8- x 2-inch baking dish; set aside.

Place butter in a 4-cup glass measure. Microwave at HIGH 55 seconds or until melted. Add brown sugar, mustard, and cranberry sauce; microwave at HIGH 2 to 3 minutes or until thoroughly heated. Spoon cranberry mixture over fruit. Microwave, uncovered, at HIGH 7 to 8 minutes or until thoroughly heated.
Shirley M. Draper
Winter Park, Florida

CRANBERRY CLOUD

2 cups fresh cranberries
2 cups miniature marshmallows
¾ cup sugar
2 cups unpeeled, cubed green apple
½ cup seedless green grapes
½ cup coarsely chopped walnuts, toasted
1 cup whipping cream, whipped
Lettuce leaves

Position knife blade in food processor bowl; add cranberries. Cover with lid, and process until coarsely ground. Combine cranberries, marshmallows, and sugar in a large bowl; stir gently. Cover and chill at least 1½ hours.

Add apple, grapes, and walnuts; stir gently. Fold in whipped cream; cover and chill at least 1 hour. Serve on lettuce leaves. Yield: 6 to 8 servings. *Donna Tolin*
Bartlesville, Oklahoma

FROSTED CRANBERRY SALAD

1 (15¼-ounce) can unsweetened, crushed pineapple, undrained
1 (6-ounce) package lemon-flavored gelatin
1 (16-ounce) can whole-berry cranberry sauce
1 cup ginger ale
1 cup chopped celery
1 (8-ounce) package cream cheese, softened
1 (8-ounce) container frozen whipped topping, thawed
½ cup chopped pecans, toasted

Drain pineapple, reserving juice; set pineapple aside. Add enough water to juice to measure 2 cups. Bring to boil, and remove from heat. Add gelatin, stirring until gelatin dissolves. Add cranberry sauce, stirring until blended. Stir in ginger ale. Chill until the consistency of unbeaten egg white; fold in reserved pineapple and celery. Spoon mixture into a lightly oiled 13- x 9- x 2-inch dish; cover and chill until firm.

Beat cream cheese at medium speed of electric mixer until light and fluffy; fold in whipped topping. Spread mixture evenly over salad, and sprinkle with pecans. Cover and chill until firm. Yield: 15 servings.

Mrs. Thomas F. Everett
Blackville, South Carolina

Elegant Charlotte Russe

"I can't remember a Christmas or Thanksgiving without Charlotte Russe," says Mrs. Ansel Wheeler of Montgomery. "I guess we have it 'cause Momma liked it. And you know, I can remember when the men wouldn't eat it. Now some of them clean the bowl."

Serving Charlotte Russe is a holiday tradition for many Southern families. Several readers shared their "very old family recipe"; most were very similar to Mrs. Wheeler's, differing only in the amount of sugar and the type of liquor. Bourbon and sherry are used most often, but rum was mentioned as well. Some families choose to flavor the creamy custard with vanilla or almond extract, rather than liquor.

CHARLOTTE RUSSE

1 envelope unflavored gelatin
½ cup cold water
4 eggs, separated
1 cup sugar
¼ cup bourbon
2 cups whipping cream
17 to 20 ladyfingers
Garnishes: candied violets, fresh mint

Sprinkle gelatin over cold water in a small saucepan; let stand 1 minute. Cook over low heat until gelatin dissolves; cool slightly.

Beat egg yolks and sugar in a large bowl at medium speed of an electric mixer until thick and lemon colored. Stir in bourbon. Gradually add dissolved gelatin, stirring constantly.

Beat egg whites (at room temperature) until stiff, but not dry. Fold into yolk mixture. Beat whipping cream until soft peaks form. Fold into egg mixture.

Split ladyfingers in half lengthwise; line a 3-quart glass bowl with ladyfingers. Pour in filling; cover and chill at least 8 hours. Garnish, if desired. Yield: 10 to 12 servings.

Mrs. Ansel Wheeler
Montgomery, Alabama

PINEAPPLE CHARLOTTE

1 (15¼-ounce) can sliced pineapple, undrained
¼ cup sugar
1 tablespoon cornstarch
2½ cups milk
4 egg yolks, beaten
1 envelope unflavored gelatin
2 egg whites
1½ cups whipping cream
3 tablespoons sugar
1 (3-ounce) package ladyfingers

Drain pineapple, reserving ⅔ cup juice. Chop pineapple slices, reserving 5 slices for garnish.

Combine ¼ cup sugar and cornstarch in a heavy saucepan; add milk and egg yolks. Cook over medium heat, stirring constantly, until mixture comes to a boil. Boil 1 minute.

Sprinkle gelatin over reserved pineapple juice; let stand 1 minute. Slowly stir into custard mixture. Cool to room temperature.

Beat egg whites (at room temperature) until stiff peaks form. Beat whipping cream until foamy; gradually add 3 tablespoons sugar, beating until soft peaks form. Reserve about 2 cups whipped cream. Fold remaining whipped cream, beaten egg whites, and chopped pineapple into custard mixture.

Split ladyfingers in half lengthwise; line a 2½-quart glass bowl with ladyfingers. Pour in filling; cover and chill at least 8 hours. Garnish with reserved whipped cream and pineapple slices. Yield: 8 to 10 servings.

Rublelene Singleton
Scotts Hill, Tennessee

Tip: *Raw eggs separate more easily while still cold from the refrigerator, but let whites reach room temperature in order to get maximum volume when beating.*

DECEMBER

Christmastime inspires entertaining. And whether you're hosting an open house, a luncheon, or a dinner, a special occasion deserves a special finale. Choose from our collection of 25 all-time favorite desserts, including the Hummingbird Cake, the most frequently requested Southern Living *recipe. This sampler of desserts includes cakes and pies, cookies and candies, each spectacular enough to earn rave reviews at any gathering. With all of these outstanding recipes, why not plan a dessert buffet? It just may become your favorite form of holiday entertaining.*

Side Dishes With A Holiday Dash

Here's the formula for a successful holiday meal. Simply select your favorite entrée—perhaps a turkey, pork loin roast, or beef tenderloin—and add a crunchy salad, two or more fruits or vegetables, bread, and a delectable dessert. Now, what to choose for the side dishes? These recipes offer a wide variety of color and flavor.

When planning a menu, remember to include an array of colors, shapes, and textures. For example, cut carrots in julienne strips or slice them on the diagonal if you already have something round on the plate. When one vegetable is a starch—Garlic-Parsley Potatoes, for instance—select a vegetable such as asparagus, carrots, or green beans to serve alongside it. If Holiday Sweet Potato Bake or another side dish with a mashed vegetable is on the menu, pair it with a firm vegetable or fruit salad to vary the texture.

Not every dish has to be a fancy recipe. If a menu already has a wide array of flavors, simply add a steamed vegetable, such as zucchini, or a simple green salad to serve alongside some of the recipes here.

Remember to garnish, too, especially for holiday meals. Asparagus With Cream Sauce is a delicate, lightly flavored recipe that deserves a garnish with just a hint of color. Simply twist pimiento into a rosette and add a parsley sprig to make the dish look extra special. Cherry tomatoes, lemon or lime slices, and watercress are also easy garnishes to add in a moment's time.

CALICO SQUASH CASSEROLE

1 pound yellow squash, sliced
½ pound zucchini, sliced
1 cup water
½ cup chopped onion
¼ cup chopped green pepper
3 tablespoons chopped green onions
¼ cup butter or margarine, melted and divided
1 cup herb-seasoned stuffing mix
1 (10¾-ounce) can cream of chicken soup, undiluted
1 (8-ounce) can water chestnuts, drained and chopped
½ cup plain low-fat yogurt
¼ cup chopped pimiento
1 large carrot, grated
½ teaspoon salt
¼ teaspoon pepper

Combine first 3 ingredients in a medium saucepan; bring to a boil. Cover, reduce heat, and simmer 8 minutes or until squash is tender. Drain and set aside.

Sauté onion, green pepper, and green onions in 1 tablespoon butter until tender; set aside.

Combine stuffing mix and remaining 3 tablespoons butter in a large bowl; reserve ⅓ cup mixture.

Combine squash mixture, onion mixture, soup, and remaining ingredients; spoon mixture into a lightly greased 12- x 8- x 2-inch baking dish. Sprinkle with reserved stuffing mixture. Bake at 350° for 30 minutes or until casserole is thoroughly heated. Yield: 6 to 8 servings.

Betty J. Casey
Montgomery, Alabama

GARLIC-PARSLEY POTATOES

3 pounds medium-size red potatoes, unpeeled and sliced
¼ cup olive oil
8 cloves garlic, minced
1 teaspoon salt
½ teaspoon freshly ground pepper
2 tablespoons chopped fresh parsley, divided

Combine first 5 ingredients; toss to coat well. Layer half of mixture in a lightly greased 12- x 8- x 2-inch dish. Sprinkle with half of parsley. Layer remaining mixture. Cover and bake at 350° for 45 minutes or until tender. Uncover; sprinkle with remaining parsley. Yield: 8 servings.

Elizabeth M. Haney
Dublin, Virginia

HOLIDAY SWEET POTATO BAKE

2 (16-ounce) cans cut sweet
   potatoes, drained
⅓ cup evaporated milk
⅓ cup apricot brandy or brandy
¼ cup butter or margarine,
   melted
2 tablespoons brown sugar
1 teaspoon ground cinnamon
¼ teaspoon salt
1 (15¼-ounce) can crushed
   pineapple, drained
1 cup chopped pecans, divided
½ cup golden raisins
½ cup flaked coconut
1 cup miniature marshmallows

Combine first 7 ingredients in a mixing bowl; beat at low speed of an
electric mixer until blended. Stir in
pineapple, ½ cup pecans, raisins, and
coconut; spoon into a lightly greased
8-inch square baking dish. Sprinkle
with remaining ½ cup pecans. Bake
at 350° for 25 minutes; sprinkle with
marshmallows, and bake an additional
5 minutes. Yield: 8 servings.
Linda Creek
Jasper, Tennessee

MUSTARD FRUIT BAKE

1 (16-ounce) can sliced peaches,
   drained
1 (15¼-ounce) can pineapple
   chunks, drained
½ cup pitted prunes (optional)
½ cup firmly packed brown sugar
¼ cup butter or margarine
2 teaspoons prepared mustard
2 medium bananas, cut into
   1-inch slices

Combine sliced peaches, pineapple
chunks, and, if desired, prunes in a
lightly greased 8-inch square baking
dish. Combine brown sugar, butter,
and mustard in a small saucepan;
cook over low heat until butter
melts, stirring constantly. Pour mixture over fruit. Bake, uncovered, at

350° for 25 minutes. Stir in bananas,
and bake an additional 5 minutes.
Serve immediately. Yield: 6 to 8
servings.
Eugenia W. Bell
Louisville, Kentucky

CRANBERRY RING

2 (3-ounce) packages
   raspberry-flavored gelatin
3 cups boiling water
1 (16-ounce) can whole-berry
   cranberry sauce
¼ teaspoon ground cinnamon
⅛ teaspoon ground cloves
2 tablespoons grated orange rind
2 oranges, peeled, sectioned, and
   diced
1 Red Delicious apple, unpeeled
   and diced

Dissolve gelatin in boiling water in a
large bowl; add cranberry sauce and
next 3 ingredients, stirring until
blended. Chill mixture until the consistency of unbeaten egg white. Fold
in fruit. Pour mixture into a lightly
oiled 6-cup ring mold; cover and chill
until firm. Yield: 10 to 12 servings.
Dorothy C. Taylor
Palm City, Florida

MINT-GLAZED CARROTS AND PEAS

1 pound carrots, scraped and
   thinly sliced
2 tablespoons butter or margarine
¼ cup sugar
1 to 2 tablespoons jellied mint
   sauce
⅛ teaspoon pepper
1 (10-ounce) package frozen
   English peas, thawed
1 tablespoon chopped fresh
   parsley (optional)

Cook carrots in boiling water to
cover 5 minutes. Drain and set aside.

Combine butter, sugar, jellied mint
sauce, and pepper in a medium
saucepan; cook over low heat, stirring constantly, 1 minute or until
sugar dissolves. Gently stir in carrots
and peas; cook over low heat, uncovered, 6 minutes or until carrots are
crisp-tender, stirring occasionally.
Spoon into a serving bowl; sprinkle
with parsley, if desired. Yield: 6
servings.
Suzan L. Wiener
Spring Hill, Florida

ASPARAGUS WITH CREAM SAUCE

2 pounds fresh asparagus spears
1 tablespoon butter or margarine
1½ tablespoons all-purpose flour
½ cup chicken broth
½ cup half-and-half
2 tablespoons Dijon mustard
1 teaspoon fresh lemon juice
¼ teaspoon freshly ground pepper
Garnishes: pimiento rose, fresh
   parsley sprig

Snap off tough ends of asparagus; remove scales from stalks with a knife
or vegetable peeler, if desired.
Cover and cook asparagus in a small
amount of boiling water 6 to 8 minutes or until crisp-tender; drain. Arrange in a serving dish; keep warm.

  Melt butter in a small saucepan
over low heat; add flour, stirring until
smooth. Cook 1 minute, stirring constantly. Gradually add chicken broth
and half-and-half; cook over medium
heat, stirring constantly, until thickened and bubbly. Stir in mustard,
lemon juice, and pepper. Spoon over
asparagus. Garnish, if desired. Yield:
8 servings.
Gwen Louer
Roswell, Georgia

SESAME SPINACH SALAD

¼ cup vegetable oil
2 tablespoons white wine vinegar
2 tablespoons chopped fresh
  parsley
1 teaspoon Beau Monde seasoning
¼ teaspoon salt
¼ teaspoon pepper
¼ teaspoon dried whole summer
  savory
1 pound spinach
1 tablespoon sesame seeds,
  toasted
1 cup croutons

Combine first 7 ingredients in a jar; cover tightly, and shake vigorously.

Remove stems from spinach; wash leaves thoroughly, and pat dry. Tear into bite-size pieces. Combine spinach and sesame seeds in a bowl; add dressing, and toss gently. Sprinkle with croutons. Yield: 4 to 6 servings.   *Rosemarie Eggenberger*
Aiken, South Carolina

BROCCOLI SALAD

½ cup sour cream
⅓ cup mayonnaise or salad
  dressing
3 tablespoons apple-cider vinegar
¾ teaspoon celery seeds
¾ teaspoon dry mustard
¼ teaspoon salt
Pinch of white pepper
1½ pounds fresh broccoli
1 bunch green onions, cut into
  ½-inch pieces
1 cup pimiento-stuffed olives,
  sliced
1 (8-ounce) can sliced water
  chestnuts, drained

Combine first 7 ingredients in a small bowl; set aside.

Trim off large leaves of broccoli, and remove tough ends of lower stalks; wash broccoli thoroughly. Cut stalks into ¼-inch slices. Cut remaining broccoli into flowerets; place in a large salad bowl. Add green onions and remaining ingredients. Pour dressing over top; toss gently to coat. Cover and chill 1 hour. Yield: 8 to 10 servings.   *Louise McGrotha*
Columbus, Georgia

QUICK!

Easy Appetizers

Whether you're taking an appetizer to a holiday gathering or serving one to guests in your home, ease of preparation is an important consideration. Here are several recipes that can be made with minimal effort yet yield maximum rewards.

Delectable Chutney-Bacon Brie can be heated in either a microwave or conventional oven. Serve it with a variety of unsalted crackers or apple and pear wedges.

SUPER SEAFOOD DIP

1 (7-ounce) can medium-size
  shrimp, drained
1 (4-ounce) can sliced ripe olives,
  drained
1 hard-cooked egg, finely chopped
1½ cups sour cream
⅓ cup picante sauce
2 teaspoons lemon juice
1 (0.6-ounce) package Italian
  salad dressing mix

Combine all ingredients; serve with pita or bagel chips. Yield: 2¾ cups.
Ranae Phelps
Dallas, Texas

CRABMEAT-HORSERADISH SPREAD

1 (8-ounce) package cream
  cheese, softened
2 to 3 tablespoons picante sauce
2 teaspoons prepared horseradish
1 (6¼-ounce) can crabmeat,
  drained

Combine first 3 ingredients; beat at medium speed of an electric mixer until smooth. Stir in crabmeat. Serve spread with assorted crackers. Yield: 1½ cups.   *Edna Hamilton*
Jefferson, Texas

CHUTNEY-BACON BRIE

1 (15-ounce) mini-Brie
½ cup chutney
¼ cup bacon bits

Remove rind from top of cheese, cutting to within ½ inch of outside edges. Place cheese on a microwave-safe dish, and spread chutney over top; sprinkle with bacon bits. Microwave, uncovered, at HIGH 1½ to 2 minutes or until Brie softens to desired consistency, giving dish a half-turn after 1 minute. Serve with unsalted crackers or fruit. Yield: 12 to 15 appetizer servings.

Conventional Directions: Prepare as directed, except to bake at 325° for 20 minutes in a quiche dish.
Cynthia Altman
Johnsonville, South Carolina

MEXICAN ARTICHOKE DIP

1 (14-ounce) can artichoke
  hearts, drained and chopped
1 (4-ounce) can chopped green
  chiles, undrained
1 cup grated Parmesan cheese
1 cup mayonnaise or salad
  dressing

Combine all ingredients; spoon into a lightly greased 1-quart baking dish. Bake at 350° for 15 to 20 minutes or until mixture is thoroughly heated. Serve immediately with tortilla chips. Yield: 3 cups.

Microwave Directions: Combine all ingredients; spoon into a lightly greased 1-quart baking dish. Cover with wax paper; microwave at ME-DIUM (50% power) 7 to 8 minutes or until mixture is thoroughly heated, stirring twice.   *Sondra J. Green*
Midlothian, Virginia

HEARTS OF PALM SPREAD

1 (14-ounce) can hearts of palm, drained and chopped
1 cup (4 ounces) shredded mozzarella cheese
¾ cup mayonnaise or salad dressing
½ cup grated Parmesan cheese
¼ cup sour cream
2 tablespoons minced green onions

Combine all ingredients; spoon into a lightly greased 9-inch quiche dish. Bake at 350° for 20 minutes or until bubbly. Serve with crackers. Yield: about 2 cups.

Microwave Directions: Combine all ingredients; spoon into a lightly greased 9-inch quiche dish. Cover with wax paper; microwave at ME-DIUM (50% power) 7 to 8 minutes or until thoroughly heated, stirring once halfway through cooking time.
Ursula Hennessy
Springfield, Virginia

Cranberries: Jewels Of The Season

What would the holidays be like without cranberries? Less nutritious for one thing. Ruby-red cranberries add dietary fiber, potassium, and vitamin C to dishes without adding many calories. In addition, these plump little bundles are loaded with character, color, and flavor.

The natural tartness of cranberries can be tamed with sugar—though not too much or it will detract from their distinctive flavor. Cooking them with other naturally sweet fruits, such as apples, oranges, or bananas, subdues the sourness of cranberries while leaving a tangy taste.

As cranberries cook, their skins burst to reveal the fruit inside. Their high pectin content makes them thicken and gel as they cool, thus omitting the need for a thickening agent in many cases.

It seems a shame to relegate cranberries to only one season. Try freezing several packages for use throughout the year, or refrigerate them for up to four months.

CRANBERRY PORK

1 cup chopped fresh cranberries
¼ cup cranberry juice cocktail
3 tablespoons brown sugar
1 teaspoon grated orange rind
½ teaspoon ground allspice
4 (4-ounce) boneless pork loin chops
Vegetable cooking spray

Combine first 5 ingredients in a small saucepan. Bring to a boil; reduce heat, and simmer 5 to 10 minutes or until cranberries are tender, stirring

often. Remove from heat, and keep sauce warm.

Trim fat from pork. Coat a large nonstick skillet with cooking spray; place over medium-high heat until hot. Add chops, and cook 5 to 6 minutes on each side or until meat thermometer registers 160°. Transfer to a serving dish; spoon cranberry sauce over pork chops, and serve. Yield: 4 servings (253 calories per 3 ounces cooked meat with 2 tablespoons sauce).

☐ *24.4 grams protein, 11.4 grams fat, 12.3 grams carbohydrate, 77 milligrams cholesterol, 62 milligrams sodium, and 15 milligrams calcium.*

CRANBERRIES JUBILEE
(pictured on page 297)

1 (12-ounce) package fresh cranberries
1 (10.25-ounce) jar reduced-sugar strawberry jam
1 teaspoon grated orange rind
⅓ cup brandy
2 tablespoons brandy
7 cups vanilla-flavored low-fat frozen yogurt

Combine first 4 ingredients in a saucepan. Bring to a boil over medium heat; cook 5 minutes, stirring constantly, or until cranberries pop and sauce begins to thicken (do not overcook). Remove from heat, and let cool slightly.

Place 2 tablespoons brandy in a small, long-handled saucepan; heat just until warm (do not boil). Remove from heat. Ignite brandy, and pour over cranberries; stir until flames die down. Serve immediately over frozen yogurt. Yield: 14 servings (155 calories per 2 tablespoons sauce over ½ cup yogurt).

☐ *3.1 grams protein, 2 grams fat, 28 grams carbohydrate, 10 milligrams cholesterol, 50 milligrams sodium, and 99 milligrams calcium.*

CRANBERRY-AND-APPLE COBBLER

¾ cup firmly packed brown sugar
2½ tablespoons quick-cooking tapioca
½ cup water
1 teaspoon vanilla extract
5 cups sliced cooking apples
2 cups fresh cranberries
Vegetable cooking spray
Lattice Crust

Combine first 4 ingredients in a large bowl; add apples and cranberries, tossing to coat. Spoon into a 12- x 8- x 2-inch baking dish coated with cooking spray; set aside.

Arrange crust over fruit in a lattice design. Bake at 425° for 15 minutes. Reduce temperature to 350°, and bake 30 minutes. Serve warm. Yield: 10 servings (199 calories per ½-cup serving).

☐ *1.5 grams protein, 4.9 grams fat, 38.4 grams carbohydrate, 0 milligrams cholesterol, 51 milligrams sodium, and 21 milligrams calcium.*

Lattice Crust

1 cup all-purpose flour
¼ cup corn oil margarine
2 to 3 tablespoons cold water

Place flour in a small bowl; cut in margarine with a pastry blender until mixture resembles coarse meal. Sprinkle water evenly over surface of mixture; stir with a fork until dry ingredients are moistened. Shape into a ball; gently press between 2 sheets of heavy-duty plastic wrap into a 4-inch circle. Chill 15 minutes.

Roll dough to a 12- x 8-inch rectangle. Freeze 5 minutes. Remove top sheet of plastic wrap; cut into strips to fit baking dish. Yield: crust for 1 cobbler.

CRANBERRY-BANANA BREAD

2 cups fresh cranberries
½ cup firmly packed brown sugar
¼ cup vegetable oil
1 egg
2 egg whites
1¾ cups all-purpose flour
2 teaspoons baking powder
¼ teaspoon baking soda
½ teaspoon salt
1 cup mashed banana
Vegetable cooking spray

Place cranberries in a medium saucepan. Cover and cook over medium heat 5 minutes or until cranberries begin to pop. Uncover and remove from heat.

Combine sugar and oil in a medium bowl; beat at medium speed of an electric mixer 2 minutes or until well blended. Add egg and egg whites; beat until light and lemon colored.

Combine dry ingredients; add to creamed mixture alternately with banana, mixing well after each addition. Fold in cranberries.

Pour batter into a 9- x 5- x 3-inch loafpan coated with cooking spray. Bake at 350° for 55 to 60 minutes or until bread tests done, shielding with aluminum foil the last 15 minutes. Cool in pan 10 minutes; remove from pan, and let cool on a wire rack. Yield: 18 servings (117 calories per ½-inch slice).

☐ *2.1 grams protein, 3.5 grams fat, 19.5 grams carbohydrate, 12 milligrams cholesterol, 121 milligrams sodium, and 34 milligrams calcium.*

Tip: *Always measure ingredients accurately. Level dry ingredients in a cup with a knife edge or a spoon handle. Measure liquids in a cup so that the fluid is level with the top of the measuring line. Measure solid shortening by packing it firmly in a graduated measuring cup.*

MINIATURE CRANBERRY MUFFINS

1 cup fresh cranberrries, chopped
1 cup all-purpose flour, divided
½ cup whole wheat flour
1 teaspoon baking powder
½ teaspoon baking soda
⅓ cup sugar
1 cup orange juice
½ cup morsels of wheat bran cereal
2 tablespoons vegetable oil
1 egg, slightly beaten
1 teaspoon vanilla extract
Vegetable cooking spray

Toss chopped cranberries with ¼ cup all-purpose flour; set aside. Combine remaining all-purpose flour, whole wheat flour, baking powder, soda, and sugar in a large mixing bowl; make a well in center of mixture. Combine orange juice and next 4 ingredients in a small bowl; add to dry mixture, stirring just until moistened. Stir in cranberry mixture.

Spoon into miniature (1¾-inch) muffin pans coated with cooking spray, filling three-fourths full. Bake at 350° for 10 to 12 minutes. Yield: 3 dozen (42 calories per muffin).

☐ *1 gram protein, 1 gram fat, 7.8 grams carbohydrate, 6 milligrams cholesterol, 29 milligrams sodium, and 11 milligrams calcium.*

Melanie Keaton
Richmond, Kentucky

LIGHT MENU

A Menu For The Two Of You

Take time out during the holidays to share this special meal with someone dear to you. It boasts an appealing assortment of flavors and an eye-catching look without all the calories and fat that usually accompany special occasions.

Beef Tenderloin For Two
Twice-Baked Potato
Commercial whole wheat roll
Strawberry-Yogurt Dessert

BEEF TENDERLOIN FOR TWO

2 (4-ounce) beef tenderloin steaks
1 large clove garlic, crushed
¼ teaspoon cracked pepper
¾ cup canned ready-to-serve beef
   broth
2 tablespoons Madeira wine
2 cups sliced fresh mushrooms
1 cup fresh whole green beans
2 small tomatoes, cut into
   wedges
Vegetable cooking spray

Rub both sides of steaks with garlic, and sprinkle with pepper; set aside.

Combine beef broth and Madeira in a medium skillet; bring to a boil over medium heat. Add mushrooms and green beans, keeping them separated. Cover, reduce heat, and simmer 7 minutes or until beans are crisp-tender. Add tomatoes; heat thoroughly.

Place steaks on rack coated with cooking spray; place in broiler pan. Broil 6 inches from heat 5 minutes on each side or until meat thermometer registers 140° (rare), 150° (medium-rare), or 160° (medium).

Arrange vegetables on serving plates, reserving liquid; place steak on mushrooms. Reduce reserved liquid over high heat to 1 tablespoon; drizzle over steaks. Yield: 2 servings (251 calories per serving).

☐ *29.4 grams protein, 9.1 grams fat, 14.4 grams carbohydrate, 80 milligrams cholesterol, 361 milligrams sodium, and 50 milligrams calcium.*
Mrs. Joe Mann
Pearsall, Texas

TWICE-BAKED POTATO

1 (12-ounce) baking potato
3 tablespoons light process cream
   cheese product
3 tablespoons plain nonfat yogurt
2 teaspoons chopped fresh chives
   or ¾ teaspoon freeze-dried
   chives
⅛ teaspoon salt
¼ teaspoon pepper
⅛ teaspoon paprika

Wash potato; prick several times with a fork. Place potato on a paper towel in microwave oven. Microwave at HIGH 4 to 6 minutes. Let potato stand 5 minutes. Cut potato in half lengthwise; carefully scoop out pulp, leaving shells intact. Combine potato pulp, cream cheese, and next 4 ingredients. Stuff shells with potato mixture; sprinkle evenly with paprika. Place on a microwave-safe plate; microwave at HIGH 1 minute or until hot. Yield: 2 servings (185 calories per serving).

☐ *7.2 grams protein, 3.8 grams fat, 31.5 grams carbohydrate, 13 miligrams cholesterol, 294 milligrams sodium, and 96 milligrams calcium.*

STRAWBERRY-YOGURT DESSERT

1 cup fresh strawberries
1 (8-ounce) carton strawberry
   low-fat yogurt
1 egg white
⅛ teaspoon cream of tartar
Garnish: strawberry fans

Place 1 cup strawberries in container of an electric blender; cover and process until smooth. Remove to a small bowl; stir in yogurt with a wire whisk.

Beat egg white (at room temperature) and cream of tartar at high speed of an electric mixer until stiff peaks form; fold into strawberry mixture. Spoon evenly into 4 individual

dessert dishes; chill until firm. Garnish, if desired. Yield: 4 servings (84 calories per serving).

☐ *3.6 grams protein, 0.9 gram fat, 16 grams carbohydrate, 6 milligrams cholesterol, 81 milligrams sodium, and 96 milligrams calcium.*

Heart-Smart Pumpkin Pie

Perhaps more than any other course of a holiday meal, dessert has a traditional feel. And in the South a holiday meal wouldn't seem complete without pumpkin or sweet potato pie. However, the sugar, butter, eggs, and whole milk used in its preparation run contrary to healthy eating.

With just a few changes in ingredients and adjustments in cooking techniques, we created this New-Fashioned Pumpkin Pie. It has the rich flavor of traditional pumpkin pie without all the fat and calories. We think you'll be pleasantly surprised with this deliciously healthy version of an old-time favorite. If sweet potato pie is more to your liking, simply substitute cooked, mashed sweet potatoes for pumpkin.

NEW-FASHIONED PUMPKIN PIE
(pictured on page 304)

2 envelopes unflavored gelatin
1 cup evaporated skimmed milk
1 cup canned or mashed cooked
  pumpkin
½ teaspoon pumpkin pie spice
¼ teaspoon grated orange rind
¾ cup plain nonfat yogurt
2 egg whites
⅛ teaspoon salt
⅔ cup firmly packed brown sugar
Gingersnap Crust
1 tablespoon chopped pecans,
  toasted
Garnish: orange rind curl

Sprinkle gelatin over milk in a heavy saucepan; let stand 1 minute. Cook over low heat, stirring constantly, until gelatin dissolves. Add pumpkin, pie spice, and grated orange rind; stir well. Chill until the consistency

of unbeaten egg white. Fold in yogurt (at room temperature).

Beat egg whites (at room temperature) and salt at medium speed of an electric mixer until soft peaks form. Add brown sugar, a little at a time, and beat until stiff peaks form. Fold egg white mixture into pumpkin mixture. Pour mixture into Gingersnap Crust, and chill. Before serving, sprinkle pie with pecans, and garnish, if desired. Yield: 8 servings (200 calories per slice).

□ *7 grams protein, 5.3 grams fat, 32.2 grams carbohydrate, 5 milligrams cholesterol, 157 milligrams sodium, and 179 milligrams calcium.*

Gingersnap Crust

1 cup gingersnap crumbs
2 tablespoons margarine, melted
Vegetable cooking spray

Combine crumbs and melted margarine in a small bowl; stir well. Firmly press mixture into a 9-inch pieplate coated with cooking spray. Yield: one 9-inch crust.

COMPARE THE NUTRIENTS (per serving)		
	Traditional	Light
Calories	454	200
Fat	28.2g	5.3g
Cholesterol	83mg	5mg

Pair Citrus And Cream

It's not just for breakfast anymore! Jeanne S. Hotaling of Augusta, Georgia, uses orange juice in her sinfully rich Frosty Orange Pie, a frozen treat just right for a ladies' luncheon or even an extra-special dessert for the family.

FROSTY ORANGE PIE

3 egg yolks
¼ cup sugar
¼ cup plus 2 tablespoons frozen
  orange juice concentrate,
  thawed and undiluted
2 tablespoons water
3 egg whites
⅓ cup sugar
1 cup whipping cream, whipped
Graham cracker crust (recipe
  follows)
Garnish: whipped cream

Combine first 4 ingredients in top of a double boiler; bring water in bottom of double boiler to a boil. Cook, stirring constantly, until egg mixture is thickened and thermometer reaches 165° (about 15 minutes). Pour egg mixture into a large bowl. Cover and chill until mixture is cool, stirring occasionally.

Beat egg whites (at room temperature) at medium speed of an electric mixer until soft peaks form. Gradually add ⅓ cup sugar, 1 tablespoon at a time, beating until stiff peaks form. Fold egg whites into chilled egg mixture. Fold in whipped cream; spoon into chilled crust. Garnish by piping additional whipped cream around edges; sprinkle with 2 tablespoons crumbs reserved from graham cracker crust. Freeze. Remove from freezer about 15 minutes before serving. Yield: one 9-inch pie.

Graham Cracker Crust

1½ cups graham cracker crumbs
¼ cup sifted powdered sugar
1 teaspoon ground cinnamon
¼ cup plus 2 tablespoons butter
  or margarine, melted

Combine all ingredients; mix well. Reserve 2 tablespoons crumb mixture, and set aside. Firmly press crumb mixture evenly over bottom and sides of a 9-inch pieplate. Bake at 300° for 15 minutes; chill thoroughly. Yield: one 9-inch crust.

Plump cranberries burst with flavor in Cranberries Jubilee (page 293), a spectacular dessert.

Believe it or not, two spice layers and one plain layer come from just one batter for Japanese Fruitcake (page 252).

Serve Hot Chocolate Deluxe (page 272) dolloped with whipped cream and sprinkled with chocolate shavings.

Almond Cream Confections, Milk Chocolate Pound Cake, and Ice-Cream Pie Spectacular (shown clockwise from top) can be served year-round to make ordinary days as special as Christmas. (Recipes begin on page 305.)

Lay a holiday smorgasbord of sweets
on your sideboard with (from left)
Million Dollar Pound Cake,
Chocolate-Glazed Triple-Layer
Cheesecake, Black Walnut Cake,
Choco-Mallow Brownies,
Chocolate-Tipped Butter Cookies,
Pecan Pie, and Coconut Cream Pie.
(Recipes begin on page 305.)

The rich holiday flavors of fruits, nuts, and spices in The Compromise Cake (page 253) are sure to make everyone happy.

One of the best parts of holiday preparation is planning special desserts. In this collection, there's something for everyone, with (from left) Caramel Cake, Roasted Pecan Clusters, Cream Cheese Tarts, and Sweetheart Fudge Pie. (Recipes begin on page 305.)

It's hard to pick just one favorite dessert from this offering: (clockwise from front) Swedish Heirloom Cookies, Chocolate-Peanut Butter Fudge, Light Fruitcake, Pecan Cobbler Supreme, Holiday Coconut Cake, Perfect Chocolate Cake, Crispy Oat Cookies, and Deluxe Lemon Meringue Pie. (Recipes begin on page 305.)

Health-conscious eaters will find the rich flavor of New-Fashioned Pumpkin Pie (page 296) rivals that of its traditional counterpart.

Our All-Time Best Desserts

We always suspected that Southerners had a sweet tooth. And the tally from ballots that ran in the magazine last year asking for your favorite *Southern Living* recipes confirms our suspicion. The overwhelming response was for desserts. Votes came in for all types of goodies, from cakes to pies to cookies to ice cream. So we narrowed all the votes down to the top 25, in honor of our Silver Jubilee.

Interestingly, your votes mirrored the letters we've received from readers throughout the years. We'd rate the Hummingbird Cake as our all-time most requested recipe, and you voted it your number one choice, too. And reading the titles of other recipes for which readers voted seemed like reviewing the letters we've received all these years.

Here we've reprinted the recipes as they originally ran in the magazine except for a few minor editing changes to update package sizes and cut back on fat, sugar, and sodium where possible to reflect current trends. We hope you enjoy sampling these recipes.

■ Here it is—your all-time favorite recipe—**Hummingbird Cake!** It got the most votes of all and has won blue ribbons at several county fairs across the South since it ran in February 1978, according to letters sent by readers.

HUMMINGBIRD CAKE
(pictured on back cover)

3 cups all-purpose flour
1 teaspoon baking soda
½ teaspoon salt
2 cups sugar
1 teaspoon ground cinnamon
3 eggs, beaten
¾ cup vegetable oil
1½ teaspoons vanilla extract
1 (8-ounce) can crushed
   pineapple, undrained
1 cup chopped pecans
1¾ cups mashed bananas
½ cup chopped pecans
Cream Cheese Frosting

Combine first 5 ingredients in a large bowl; add eggs and oil, stirring until dry ingredients are moistened. Do not beat. Stir in vanilla, pineapple, 1 cup pecans, and bananas.

Pour batter into 3 greased and floured 9-inch round cakepans. Bake at 350° for 23 to 28 minutes or until a wooden pick inserted in center comes out clean. Cool in pans 10 minutes; remove from pans, and let cool completely on wire racks.

Stir ½ cup pecans into Cream Cheese Frosting, if desired, or reserve them to sprinkle over top of frosted cake. Spread frosting between layers and on top and sides of cake. Yield: one 3-layer cake.

Cream Cheese Frosting

½ cup butter or margarine,
   softened
1 (8-ounce) package cream
   cheese, softened
1 (16-ounce) package powdered
   sugar, sifted
1 teaspoon vanilla extract

Cream butter and cream cheese. Gradually add powdered sugar, beat until mixture is light and fluffy. Stir in vanilla. Yield: enough for one 3-layer cake.
          Mrs. L. H. Wiggins
     Greensboro, North Carolina

■ Readers originally found **Coconut-Cream Cheese Pound Cake** in a November 1985 story about foods that travel well to potluck dinners. The added ingredients put this recipe in a different category from traditional pound cakes; it's extra rich and flavorful.

COCONUT-CREAM CHEESE
POUND CAKE

½ cup butter or margarine,
   softened
½ cup shortening
1 (8-ounce) package cream
   cheese, softened
3 cups sugar
6 eggs
3 cups all-purpose flour
¼ teaspoon baking soda
¼ teaspoon salt
1 (6-ounce) package frozen
   coconut, thawed
1 teaspoon vanilla extract
1 teaspoon coconut flavoring

Cream butter, shortening, and cream cheese; gradually add sugar, beating well at medium speed of an electric mixer. Add eggs, one at a time, beating after each addition.

Combine flour, soda, and salt; add to creamed mixture, stirring just until blended. Stir in coconut and remaining ingredients.

Pour batter into a greased and floured 10-inch tube pan. Bake at 325° for 1½ hours or until a wooden pick inserted in center of cake comes out clean. Cool in pan 10 to 15 minutes; remove from pan, and let cool completely on a wire rack. Yield: one 10-inch cake.
            Pat Belcher
        Woodstock, Georgia

■ We're not surprised that **Million Dollar Pound Cake** appeared on your ballots as a favorite. Originally running in September 1978, it's one of the best traditional pound cakes we've ever tested, and many of our home economists like to prepare it in their homes.

■ Spotlighted in a photograph in the 1976 Christmas issue of the magazine, **Milk Chocolate Pound Cake** tastes as good today as it did when it originally ran. We've made adjustments to account for the change in ounce size of the milk chocolate candy bars, but the cake remains rich and chocolaty.

MILLION DOLLAR POUND CAKE

(pictured on pages 300 and 301)

1 pound butter, softened
3 cups sugar
6 eggs
4 cups all-purpose flour
¾ cup milk
1 teaspoon almond extract
1 teaspoon vanilla extract

Cream butter in a large mixing bowl; gradually add sugar, beating well at medium speed of an electric mixer. Add eggs, one at a time, beating after each addition.

Add flour to creamed mixture alternately with milk, beginning and ending with flour. Mix just until blended after each addition. Stir in flavorings.

Pour batter into a greased and floured 10-inch tube pan. Bake at 300° for 1 hour and 40 minutes or until a wooden pick inserted in center of cake comes out clean.

Cool cake in pan 10 to 15 minutes; remove cake from pan, and let cool completely on a wire rack. Yield: one 10-inch cake.

Mrs. Billy Mack Burk
Leesburg, Alabama

MILK CHOCOLATE POUND CAKE

(pictured on page 299)

1 cup butter or margarine,
  softened
1½ cups sugar
4 eggs
6 (1.55-ounce) milk chocolate
  candy bars, melted
2½ cups all-purpose flour
¼ teaspoon baking soda
Pinch of salt
1 cup buttermilk
1 cup chopped pecans
1 (5½-ounce) can chocolate syrup
2 teaspoons vanilla extract
Powdered sugar (optional)

Cream butter; gradually add 1½ cups sugar, beating well at medium speed of an electric mixer. Add eggs, one at a time, beating after each addition. Add melted candy bars.

Combine flour, soda, and salt in a small bowl; add to chocolate mixture alternately with buttermilk, beginning and ending with flour mixture. Mix just until blended after each addition. Add pecans, chocolate syrup, and vanilla, blending well.

Pour batter into a greased and floured 10-inch Bundt or tube pan. Bake at 325° for 1 hour and 15 minutes or until a wooden pick inserted in center of cake comes out clean. Cool in pan 10 to 15 minutes; remove from pan, and cool completely on a wire rack. Sift a small amount of powdered sugar over cake, if desired. Yield: one 10-inch cake.

Rosalie Pope
Texarkana, Arkansas

Cake Tips

■ For a successful cake, measure all the ingredients accurately, follow the recipe without making any substitutions, and use the pan sizes recommended in the recipe.

■ For best results in cake baking, let eggs, butter, and milk reach room temperature before mixing.

■ To test for doneness in baking a butter or margarine cake, insert a wooden pick or wire cake tester into the center of the cake in at least two places. The tester should come out clean if the cake is done. The cake should be beginning to shrink from the pan's sides. If the cake is pressed with a finger in the center, it should come back into shape at once. If cake tests done, remove from oven and invert cakepan 5 minutes (or time specified in the directions); loosen the cake from the sides and bottom of the pan. Invert it onto a plate or cake rack and turn it right side up on another cake rack so that air may circulate around it. This prevents sogginess.

■ To keep the plate neat while frosting a cake, place three or four strips of wax paper over the edges of the plate. Position the cake on the plate, and fill and frost it; then carefully pull out the wax paper strips.

■ Do not grease pans for angel food and true sponge cakes. These batters need to cling to the side of the pan to reach their full height.

■ When Ethelwyn Langston sent this recipe, she jotted a note that said she felt like she was in heaven when she ate this caramel frosting. Lots of folks must have sampled **Caramel Cake** as soon as it appeared in March 1989 and agreed with her because our first ballot ran only two months later.

CARAMEL CAKE
(pictured on page 302)

1 (8-ounce) carton sour cream
¼ cup milk
1 cup butter, softened
2 cups sugar
4 eggs
2¾ cups all-purpose flour
2 teaspoons baking powder
½ teaspoon salt
1 teaspoon vanilla extract
1 teaspoon rum extract (optional)
Caramel Frosting

Combine sour cream and milk. Cream butter; gradually add sugar, beating well at medium speed of an electric mixer. Add eggs, one at a time, beating well after each addition.

Combine flour, baking powder, and salt; add to creamed mixture alternately with sour cream mixture, beginning and ending with flour mixture. Mix after each addition. Stir in vanilla and, if desired, rum extract.

Pour batter into 2 greased and floured 9-inch round cakepans. Bake at 350° for 30 to 35 minutes or until a wooden pick inserted in center comes out clean. Cool in pans 10 minutes; remove from pans, and cool completely on wire racks. Spread Caramel Frosting between layers and on top and sides of cake. Yield: one 2-layer cake.

Caramel Frosting

3 cups sugar, divided
1 tablespoon all-purpose flour
1 cup milk
¾ cup butter or margarine
1 teaspoon vanilla extract

Sprinkle ½ cup sugar in a shallow, heavy 3½-quart Dutch oven; cook over medium heat, stirring constantly, until sugar melts (sugar will clump) and syrup is light golden brown. Remove from heat.

Combine remaining 2½ cups sugar and flour in a large saucepan, stirring well; add milk, and bring to a boil, stirring constantly.

Gradually pour about one-fourth of hot mixture into caramelized sugar, stirring constantly; add remaining hot mixture (mixture will lump, but continue stirring until smooth).

Return mixture to heat; cover and cook over low heat 2 minutes. Uncover and cook, without stirring, over medium heat until a candy thermometer reaches 238°. Add butter, stirring to blend. Remove from heat, and cool, without stirring, until temperature drops to 110° (about 1 hour). Add vanilla, and beat with a wooden spoon or at medium speed of an electric mixer, until of spreading consistency (about 20 minutes). Yield: enough for one 2-layer cake.

Ethelwyn Langston
Birmingham, Alabama

■ Since **Perfect Chocolate Cake** ran in our September 1977 issue, it has kept a steady stream of letters coming in requesting reprints.

PERFECT CHOCOLATE CAKE
(pictured on cover and page 303)

1 cup cocoa
2 cups boiling water
1 cup butter or margarine, softened
2½ cups sugar
4 eggs
2¾ cups all-purpose flour
2 teaspoons baking soda
½ teaspoon baking powder
½ teaspoon salt
1½ teaspoons vanilla extract
Whipped Cream Filling
Perfect Chocolate Frosting

Combine cocoa and boiling water, stirring until smooth; set aside.

Cream butter; gradually add sugar, beating well at medium speed of an electric mixer. Add eggs, one at a time, beating well after each addition.

Combine flour, soda, baking powder, and salt in a medium bowl; add to creamed mixture alternately with cocoa mixture, beating at low speed of electric mixer, beginning and ending with flour mixture. Stir in vanilla. Do not overbeat.

Pour batter into 3 greased and floured 9-inch round cakepans. Bake at 350° for 20 to 25 minutes or until a wooden pick inserted in center comes out clean. Cool in pans 10 minutes; remove from pans, and cool completely on wire racks.

Spread Whipped Cream Filling between layers; spread Perfect Chocolate Frosting on top and sides of cake. Refrigerate until ready to serve. Yield: one 3-layer cake.

Whipped Cream Filling

1 cup whipping cream
1 teaspoon vanilla extract
¼ cup sifted powdered sugar

Beat whipping cream and vanilla until foamy; gradually add powdered sugar, beating until soft peaks form. Chill. Yield: about 2 cups.

Perfect Chocolate Frosting

1 (6-ounce) package semisweet chocolate morsels
½ cup half-and-half
¾ cup butter or margarine
2½ cups sifted powdered sugar

Combine first 3 ingredients in a heavy saucepan; cook over medium heat, stirring until chocolate melts. Remove from heat; add powdered sugar, mixing well.

Set saucepan in ice, and beat at low speed of an electric mixer until frosting holds its shape and loses its gloss. Add a few more drops of half-and-half if needed to make spreading consistency. Yield: 2½ cups.

Dondee Gage Steves
San Antonio, Texas

■ The November 1980 photograph of **Black Walnut Cake** must have caught the eye of a lot of cake lovers because the recipe generated much response. Black walnuts dot both the layers and frosting of this cake.

BLACK WALNUT CAKE

(pictured on pages 300 and 301)

½ cup butter or margarine, softened
½ cup shortening
2 cups sugar
5 eggs, separated
1 cup buttermilk
1 teaspoon baking soda
2 cups all-purpose flour
1 teaspoon vanilla extract
1 cup chopped black walnuts
1 (3-ounce) can flaked coconut
½ teaspoon cream of tartar
Cream Cheese Frosting
Chopped black walnuts

Cream butter and shortening; gradually add sugar, beating well at medium speed of an electric mixer. Add egg yolks, one at a time, beating well after each addition.

Combine buttermilk and soda; stir until soda dissolves.

Add flour to creamed mixture alternately with buttermilk mixture, beginning and ending with flour. Mix after each addition. Stir in vanilla. Add 1 cup walnuts and coconut, stirring well.

Beat egg whites (at room temperature) and cream of tartar until stiff peaks form; fold into batter.

Pour batter into 3 greased and floured 9-inch round cakepans. Bake at 350° for 22 to 25 minutes or until a wooden pick inserted in center comes out clean. Cool in pans 10 minutes; remove from pans, and let cool completely on wire racks.

Spread Cream Cheese Frosting between layers and on top and sides of cake; press additional chopped walnuts onto sides of cake. Yield: one 3-layer cake.

Cream Cheese Frosting

¾ cup butter, softened
1 (8-ounce) package cream cheese, softened
1 (3-ounce) package cream cheese, softened
6¾ cups sifted powdered sugar
1½ teaspoons vanilla extract

Cream butter and cream cheese; gradually add powdered sugar, beating until mixture is light and fluffy. Stir in vanilla. Yield: enough for one 3-layer cake.

Mrs. Leslie L. Jones
Richmond, Kentucky

■ In addition to being revered by readers, **Holiday Coconut Cake** is special to the folks on our foods staff. For many years, in fact, this cake has been a favorite of our Senior Foods Editor—the recipe was sent in by her mother for our December 1977 issue!

HOLIDAY COCONUT CAKE

(pictured on page 303)

⅓ cup shortening
⅓ cup butter or margarine, softened
1¾ cups sugar
3 cups sifted cake flour
1 tablespoon plus ½ teaspoon baking powder
¾ teaspoon salt
1⅓ cups milk
2 teaspoons vanilla extract
4 egg whites
Lemon Filling
Fluffy Frosting
Freshly grated coconut

Cream shortening and butter; gradually add sugar, beating well at medium speed of an electric mixer.

Combine flour, baking powder, and salt; add to creamed mixture alternately with milk, beginning and ending with flour mixture. Mix after each addition. Stir in vanilla.

Beat egg whites (at room temperature) until stiff peaks form. Gently fold into batter.

Pour batter into 3 greased and floured 9-inch round cakepans. Bake at 350° for 22 to 25 minutes or until a wooden pick inserted in center comes out clean. Cool in pans 10 minutes; remove from pans, and cool completely on wire racks.

Spread Lemon Filling between layers; spread Fluffy Frosting on top and sides of cake. Sprinkle cake with coconut. Yield: one 3-layer cake.

Lemon Filling

1 cup sugar
¼ cup cornstarch
1 cup water
2 egg yolks, beaten
2 tablespoons butter or margarine
1 tablespoon grated lemon rind
3 tablespoons lemon juice

Combine sugar and cornstarch in a heavy saucepan; add water, stirring well. Cook over medium heat, stirring constantly, until mixture thickens and boils. Boil 1 minute.

Gradually stir about one-fourth of hot mixture into egg yolks; add to remaining hot mixture, stirring constantly. Return to a boil; cook 1 minute or until candy thermometer registers 165°, stirring constantly. Remove from heat; stir in butter and remaining ingredients. Cool filling completely before spreading. Yield: 1¾ cups.

Fluffy Frosting

1 cup sugar
⅓ cup water
2 tablespoons light corn syrup
2 egg whites
¼ cup sifted powdered sugar
1 teaspoon vanilla extract

Combine first 3 ingredients in a heavy saucepan; cook over medium heat, stirring constantly, until clear.

Cook, without stirring, until candy thermometer registers 236°.

Beat egg whites (at room temperature) until soft peaks form; continue to beat, slowly adding syrup mixture. Add powdered sugar and vanilla; continue beating until stiff peaks form and frosting is thick enough to spread. Yield: 2½ cups.

Katherine Wickstrom
Pelham, Alabama

■ Lots of Southerners make fruitcake every Christmas, and readers have consistently requested copies of **Light Fruitcake** since its debut in November 1977. Here it is again, just in time for another season of holiday baking.

LIGHT FRUITCAKE
(pictured on page 303)

1½ cups butter, softened
1½ cups sugar
1 tablespoon vanilla extract
1 tablespoon lemon extract
7 eggs, separated
3 cups all-purpose flour
1½ pounds diced yellow, green, and red candied pineapple (about 3 cups)
1 pound red and green candied cherries (about 2 cups)
¼ pound diced candied citron (about ½ cup)
½ pound golden raisins (about 1½ cups)
3 cups pecan halves
1 cup black walnuts, coarsely chopped
½ cup all-purpose flour
Additional candied fruit and nuts (optional)
¼ cup brandy
Additional brandy

Make a liner for a 10-inch tube pan by drawing a circle with an 18-inch diameter on a piece of brown paper. (Do not used recycled paper.) Cut out circle; set pan in center, and draw around base of pan and inside tube. Fold circle into eighths, having the drawn lines on the outside.

Cut off tip end of circle along inside drawn line. Unfold paper; cut along folds to the outside drawn line. From another piece of brown paper, cut another circle with a 10-inch diameter; grease and set aside. Place the 18-inch liner in pan; grease and set aside.

Cream butter; gradually add sugar, beating well at medium speed of an electric mixer. Stir in flavorings. Beat egg yolks; alternately add yolks and 3 cups flour to creamed mixture.

Combine candied pineapple, cherries, citron, golden raisins, pecans, and walnuts in a bowl; dredge with ½ cup flour, stirring to coat well. Stir mixture into batter. Beat egg whites (at room temperature) until stiff peaks form; fold into batter.

Spoon batter into prepared pan. Arrange additional candied fruit and nuts on top of batter, if desired. Cover pan with 10-inch brown paper circle, greased side down. Bake at 250° for about 4 hours or until cake tests done. Remove from oven. Take off paper cover, and slowly pour ¼ cup brandy evenly over cake; cool completely on wire rack.

Remove cake from pan; peel paper liner from cake. Wrap cake in brandy-soaked cheesecloth. Store in an airtight container in a cool place up to 3 weeks; pour a small amount of brandy over cake each week. Yield: one 10-inch cake.

Mrs. Robert L. Perry
Richmond, Virginia

Tip: *Have your oven thermostat professionally checked at least once a year. Another way to occasionally check oven temperature is to prepare a cake mix according to package directions; the cake should bake the entire recommended time and test done. (A wooden pick inserted in the center should come out clean.)*

■ This winner, **Choco-Mallow Brownies,** from September 1987 is laced with melted marshmallows and topped with a rich chocolate frosting.

CHOCO-MALLOW BROWNIES
(pictured on pages 300 and 301)

½ cup butter or margarine, softened
1 cup sugar
2 eggs
¾ cup all-purpose flour
½ teaspoon baking powder
Pinch of salt
3 tablespoons cocoa
1 teaspoon vanilla extract
½ cup chopped pecans
2 cups miniature marshmallows
Chocolate Frosting

Cream butter; gradually add sugar, beating well at medium speed of an electric mixer. Add eggs, one at a time, beating after each addition.

Combine flour and next 3 ingredients; add to creamed mixture, stirring well. Stir in vanilla and pecans. Spoon into a greased and floured 9-inch square pan. Bake at 350° for 18 to 20 minutes. Remove from oven; sprinkle with marshmallows. Cover with aluminum foil, and let stand 5 minutes or until marshmallows melt.

Spread Chocolate Frosting on top of warm brownies. Cool and cut into 1½-inch squares. Yield: 3 dozen.

Chocolate Frosting

¼ cup butter or margarine, melted
2 cups sifted powdered sugar
3 tablespoons cocoa
4 to 5 tablespoons half-and-half

Combine butter, sugar, and cocoa in a mixing bowl. Gradually add half-and-half, beating at medium speed of an electric mixer until frosting reaches spreading consistency. Yield: enough for 9-inch pan of brownies.

Doris Ramsey
Martinsville, Virginia

When Mrs. Randy Bryant sent this recipe to us for **Chocolate-Glazed Triple-Layer Cheesecake,** she had no idea what a hit it would make with our foods staff. Since it appeared in our December 1986 issue, we've made it in our homes and served it at company-sponsored functions. Many readers have written for reprints of it, too.

CHOCOLATE-GLAZED TRIPLE-LAYER CHEESECAKE
(pictured on pages 300 and 301)

1 (8½-ounce) package chocolate wafer cookies, crushed (about 2 cups)
¾ cup sugar, divided
¼ cup plus 1 tablespoon butter or margarine, melted
2 (8-ounce) packages cream cheese, softened and divided
3 eggs
1 teaspoon vanilla extract, divided
2 (1-ounce) squares semisweet chocolate, melted
1⅓ cups sour cream, divided
⅓ cup firmly packed dark brown sugar
1 tablespoon all-purpose flour
¼ cup chopped pecans
5 ounces cream cheese, softened
¼ teaspoon almond extract
Chocolate Glaze
Garnish: chocolate leaves

Combine cookie crumbs, ¼ cup sugar, and butter; blend well. Press onto bottom and 2 inches up sides of a 9-inch springform pan. Set aside.

Combine 1 (8-ounce) package cream cheese and ¼ cup sugar; beat at medium speed of an electric mixer until fluffy. Add 1 egg and ¼ teaspoon vanilla; beat well. Stir in melted chocolate and ⅓ cup sour cream. Spoon over chocolate crust.

Combine remaining (8-ounce) package cream cheese, brown sugar, and flour; beat until fluffy. Add 1 egg and ½ teaspoon vanilla; beat well. Stir in pecans. Spoon over chocolate layer.

Combine 5 ounces cream cheese and remaining ¼ cup sugar; beat until fluffy. Add remaining egg, and beat well. Stir in remaining 1 cup sour cream, ¼ teaspoon vanilla, and almond extract. Spoon gently over pecan layer.

Bake at 325° for 1 hour. Turn oven off, and leave cheesecake in oven 30 minutes; open door of oven, and leave cheesecake in oven an additional 30 minutes. Cool. Cover and chill at least 8 hours. Remove from pan. Spread warm Chocolate Glaze over cheesecake. Garnish, if desired. Yield: 10 to 12 servings.

Chocolate Glaze

6 (1-ounce) squares semisweet chocolate
¼ cup butter or margarine
¾ cup sifted powdered sugar
2 tablespoons water
1 teaspoon vanilla extract

Combine chocolate and butter in top of a double boiler; bring water to a boil. Reduce heat to low; cook until chocolate melts. Remove from heat; stir in remaining ingredients. Stir until smooth. Spread over cheesecake while glaze is warm. Yield: enough for one 9-inch cheesecake.
Mrs. Randy Bryant
Franklin, Virginia

A bumper crop of pecans one crisp autumn brought a bumper crop of recipe ideas for this reader. A love for homemade candy led to her creation of **Roasted Pecan Clusters,** and we passed on the sweet secret in October 1985.

ROASTED PECAN CLUSTERS
(pictured on page 302)

3 tablespoons butter or margarine
3 cups pecan pieces
12 (1-ounce) squares chocolate-flavored candy coating

Melt butter in a 15- x 10- x 1-inch jellyroll pan. Spread pecans evenly in pan. Bake at 300° for 30 minutes, stirring every 10 minutes.

Place candy coating in top of a double boiler; bring water to a boil. Reduce heat to low, and cook until coating melts. Cool 2 minutes; add pecans, and stir until coated. Drop by rounded teaspoonfuls onto wax paper. Cool completely. Yield: about 4 dozen.
Margaret Haegelin
Hondo, Texas

Good enough to stand on its own, this recipe was highlighted in September 1987. The foods staff was excited to have the treats again last Christmas when Jean Liles, our Senior Foods Editor, contributed **Almond Cream Confections** for our annual "sweets swap."

ALMOND CREAM CONFECTIONS
(pictured on cover and page 299)

½ cup butter
¼ cup sugar
2 tablespoons cocoa
2 teaspoons vanilla extract
¼ teaspoon salt
1 egg, slightly beaten
1 cup slivered almonds, toasted and chopped
1¾ cups vanilla wafer crumbs
½ cup flaked coconut
Cream Filling
2 (1-ounce) squares semisweet chocolate

Combine first 6 ingredients in a heavy saucepan; cook over low heat, stirring constantly, until butter melts and mixture begins to thicken. Remove from heat; add almonds, vanilla wafer crumbs, and coconut, stirring well. Press firmly into an ungreased 9-inch square pan; cover and chill.

Spread Cream Filling over almond mixture; cover and chill. Cut into 1½-inch squares. Remove from pan, and place about ½ inch apart on a baking sheet.

Place chocolate in a zip-top heavy-duty plastic bag; seal. Submerge in hot water until chocolate melts. Snip a tiny hole in end of bag with scissors; drizzle over Cream Filling. Yield: 3 dozen.

Cream Filling

⅓ cup butter, softened
3 to 4 tablespoons milk
½ teaspoon vanilla extract
3 cups sifted powdered sugar

Cream butter at high speed of electric mixer. Add milk and vanilla. Slowly add sugar; mix until smooth. Yield: about 2 cups.   *Jean Carriger*
Lakeland, Florida

■ We bet lots of Christmas care packages have included **Chocolate-Peanut Butter Fudge** since the recipe and mailing tips were printed in our November 1987 "Holiday Dinners" special section. It's great for serving or sending.

CHOCOLATE-PEANUT BUTTER FUDGE
(pictured on page 303)

2½ cups sugar
¼ cup cocoa
1 cup milk
1 tablespoon light corn syrup
½ cup butter or margarine, divided
1 cup chopped pecans
½ cup peanut butter
2 teaspoons vanilla extract

Combine first 4 ingredients in a Dutch oven; cook over medium heat,

stirring constantly, until sugar dissolves. Add 2 tablespoons butter; stir until butter melts. Cover and boil mixture 3 minutes.

Remove cover, and continue to cook, without stirring, until mixture reaches soft ball stage (234°). Remove from heat, and without stirring, add remaining butter, pecans, peanut butter, and vanilla. Cool 10 minutes.

Beat mixture until well blended, and pour immediately into a buttered 9-inch square pan. Cool and cut fudge into 1½-inch squares. Yield: 3 dozen.   *Carolyn Webb*
Jackson, Mississippi

■ The recipe for **Crispy Oat Cookies** arrived labeled as "The World's Best Cookie." We can't speak for the whole world, but we will say this treat from August 1988 is one of the South's best cookies for sure.

CRISPY OAT COOKIES
(pictured on page 303)

1 cup butter or margarine, softened
1 cup sugar
1 cup firmly packed brown sugar
1 egg
1 cup vegetable oil
1 teaspoon vanilla extract
3½ cups all-purpose flour
1 teaspoon baking soda
½ teaspoon salt
1 cup regular oats, uncooked
1 cup crushed corn flakes cereal
½ cup flaked coconut
½ cup chopped pecans or walnuts

Cream butter; gradually add sugars, beating well at medium speed of an electric mixer. Add egg, and beat well; add oil and vanilla, mixing well.

Combine flour, soda, and salt; add to creamed mixture, mixing well. Stir in oats and remaining ingredients.

Shape dough into 1-inch balls. Place on ungreased cookie sheets, and flatten each ball with tines of a fork. Bake at 325° for 15 minutes. Cool slightly; remove from cookie sheets, and cool. Yield: 10 dozen.
Dorothy C. Taylor
Palm City, Florida

■ These favorite cookies took us back to June 1981 when we were still using black-and-white photography. Today the flavor of **Swedish Heirloom Cookies** is as good as ever, but you'll agree they're even more appetizing in color.

SWEDISH HEIRLOOM COOKIES
(pictured on page 303)

½ cup shortening
½ cup butter or margarine, softened
1 cup sifted powdered sugar
½ teaspoon salt
2 cups all-purpose flour
1 tablespoon water
1 tablespoon vanilla extract
1¼ cups ground almonds
Powdered sugar

Cream shortening and butter at medium speed of an electric mixer until light and fluffy. Add 1 cup powdered sugar and salt; mix well. Stir in flour. Add water, vanilla, and almonds, stirring well. Shape dough into 1-inch balls. Place on ungreased cookie sheets, and flatten. Bake at 325° for 12 to 15 minutes or until done. Dredge warm cookies in powdered sugar. Yield: 4 dozen.
Mrs. J. W. Montgomery
Kinston, North Carolina

■ In 1984, a handwritten card landed in our test kitchens with no name and address attached. We tried **Chocolate-Tipped Butter Cookies,** which were an instant hit in our November "Holiday Dinners" special section. Today they rank as an all-time favorite, and our anonymous reader remains a mystery.

CHOCOLATE-TIPPED BUTTER COOKIES

(pictured on cover and pages 300 and 301)

1 cup butter or margarine, softened
½ cup sifted powdered sugar
1 teaspoon vanilla extract
2 cups all-purpose flour
1 (6-ounce) package semisweet chocolate morsels
1 tablespoon shortening
½ cup finely chopped pecans

Cream butter; gradually add sugar, beating until light and fluffy. Stir in vanilla. Gradually add flour; mix well.

Shape dough into 2½- x ½-inch sticks. Place on ungreased cookie sheets. Flatten three-quarters of each cookie lengthwise with tines of a fork to ¼-inch thickness. Bake at 350° for 12 to 14 minutes. Remove to wire racks to cool.

Combine chocolate morsels and shortening in top of a double boiler; bring water to a boil. Reduce heat to low; cook until chocolate melts, stirring occasionally. Remove double boiler from heat, leaving chocolate mixture over hot water.

Dip unflattened tips of cookies in warm chocolate to coat both sides; roll tips in chopped pecans. Place cookies on wire racks until chocolate is firm.

Arrange cookies between layers of wax paper in an airtight container; store in a cool place. Yield: 4 dozen.

■ We've featured over two dozen new variations of pecan pie since this one first appeared in November 1975, but when pressed for a clear choice, this basic Southern **Pecan Pie** is the best.

PECAN PIE

(pictured on cover and pages 300 and 301)

1 cup sugar
1 cup light corn syrup
⅓ cup butter or margarine
4 eggs, beaten
1 teaspoon vanilla extract
¼ teaspoon salt
1 unbaked 9-inch pastry shell
1 to 1¼ cups pecan halves

Combine first 3 ingredients in a medium saucepan. Cook over low heat, stirring constantly, until sugar dissolves and butter melts; let cool slightly. Add eggs, vanilla, and salt to mixture, stirring well. Pour filling into pastry shell, and top with pecan halves. Bake at 325° for 50 to 55 minutes. Yield: one 9-inch pie.

Jane Brittain
Gadsden, Alabama

■ Cheesecake fans have raved about **Cream Cheese Tarts** as an innovative way to serve their favorite dessert since it ran in March 1984. The individual tarts are popular for parties and easy to make with a short list of ingredients.

CREAM CHEESE TARTS

(pictured on page 302)

2 (8-ounce) packages cream cheese, softened
1 cup sugar
2 eggs
1 teaspoon vanilla extract
12 vanilla wafers
Blueberry pie filling

Beat cream cheese at medium speed of an electric mixer until light and fluffy. Gradually add sugar, mixing well. Add eggs, one at a time, beating well after each addition. Stir in vanilla.

Place a vanilla wafer in each paper-lined cup of a muffin pan. Spoon cream cheese mixture over wafers, filling cups full. Bake at 350° for 20 minutes. Leave in muffin pan, and chill overnight. To serve, top with a small amount of blueberry pie filling. Yield: 12 servings.

Rebecca T. Wine
Florence, Alabama

■ In a September 1987 article revealing the secrets to a good cream pie, we selected this reader's recipe as a foolproof formula for a sweet Southern favorite. You, too, can make **Coconut Cream Pie** with confidence.

COCONUT CREAM PIE

(pictured on pages 300 and 301)

¾ cup sugar
¼ cup cornstarch
¼ teaspoon salt
2 cups milk
3 egg yolks
2 tablespoons butter or margarine
1 teaspoon vanilla extract
1 cup flaked coconut
1 baked 9-inch pastry shell
1 cup whipping cream
¼ cup sifted powdered sugar
Garnish: toasted flaked coconut

Combine first 3 ingredients in a heavy saucepan; gradually stir in milk. Cook over medium heat, stirring constantly, until thickened and bubbly. Cook 1 minute.

Beat egg yolks; gradually stir about one-fourth of hot mixture into yolks; add to remaining hot mixture, stirring constantly. Cook, stirring constantly, 30 seconds. Remove from heat; stir in butter, vanilla, and 1 cup flaked coconut. Pour into pastry shell. Cool completely; cover and chill 1 to 2 hours.

Beat whipping cream at high speed of an electric mixer until foamy; gradually add powdered sugar, 1 tablespoon at a time, beating until soft peaks form. Pipe sweetened whipped cream onto pie. Garnish, if desired. Yield: one 9-inch pie.

Debbie Dermid
Horse Shoe, North Carolina

■ While most of our recipes come from readers, occasionally our staff can't resist putting a finger in the pie. This classic, **Deluxe Lemon Meringue Pie,** is an in-house production we first shared with you in August 1981.

DELUXE LEMON MERINGUE PIE
(pictured on page 303)

1½ cups sugar
⅓ cup cornstarch
¼ teaspoon salt
1½ cups cold water
½ cup lemon juice
5 eggs, separated
2 tablespoons butter or margarine
1 to 3 teaspoons grated lemon rind
1 baked 9-inch pastry shell
¼ teaspoon cream of tartar
½ cup plus 2 tablespoons sugar
½ teaspoon vanilla extract

Combine first 3 ingredients in a large heavy saucepan; mix well. Gradually add water and lemon juice, stirring until mixture is smooth.

Beat egg yolks until thick and lemon colored; gradually stir into lemon mixture. Add butter, and cook over medium heat, stirring constantly, until thickened and bubbly.

Cook 1 minute, stirring continuously. Remove from heat; stir in lemon rind. Pour into pastry shell.

Beat egg whites (at room temperature) and cream of tartar at high speed of an electric mixer just until foamy. Gradually add ½ cup plus 2 tablespoons sugar, 1 tablespoon at a time, beating until stiff peaks form and sugar dissolves (2 to 4 minutes). Beat in vanilla, and spread meringue over hot filling, sealing to edge of pastry. Bake at 350° for 12 to 15 minutes or until golden brown. Cool to room temperature. Yield: one 9-inch pie.

■ A staff and reader favorite since it appeared in June 1977, **Peach Cobbler Supreme** is Southern dessert at its best. It's hard to improve on perfection, but a scoop of homemade vanilla ice cream on top somehow makes it even better.

PEACH COBBLER SUPREME
(pictured on page 303)

About 8 cups sliced fresh peaches
2 cups sugar
2 to 4 tablespoons all-purpose flour
½ teaspoon ground nutmeg
1 teaspoon almond or vanilla extract
⅓ cup butter or margarine
Pastry for double-crust pie

Combine first 4 ingredients in a Dutch oven; set aside until syrup forms. Bring peach mixture to a boil; reduce heat to low, and cook 10 minutes or until tender. Remove from heat; add almond extract and butter, stirring until butter melts.

Roll half of pastry to ⅛-inch thickness on a lightly floured surface; cut into an 8-inch square. Spoon half of peaches into a lightly buttered 8-inch square baking dish; top with pastry

square. Bake at 425° for 14 minutes or until lightly browned. Spoon remaining peaches over baked pastry square.

Roll remaining pastry to ⅛-inch thickness, and cut into 1-inch strips; arrange in lattice design over peaches. Bake at 425° for 15 to 18 minutes or until browned. Yield: 8 servings.

■ Decadence at its best, **Sweetheart Fudge Pie** was originally this reader's Valentine to friends and family. However, we found this rich chocolate indulgence endearing anytime of year and printed it in the December 1986 issue.

SWEETHEART FUDGE PIE
(pictured on page 302)

½ cup butter or margarine, softened
¾ cup firmly packed brown sugar
3 eggs
1 (12-ounce) package semisweet chocolate morsels, melted
2 teaspoons instant coffee granules
1 teaspoon rum extract
½ cup all-purpose flour
1 cup coarsely chopped walnuts
1 unbaked 9-inch pastry shell
Garnishes: piped whipped cream and chopped walnuts

Cream butter; gradually add brown sugar, beating at medium speed of an electric mixer until light and fluffy. Add eggs, one at a time, beating well after each addition. Add melted chocolate, coffee granules, and rum extract; mix well. Stir in flour and 1 cup chopped walnuts.

Pour mixture into pastry shell. Bake at 375° for 25 minutes; cool completely. Chill. Garnish, if desired. Yield: one 9-inch pie.

Peggy H. Amos
Martinsville, Virginia

■ Some say ice cream is best served plain in a cone, but this reader took a fancier approach back in August 1978. Her recipe for **Ice-Cream Pie Spectacular** with its rich Brown Sugar Sauce is still a winner.

■ Buried in the middle of an August 1980 story that gave nine recipes for ice cream, readers quickly singled out **Deluxe Peach Ice Cream** as a favorite. We think you'll like it, too.

From Our Kitchen To Yours

In the past year we have received thousands of questions from our readers. To give you a sampling, here are some of the most frequently asked questions of 1990 along with our answers.

ICE-CREAM PIE SPECTACULAR
(pictured on page 299)

1 cup graham cracker crumbs
½ cup chopped walnuts
¼ cup butter or margarine, melted
1 pint coffee ice cream, softened
1 pint vanilla ice cream, softened
Brown Sugar Sauce

Combine graham cracker crumbs, walnuts, and butter, stirring well. Press mixture firmly into a buttered 9-inch pieplate. Bake at 375° for 8 minutes; cool.

Spoon coffee ice cream into cool crust, spreading evenly; freeze until almost firm. Spread vanilla ice cream over coffee ice-cream layer, and freeze until firm. Spoon warm Brown Sugar Sauce over slices. Yield: one 9-inch pie.

Brown Sugar Sauce

3 tablespoons butter or margarine
1 cup firmly packed brown sugar
½ cup half-and-half
1 cup chopped walnuts
1 teaspoon vanilla extract

Melt butter in a heavy saucepan over low heat; add brown sugar. Cook 5 to 6 minutes, stirring constantly. Remove from heat, and gradually stir in half-and-half. Return pan to heat, and cook 1 minute. Remove from heat again; stir in walnuts and vanilla. Yield: about 1½ cups.

Katharine E. Barrett
Burke, Virginia

DELUXE PEACH ICE CREAM

6 cups mashed peaches
1 cup sugar
3 eggs
1½ cups sugar
2 tablespoons all-purpose flour
½ teaspoon salt
1 quart milk
1 cup whipping cream
1 tablespoon vanilla extract

Combine peaches and 1 cup sugar; stir well, and set aside.

Beat eggs at medium speed of an electric mixer until frothy. Combine 1½ cups sugar, flour, and salt; stir well. Gradually add sugar mixture to eggs; beat until thickened. Add milk; mix well.

Pour egg mixture into a large saucepan. Cook over low heat, stirring constantly, until mixture thickens and coats a metal spoon (about 15 minutes). Remove from heat, and set pan in cold water; stir gently until cool. Stir in cream, vanilla, and peaches.

Pour mixture into freezer container of a 1-gallon electric freezer. Freeze according to manufacturer's instructions. Let ripen at least 1 hour. Yield: about 1 gallon.

Florence L. Costello
Chattanooga, Tennessee

Tip: *Make certain your refrigerator or freezer is cold enough. Refrigerator temperature should be maintained at 34°F to 40°F, and freezer temperature at 0°F or lower. To allow the cold air to circulate freely, make sure that foods are not overcrowded.*

■ **Can butter and margarine products be substituted in baked goods?** Products that are labeled spread, reduced-calorie, liquid, or soft-style tub butter or margarine contain less fat than regular butter or margarine. Therefore, if substituted, these products do not always produce satisfactory results. For example, corn-oil margarine makes a softer cookie dough; the dough needs to chill three hours before slicing or at least five hours before rolling. Air or some inert gas is beaten into whipped butter to increase the volume and make spreading easier, so that adjustments need to be made when substituting. Usually 1½ cups whipped margarine equals 1 cup regular margarine. Because reduced-calorie margarine has a higher water content than regular margarine, it isn't always suitable for baking.

■ **What are some foods that can be prepared ahead and frozen?** Main-dish casseroles can be frozen up to three months; however, recipes containing creamed cottage cheese, hard-cooked egg, cheese, and mayonnaise do not always freeze well. Before reheating a frozen casserole, thaw it in the refrigerator overnight or in the microwave.

Unbaked fruit pies will freeze up to eight months; bake unthawed pies at 400° for approximately 1 hour and 15 minutes. Baked fruit pies will freeze up to two months; thaw in a 375° oven for 30 minutes.

Baked cookies can be frozen up to eight months; to thaw crisp cookies, remove them from the container.

Unfrosted cakes can be frozen up to five months; thaw in the wrapper at room temperature about one hour.

Cakes with a creamy-type frosting will freeze up to three months; to thaw cake, unwrap, and let stand at room temperature two to three hours. Thaw cakes with a whipped cream or cream cheese frosting unwrapped in the refrigerator for about four hours. Cheesecakes can be frozen up to one month. Fruitcakes will freeze up to one year.

Baked bread can be frozen up to three months, but raw dough should not be frozen unless specified in the recipe. Thaw foil-wrapped bread at room temperature for two to three hours, or bake wrapped at 350° for 20 to 30 minutes.

Stir In The Champagne

Gifts of champagne and sparkling wines should be savored, not saved. The sparkle makes them unique, and unlike some wines, champagne and sparkling wines do not improve with age. We offer these recipes for you to finish off a freshly opened bottle or to use any unopened bottles you may have on hand.

BERRY MIMOSA SAUCE

1 cup orange juice
1½ tablespoons cornstarch
½ cup dry champagne
2 tablespoons honey
1 cup raspberries or strawberries

Combine orange juice and cornstarch in a medium saucepan; whisk until blended. Stir in champagne. Bring to a boil; reduce heat, and cook 1 minute. Stir in honey and berries. Serve over cake, ice cream, or French toast. Yield: 2 cups.

CHAMPAGNE ICE

1½ cups sugar
3 cups water
1½ tablespoons grated lemon rind
⅓ cup fresh lemon juice
2 (750-milliliter) bottles champagne

Combine all ingredients in freezer can of a 1-gallon hand-turned or electric freezer; stir well. Freeze according to manufacturer's instructions. Ice cream may be ripened for 1 hour, if desired. Yield: 2½ quarts.

STRAWBERRY CHAMPAGNE PUNCH

3 (6-ounce) cans frozen lemonade, thawed and undiluted
5 cups water
1 pint fresh strawberries, sliced
1 quart ginger ale, chilled
2 (750-milliliter) bottles dry champagne, chilled

Combine first 3 ingredients; chill 4 hours. Gently stir in ginger ale and champagne just before serving. Yield: 4½ quarts.
Beth McClain
Grand Prairie, Texas

An Easy But Superb Dinner For Four

A good dinner feeds more than just the stomach. It satisfies the soul and invites the best of conversations. During the holiday season, a time of abundant food and sharing, that's truer than ever.

With that in mind, we've gathered some of our readers' easy-to-make recipes into a menu that will do more than simply satisfy hunger. Glazed

Pork Tenderloin borrows rich flavor from a marinade of allspice and honey. Sprinkled with basil, Parmesan cheese, and pepper, potato halves are quickly baked in the microwave oven for Basil-Cheese Potatoes. Bright red tomato wedges color Bean-and-Tomato Skillet, while the bay leaf and green beans in the recipe scent the air with a savory aroma as they cook. Easy Custard With Nutmeg bakes during the meal and is served for dessert. Come, you're invited for dinner.

Glazed Pork Tenderloin
Bean-and-Tomato Skillet
Basil-Cheese Potatoes
Commercial whole wheat rolls
Easy Custard With Nutmeg
Tea or coffee

GLAZED PORK TENDERLOIN

¼ cup orange juice
2 tablespoons honey
½ teaspoon ground allspice
2 (½-pound) pork tenderloins

Combine first 3 ingredients. Place tenderloins in a large shallow dish. Pour orange juice mixture over tenderloins; cover and chill 2 to 4 hours, turning occasionally.

Remove tenderloins from marinade, reserving marinade; place on a rack in a shallow roasting pan. Insert meat thermometer into thickest part of tenderloin, making sure it does not touch fat. Bake at 350° for 25 to 30 minutes or until meat thermometer registers 160°, basting occasionally with marinade. Yield: 4 servings.

Tip: *Roll lemons, oranges, and grapefruit on a counter before cutting to soften; you will get more juice.*

BEAN-AND-TOMATO SKILLET

2 tablespoons vegetable oil
1 (9-ounce) package frozen whole
  green beans
2 small onions, sliced
2 tablespoons water
1 teaspoon sugar
1 bay leaf
2 large tomatoes, peeled and cut
  into wedges

Heat oil in a large skillet; add remaining ingredients except tomatoes, and stir well. Cover and cook over medium heat 10 minutes; remove bay leaf. Place tomato wedges on mixture. Cover and cook an additional 7 minutes. Yield: 4 servings.

Sarah Watson
Knoxville, Tennessee

BASIL-CHEESE POTATOES

2 large baking potatoes, unpeeled
1 teaspoon butter or margarine,
  melted
1 teaspoon lemon juice
2 tablespoons grated Parmesan
  cheese
½ teaspoon dried whole basil
¼ teaspoon pepper

Slice potatoes in half lengthwise. Combine butter and lemon juice; brush cut surface of potatoes with mixture. Combine cheese, basil, and pepper; sprinkle on top of potatoes.

Place potato halves, cut side up, on a 12-inch pizza plate; cover loosely with wax paper. Microwave at HIGH 14 to 16 minutes, giving plate a half-turn after 7 minutes. Let stand 2 minutes. Yield: 4 servings.

Tip: *Add salt to taste after cooking to prevent dark spots from forming on microwaved vegetables.*

EASY CUSTARD WITH NUTMEG

½ cup sugar
3 eggs
⅓ cup sugar
½ teaspoon vanilla extract
¼ teaspoon ground nutmeg
2 cups milk

Cook ½ cup sugar in a heavy skillet over medium heat until golden brown, stirring constantly. Pour syrup into four 10-ounce custard cups; set aside.

Combine eggs, ⅓ cup sugar, vanilla, and nutmeg; gradually add milk, beating well. Pour mixture evenly into custard cups. Place cups in a 13- x 9- x 2-inch pan; pour hot water to a depth of 1 inch into pan. Cover with aluminum foil, and bake at 350° for 40 to 45 minutes or until a knife inserted in center comes out clean. Remove from water, and cool. To serve, loosen edge of custard with a spatula; invert onto plates. Yield: 4 servings. *Jennie Kinnard*
Mabank, Texas

Entrées For Any Occasion

You're sure to need many types of menus to match the busy days ahead. Here's a group of entrée recipes planned to meet every need during the holidays, from quick family meals to more formal entertaining.

Sweet-and-Sour Pork is a nice, easy choice for the family. It's so simple you can stir it up in less than 30 minutes but so filling that it can be a one-dish meal. When a couple of friends join you, put Baked Flounder on the menu. This extra-flavorful recipe offers convenience, as well as a choice of conventional or microwave directions.

And if you're still tired of turkey left from Thanksgiving, Stuffed Country Ham makes a nice option for the big meal on Christmas Day (especially if you were lucky enough to receive one as a gift). The recipe will probably make enough to feed all the relatives, too.

BAKED FLOUNDER

4 flounder fillets (about 1 pound)
2 tablespoons chopped onion
½ teaspoon salt
⅛ teaspoon freshly ground pepper
⅓ cup apple juice
2 tablespoons dry white wine
2 tablespoons lemon juice
2 tablespoons butter or margarine
2 tablespoons all-purpose flour
¼ cup whipping cream
¼ cup freshly grated Parmesan
  cheese
Minced fresh parsley

Arrange fillets in a lightly greased 12- x 8- x 2-inch baking dish. Sprinkle with onion, salt, and pepper.

Combine apple juice, wine, and lemon juice; pour over fish. Cover and bake at 350° for 25 to 30 minutes or until fish flakes easily when tested with a fork. Transfer fish to a serving platter. Strain and reserve ⅔ cup liquid.

Melt butter in a heavy saucepan over low heat; add flour, stirring until smooth. Cook 1 minute, stirring constantly. Gradually add whipping cream and reserved ⅔ cup liquid. Cook over medium heat, stirring constantly, until mixture is thickened and bubbly; pour over fish. Sprinkle with Parmesan cheese and parsley. Yield: 4 servings.

Microwave Directions: Arrange fillets, with thicker portions to the outside, in a lightly greased 12- x 8- x 2-inch baking dish. Sprinkle with onion, salt, and pepper.

Combine apple juice, wine, and lemon juice; pour over fish. Cover with heavy-duty plastic wrap; fold back a small corner of wrap to allow steam to escape. Microwave at HIGH 8 to 10 minutes or until fish flakes easily when tested with a fork, giving dish a half-turn after 4 minutes. Transfer fish to a serving platter. Strain and reserve ⅔ cup liquid.

Place butter in a 2-cup glass measure; microwave at HIGH 45 seconds or until melted. Add flour, stirring until smooth. Gradually add whipping cream and reserved liquid, stirring well. Microwave at HIGH 3 minutes or until thickened and bubbly, stirring at 1-minute intervals; pour over fish. Sprinkle with Parmesan cheese and parsley.

Betty Manente
Lighthouse Point, Florida

SHRIMP-AND-SCALLOP SAUTÉ WITH PECAN RICE

½ pound unpeeled medium-size
  fresh shrimp
1 (10½-ounce) can condensed
  beef broth, undiluted and
  divided
⅓ cup beer
½ pound bay scallops
¼ cup coarsely chopped pecans
2 tablespoons butter or
  margarine, melted
¾ cup long-grain rice, uncooked
¼ cup chopped onion
⅛ teaspoon ground turmeric
1 cup water
1 clove garlic, minced
¼ teaspoon crushed red pepper
2 tablespoons butter or
  margarine, melted
1 tablespoon cornstarch

Peel and devein shrimp. Combine ½ cup broth and beer in a shallow dish; add shrimp and scallops. Cover and refrigerate 1 hour, stirring seafood occasionally.

Sauté pecans in 2 tablespoons butter in a saucepan over medium heat until pecans are browned. Remove pecans with a slotted spoon; set

aside. Add rice, onion, and turmeric to pan drippings; cook over medium heat, stirring constantly, 1 minute. Add remaining beef broth and water; bring to a boil. Cover, reduce heat, and simmer 20 minutes or until liquid is absorbed and rice is tender. Stir in pecans.

Remove shrimp and scallops from marinade, reserving marinade. Cook seafood, garlic, and red pepper in 2 tablespoons butter in a skillet over medium heat 2 to 3 minutes or until seafood is done, stirring frequently.

Add cornstarch to reserved marinade, stirring well; add to shrimp and scallops. Bring to a boil; cook 1 minute or until slightly thickened, stirring constantly. Serve over pecan rice. Yield: 3 servings.

Shirley M. Draper
Winter Park, Florida

STUFFED COUNTRY HAM

1 (12-pound) uncooked country
  ham
2 cups chopped fresh parsley
1 large onion, minced
1 pound bacon, cooked and
  crumbled
1 cup soft breadcrumbs, toasted
1 egg, beaten
3 tablespoons prepared mustard
3 tablespoons brown sugar
2 tablespoons dried whole thyme
1 teaspoon celery seeds
1 teaspoon red pepper
1 teaspoon pepper

Place country ham in a large container. Cover ham with water, and let soak 24 hours. Pour off water. Scrub ham in warm water with a stiff brush, and rinse well.

Place ham in a large cooking container, and cover with hot water. Bring to a boil; cover, reduce heat, and simmer 2 hours or until meat thermometer registers 142°. (Make sure thermometer does not touch fat or bone.) Drain ham, and let cool. Trim skin from ham. Cut slits into ham in a diamond pattern, cutting 1½ inches deep and 1½ inches apart.

Combine remaining in[...] stir well. Stuff vegetable m[...] slits. Place ham in a ro[...] and bake, uncovered, at [...] hour or until browned[...] servings.   *Helen Co[...]*
New Orle[...]

SWEET-AND-SOUR PORK

1 (8¼-ounce) can pineapple
  chunks, undrained
2 (¾-pound) pork tenderloins, cut
  into ¾-inch cubes
¾ cup chopped onion
2 tablespoons vegetable oil
2 tablespoons lemon juice
2 tablespoons brown sugar
1 tablespoon cornstarch
1 tablespoon soy sauce
½ teaspoon salt
⅛ teaspoon ground ginger
⅛ teaspoon pepper
1 small green pepper, cut into
  strips
1 (6-ounce) package frozen snow
  pea pods, thawed
Hot cooked rice

Drain pineapple, reserving juice. Set both aside.

Sauté pork and onion in a large skillet in hot oil 10 to 12 minutes or until pork is done. Combine reserved pineapple juice, lemon juice, and next 6 ingredients, stirring well. Add juice mixture and green pepper to skillet; cook over medium heat 1 to 2 minutes or until sauce is thickened, stirring constantly. Add pineapple and snow peas; cook 2 minutes or until thoroughly heated, stirring occasionally. Serve over rice. Yield: 6 servings.   *Mrs. Robert L. Scofield*
Clarksville, Tennessee

MARINATED RIB-EYE ROAST

½ cup dry red wine
¼ cup vegetable oil
3 tablespoons white vinegar
⅓ cup chopped green onions
⅓ cup chopped celery
¼ cup chopped green pepper
1 (0.7-ounce) envelope Italian or garlic salad dressing mix
1½ teaspoons Worcestershire sauce
1 (5- to 6-pound) boneless rib-eye roast, trimmed

Combine first 8 ingredients, mixing well. Place roast in a large shallow dish; pour wine mixture over roast. Cover and marinate 8 hours in refrigerator, turning occasionally.

Remove roast from marinade; discard marinade. Place roast in a shallow pan; insert meat thermometer, making sure it does not touch fat. Bake at 325° for 2 hours or until thermometer registers 140° (rare) or 160° (medium). Yield: 12 to 15 servings.   *Betsy Rose*
Greensboro, North Carolina

DIJON CHICKEN WITH PASTA

6 chicken breast halves
¾ cup butter or margarine, softened
⅓ cup sliced green onions
¼ cup chopped fresh parsley
3½ tablespoons Dijon mustard
12 ounces uncooked fettuccine
Garnish: fresh parsley sprigs

Loosen skin from breast halves, forming a pocket without detaching skin. Set aside.

Combine butter and next 3 ingredients, mixing well. Place 1½ tablespoons butter mixture under skin of each piece of chicken; reserve remaining mixture. Place chicken, skin side up, in a lightly greased 13- x 9- x 2-inch baking dish. Bake at 350° for 1 hour, basting occasionally with pan drippings.

Cook fettuccine according to package directions; drain and return to Dutch oven. Add remaining butter mixture, tossing well. Serve with chicken. Garnish, if desired. Yield: 6 servings.   *Mary Helen Hackney*
Greenville, North Carolina

Stir Leftovers Into A Salad

Most of us have meat and poultry left over from holiday meals. For an easy alternative to plain sandwiches, try turning those leftovers into a tasty salad.

You can use either chicken or turkey in Fruited Chicken Salad. Apple, celery, and walnuts give it a crunchy goodness that's hard to beat. Served on lettuce leaves or croissants, this salad makes a tasty entrée for lunch or dinner.

FRUITED CHICKEN SALAD

1½ cups chopped cooked chicken or turkey
1 cup chopped unpeeled apple
¾ cup chopped celery
½ cup chopped walnuts
1 (3-ounce) package cream cheese, softened
½ cup sour cream
3 tablespoons pineapple juice
¼ teaspoon salt
⅛ teaspoon white pepper

Combine first 4 ingredients. Combine cream cheese and remaining ingredients; mix well. Add to chicken mixture, stirring well. Cover and chill. Yield: 6 servings.   *Mrs. L. Mayer*
Richmond, Virginia

TURKEY SALAD

2½ cups diced cooked turkey or chicken
1 cup diced celery
½ cup raisins
2 green onions, thinly sliced
½ cup mayonnaise or salad dressing
¼ cup chopped fresh parsley
1 tablespoon dry white wine
½ teaspoon dried whole tarragon
¼ teaspoon salt
¼ teaspoon pepper
½ cup slivered almonds, toasted

Combine first 4 ingredients; set aside. Combine mayonnaise, parsley, wine, tarragon, salt, and pepper; fold into turkey mixture. Stir in almonds before serving. Yield: 4 servings.
Mrs. K. W. Kenney
Richmond, Virginia

ROAST BEEF SALAD

1 cup cubed cooked roast beef
1 cup cubed Cheddar cheese
1 medium cucumber, sliced
½ cup sliced green onions
1 tablespoon minced fresh dillweed or 1 teaspoon dried whole dillweed
⅔ cup commercial cucumber salad dressing
1 tablespoon white vinegar
1 tablespoon prepared horseradish
1 avocado, cut into wedges
1 medium tomato, cut into wedges
Lettuce leaves

Combine first 5 ingredients, and toss gently; set aside. Combine cucumber salad dressing, vinegar, and horseradish; pour over roast beef mixture, and toss gently. Cover and chill.

Arrange avocado and tomato wedges on individual lettuce-lined plates; spoon salad onto plates. Serve immediately. Yield: 4 servings.   *Ethel Jernegan*
Savannah, Georgia

COLORFUL HAM-AND-RICE SALAD

1 cup long-grain rice, uncooked
1 (10-ounce) package frozen
    English peas, thawed and
    drained
1 cup cooked ham strips
4 ounces Swiss cheese, cut into
    1- x ¼-inch strips
¾ cup mayonnaise or salad
    dressing
½ cup chopped dill pickle
¼ cup chopped onion
½ teaspoon dried dillweed
½ teaspoon salt
¼ teaspoon pepper
Lettuce leaves
Garnish: tomato wedges

Cook rice according to package directions, omitting salt; cool. Combine rice and next 9 ingredients, stirring until mixed. Cover and chill thoroughly. Serve on lettuce leaves, and garnish, if desired. Yield: 6 servings.   *Sharry Swann*
Tifton, Georgia

LAYERED OVERNIGHT SALAD

3 cups shredded iceberg lettuce
1 cup sliced carrot
1 cup sliced cucumber
1 cup coarsely shredded red
    cabbage
4 cups cooked macaroni
3 hard-cooked eggs, sliced
1 small purple onion, thinly
    sliced and separated into rings
1 cup julienne-sliced ham
1 (10-ounce) package frozen
    English peas, thawed and
    drained
½ cup (2 ounces) shredded
    Cheddar cheese
½ cup (2 ounces) shredded
    Monterey Jack cheese
Dressing (recipe follows)
2 tablespoons chopped fresh
    parsley

Layer first 11 ingredients in order given in a large salad bowl. Spread dressing over top, sealing to edge of bowl. Cover tightly; refrigerate 8

hours. Sprinkle salad with parsley before serving. Yield: 6 servings.

Dressing

1 cup mayonnaise or salad
    dressing
½ cup sour cream
¼ cup sliced green onions
2 to 3 teaspoons spicy mustard
1 teaspoon sugar
¼ teaspoon salt
¼ teaspoon white pepper

Combine all ingredients; stir well. Yield: 1⅔ cups.   *Carol S. Noble*
Burgaw, South Carolina

After The Slopes, The Feast

It's time to head for the slopes. Whether you drive to the Southern mountains or fly out West, this menu has ingredients you can pack in the car or buy at the grocery store upon arrival at your skiing destination.

Sea-and-Ski Cocktail Mix
Chili-Chicken Stew
Commercial coleslaw
Seasoned Cornbread
Brownie Chip Cookies

SEA-AND-SKI COCKTAIL MIX

1 (12-ounce) package bite-size
    crispy rice squares
1 (7-ounce) package toasted
    oat O-shaped cereal
1 (10-ounce) package thin pretzel
    sticks
2 cups butter or margarine,
    melted
1 teaspoon hot sauce
1¼ teaspoons garlic salt
2 (12-ounce) cans salted mixed
    nuts

Divide cereals and pretzels into 2 large roasting pans. Combine butter, hot sauce, and garlic salt; pour over cereal mixtures, stirring until all pieces are evenly coated. Bake at 200° for 1½ hours, stirring every 30 minutes. Add nuts, and bake an additional 45 minutes. Yield: 4 quarts.
Carolyn McCue
Oklahoma City, Oklahoma

CHILI-CHICKEN STEW

6 chicken breast halves, boned
    and skinned
1 medium onion, chopped
1 medium green pepper, chopped
2 cloves garlic, minced
1 tablespoon vegetable oil
2 (14½-ounce) cans stewed
    tomatoes, undrained and
    chopped
1 (15-ounce) can pinto beans,
    drained
⅔ cup picante sauce
1 teaspoon chili powder
1 teaspoon ground cumin
½ teaspoon salt
Shredded Cheddar cheese, sour
    cream, diced avocado, and
    sliced green onions

Cut chicken into 1-inch squares. Cook chicken, onion, chopped green pepper, and garlic in hot oil in a Dutch oven until lightly browned. Add tomatoes and next 5 ingredients; cover, reduce heat, and simmer 20 minutes. Top individual servings with remaining ingredients. Yield: 6 servings.   *Joan Voan*
Shepherd, Texas

Tip: *Check foods closely as you are shopping to be sure they are not spoiled. Do not buy cans that are badly dented, leaking, or bulging at the ends. Do not select packages which have broken seals.*

SEASONED CORNBREAD

1 (8½-ounce) package corn muffin
   mix
½ teaspoon poultry seasoning
1 egg, beaten
⅔ cup milk

Combine muffin mix and poultry seasoning; add egg and milk, stirring just until dry ingredients are moistened. Pour batter into a well-greased 8-inch square baking dish; bake at 400° for 18 to 20 minutes or until golden brown. Yield: 9 servings.

Carolyne M. Carnevale
Ormond Beach, Florida

BROWNIE CHIP COOKIES

1 (23.7-ounce) package brownie
   mix
2 eggs
⅓ cup vegetable oil
1 (6-ounce) package semisweet
   chocolate morsels
½ cup chopped pecans

Combine brownie mix, eggs, and oil; beat about 50 strokes with a spoon. Stir in chocolate morsels and pecans. Drop dough by rounded teaspoonfuls onto greased cookie sheets. Bake at 350° for 10 to 12 minutes. Cool slightly (about 2 minutes) on cookie sheets. Remove to wire racks, and let cool completely. Yield: about 6 dozen.   *Glenda Chambers*
Woodstock, Georgia

Tip: *For perfectly shaped round cookies, pack homemade refrigerator cookie dough into clean 6-ounce juice cans (don't remove bottoms) and freeze dough. Thaw cookie dough about 15 minutes; then open bottom of can and push up, using the top edge as a cutting guide.*

Roast Turkey: Something To Squawk About

If you're chicken about cooking turkey, fear no more. It's not as difficult as you might think. Following the steps here and using good judgment about food safety ensure a feather for your cap.

Frozen, Fresh, or Pre-cooked

Many kinds of turkey are available during the holiday season; select what you want according to your needs. You can buy a frozen turkey of any size early, but keep it frozen until one to four days before cooking. (For how long it will take to thaw, see our chart below.)

If you prefer not to have a turkey taking up space in your refrigerator as it thaws, order a fresh one ahead of time (one to two days before cooking). Don't buy fresh turkeys that have been stuffed with dressing at the deli; bacteria grows easily in the cavity of a fresh, stuffed turkey if it sits long. Instead, stuff your turkey at home and cook immediately, or bake the dressing separately in a baking dish.

Pre-cooked turkey is available for the truly busy host or hostess. Serve these turkeys immediately, if possible; if not, remove dressing from the cavity of the turkey and refrigerate both. The meat will keep in the refrigerator for three to four days, the stuffing for one or two days. To reheat, bake the turkey at 325° to 350°

Thawing Times for Whole Turkey

Weight of Turkey	In Refrigerator	In Cold Water
8 to 12 pounds	1 to 2 days	4 to 6 hours
12 to 16 pounds	2 to 3 days	6 to 9 hours
16 to 20 pounds	3 to 4 days	9 to 11 hours
20 to 24 pounds	4 to 5 days	11 to 12 hours

Note: If the cold water method is used, change water every 30 minutes. After thawing for either method, remove neck and giblets, wash turkey inside and outside with cold water, and drain well. **Wash hands, utensils, sink, counter, and anything else that touches raw turkey with hot, soapy water.**

Timetable for Roasting
Fresh or Thawed Turkey in a 325° Oven

Weight (pounds)	Unstuffed (hours)	Stuffed (hours)
6 to 8	2¼ to 3¼	3 to 3½
8 to 12	3 to 4	3½ to 4½
12 to 16	3½ to 4½	4½ to 5½
16 to 20	4 to 5	5½ to 6½
20 to 24	4½ to 5½	6½ to 7
24 to 28	5 to 6½	7 to 8½

for 10 minutes per pound or until a meat thermometer inserted in the bird registers 160°.

The Big Chill Ends

A microwave oven shortens the amount of time a turkey spends thawing. Check the microwave oven manufacturer's instructions for the size turkey that will fit in your oven, the minutes per pound, and the power level to use for thawing. Turkey may also be thawed in the refrigerator or in cold water. Don't thaw turkey at room temperature; harmful bacteria can grow.

How to Roast a Turkey

You may have seen this recipe before. It's our standard, never-fail recipe for roast turkey.

ROAST TURKEY

1 whole turkey
Salt (optional)
Vegetable oil or melted butter or
 margarine

Remove giblets and neck from turkey; reserve for other uses, if desired. Rinse turkey thoroughly with cold water; pat dry. Sprinkle cavity with salt for unstuffed turkey. If stuffing is desired, lightly stuff dressing into body cavities of turkey. If excess skin around tail has been cut away, tuck legs under flap of skin around tail. If excess skin is intact, close cavity with skewers, and truss. Tie ends of legs to tail with cord. Lift wingtips up and over back, and tuck under turkey.

Place turkey on a roasting rack, breast side up; brush entire turkey with oil. Insert meat thermometer in meaty part of thigh, making sure it does not touch bone. Bake at 325° until meat thermometer reaches 185° (see Timetable for Roasting). If turkey starts browning too much, cover loosely with aluminum foil.

When turkey is two-thirds done, cut the cord or band of skin holding the drumstick ends to the tail; this will ensure that the thighs are

cooked internally. Turkey is done when drumsticks are easy to move up and down. Let stand 15 minutes before carving. Yield: Plan to buy 1½ pounds frozen or fresh, uncooked turkey per person; buy 1¼ pounds pre-cooked turkey per person.

Love That Turkey Sandwich

Turkey eating doesn't end with the holiday dinner. For many food enthusiasts, the turkey sandwich that follows the big meal is the best part of a family dinner. To be sure your loved ones eat safe leftovers, never leave food, including turkey, at room temperature for over two hours. For a buffet party, prepare food trays ahead of time, and keep them in your refrigerator until needed. Replenish food trays, as needed.

After dinner is over, remove any stuffing from the bird, and refrigerate both. Insist that snackers retrieve turkey slices from the refrigerator—not the table. The risk of food poisoning is too great to leave the meat out all afternoon and evening. Leftover turkey will keep in the refrigerator three or four days; dressing and gravy keep only one to two days. It is also important to make sure you bring leftover gravy to a rolling boil before serving.

Tip: *Keep butter, margarine, and fat drippings tightly covered in the refrigerator. Vegetable shortening can be kept covered at room temperature. Homemade salad dressing should be kept in the refrigerator; mayonnaise and commercial salad dressings should be refrigerated after opening. Foods mixed with mayonnaise, such as potato salad or egg salad, should be refrigerated and used within a couple of days.*

Bread With Italian Roots

Focaccia, an unadorned cousin to pizza, has been around since medieval times. Traditionally it's a hearth-baked bread with a sprinkling of salt, a few drops of olive oil, and perhaps a little chopped onion.

Patricia Saylor of Crofton, Maryland, makes her Mustard-and-Onion Focaccia spicier than the authentic version. In addition to the traditional toppings, she adds Dijon mustard, red pepper, and black pepper. And to save time, she takes advantage of frozen bread dough.

MUSTARD-AND-ONION FOCACCIA

1 medium onion, sliced and cut
 into quarters
1 tablespoon butter or margarine,
 melted
¼ cup Dijon mustard
⅛ teaspoon red pepper
1 (16-ounce) loaf frozen bread
 dough, thawed
1 tablespoon olive oil
⅛ teaspoon salt
Dash of black pepper

Sauté onion in butter until tender; set aside.

Combine mustard and red pepper; set aside. Place bread dough on a lightly floured large baking sheet; roll to a 15- x 10-inch rectangle. Brush dough with olive oil; spread mustard mixture over dough. Arrange onion evenly over mustard. Sprinkle with salt and black pepper. Bake at 400° for 15 to 18 minutes or until golden. Cut into rectangles. Yield: 6 to 8 servings.

Sip The Holiday Spirit

Break the ice at your next holiday party with these delightful frozen beverages. Perfect for entertaining, these recipes can be made days before your event, leaving you plenty of time to tend to last-minute details before your guests arrive.

WHITE SANGRÍA SLUSH

1 (12-ounce) can frozen lemonade
  concentrate, thawed and
  undiluted
1 (6-ounce) can frozen orange
  juice concentrate, thawed and
  undiluted
1½ cups water
1 (750-milliliter) bottle Chablis or
  other dry white wine, chilled
1 (10-ounce) bottle club soda,
  chilled
Garnishes: lemon, lime, or orange
  slices

Combine first 3 ingredients in a 13- x 9- x 2-inch pan; freeze until firm. To serve, spoon slush mixture into a large pitcher. Add wine and club soda; stir gently until slushy. If desired, place a fruit slice on rim of each glass. Yield: 2 quarts.

Mrs. William Huffcut
Pensacola, Florida

PEACH DAIQUIRIS

1 (10-ounce) package frozen
  peaches
1 (6-ounce) can frozen lemonade
  concentrate, thawed and
  undiluted
1 cup water
¾ cup rum

Combine all ingredients in container of an electric blender; process until smooth. Spoon into a freezer container, and freeze. Let stand at room temperature 15 minutes or until slushy before serving. Yield: 1 quart.

Note: One 10-ounce package frozen strawberries may be substituted for peaches, if desired. *Violet Nelson*
Columbia, South Carolina

CHAMPAGNE FRUIT SLUSH

2 cups sugar
3 cups boiling water
3 bananas, quartered
1 (8-ounce) can sliced peaches,
  undrained
1 (12-ounce) can frozen orange
  juice concentrate, thawed and
  undiluted
1 (6-ounce) can frozen lemonade
  concentrate, thawed and
  undiluted
1 (46-ounce) can pineapple juice
3 (750-milliliter) bottles
  champagne, chilled

Combine sugar and boiling water, stirring until sugar dissolves. Cool. Combine bananas and peaches in container of an electric blender; process until smooth. Combine sugar syrup, banana mixture, orange juice concentrate, lemonade concentrate, and pineapple juice in a large container. Freeze until firm.

To serve, partially thaw frozen mixture. Place in a punch bowl, and break into chunks. Add champagne; stir gently until slushy. Yield: about 6 quarts. *Kathy Hunt*
Dallas, Texas

SLUSH WITH A PUNCH

¾ cup sugar
7 cups water
1 (12-ounce) can frozen lemonade
  concentrate, thawed and
  undiluted
1 (12-ounce) can frozen orange
  juice concentrate, thawed and
  undiluted
1 (6-ounce) can frozen pineapple
  juice concentrate, thawed and
  undiluted
1 to 1½ cups coconut liqueur
5 to 6 cups lemon-lime
  carbonated beverage, chilled

Combine sugar and water in a saucepan; bring to a boil, stirring until sugar dissolves. Cool. Add concentrates and liqueur, stirring well. Pour mixture into a large container, and freeze.

To serve, spoon about 1 cup slush mixture into a glass. Add ½ cup lemon-lime beverage, stirring until slushy. Yield: 1 gallon.

Merle R. Downs
Tryon, North Carolina

AMARETTO SLUSH

1 cup boiling water
3 regular-size tea bags
3½ cups water
1½ cups amaretto
1 cup sugar
1 (6-ounce) can frozen orange
  juice concentrate, thawed and
  undiluted
1 (6-ounce) can frozen lemonade
  concentrate, thawed and
  undiluted
2 (33.8-ounce) bottles ginger ale,
  chilled

Pour boiling water over tea bags; cover and let stand 5 minutes. Remove tea bags; discard. Transfer tea to a 2-quart freezer container. Stir in 3½ cups water and next 4 ingredients. Cover and freeze until firm.

To serve, partially thaw until slushy. Pour equal parts of slush mixture and ginger ale into serving glasses. Yield: 1 gallon.

Barbara Bolden
Eden, North Carolina

Ease Into Morning

Getting out of a cozy bed on frosty mornings will be easy when you know one of these breakfast treats is your reward. Tropical Coffee Cake's subtle sunny flavors of orange and coconut will have you warmed up to winter in no time.

After a merry round of package opening on Christmas morning, hungry grownups will appreciate Sweet Potato Waffles With Orange Butter as a thoughtful gift from the kitchen.

TROPICAL COFFEE CAKE

½ cup chopped pecans
½ cup flaked coconut
¼ cup sugar
2 teaspoons grated orange rind
1 teaspoon ground cinnamon
½ cup butter or margarine, softened
1 cup sugar
2 eggs
1 (8-ounce) carton sour cream
1 teaspoon vanilla extract
2 cups all-purpose flour
1 teaspoon baking soda
1 teaspoon baking powder
Dash of salt

Combine first 5 ingredients in a small bowl; set aside.

Cream butter; gradually add 1 cup sugar, beating at medium speed of an electric mixer. Add eggs, one at a time, beating after each addition. Add sour cream and vanilla.

Combine flour, soda, baking powder, and salt; add to creamed mixture, beating well. Spoon half of batter into a greased 9-inch square pan; sprinkle with half of pecan mixture. Repeat procedure with batter and pecan mixture. Gently swirl with a knife to create a marbled effect. Bake at 350° for 35 minutes or until a wooden pick inserted in center comes out clean. Yield: 9 to 12 servings.

Andra Temple
Dothan, Alabama

SWEET POTATO WAFFLES WITH ORANGE BUTTER

2 cups all-purpose flour
1 tablespoon baking powder
½ teaspoon salt
Dash of cream of tartar
3 eggs, separated
1½ cups cooked mashed sweet potatoes
1 cup milk
¼ cup firmly packed brown sugar
¼ cup butter or margarine, melted
2 tablespoons grated orange rind
Orange Butter
Garnish: orange slices

Combine first 4 ingredients in a large bowl; set aside.

Combine egg yolks, sweet potatoes, milk, brown sugar, butter, and grated rind; stir into flour mixture. Beat egg whites (at room temperature) until stiff peaks form; carefully fold into batter (batter will be thick). Spread batter on a preheated oiled waffle iron, and cook until lightly browned. Serve waffles with Orange Butter and honey. Garnish, if desired. Yield: 8 (8-inch) waffles.

Orange Butter

½ cup butter or margarine, softened
1 tablespoon grated orange rind

Combine butter and orange rind; beat at medium speed of an electric mixer until blended. Yield: ½ cup.

Ella C. Stivers
Houston, Texas

PUMPKIN DOUGHNUT DROPS

½ cup sugar
1 teaspoon ground cinnamon
1½ cups all-purpose flour
1 tablespoon baking powder
½ teaspoon salt
⅓ cup sugar
¼ teaspoon ground cinnamon
¼ teaspoon ground nutmeg
¼ teaspoon ground ginger
1 egg, beaten
½ cup canned or cooked mashed pumpkin
¼ cup milk
2 tablespoons vegetable oil
½ teaspoon vanilla extract
Vegetable oil

Combine ½ cup sugar and 1 teaspoon cinnamon; set aside.

Combine flour and next 6 ingredients in a medium bowl. Combine egg, pumpkin, milk, 2 tablespoons vegetable oil, and vanilla. Add to flour mixture, stirring just until dry ingredients are moistened.

Pour oil to a depth of 2 inches into a heavy saucepan; heat to 375°. Carefully drop pumpkin mixture by level tablespoonfuls into oil; fry until golden brown, turning once. Drain on paper towels, and roll in sugar-cinnamon mixture. Serve immediately. Yield: about 1½ dozen.

Edith Askins
Greenville, Texas

Tip: *The secret of good muffins is in the mixing. Combine all the dry ingredients in a bowl, and form a well in the center of the mixture. Add the liquid all at once, and stir only enough to moisten the dry ingredients. The mixture will be lumpy, but further mixing will make the muffins tough.*

Roots Of Southern Food

by John Egerton

Imagine being in charge of a kitchen somewhere in the South when word is received that the United Nations General Assembly is coming to dinner—more than 1,500 delegates and guests altogether, representing a panoramic spectrum of cultural backgrounds and palates.

A daunting prospect, to say the least—but not too much for a team of world-class Southern cooks. Such a challenge arose in Nashville back in 1976 when the United Nations, for the first time in its history, made an en masse excursion away from its headquarters. The local planners of a Nashville summer banquet for the world body considered and dismissed a multitude of menu proposals highlighting various international gourmet cuisines. Finally, wiser heads prevailed, and the designated hostess/caterer, Phila Hach of Clarksville, Tennessee, was asked to prepare and serve a classic and traditional Southern country feast.

And so it was that in the shadow of the Parthenon in the city that for more than a century has called itself "the Athens of the South," envoys from 125 nations of the world came to dine on country ham, catfish and hush puppies, fried chicken, green beans with ham hock, corn on the cob, potato salad, coleslaw, cucumber pickles, deviled eggs, cornbread, yeast rolls, beaten biscuits, watermelon, cantaloupe, iced tea, sweet milk, buttermilk, orange juice, mint juleps, pecan pie, chess pie, and various other treasures of Southern culinary history.

If such an occasion had arisen in 1876 or even 1676, many of the same foods might have been served—the ham, the fish, the chicken, the corn and beans, the melons, the bread. Throughout most of the five centuries since the time of Columbus, the South has evolved a distinctive cookery that has consistently reflected its culture. Here, perhaps more than anywhere, the old maxim applies: We are what we eat.

Pork Meets Corn

Right from the first, Spanish and English explorers both introduced and discovered good things to eat when they came ashore in present-day Virginia, the Carolinas, Georgia, Florida, and the islands farther south, and that process of exchange and cross-fertilization continued with the later arrival of other Europeans and Africans. Together with the Native American populations of the coastal region, the emigrants from other lands sowed the symbolic and literal seeds from which sprang the roots of a diverse cuisine now widely known and loved as Southern cooking. Under that broad umbrella, numerous styles of food preparation have thrived—Creole and Acadian, coastal and mountain, country and soul, ethnic and indigenous, traditional and modern, plain and fancy, uptown and down-home.

Corn was already here when pork arrived on the hoof by ship from Spain. The Indians also had beans, peas, squash, onions, greens, and various kinds of fruits, berries, and nuts to offer, as well as woods that teemed with wild game and waters that abounded with seafood. Over the span of a century or more, the newcomers contributed livestock, wheat and oats, cabbages and yams, okra and black-eyed peas, peanuts, potatoes, tomatoes, oranges, rice, melons, chocolate, coffee, tea, and other foodstuffs.

And in this fertile atmosphere, where plentiful rain and sun and the turning of the seasons combined to create an ideal environment in which almost anything could grow, the South became primarily an agricultural land, the garden of a young nation. With all the necessary native and imported raw materials at hand, it was but one step further to the creation of an eclectic and distinguished regional cuisine. All that was needed to make great cookery was great cooks—and, as it turned out, the South had those too.

Cooking is a creative talent, an art, a science—and, some would say, more a gift than an acquired skill. Great cooks are commonly described as "natural born," not made. Somehow, as if by an unwritten formula of apportionment, the South seems to have received more than its share of kitchen virtuosos. Natives and immigrants, blacks and whites, women and men have all brought to the kitchen enough wisdom and instinct and sure-handed control to make Southern cooking stand out above all the other regional culinary styles in the nation.

More than natural law accounts for this wealth of talent; there are some historical explanations as well. Slavery was a major factor in the evolution of black cooks. The women and men of African heritage who did the lion's share of cooking and serving for generations were the primary creators of what we now celebrate as Southern cooking. It was they, more than any others, who transformed the rudimentary staples of a pioneer culture into the refined dishes and the sumptuous feasts that came to epitomize Southern hospitality.

Poverty was another historical condition that influenced the evolution of Southern food. At least twice in American history, in the traumatic eras of the Civil War and the Great Depression, the masses of Southern people, whatever their race or class, experienced hunger firsthand. Often their very survival depended on the inventive and improvisational talents of fishers and hunters, gardeners and foragers—and most of all, cooks.

Out of these somber periods of Southern history—periods of slavery, segregation, poverty—came legions of great cooks and the classic dishes

they created. This puzzling anomaly has a striking parallel in another of the region's indigenous creations: music. The original music of the South—the blues, spirituals, jazz, country, gospel—is a collective art form born of hard times. From the depths of pain and heartbreak, local musicians brought forth expressive sounds of beauty that lingered in the mind, and the quality of their music caused it to spread around the nation and around the world.

And so it is with Southern food. It, too, was born out of strife and travail and suffering, then tempered by servitude, and flavored by poverty and injustice. But the black and white women as well as the black men who took the little bit of latitude they had for inventiveness and produced divine dishes of the highest order, transcended the barriers of race and class and sex that surrounded them.

Their food was delightful, memorable; like the music, it proved to have a timeless and universal appeal—and now, long years later, we still declare its excellence, and praise those who created it.

Up from Adversity

These are the paradoxical roots of Southern food. No culture can cut itself off from its history, and no amount of romantic embellishment can change that. Divisions of race and class and the physical and psychological isolation of this region from the rest of the nation were all facts of life in the Southern past.

But it is also true that every culture is a complex amalgam of positive and negative parts—and in the South, food has always been one of the most positive and enduring reflections of the region's character. In practically every good and lasting memory any Southerner holds—of family and friends, of home and countryside, of school and church, of joyful and even solemn occasions—food is there, working through all the senses to leave a powerful and permanent impression.

No wonder, then, that Southern food is often celebrated in verse and

song, novels and short stories, art and theater, serious essays and humorous expressions. Consider, for example, this declaration by the ladies of the Methodist Church in Maysville, Kentucky, in their 1884 cookbook: "Bad dinners go hand in hand with total depravity, while a well-fed man is already half saved." It is not altogether clear which was their more compelling mission—good dinners or salvation.

Soprano Leontyne Price is a world-renowned opera star far removed from her Mississippi roots—but, she says, images of home still are "rampant in my memories," and foremost among them are catfish, cornbread, turnip greens, and fried chicken. Living closer to home but similarly appreciative is author Reynolds Price. Drinking deep from his own North Carolina well of family dinner-table recollections, he etched this vivid scene in his recent novel, *Good Hearts:*

It was Mama's usual light lunch—the turkey with cornbread dressing and cranberry sauce, country ham, corn pudding, snaps and little butterbeans she'd put up last July, spiced peaches, cold crisp watermelon-rind pickles, macaroni and cheese, creamed potatoes and gravy, then her own angelfood cake and ambrosia. Every mouthful made the only way, from the naked pot upward by hand. I hadn't eaten with her since the Fourth of July, and it was a real shock to my tongue—that many kind flavors, all happening at once like good deeds intended for me. Whenever I compliment her on it, she just says, "It's the only way I know to cook."

It takes a Southerner—and a writer of Reynolds Price's caliber—to construct a passage like that. As the saying goes, you have to have been there to grasp the full picture. Price's "Mama" and all the other Mamas of the South have elevated dinners like the one he describes to the highest level of quality, and in so doing have earned for themselves a measure of immortality.

Cookery and History

In every great history there are larger-than-life characters, dramatic events, hallowed places, mythic tales of stirring adventures. By these measures, the story of Southern food and its place in the culture certainly qualifies as a compelling drama, an epic of pathos and humor with a cast of millions. Look back at the record and you can see how central this cook's-eye view has been to the larger story of Southern history.

It was food that brought Native Americans and Europeans together, and it was food that drove them apart. They met at Jamestown in 1607 over pork and corn and roast oysters, and in the "starving times" of subsequent winters it was also corn—or rather the lack of it—over which they fought.

The plantations that rose up in the Coastal South and later in the interior became temples of a hospitality so lavish that visitors went away marveling at the gastronomic spectacle. France, with all its culinary renown, had nothing on the elegant feasts presided over by these Southern gentlemen and ladies, and as for England, its cookery seemed hardly worth comparing.

Thomas Jefferson, the agrarian gentleman and gourmet who served as governor of Virginia and minister to France before his election as President, probably did more than any other Southerner in history to establish the importance of food in the culture. (In one of his least applauded acts as governor, Jefferson enraged the butchers of Richmond by sending his agents into the countryside to buy up market-bound hogs. When he later offered the animals for sale at an inflated monopoly price, the butchers marched to the home of their "Hog Governor" and festooned his picket fence with chitterlings.)

While serving in France in the mid-1780s, Jefferson traveled extensively in Europe and always showed the keenest interest in food. On his return to Virginia, he introduced Southern and American eaters to vanilla extract, olives and olive oil, wines from France, pasta from Italy, waffles (and a waffle iron) from Holland, and recipes for such culinary treasures as ice cream, meringues, and oil-and-vinegar salad dressing. His garden at Monticello was the most extensive vegetable plot in the United States, an experimental farm where new varieties of plants were constantly being tried and their performance meticulously recorded.

Though his tastes encompassed far more than the cookery of the South, Jefferson did much to spread the popularity of this food by serving and savoring such regional specialties as Virginia ham, Chesapeake crabs, shad, sweet potatoes, black-eyed peas, turnip greens, and roasted Indian corn. In order to appreciate what a lasting contribution that was, consider this: Two centuries have passed since the age of Jefferson, and now most of the nation's hogs and corn grow in the Midwest, but if you're looking for genuine country ham and barbecue or for roasting ears and cornbread—not to mention bourbon whiskey—the best place to find them is still here in the South.

First in Cookbooks

Even before Thomas Jefferson planted his garden, the first cookbook to be published in America was brought out by William Parks, a printer in Williamsburg, Virginia. That 1742 volume was actually a reprint of a London cookery book that had little applicability in the colonies, but it did pave the way for others to come, and it also established the South as the American leader in cookbooks, a position that it has never relinquished.

The first truly American-and-Southern cookbook was *The Virginia House-Wife*, by Mary Randolph. Published in 1824, it became a model for other "housewife" books (one from Kentucky in 1839, another from South Carolina in 1847), and food historians consider it the most influential American cookbook of the entire 19th century.

The Dixie Cook-Book, a comprehensive volume of more than 1,300 pages, was published in Atlanta in 1883 and dedicated "to the mothers, wives, and daughters of the 'Sunny South,' who have so bravely faced the difficulties which new social conditions have imposed on them as mistresses of Southern homes, and on whose courage and fidelity in good or ill fortune the future of their beloved land must depend." The *Dixie* was one of many postwar volumes that aimed to instruct women in the basics of cookery.

It was also in 1885 that Lafcadio Hearn, a journalist in New Orleans, anonymously wrote *La Cuisine Creole,* the first major cookbook from that leading food city of the South. By the turn of the century, when the editors of *The Times-Picayune,* a New Orleans newspaper, issued the now-classic *Picayune's Creole Cook Book,* the city's reputation for good food and good times had long since been established in the South and around the nation.

Names and places in the history of food in 19th-century New Orleans still resonate with meaning: Antoine's, a famous reataurant then and now; the St. Charles Hotel in the French Quarter; Elizabeth Kettenring Bégué, the cook and hostess who for all practical purposes invented brunch; legions of entrepreneurs and cooks who made steamboat dining on the Mississippi and Pullman diners on the railroads so appealing; and, perhaps most important of all, the food itself—such mystical and wonderful creations as bouillabaisse, a delectable seafood stew of French inspiration; filé gumbo, a magical union of Choctaw and African cookery; and pralines, a caramelized sugar-and-pecan confection that may be as old as New Orleans itself.

Creoles, contrary to popular belief, were not social aristocrats but simply the first generation New Orleans-born sons and daughters of immigrants (French, Spanish, African, whatever). By that populist definition, the term embraced all that has come to be regarded as distinctly New Orleanian—and that takes generations of distinguished cooks and delectable dishes.

Louisiana, by all odds the most food-conscious and cuisine-rich state in the nation, has given us two of the most distinctive cooking styles to be found anywhere in the world. New Orleans-born Creole and bayou-born Acadian (Cajun) are like city and country cousins, the one rich and elegant and sophisticated, the other earthy, spicy, straightforward—and both of them confidently, even arrogantly, superior. With all due allowances for oversimplification, Creole and Cajun styles are like nonidentical twins in a family of gifted overachievers: obviously different, obviously kin, and obviously excellent.

Southern Hostelries

In the early decades of the 20th century, New Orleans solidified its position as a dining mecca with the rise of such restaurants as Arnaud's and Galatoire's—both still thriving. Elsewhere in the South, a host of other institutions dedicated to fine food were building solid reputations of their own. Hotels such as The Peabody in Memphis, the Hermitage in Nashville, the Seelbach in Louisville, The Tutwiler in Birmingham, and the Adolphus in Dallas often rivaled the best of New Orleans and cities outside the region. In recent years, all of these hotels have been restored to their original splendor, and again offer excellent fare.

Southern inns were immensely popular too, from the famous edifice in Williamsburg and others in small-town Virginia to the Grove Park in Asheville and a host of little gems, among them Boone Tavern in Berea, Kentucky; House by the Road in Ashburn, Georgia; Inn by the Sea at Pass Christian, Mississippi; the Purefoy Hotel in Talladega, Alabama; the Sedberry Hotel in McMinnville, Tennessee; and the Old Stage Coach, in the heart of Arkansas. Many of the old lodges are gone now, but some, such as the Williamsburg and Grove Park Inns and Boone Tavern, have not only survived but seemingly have improved with age.

Aside from hostelries, there were numerous Southern dining places that developed a loyal and far-flung clientele. Weidmann's in Meridian, Mississippi, was and is such a place, and the same can be said for Tampa's famed Spanish restaurant, Columbia, and for the venerable Bright Star in Bessemer, Alabama. The Morrison's cafeteria chain got its start in Mobile in 1920 and is still headquartered there, and Krystal, one of the earliest of fast-food hamburger chains, was founded in Chattanooga in 1932.

Another trailblazer in the field of food was Piggly Wiggly, the store that pioneered the concept of self-service grocery shopping. This first supermarket was established in Memphis in 1916 and remains a prominent Southern institution, one of several chains in the competitive supermarket field.

Clearly, the South has contributed more than its proportional share to the social and cultural unfolding of American food history. Of particular importance in this regard have been some outstanding individual contributions by natives of the region. Kentucky, to cite one notable example, has given us journalist/humorist Irvin S. Cobb, who often wrote about food and drink; travel guide and restaurant critic Duncan Hines, who parlayed his guidebooks into a sprawling network of food-related enterprises; historian Thomas D. Clark, one of the few of his profession to treat food as a subject worthy of scrutiny; and a small army of excellent cookbook writers, from Jennie Benedict and

Emma Allen Hayes (one of the nation's first black food-book authors, in 1912) to authors Marion Flexner, Cissy Gregg, Lillian Marshall, and Camille Glenn.

Martha McCulloch-Williams came within a few miles of being born a Kentuckian; her plantation home was just across the state line in Tennessee. In 1913, when she was a 65-year-old writer long removed to New York, she produced from memory an account of her early years that survives now as a classic, one of the first narrative cookbooks ever written. Far more than a mere collection of recipes, *Dishes & Beverages of the Old South* is a revealing social history. Numerous others have followed with outstanding narratives of their own, adding much to the public understanding of Southern history.

And as for straightforward recipe collections of the highest quality, there are literally scores, hundreds of them, as the mere mention of a few authors will signify: Henrietta Dull, Marion Brown, Winifred G. Cheney, Mary Land, Lena Richard, Craig Claiborne, Jeanne Voltz, Lena Sturges, Kathryn T. Windham, Sallie Hill, Cleora Butler, Paul Prudhomme, Justin Wilson, Nathalie Dupree.

Change and Tradition

An endless succession of transformations has swept through the South since the end of World War II, and not least among them has been a series of major modifications of what and how people eat. This is not just a Southern phenomenon, of course; it's national, even international.

Fast-food chains, new technology, the movement of women into the workplace, the decline of the agricultural economy, the rise of television and other marketing tools, advances in medical science, concern about health and nutrition—these and other developments have combined to revolutionize eating habits. People eat out much more than previously, and what they eat is different—more highly processed, more chemically altered, lower in fat, higher in fiber, changed (and, overall, probably less appealing) in taste. Along with these changes have come new labels for food products. Terms such as "natural" and "light" are often used to describe modern food, though their meaning is not always clear.

Change is inevitable and necessary; growth is not possible without it. More often than not, change is also unsettling, a mixture of positive and negative elements, of gains and losses. Again, Southern food is illustrative: Greater freedoms and higher living standards are certainly desirable improvements, one manifestation of which is the sharp increase in restaurant dining—but another is the decline of home cooking, and with it the fading importance of the dinner table as a family council site and of meals in general as a unifying ritual in the American home. Women cook less, and that's good news for them; men may actually cook more, and that's a gain too. But both men and women combined have less time than ever to devote to one of life's most satisfying and civilizing pleasures: the preparing and sharing of food and drink with others who appreciate its many virtues.

In the years to come, there will no doubt be a continuing movement away from having the homegrown, home-cooked, home-served meals that once were the South's only option. Over and beyond the time and trouble they require, the dishes themselves now raise caution flags among health-conscious eaters. Sugar and cream, butter and eggs, salt and pork seasonings produce richer and heavier foods than today's lifestyles require, and increasingly, admonitions against such ingredients are being heard.

But food habits are powerful, and the positive traditions associated with eating in the South are too satisfying and pervasive to simply vanish. It's one thing to make sensible modifications in eating patterns and diet; it's something else altogether to throw out the heritage and the incomparable Southern dishes with the dishwater. The regional traditions that gave identity and character and quality to the foods of our foremothers and fathers have a staying power that has survived the centuries; it seems safe to conclude that they will endure for yet a while longer.

Appendices

MICROWAVE COOKING CHART

Food Item	Amounts	Time	Procedure
Beverages			
Boiling Water (for tea)	½ cup	1½ to 2½ minutes	Place in a glass measure and microwave, uncovered, at HIGH until boiling.
	1 cup	2 to 3½ minutes	
	2 cups	4 to 5½ minutes	
Hot Milk (for cocoa)	½ cup	1 to 2 minutes	Place in a glass measure and microwave, uncovered, at HIGH until thoroughly heated (do not boil).
	1 cup	2 to 3½ minutes	
	2 cups	4 to 5 minutes	
Cereal			
Quick Cooking Oats	⅓ cup	2 to 3 minutes	Place in a serving bowl; add ¾ cup water. Microwave, uncovered, at HIGH until boiling.
Conveniences			
Toasting Almonds, Peanuts, Pecans, Walnuts	¼ cup	2 to 4 minutes	Spread in a pieplate and microwave, uncovered, at HIGH until lightly toasted.
	½ cup	3 to 4 minutes	
	1 cup	4 to 5 minutes	
Toasting Coconut	½ cup	2 to 3 minutes	Spread in a pieplate and microwave, uncovered, at HIGH until lightly toasted (will darken upon standing).
Melting Chocolate Morsels	1 cup	3 to 3½ minutes	Place in a glass measure and microwave, uncovered, at MEDIUM (50% power) until softened. Stir well.
Cheese and Butter			
Melting Butter or Margarine	¼ cup	55 seconds	Place in a glass measure and microwave, uncovered, at HIGH until melted.
	½ cup	1 minute	
	1 cup	1½ to 2 minutes	
Softening Cream Cheese	3-ounce package	30 to 40 seconds	Place in a glass measure and microwave, uncovered, at HIGH until softened.
	8-ounce package	45 seconds to 1 minute	
Fish and Shellfish			
Fish Fillets	4 (4-ounce)	5 to 8 minutes	Place in a baking dish. Cover and microwave at HIGH until fish flakes easily when tested with a fork.
Shrimp, peeled	1 pound	3 to 5 minutes	Place in a baking dish. Cover and microwave at HIGH until tender and pink.
Meat			
Ground Beef	1 pound	5 to 8 minutes	Place in a baking dish. Cover and microwave at HIGH until no longer pink.
Bacon	2 slices	2 to 3 minutes	Place on a bacon rack. Cover with paper towels and microwave at HIGH until crisp.
	4 slices	3½ to 4½ minutes	
	6 slices	5 to 7 minutes	
Frankfurters	1 link	25 to 30 seconds	Pierce each link with a fork. Place in a baking dish. Cover and microwave at HIGH until thoroughly heated.
	2 links	30 seconds to 1 minute	
Poultry			
Whole Broiler-Fryer	1 (3-pound)	40 to 50 minutes	Place on a rack in a baking dish. Cover and microwave at MEDIUM (50% power) until drumsticks are easy to move.
Cut-up Broiler-Fryer	3 pounds	18 to 20 minutes	Place in a baking dish. Cover and microwave at HIGH until tender.

EQUIVALENT WEIGHTS AND MEASURES

Food	Weight or Count	Measure or Yield
Apples	1 pound (3 medium)	3 cups sliced
Bacon	8 slices cooked	½ cup crumbled
Bananas	1 pound (3 medium)	2½ cups sliced, or about 2 cups mashed
Bread	1 pound	12 to 16 slices
	About 1½ slices	1 cup soft crumbs
Butter or margarine	1 pound	2 cups
	¼-pound stick	½ cup
Cabbage	1 pound head	4½ cups shredded
Candied fruit or peels	½ pound	1¼ cups chopped
Carrots	1 pound	3 cups shredded
Cheese, American or Cheddar	1 pound	About 4 cups shredded
cottage	1 pound	2 cups
cream	3-ounce package	6 tablespoons
Chocolate morsels	6-ounce package	1 cup
Cocoa	1 pound	4 cups
Coconut, flaked or shredded	1 pound	5 cups
Coffee	1 pound	80 tablespoons (40 cups perked)
Corn	2 medium ears	1 cup kernels
Cornmeal	1 pound	3 cups
Crab, in shell	1 pound	¾ to 1 cup flaked
Crackers, chocolate wafers	19 wafers	1 cup crumbs
graham crackers	14 squares	1 cup fine crumbs
saltine crackers	28 crackers	1 cup finely crushed
vanilla wafers	22 wafers	1 cup finely crushed
Cream, whipping	1 cup (½ pint)	2 cups whipped
Dates, pitted	1 pound	3 cups chopped
	8-ounce package	1½ cups chopped
Eggs	5 large	1 cup
whites	8 to 11	1 cup
yolks	12 to 14	1 cup
Flour, all-purpose	1 pound	3½ cups
cake	1 pound	4¾ to 5 cups sifted
whole wheat	1 pound	3½ cups unsifted
Green pepper	1 large	1 cup diced
Lemon	1 medium	2 to 3 tablespoons juice; 2 teaspoons grated rind
Lettuce	1 pound head	6¼ cups torn
Lime	1 medium	1½ to 2 tablespoons juice; 1½ teaspoons grated rind
Macaroni	4 ounces (1 cup)	2¼ cups cooked
Marshmallows	11 large	1 cup
	10 miniature	1 large marshmallow
Marshmallows, miniature	½ pound	4½ cups
Milk, evaporated	5.33-ounce can	⅔ cup
evaporated	13-ounce can	1⅝ cups
sweetened condensed	14-ounce can	1¼ cups
Mushrooms	3 cups raw (8 ounces)	1 cup sliced cooked
Nuts, almonds	1 pound	1 to 1¾ cups nutmeats
	1 pound shelled	3½ cups nutmeats
peanuts	1 pound	2¼ cups nutmeats
	1 pound shelled	3 cups
pecans	1 pound	2¼ cups nutmeats
	1 pound shelled	4 cups
walnuts	1 pound	1⅔ cups nutmeats
	1 pound shelled	4 cups
Oats, quick-cooking	1 cup	1¾ cups cooked
Onion	1 medium	½ cup chopped
Orange	1 medium	⅓ cup juice; 2 tablespoons grated rind
Peaches	2 medium	1 cup sliced

EQUIVALENT WEIGHTS AND MEASURES *(continued)*

Food	Weight or Count	Measure or Yield
Pears	2 medium	1 cup sliced
Potatoes, white	3 medium	2 cups cubed cooked or 1¾ cups mashed
sweet	3 medium	3 cups sliced
Raisins, seedless	1 pound	3 cups
Rice, long-grain	1 cup	3 to 4 cups cooked
pre-cooked	1 cup	2 cups cooked
Shrimp, raw in shell	1½ pounds	2 cups (¾ pound) cleaned, cooked
Spaghetti	7 ounces	About 4 cups cooked
Strawberries	1 quart	4 cups sliced
Sugar, brown	1 pound	2⅓ cups firmly packed
powdered	1 pound	3½ cups unsifted
granulated	1 pound	2 cups

HANDY SUBSTITUTIONS

Ingredient Called For	Substitution
1 cup self-rising flour	1 cup all-purpose flour plus 1 teaspoon baking powder and ½ teaspoon salt
1 cup cake flour	1 cup sifted all-purpose flour minus 2 tablespoons
1 cup all-purpose flour	1 cup cake flour plus 2 tablespoons
1 teaspoon baking powder	½ teaspoon cream of tartar plus ¼ teaspoon soda
1 tablespoon cornstarch or arrowroot	2 tablespoons all-purpose flour
1 tablespoon tapioca	1½ tablespoons all-purpose flour
2 large eggs	3 small eggs
1 egg	2 egg yolks (for custard)
1 egg	2 egg yolks plus 1 tablespoon water (for cookies)
1 (8-ounce) carton commercial sour cream	1 tablespoon lemon juice plus evaporated milk to equal 1 cup; or 3 tablespoons butter plus ⅞ cup sour milk
1 cup yogurt	1 cup buttermilk or sour milk
1 cup sour milk or buttermilk	1 tablespoon vinegar or lemon juice plus sweet milk to equal 1 cup
1 cup fresh milk	½ cup evaporated milk plus ½ cup water
1 cup fresh milk	3 to 5 tablespoons nonfat dry milk solids in 1 cup water
1 cup honey	1¼ cups sugar plus ¼ cup water
1 (1-ounce) square unsweetened chocolate	3 tablespoons cocoa plus 1 tablespoon butter or margarine
1 tablespoon fresh herbs	1 teaspoon dried herbs or ¼ teaspoon powdered herbs
¼ cup chopped fresh parsley	1 tablespoon dried parsley flakes
1 teaspoon dry mustard	1 tablespoon prepared mustard
1 pound fresh mushrooms	6 ounces canned mushrooms

EQUIVALENT MEASUREMENTS

3 teaspoons...............	1 tablespoon	2 cups.....................	1 pint (16 fluid ounces)
4 tablespoons..............	¼ cup	4 cups.....................	1 quart
5⅓ tablespoons..............	⅓ cup	4 quarts	1 gallon
8 tablespoons..............	½ cup	⅛ cup........................	2 tablespoons
16 tablespoons..............	1 cup	⅓ cup........................	5 tablespoons plus 1 teaspoon
2 tablespoons (liquid).....	1 ounce	⅔ cup........................	10 tablespoons plus 2 teaspoons
1 cup	8 fluid ounces	¾ cup........................	12 tablespoons

CHEESE SELECTION GUIDE

Cheese	Flavor, Texture, and Color	Used For	Goes With
American	Very mild; creamy yellow	Sandwiches, snacks	Crackers, bread
Bel Paese (Italy)	Mild; spongy; creamy yellow interior	Dessert, snacks	Fresh fruit, crusty French bread
Brie (France)	Sharper than Camembert; soft, creamy, with edible crust	Dessert, snacks	Fresh fruit
Blue (France)	Piquant, spicy; marbled, blue veined, semisoft; creamy white	Dessert, dips, salads, appetizers, cheese trays	Fresh fruit, bland crackers
Brick (United States)	Mild; semisoft; cream-colored to orange	Sandwiches, appetizers, cheese trays	Crackers, bread
Camembert (France)	Mild to pungent; edible crust; creamy yellow	Dessert, snacks	Especially good with tart apple slices
Cheddar (England) (United States)	Mild to sharp; cream-colored to orange	Dessert, sandwiches, salads, appetizers, cheese trays; use as an ingredient in cooking	Especially good with apples or pears
Chèvre (French)	Goat cheese; very pungent; creamy	Relishes, appetizers, sauces	Crackers, fruit
Cottage Cheese (United States)	Mild; soft, moist, large or small curd; white	Appetizers, fruit salads, snacks; use as an ingredient in cooking	Canned or fresh fruit
Cream Cheese (United States)	Mild; buttery, soft, smooth; white	Dessert, sandwiches, salads; use as an ingredient in cooking	Jelly and crackers
Edam (Holland)	Mild; firm with red wax coating	Dessert, appetizers, cheese tray	Fresh fruit
Feta (Greece)	Salty; crumbly, but sliceable; snow white	Appetizers; use as an ingredient in cooking	Greek salad
Fontina (Italy)	Nutty; semisoft to hard	Dessert, appetizers, sandwiches	Fresh fruit, crackers, bread
Gjetost (Norway)	Sweetish; firm, smooth; caramel-colored	Appetizers	Crackers
Gouda (Holland)	Mild, nutty; softer than Edam, with or without red wax coating	Dessert, appetizers	Fresh fruit, crackers
Gruyère (Switzerland)	Nutty; similar to swiss; firm with tiny holes	Dessert, appetizers	Fresh fruit
Jarlsberg (Norway)	Mild, nutty; firm	Sandwiches, snacks	Fresh fruit, bread
Havarti (Denmark)	Mild; rich and creamy	Snacks, sandwiches	Crackers, bread, fresh fruit
Liederkranz (United States)	Robust; texture of heavy honey, edible light-orange crust	Dessert, snacks	Fresh fruit, matzo, pumpernickel, sour rye, thinly sliced onion
Limburger (Belgium)	Robust, aromatic; soft, smooth; creamy white	Dessert	Fresh fruit, dark bread, bland crackers
Monterey Jack (United States)	Mild; semisoft; creamy white	Snacks, sandwiches, sauces, casseroles	Bread, crackers
Mozzarella (Italy)	Delicate, mild; semisoft; creamy white	Pizza; use as an ingredient in cooking	Italian foods
Muenster (Germany)	Mild to mellow; semisoft	Sandwiches, cheese trays	Crackers, bread
Parmesan (Italy)	Sharp, piquant; hard, brittle body; light yellow	Use grated as an ingredient in cooking; table use: young cheese, not aged	Italian foods; combine with Swiss for sauces
Pineapple Cheese (United States)	Sharp; firm, pineapple-shaped	Dessert, appetizers, salads, snacks	Fresh fruit
Port Salut (France)	Mellow to robust, fresh buttery flavor; semisoft	Dessert, appetizers, cheese trays	Fresh fruit, crackers

CHEESE SELECTION GUIDE *(continued)*

Cheese	Flavor, Texture, and Color	Used For	Goes With
Provolone (Italy)	Mild to sharp, usually smoked, salty; hard; yellowish-white	Dessert, appetizers; use as an ingredient in cooking	Italian foods
Ricotta (Italy)	Bland but semisweet; soft; creamy white	An ingredient in main dishes, filling, or pastries	Fresh fruit
Romano (Italy)	Sharp; hard, brittle body; light yellow	Use grated as an ingredient in cooking; table use: young cheese, not aged	Italian foods, salads, sauces
Roquefort (France)	Sharp; semisoft, sometimes crumbly; blue veined	Desserts, dips, salads, appetizers	Bland crackers, fresh fruit, demitasse
Stilton (England)	Semisoft; slightly more crumbly than blue; blue veined	Dessert, cheese trays, dips, salads	Fresh fruit, bland crackers
Swiss (Switzerland)	Sweetish; nutty with large holes; pale yellow	Dessert, cheese trays, salads, sandwiches, appetizers, use as an ingredient in cooking	Fresh fruit, squares of crusty French bread

WINE SELECTION GUIDE

Type of Wine	Specific Wine	Serve With	Temperature	When to Serve
Appetizer	Sherry (dry), Port Vermouth (dry)	Appetizers, nuts, cheese	Chilled, room temperature, over ice	Before dinner
Table Wines (white)	Rhine, Chablis, Sauterne, Light Muscat, Riesling, White Chianti	Fish, seafood, poultry, cheese, lamb, veal, eggs, lighter foods, pork (except ham)	Chilled	With dinner; any time, with or without food
Table Wines (red)	Rosé	Curry, patio parties, Chinese food, any food	Slightly chilled	With dinner; any time, with or without food
	Claret	Game, Italian food, beef, Hawaiian food	Slightly chilled	With dinner
	Chianti	Red meat, cheese, roasts, game, Italian food	Slightly chilled	With dinner
	Burgundy	Cheese, Italian food, game, ham, heartier foods, roasts, steaks	Slightly chilled	With dinner; any time, with or without food
Sparkling Wines	Champagne, dry	Appetizers, fish, seafood, poultry, main courses, desserts, cheese, any festive meal	Chilled	Any time, with or without food
Dessert Wines	Port, Muscatel, Tokay, Champagne (sweet), Sherry (cream), Madeira (sweet), Sauterne, Marsala, Malaga	Desserts, fruit, nuts, cheeses, cakes, pastries	Cool or room temperature	After dinner with dessert

Recipe Title Index

An alphabetical listing of every recipe by exact title
All microwave recipe page numbers are preceded by an "M"

Acadian Stuffed Pitas, 177
Almond-Chicken Salad Shanghai, 160
Almond Cream Confections, 310
Almond Crescent Rolls, 283
Almond Delight Dip, 226
Almond Muffins, 87
Amaretto, 272
Amaretto-Hot Fruit Compote, 250
Amaretto-Irish Cream Cheesecake, 266
Amaretto Pears with Meringue, M58
Amaretto Slush, 322
Angel Biscuits, 28
Angel Food Cake with Amaretto-Almond
  Sauce, 199
Apple-Barbecue Spareribs, 160
Apple Cooler, 14
Apple-Date-Nut Ring, 212
Apple-Oatmeal Cookies, 218
Applesauce, 255
Applesauce Drop Doughnuts, 70
Applesauce-Pecan Bread, 66
Apricot Crescents, 181
Apricot-Filled Chocolate Torte, 107
Apricot Mint Cooler, 165
Apricot Sponge Torte, 59
Artichoke-Cheese Strata, 236
Artichoke Hearts with Lemon, 98
Asparagus Vinaigrette, 82, 138
Asparagus with Cream Sauce, 291
Asparagus with Curry Sauce, 17

Back-Home Tea Cakes, 156
Bacon-and-Tomato Dip, 147
Bacon, Pimiento, and Cheese Hoagies, 144
Baked Apples à l'Orange, 280
Baked Flounder, 316
Baked Halibut with Champagne Sauce, 29
Baked Ham with Orange-Honey Glaze, 53
Baked New Potatoes, 90
Baked Oysters Bienville, 27
Baked Sausage Patties, 82
Baked Spinach Tomatoes, 92
Banana-Blueberry Smoothie, 104
Banana Milkshake, 179
Barbecued Short Ribs, 148
Barbecued Shrimp, 28
Barley-Broccoli Salad, 135
Basic Cupcake Muffins, 87
Basic Light Cake, 107
Basil and Cream Sauce, 118
Basil-Cheese Potatoes, M316
Basil Sauce, 85
Basting Sauce, 120
Bay Laurel Peaches, 124
Bean-and-Tomato Skillet, 316
Beef Kabobs with Vegetables, 148
Beef Stew, 230

Beef Tenderloin for Two, 295
Beef Tenderloin Picnic Sandwiches, 91
Beef with Asparagus, 100
Beet Aspic, 123
Bellini Spritzers, 110
Berry Mimosa Sauce, 315
Best-Ever Yeast Rolls, 46
Biscuits with Country Ham, 93
Blackened Red Snapper, 27
Black-Eyed Pea Salad, 173
Black-Eyed Peas with Rice, 208
Black Pepper Cheese Logs, 61
Black Walnut Cake, 308
Blueberry-Sour Cream Cake, 140
Blue Cheese Dressing, 286
Blue Cheese Sauce, 142
Blue Cheese Spread, 215
Blue Cheese Vinaigrette, 55, 280
Bluegrass Chocolate Tarts, 84
Blushing Pink Soda, 104
Boiled Frosting, 45
Bourbon Balls, 83
Bourbon Steak, 148
Bourbon Yams, 232
Breaded Catfish with Creole Sauce, 28
Bread Pudding, 219
Bread Pudding with Whiskey Sauce, 230
Breakfast Burritos, 192
Breakfast Pizza, 140, 178
Broccoli-and-Chicken Soup, 202
Broccoli-Chicken Salad, 129
Broccoli-Ham au Gratin, 239
Broccoli 'n' Cauliflower Salad, 32
Broccoli Salad, 292
Brownie Chip Cookies, 320
Brown Meat Stock, 31
Brown Rice Pilaf, 136
Brown Sugar Sauce, 314
Brunch Pears with Blue Cheese Sauce, 142
Brussels Sprouts in Mustard Sauce, 228
Buckin' Bronco Cookies, 95
Burgundy Eye-of-Round, 243
Burgundy Round Steak over Rice, M33
Burrito Rollups, 119
Butterbeans, 166
Butter Crust, 173
Butternut Squash Pudding, M19
Butter Pecan Turtle Bars, 70
Butterscotch Pinwheels, 49
Buttery Brown Sugar Dip with Fruit, 243

Caesar's Fish, 76
Calico Squash Casserole, 290
Cappuccino Mix, 87
Carambola-Yogurt Calypso, 169
Caramel Brie with Fresh Fruit, 266

Caramel Cake, 307
Caramel-Crowned Flans, 227
Caramel Frosting, 307
Carrot Cream Soup, 210
Catfish Gumbo, 278
Cauliflower Soufflé, 17
Cauliflower Soup, 211
Champagne Fruit Slush, 322
Champagne Ice, 315
Champagne Jelly, 248
Champagne Sauce, 29
Charlotte Russe, 288
Cheese-Apricot Sweet Rolls, 195
Cheese Grits, 102
Cheese Loaf, 93
Cheese Sauce, 235
Cheese-Stuffed Onions, 34
Cheesy Breakfast Sandwiches, 140
Cheesy Country Ham Puff, 88
Cheesy Fried Eggplant, 75
Cherry-Nut Muffins, 87
Chervil-and-Savory Sauce, 117
Chess Tarts, 83
Chicken-and-Sausage Gumbo, 256
Chicken-and-Tomatoes over Fettuccine, 204
Chicken-Apple Salad, 216
Chicken Breasts with Curried Peppers, 227
Chicken Chow Mein, 68
Chicken Cornbread Dressing, 159
Chicken Creole, 146
Chicken Curry Sauce, 117
Chicken Enchiladas, 121
Chicken Fajitas, 204
Chicken-Fruit Salad, 234
Chicken Gumbo, 26
Chicken-Rice Medaillons in Pepper Pesto, 97
Chicken Salad Oriental, 146
Chicken Salad Ring, 123
Chicken-Spaghetti Salad, 146
Chicken with Artichokes and Mushrooms, 35
Chili Casserole, 176
Chili-Cheese Dip, 225
Chili-Cheese Potatoes, M62
Chili-Chicken Stew, 319
Chili in Pastry Cups, 68
Chilled Carrot-Mint Soup, M168
Chilled Dilly Peas, 143
Chinese Chicken Stir-Fry, 100
Chives-Grits Timbales, 172
Chocolate Angel Food Cake, 111
Chocolate Buttercream Cake, 108
Chocolate-Cheese Filling, 47
Chocolate Chip-Banana Bread, 267
Chocolate Chip Cookies, 193
Chocolate Chip Muffins, 87
Chocolate-Coconut Squares, 70
Chocolate Crust, M15
Chocolate-Drizzled Pineapple with Raspberry
  Sauce, 57

Chocolate Frosting, 194, 252, 265, 284, 309
Chocolate Glaze, 310
Chocolate-Glazed Triple-Layer
  Cheesecake, 310
Chocolate-Mint Parfaits, M15
Chocolate-Mint Whipped Cream Cake, 265
Chocolate-Peanut Butter Fudge, 311
Chocolate-Peanut Butter Snacks, 226
Chocolate Pecan Pie, 184
Chocolate Pound Cake with Frosting, 284
Chocolate Sauce, 57
Chocolate-Tipped Butter Cookies, 312
Choco-Mallow Brownies, 309
Chunky Salsa, 206
Chutney-Bacon Brie, M292
Cinnamon Apple Rings, 250
Cinnamon-Cheese Filling, 46
Cinnamon-Oat Bread, 135
Cinnamon Popovers, 66
Citrus Spinach Salad, 59
Clam Chowder, 202
Clam Puffs, 60
Cocktail Sauce, 242
Cocktail Smoky Links, 168
Cocoa Crown Cake, 107
Coconut-Cream Cheese Pound Cake, 305
Coconut Cream Pie, 312
Coconut Crunch Pie, 105
Coconut Kisses, 106
Coconut-Pecan Coils, 196
Colcannon, 64
Cold Spiced Fruit, 269
Colored Frostings, 21
Colored Sugars, 21
Colorful Ham-and-Rice Salad, 319
Colorful Tossed Salad, 55
Commissary Barbecue Beans, 120
Congealed Cranberry Salad, 124
Cooked Salad Dressing, 231
Corn-and-Bean Casserole, 208
Corn-and-Pea Salad, 181
Corn Chowder, 202
Cornish Hens with Fruited Stuffing, 191
Cornmeal Pastry Cups, 69
Corn Pudding, 219
Corn Sticks, 214
Country Ham Sauce, 117
Country Ham with Brown Sugar Coating, 88
Crab Cakes, 71
Crabmeat-Horseradish Spread, 292
Crabmeat Mousse, 190
Crab, Shrimp, and Artichoke au Gratin, 240
Cranapple Wine, 272
Cranberries Jubilee, 293
Cranberry-and-Apple Cobbler, 294
Cranberry-Banana Bread, 294
Cranberry Cloud, 287
Cranberry Coffee Cake, 159
Cranberry Cream, 66
Cranberry Leg of Lamb, 52
Cranberry-Mustard Fruit Bake, 287
Cranberry-Orange Delight, 168
Cranberry Pork, 293
Cranberry Pork Chops, 53
Cranberry Ring, 291
Crawfish Étouffée, 103
Cream Cheese Chicken Breasts, 234
Cream Cheese-Crabmeat Mold, 71
Cream Cheese Filling, 170
Cream Cheese Frosting, 305, 308
Cream Cheese Tarts, 312

Creamed Sweetbreads, 82
Cream Filling, 311
Cream of Celery Soup, 210
Cream of Corn Soup, 210
Cream of Spinach Soup, 211
Cream Pea Soup, 211
Creamy Baked Corn, 60
Creamy Corn, 207
Creamy French Dressing, 286
Creamy Holiday Fruit Salad, 251
Creamy Onion Soup, 211
Creamy Raisin Spread, 36
Creamy Scrambled Eggs, 82
Creamy Shrimp Curry, 145
Creamy Turkey Divan, M34
Creole Rice, 183
Creole Sauce, 28
Crêpes, 157
Crispy-Chewy Molasses Cookies, 218
Crispy Oat Cookies, 311
Crispy Walnut Chicken, 89
Crunchy Peanut Granola, 48
Crunchy Pea Salad, 143
Cucumber Dressing, 144
Cucumber Sandwiches, 81
Cucumber-Tomato Salad, 144
Curried Carrots and Pineapple, 228
Curried Chicken Cheesecake, 174
Curried Onions, 34
Curried Rice, 183
Curried Sour Cream Sauce, 174

Daisy Biscuits, 86
Date Squares, 49
Decorative Tea Cakes, 156
Deep-Dish Cheesecake Coffee Cake, 50
Deep-Fried Okra, 154
Deluxe Lemon Meringue Pie, 313
Deluxe Peach Ice Cream, 314
Dijon Chicken with Pasta, 318
Dilled Carrots, 17
Dilled Cucumber Soup, M167
Dilled Zucchini Soup, 88
Dilly Chicken, 65
Double-Crust Chicken Pot Pie, 220
Down-Home Vegetable Soup, 32
Dried Tomato-Cheese Spread, 204
Dried Tomato-Cheese Tart, 203
Dried Tomato-Cream Soup, 203
Dried Tomato Pesto, 204
Dried Tomato Spaghetti Sauce, 202
Dropped Tea Cakes, 156
Dry Spices, 120

Easy Beef Tenderloin, 268
Easy Caramel Rolls, 195
Easy Custard with Nutmeg, 316
Easy Herb Biscuits, 283
Easy Microwave Chicken Broth, M167
Easy Monkey Bread, 214
Easy Pickled Cucumber Rounds, 143
Easy Pocket Pizzas, 168
Easy Red Beans and Rice, 220
Easy Texas Chili, 201
Eggnog Pound Cake, 253

Eggplant Dressing, 236
Eggplant Salad, 99
Eggs Bel-Mar, 92
Elf Gorp, 270
Emerald Sauce, 63
English Pea Salad, 143

Fajita in a Pita, 177
Fettuccine with Broccoli, 97
Fiery Fried Stuffed Jalapeños, 118
Fluffy Frosting, 308
Fluffy White Filling, 252
Fluffy White Frosting, 105
Fontina-Baked Chicken, 64
Four-Fruit Wassail, 22
Freezer Dinner Rolls, 251
French Coconut Pie, 162
French Green Beans, 208
French Onion Soup, 31
French Toast with Grand Marnier Fruit
  Sauce, 93
Fresh Fruit Salad with Orange Cream, 126
Fresh Fruit Tart, 58
Fresh Fruit with Honey-Sour Cream
  Dip, 180
Fresh Mushroom Soup, 190
Fresh Strawberries with Cream Dip, 86
Fried Cauliflower, 18
Front Porch Lemonade, 156
Frosted Chocolate Snack Cake, 194
Frosted Cranberry Salad, 288
Frosty Lime Fizz, 104
Frosty Orange Pie, 296
Frozen Chocolate Roulage, 56
Frozen Fresh Peach Yogurt, 139
Fruited Acorn Squash, 228
Fruited Chicken Salad, 318
Fruited Pot Roast, 211
Fruited Rice Mix, 267
Fruit-Glazed Cheesecake, 162
Fruit-on-a-Pick, 179

Garlic-Chive Butter Sauce, 96
Garlic Grilled Pork Tenderloin, 172
Garlic-Parsley Potatoes, 290
Gazebo Cheese Soup, 158
Ginger Dressing, 160
Ginger-Nut Chicken, M33
Gingersnap Crust, 296
Glazed Ham Loaf, 212
Glazed Orange Rolls, 194
Glazed Pork Tenderloin, 315
Glazed Sweet Bread Wreath, 192
Glazed Sweet Potato Casserole, 250
Goat Cheese and Greens, 54
Golden Bread, 47
Golden Pound Cake, 284
Gouda Cheese Spread, 36
Graham Cracker Crust, 296
Grand Marnier Fruit Sauce, 93
Grandma's Ambrosia, 254
Grandma's Tea Cakes, 156
Grapefruit Drink, 84
Greek Lemon Chicken, 65
Greek Salad Dressing, 286

Green Chile Quesadillas, 121
Green Peppercorn Butter, 117
Grilled Catfish Cajun-Style, 129
Grilled Catfish with Red Salsa, 172
Grilled Corn-on-the-Cob, 166
Grilled Flank Steak with Sweet Peppers, 138
Grilled Marinated Grouper, 166
Grilled Pork with Salsa, 128
Grilled Tuna Steaks, 129
Grouper with Sautéed Vegetables, M233
Guacamole, 205
Guacamole Spread, 119

Haddock Fillets in White Wine, 76
Ham and Apricots, 53
Ham-and-Asparagus Cheesecake, 174
Ham-and-Cheese Pita Pockets, 271
Ham-and-Pasta Salad, 128
Ham Loaves, 235
Ham-Pecan-Blue Cheese Pasta Salad, 62
Ham Pinwheels, 235
Ham Pot Pie, 25
Harvest Pumpkin Bread, M215
Hawaiian Banana Cream Pie, 105
Healthy Heroes, 177
Hearts of Palm Spread, 293
Herb Butter Zucchini Fans, 201
Herbed Cornbread, 214
Herbed Eggplant Soup, 173
Holiday Brew, 272
Holiday Coconut Cake, 308
Holiday Coffee, 273
Holiday Ham Slice with Cinnamon Apple
    Rings, 250
Holiday Sweet Potato Bake, 291
Homemade Mayonnaise, 81
Homemade Picante Sauce, 205
Homemade Texas Chips with Guacamole
    Spread, 119
Honey-and-Herb Grilled Pork, 148
Honey-Baked Apple Dessert, M213
Honey-Glazed Apples, 125
Honey-Mustard Dressing, 55, 111, 146
Honey-Mustard Glazed Lamb, 52
Honey-Pecan Finger Pies, 184
Hopping John, 12
Horseradish Cream, 96
Horseradish Spread, 243
Hot Apple Cider, 21, 225
Hot Chocolate Deluxe, 272
Hot Cranapple Glogg, 22
Hot Fruit Compote, 124
Hot Nut Crackers, 206
Hot Pineapple Nectar, 21
Hummingbird Cake, 305
Hurry-Up Yeast Rolls, 90

Ice Cream Bombe, 269
Ice-Cream Pie Spectacular, 314
Icy-Spicy Mexican Tomato Soup, 155
Individual Chicken Bake, 279
Irish Soda Bread, 214
Irish Stew, 64
Italian Casserole, 238
Italian Crêpes, 157
Italian Garden Harvest Soup, M167
Italian Green Beans, 164

Italian Sauce, 67
Italian-Stuffed Eggplant, 74

Jambalaya, 26
Japanese Fruitcake, 252
Jicama-Orange Salad, 122
Jiffy Spanish Rice, 176
John Wills's Baby Loin Back Ribs, 120
Julienne Zucchini and Carrots, 14

Kentucky Ham 'n' Angel Biscuits, 83
Kidney Bean Casserole, 136
Kid-Pleasin' Chocolate Mousse, 271
Kid's Cooler, 95
King Cake, 20
Koulourakia, 193
Kumquat Marmalade, 48

Lady Baltimore Cake, 45
Lamb Chops with Herbs, 164
Lamb Pie, 26
Lasagna in a Bun, 176
Lasagna Maria, 191
Latkes, 254
Lattice Crust, 294
Layered Overnight Salad, 319
Layered Tomato Aspic, 99
Leafy Cheese Sandwiches, 56
Leeks in Dilled Lemon-Butter, M98
Lemon-Apricot Filling, 105
Lemon-Buttered New Potatoes, 268
Lemon Cloud Mousse, 90
Lemon-Coconut Frosting, 253
Lemon Curd with Berries, 102
Lemon Filling, 308
Lemon-Garlic Chicken, 35
Lemon Velvet, 15
Lemony Potato Wedges, M61
Lentils-and-Rice Salad, 197
Lentil Spaghetti Sauce, 198
Leonard's-Style Onion Rings, 120
Light Fruitcake, 309
Lightnin' Cheese Biscuits, 283
Light Poultry Stock, 31
Light Tortilla Chips, 278
Lime Slush Punch, 273
Limping Susan, 155
Lobster Medallions in Garlic-Chive Butter
    Sauce, 96
Lobster Salad, 69
Lord Baltimore Cake, 45
Louisiana Crawfish Dressing, 103
Luncheon Pasta Salad, 191
Luscious Flan, 56
Luscious Lemon Cheesecake, M196

Macaroni and Cheese, 30
Maple-Bran Muffins, 66
Maple Cream Coffee Treat, 50
Marinated Asparagus and Hearts
    of Palm, 91
Marinated Cheese, 244
Marinated Chicken Breasts, 54

Marinated Chicken Strips and
    Vegetables, 110
Marinated Legumes, 197
Marinated Mushroom Salad, 181
Marinated Rib-Eye Roast, 318
Marinated Vegetables Italian, 242
Marinated Zucchini Salad, 32
Marshmallow Popcorn Balls, 226
Mayonnaise Rolls, 283
Meatballs with Pineapple and Peppers, 145
Medaillons of Beef with Horseradish
    Cream, 96
Mediterranean Salad, 99
Melon-Berry Salad, 180
Mesclun with Tarragon Dressing, 55
Mexican Artichoke Dip, 292
Mexican Beef Roll-Ups, 176
Mexican Cheese Spread, 119
Mexican Hush Puppies, 214
Mexican Kidney Beans, 205
Mexi-Style, Oven-Fried Fish, 76
Mex-Tex Soup, 278
Microwave Chef Salad, M146
Microwave Chocolate Pie, M15
Microwave Mexican Casserole, M231
Milk Chocolate Pound Cake, 306
Million Dollar Pound Cake, 306
Miniature Carrot Cakes, 94
Miniature Cheesecakes, 170
Miniature Cranberry Muffins, 294
Miniature Derby Tarts, 92
Mini-Teriyaki Meat Loaf, 69
Minted Peas and Peppers, M99
Mint-Glazed Carrots and Peas, 291
Mint Juleps, 81
Mint Syrup, 89
Mint Tea, 89
Mirliton Balls, 217
Mixed Fruit Punch, 207
Mixed Green Salad, 230
Mixed Greens with Blue Cheese
    Vinaigrette, 280
Moussaka, 68
Mulled Grape Juice, 21
Mushroom-Rice Soup, 32
Mussels Linguine, M112
Mustard-and-Onion Focaccia, 321
Mustard Fruit Bake, 291
Mustard Sauce, 19, 97

Nana's Chicken Pie, 25
New-Fashioned Pumpkin Pie, 296
New Potato Medley, 279
No-Crust Spinach Quiche, 142
Novelty Layer Squares, 70
Nutty Granola, 95
Nutty Wheat Loaf, 65

Oatmeal Cherry-Apple Crisp, M16
Oatmeal-Chocolate Chippers, 218
Okra-Corn-and-Tomato Vinaigrette, 173
Okra Salad, 155
Old-Fashioned Cinnamon Rolls, 196
Old-Fashioned Corn Sticks, 232
Old-Fashioned Crab Soup, 71
Old-Fashioned Rock Cream with
    Strawberries, 125

One-Foot-in-the-Fire Fudge Cake, 252
Onion Crescent Crunch Sticks, 206
Onion-Herb Bread, 165
Onion Kuchen, 34
Open-Faced Jalapeño Heroes, 144
Orange Butter, 323
Orange Butter Glaze, 194
Orange-Cheese Filling, 47
Orange-Coconut Pie, 90
Orange Cream, 126
Orange-Glazed Carrots, M98
Orange Juicy, 178
Orange-Turkey Slices, 53
Oriental Pasta Salad, 63
Oriental Pork Chops, 212
Oriental Shrimp and Rice, 183
Oven-Baked French Toast, 192
Oven-Braised Country Ham, 87
Oven-Fried Chicken Chimichangas, 175
Oven-Fried Snapper, 75
Overnight Vegetable Salad, 33

Papaya Shake, 169
Paprika Cornbread, 213
Parmesan Popovers, 66
Parmesan Potatoes, M62
Parslied Chicken Bake, 65
Parslied Corn, 155
Party Nibbles, 249
Party Reubens, 61
Passion Fruit Punch, 169
Passover Linzer Torte, 106
Passover Sponge Cake, 106
Pasta Salad, 62, 91
Pasta with Catfish and Artichokes, 123
Patio Potato Salad, 160
Peach-and-Kiwi Salad, 180
Peach Cobbler, 219
Peach Cobbler Supreme, 313
Peach Cream Tart, 173
Peach Daiquiris, 322
Peach Dressing, 180
Peach Filling, 107
Peach-Glazed Carrots, 13
Peach Petals, 104
Peach Sherbet, 179
Peachy Almond-Butter Cake, 107
Peachy Chicken, 212
Peachy Cream Cheese Spread, M215
Pear Honey, 159
Pecan Chicken, 54
Pecan Pie, 312
Pecan Squares, 69
Pecan Tart with Praline Cream, 256
Peppermint-Eggnog Punch, 273
Pepper-Mushroom Medley, 98
Pepper Pesto, 97
Peppy Prune Relish, 227
Perfect Chocolate Cake, 307
Perfect Chocolate Frosting, 307
Perky Cinnamon-Apple Juice, 22
Pesto-and-Cream Cheese Round, 242
Pesto Potato Salad, 164
Pineapple-Banana Slush, 14
Pineapple Charlotte, 288
Pineapple Cooler, 207
Pineapple Soda, 179
Pizza Cookie, 49
Poached Fish with Vegetables, 18

Poached Pears with Dark Chocolate
Sauce, M141
Poached Plums, M141
Poached Salmon with Emerald Sauce, 63
Pork Chop-Vegetable Casserole, 208
Pork Chow Mein, 101
Pork Marsala, 35
Pork Medaillons in Mustard Sauce, 96
Potato Salad, 122
Powdered Sugar Glaze, 95
Praline Buns, 195
Praline Freeze, 48
Pralines, 48
Presto Pasta Salad, 63
Pretty Pepper Kabobs, 166
Pumpkin Doughnut Drops, 323
Pumpkin Pudding, M20

Quick Breakfast Sweet Rolls, 195
Quick Chicken, 117
Quick Clam Linguine, 233
Quick Corn Relish, 13
Quick Crouton Bread, 138
Quick Crunchy Flounder, 76
Quick Eggplant Slices, 75
Quick Fruit Dip, 110
Quick Garlic Bread, 283
Quick Nacho Dip, 168
Quick Upside Down Cake, 219

Rainbow Pepper Topping, 117
Raisin Filling, 86
Raisin Pastry Bites, 86
Ranch-Style Dip, 138
Raspberry Filling, 111
Raspberry Party Puffs, 170
Raspberry Swirl Cookies, 111
Ratatouille Pasta Salad, 74
Red-and-Green Salad, 55
Red Beans and Rice, 27
Red Salsa, 172
Red, White, and Green Salad, 18
Reuben Casserole, 240
Reuben Cheesecake, 175
Ribs with Blender Barbecue Sauce, 12
Rice à l'Orange, 236
Roast Beef Salad, 318
Roast Duckling with Tangerine Stuffing, 16
Roasted New Potatoes, 138
Roasted Pecan Clusters, 310
Roasted Pepper-and-Chicken Soup, 58
Roasted Red Pepper and Watercress
Salad, 55
Roast Turkey, 321
Robust Salad, 181
Romano Onion Bake, 98
Rosy Raspberry Fizz, 179
Roulage, 266
Rum-Nut Muffins, 87

Salad Dressing, 161
Salami Rollups, 226
Salmon Fettuccine, 123
Santa's Slush, 271
Saucy Meatballs, 122

Sausage-and-Cornbread Pie, 25
Sausage-Apple Balls, 85
Sausage-Cheese Grits, 238
Sausage Quesadillas, 118
Sausage-Stuffed French Loaf, 19
Savory Pastry, 24
Savory Southern Chicken Pie, 24
Scalloped Oysters, 249
Scallops and Wild Rice, 129
Scarlet Sipper, 198
Sea-and-Ski Cocktail Mix, 319
Seafood and Pasta, 234
Seafood Gumbo, 154
Seafood Pasta Salad, 62
Seafood Salad, 88
Seasoned Cornbread, 320
Sesame Spinach Salad, 292
Sherried Fruit Mold, 124
Shortcut Chicken and Rice, 220
Shrimp-and-Noodle Casserole, 240
Shrimp-and-Scallop Sauté with Pecan
Rice, 317
Shrimp Creole, M220
Shrimp Dee-Lish, 216
Shrimp Étouffée, 229
Shrimp Rémoulade, 255
Shrimp Salad Sandwiches, 178
Shrimp Versailles, 233
Simple Beef Burgundy, 234
Skillet Cabbage, 229
Skillet Cornbread, 13
Slush with a Punch, 322
Smoked Turkey, 249
Smoked Turkey Medley, 128
Smoked Turkey Pasta Primavera, 84
Snowflake Biscuits, 158
Snow Peas with Red Pepper, 102
Snowy Chocolate Bites, 47
Soufflé Potatoes, 14
Sour Cream Muffins, 283
Sour Cream Pancakes with Fruit
Topping, 142
Sour Cream Yeast Rolls, 17
Sourdough Wedges, 199
Southern Long Island Iced Tea, 207
Southern Rice, 250
Southwestern Rice, 121
Spanish Rice, 183
Sparkling Gin Cooler, 272
Special Derby Brownies, 94
Special Green Beans, 268
Special Pizza Crust, 139
Speedy Crabmeat Imperial, M112
Speedy Sweet Potato Pie, 219
Spicy Bloody Marys, 207
Spicy Cornbread Muffins, 59
Spicy Egg Roll-Ups, 140
Spicy Ham Patties, 235
Spicy-Hot Black-Eyed Peas, 135
Spicy Poached Apples, M141
Spicy Tortilla Soup, 32
Spinach-Apple Salad, 89
Spinach Pesto Cheesecake, 175
Spinach Salad with Honey Dressing, 16
Split Pea Soup, 198
Spoonbread, 200
Sprout Salad, 137
Spumoni Charlotte, 193
Squash Casserole, 161
Squash Delight, 236
Squash Nosh, 147

Steak lo Mein, 100
Steamed Vegetable Medley, 29
Stir-Fried Vegetables, 136
Strawberries Dipped in White Chocolate, 83
Strawberries 'n' Cream, 30
Strawberries with Lemon Cream, 170
Strawberry Champagne Punch, 315
Strawberry Daiquiris, 125
Strawberry Punch, 273
Strawberry Spritzer, 14
Strawberry Topping, 142
Strawberry-Yogurt Dessert, 295
Stuffed Country Ham, 317
Stuffed Flank Steak with Noodles, 101
Stuffed Mirlitons, 217
Stuffed Scalloped Tomatoes, 29
Stuffed Squash Mexican, 200
Stuffed White Squash, M201
Sufganiyot (Jelly-Filled Doughnuts), 255
Sugar Glaze, 47
Super Seafood Dip, 292
Swedish Heirloom Cookies, 311
Sweet-and-Sour Baked Onions, 34
Sweet-and-Sour Burgers, 128
Sweet-and-Sour Chicken, 161
Sweet-and-Sour Chicken Nuggets, 168
Sweet-and-Sour Chicken Wings, 206
Sweet-and-Sour Pork, 317
Sweet-and-Sour Shrimp, M112
Sweet-Filled Yeast Loaves, 46
Sweetheart Fudge Pie, 313
Sweet Kugel, 254
Sweet Pinwheel Rolls, 46
Sweet Potatoes-and-Apple Casserole, 228
Sweet Potato Waffles with Orange
   Butter, 323
Sweet Sauce, 120
Sweet Yeast Braid, 46
Swiss Alpine Quiche, 18
Swiss Cheese Spread, 60
Swiss Chicken Casserole, 67

Tacoritos, 133
Taco Salad, 20
Tangerine Stuffing, 16
Tangy Sauce for Fruit, 161
Tarragon Chicken Salad, 199
Tarragon Dressing, 55
Tart Crust, 58
Tart Pastry, 92
Tart Shells, 84
Tasty Rolls, 85
Tea Punch, 143, 207
Texas Ranch Beans, 198
Texas Star Pecan Pie, 184
Tex-Mex Meat Loaf for Two, 234
The Compromise Cake, 253
Thick-and-Creamy Dip, 271
Toasted Coconut Pie, 105
Tomato Juice Cocktail, 12
Tortilla Soup, 201
Tropical Coffee Cake, 323
Tropical Fruit Punch, 169
Tropical Punch, 207
Tropical Smoothie, 169
Tropical Spinach Salad, 231
Turkey-Apple Salad, 181
Turkey Barbecue, 158
Turkey Hero with Garlic Sauce, 145
Turkey-in-the-Slaw Sandwich, 177
Turkey Nachos, 118
Turkey-Noodle-Poppyseed Casserole, 239
Turkey Pot Pie, 24
Turkey-Rice Soup, 89
Turkey Salad, 318
Turkey-Tomato Stew, 279
Turkey-Vegetable Pizza, 139
Turnip Greens, 13, 232
Twice-Baked Potato, M295
Two-Cheese Tortilla Snack, 119

Unforgettable Coconut Cake, 104

Vanilla Poached Pears, 57
Vegetable Burritos, 134
Vegetable Relish, 147
Vegetable Spread, 144
Vegetable Stock, 31
Very Berry Sorbet, 85
Vinaigrette Dressing, 173

Wassail, 273
Watercress Sandwiches, 82
Watermelon-Berry Slush, 137
Watermelon-Cherry Compote, 180
Whipped Cream Filling, 265, 307
Whipping Cream Pound Cake, 284
Whiskey Punch, 64
Whiskey Sauce, 230
White Bean Soup, 201
White Grape Punch, 15
White Sangría Slush, 322
Whole Wheat-Apple Crumble, M213
Whole Wheat Popovers, 66
Whole Wheat Rolls, 111
Wide-Eyed Pizzas, 94
Williamsburg Turkey Soup, 287
Wine Pâté, 36

Yellow Birds, 103
Yogurt-Muesli Muffins, 215
Yogurt-Sesame Chicken, 216
Yule Street Truffles, 242

Zesty Deviled Chicken, 232
Zesty Marinated Salad, 90
Zippy Shrimp Spread, 36
Zippy Steak and Gravy, 35
Zucchini Fries, 147

Month-by-Month Index

An alphabetical listing within the month of every food article and accompanying recipes
All microwave recipe page numbers are preceded by an "M"

JANUARY

A Lesson On Poaching Fish, 18
Poached Fish with Vegetables, 18
Entertaining Is Easy For This Man, 16
Asparagus with Curry Sauce, 17
Dilled Carrots, 17
Roast Duckling with Tangerine
Stuffing, 16
Sour Cream Yeast Rolls, 17
Spinach Salad with Honey Dressing, 16
Fast And Fabulous Finales, M15
Chocolate-Mint Parfaits, M15
Microwave Chocolate Pie, M15
Oatmeal Cherry-Apple Crisp, M16
From Our Kitchen To Yours, 22
First Aid for Kitchen Burns, 22
Here's To The Lucky Year Ahead, 12
Hopping John, 12
Ribs with Blender Barbecue Sauce, 12
Skillet Cornbread, 13
Tomato Juice Cocktail, 12
Turnip Greens, 13
Microwave Puddings, M19
Butternut Squash Pudding, M19
Pumpkin Pudding, M20
Quenchers: Cool And Light, 14
Apple Cooler, 14
Lemon Velvet, 15
Pineapple-Banana Slush, 14
Strawberry Spritzer, 14
White Grape Punch, 15
Serve Vegetables, 13
Julienne Zucchini and Carrots, 14
Peach-Glazed Carrots, 13
Quick Corn Relish, 13
Soufflé Potatoes, 14
Sip A Hot Cider, 21
Four-Fruit Wassail, 22
Hot Apple Cider, 21
Hot Cranapple Glogg, 22
Hot Pineapple Nectar, 21
Mulled Grape Juice, 21
Perky Cinnamon-Apple Juice, 22
Super Bowl Sandwich, 19
Sausage-Stuffed French Loaf, 19
Taco Salad For Two, 20
Taco Salad, 20
The Jeweled Crown Of Mardi Gras, 20
King Cake, 20
**Wonderful Ways With Broccoli And
Cauliflower, 17**
Cauliflower Soufflé, 17
Fried Cauliflower, 18
Red, White, and Green Salad, 18
Swiss Alpine Quiche, 18

FEBRUARY

A Heart-Healthy Menu For Two, 29
Baked Halibut with Champagne
Sauce, 29
Steamed Vegetable Medley, 29
Strawberries 'n' Cream, 30
Stuffed Scalloped Tomatoes, 29
A Novel Look At Nobility, 45
Lady Baltimore Cake, 45
Lord Baltimore Cake, 45
Cookie By The Slice, 49
Pizza Cookie, 49
Cook It Light, Cook It Cajun, 26
Angel Biscuits, 28
Baked Oysters Bienville, 27
Barbecued Shrimp, 28
Blackened Red Snapper, 27
Breaded Catfish with Creole Sauce, 28
Chicken Gumbo, 26
Jambalaya, 26
Red Beans and Rice, 27
Dinner In A Skillet, 35
Chicken with Artichokes and
Mushrooms, 35
Lemon-Garlic Chicken, 35
Pork Marsala, 35
Zippy Steak and Gravy, 35
From Our Kitchen To Yours, 50
Basic Guide for a Well-Equipped
Kitchen, 50
**Homemade Soups—Warm And
Delicious, 31**
Down-Home Vegetable Soup, 32
French Onion Soup, 31
Mushroom-Rice Soup, 32
Spicy Tortilla Soup, 32
**Homemade Stocks Make Savory Soups
And Stews, 30**
Brown Meat Stock, 31
Light Poultry Stock, 31
Vegetable Stock, 31
**One Recipe, Three Batches Of
Bread, 46**
Best-Ever Yeast Rolls, 46
Pastries For Breakfast, 49
Butterscotch Pinwheels, 49
Date Squares, 49
Deep-Dish Cheesecake Coffee
Cake, 50
Maple Cream Coffee Treat, 50
Pralines For Dessert, 48
Praline Freeze, 48
Put The Chill On Winter Salads, 32
Broccoli 'n' Cauliflower Salad, 32
Marinated Zucchini Salad, 32
Overnight Vegetable Salad, 33
**Savory Dough Conceals
The Cheese, 47**
Golden Bread, 47

Savory Pot Pies, 24
Ham Pot Pie, 25
Lamb Pie, 26
Nana's Chicken Pie, 25
Sausage-and-Cornbread Pie, 25
Savory Southern Chicken Pie, 24
Turkey Pot Pie, 24
Serve Onions On The Side, 34
Cheese-Stuffed Onions, 34
Curried Onions, 34
Onion Kuchen, 34
Sweet-and-Sour Baked
Onions, 34
Snack-In-The-Box, 47
Crunchy Peanut Granola, 48
Snowy Chocolate Bites, 47
**Tease Appetites With A Party
Spread, 36**
Creamy Raisin Spread, 36
Gouda Cheese Spread, 36
Wine Pâté, 36
Zippy Shrimp Spread, 36
Treat Yourself To Kumquats, 48
Kumquat Marmalade, 48
**Trimmed-Down Macaroni And
Cheese, 30**
Macaroni and Cheese, 30
Weeknight Entrées, M33
Burgundy Round Steak
over Rice, M33
Creamy Turkey Divan, M34
Ginger-Nut Chicken, M33

MARCH

A Healthier Corn Pudding, 60
Creamy Baked Corn, 60
A Wellspring Of Entrée Ideas, 52
Baked Ham with Orange-Honey
Glaze, 53
Cranberry Leg of Lamb, 52
Cranberry Pork Chops, 53
Ham and Apricots, 53
Honey-Mustard Glazed Lamb, 52
Marinated Chicken Breasts, 54
Orange-Turkey Slices, 53
Pecan Chicken, 54
**Bar Cookies Are Welcome
Anytime, 69**
Butter Pecan Turtle Bars, 70
Chocolate-Coconut Squares, 70
Novelty Layer Squares, 70
Pecan Squares, 69
**Beefed Up Dishes For
Globe-Trotters, 68**
Chili in Pastry Cups, 68
Mini-Teriyaki Meat Loaf, 69
Moussaka, 68

MARCH
(continued)

Crab—A Southern Delicacy, 71
    Crab Cakes, 71
    Cream Cheese-Crabmeat Mold, 71
    Old-Fashioned Crab Soup, 71
Crispy, Delicious Popovers, 66
    Cinnamon Popovers, 66
    Parmesan Popovers, 66
    Whole Wheat Popovers, 66
Cure The Chicken Doldrums, 64
    Dilly Chicken, 65
    Fontina-Baked Chicken, 64
    Greek Lemon Chicken, 65
    Parslied Chicken Bake, 65
From Our Kitchen To Yours, 72
    What to Look for on Food Labels, 72
Make Ahead And Freeze, 67
    Chicken Chow Mein, 68
    Italian Sauce, 67
    Swiss Chicken Casserole, 67
Plan The Meal Around Healthy Soup, 58
    Apricot Sponge Torte, 59
    Citrus Spinach Salad, 59
    Roasted Pepper-and-Chicken Soup, 58
    Spicy Cornbread Muffins, 59
Potatoes In Minutes, M61
    Chili-Cheese Potatoes, M62
    Lemony Potato Wedges, M61
    Parmesan Potatoes, M62
Quick Breads, Faster Than Yeast, 65
    Applesauce-Pecan Bread, 66
    Maple-Bran Muffins, 66
    Nutty Wheat Loaf, 65
Spectacular Light Desserts, 56
    Amaretto Pears with Meringue, M58
    Chocolate-Drizzled Pineapple with Raspberry Sauce, 57
    Fresh Fruit Tart, 58
    Frozen Chocolate Roulage, 56
    Luscious Flan, 56
    Vanilla Poached Pears, 57
Sporty Appetizers For Active Appetites, 60
    Black Pepper Cheese Logs, 61
    Clam Puffs, 60
    Party Reubens, 61
    Swiss Cheese Spread, 60
The Best Of Seafood In A Salad, 69
    Lobster Salad, 69
The Luck Of The Irish To You, 63
    Colcannon, 64
    Irish Stew, 64
    Poached Salmon with Emerald Sauce, 63
    Whiskey Punch, 64
Time Enough For Doughnuts, 70
    Applesauce Drop Doughnuts, 70
Toss A Pasta Salad, 62
    Ham-Pecan-Blue Cheese Pasta Salad, 62
    Oriental Pasta Salad, 63
    Pasta Salad, 62
    Presto Pasta Salad, 63
    Seafood Pasta Salad, 62
Toss The Salad, But Don't Mix Up The Greens, 54
    Colorful Tossed Salad, 55
    Goat Cheese and Greens, 54
    Leafy Cheese Sandwiches, 56
    Mesclun with Tarragon Dressing, 55
    Red-and-Green Salad, 55
    Roasted Red Pepper and Watercress Salad, 55

APRIL
BRUNCHES & LUNCHES, 81
A Lunch For A Southern Celebration, 89
    Baked New Potatoes, 90
    Crispy Walnut Chicken, 89
    Hurry-Up Yeast Rolls, 90
    Lemon Cloud Mousse, 90
    Mint Tea, 89
    Orange-Coconut Pie, 90
    Zesty Marinated Salad, 90
Country Ham, From Start To Finish, 87
    Cheesy Country Ham Puff, 88
    Country Ham with Brown Sugar Coating, 88
    Oven-Braised Country Ham, 87
Invite Friends To A Coffee, 85
    Basic Cupcake Muffins, 87
    Cappuccino Mix, 87
    Daisy Biscuits, 86
    Fresh Strawberries with Cream Dip, 86
    Raisin Pastry Bites, 86
    Sausage-Apple Balls, 85
Kids Kindle The Derby Spirit, 94
    Buckin' Bronco Cookies, 95
    Kid's Cooler, 95
    Wide-Eyed Pizzas, 94
Lunches, Boxed To Go, 91
    Beef Tenderloin Picnic Sandwiches, 91
    Marinated Asparagus and Hearts of Palm, 91
    Miniature Derby Tarts, 92
    Pasta Salad, 91
Reach For The Granola, 95
    Nutty Granola, 95
Share This Menu With Friends, 84
    Grapefruit Drink, 84
    Smoked Turkey Pasta Primavera, 84
    Tasty Rolls, 85
    Very Berry Sorbet, 85
Soup And Salad Specials, 88
    Dilled Zucchini Soup, 88
    Seafood Salad, 88
    Spinach-Apple Salad, 89
    Turkey-Rice Soup, 89
The Races Start With Brunch, 92
    Baked Spinach Tomatoes, 92
    Biscuits with Country Ham, 93
    Cheese Loaf, 93
    Eggs Bel-Mar, 92
    French Toast with Grand Marnier Fruit Sauce, 93
    Miniature Carrot Cakes, 94
    Special Derby Brownies, 94
Toast The Morning, And Greet Midday, 81
    Asparagus Vinaigrette, 82
    Baked Sausage Patties, 82
    Bluegrass Chocolate Tarts, 84
    Bourbon Balls, 83
    Chess Tarts, 83
    Creamed Sweetbreads, 82
    Creamy Scrambled Eggs, 82
    Cucumber Sandwiches, 81
    Kentucky Ham 'n' Angel Biscuits, 83
    Mint Juleps, 81
    Strawberries Dipped in White Chocolate, 83
    Watercress Sandwiches, 82

Desserts Tailored For Passover, 106
    Passover Linzer Torte, 106
    Passover Sponge Cake, 106
Fancy Cakes From Basic Layers, 106
    Apricot-Filled Chocolate Torte, 107
    Basic Light Cake, 107
    Chocolate Buttercream Cake, 108
    Cocoa Crown Cake, 107
    Peachy Almond-Butter Cake, 107
From Our Kitchen To Yours, 108
    Techniques for Using a Decorating Bag, 108
Hats Off To Spring Beverages, 103
    Banana-Blueberry Smoothie, 104
    Blushing Pink Soda, 104
    Frosty Lime Fizz, 104
    Peach Petals, 104
    Yellow Birds, 103
Medaillons Make A Showy Entrée, 96
    Chicken-Rice Medaillons in Pepper Pesto, 97
    Lobster Medaillons in Garlic-Chive Butter Sauce, 96
    Medaillons of Beef with Horseradish Cream, 96
    Pork Medaillons in Mustard Sauce, 96
Not Such A Tough Nut To Crack, 104
    Coconut Crunch Pie, 105
    Coconut Kisses, 106
    Hawaiian Banana Cream Pie, 105
    Toasted Coconut Pie, 105
    Unforgettable Coconut Cake, 104
Outstanding Standbys, 99
    Eggplant Salad, 99
    Layered Tomato Aspic, 99
    Mediterranean Salad, 99
Rely On Fish Fillets, 75
    Caesar's Fish, 76
    Haddock Fillets in White Wine, 76
    Mexi-Style, Oven-Fried Fish, 76
    Oven-Fried Snapper, 75
    Quick Crunchy Flounder, 76
Serve A Hearty Supper, 101
    Lemon Curd with Berries, 102
    Snow Peas with Red Pepper, 102
    Stuffed Flank Steak with Noodles, 101
Sit Down To Some Crawfish, 102
    Crawfish Étouffée, 103
    Louisiana Crawfish Dressing, 103
Something Different With Steak, 97
    Artichoke Hearts with Lemon, 98
    Fettuccine with Broccoli, 97
    Pepper-Mushroom Medley, 98
    Romano Onion Bake, 98
Tease The Palate With Eggplant, 74
    Cheesy Fried Eggplant, 75
    Italian-Stuffed Eggplant, 74
    Quick Eggplant Slices, 75
    Ratatouille Pasta Salad, 74

The Microwave Is A Natural For
  Vegetables, M98
    Leeks in Dilled Lemon-Butter, M98
    Minted Peas and Peppers, M99
    Orange-Glazed Carrots, M98
Toss A Healthy Stir-Fry, 100
    Beef with Asparagus, 100
    Chinese Chicken Stir-Fry, 100
    Pork Chow Mein, 101
    Steak lo Mein, 100
Trimmed-Down Cheese Grits, 102
    Cheese Grits, 102

                MAY
Better-Than-Ever Potato Salad, 122
    Potato Salad, 122
Blue-Ribbon Cookies, 111
    Raspberry Swirl Cookies, 111
Celebrate Cinco De Mayo, 121
    Chicken Enchiladas, 121
    Green Chile Quesadillas, 121
    Jicama-Orange Salad, 122
    Southwestern Rice, 121
Embellish Pasta For An Entrée, 122
    Pasta with Catfish and
        Artichokes, 123
    Salmon Fettuccine, 123
    Saucy Meatballs, 122
Enjoy Barbecue, Memphis Style, 120
    Commissary Barbecue Beans, 120
    John Wills's Baby Loin
        Back Ribs, 120
    Leonard's-Style Onion Rings, 120
Feast On Fresh Strawberries, 125
    Fresh Fruit Salad with Orange
        Cream, 126
    Old-Fashioned Rock Cream with
        Strawberries, 125
    Strawberry Daiquiris, 125
From Our Kitchen To Yours, 126
    Versatile Kitchen Gadgets, 126
Host A Healthy Springtime
  Get-Together, 110
    Bellini Spritzers, 110
    Chocolate Angel Food Cake, 111
    Marinated Chicken Strips and
        Vegetables, 110
    Quick Fruit Dip, 110
    Whole Wheat Rolls, 111
Make A Meal Of Tex-Mex
  Appetizers, 118
    Burrito Rollups, 119
    Fiery Fried Stuffed Jalapeños, 118
    Homemade Texas Chips with
        Guacamole Spread, 119
    Mexican Cheese Spread, 119
    Sausage Quesadillas, 118
    Turkey Nachos, 118
    Two-Cheese Tortilla Snack, 119
Mold A Salad Ahead Of Time, 123
    Beet Aspic, 123
    Chicken Salad Ring, 123
    Congealed Cranberry Salad, 124
    Sherried Fruit Mold, 124
Serve Fruit On The Side, 124
    Bay Laurel Peaches, 124
    Honey-Glazed Apples, 125
    Hot Fruit Compote, 124

Shellfish: Fast And Flavorful, M112
    Mussels Linguine, M112
    Speedy Crabmeat Imperial, M112
    Sweet-and-Sour Shrimp, M112
Team Chicken And Sauces, 117
    Basil and Cream Sauce, 118
    Chervil-and-Savory Sauce, 117
    Chicken Curry Sauce, 117
    Country Ham Sauce, 117
    Green Peppercorn Butter, 117
    Quick Chicken, 117
    Rainbow Pepper Topping, 117

                JUNE
A Hero, Any Way You Stack It, 144
    Bacon, Pimiento, and Cheese
        Hoagies, 144
    Open-Faced Jalapeño Heroes, 144
    Turkey Hero with Garlic Sauce, 145
Appetizers From The Vegetable
  Patch, 147
    Bacon-and-Tomato Dip, 147
    Squash Nosh, 147
    Vegetable Relish, 147
    Zucchini Fries, 147
A Taste Of English Peas In A
  Salad, 143
    Chilled Dilly Peas, 143
    Crunchy Pea Salad, 143
    English Pea Salad, 143
Burstin' With Blueberries, 140
    Blueberry-Sour Cream Cake, 140
Chicken Salad, Better Than Ever, 146
    Chicken Salad Oriental, 146
    Chicken-Spaghetti Salad, 146
    Microwave Chef Salad, M146
Fired Up About Grilled Entrées, 148
    Barbecued Short Ribs, 148
    Beef Kabobs with Vegetables, 148
    Bourbon Steak, 148
    Honey-and-Herb Grilled Pork, 148
From Our Kitchen To Yours, 130
    Buying, Storing, and Cooking Fish, 130
Meaty Ways With Rice, 145
    Chicken Creole, 146
    Creamy Shrimp Curry, 145
    Meatballs with Pineapple and
        Peppers, 145

ON THE LIGHT SIDE, 131
A Fiesta Of Mexican Food, 133
    Tacoritos, 133
    Vegetable Burritos, 134
A Heart-Healthy Feast For
  Guests, 137
    Asparagus Vinaigrette, 138
    Frozen Fresh Peach Yogurt, 139
    Grilled Flank Steak with Sweet
        Peppers, 138
    Quick Crouton Bread, 138
    Ranch-Style Dip, 138
    Roasted New Potatoes, 138
    Watermelon-Berry Slush, 137
Do Your Heart A Favor; Adopt A
  Healthy Lifestyle, 131
    Information on Cholesterol and
        Fats, 131
Fiber For Your Arteries, 134
    Barley-Broccoli Salad, 135
    Brown Rice Pilaf, 136

Cinnamon-Oat Bread, 135
Kidney Bean Casserole, 136
Spicy-Hot Black-Eyed Peas, 135
Homegrown Sprouts, 136
    Sprout Salad, 137
    Stir-Fried Vegetables, 136
Pizza Goes Light, 139
    Turkey-Vegetable Pizza, 139
Triglycerides: Why Are They
  Important?, 134
    Understanding Triglyceride
        Levels, 134

Picture Perfect, From Garden To
  Table, 142
    Brunch Pears with Blue Cheese
        Sauce, 142
    No-Crust Spinach Quiche, 142
    Sour Cream Pancakes with Fruit
        Topping, 142
    Tea Punch, 143
Poaching Imparts Flavor, M141
    Poached Pears with Dark Chocolate
        Sauce, M141
    Poached Plums, M141
    Spicy Poached Apples, M141
Relax! The Entrées Are Easy, 128
    Broccoli-Chicken Salad, 129
    Grilled Catfish Cajun-Style, 129
    Grilled Pork with Salsa, 128
    Grilled Tuna Steaks, 129
    Ham-and-Pasta Salad, 128
    Scallops and Wild Rice, 129
    Smoked Turkey Medley, 128
    Sweet-and-Sour Burgers, 128
These Eggs Can't Be Beat, 140
    Breakfast Pizza, 140
    Cheesy Breakfast Sandwiches, 140
    Spicy Egg Roll-Ups, 140
The Time Is Ripe For
  Cucumbers, 143
    Cucumber Dressing, 144
    Cucumber-Tomato Salad, 144
    Easy Pickled Cucumber Rounds, 143
    Vegetable Spread, 144

                JULY
Drinks With A Taste Of The
  Tropics, 169
    Carambola-Yogurt Calypso, 169
    Papaya Shake, 169
    Passion Fruit Punch, 169
    Tropical Fruit Punch, 169
    Tropical Smoothie, 169
Herbs—Nature's Own
  Seasonings, 164
    Apricot Mint Cooler, 165
    Italian Green Beans, 164
    Lamb Chops with Herbs, 164
    Onion-Herb Bread, 165
    Pesto Potato Salad, 164
Invite Friends For A Healthy
  Cookout, 166
    Grilled Corn-on-the-Cob, 166
    Grilled Marinated Grouper, 166
    Pretty Pepper Kabobs, 166
Lean Butterbeans, 166
    Butterbeans, 166

JULY
(continued)

Play It Cool With Soup, M167
Chilled Carrot-Mint Soup, M168
Dilled Cucumber Soup, M167
Easy Microwave Chicken Broth, M167
Italian Garden Harvest Soup, M167
Sauces Take The Lead, 168
Cocktail Smoky Links, 168
Cranberry-Orange Delight, 168
Easy Pocket Pizzas, 168
Quick Nacho Dip, 168
Sweet-and-Sour Chicken Nuggets, 168
Summer's Sweet Traditions, 156
Back-Home Tea Cakes, 156
Decorative Tea Cakes, 156
Dropped Tea Cakes, 156
Front Porch Lemonade, 156
Grandma's Tea Cakes, 156

SUMMER SUPPERS, 157
A Taste Of Tennessee, 161
French Coconut Pie, 162
Fruit-Glazed Cheesecake, 162
Squash Casserole, 161
Sweet-and-Sour Chicken, 161
Tangy Sauce for Fruit, 161
From Generation To Generation, 163
Ideas for Memorabilia and Mementos
for Your Family Reunion, 163
Gather Around The Porter Table, 158
Chicken Cornbread Dressing, 159
Cranberry Coffee Cake, 159
Pear Honey, 159
Turkey Barbecue, 158
Publish Your Family Recipes, 163
A Guide to Publishing a Family
Cookbook, 163
Reunion Samplings, 160
Almond-Chicken Salad Shanghai, 160
Apple-Barbecue Spareribs, 160
Patio Potato Salad, 160
*Stop Talking And Start
Planning!, 162*
Tips for Planning Your Family
Reunion, 162
Treasured Reunion Recipes, 157
Gazebo Cheese Soup, 158
Italian Crêpes, 157
Snowflake Biscuits, 158

The Best Berries Of The Season, 170
Miniature Cheesecakes, 170
Raspberry Party Puffs, 170
Strawberries with Lemon Cream, 170
**Vegetables That Signal The
Season, 154**
Deep-Fried Okra, 154
Icy-Spicy Mexican Tomato Soup, 155
Limping Susan, 155
Okra Salad, 155
Parslied Corn, 155
Seafood Gumbo, 154

AUGUST
A Breakfast For Kids, 178
Breakfast Pizza, 178
Fruit-on-a-Pick, 179
Orange Juicy, 178
A Peach Of A Sherbet, 179
Peach Sherbet, 179
Around The World With Rice, 183
Creole Rice, 183
Curried Rice, 183
Oriental Shrimp and Rice, 183
Spanish Rice, 183
**Celebrating The Fruits Of
Summer, 180**
Fresh Fruit with Honey-Sour Cream
Dip, 180
Melon-Berry Salad, 180
Peach-and-Kiwi Salad, 180
Watermelon-Cherry Compote, 180
**Contemporary Cuisine With A Southern
Accent, 172**
Black-Eyed Pea Salad, 173
Chives-Grits Timbales, 172
Garlic Grilled Pork Tenderloin, 172
Grilled Catfish with Red Salsa, 172
Herbed Eggplant Soup, 173
Okra-Corn-and-Tomato Vinaigrette, 173
Peach Cream Tart, 173
From Our Kitchen To Yours, 182
Guidelines for Setting the Table, 182
Healthy Sandwiches That Satisfy, 176
Acadian Stuffed Pitas, 177
Fajita in a Pita, 177
Healthy Heroes, 177
Lasagna in a Bun, 176
Shrimp Salad Sandwiches, 178
Turkey-in-The-Slaw Sandwich, 177
In The Mood For A Soda?, 179
Banana Milkshake, 179
Pineapple Soda, 179
Rosy Raspberry Fizz, 179
New Choices For Cheesecake, 174
Curried Chicken Cheesecake, 174
Ham-and-Asparagus Cheesecake, 174
Reuben Cheesecake, 175
Spinach Pesto Cheesecake, 175
Olé, It's Mexican, 175
Chili Casserole, 176
Jiffy Spanish Rice, 176
Mexican Beef Roll-Ups, 176
Oven-Fried Chicken Chimichangas, 175
Pastries Are Her Cup Of Tea, 181
Apricot Crescents, 181
Pecans Make The Pie, 184
Chocolate Pecan Pie, 184
Honey-Pecan Finger Pies, 184
Texas Star Pecan Pie, 184
**Toss Around New Ideas For
Salads, 180**
Corn-and-Pea Salad, 181
Marinated Mushroom Salad, 181
Robust Salad, 181
Turkey-Apple Salad, 181

SEPTEMBER
**A Banker Lends His Culinary
Talents, 204**
Chicken Fajitas, 204
Guacamole, 205

Homemade Picante Sauce, 205
Mexican Kidney Beans, 205
A Healthy Salute To Summer, 198
Angel Food Cake with Amaretto-Almond
Sauce, 199
Scarlet Sipper, 198
Sourdough Wedges, 199
Tarragon Chicken Salad, 199
Appetizers To Cheer For, 206
Chunky Salsa, 206
Hot Nut Crackers, 206
Onion Crescent Crunch Sticks, 206
Sweet-and-Sour Chicken Wings, 206
**Dried Tomatoes Burst With
Flavor, 202**
Chicken-and-Tomatoes over
Fettuccine, 204
Dried Tomato-Cheese Spread, 204
Dried Tomato-Cheese Tart, 203
Dried Tomato-Cream Soup, 203
Dried Tomato Pesto, 204
Dried Tomato Spaghetti Sauce, 202
From Our Kitchen To Yours, 205
Creative Centerpieces, 205
Here's To The Game, 206
Mixed Fruit Punch, 207
Pineapple Cooler, 207
Southern Long Island Iced Tea, 207
Spicy Bloody Marys, 207
Tea Punch, 207
Tropical Punch, 207
Ladle Up Some Soup, 201
Broccoli-and-Chicken Soup, 202
Clam Chowder, 202
Corn Chowder, 202
Easy Texas Chili, 201
Tortilla Soup, 201
White Bean Soup, 201
**Meet Our Cooks Across The
South, 190**
Breakfast Burritos, 192
Chocolate Chip Cookies, 193
Cornish Hens with Fruited
Stuffing, 191
Crabmeat Mousse, 190
Fresh Mushroom Soup, 190
Frosted Chocolate Snack Cake, 194
Glazed Sweet Bread Wreath, 192
Koulourakia, 193
Lasagna Maria, 191
Luncheon Pasta Salad, 191
Oven-Baked French Toast, 192
Spumoni Charlotte, 193
Microwave Cheesecake, M196
Luscious Lemon Cheesecake, M196
Serve This Bread With A Spoon, 200
Spoonbread, 200
Speedy Vegetables, 207
Black-Eyed Peas with Rice, 208
Corn-and-Bean Casserole, 208
Creamy Corn, 207
French Green Beans, 208
Pork Chop-Vegetable
Casserole, 208
**Spilling The Beans About
Legumes, 197**
Lentils-and-Rice Salad, 197
Lentil Spaghetti Sauce, 198
Marinated Legumes, 197
Split Pea Soup, 198
Texas Ranch Beans, 198

Squash Side Dishes To Savor, 200
    Herb Butter Zucchini Fans, 201
    Stuffed Squash Mexican, 200
    Stuffed White Squash, M201
Sweet Rolls On The Rise, 194
    Cheese-Apricot Sweet Rolls, 195
    Coconut-Pecan Coils, 196
    Easy Caramel Rolls, 195
    Glazed Orange Rolls, 194
    Old-Fashioned Cinnamon Rolls, 196
    Praline Buns, 195
    Quick Breakfast Sweet Rolls, 195

OCTOBER

A Healthy Meal With A Cajun
  Flair, 229
    Bread Pudding with Whiskey Sauce, 230
    Mixed Green Salad, 230
    Shrimp Étouffée, 229
Artichokes Fill This Strata, 236
    Artichoke-Cheese Strata, 236
A Southern Menu With A Few
  Surprises, 232
    Bourbon Yams, 232
    Old-Fashioned Corn Sticks, 232
    Turnip Greens, 232
    Zesty Deviled Chicken, 232
Beef Stew Minus All The Fat, 230
    Beef Stew, 230
Classic Creations With Cornmeal, 213
    Corn Sticks, 214
    Herbed Cornbread, 214
    Mexican Hush Puppies, 214
    Paprika Cornbread, 213
Crazy About Caramel, 227
    Caramel-Crowned Flans, 227
Fiesta Supper In A Snap, M231
    Microwave Mexican Casserole, M231
Fight Cancer With Your Fork, 228
    Brussels Sprouts in Mustard Sauce, 228
    Curried Carrots and Pineapple, 228
    Fruited Acorn Squash, 228
    Skillet Cabbage, 229
    Sweet Potatoes-and-Apple
      Casserole, 228
From Our Kitchen To Yours, 225
    Etiquette at the Dinner Table, 225
Fruit Makes It Fancy, 211
    Fruited Pot Roast, 211
    Glazed Ham Loaf, 212
    Oriental Pork Chops, 212
    Peachy Chicken, 212
Ham With New Appeal, 235
    Ham Loaves, 235
    Ham Pinwheels, 235
    Spicy Ham Patties, 235
Introducing Mirlitons, 217
    Mirliton Balls, 217
    Stuffed Mirlitons, 217
It's Apple Season, 212
    Apple-Date-Nut Ring, 212
    Honey-Baked Apple Dessert, M213
    Whole Wheat-Apple Crumble, M213
Ladle Up The Cream Of The Crop, 210
    Carrot Cream Soup, 210
    Cauliflower Soup, 211
    Cream of Celery Soup, 210
    Cream of Corn Soup, 210

Cream of Spinach Soup, 211
Cream Pea Soup, 211
Creamy Onion Soup, 211
No Trick To Treats For Teens, 225
    Almond Delight Dip, 226
    Chili-Cheese Dip, 225
    Chocolate-Peanut Butter Snacks, 226
    Hot Apple Cider, 225
    Marshmallow Popcorn Balls, 226
    Salami Rollups, 226
Pick An Entrée For Two, 234
    Chicken-Fruit Salad, 234
    Cream Cheese Chicken Breasts, 234
    Simple Beef Burgundy, 234
    Tex-Mex Meat Loaf for Two, 234
Plump And Delicious, 227
    Chicken Breasts with Curried
      Peppers, 227
    Peppy Prune Relish, 227
Quick Southern Classics, 218
    Bread Pudding, 219
    Corn Pudding, 219
    Double-Crust Chicken Pot Pie, 220
    Easy Red Beans and Rice, 220
    Peach Cobbler, 219
    Quick Upside Down Cake, 219
    Shortcut Chicken and Rice, 220
    Shrimp Creole, M220
    Speedy Sweet Potato Pie, 219
Side Dishes That Satisfy, 236
    Eggplant Dressing, 236
    Rice à l'Orange, 236
    Squash Delight, 236
Supper From The Sea, 233
    Grouper with Sautéed
      Vegetables, M233
    Quick Clam Linguine, 233
    Seafood and Pasta, 234
    Shrimp Versailles, 233
Sweet Send-Offs, 218
    Apple-Oatmeal Cookies, 218
    Crispy-Chewy Molasses
      Cookies, 218
    Oatmeal-Chocolate Chippers, 218
Tastefully Tossed Salad, 231
    Tropical Spinach Salad, 231
Usher In Autumn With Breads, 214
    Easy Monkey Bread, 214
    Harvest Pumpkin Bread, M215
    Irish Soda Bread, 214
Yogurt Adds Culture To These
  Dishes, 215
    Blue Cheese Spread, 215
    Chicken-Apple Salad, 216
    Shrimp Dee-Lish, 216
    Yogurt-Muesli Muffins, 215
    Yogurt-Sesame Chicken, 216

NOVEMBER

A Passion For Pound Cake, 284
    Chocolate Pound Cake with
      Frosting, 284
    Golden Pound Cake, 284
    Whipping Cream Pound Cake, 284
Choose A Better Salad, 286
    Blue Cheese Dressing, 286
    Creamy French Dressing, 286
    Greek Salad Dressing, 286

Company's Coming For Casseroles, 238
    Broccoli-Ham au Gratin, 239
    Crab, Shrimp, and Artichoke au
      Gratin, 240
    Italian Casserole, 238
    Reuben Casserole, 240
    Sausage-Cheese Grits, 238
    Shrimp-and-Noodle Casserole, 240
    Turkey-Noodle Poppyseed
      Casserole, 239
Crimson Cranberries, 287
    Cranberry Cloud, 287
    Cranberry-Mustard Fruit Bake, 287
    Frosted Cranberry Salad, 288
Elegant Charlotte Russe, 288
    Charlotte Russe, 288
    Pineapple Charlotte, 288

HOLIDAY DINNERS, 241
Accent With Light, 282
    Set a Holiday Mood with Lights, 282
A Clear Look At Glassware, 274
    Glassware Identified and
      Illustrated, 274
A Grand Finale, 265
    Chocolate-Mint Whipped Cream
      Cake, 265
*Beverages Brewed For The
  Season, 272*
    Amaretto, 272
    Cranapple Wine, 272
    Holiday Brew, 272
    Hot Chocolate Deluxe, 272
    Sparkling Gin Cooler, 272
Beverages For All Ages, 273
    Holiday Coffee, 273
    Lime Slush Punch, 273
    Peppermint-Eggnog Punch, 273
    Strawberry Punch, 273
    Wassail, 273
Decorate The Door Naturally, 280
    How to Create a Holiday Decoration
      for Your Door, 280
*Dinner For The
  Health-Conscious, 279*
    Baked Apples à l'Orange, 280
    Individual Chicken Bake, 279
    Mixed Greens with Blue Cheese
      Vinaigrette, 280
    New Potato Medley, 279
*Dishes That Make Holiday
  Tradition, 249*
    Amaretto-Hot Fruit Compote, 250
    Freezer Dinner Rolls, 251
    Glazed Sweet Potato Casserole, 250
    Holiday Ham Slice with Cinnamon
      Apple Rings, 250
    Scalloped Oysters, 249
    Smoked Turkey, 249
    Southern Rice, 250
Drop By For Dessert, 266
    Amaretto-Irish Cream Cheesecake, 266
    Caramel Brie with Fresh Fruit, 266
    Roulage, 266
*Entertain Young Adults With A
  Festive Menu, 268*
    Cold Spiced Fruit, 269
    Easy Beef Tenderloin, 268
    Ice Cream Bombe, 269
    Lemon-Buttered New Potatoes, 268
    Special Green Beans, 268

NOVEMBER
(continued)

From Our Kitchen To Yours, 276
How to Entertain with
Confidence, 276
Gifts Say "Thank You," 267
Chocolate Chip-Banana Bread, 267
Fruited Rice Mix, 267
Holiday Entertaining At Its Best, 241
Burgundy Eye-of-Round, 243
Buttery Brown Sugar Dip with
Fruit, 243
Cocktail Sauce, 242
Horseradish Spread, 243
Marinated Cheese, 244
Marinated Vegetables Italian, 242
Pesto-and-Cream Cheese Round, 242
Yule Street Truffles, 242
Innovative Invitations, 277
How to Create Your Own
Party Invitations, 277
Invite Kids To The Party, 269
Elf Gorp, 270
Ham-and-Cheese Pita Pockets, 271
Kid-Pleasin' Chocolate Mousse, 271
Santa's Slush, 271
Thick-and-Creamy Dip, 271
It's Easy To Host A Buffet, 246
How to Plan and Host a Buffet, 246
Longing For Louisiana Flavor, 255
Chicken-and-Sausage Gumbo, 256
Pecan Tart with Praline Cream, 256
Shrimp Rémoulade, 255
Open House Planning Guide, 244
A Step-by-Step Party Planner, 244
Set The Mood For A Party, 247
Champagne Jelly, 248
Party Nibbles, 249
Simmer A Pot Of Soup, 278
Catfish Gumbo, 278
Mex-Tex Soup, 278
Turkey-Tomato Stew, 279
Taste A Sentimental Journey, 251
Creamy Holiday Fruit Salad, 251
Eggnog Pound Cake, 253
Grandma's Ambrosia, 254
Japanese Fruitcake, 252
One-Foot-in-the-Fire Fudge
Cake, 252
The Compromise Cake, 253
*Tasty, Timeless Hanukkah
Treats,* 254
Applesauce, 255
Latkes, 254
Sufganiyot (Jelly-Filled
Doughnuts), 255
Sweet Kugel, 254

Making The Best Pound Cakes, 285
Tips to Ensure Delicious Pound
Cakes, 285

No-Fret Breads, 283
Almond Crescent Rolls, 283
Easy Herb Biscuits, 283
Lightnin' Cheese Biscuits, 283
Mayonnaise Rolls, 283
Quick Garlic Bread, 283
Sour Cream Muffins, 283
Tasty Turkey Soup, 287
Williamsburg Turkey Soup, 287

DECEMBER
After The Slopes, The Feast, 319
Brownie Chip Cookies, 320
Chili-Chicken Stew, 319
Sea-and-Ski Cocktail Mix, 319
Seasoned Cornbread, 320
**A Menu For The Two
Of You,** 294
Beef Tenderloin for Two, 295
Strawberry-Yogurt Dessert, 295
Twice-Baked Potato, M295
**An Easy But Superb Dinner For
Four,** 315
Basil-Cheese Potatoes, M316
Bean-and-Tomato Skillet, 316
Easy Custard with Nutmeg, 316
Glazed Pork Tenderloin, 315
Bread With Italian Roots, 321
Mustard-and-Onion Focaccia, 321
**Cranberries: Jewels Of The
Season,** 293
Cranberries Jubilee, 293
Cranberry-and-Apple Cobbler, 294
Cranberry-Banana Bread, 294
Cranberry Pork, 293
Miniature Cranberry Muffins, 294
Ease Into Morning, 323
Pumpkin Doughnut Drops, 323
Sweet Potato Waffles with Orange
Butter, 323
Tropical Coffee Cake, 323
Easy Appetizers, 292
Chutney-Bacon Brie, M292
Crabmeat-Horseradish Spread, 292
Hearts of Palm Spread, 293
Mexican Artichoke Dip, 292
Super Seafood Dip, 292
Entrées For Any Occasion, 316
Baked Flounder, 316
Dijon Chicken with Pasta, 318
Marinated Rib-Eye Roast, 318
Shrimp-and-Scallop Sauté with Pecan
Rice, 317
Stuffed Country Ham, 317
Sweet-and-Sour Pork, 317
From Our Kitchen To Yours, 314
Answers to Frequently Asked Questions
from Readers, 314
Heart-Smart Pumpkin Pie, 296
New-Fashioned Pumpkin Pie, 296

Our All-Time Best Desserts, 305
Almond Cream Confections, 310
Black Walnut Cake, 308
Caramel Cake, 307
Chocolate-Glazed Triple-Layer
Cheesecake, 310
Chocolate-Peanut Butter Fudge, 311
Chocolate-Tipped Butter
Cookies, 312
Choco-Mallow Brownies, 309
Coconut-Cream Cheese Pound
Cake, 305
Coconut Cream Pie, 312
Cream Cheese Tarts, 312
Crispy Oat Cookies, 311
Deluxe Lemon Meringue Pie, 313
Deluxe Peach Ice Cream, 314
Holiday Coconut Cake, 308
Hummingbird Cake, 305
Ice-Cream Pie Spectacular, 314
Light Fruitcake, 309
Milk Chocolate Pound Cake, 306
Million Dollar Pound Cake, 306
Peach Cobbler Supreme, 313
Pecan Pie, 312
Perfect Chocolate Cake, 307
Roasted Pecan Clusters, 310
Swedish Heirloom Cookies, 311
Sweetheart Fudge Pie, 313
Pair Citrus And Cream, 296
Frosty Orange Pie, 296
**Roast Turkey: Something To Squawk
About,** 320
Roast Turkey, 321
**Side Dishes With A Holiday
Dash,** 290
Asparagus with Cream Sauce, 291
Broccoli Salad, 292
Calico Squash Casserole, 290
Cranberry Ring, 291
Garlic-Parsley Potatoes, 290
Holiday Sweet Potato Bake, 291
Mint-Glazed Carrots and Peas, 291
Mustard Fruit Bake, 291
Sesame Spinach Salad, 292
Sip The Holiday Spirit, 322
Amaretto Slush, 322
Champagne Fruit Slush, 322
Peach Daiquiris, 322
Slush with a Punch, 322
White Sangría Slush, 322
Stir In The Champagne, 315
Berry Mimosa Sauce, 315
Champagne Ice, 315
Strawberry Champagne
Punch, 315
Stir Leftovers Into A Salad, 318
Colorful Ham-and-Rice Salad, 319
Fruited Chicken Salad, 318
Layered Overnight Salad, 319
Roast Beef Salad, 318
Turkey Salad, 318

General Recipe Index

A listing of every recipe by food category and/or major ingredient
All microwave recipe page numbers are preceded by an "M"

Almonds
Cake, Peachy Almond-Butter, 107
Confections, Almond Cream, 310
Dip, Almond Delight, 226
Muffins, Almond, 87
Rolls, Almond Crescent, 283
Salad Shanghai, Almond-Chicken, 160
Sauce, Angel Food Cake with
    Amaretto-Almond, 199
Ambrosia
Grandma's Ambrosia, 254
Appetizers
Burrito Rollups, 119
Cheese
    Brie, Chutney-Bacon, M292
    Brie with Fresh Fruit, Caramel, 266
    Cream Cheese Round,
      Pesto-and-, 242
    Logs, Black Pepper Cheese, 61
    Marinated Cheese, 244
    Mold, Cream Cheese-Crabmeat, 71
    Quesadillas, Green Chile, 121
Chicken Wings, Sweet-and-Sour, 206
Chili in Pastry Cups, 68
Chips with Guacamole Spread, Homemade
    Texas, 119
Chocolate Bites, Snowy, 47
Chocolate-Peanut Butter Snacks, 226
Clam Puffs, 60
Crackers, Hot Nut, 206
Dips
    Almond Delight Dip, 226
    Artichoke Dip, Mexican, 292
    Bacon-and-Tomato Dip, 147
    Brown Sugar Dip with Fruit,
      Buttery, 243
    Chili-Cheese Dip, 225
    Fruit Dip, Quick, 110
    Nacho Dip, Quick, 168
    Orange Cream, 126
    Ranch-Style Dip, 138
    Seafood Dip, Super, 292
    Thick-and-Creamy Dip, 271
Eggplant, Cheesy Fried, 75
Eye-of-Round, Burgundy, 243
Fruit with Honey-Sour Cream Dip,
    Fresh, 180
Gorp, Elf, 270
Granola, Nutty, 95
Jalapeños, Fiery Fried Stuffed, 118
Links, Cocktail Smoky, 168
Mirliton Balls, 217
Mix, Sea-and-Ski Cocktail, 319
Mousse, Crabmeat, 190
Nachos, Turkey, 118
Nibbles, Party, 249
Onion Crescent Crunch Sticks, 206
Oysters Bienville, Baked, 27
Pâté, Wine, 36

Popcorn Balls, Marshmallow, 226
Raspberry Party Puffs, 170
Reubens, Party, 61
Salami Rollups, 226
Salsa, Chunky, 206
Sandwiches, Cucumber, 81
Sandwiches, Watercress, 82
Sausage-Apple Balls, 85
Sausage Quesadillas, 118
Spreads
    Blue Cheese Spread, 215
    Cheese Spread, Mexican, 119
    Crabmeat-Horseradish Spread, 292
    Gouda Cheese Spread, 36
    Guacamole Spread, 119
    Hearts of Palm Spread, 293
    Horseradish Spread, 243
    Raisin Spread, Creamy, 36
    Shrimp Spread, Zippy, 36
    Swiss Cheese Spread, 60
    Tomato-Cheese Spread, Dried, 204
    Vegetable Spread, 144
Squash Nosh, 147
Strawberries with Lemon Cream, 170
Tortilla Snack, Two-Cheese, 119
Vegetables Italian, Marinated, 242
Zucchini Fries, 147
Apples
Baked Apples à l'Orange, 280
Balls, Sausage-Apple, 85
Casserole, Sweet Potatoes-and-Apple, 228
Cider, Hot Apple, 21, 225
Cobbler, Cranberry-and-Apple, 294
Cookies, Apple-Oatmeal, 218
Cooler, Apple, 14
Crisp, Oatmeal Cherry-Apple, M16
Crumble, Whole Wheat-Apple, M213
Date-Nut Ring, Apple-, 212
Dessert, Honey-Baked Apple, M213
Glazed Apples, Honey-, 125
Juice, Perky Cinnamon-Apple, 22
Poached Apples, Spicy, M141
Rings, Cinnamon Apple, 250
Salad, Chicken-Apple, 216
Salad, Spinach-Apple, 89
Salad, Turkey-Apple, 181
Spareribs, Apple-Barbecue, 160
Applesauce
Applesauce, 255
Bread, Applesauce-Pecan, 66
Doughnuts, Applesauce Drop, 70
Apricots
Cooler, Apricot Mint, 165
Crescents, Apricot, 181
Filling, Lemon-Apricot, 105
Ham and Apricots, 53
Rolls, Cheese-Apricot Sweet, 195
Torte, Apricot-Filled Chocolate, 107
Torte, Apricot Sponge, 59

Artichokes
au Gratin, Crab, Shrimp, and
    Artichoke, 240
Chicken with Artichokes and
    Mushrooms, 35
Dip, Mexican Artichoke, 292
Lemon, Artichoke Hearts with, 98
Pasta with Catfish and Artichokes, 123
Strata, Apricot-Cheese, 236
Asparagus
Beef with Asparagus, 100
Cheesecake, Ham-and-Asparagus, 174
Cream Sauce, Asparagus with, 291
Curry Sauce, Asparagus with, 17
Marinated Asparagus and Hearts of
    Palm, 91
Vinaigrette, Asparagus, 82, 138
Aspic
Beet Aspic, 123
Tomato Aspic, Layered, 99
Avocados
Guacamole, 205
Guacamole Spread, 119

Bacon
Brie, Chutney-Bacon, M292
Dip, Bacon-and-Tomato, 147
Hoagies, Bacon, Pimiento, and
    Cheese, 144
Bananas
Bread, Chocolate Chip-Banana, 267
Bread, Cranberry-Banana, 294
Milkshake, Banana, 179
Pie, Hawaiian Banana Cream, 105
Slush, Pineapple-Banana, 14
Smoothie, Banana-Blueberry, 104
Barbecue
Beans, Commissary Barbecue, 120
Ribs, Barbecued Short, 148
Ribs, John Wills's Baby Loin Back, 120
Sauces
    Basting Sauce, 120
    Blender Barbecue Sauce, Ribs
      with, 12
    Sweet Sauce, 120
Shrimp, Barbecued, 28
Spareribs, Apple-Barbecue, 160
Turkey Barbecue, 158
Barley
Salad, Barley-Broccoli, 135
Beans
Barbecue Beans, Commissary, 120
Butterbeans, 166
Green
    Casserole, Corn-and-Bean, 208
    French Green Beans, 208

Beans, Green
(continued)

Italian Green Beans, 164
Special Green Beans, 268
Tomato Skillet, Bean-and-, 316
Kidney Bean Casserole, 136
Kidney Beans, Mexican, 205
Legumes, Marinated, 197
Lentils-and-Rice Salad, 197
Lentil Spaghetti Sauce, 198
Red Beans and Rice, 27
Red Beans and Rice, Easy, 220
Texas Ranch Beans, 198
White Bean Soup, 201

Beef
Asparagus, Beef with, 100
Burgundy, Simple Beef, 234
Corned Beef
Reuben Casserole, 240
Reuben Cheesecake, 175
Reubens, Party, 61
Kabobs with Vegetables, Beef, 148
Medaillons of Beef with Horseradish
Cream, 96
Ribs, Barbecued Short, 148
Roasts
Eye-of-Round, Burgundy, 243
Pot Roast, Fruited, 211
Rib-Eye Roast, Marinated, 318
Roll-Ups, Mexican Beef, 176
Salad, Roast Beef, 318
Steaks
Bourbon Steak, 148
Flank Steak with Noodles,
Stuffed, 101
Flank Steak with Sweet Peppers,
Grilled, 138
lo Mein, Steak, 100
Round Steak over Rice,
Burgundy, M33
Zippy Steak and Gravy, 35
Stew, Beef, 230
Stew, Irish, 64
Stock, Brown Meat, 31
Tenderloin, Easy Beef, 268
Tenderloin for Two, Beef, 295
Tenderloin Picnic Sandwiches,
Beef, 91

Beef, Ground
Burgers, Sweet-and-Sour, 128
Casserole, Microwave
Mexican, M231
Chili
Easy Texas Chili, 201
Pastry Cups, Chili in, 68
Crêpes, Italian, 157
Dip, Quick Nacho, 168
Lasagna in a Bun, 176
Meatballs
Pineapple and Peppers, Meatballs
with, 145
Saucy Meatballs, 122
Meat Loaf
Mini-Teriyaki Meat Loaf, 69
Tex-Mex Meat Loaf for
Two, 234
Moussaka, 68
Salad, Taco, 20
Sauce, Italian, 67
Tacoritos, 133

Beets
Aspic, Beet, 123
Salad, Red-and-Green, 55
Beverages
Alcoholic
Amaretto, 272
Amaretto Slush, 322
Bellini Spritzers, 110
Bloody Marys, Spicy, 207
Champagne Fruit Slush, 322
Chocolate Deluxe, Hot, 272
Cranapple Glogg, Hot, 22
Cranapple Wine, 272
Daiquiris, Peach, 322
Daiquiris, Strawberry, 125
Gin Cooler, Sparkling, 272
Mint Juleps, 81
Peach Petals, 104
Punch, Strawberry Champagne, 315
Punch, Whiskey, 64
Sangría Slush, White, 322
Slush with a Punch, 322
Tea, Southern Long Island Iced, 207
Wassail, Four-Fruit, 22
Yellow Birds, 103
Apple Cider, Hot, 21, 225
Apple Cooler, 14
Apple Juice, Perky Cinnamon-, 22
Apricot Mint Cooler, 165
Banana-Blueberry Smoothie, 104
Cappuccino Mix, 87
Carambola-Yogurt Calypso, 169
Coffee, Holiday, 273
Grapefruit Drink, 84
Grape Juice, Mulled, 21
Holiday Brew, 272
Kid's Cooler, 95
Lemonade, Front Porch, 156
Lemon Velvet, 15
Lime Fizz, Frosty, 104
Milkshake, Banana, 179
Orange Juicy, 178
Pineapple-Banana Slush, 14
Pineapple Cooler, 207
Pineapple Nectar, Hot, 21
Pineapple Soda, 179
Pink Soda, Blushing, 104
Punch. *See also* Beverages/Alcoholic.
Fruit Punch, Mixed, 207
Fruit Punch, Passion, 169
Fruit Punch, Tropical, 169
Lime Slush Punch, 273
Peppermint-Eggnog Punch, 273
Strawberry Punch, 273
Tea Punch, 143, 207
Tropical Punch, 207
White Grape Punch, 15
Raspberry Fizz, Rosy, 179
Scarlet Sipper, 198
Shake, Papaya, 169
Slush, Santa's, 271
Strawberry Spritzer, 14
Syrup, Mint, 89
Tea, Mint, 89
Tomato Juice Cocktail, 12
Tropical Smoothie, 169
Wassail, 273
Watermelon-Berry Slush, 137
Biscuits
Angel Biscuits, 28
Cheese Biscuits, Lightnin', 283

Country Ham, Biscuits with, 93
Daisy Biscuits, 86
Ham 'n' Angel Biscuits, Kentucky, 83
Herb Biscuits, Easy, 283
Snowflake Biscuits, 158
Blueberries
Cake, Blueberry-Sour Cream, 140
Lemon Curd with Berries, 102
Salad, Melon-Berry, 180
Smoothie, Banana-Blueberry, 104
Bran
Muffins, Maple-Bran, 66
Breads. *See also* specific types.
Applesauce-Pecan Bread, 66
Cheese Loaf, 93
Chocolate Chip-Banana Bread, 267
Cranberry-Banana Bread, 294
Crouton Bread, Quick, 138
Focaccia, Mustard-and-Onion, 321
Garlic Bread, Quick, 283
Irish Soda Bread, 214
Koulourakia, 193
Popovers, Cinnamon, 66
Popovers, Parmesan, 66
Popovers, Whole Wheat, 66
Pudding, Bread, 219
Pudding with Whiskey Sauce,
Bread, 230
Pumpkin Bread, Harvest, M215
Sourdough Wedges, 199
Spoonbread, 200
Wheat Loaf, Nutty, 65
Yeast
Apple-Date-Nut Ring, 212
Braid, Sweet Yeast, 46
Cinnamon-Oat Bread, 135
Golden Bread, 47
Loaves, Sweet-Filled Yeast, 46
Monkey Bread, Easy, 214
Onion-Herb Bread, 165
Sweet Bread Wreath, Glazed, 192
Broccoli
au Gratin, Broccoli-Ham, 239
Divan, Creamy Turkey, M34
Fettuccine with Broccoli, 97
Salad, Barley-Broccoli, 135
Salad, Broccoli, 292
Salad, Broccoli-Chicken, 129
Salad, Broccoli 'n' Cauliflower, 32
Salad, Red, White, and Green, 18
Soup, Broccoli-and-Chicken, 202
Brussels Sprouts
Mustard Sauce, Brussels
Sprouts in, 228
Burritos
Breakfast Burritos, 192
Rollups, Burrito, 119
Vegetable Burritos, 134
Butter
Green Peppercorn Butter, 117
Orange Butter, 323
Butterscotch
Pinwheels, Butterscotch, 49

Cabbage
Colcannon, 64
Skillet Cabbage, 229
Cakes. *See also* Breads, Cookies.
Almond-Butter Cake, Peachy, 107
Angel Food
Amaretto-Almond Sauce, Angel Food
Cake with, 199
Chocolate Angel Food Cake, 111
Blueberry-Sour Cream Cake, 140
Caramel Cake, 307
Carrot Cakes, Miniature, 94
Cheesecakes
Amaretto-Irish Cream
Cheesecake, 266
Chicken Cheesecake, Curried, 174
Fruit-Glazed Cheesecake, 162
Ham-and-Asparagus Cheesecake, 174
Lemon Cheesecake, Luscious, M196
Miniature Cheesecakes, 170
Reuben Cheesecake, 175
Spinach Pesto Cheesecake, 175
Triple-Layer Cheesecake,
Chocolate-Glazed, 310
Chocolate
Buttercream Cake, Chocolate, 108
Cocoa Crown Cake, 107
Fudge Cake,
One-Foot-in-the-Fire, 252
Perfect Chocolate Cake, 307
Snack Cake, Frosted Chocolate, 194
Torte, Apricot-Filled Chocolate, 107
Whipped Cream Cake,
Chocolate-Mint, 265
Coconut
Holiday Coconut Cake, 308
Unforgettable Coconut Cake, 104
Coffee Cakes
Cheesecake Coffee Cake,
Deep-Dish, 50
Cranberry Coffee Cake, 159
Tropical Coffee Cake, 323
Compromise Cake, The, 253
Fruitcakes
Japanese Fruitcake, 252
Light Fruitcake, 309
Hummingbird Cake, 305
King Cake, 20
Lady Baltimore Cake, 45
Light Cake, Basic, 107
Lord Baltimore Cake, 45
Pound
Chocolate Pound Cake with
Frosting, 284
Coconut-Cream Cheese Pound
Cake, 305
Eggnog Pound Cake, 253
Golden Pound Cake, 284
Milk Chocolate Pound Cake, 306
Million Dollar Pound Cake, 306
Whipping Cream Pound Cake, 284
Sponge Cake, Passover, 106
Torte, Apricot Sponge, 59
Torte, Passover Linzer, 106
Upside Down Cake, Quick, 219
Walnut Cake, Black, 308
Candies
Bourbon Balls, 83
Fudge, Chocolate-Peanut Butter, 311
Pecan Clusters, Roasted, 310
Truffles, Yule Street, 242

Cantaloupe. *See* Melons.
Caramel
Brie with Fresh Fruit, Caramel, 266
Cake, Caramel, 307
Flans, Caramel-Crowned, 227
Frosting, Caramel, 307
Rolls, Easy Caramel, 195
Carrots
Cakes, Miniature Carrot, 94
Curried Carrots and Pineapple, 228
Dilled Carrots, 17
Glazed Carrots and Peas, Mint-, 291
Glazed Carrots, Orange-, M98
Glazed Carrots, Peach-, 13
Julienne Zucchini and Carrots, 14
Soup, Carrot Cream, 210
Soup, Chilled Carrot-Mint, M168
Casseroles
Broccoli-Ham au Gratin, 239
Chili Casserole, 176
Eggs Bel-Mar, 92
Italian Casserole, 238
Kidney Bean Casserole, 136
Meat
Mexican Casserole, Microwave, M231
Moussaka, 68
Pork Chop-Vegetable Casserole, 208
Poultry
Chicken Casserole, Swiss, 67
Chicken, Fontina-Baked, 64
Turkey-Noodle-Poppyseed
Casserole, 239
Reuben Casserole, 240
Rice, Spanish, 183
Seafood
Crab, Shrimp, and Artichoke au
Gratin, 240
Shrimp-and-Noodle Casserole, 240
Vegetable
Corn-and-Bean Casserole, 208
Corn, Creamy Baked, 60
Potatoes, Parmesan, M62
Squash Casserole, 161
Squash Casserole, Calico, 290
Sweet Potato Bake, Holiday, 291
Sweet Potato Casserole, Glazed, 250
Sweet Potatoes-and-Apple
Casserole, 228
Cauliflower
Fried Cauliflower, 18
Salad, Broccoli 'n' Cauliflower, 32
Salad, Red, White, and Green, 18
Soufflé, Cauliflower, 17
Soup, Cauliflower, 211
Celery
Soup, Cream of Celery, 210
Cheese. *See also* Appetizers/Cheese.
Breads
Biscuits, Lightnin' Cheese, 283
Loaf, Cheese, 93
Popovers, Parmesan, 66
Rolls, Cheese-Apricot Sweet, 195
Burritos, Breakfast, 192
Cake, Coconut-Cream Cheese Pound, 305
Cake, Deep-Dish Cheesecake Coffee, 50
Casseroles
Broccoli-Ham au Gratin, 239
Chicken, Fontina-Baked, 64
Crab, Shrimp, and Artichoke au
Gratin, 240
Lasagna Maria, 191

Mexican Casserole, Microwave, M231
Reuben Casserole, 240
Swiss Chicken Casserole, 67
Chicken Breasts, Cream Cheese, 234
Country Ham Puff, Cheesy, 88
Crackers, Hot Nut, 206
Dressing, Blue Cheese, 286
Frosting, Cream Cheese, 305, 308
Goat Cheese and Greens, 54
Grits, Cheese, 102
Grits, Sausage-Cheese, 238
Hoagies, Bacon, Pimiento, and Cheese, 144
Lasagna in a Bun, 176
Macaroni and Cheese, 30
Marinated Cheese, 244
Pita Pockets, Ham-and-Cheese, 271
Quesadillas, Sausage, 118
Quiche, Swiss Alpine, 18
Salad, Ham-Pecan-Blue Cheese Pasta, 62
Sandwiches, Cheesy Breakfast, 140
Sandwiches, Leafy Cheese, 56
Sauces
Blue Cheese Sauce, 142
Cheese Sauce, 235
Soup, Gazebo Cheese, 158
Spreads and Fillings
Blue Cheese Spread, 215
Chocolate-Cheese Filling, 47
Cinnamon-Cheese Filling, 46
Cranberry Cream, 66
Cream Cheese Filling, 170
Cream Cheese Spread, Peachy, M215
Gouda Cheese Spread, 36
Mexican Cheese Spread, 119
Orange-Cheese Filling, 47
Swiss Cheese Spread, 60
Strata, Artichoke-Cheese, 236
Tart, Dried Tomato-Cheese, 203
Tarts, Cream Cheese, 312
Tortilla Snack, Two-Cheese, 119
Vegetables
Eggplant, Cheesy Fried, 75
Onion Bake, Romano, 98
Onions, Cheese-Stuffed, 34
Potatoes, Basil-Cheese, M316
Potatoes, Chili-Cheese, M62
Potatoes, Parmesan, M62
Vinaigrette, Blue Cheese, 55, 280
Cheesecakes. *See* Cakes/Cheesecakes.
Cherries
Compote, Watermelon-Cherry, 180
Crisp, Oatmeal Cherry-Apple, M16
Muffins, Cherry-Nut, 87
Chicken
Artichokes and Mushrooms, Chicken
with, 35
Baked Chicken, Fontina-, 64
Bake, Individual Chicken, 279
Bake, Parslied Chicken, 65
Broth, Easy Microwave Chicken, M167
Casserole, Swiss Chicken, 67
Cheesecake, Curried Chicken, 174
Chimichangas, Oven-Fried Chicken, 175
Chow Mein, Chicken, 68
Cream Cheese Chicken Breasts, 234
Creole, Chicken, 146
Deviled Chicken, Zesty, 232
Dijon Chicken with Pasta, 318
Dilly Chicken, 65
Dressing, Chicken Cornbread, 159
Enchiladas, Chicken, 121

Chicken

(continued)

Fajita in a Pita, 177
Fajitas, Chicken, 204
Fettuccine, Chicken-and-Tomatoes
  over, 204
Ginger-Nut Chicken, M33
Greek Lemon Chicken, 65
Gumbo, Chicken, 26
Gumbo, Chicken-and-Sausage, 256
Jambalaya, 26
Lemon-Garlic Chicken, 35
Marinated Chicken Breasts, 54
Marinated Chicken Strips and
  Vegetables, 110
Medaillons in Pepper Pesto,
  Chicken-Rice, 97
Peachy Chicken, 212
Pecan Chicken, 54
Peppers, Chicken Breasts with
  Curried, 227
Pie, Nana's Chicken, 25
Pie, Savory Southern Chicken, 24
Pitas, Acadian Stuffed, 177
Pot Pie, Double-Crust Chicken, 220
Quick Chicken, 117
Rice, Shortcut Chicken and, 220
Salads
    Almond-Chicken Salad
      Shanghai, 160
    Apple Salad, Chicken-, 216
    Broccoli-Chicken Salad, 129
    Fruited Chicken Salad, 318
    Fruit Salad, Chicken, 234
    Oriental, Chicken Salad, 146
    Ring, Chicken Salad, 123
    Spaghetti Salad, Chicken-, 146
    Tarragon Chicken Salad, 199
Sauce, Chicken Curry, 117
Soup, Broccoli-and-Chicken, 202
Soup, Roasted Pepper-and-Chicken, 58
Stew, Chili-Chicken, 319
Stir-Fry, Chinese Chicken, 100
Stock, Light Poultry, 31
Sweet-and-Sour Chicken, 161
Sweet-and-Sour Chicken Nuggets, 168
Sweet-and-Sour Chicken Wings, 206
Walnut Chicken, Crispy, 89
Yogurt-Sesame Chicken, 216
Chili
Casserole, Chili, 176
Easy Texas Chili, 201
Pastry Cups, Chili in, 68
Chocolate
Bars and Cookies
    Brownie Chip Cookies, 320
    Brownies, Choco-Mallow, 309
    Butter Cookies,
      Chocolate-Tipped, 312
    Butter Pecan Turtle Bars, 70
    Chip Cookies, Chocolate, 193
    Coconut Squares, Chocolate-, 70
    Derby Brownies, Special, 94
    Oatmeal-Chocolate Chippers, 218
Bites, Snowy Chocolate, 47
Bread, Chocolate Chip-Banana, 267
Cakes and Tortes
    Angel Food Cake, Chocolate, 111
    Apricot-Filled Chocolate Torte, 107
    Buttercream Cake, Chocolate, 108

Cheesecake, Chocolate-Glazed
  Triple-Layer, 310
Cocoa Crown Cake, 107
Fudge Cake,
  One-Foot-in-the-Fire, 252
Perfect Chocolate Cake, 307
Pound Cake, Milk Chocolate, 306
Pound Cake with Frosting,
  Chocolate, 284
Snack Cake, Frosted Chocolate, 194
Whipped Cream Cake,
  Chocolate-Mint, 265
Candies
    Bourbon Balls, 83
    Fudge, Chocolate-Peanut Butter, 311
    Pecan Clusters, Roasted, 310
    Truffles, Yule Street, 242
Crust, Chocolate, M15
Frostings, Fillings, and Toppings
    Cheese Filling, Chocolate-, 47
    Frosting, Chocolate, 194, 252, 265,
      284, 309
    Glaze, Chocolate, 310
    Perfect Chocolate Frosting, 307
Hot Chocolate Deluxe, 272
Mousse, Kid-Pleasin' Chocolate, 271
Muffins, Chocolate Chip, 87
Parfaits, Chocolate-Mint, M15
Pies and Tarts
    Bluegrass Chocolate Tarts, 84
    Fudge Pie, Sweetheart, 313
    Microwave Chocolate Pie, M15
    Pecan Pie, Chocolate, 184
Pineapple with Raspberry Sauce,
  Chocolate-Drizzled, 57
Roulage, 266
Roulage, Frozen Chocolate, 56
Sauces
    Chocolate Sauce, 57
    Dark Chocolate Sauce, Poached Pears
      with, M141
Snacks, Chocolate-Peanut Butter, 226
Strawberries Dipped in White
  Chocolate, 83
Chowders
Clam Chowder, 202
Corn Chowder, 202
Clams
Chowder, Clam, 202
Linguine, Quick Clam, 233
Puffs, Clam, 60
Coconut
Ambrosia, Grandma's, 254
Cake, Coconut-Cream Cheese Pound, 305
Cake, Holiday Coconut, 308
Cake, Unforgettable Coconut, 104
Frosting, Lemon-Coconut, 253
Kisses, Coconut, 106
Pecan Coils, Coconut-, 196
Pie, Coconut Cream, 312
Pie, Coconut Crunch, 105
Pie, French Coconut, 162
Pie, Orange-Coconut, 90
Pie, Toasted Coconut, 105
Squares, Chocolate-Coconut, 70
Coffee
Holiday Coffee, 273
Cookies
Bars and Squares
    Almond Cream Confections, 310
    Brownies, Choco-Mallow, 309

Brownies, Special Derby, 94
    Butter Pecan Turtle Bars, 70
    Chocolate-Coconut Squares, 70
    Layer Squares, Novelty, 70
    Pecan Squares, 69
Buckin' Bronco Cookies, 95
Butter Cookies, Chocolate-Tipped, 312
Drop
    Apple-Oatmeal Cookies, 218
    Brownie Chip Cookies, 320
    Chocolate Chip Cookies, 193
    Coconut Kisses, 106
    Molasses Cookies, Crispy-Chewy, 218
    Oatmeal-Chocolate Chippers, 218
    Tea Cakes, Dropped, 156
Oat Cookies, Crispy, 311
Rolled
    Raspberry Swirl Cookies, 111
    Tea Cakes, Back-Home, 156
    Tea Cakes, Decorative, 156
    Tea Cakes, Grandma's, 156
Swedish Heirloom Cookies, 311
Cooking Light. *See* On The Light Side.
Corn
Baked Corn, Creamy, 60
Casserole, Corn-and-Bean, 208
Chowder, Corn, 202
Cob, Grilled Corn-on-the-, 166
Creamy Corn, 207
Limping Susan, 155
Parslied Corn, 155
Pudding, Corn, 219
Relish, Quick Corn, 13
Salad, Corn-and-Pea, 181
Soup, Cream of Corn, 210
Vinaigrette, Okra-Corn-and-Tomato, 173
Cornbreads
Dressing, Chicken Cornbread, 159
Herbed Cornbread, 214
Hush Puppies, Mexican, 214
Muffins, Spicy Cornbread, 59
Paprika Cornbread, 213
Pie, Sausage-and-Cornbread, 25
Seasoned Cornbread, 320
Skillet Cornbread, 13
Sticks, Corn, 214
Sticks, Old-Fashioned Corn, 232
Cornish Hens
Fruited Stuffing, Cornish Hens
  with, 191
Crab
au Gratin, Crab, Shrimp, and
  Artichoke, 240
Cakes, Crab, 71
Imperial, Speedy Crabmeat, M112
Mold, Cream Cheese-Crabmeat, 71
Mousse, Crabmeat, 190
Soup, Old-Fashioned Crab, 71
Spread, Crabmeat-Horseradish, 292
Crackers
Hot Nut Crackers, 206
Cranberries
Bread, Cranberry-Banana, 294
Cloud, Cranberry, 287
Cobbler, Cranberry-and-Apple, 294
Coffee Cake, Cranberry, 159
Cream, Cranberry, 66
Fruit Bake, Cranberry-Mustard, 287
Jubilee, Cranberries, 293
Lamb, Cranberry Leg of, 52
Muffins, Miniature Cranberry, 294

Orange Delight, Cranberry-, 168
Pork Chops, Cranberry, 53
Pork, Cranberry, 293
Ring, Cranberry, 291
Salad, Congealed Cranberry, 124
Salad, Frosted Cranberry, 288
Crawfish
Dressing, Louisiana Crawfish, 103
Étouffée, Crawfish, 103
Crêpes
Crêpes, 157
Italian Crêpes, 157
Cucumbers
Dressing, Cucumber, 144
Pickled Cucumber Rounds, Easy, 143
Salad, Cucumber-Tomato, 144
Sandwiches, Cucumber, 81
Soup, Dilled Cucumber, M167
Curry
Carrots and Pineapple, Curried, 228
Chicken Cheesecake, Curried, 174
Onions, Curried, 34
Peppers, Chicken Breasts with
    Curried, 227
Rice, Curried, 183
Sauce, Asparagus with Curry, 17
Sauce, Chicken Curry, 117
Sauce, Curried Sour Cream, 174
Shrimp Curry, Creamy, 145
Custards
Easy Custard with Nutmeg, 316
Flan, Luscious, 56
Flans, Caramel-Crowned, 227

Dates
Apple-Date-Nut Ring, 212
Squares, Date, 49
Desserts. *See also* specific types.
Apple Crumble, Whole
    Wheat-, M213
Apple Dessert, Honey-Baked, M213
Charlotte, Pineapple, 288
Charlotte Russe, 288
Charlotte, Spumoni, 193
Cranberries Jubilee, 293
Frozen
        Bombe, Ice Cream, 269
        Chocolate Roulage, Frozen, 56
Kugel, Sweet, 254
Lemon Curd with Berries, 102
Oatmeal Cherry-Apple Crisp, M16
Parfaits, Chocolate-Mint M15
Pears, Vanilla Poached, 57
Pears with Dark Chocolate Sauce,
    Poached, M141
Pears with Meringue, Amaretto, M58
Pineapple with Raspberry Sauce,
    Chocolate-Drizzled, 57
Roulage, 266
Sauces
        Berry Mimosa Sauce, 315
        Brown Sugar Sauce, 314
        Chocolate Sauce, 57
        Whiskey Sauce, 230
Strawberries 'n' Cream, 30
Strawberries, Old-Fashioned Rock Cream
    with, 125
Strawberry-Yogurt Dessert, 295

Doughnuts
Applesauce Drop Doughnuts, 70
Pumpkin Doughnut Drops, 323
Sufganiyot (Jelly-Filled Doughnuts), 255
Dressing. *See* Stuffings and Dressings.
Duck and Duckling
Roast Duckling with Tangerine Stuffing, 16

Eggnog
Cake, Eggnog Pound, 253
Punch, Peppermint-Eggnog, 273
Eggplant
Dressing, Eggplant, 236
Fried Eggplant, Cheesy, 75
Moussaka, 68
Salad, Eggplant, 99
Slices, Quick Eggplant, 75
Soup, Herbed Eggplant, 173
Stuffed Eggplant, Italian-, 74
Eggs
Bel-Mar, Eggs, 92
Roll-Ups, Spicy Egg, 140
Scrambled Eggs, Creamy, 82
Enchiladas
Chicken Enchiladas, 121

Fajitas
Chicken Fajitas, 204
Pita, Fajita in a, 177
Fettuccine
Broccoli, Fettuccine with, 97
Chicken-and-Tomatoes over
    Fettuccine, 204
Salmon Fettuccine, 123
Fillings. *See* Frostings.
Fish. *See also* specific types and Seafood.
Caesar's Fish, 76
Catfish and Artichokes, Pasta with, 123
Catfish Cajun-Style, Grilled, 129
Catfish Gumbo, 278
Catfish with Creole Sauce, Breaded, 28
Catfish with Red Salsa, Grilled, 172
Flounder, Baked, 316
Flounder, Quick Crunchy, 76
Grouper, Grilled Marinated, 166
Grouper with Sautéed Vegetables, M233
Haddock Fillets in White Wine, 76
Halibut with Champagne Sauce, Baked, 29
Oven-Fried Fish, Mexi-Style, 76
Poached Fish with Vegetables, 18
Red Snapper, Blackened, 27
Snapper, Oven-Fried, 75
Food Processor
Guacamole, 205
Pesto, Pepper, 97
Sauce, Homemade Picante, 205
Soufflé, Cauliflower, 17
French Toast
Grand Marnier Fruit Sauce, French Toast
    with, 93
Oven-Baked French Toast, 192
Frostings, Fillings, and Toppings
Boiled Frosting, 45
Caramel Frosting, 307
Chocolate-Cheese Filling, 47

Chocolate Frosting, 194, 252, 265,
    284, 309
Chocolate Frosting, Perfect, 307
Chocolate Glaze, 310
Cinnamon-Cheese Filling, 46
Colored Frostings, 21
Cream Cheese Filling, 170
Cream Cheese Frosting, 305, 308
Cream Filling, 311
Fluffy Frosting, 308
Fluffy White Filling, 252
Fluffy White Frosting, 105
Horseradish Cream, 96
Lemon-Apricot Filling, 105
Lemon-Coconut Frosting, 253
Lemon Filling, 308
Mint Syrup, 89
Orange Butter Glaze, 194
Orange-Cheese Filling, 47
Peach Filling, 107
Pepper Topping, Rainbow, 117
Powdered Sugar Glaze, 95
Raisin Filling, 86
Raspberry Filling, 111
Strawberry Topping, 142
Sugar Glaze, 47
Sugars, Colored, 21
Whipped Cream Filling, 265, 307
Fruit. *See also* specific types.
Bake, Cranberry-Mustard
    Fruit, 287
Bake, Mustard Fruit, 291
Brie with Fresh Fruit,
    Caramel, 266
Brown Sugar Dip with Fruit,
    Buttery, 243
Cheesecake, Fruit-Glazed, 162
Compote, Amaretto-Hot
    Fruit, 250
Compote, Hot Fruit, 124
Dip, Quick Fruit, 110
Fruitcakes
        Japanese Fruitcake, 252
        Light Fruitcake, 309
Honey-Sour Cream Dip, Fresh Fruit
    with, 180
Pick, Fruit-on-a-, 179
Pot Roast, Fruited, 211
Punch, Mixed Fruit, 207
Punch, Passion Fruit, 169
Punch, Tropical Fruit, 169
Rice Mix, Fruited, 267
Salads
        Chicken Fruit Salad, 234
        Chicken Salad, Fruited, 318
        Creamy Holiday Fruit Salad, 251
        Mold, Sherried Fruit, 124
        Orange Cream, Fresh Fruit Salad
            with, 126
Sauce for Fruit, Tangy, 161
Sauce, Grand Marnier Fruit, 93
Slush, Champagne Fruit, 322
Spiced Fruit, Cold, 269
Stuffing, Cornish Hens with
    Fruited, 191
Tart, Fresh Fruit, 58

Granola
Nutty Granola, 95
Peanut Granola, Crunchy, 48
Grapefruit
Drink, Grapefruit, 84
Grapes
Juice, Mulled Grape, 21
Punch, White Grape, 15
Greens
Turnip Greens, 13, 232
Grits
Cheese Grits, 102
Sausage-Cheese Grits, 238
Timbales, Chives-Grits, 172
Gumbos
Catfish Gumbo, 278
Chicken-and-Sausage Gumbo, 256
Chicken Gumbo, 26
Seafood Gumbo, 154

Ham. *See also* Pork.
Apricots, Ham and, 53
au Gratin, Broccoli-Ham, 239
Baked Ham with Orange-Honey Glaze, 53
Biscuits, Kentucky Ham 'n' Angel, 83
Cheesecake, Ham-and-Asparagus, 174
Country Ham
Biscuits with Country Ham, 93
Brown Sugar Coating, Country Ham with, 88
Oven-Braised Country Ham, 87
Puff, Cheesy Country Ham, 88
Sauce, Country Ham, 117
Stuffed Country Ham, 317
Loaf, Glazed Ham, 212
Loaves, Ham, 235
Patties, Spicy Ham, 235
Pie, Ham Pot, 25
Pinwheels, Ham, 235
Pita Pockets, Ham-and-Cheese, 271
Salad, Colorful Ham-and-Rice, 319
Salad, Ham-and-Pasta, 128
Salad, Ham-Pecan-Blue Cheese Pasta, 62
Slice with Cinnamon Apple Rings, Holiday Ham, 250
Hearts of Palm
Marinated Asparagus and Hearts of Palm, 91
Spread, Hearts of Palm, 293
Honey
Dressing, Honey-Mustard, 55, 111, 146
Dressing, Spinach Salad with Honey, 16
Pear Honey, 159
Honeydew. *See* Melons.
Hors d'Oeuvres. *See* Appetizers.

Ice Creams and Sherbets
Berry Sorbet, Very, 85
Beverages
Pineapple Soda, 179
Pink Soda, Blushing, 104
Raspberry Fizz, Rosy, 179
Bombe, Ice Cream, 269
Champagne Ice, 315
Peach Ice Cream, Deluxe, 314

Peach Sherbet, 179
Pie Spectacular, Ice-Cream, 314
Praline Freeze, 48

Jams and Jellies
Champagne Jelly, 248
Kumquat Marmalade, 48
Jicama
Salad, Jicama-Orange, 122

Kabobs
Beef Kabobs with Vegetables, 148
Pepper Kabobs, Pretty, 166
Shrimp, Barbecued, 28
Kiwifruit
Salad, Peach-and-Kiwi, 180

Lamb
Chops with Herbs, Lamb, 164
Glazed Lamb, Honey-Mustard, 52
Leg of Lamb, Cranberry, 52
Pie, Lamb, 26
Lasagna
Bun, Lasagna in a, 176
Maria, Lasagna, 191
Leeks
Dilled Lemon-Butter, Leeks in, M98
Lemon
Artichoke Hearts with Lemon, 98
Beverages
Front Porch Lemonade, 156
Velvet, Lemon, 15
Chicken, Greek Lemon, 65
Chicken, Lemon-Garlic, 35
Desserts
Cheesecake, Luscious Lemon, M196
Cream, Strawberries with Lemon, 170
Curd with Berries, Lemon, 102
Filling, Lemon, 308
Filling, Lemon-Apricot, 105
Frosting, Lemon-Coconut, 253
Mousse, Lemon Cloud, 90
Pie, Deluxe Lemon Meringue, 313
Potatoes, Lemon-Buttered New, 268
Potato Wedges, Lemony, M61
Lime
Fizz, Frosty Lime, 104
Punch, Lime Slush, 273
Linguine
Clam Linguine, Quick, 233
Mussels Linguine, M112
Lobster
Medaillons in Garlic-Chive Butter Sauce, Lobster, 96
Salad, Lobster, 69

Macaroni
Cheese, Macaroni and, 30
Marshmallows
Brownies, Choco-Mallow, 309
Popcorn Balls, Marshmallow, 226
Mayonnaise
Homemade Mayonnaise, 81
Meatballs
Pineapple and Peppers, Meatballs with, 145
Saucy Meatballs, 122
Meat Loaf. *See* Beef, Ground/Meat Loaf.
Melons
Salad, Melon-Berry, 180
Watermelon-Berry Slush, 137
Watermelon-Cherry Compote, 180
Meringues
Coconut Kisses, 106
Pears with Meringue, Amaretto, 58
Microwave
Appetizers
Brie, Chutney-Bacon, M292
Dip, Mexican Artichoke, M292
Apples, Honey-Glazed, M125
Apples, Spicy Poached, M141
Bread, Harvest Pumpkin, M215
Desserts
Apple Crumble, Whole Wheat-, M213
Apple Dessert, Honey-Baked, M213
Cheesecake, Luscious Lemon, M196
Chocolate-Mint Parfaits, M15
Crust, Chocolate, M15
Oatmeal Cherry-Apple Crisp, M16
Pears with Dark Chocolate Sauce, Poached, M141
Pie, Microwave Chocolate, M15
Plums, Poached, M141
Pudding, Butternut Squash, M19
Pudding, Pumpkin, M20
Truffles, Yule Street, M242
Fruit Bake, Cranberry-Mustard, M287
Fruit Compote, Hot, M124
Main Dishes
Broccoli-Ham au Gratin, M239
Casserole, Microwave Mexican, M231
Chicken, Ginger-Nut, M33
Crabmeat Imperial, Speedy, M112
Crab, Shrimp, and Artichoke au Gratin, M240
Flounder, Baked, M316
Grits, Sausage-Cheese, M238
Grouper with Sautéed Vegetables, M233
Mussels Linguine, M112
Round Steak over Rice, Burgundy, M33
Shrimp Creole, M220
Shrimp, Sweet-and-Sour, M112
Turkey Divan, Creamy, M34
Peaches, Bay Laurel, M124
Relish, Quick Corn, M13
Rice, Jiffy Spanish, M176
Salad, Microwave Chef, M146
Soups and Stews
Carrot-Mint Soup, Chilled, M168
Chicken Broth, Easy Microwave, M167
Cucumber Soup, Dilled, M167
Garden Harvest Soup, Italian, M167

Spreads
Cream Cheese Spread, Peachy, M215
Hearts of Palm Spread, M293
Vegetables
Carrots, Orange-Glazed, M98
Carrots, Peach-Glazed, M13
Corn-and-Bean Casserole, M208
Corn, Parslied, M155
Green Beans, French, M208
Leeks in Dilled Lemon-Butter, M98
Peas and Peppers, Minted, M99
Potatoes, Basil-Cheese, M316
Potatoes, Chili-Cheese, M62
Potatoes, Parmesan, M62
Potatoes, Soufflé, M14
Potato, Twice-Baked, M295
Potato Wedges, Lemony, M61
Squash Mexican, Stuffed, M200
Squash, Stuffed White, M201
Zucchini and Carrots, Julienne, M14

Mousses
Chocolate Mousse, Kid-Pleasin', 271
Crabmeat Mousse, 190
Lemon Cloud Mousse, 90

Muffins
Almond Muffins, 87
Basic Cupcake Muffins, 87
Bran Muffins, Maple-, 66
Cherry-Nut Muffins, 87
Chocolate Chip Muffins, 87
Cornbread Muffins, Spicy, 59
Cranberry Muffins, Miniature, 294
Rum-Nut Muffins, 87
Sour Cream Muffins, 283
Yogurt-Muesli Muffins, 215

Mushrooms
Chicken with Artichokes and
Mushrooms, 35
Pepper-Mushroom Medley, 98
Salad, Marinated Mushroom, 181
Soup, Fresh Mushroom, 190
Soup, Mushroom-Rice, 32

Mustard
Dressing, Honey-Mustard, 55, 111, 146
Fruit Bake, Mustard, 291
Sauce, Mustard, 19, 97

Noodles
Casserole, Shrimp-and-Noodle, 240
Casserole, Turkey-Noodle-Poppyseed, 239
Kugel, Sweet, 254

Oatmeal
Chocolate Chippers, Oatmeal-, 218
Cookies, Apple-Oatmeal, 218
Cookies, Crispy Oat, 311
Crisp, Oatmeal Cherry-Apple, M16

Okra
Deep-Fried Okra, 154
Salad, Okra, 155
Vinaigrette, Okra-Corn-and-Tomato, 173

Onions
Baked Onions, Sweet-and-Sour, 34
Bake, Romano Onion, 98
Bread, Onion-Herb, 165

Crunch Sticks, Onion Crescent, 206
Curried Onions, 34
Focaccia, Mustard-and-Onion, 321
Kuchen, Onion, 34
Rings, Leonard's-Style Onion, 120
Soup
Creamy Onion Soup, 211
French Onion Soup, 31
Stuffed Onions, Cheese-, 34
On The Light Side
Appetizers
Dip, Quick Fruit, 110
Dip, Ranch-Style, 138
Oysters Bienville, Baked, 27
Beverages
Apple Cooler, 14
Apricot Mint Cooler, 165
Bellini Spritzers, 110
Lemon Velvet, 15
Orange Juicy, 178
Pineapple-Banana Slush, 14
Punch, White Grape, 15
Scarlet Sipper, 198
Strawberry Spritzer, 14
Watermelon-Berry Slush, 137
Breads
Biscuits, Angel, 28
Cinnamon-Oat Bread, 135
Cranberry-Banana Bread, 294
Crouton Bread, Quick, 138
Muffins, Miniature
Cranberry, 294
Muffins, Spicy Cornbread, 59
Onion-Herb Bread, 165
Rolls, Whole Wheat, 111
Sourdough Wedges, 199
Spoonbread, 200
Desserts
Apples à l'Orange, Baked, 280
Cake, Chocolate Angel Food, 111
Cake with Amaretto-Almond Sauce,
Angel Food, 199
Cobbler, Cranberry-and-Apple, 294
Cranberries Jubilee, 293
Crust, Gingersnap, 296
Crust, Lattice, 294
Flan, Luscious, 56
Lemon Curd with Berries, 102
Pears, Vanilla Poached, 57
Pears with Meringue,
Amaretto, M58
Pie, New-Fashioned Pumpkin, 296
Pineapple with Raspberry Sauce,
Chocolate-Drizzled, 57
Pudding with Whiskey Sauce,
Bread, 230
Roulage, Frozen Chocolate, 56
Sherbet, Peach, 179
Strawberries 'n' Cream, 30
Strawberry-Yogurt Dessert, 295
Tart, Fresh Fruit, 58
Torte, Apricot Sponge, 59
Yogurt, Frozen Fresh Peach, 139
Fruit-on-a-Pick, 179
Grits, Cheese, 102
Main Dishes
Beans and Rice, Red, 27
Beef Tenderloin for Two, 295
Beef with Asparagus, 100
Catfish with Creole Sauce,
Breaded, 28

Chicken Bake, Individual, 279
Chicken Enchiladas, 121
Chicken Gumbo, 26
Chicken Stir-Fry, Chinese, 100
Chicken Strips and Vegetables,
Marinated, 110
Fajita in a Pita, 177
Flank Steak with Noodles,
Stuffed, 101
Flank Steak with Sweet Peppers,
Grilled, 138
Grouper, Grilled Marinated, 166
Halibut with Champagne Sauce,
Baked, 29
Jambalaya, 26
Lamb Chops with Herbs, 164
Lasagna in a Bun, 176
Pizza, Breakfast, 178
Pizza, Turkey-Vegetable, 139
Pork Chow Mein, 101
Pork, Cranberry, 293
Red Snapper, Blackened, 27
Shrimp, Barbecued, 28
Shrimp Étouffée, 229
Steak lo Mein, 100
Tacoritos, 133
Pizza Crust, Special, 139
Quesadillas, Green Chile, 121
Rice Pilaf, Brown, 136
Rice, Southwestern, 121
Salad Dressings
Blue Cheese Vinaigrette, 280
Honey-Mustard Dressing, 111
Salads
Barley-Broccoli Salad, 135
Green Salad, Mixed, 230
Greens with Blue Cheese Vinaigrette,
Mixed, 280
Jicama-Orange Salad, 122
Legumes, Marinated, 197
Lentils-and-Rice Salad, 197
Potato Salad, 122
Potato Salad, Pesto, 164
Spinach Salad, Citrus, 59
Sprout Salad, 137
Tarragon Chicken Salad, 199
Sandwiches
Heroes, Healthy, 177
Pitas, Acadian Stuffed, 177
Shrimp Salad Sandwiches, 178
Turkey-in-the-Slaw
Sandwich, 177
Sauces and Gravies
Champagne Sauce, 29
Chocolate Sauce, 57
Creole Sauce, 28
Spaghetti Sauce, Lentil, 198
Whiskey Sauce, 230
Soups and Stews
Beef Stew, 230
Gumbo, Catfish, 278
Mex-Tex Soup, 278
Pepper-and-Chicken Soup,
Roasted, 58
Split Pea Soup, 198
Turkey-Tomato Stew, 279
Tortilla Chips, Light, 278
Vegetables
Acorn Squash, Fruited, 228
Asparagus Vinaigrette, 138
Beans, Texas Ranch, 198

On The Light Side, Vegetables
(continued)

    Black-Eyed Peas, Spicy Hot, 135
    Brussels Sprouts in Mustard Sauce, 228
    Burritos, Vegetable, 134
    Butterbeans, 166
    Cabbage, Skillet, 229
    Carrots and Pineapple, Curried, 228
    Corn, Creamy Baked, 60
    Corn-on-the-Cob, Grilled 166
    Green Beans, Italian, 164
    Kidney Bean Casserole, 136
    New Potatoes, Roasted, 138
    New Potato Medley, 279
    Pepper Kabobs, Pretty, 166
    Potato, Twice-Baked, M295
    Snow Peas with Red Pepper, 102
    Steamed Vegetable Medley, 29
    Stir-Fried Vegetables, 136
    Sweet Potatoes-and-Apple
      Casserole, 228
    Tomatoes, Stuffed Scalloped, 29
Oranges
  Butter, Orange, 323
  Carrots, Orange-Glazed, M98
  Cream, Orange, 126
  Desserts
    Pie, Frosty Orange, 296
    Pie, Orange-Coconut, 90
  Filling, Orange-Cheese, 47
  Glaze, Orange Butter, 194
  Juicy, Orange, 178
  Rice à l'Orange, 236
  Rolls, Glazed Orange, 194
  Salads
    Cranberry-Orange Delight, 168
    Jicama-Orange Salad, 122
  Turkey Slices, Orange-, 53
Oysters
  Baked Oysters Bienville, 27
  Scalloped Oysters, 249

Pancakes
  Latkes, 254
  Sour Cream Pancakes with Fruit
    Topping, 142
Pastas. *See also* specific types.
  Catfish and Artichokes, Pasta with, 123
  Chicken with Pasta, Dijon, 318
  Primavera, Smoked Turkey Pasta, 84
  Salad, Ham-and-Pasta, 128
  Salad, Ham-Pecan-Blue Cheese Pasta, 62
  Salad, Luncheon Pasta, 191
  Salad, Oriental Pasta, 63
  Salad, Pasta, 62, 91
  Salad, Presto Pasta, 63
  Salad, Ratatouille Pasta, 74
  Salad, Seafood Pasta, 62
  Seafood and Pasta, 234
Pâté. *See* Appetizers/Pâté.
Peaches
  Bay Laurel Peaches, 124
  Bellini Spritzers, 110
  Cake, Peachy Almond-Butter, 107
  Chicken, Peachy, 212
  Cobbler, Peach, 219
  Cobbler Supreme, Peach, 313
  Daiquiris, Peach, 322

Dressing, Peach, 180
Filling, Peach, 107
Ice Cream, Deluxe Peach, 314
Petals, Peach, 104
Salad, Peach-and-Kiwi, 180
Sherbet, Peach, 179
Spread, Peachy Cream Cheese, M215
Tart, Peach Cream, 173
Yogurt, Frozen Fresh Peach, 139
Peanut Butter
  Fudge, Chocolate-Peanut Butter, 311
  Snacks, Chocolate-Peanut Butter, 226
Peanuts
  Chicken, Ginger-Nut, M33
  Granola, Crunchy Peanut, 48
Pears
  Amaretto Pears with Meringue, M58
  Blue Cheese Sauce, Brunch Pears
    with, 142
  Honey, Pear, 159
  Poached Pears, Vanilla, 57
  Poached Pears with Dark Chocolate
    Sauce, M141
Peas
  Black-Eyed
    Hopping John, 12
    Rice, Black-Eyed Peas with, 208
    Salad, Black-Eyed Pea, 173
    Spicy-Hot Black-Eyed Peas, 135
  English
    Carrots and Peas, Mint-Glazed, 291
    Chilled Dilly Peas, 143
    Salad, Corn-and-Pea, 181
    Salad, Crunchy Pea, 143
    Salad, English Pea, 143
  Snow
    Peppers, Minted Peas and, M99
    Red Pepper, Snow Peas with, 102
  Soup, Cream Pea, 211
  Soup, Split Pea, 198
Pecans
  Bars, Butter Pecan Turtle, 70
  Bread, Applesauce-Pecan, 66
  Chicken, Pecan, 54
  Clusters, Roasted Pecan, 310
  Coconut-Pecan Coils, 196
  Granola, Nutty, 95
  Muffins, Cherry-Nut, 87
  Muffins, Rum-Nut, 87
  Pie, Chocolate Pecan, 184
  Pie, Pecan, 312
  Pies, Honey-Pecan Finger, 184
  Pie, Texas Star Pecan, 184
  Pralines, 48
  Rice, Shrimp-and-Scallop Sauté with
    Pecan, 317
  Salad, Ham-Pecan-Blue Cheese Pasta, 62
  Squares, Pecan, 69
  Tart with Praline Cream, Pecan, 256
Peppers
  Curried Peppers, Chicken Breasts
    with, 227
  Flank Steak with Sweet Peppers,
    Grilled, 138
  Jalapeño
    Open-Faced Jalapeño Heroes, 144
    Stuffed Jalapeños, Fiery Fried, 118
  Kabobs, Pretty Pepper, 166
  Meatballs with Pineapple and Peppers, 145
  Medley, Pepper-Mushroom, 98
  Peas and Peppers, Minted, M99

Pesto, Pepper, 97
Red Pepper and Watercress Salad,
  Roasted, 55
Red Pepper, Snow Peas with, 102
Soup, Roasted Pepper-and-Chicken, 58
Topping, Rainbow Pepper, 117
Pickles and Relishes
  Corn Relish, Quick, 13
  Cucumber Rounds, Easy Pickled, 143
  Prune Relish, Peppy, 227
  Vegetable Relish, 147
Pies and Pastries
  Banana Cream Pie, Hawaiian, 105
  Chocolate
    Fudge Pie, Sweetheart, 313
    Microwave Chocolate Pie, M15
  Cobblers
    Cranberry-and-Apple Cobbler, 294
    Peach Cobbler, 219
    Peach Cobbler Supreme, 313
  Coconut Cream Pie, 312
  Coconut Crunch Pie, 105
  Coconut Pie, French, 162
  Coconut Pie, Toasted, 105
  Ice-Cream Pie Spectacular, 314
  Lemon Meringue Pie, Deluxe, 313
  Main Dish
    Chicken Pie, Nana's, 25
    Chicken Pie, Savory Southern, 24
    Chicken Pot Pie, Double-Crust, 220
    Ham Pot Pie, 25
    Lamb Pie, 26
    Sausage-and-Cornbread Pie, 25
    Turkey Pot Pie, 24
  Maple Cream Coffee Treat, 50
  Orange-Coconut Pie, 90
  Orange Pie, Frosty, 296
  Pastries and Crusts
    Butter Crust, 173
    Chocolate Crust, M15
    Cornmeal Pastry Cups, 69
    Gingersnap Crust, 296
    Graham Cracker Crust, 296
    Lattice Crust, 294
    Savory Pastry, 24
    Tart Crust, 58
    Tart Pastry, 92
    Tart Shells, 84
  Pecan
    Chocolate Pecan Pie, 184
    Honey-Pecan Finger Pies, 184
    Pecan Pie, 312
    Texas Star Pecan Pie, 184
  Pumpkin Pie, New-Fashioned, 296
  Raisin Pastry Bites, 86
  Raspberry Party Puffs, 170
  Sweet Potato Pie, Speedy, 219
  Tarts
    Chess Tarts, 83
    Chocolate Tarts, Bluegrass, 84
    Cream Cheese Tarts, 312
    Derby Tarts, Miniature, 92
    Fruit Tart, Fresh, 58
    Peach Cream Tart, 173
    Pecan Tart with Praline Cream, 256
    Tomato-Cheese Tart, Dried, 203

Pimiento
Hoagies, Bacon, Pimiento, and
Cheese, 144
Pineapple
Charlotte, Pineapple, 288
Chocolate-Drizzled Pineapple with
Raspberry Sauce, 57
Cooler, Pineapple, 207
Curried Carrots and Pineapple, 228
Meatballs with Pineapple and Peppers, 145
Nectar, Hot Pineapple, 21
Slush, Pineapple-Banana, 14
Soda, Pineapple, 179
Pizza
Breakfast Pizza, 140, 178
Cookie, Pizza, 49
Crust, Special Pizza, 139
Pocket Pizzas, Easy, 168
Turkey-Vegetable Pizza, 139
Wide-Eyed Pizzas, 94
Plums
Poached Plums, M141
Popcorn
Balls, Marshmallow Popcorn, 226
Pork. *See also* Bacon, Ham, Sausage.
Chops
Cranberry Pork, 293
Cranberry Pork Chops, 53
Oriental Pork Chops, 212
Vegetable Casserole, Pork
Chop-, 208
Chow Mein, Pork, 101
Grilled Pork, Honey-and-Herb, 148
Ribs
Apple-Barbecue Spareribs, 160
Baby Loin Back Ribs, John
Wills's, 120
Barbecue Sauce, Ribs with
Blender, 12
Sweet-and-Sour Pork, 317
Tenderloin
Glazed Pork Tenderloin, 315
Grilled Pork Tenderloin, Garlic, 172
Grilled Pork with Salsa, 128
Marsala, Pork, 35
Medaillons in Mustard Sauce,
Pork, 96
Potatoes
Baked
New Potatoes, Baked, 90
Twice-Baked Potato, M295
Basil-Cheese Potatoes, M316
Chili-Cheese Potatoes, M62
Colcannon, 64
Garlic-Parsley Potatoes, 290
Latkes, 254
Lemony Potato Wedges, M61
New Potatoes, Lemon-Buttered, 268
New Potatoes, Roasted, 138
New Potato Medley, 279
Parmesan Potatoes, M62
Salads
Patio Potato Salad, 160
Pesto Potato Salad, 164
Potato Salad, 122
Soufflé Potatoes, 14
Potatoes, Sweet
Bake, Holiday Sweet Potato, 291
Casserole, Glazed Sweet Potato, 250
Casserole, Sweet Potatoes-and-Apple, 228
Pie, Speedy Sweet Potato, 219

Waffles with Orange Butter, Sweet
Potato, 323
Yams, Bourbon, 232
Pralines
Buns, Praline, 195
Freeze, Praline, 48
Pralines, 48
Prunes
Relish, Peppy Prune, 227
Puddings. *See also* Custards.
Bread Pudding, 219
Bread Pudding with Whiskey
Sauce, 230
Butternut Squash Pudding, M19
Corn Pudding, 219
Pumpkin Pudding, M20
Pumpkin
Bread, Harvest Pumpkin, M215
Doughnut Drops, Pumpkin, 323
Pie, New-Fashioned Pumpkin, 296
Pudding, Pumpkin, M20

Quiches
Spinach Quiche, No-Crust, 142
Swiss Alpine Quiche, 18
QUICK!
Appetizers
Dip, Quick Nacho, 168
Links, Cocktail Smoky, 168
Breads
Biscuits, Easy Herb, 283
Biscuits, Lightnin' Cheese, 283
Garlic Bread, Quick, 283
Muffins, Sour Cream, 283
Rolls, Almond Crescent, 283
Rolls, Mayonnaise, 283
Butter, Green Peppercorn, 117
Egg Roll-Ups, Spicy, 140
Main Dishes
Beef Roll-Ups, Mexican, 176
Chicken Chimichangas,
Oven-Fried, 175
Chicken, Lemon-Garlic, 35
Chicken Nuggets,
Sweet-and-Sour, 168
Chicken, Quick, 117
Chicken with Artichokes and
Mushrooms, 35
Chili Casserole, 176
Chili, Easy Texas, 201
Fish, Caesar's, 76
Fish, Mexi-Style,
Oven-Fried, 76
Flounder, Quick Crunchy, 76
Grouper with Sautéed
Vegetables, 233
Haddock Fillets in White
Wine, 76
Linguine, Quick Clam, 233
Pizza, Breakfast, 140
Pizzas, Easy Pocket, 168
Pork Marsala, 35
Seafood and Pasta, 234
Shrimp Versailles, 233
Snapper, Oven-Fried, 75
Steak and Gravy, Zippy, 35
Relish, Quick Corn, 13
Rice, Jiffy Spanish, 176

Salads
Cranberry-Orange Delight, 168
Ham-Pecan-Blue Cheese Pasta
Salad, 62
Pasta Salad, 62
Pasta Salad, Oriental, 63
Pasta Salad, Presto, 63
Seafood Pasta Salad, 62
Sandwiches, Cheesy Breakfast, 140
Sauces and Gravies
Basil and Cream Sauce, 118
Chervil-and-Savory Sauce, 117
Chicken Curry Sauce, 117
Country Ham Sauce, 117
Soups and Stews
Broccoli-and-Chicken Soup, 202
Chowder, Clam, 202
Chowder, Corn, 202
Tortilla Soup, 201
White Bean Soup, 201
Topping, Rainbow Pepper, 117
Vegetables
Carrots, Peach-Glazed, 13
Potatoes, Soufflé, 14
Zucchini and Carrots, Julienne, 14

Raisins
Filling, Raisin, 86
Pastry Bites, Raisin, 86
Spread, Creamy Raisin, 36
Raspberries
Cookies, Raspberry Swirl, 111
Filling, Raspberry, 111
Fizz, Rosy Raspberry, 179
Lemon Curd with Berries, 102
Party Puffs, Raspberry, 170
Sauce, Berry Mimosa, 315
Watermelon-Berry Slush, 137
Relishes. *See* Pickles and Relishes.
Rice
à l'Orange, Rice, 236
Beans and Rice, Easy Red, 220
Beans and Rice, Red, 27
Black-Eyed Peas with Rice, 208
Brown Rice Pilaf, 136
Chicken and Rice, Shortcut, 220
Creole Rice, 183
Curried Rice, 183
Medaillons in Pepper Pesto,
Chicken-Rice, 97
Mix, Fruited Rice, 267
Pecan Rice, Shrimp-and-Scallop Sauté
with, 317
Salads
Ham-and-Rice Salad, Colorful, 319
Lentils-and-Rice Salad, 197
Shrimp and Rice, Oriental, 183
Soup, Mushroom-Rice, 32
Soup, Turkey-Rice, 89
Southern Rice, 250
Southwestern Rice, 121
Spanish Rice, 183
Spanish Rice, Jiffy, 176
Wild Rice, Scallops and, 129
Rolls and Buns. *See also* Breads.
Butterscotch Pinwheels, 49
Caramel Rolls, Easy, 195
Cheese-Apricot Sweet Rolls, 195

Rolls and Buns
(continued)

Cinnamon Rolls, Old-Fashioned, 196
Coconut-Pecan Coils, 196
Crescent Rolls, Almond, 283
Crescents, Apricot, 181
Freezer Dinner Rolls, 251
Mayonnaise Rolls, 283
Orange Rolls, Glazed, 194
Pinwheel Rolls, Sweet, 46
Praline Buns, 195
Sour Cream Yeast Rolls, 17
Sweet Rolls, Quick Breakfast, 195
Tasty Rolls, 85
Whole Wheat Rolls, 111
Yeast Rolls, Best-Ever, 46
Yeast Rolls, Hurry-Up, 90

Salad Dressings
Blue Cheese Dressing, 286
Blue Cheese Vinaigrette, 55, 280
Cooked Salad Dressing, 231
Cucumber Dressing, 144
French Dressing, Creamy, 286
Ginger Dressing, 160
Greek Salad Dressing, 286
Honey Dressing, Spinach Salad
   with, 16
Honey-Mustard Dressing, 55, 111, 146
Orange Cream, 126
Peach Dressing, 180
Salad Dressing, 161
Tarragon Dressing, 55
Vinaigrette Dressing, 173
Salads
Ambrosia, Grandma's, 254
Asparagus Vinaigrette, 138
Aspic
   Beet Aspic, 123
   Tomato Aspic, Layered, 99
Barley-Broccoli Salad, 135
Broccoli 'n' Cauliflower Salad, 32
Broccoli Salad, 292
Chef Salad, Microwave, M146
Chicken
   Almond-Chicken Salad
      Shanghai, 160
   Apple Salad, Chicken-, 216
   Broccoli-Chicken Salad, 129
   Fruited Chicken Salad, 318
   Fruit Salad, Chicken, 234
   Oriental, Chicken Salad, 146
   Spaghetti Salad, Chicken-, 146
   Tarragon Chicken Salad, 199
Congealed
   Chicken Salad Ring, 123
   Cranberry-Orange Delight, 168
   Cranberry Ring, 291
   Cranberry Salad,
      Congealed, 124
   Cranberry Salad, Frosted, 288
   Fruit Mold, Sherried, 124
Corn-and-Pea Salad, 181
Cranberry Cloud, 287
Cucumber-Tomato Salad, 144
Eggplant Salad, 99
English Pea Salad, 143

Fruit
   Creamy Holiday Fruit Salad, 251
   Orange Cream, Fresh Fruit Salad
      with, 126
Green
   Goat Cheese and Greens, 54
   Mediterranean Salad, 99
   Mesclun with Tarragon Dressing, 55
   Mixed Green Salad, 230
   Mixed Greens with Blue Cheese
      Vinaigrette, 280
   Red-and-Green Salad, 55
   Robust Salad, 181
   Tossed Salad, Colorful, 55
   Watercress Salad, Roasted Red
      Pepper and, 55
Ham-and-Pasta Salad, 128
Ham-and-Rice Salad, Colorful, 319
Jicama-Orange Salad, 122
Layered Overnight Salad, 319
Legumes, Marinated, 197
Lentils-and-Rice Salad, 197
Lobster Salad, 69
Marinated Salad, Zesty, 90
Melon-Berry Salad, 180
Mushroom Salad, Marinated, 181
Okra-Corn-and-Tomato Vinaigrette, 173
Okra Salad, 155
Pasta Salad, 62, 91
Pasta Salad, Ham-Pecan-Blue Cheese, 62
Pasta Salad, Luncheon, 191
Pasta Salad, Oriental, 63
Pasta Salad, Presto, 63
Pasta Salad, Ratatouille, 74
Pasta Salad, Seafood, 62
Peach-and-Kiwi Salad, 180
Pea Salad, Black-Eyed, 173
Pea Salad, Crunchy, 143
Potato
   Patio Potato Salad, 160
   Pesto Potato Salad, 164
   Salad, Potato, 122
Red, White, and Green Salad, 18
Roast Beef Salad, 318
Seafood Salad, 88
Shrimp Rémoulade, 255
Shrimp Salad Sandwiches, 178
Spinach-Apple Salad, 89
Spinach Salad, Citrus, 59
Spinach Salad, Sesame, 292
Spinach Salad, Tropical, 231
Spinach Salad with Honey Dressing, 16
Sprout Salad, 137
Taco Salad, 20
Turkey-Apple Salad, 181
Turkey Salad, 318
Vegetable
   Overnight Vegetable Salad, 33
   Zucchini Salad, Marinated, 32
Salmon
Fettuccine, Salmon, 123
Poached Salmon with Emerald Sauce, 63
Sandwiches
Bacon, Pimiento, and Cheese
   Hoagies, 144
Beef Tenderloin Picnic Sandwiches, 91
Breakfast Sandwiches, Cheesy, 140
Cheese Sandwiches, Leafy, 56
Cucumber Sandwiches, 81
Heroes, Healthy, 177
Jalapeño Heroes, Open-Faced, 144

Pita Pockets, Ham-and-Cheese, 271
Pitas, Acadian Stuffed, 177
Reubens, Party, 61
Sausage-Stuffed French Loaf, 19
Shrimp Salad Sandwiches, 178
Turkey Hero with Garlic Sauce, 145
Turkey-in-the-Slaw Sandwich, 177
Watercress Sandwiches, 82
Sauces. *See also* Desserts/Sauces.
Basil and Cream Sauce, 118
Basil Sauce, 85
Blue Cheese Sauce, 142
Champagne Sauce, 29
Cheese Sauce, 235
Chervil-and-Savory Sauce, 117
Chicken Curry Sauce, 117
Cocktail Sauce, 242
Country Ham Sauce, 117
Creole Sauce, 28
Curried Sour Cream Sauce, 174
Curry Sauce, Asparagus with, 17
Emerald Sauce, 63
Fruit Sauce, Grand Marnier, 93
Fruit, Tangy Sauce for, 161
Garlic-Chive Butter Sauce, 96
Garlic Sauce, Turkey Hero with, 145
Italian Sauce, 67
Mustard Sauce, 19, 97
Pesto, Dried Tomato, 204
Pesto, Pepper, 97
Picante Sauce, Homemade, 205
Salsa, Chunky, 206
Salsa, Red, 172
Spaghetti Sauce, Dried Tomato, 202
Spaghetti Sauce, Lentil, 198
Sausage
Baked Sausage Patties, 82
Balls, Sausage-Apple, 85
Burritos, Breakfast, 192
Casserole, Italian, 238
Cocktail Smoky Links, 168
Grits, Sausage-Cheese, 238
Gumbo, Chicken-and-Sausage, 256
Lasagna Maria, 191
Loaf, Sausage-Stuffed French, 19
Pie, Sausage-and-Cornbread, 25
Quesadillas, Sausage, 118
Roll-Ups, Spicy Egg, 140
Salami Rollups, 226
Scallops
Sauté with Pecan Rice,
   Shrimp-and-Scallop, 317
Wild Rice, Scallops and, 129
Seafood. *See also* specific types and Fish.
Dip, Super Seafood, 292
Gumbo, Seafood, 154
Mussels Linguine, M112
Pasta, Seafood and, 234
Salad, Seafood, 88
Salad, Seafood Pasta, 62
Sherbets. *See* Ice Creams and Sherbets.

Shrimp
au Gratin, Crab, Shrimp, and
Artichoke, 240
Barbecued Shrimp, 28
Casserole, Shrimp-and-Noodle, 240
Creole, Shrimp, M220
Curry, Creamy Shrimp, 145
Dee-Lish, Shrimp, 216
Étouffée, Shrimp, 229
Rémoulade, Shrimp, 255
Rice, Oriental Shrimp and, 183
Salad Sandwiches, Shrimp, 178
Sauté with Pecan Rice,
Shrimp-and-Scallop, 317
Spread, Zippy Shrimp, 36
Sweet-and-Sour Shrimp, M112
Versailles, Shrimp, 233
Soufflés
Cauliflower Soufflé, 17
Potatoes, Soufflé, 14
Soups. *See also* Chili, Chowders, Gumbos,
Stews.
Broccoli-and-Chicken Soup, 202
Carrot Cream Soup, 210
Carrot-Mint Soup, Chilled, M168
Cauliflower Soup, 211
Celery Soup, Cream of, 210
Cheese Soup, Gazebo, 158
Chicken Broth, Easy
Microwave, M167
Corn Soup, Cream of, 210
Crab Soup, Old-Fashioned, 71
Cucumber Soup, Dilled, M167
Eggplant Soup, Herbed, 173
Garden Harvest Soup, Italian, M167
Mushroom-Rice Soup, 32
Mushroom Soup, Fresh, 190
Onion Soup, Creamy, 211
Onion Soup, French, 31
Pea Soup, Cream, 211
Pepper-and-Chicken Soup, Roasted, 58
Spinach Soup, Cream of, 211
Stock, Brown Meat, 31
Stock, Light Poultry, 31
Stock, Vegetable, 31
Tomato-Cream Soup, Dried, 203
Tomato Soup, Icy-Spicy Mexican, 155
Tortilla Soup, 201
Tortilla Soup, Spicy, 32
Turkey-Rice Soup, 89
Turkey Soup, Williamsburg, 287
Vegetable Soup, Down-Home, 32
White Bean Soup, 201
Zucchini Soup, Dilled, 88
Spaghetti
Casserole, Italian, 238
Salad, Chicken-Spaghetti, 146
Spice
Dry Spices, 120
Spinach
Cheesecake, Spinach Pesto, 175
Quiche, No-Crust Spinach, 142
Salads
Apple Salad, Spinach-, 89
Citrus Spinach Salad, 59
Honey Dressing, Spinach Salad with, 16
Sesame Spinach Salad, 292
Tropical Spinach Salad, 231
Sauce, Emerald, 63
Soup, Cream of Spinach, 211
Tomatoes, Baked Spinach, 92

Spreads. *See also* Appetizers/Spreads.
Cheese Spread, Gouda, 36
Cheese Spread, Mexican, 119
Crabmeat-Horseradish Spread, 292
Cream Cheese Spread,
Peachy, M215
Guacamole Spread, 119
Hearts of Palm Spread, 293
Horseradish Spread, 243
Raisin Spread, Creamy, 36
Shrimp Spread, Zippy, 36
Swiss Cheese Spread, 60
Tomato-Cheese Spread, Dried, 204
Vegetable Spread, 144
Sprouts
Salad, Sprout, 137
Squash. *See also* Zucchini.
Acorn Squash, Fruited, 228
Butternut Squash Pudding, M19
Casserole, Calico Squash, 290
Casserole, Squash, 161
Delight, Squash, 236
Mirliton Balls, 217
Mirlitons, Stuffed, 217
Yellow
Nosh, Squash, 147
Stuffed Squash Mexican, 200
White Squash, Stuffed, M201
Stews. *See also* Chili, Gumbos, Soups.
Beef Stew, 230
Chicken Stew, Chili-, 319
Irish Stew, 64
Turkey-Tomato Stew, 279
Strawberries
Cream Dip, Fresh Strawberries
with, 86
Cream, Strawberries 'n', 30
Daiquiris, Strawberry, 125
Dessert, Strawberry-Yogurt, 295
Lemon Cream, Strawberries
with, 170
Punch, Strawberry, 273
Punch, Strawberry Champagne, 315
Rock Cream with Strawberries,
Old-Fashioned, 125
Sauce, Berry Mimosa, 315
Sorbet, Very Berry, 85
Spritzer, Strawberry, 14
Topping, Strawberry, 142
White Chocolate, Strawberries
Dipped in, 83
Stuffings and Dressings
Chicken Cornbread Dressing, 159
Crawfish Dressing, Louisiana, 103
Eggplant Dressing, 236
Fruited Stuffing, Cornish Hens
with, 191
Tangerine Stuffing, 16

Sweet-and-Sour
Burgers, Sweet-and-Sour, 128
Chicken Nuggets, Sweet-and-Sour, 168
Chicken, Sweet-and-Sour, 161
Chicken Wings, Sweet-and-Sour, 206
Onions, Sweet-and-Sour Baked, 34
Pork, Sweet-and-Sour, 317
Shrimp, Sweet-and-Sour, M112

Tacos. *See also* Burritos, Enchiladas,
Tortillas.
Salad, Taco, 20
Tea
Long Island Iced Tea, Southern, 207
Mint Tea, 89
Punch, Tea, 143, 207
Timbales
Grits Timbales, Chives-, 172
Tomatoes
Aspic, Layered Tomato, 99
Baked Spinach Tomatoes, 92
Bean-and-Tomato Skillet, 316
Cocktail, Tomato Juice, 12
Dip, Bacon-and-Tomato, 147
Dried Tomato-Cheese Spread, 204
Dried Tomato-Cheese Tart, 203
Dried Tomato-Cream Soup, 203
Dried Tomato Pesto, 204
Dried Tomato Spaghetti Sauce, 202
Fettuccine, Chicken-and-Tomatoes
over, 204
Salad, Cucumber-Tomato, 144
Salad, Red, White, and Green, 18
Salsa, Chunky, 206
Salsa, Red, 172
Sauce, Homemade Picante, 205
Soup, Icy-Spicy Mexican Tomato, 155
Stew, Turkey-Tomato, 279
Stuffed Scalloped Tomatoes, 29
Vinaigrette, Okra-Corn-and-Tomato, 173
Tortillas
Beef Roll-Ups, Mexican, 176
Burritos, Breakfast, 192
Cheese Tortilla Snack, Two-, 119
Chips, Light Tortilla, 278
Quesadillas, Sausage, 118
Soup, Spicy Tortilla, 32
Soup, Tortilla, 201
Tacoritos, 133
Tuna
Steaks, Grilled Tuna, 129
Turkey
Barbecue, Turkey, 158
Casserole, Turkey-Noodle-Poppyseed, 239
Divan, Creamy Turkey, M34
Garlic Sauce, Turkey Hero with, 145
Nachos, Turkey, 118
Pie, Turkey Pot, 24
Pizza, Turkey-Vegetable, 139
Primavera, Smoked Turkey Pasta, 84
Roast Turkey, 321
Salad, Turkey, 318
Salad, Turkey-Apple, 181
Sandwich, Turkey-in-the-Slaw, 177
Slices, Orange-Turkey, 53
Smoked Turkey, 249
Smoked Turkey Medley, 128
Soup, Turkey-Rice, 89

Turkey
(continued)

Soup, Williamsburg Turkey, 287
Stew, Turkey-Tomato, 279
Stock, Light Poultry, 31
Turnips
Greens, Turnip, 13, 232

Vanilla
Pears, Vanilla Poached, 57
Veal
Stock, Brown Meat, 31
Sweetbreads, Creamed, 82
Vegetables. *See also* specific types.
Beef Kabobs with Vegetables, 148
Burritos, Vegetable, 134
Chicken Strips and Vegetables,
Marinated, 110
Fish with Vegetables, Poached, 18
Limping Susan, 155
Marinated Vegetables Italian, 242

Pizza, Turkey-Vegetable, 139
Relish, Vegetable, 147
Salads
Overnight Vegetable Salad, 33
Ratatouille Pasta Salad, 74
Sautéed Vegetables, Grouper with, M233
Soup, Down-Home Vegetable, 32
Spread, Vegetable, 144
Steamed Vegetable Medley, 29
Stir-Fried Vegetables, 136
Stock, Vegetable, 31
Turkey Pasta Primavera, Smoked, 84

Waffles
Sweet Potato Waffles with Orange
Butter, 323
Walnuts
Apple-Date-Nut Ring, 212
Cake, Black Walnut, 308
Chicken, Crispy Walnut, 89
Loaf, Nutty Wheat, 65
Watermelon. *See* Melons.

Wild Rice. *See* Rice/Wild Rice.
Wok Cooking
Chicken Stir-Fry, Chinese, 100
Vegetables, Stir-Fried, 136

Yogurt
Carambola-Yogurt Calypso, 169
Chicken, Yogurt-Sesame, 216
Dessert, Strawberry-Yogurt, 295
Muffins, Yogurt-Muesli, 215
Peach Yogurt, Frozen
Fresh, 139

Zucchini
Fans, Herb Butter Zucchini, 201
Fries, Zucchini, 147
Julienne Zucchini and Carrots, 14
Salad, Marinated Zucchini, 32
Soup, Dilled Zucchini, 88

Favorite Recipes

Record your favorite recipes below for quick and handy reference.

Appetizers	Source/Page	Remarks

Beverages	Source/Page	Remarks

Breads Source/Page Remarks

Desserts Source/Page Remarks

Main Dishes	Source/Page	Remarks

Salads	Source/Page	Remarks

Soups and Stews   Source/Page   Remarks

Vegetables and Side Dishes   Source/Page   Remarks